NEW PERSPECTIVES ON INDUSTRIAL POLICY FOR A MODERN BRITAIN

NEW PERSPECTIVES ON INDUSTRIAL POLICY FOR A MODERN BRITAIN

Edited by

DAVID BAILEY, KEITH COWLING,
AND PHILIP R. TOMLINSON

OXFORD
UNIVERSITY PRESS

OXFORD
UNIVERSITY PRESS

Great Clarendon Street, Oxford, OX2 6DP,
United Kingdom

Oxford University Press is a department of the University of Oxford.
It furthers the University's objective of excellence in research, scholarship,
and education by publishing worldwide. Oxford is a registered trade mark of
Oxford University Press in the UK and in certain other countries

First Edition published in 2015

Impression: 1

Published in the United States of America by Oxford University Press
198 Madison Avenue, New York, NY 10016, United States of America

British Library Cataloguing in Publication Data
Data available

Library of Congress Control Number: 2014953674

ISBN 978-0-19-870620-5

Printed and bound by
CPI Group (UK) Ltd, Croydon, CR0 4YY

For Mikey, Oliver, and Ruby

FOREWORD

I welcome the publication of this volume on industrial policy. It offers a range of views on what a new industrial policy could look like. And without agreeing with the viewpoints in every chapter, I welcome this contribution to the debate. Indeed, as I noted in the *Wright Review of Advanced Manufacturing*, Britain needs a modern active industrial policy.

This is not about government 'picking winners', investing long-term capital in large companies, or trying to plan the economy. Rather, it is about focusing on improving the environment in which companies operate, recognizing the positive influence that government can have, and working together to tackle the challenges. For twenty years the manufacturing sector was thought of as 'beached' by successive governments: left behind by the tide of our economic history. More recently we have had a reawakening to the sector's importance and potential, and as a result we have seen the right direction of travel in policy terms. But there remain some important policy gaps that we need fill in an evolutionary sort of way.

In particular, industrial policy needs to be strategic, long-term, and stable, because major investment decisions are taken with a view to the long term. For example, the decision to build a new automotive engine plant in the UK means the site is likely to be used for this purpose for at least twenty-five or thirty years. So the degree of perceived policy stability is extremely important, and cross-party consensus should be sought wherever possible. Our adversarial political culture, the electoral cycle, and the churn of government ministers all militate against this. So I propose two specific measures to stabilize the system.

The first relates to the innovation system, where I recommend the institution of a regular five-yearly review across the whole of innovation policy, with a ten-year horizon. This strategic review of innovation support would consider all the major areas of government activity and spending related to innovation, as well as the numerous programmes focused on particular innovation activities, technologies, and processes. It would be the vehicle for evaluating the effectiveness and value for money of public support for innovation; considering the balance between its various different elements, ensuring we are targeting the right sectors, activities and technologies, and setting priorities for the coming ten years.

I recommend a second similar review across the wider system of industrial policy. At present the government identifies eleven key industry sectors, each of which has a sector council and sector strategy. A five-yearly strategic review of industrial policy would evaluate the success of the existing industrial sector strategies; ensure that the identified sectors and themes are still appropriate, and identify the key strategic priorities looking forward ten years. At the moment the sector strategies lack sufficiently SMART objectives against which they can be properly evaluated, and this should be rectified quickly.

The same need for stability applies to the institutions that support industry nationally—the industry sector councils—and the bodies that support local and regional development: the Local Economic Partnerships. Evolution (not revolution) and devolution should be the watchwords for these national and local institutions: we should be seeking to develop the existing bodies and devolve as much power, funding, and responsibility to them as possible.

Some Key Recommendations

Politicians and policy-makers should see manufacturing through the lens of business investment decisions and focus on creating a globally competitive investment environment in the UK.

The UK should position itself as one of the leaders of the advanced economies on climate change, but must avoid unilateral regulatory costs that drive activity to other jurisdictions. There needs to be a wide-ranging strategic review of environmental energy regulation to reduce costs, improve simplicity for companies, and create long-term stability.

Government should commit to creating a globally competitive business taxation regime, taking into account the cumulative impact of all business taxes including the headline rate of Corporation Tax. The next move should be to increase and then stabilize the value of capital allowances to incentivise productive investment. A comprehensive review of business property taxation should be undertaken.

Additional spending on science and technology should be the first priority for any additional public resources to support advanced manufacturing. At the moment the large science budget is ring-fenced. We should extend this ring-fence to include both the science resource budget and the technology budget administered by the Technology Strategy Board, and increase this total as soon as possible.

The Catapult technology centres are a promising initiative and should be protected until they can be properly evaluated. They should focus on deepening the links they create between the scientific research community and businesses, especially small and medium-sized businesses. We should not increase the number of Catapults or individual centres without a corresponding increase in funding.

We must double the number of apprentices qualifying in manufacturing related skills at level 3 or above by the end of the next Parliament. Employers should have full ownership of the standards and funding for apprenticeships, and the sector councils should take on responsibilities for expanding supply.

We must also double the supply of engineering and other manufacturing-related degree places for UK domiciled students by the end of the next Parliament. To address our urgent higher-level skills needs, we must revisit visa arrangements to allow highly skilled non-EU graduates to work more easily in UK manufacturing roles. In addition we must continue to grow the pipeline of enthusiastic and well-qualified young people— especially women—who want to study manufacturing-related degrees.

Businesses need to exercise acumen and creativity in seeking funding. More competition in the banking sector would help push the mainstream lenders into more imaginative and more proactive lending practices. But the onus lies on the banks themselves to rebuild their balance sheets whilst taking the opportunities of funding the growing advanced manufacturing sector.

A new British Business Bank should act as the delivery mechanism for all the public funding schemes available to business. It should provide access to meaningful amounts of new funding, through an efficient and timely decision-making process. It should be the single 'front door' for all public funding schemes whilst simplifying and reducing them in number.

As noted, there should be a regular five-yearly strategic review of innovation support, with a ten-year horizon, carried out at the beginning of each Parliament. It would consider all the major areas of government activity and spending related to innovation as well as the numerous programmes focused on particular innovation activities, technologies and processes. It would be the vehicle for evaluating the effectiveness and value for money of public support for innovation, making sure that we are targeting the right sectors, activities and technologies, and setting priorities for the coming ten years.

Finally, there should be a similar five-yearly strategic review of industrial policy to evaluate the success of the existing industrial sector strategies; ensure that the identified sectors and themes are still appropriate, and identify the key strategic priorities looking forward ten years.

Mike Wright
Author of the *Wright Review of Advanced Manufacturing*

Contents

List of Figures   xv
List of Tables   xvii
Contributors   xix

1. Introduction: New Perspectives on Industrial Policy for a
   Modern Britain   1
   David Bailey, Keith Cowling, and Philip R. Tomlinson

PART 1: PERSPECTIVES ON INDUSTRIAL POLICY

2. DIP-ly Speaking: Debunking Ten Myths, and a Business
   Strategy-Informed Developmental Industrial Policy   17
   Christos Pitelis

3. Industrial Policy: International Experiences   41
   David Coates

4. Reframing Industrial Policy   60
   Andrew Bowman, Julie Froud, Sukhdev Johal, Adam Leaver,
   and Karel Williams

5. The Role of Industrial Policy: Lessons from Asia   79
   Mushtaq Khan

PART 2: FINANCE FOR INDUSTRY, ENTREPRENEURSHIP, AND INNOVATION

6. Finance and Industrial Strategy   101
   Malcolm Sawyer

7. Financial Architecture and Industrial Policy: Alternative
   Ownership Structures and the Role of Mutuals   116
   Jonathan Michie

8. Harnessing the Private Sector to Enhance Industrial Innovation   131
   GORDON MURRAY, WEIXI LIU, AND MARC COWLING

9. How to Make 'Smart' Innovation-Led Growth Also
   'Inclusive' Growth   170
   MARIANA MAZZUCATO

PART 3: EMPLOYMENT ISSUES AND
INDUSTRIAL POLICY

10. Skills and Training for a More Innovation-Intensive Economy   183
    FRANCIS GREEN AND GEOFF MASON

11. Beyond a Human Capital Approach to Education and the Labour
    Market: The Case for Industrial Policy   206
    PHILLIP BROWN, SIN YI CHEUNG, AND HUGH LAUDER

12. Workers' Voice in Company Decision-Making   225
    JANET WILLIAMSON AND TIM PAGE

13. Employment Rights and Industrial Policy   241
    PAUL L. LATREILLE AND RICHARD SAUNDRY

PART 4: INDUSTRIAL POLICY AND
REGIONAL DEVELOPMENT

14. An Industrial Strategy for UK Cities   263
    DAVID BAILEY, KEITH COWLING, AND PHILIP R. TOMLINSON

15. Mind the Gap! What Might a Place-Based Industrial and
    Regional Policy Look Like?   287
    DAVID BAILEY, PAUL HILDRETH, AND LISA DE PROPRIS

PART 5: REGULATION, FDI, AND
INDUSTRIAL POLICY

16. Regulation and Governance of Public Utilities   311
    MICHAEL WATERSON

17. Refining Inward Investment Policy: Maximizing the Returns to Limited Funds   327

NIGEL DRIFFIELD, SANDRA LANCHEROS, AND YAMA TEMOURI

18. Takeovers and Takeover Policy   343

AJIT SINGH, GURMAIL SINGH, DAVID BAILEY, AND HELENA LENIHAN

PART 6: INDUSTRIAL POLICY AND SUSTAINABLE DEVELOPMENT

19. Industrial Policy for a Sustainable Growth Path   365

KARL AIGINGER

20. Industrial Policy: A Green Agenda   395

DAN COFFEY AND CAROLE THORNLEY

Author Index   421
General Index   431

List of Figures

4.1   Share of the Growth (%) in Real Original Income between 1979 and 2012 in Economically Active Households   68

4.2   Annual Change in Real Original Income (£) of Economically Active Households   68

4.3   Share of Nominal GVA Growth (%) by Region   69

4.4   Regional GVA as a Percentage of London's GVA, 1989–2012   70

8.1   Share of Venture Capital Investments as a Percentage of Total PE/VC Investments for US, UK, and Australia   139

8.2   Venture Capital Investments in Australia   139

8.3   Annual Australian Private Equity and Venture Capital Investments   140

8.4   Australian Follow-On Venture Capital Investments by Stage   150

8.5   IPO Share Price Performance of IIF Supported Firms   151

9.1   National Institutes of Health R&D Funding   171

9.2   Number of Early Stage and Seed Funding Awards, SBIR, and Venture Capital   172

11.1   Male A-level and Degree Graduates' Hourly Earnings 2009–11   214

11.2   Male A-level and Degree Graduates' Hourly Earnings 1999–2001   214

11.3   Female A-level and Degree Graduates' Hourly Earnings 2009–11   215

11.4   Female A-level and Degree Graduates' Hourly Earnings 1999–2001   215

13.1   UK Indicators of Economic Performance 2001–13   243

13.2   Employment Tribunal Receipts April 2012–March 2014   248

17.1   Financial Assistance to UK-Owned and Foreign Firms in the Assisted Areas of Great Britain: 1991–2000 and 2001–13   330

19.1   Current Account and Growth of Real GDP   368

19.2   Share of Manufacturing (Current Prices) and Growth of Real GDP   369

19.3   Depth of the Crisis vs 'Industrial Base'   369

19.4   Share of Manufacturing from 1960 to 2012: Countries with a Strong Decline Nominal Value; in % of GDP   378

19.5   Share of Manufacturing 1960 to 2012: Countries with a Smaller Decline
       Nominal Value; in % of GDP   379

19.6   Share of Manufacturing 1960 to 2012: EU–15, USA, Japan Nominal
       Value; in % of GDP   380

20.1   North East LCEA Electric Vehicle Cluster   413

List of Tables

6.1	Savings and Investment in the UK	106
8.1	IIF Programme Effectiveness	141
8.2	Operating Characteristics of Hybrid VC Funds	142
8.3	Variable Definitions	146
8.4	Summary Statistics for Australian Risk Capital Investment by Type of VC Provider	147
8.5	Stage of Investment for IIF Supported Businesses	148
8.6	Pair-Wise Correlations between Variables	149
8.7	Poisson Regression: Number of Staged Investments	153
8.8	OLS Regression: Years to Investment and Total Equity Investment	155
8.9	Multinomial Logistic Regression: Probability of IIF/IIF Affiliate Investment	158
8.10	Probit Regressions: Exit Outcomes	160
10.1	Single Occupation Most Affected by Skill Updating Needs, UK Commission's Employers Skills Survey, 2013	188
10.2	Human Resources in Science and Technology (HRST) as a Percentage of Total Employment, 2012	190
10.3	Apprenticeship Programme Starts, England, 2012–13, Analyzed by Sector Subject Area and Rate of Growth Since 2002–3	196
12.1	The European Participation Index (2008–9 Data)	232
14.1	The UK's Largest Cities: A Comparative Economic Picture	272
19.1	Share of Manufacturing and the Dynamic of Industrial Production	371
19.2	European and US Sector Balances and Export Share	387
20.1	Alternative Vehicle Technology Policy Array	412

Contributors

Karl Aiginger has been the Director of the WIFO since 2005. His research areas are industrial economics, competitiveness and strategies of firms, regions and countries. For many years he was responsible for the background reports to the European Commission on industrial competitiveness. He has also been a visiting professor at Stanford University, MIT, and UCLA. He also teaches at the Vienna University of Economic and Business Administration and is an honorary professor at the University of Linz. He is Editor of the *Journal of Industry, Competition and Trade* (JICT) and is the coordinator of the FP7 funded research project 'WWW for Europe – a new growth path for Europe'.

David Bailey is Professor of Industrial Strategy at Aston Business School. He has written extensively on industrial and regional policy, especially in relation to manufacturing and the auto industry. His recent research has been funded by a number of state and private organizations including the ESRC. He recently undertook an INTERREG project on the role of FDI in cluster upgrading, and is an Area Coordinator (on industrial policy) for the FP7 project WWW for Europe (Welfare, Wealth, Work). He is a regular blogger, newspaper columnist, and media commentator. He was Chair of the Regional Studies Association between 2006 and 2012 and is now an Honorary Vice-Chair, and an Editor of the journals *Regional Studies* and *Policy Studies*.

Andrew Bowman is a postdoctoral Research Associate at the Economic and Social Research Council funded Centre for Research on Socio-Cultural Change (CRESC) at the University of Manchester. Prior to this he wrote his PhD thesis at the University of Manchester's Centre for the History of Science, Technology and Medicine. His research with CRESC has focused on issues surrounding modern industrial policy, financialization, and public utilities. His co-authored book *The End of the Experiment: From Competition to the Foundational Economy* was published in 2014.

Phillip Brown is a Distinguished Research Professor in the School of Social Sciences, Cardiff University, having previously worked at the University of Kent and Cambridge. He has been a Visiting Professor at the University of British Columbia, Sciences Po in Paris, and the University of Turku. He is currently a Visiting Professor at the Centre for Skills, Performance and Productivity Research in Singapore and a Visiting Fellow at the UK Commission for Employment and Skills (UKCES). He has written, co-authored, and co-edited sixteen books including *The Global Auction: The Broken Promises of Education, Jobs and Incomes* (2011) (with Hugh Lauder and David Ashton).

Sin Yi Cheung is Senior Lecturer of Sociology in the School of Social Sciences at Cardiff University and Deputy Director of Cardiff Q-Step Centre for Excellence in Quantitative Methods Teaching. After obtaining her DPhil in Sociology at Oxford University, she taught at Oxford Brookes and Birmingham Universities. Her research is concerned with different forms of social inequalities especially the link between education and work, and among ethnic minorities in Britain. Her latest publications include refugee integration and the labour market outcomes of second generation ethno-religious minorities.

David Coates holds the Worrell Chair in Anglo-American Studies in the Department of Politics and International Affairs at Wake Forest University in North Carolina, having previously taught at the universities of York, Leeds, and Manchester (and the Open University). He has written extensively on labour politics, contemporary political economy and American public policy, and blogs regularly on *The Huffington Post*. Author of, among other books, *The Question of UK Decline* (1994), *Models of Capitalism* (2000), and *Prolonged Labour: The Slow Growth of New Labour Britain* (2005); his latest work, *America in the Shadow of Empires*, was published in December 2014.

Dan Coffey is Director of the Graduate School at Leeds University Business School, and holds degrees from Glasgow, Cambridge, and Warwick. He is the author of *The Myth of Japanese Efficiency: The World Car Industry in a Globalising Age* (2006), and co-author of *Globalization and Varieties of Capitalism* (2009). He researches auto-producing systems from both technical and social perspectives, and works also on models of capitalism and questions of sustainability. Previous work includes reports for the Italian government on policies for sustainable vehicle platforms. He is on the Steering Committee of GERPISA ('the international research network of the automobile').

Keith Cowling is Emeritus Professor of Economics at the University of Warwick. His main research interests are in industrial organization and the deficiencies of monopoly capitalism. He has played significant roles as an industrial policy adviser and published extensively in the fields of industrial economics and policy. He was the founding Editor of *International Journal of Industrial Organisation* and is author of several books, including *Monopoly Capitalism* (1982) and (with Roger Sugden), *Beyond Capitalism: Towards a New World Economic Order* (1994). He was an early President of the European Association for Research in Industrial Economics (EARIE) and a founding member of the European Union Network for Industrial Policy (EUNIP).

Marc Cowling is Professor of Entrepreneurship at Brighton Business School, having previously worked at Exeter Business School. Prior to that, he held the posts of Chief Economist at the Institute for Employment Studies and The Work Foundation. He has also held positions at Warwick Business School, Birmingham Business School, and London Business School (where he was Deputy Principal Investigator of the Global Entrepreneurship Monitor). His research focuses upon the dynamics of early stage survival and growth, the financing of SMEs and entrepreneurial businesses, labour market dynamics, and evaluating public policy. He has published widely in both economics and entrepreneurship, and he is one of the world's most highly cited researchers.

Lisa De Propris is Reader in Regional Economic Development at the Birmingham Business School where she is the Director of the Global Value Chain Research Cluster. Her main research interests focus on clusters, economic development, and global value chains. In particular, her research has been on small firms and clusters; competitiveness in clusters and regions; innovation; clusters, and foreign direct investment; re-shoring and off-shoring; regional development; knowledge economy and clusters, and creative and cultural industries. She has published extensively on European Union, regional, and industrial policy, and is currently working on two FP7-funded projects: Smart Culture; and Wealth, Work and Welfare (WWW) for Europe.

Nigel Driffield is Professor of International Business at the University of Warwick, having previously held a similar position at Aston Business School (2004–14). He has published extensively in leading journals, carried out four ESRC funded projects, and currently holds a Leverhulme fellowship focusing on the relationships between internationally mobile capital and spatially bounded agents and factors. He has also undertaken projects for the Organisation for Economic Co-operation and Development, the World Bank, European Commission, and UNCTAD, in addition to various UK government departments. Much of his work focuses upon policy related to foreign direct investment, where he has advised policy-makers at both national and, more recently, local levels.

Julie Froud is a Professor at Manchester Business School, University of Manchester. She is a member of the ESRC-funded Centre for Research in Socio-Cultural Change (CRESC) and has, with a group of colleagues, been researching financialization for more than ten years. An initial interest in financialization and corporations has been developed into a broader exploration of finance in society, including the role of elite groups in preventing a debate about finance and its reforms. Recent publications include Engelen et al., *After the Great Complacence: Financial Crisis and the Politics of Reform* (2011).

Francis Green is Professor of Work and Education Economics at the LLAKES Centre, Institute of Education. After graduating in Physics at Oxford University, he studied Economics at the London School of Economics, before writing his PhD thesis at Birkbeck College. Previously he has worked in the universities of Kingston, Massachusetts, Leicester, Leeds, and Kent. His research focuses on skills, training, work quality, and employment relations issues. His latest book, *Skills and Skilled Work: An Economic and Social Analysis*, was published in 2013.

Paul Hildreth is an independent adviser on cities, regions, and local economies, working in the UK and in Central and Eastern Europe. His background experience is in local governance and national policymaking for cities and regions. He is Visiting Policy Fellow at the Centre for Sustainable Urban and Regional Futures (SURF) at

University of Salford, Associate for the Centre for London, Board Member of the Regional Studies Association, and Non-Executive Director of Cambridge Econometrics. He is also researching for a PhD part-time at the Bartlett School of Planning at University College London.

Sukhdev Johal is Professor of Accounting & Strategy at Queen Mary, University of London. His current research interests include critical research on UK finance, how to adapt social and economic statistics to understand employment and wealth changes in the UK, how local authorities can adapt local CSR policies to promote economic democracy and local supply chains. He also works closely with CRESC. Recent co-authored books include *After the Great Complacence* (2011) and *Financialization at Work* (2008). He has also contributed to public interest reports on public policy issues such as UK rail privatization, an alternative report on UK banking reform and regional growth disparities.

Mushtaq Khan is Professor of Economics at SOAS, University of London. He has held previous positions at Corpus Christi College, Oxford, and Sidney Sussex College, Cambridge, where he was Assistant Director of Development Studies. His research focus is in institutional economics, where he has worked on social transformations, rents and rent seeking, political settlements, corruption, democratization, property rights and land reform, industrial and technology policy, 'good governance' versus 'developmental governance', and other related issues. He has worked extensively on India, Bangladesh, Thailand, Tanzania, Palestine, and South Africa and has a broader interest in South Korea, Pakistan, and Malaysia.

Sandra Lancheros is currently an Assistant Professor in Economics at the University of Nottingham Ningbo China (UNNC) specializing in microeconomics and econometrics. After completing her PhD at the University of Nottingham UK in 2012 she was appointed a Research Fellow at Aston University, UK. Her research interests are in the areas of international trade and foreign direct investment, innovation and applied econometrics.

Paul L. Latreille is Professor of Management and Associate Dean for Learning and Teaching at the University of Sheffield and is a Visiting Professor at Westminster Business School and a Research Fellow of the IZA, Bonn. He serves on the *Professional Mediators' Association* advisory group and chairs its sub-group. His research interests are in applied labour economics and employment relations, with a focus upon workplace conflict, mediation, and Employment Tribunals. He has published extensively in leading journals and for policy-makers and regularly presents to practitioner audiences. His work has been funded by the ESRC, the Department for Business, Innovation and Skills, the Ministry of Justice and Acas, among others.

Hugh Lauder is Professor of Education and Political Economy at the University of Bath (1996 to present) and Acting Director, The Institute for Policy Research. He was formerly Dean of Education at Victoria University of Wellington. He specializes in the relationship of education to the economy and has for over ten years worked on comparative studies of national skill strategies and more recently on the global skill strategies of multinational companies. His most recent book with Phillip Brown and David Ashton is *The Global Auction: The Broken Promises of Education, Income and Jobs* (2011).

Adam Leaver is Professor at Manchester Business School and a member of the Centre for Research on Socio-cultural Change (CRESC) at the University of Manchester. His research interests include the study of financial innovation and financialization, reconceptualizing national and international economic flows to better understand regional and transnational divergence, and the sociology of pricing in collectors markets. His recent co-authored books include *After the Great Complacence* (2011), *Financialization at Work* (2008), and *Financialization and Strategy* (2006).

Helena Lenihan is an Associate Professor at the Department of Economics, Kemmy Business School, University of Limerick, Ireland. She has published extensively on industrial/enterprise development and policy, innovation policy, policy evaluation and the role of entrepreneurship/new venture creation in economic development and firm growth. She has held visiting appointments at several universities including the University of Cambridge and University of Warwick and is a life-long Visiting-Fellow at Wolfson College, University of Cambridge. She has secured funding from both academic and policymaking sources and has recently been co-PI for the Irish team on an FP7-funded project. She currently serves as the independent expert on enterprise policy evaluation for an Irish policy (Forfás) steering committee.

Weixi Liu is Associate Professor at the School of Public Economics and Administration, Shanghai University of Finance and Economics. He has previously held posts at Exeter Business School, and Renmin University of China. His primary research interests lie in small business growth dynamics, the finance of entrepreneurial firms especially high-tech young firms, and government policy on entrepreneurship and entrepreneurial finance. He has published extensively in leading academic journals, and has been commissioned by both national governments and international institutions to conduct policy-focused research on entrepreneurship policy and policy evaluation.

Geoff Mason is Principal Research Fellow at the National Institute of Economic and Social Research (NIESR) and Visiting Professor at the Institute of Education, University of London. His research interests are in the areas of education, training, labour markets, productivity, and innovation. His work on employer demand for skills and the graduate labour market has been widely cited in UK public policy debates and contributed to his being invited to work as Research Adviser to the National Skills Task Force and to serve on the Royal Society Working Group on Higher Education. Recent academic publications include articles in *Labour Economics, Education Economics, Economics of Innovation and New Technology* and *Research Policy*.

Mariana Mazzucato holds the RM Phillips chair in Economics of Innovation at SPRU in the University of Sussex. Previously she has held academic positions at the

University of Denver, London Business School, Open University, and Bocconi University. Her research—funded by the European Commission, the *Institute for New Economic Thinking* (INET) and the Ford Foundation—focuses on the relationship between financial markets, innovation, and economic growth at the company, industry, and national level and she recently published *The Entrepreneurial State: Debunking Private vs. Public Sector Myths* (2013). In 2014 she won the New Statesman SPERI prize in political economy. She advises the UK government, various EU governments and the European Commission on innovation-led growth.

Jonathan Michie is Professor of Innovation & Knowledge Exchange at the University of Oxford where he is Director of the Department for Continuing Education and President of Kellogg College. Previously he held appointments at Birmingham, Birkbeck, and Cambridge Universities. He has also been a Research Associate of the ESRC Centre for Business Research and Director of the ESRC's Contracts & Competition Programme, and been an Expert to the European Commission. His main research areas have been innovation, globalization, High Commitment Work Systems, and corporate diversity. He edited the two-volume *Reader's Guide to the Social Sciences*. He was previously on the Council of Acas and is currently on the Council of the Academy of Social Sciences.

Gordon Murray OBE is Emeritus Professor (Entrepreneurship) at the University of Exeter Business School. Since 1989, he has researched, lectured, and consulted internationally in the two related areas of Entrepreneurial Finance and the international development of the formal and informal Venture Capital Industry. Professor Murray has conducted policy-focused research for the UK, German, Finnish, Danish, Irish, and other European governments, the Australian Commonwealth, and the European Commission. He has published widely on policy issues in the provision of entrepreneurial risk finance. A particular personal interest is the establishment of a fruitful, complementary dialogue between academic researchers and policy-makers.

Tim Page is a Senior Policy Officer at the TUC, where he is responsible for industrial policy, science policy, and high performance workplaces. Tim has produced a number of policy papers for the TUC, including '*The Way of the Dragon: What can the UK learn from the rise of China and East Asia?*' (2014) and '*German Lessons*' (2012). Tim represented the TUC on the Manufacturing Forum, which was established in 2014. He is also a member of the ETUC Economic and Employment Committee. Tim previously worked as a researcher at the AEU engineering union and as a research assistant to both Ian McCartney MP and Ann Clwyd MP.

Christos Pitelis is Professor of Sustainable Global Business and Director of the Centre for International Business and Management (CIBAM), at the University of Bath and a Life Fellow at Queens' College, Cambridge. He has published extensively in world leading journals and edited ten books, and serves on several leading editorial boards.

His research focuses upon the theory of the firm, international business, global governance and global finance. He has coordinated projects for governments, the European Commission, the United Nations, USAID, the Commonwealth Secretariat, and several leading corporations. He has been a Visiting Professor in Australia, Europe, Russia, China, Latin America, and the USA, and was President of the Organisation of Small and Medium-sized Enterprises in Greece.

Richard Saundry is Associate Professor (Reader) in Human Resource and Leadership Studies at the University of Plymouth. Previously he held posts at University of Central Lancashire and the University of Leeds. He is one of the UKs leading authorities on the management of conflict at work. He is both a Research Associate and Policy Associate for the Advisory, Conciliation and Arbitration Service (Acas), where he has conducted a number of funded research projects in relation to workplace conflict. He has also conducted research into trade union revitalization and union learning receiving funding from the ESRC, TUC, and UNISON. He has published a wide range of peer reviewed journal articles and policy reports.

Malcolm Sawyer is Emeritus Professor of Economics, University of Leeds, UK. He is the lead co-ordinator for the EU-funded 8-million-euro five-year project, Financialisation Economy Society and Sustainable Development (www.fessud.eu). He established and is managing editor of *International Review of Applied Economics*, and the editor of the book series *New Directions in Modern Economics*. He has authored twelve and edited over thirty books. He has also published over 100 papers in leading journals on a wide range of topics including recent papers on financialization, fiscal policies, alternative monetary policies, path dependency, public private partnerships, and conceptualizing labour supply and unemployment.

Ajit Singh is Professor Emeritus of Economics at the University of Cambridge, where he has been a member of faculty since 1965. He is one of the world's most renowned Indian-born economists, having published seventeen books and over 200 papers in world leading journals, making a substantial contribution to the study of the modern business enterprise, mergers and acquisitions, de-industrialization in advanced and emerging economies and globalization. He has been a senior economic adviser to the governments of Mexico and Tanzania, the ILO, UNCTAD, UNIDO, the World Bank, and the International Finance Corporation. He is an Academician of the UK Academy of Social Sciences. He is currently Director of Research at the Cambridge Endowment for Research in Finance.

Gurmail Singh is Professor of Economics at the Punjab University, Chandigarh. Prior to this, he was with Punjab Agricultural University, Institute for Development Communication, Khalsa College (Delhi University), and Jawaharlal Nehru University. He has been consultant to a number of organizations including the Planning Commission-Government of India, the International Labour Organization, and the Government of Punjab. Apart from this, he has been Editor-in-Chief of *Research Journal Social Sciences* and General Secretary of the Punjab Development Society. Dr Singh has authored/ co-authored books including *Impact of GATT on Punjab Agriculture* (1996); *Alternatives in Agriculture* (2001); *Indian Agriculture: Four Decades of Development (2001); Rural Development in Punjab: A Success Story Going Astray* (2008); *Understanding North-West Indian Economy* (2010); and *Economic Liberalisation and Indian Agriculture* (2012).

Yama Temouri is a Lecturer of International Business at Aston Business School, UK. His research interests are in international economics and trade, particularly the economics of multinational enterprises and its impacts on host and home economies. He is particularly interested in issues relating to productivity, outsourcing/offshoring activities, and employment dynamics. His current work looks at the extent to which differences in institutional quality across countries determine the types of activity undertaken by multinationals and how equity in joint ventures is shared with local host partner firms. He also analyses the performance of exporting and high-growth firms. His work has been published in numerous international peer-reviewed journals.

Carole Thornley is Emeritus Professor of Employment and Public Policy at Keele Management School at Keele University. After completing a first degree while working in London, she obtained a further degree at Cambridge in economics, and wrote her PhD at Warwick. She is the co-editor of *Globalization and Precarious Forms of Production and Employment: Challenges for Workers and Unions* (2010) and co-author of *Globalization and Varieties of Capitalism* (2009). Her research interests include globalization, industrial organization, employment and public policy. She is on the Steering Committee of GERPISA ('the international research network of the automobile'). She advises trade unions and has a long association with UNISON.

Philip R. Tomlinson is Associate Professor in Business Economics at the University of Bath School of Management, where he is also a convenor for the Institute for Policy Research (IPR). His research interests predominantly focus upon economic governance, regional development, and industrial policy, where he has published extensively in some of the world's leading academic journals. He also co-edited *Crisis or Recovery in Japan: State and Industrial Economy* (2007, with David Bailey and Dan Coffey) and has contributed to several edited volumes. He has addressed the All Party Parliamentary Manufacturing Group on industrial policy and also worked closely with the British Ceramic Confederation on issues relating to the development of the ceramics industry.

Michael Waterson is Professor of Economics at the University of Warwick, where he has been since 1991. His research lies broadly within the field of industrial economics, particularly supermarket pricing and energy markets. He has held previous posts at the Universities of Reading and Newcastle and was President of the European Association for Research in Industrial Economics and Chair of the (UK) Network of Industrial Economists. He was also General Editor of the *Journal of Industrial Economics* for five years. He has published widely in a variety of areas of industrial economics in a range of journals and books. Between 2005 and 2014 he was a Member of the Competition Commission.

Karel Williams is Director of the ESRC-funded Centre for Research on Socio Cultural Change and a professor at Manchester Business School. He leads a team whose research on financial crisis and economic renewal has raised issues about the power of elites and the limits of mainstream technocratic problem framings. Their public interest reports on sectors like rail or supermarkets can be freely downloaded from the cresc.ac.uk web site. Their most recent book *The End of the Experiment?* (2014) presses the case for applying distributed intelligence to decentralized experiments in the foundational economy provision of mundane goods and services.

Janet Williamson is a Senior Policy Officer at the TUC where she is responsible for corporate governance and capital markets, including company reporting, mergers and takeovers, institutional investment, workers' capital, private equity, executive pay, and corporate social responsibility. She has written many TUC reports and submissions on these topics, including 'Workers on Board: the case for workers' voice in corporate governance' (2013). She led the work to establish the Trade Union Share Owners organization which launched in 2013. Janet has represented Labour on Global Reporting Initiative Working Groups on Governance and Remuneration and Materiality, and was a member of the AA1000 Stakeholder Engagement Standard Working Group. She holds degrees from York and Sussex Universities.

CHAPTER 1

INTRODUCTION
New Perspectives on Industrial Policy for a Modern Britain

DAVID BAILEY, KEITH COWLING,
AND PHILIP R. TOMLINSON

1.1 OVERVIEW OF INDUSTRIAL POLICY

In the aftermath of the global financial crisis (GFC) (2008) and the ensuing Great Recession (2008–13), the economic debate has begun to shift towards rebalancing the UK economy, away from an over-reliance upon consumerism and the financial sector to generate growth, towards more sustainable productive activities. Within this debate, there has been increasing recognition of a greater role for the state in pursuing an active 'industrial policy' (or 'industrial strategy') to rebalance the economy. This renewed interest in industrial policy (and state intervention in the economy more widely) reflects rising concerns among an increasing number of economic commentators and policy-makers with the neo-liberal model, which has dominated socio-economic policymaking since the late 1970s. Indeed, after over thirty-five years of largely neo-liberal policies, the UK economy is not only heavily debt-ridden (in terms of both public and private debt), but also significantly weakened by its systemic imbalances, its much reduced manufacturing capacity, and long-run deterioration in its trade balance and growing regional inequalities (Wade, 2009; Cowling and Tomlinson, 2011; Cowling et al., 2011; Hutton and Lee, 2012). In contrast, the recent comparative success of the BRICs (Brazil, Russia, India, and China), and previously acclaimed industrial policies of countries such as Japan, South Korea, Germany, and even the USA suggest an active state can (and should) play a positive role in facilitating economic growth.

There is both a strong theoretical and a (historical) evidence-based case for industrial policy, and these are clearly made in this edited volume. Interestingly, the early advocates of industrial policy originate in the United States, with Alexander Hamilton's (the First US Treasury secretary) 1791 *Report on the Subject of Manufactures*, which contained a number of 'industrial policy' proposals, aimed at developing the new US republic, and in particular, US manufacturing (see Irwin, 2004). These proposals later influenced the 'American School' of capitalist economics (*circa* 1860s–1970s), which advocated a 'national' system to promote US economic independence and (national) self-sufficiency. These ideas were also supported by the German-American economist Frederick List (1841), who provided one of the first theoretical treatises for industrial policy. In contrast to the Classical economists, List argued policy-makers should take a long-term view of economic development and intervene accordingly, especially to promote domestic manufacture and commerce, rather than relying solely upon the vagaries of the market to deliver (national) prosperity (see also Chang, 2002). Modern commentators might note parallels here with Lord Michael Heseltine, who, as President of the Board of Trade and Deputy Prime Minister, once famously promised to 'intervene before breakfast, dinner, and tea' for British industry, at the Conservative Party Conference in 1992. Lord Heseltine has long been an important advocate of state intervention to enhance national competitiveness and it was his recent report, 'No Stone Unturned: In Pursuit of Growth' (2012), that has helped to place industrial policy back on the political agenda.

Thus industrial policy, after a long hiatus, is back in vogue at regional, national, and European Union (EU) levels, driven by concerns over competitiveness, globalization, de-industrialization, unemployment, and the comparatively slow growth of the British and EU economies especially in this post-recession phase (see Bailey et al., 2012). At the same time, industrial policy has been seen as a catalyst for designing economic recovery strategies at regional, national, and EU levels as well as being a concerted strategy to develop new 'clean-tech' industries to tackle environmental challenges.

It should be noted that the EU entered the GFC scoring lower productivity growth than the US while facing an erosion of its competitiveness with respect to economies such as those of the US and Japan in top-end markets and other Asian economies in lower-end markets. As noted, the GFC highlighted the fragility of some states' and localities' economic development paths and the unbalanced nature of their economies, in terms of an over-reliance on sectors such as retail, financial services, and construction, to the detriment of manufacturing. This also suggests an accompanying need for greater economic diversity so as to avoid over-dependencies on certain sectors, and a better balance of ownerships forms (e.g. foreign and domestic, limited liability, and mutuals), so as to help better insulate economies from the financial contagion spread by globalization.

Partly as a result of the GFC, industrial policy has been 'officially' rediscovered (even if many academics had in any case continued to explore its role and significance). The European Commission (2010), for example, proposed an 'integrated' industrial policy for an era of globalization that saw competitiveness and sustainability as core pillars, and has more recently highlighted the need for an 'industrial renaissance' (European Commission, 2014). But what should be the shape of such an 'integrated' industrial policy in the wake of the GFC and how can industrial policy help deliver an industrial renaissance, rebalance economies, help support sustainable development, and catalyse new technologies and innovations whilst learning lessons from past experience and debate? In addition, how could/should such an integrated industrial policy relate to regional policy?

In part this shift to a more integrated industrial policy has been informed by developments in the academic and policymaking debate and discussion on industrial policy in recent years. This debate has moved beyond a narrow 'market failure' perspective to consider wider market and systemic failure issues that necessitate a role for industrial policy (information, coordination, missing linkages) (Rodrik, 2009) as well as a broadening to consider evolutionary/systems-based views, as Pitelis notes in this volume. And over the last decade or so, the interlinked scholarly debates on regionalism, clusters, and systemic innovation (both national and regional) have also shaped the objectives and actions of policymaking. Indeed, interventions have targeted spatially defined sets of networks of firms, attempting to leverage their value chain relationships, systemic innovation processes or their reliance on common services and goods to be delivered through collective public or private actions. Cluster policy, innovation policy, and regional policy have all supported the growth and survival of firms and industries by helping them seize the opportunities of increasingly global networks of knowledge, production, and demand.

In this regard, Aiginger (2007), for example, characterizes 'systemic industrial policy' as that which supports basic education, training, and entrepreneurship, promotes FDI and exports in catching-up economies and merges with innovation strategies, cluster policy, and dynamic competitiveness in higher income countries. It thus 'goes beyond combating market failures. It acknowledges limited knowledge of policy-makers, mutual learning and co-operation between firms, institutions and government' (Aiginger, 2007: 297). In this sense, commonly adopted definitions of industrial policy are too narrow, and there is a need to recognize that 'good practice' IP is much more holistic in its approach and focuses simultaneously on both demand and supply side factors of industrial development. It is across this terrain that this volume aims to make a contribution in the UK context.

Furthermore, unlike some naive Keynesian demand management approaches and/or neoclassical supply side policies (such as promoting 'flexible' labour markets and/or tax reform) where the tendency is to focus upon either the demand or supply side of the economy, industrial policy has the potential to offer an integrated and coordinated approach to economic management. An active industrial policy may not only create and sustain domestic employment (thus sustaining demand, via investment and consumption multipliers), but it can also raise domestic industrial capacity and capability (a supply side measure) for future growth.[1] There is, therefore, a strong case for UK industrial

---

[1] Macroeconomic fiscal approaches that merely seek to raise (consumption) demand are likely to meet domestic capacity constraints, with excess demand met by imports and global outsourcing (thus generating a subsequent fiscal and balance of payments crisis). Supply side measures largely focused upon 'labour market' flexibility will largely depress wage rates and employment stability, and will dampen demand and generally lead to stagnation.

policy to be afforded an institutional status similar to both UK monetary policy, which, since 1997, is managed through an independent Bank of England, and fiscal policy, which is monitored by the Office for Fiscal Responsibility (established in 2010). At the very least, industrial policy could be 'stabilized' through regular strategic, long-term reviews as the Wright Review (2014) has suggested.

Questions, however, arise concerning the appropriate industrial policy framework to adopt in rebalancing the UK economy. This is not easy since industrial policy is a wide-ranging concept and encompasses a range of policy instruments. These include (but are not limited to) support for 'infant industry', trade policies, science and technology policies, state procurement, regulation (and deregulation), and anti-trust policy, merger policy, policies in relation to foreign direct investment, intellectual property rights, the allocation of financial resources and, in recent years, the development of clusters and regions (see also Cimoli et al., 2009). This is an extensive set of policies and throughout history, most states across the world have employed, to varying degrees, one or more (often concurrently) of these policy instruments to support industry and growth (see Chang, 2002). For policy-makers, the salient question is to assess the scale (and probable effectiveness) of industrial policies in meeting desired objectives before their implementation (see David Coates's chapter in this volume).

One of the main aims of this book to critically inform and challenge policy-makers, policy think-tanks, industrialists, trade unions, academics, and other stakeholders in framing the future course for industrial policy in the UK, set within international perspectives. In this regard, the contributors to this book have a long-standing interest in industrial policy and their expertise has often been called upon to advise governments and policy-makers from around the world. Several of the authors of chapters in this volume have participated in the European Network on Industrial Policy (EUNIP) which has, over many years, stimulated and encouraged debates around industrial policy (see for example Bianchi et al., 1990; Sugden, 1993; Cowling, 2000; Bailey et al., 2012). Thus the following chapters offer a broad set of perspectives on the many facets of industrial policy, including reflections upon past experiences of industrial policy (from across the globe) and critically analysis and advice upon contemporary UK industrial policy issues. Early versions of these chapters were discussed at a one-day workshop held at the Marx Memorial Library, in Clerkenwell, London, held on 3 February 2014 and kindly sponsored by both the University of Bath's Institute for Policy Research and Oxford University Press. We hope the chapters in this volume stimulate further debate and lead to the UK adopting a more proactive stance in relation to rebalancing its economy and socio-economic development, more widely.

1.2 CHAPTER CONTENTS

The individual chapters of this book, subject of course to the caveat of overly simplifying lines of demarcation, divide broadly into six sections, with respect to their place within the thematic structure of the collection as a whole. The development of themes and issues is best understood via a short overview of content.

1.2.1 Part 1: Perspectives on Industrial Policy

The book begins with four chapters offering broad, reflective, historical, and contemporary perspectives on industrial policy. Chapter 2 by Christos Pitelis presents a wide critical discussion on the various perspectives and principles of developmental industrial policy (DIP) and in doing so, explores its close links with international trade policy (ITP). The chapter proceeds by then identifying and subsequently debunking ten myths-false dichotomies associated with the debate on developmental industrial policy. Instead, Pitelis proposes an alternative set of principles (for developmental industrial policy) based upon utilizing/integrating contemporary concepts, such as co-opetition, glocalization, manuservices and public–private polity partnerships. Exploring these concepts more deeply, the chapter suggests business policy and strategy can be carefully used to inform contemporary developmental industrial policy. Pitelis concludes that extant political and governance structures notwithstanding, such an approach to industrial policy could provide firms and national economies with genuine sustainable competitive advantage.

In Chapter 3, David Coates provides an evaluative review of post-Second World War industrial policy in the advanced Western economies and Japan. The chapter documents how industrial policy goals have shifted over time, with policy choices reflecting different national economic (and political) priorities and capitalist structures. There has, however, been a generic shift—across nations—towards employing a narrower set of indirect policy instruments, with the broader goal of increasing market competition. Nevertheless, in spite of the rhetoric of the dominant neo-liberal paradigm, industrial policy did continue to play an important (albeit often hidden) role, as (Western) governments continually sought to support particular sectors. The chapter concludes, sanguinely, that in the aftermath of the financial crisis (2008) and recognition the (UK) economy is unbalanced, there is once again a greater acceptance of a more focused industrial policy (although it is less clear as to what form this might take).

In Chapter 4, Andrew Bowman, Julie Froud, Sukhdev Johal, Adam Leaver, and Karel Williams are rather more sceptical of the efficacy of industrial policy to rebalance the UK economy. They raise the usual concerns about the UK's secular decline but in doing so they also argue that new industrial strategies overly focused upon promoting national systems of innovation are overly optimistic and are somewhat misplaced. The argument here is the UK lacks the policy levers to deliver a major transformation (in manufacturing performance) and that such strategies fail to account for the severity of regional and social imbalances that have become more entrenched since the late 1970s (which act as real constraints to 'rebalancing regional growth'). In contrast, they suggest a reframing of industrial policy with a focus upon the 'foundational economy' which produces everyday goods and services (such as health, education, transport, and retail banking) and is distributed according to population. To support this 'foundational economy' they call for a form of 'social licensing' for the production and delivery of such services within a more regionally focused UK economy.

The final chapter (5) in this section, by Mushtaq Khan, also recognizes the importance of ensuring innovation policies are more closely aligned with the development of domestic competitive manufacturing capabilities so as to realize the potential of new ideas (and technologies) in terms of competitive products and industrial development. In this regard, the chapter draws comparative lessons from the success and failures of industrial policy in Asia in the development of organizational and technological capabilities. The chapter points out that, while the UK (and other the Western economies) still retain a lead over many emerging (Asian) economies in the organization of innovation, de-industrialization has weakened the UK's ability to exploit the tacit knowledge embedded in the organizational routines of manufacturing firms. As a result, the UK has fallen even further behind in terms of its capacity to regain a broad base of competitive firms, and this raises the risk that successful innovation strategies will be accompanied by the offshoring of manufacturing elsewhere. In trying to acquire (or re-acquire) firm-level competitive capabilities, there is much the UK can learn from the rapid industrialization of Asian economies since the Second World War. Throughout, the chapter reminds us that, critical to the success of industrial policy, is the ability of policy-makers to correctly identify and target the most important constraints facing a particular country, and to address these problems utilizing appropriate policy instruments within specific local, political, and institutional contexts. Finally, the chapter argues that a viable industrial policy strategy should not be afraid to, in part, be 'experimentalist', with different policy instruments being trialled and policies redesigned/reformed in the light of experience.

1.2.2 Part 2: Finance for Industry, Entrepreneurship, and Innovation

Part 2 considers the UK's financial architecture and its role in the wider economy. In theory, the UK finance sector ought to facilitate productive investment in industry; yet, even before the financial crisis of 2008 began to unfold, the sector had become heavily skewed towards promoting the (short-term) interests of large global financial institutions (and global capital), which became 'too big to fail'. Malcolm Sawyer's (Chapter 6) evaluation of the UK financial sector educes these concerns, where he argues the financialization processes of the last thirty years—and the fixation on financial innovations (such as derivatives and securitization)—have been detrimental to UK industry. An industrial strategy requires a finance sector that can serve the wider economy and channel investment into socially desirable directions, which aid sustainable economic development (for example, in green technologies). For this to occur, Sawyer suggests a restructuring of the financial sector is required, which is less prone to instability (and short-termism) and more focused upon commercial banking (and allocating funds to industry). The chapter offers several proposals to achieve this, including financial transaction taxes to reduce (high frequency) speculation (and promote stability), the separation (and ring fencing) of investment and commercial banking, guided lending (towards strategic sectors) and (regional) development banks (for industry).

Such restructuring would also involve promoting a more diverse financial sector, which is the focus of Jonathan Michie's chapter (7). Diversity facilitates greater stability, since it reduces systemic risk within the financial system. Yet, since the demutualization of a number of large building societies in the 1990s, corporate diversity has declined in the UK financial sector, with deleterious consequences; not one former building society has survived as an independent company and several were 'bailed out' by the state during the financial crisis. In contrast, the remaining building society sector was relatively unscathed. For Michie, a new industrial strategy would therefore include a greater role for mutual societies—including building societies—in the financial sector (and indeed, the wider economy); since such societies have very different objectives to traditional profit-maximizing financial institutions, they may better serve local businesses and communities, while also acting as a constraint upon corporate power (in the financial sector). Michie suggests the calculation of an index (the Michie–Oughton index), to be used to measure the extent of diversity within the financial sector; such an indicator could guide policy-makers in achieving wider corporate diversity.

The financing of small and medium-sized businesses (SMEs) is particularly critical in industrial strategy, since such firms are widely recognized as being a vital component in employment creation, innovation, and growth. One of the main vehicles of finance for SMEs is venture capital, yet problems of asymmetric information, risk assessment, and the appropriation of rents (from innovation) often lead to a sub-optimal allocation of funding for early start-up firms. To address this 'financing gap', several governments across the world have set up 'hybrid' venture capital schemes, whereby the state acts as a special limited partner and channels funds into capital constrained, but high potential, young enterprises through private sector venture capital firms. In Chapter 8, Gordon Murray, Weixi Liu, and Marc Cowling explore the efficacy of the Australian scheme (the Australian Innovation Investment Fund (IIF)) through a comparative econometric study (1997–2009) of the performance of firms accessing funding from the scheme and those funded solely through private venture capital. The study's results reveal significant support for the scheme, with IIF-supported firms more likely to be start-ups in high technology-based sectors and also more likely to access follow on finance as their business grows. Critically, they also find the IFF does not 'crowd out' private venture funding. They conclude such hybrid schemes should be an important facet of industrial policy, since they can assist in developing a nation's entrepreneurial and innovation infrastructure.

The final chapter (9) in this section by Mariana Mazzucato focuses upon funding for innovation-led growth. Mazzucato argues that funding for innovation is largely a collective endeavour, whereby the state (and public funds) often play a critical role in facilitating 'open innovation'. Indeed, she argues this has particularly been the case in the US, where radical innovations—such as Apple's iPhone—have been (both directly and indirectly) supported from state investments. This demonstrates the efficacy of public and private sector collaboration in promoting 'smart' innovation; such (sectoral) initiatives are now widely regarded as 'smart' industrial policy. A problem arises in that while the state often bears the risks of such investments, it does not reap the full rewards (in part, because transnational corporations can easily reduce their tax liabilities). This is problematic, since the state is burdened with the costs of innovation, while rewards are effectively privatized; this in turn reduces the state's ability to finance future projects. Mazzucato favours a more 'inclusive' approach to innovation led growth, whereby the state retains a degree of ownership in the intellectual property created from its investments. The returns (or royalties) could then be reinvested into new growth generating projects, thus facilitating a new virtuous dynamic.

1.2.3 Part 3: Employment Issues and Industrial Policy

Part 3 of this volume considers employment issues in the context of a modern economy. In doing so, it seeks to explore how industrial policy might be utilized to provide greater opportunities for employees to participate in the workplace (and the labour market), and thus add to the vitality of the wider economy. It is now recognized that wider employee engagement—and indeed more inclusive employment practices generally—can enhance productivity and firm performance. Four elements of widening employment participation are considered: skills and training, higher education, employment rights, and employee representation on corporate boards.

In Chapter 10, Francis Green and Geoff Mason explore how skills and training policies can be tailored to enhance innovation within UK firms. In doing so, they identify a 'skills deficit' within the UK economy; that is a relatively low level of employer demand and employee supply of skills required for an innovation-led economy. Moreover, the UK also suffers from a corresponding 'training deficit' (a relatively low level of training supply and demand) which entrenches the 'skills deficit'. These deficits not only adversely affect the relative performance of the UK economy, but act as barrier in rebalancing the UK economy towards higher valued added (innovation-led) activities. The authors attribute the problem in part to misconceptions in the UK in relation to 'skill shortages' and the performance of the education system which informs managerial attitudes to training (which is largely inadequate). They suggest a new approach to skills policy, based not only upon raising high level (innovation) skills but also, as part of an integrated industrial strategy, by raising high level skills demand among employers. This in turn, should help to rebalance the economy and move it onto a higher innovation plane.

Raising the demand for high level skills (within the UK) is also an issue for Phillip Brown, Sin Yi Chueng, and Hugh Lauder. However, their chapter (11) raises concerns about 'the global auction for jobs', which is eroding the returns to investments in human capital. Focusing upon the recent expansion of higher education, and the global growth in the number of graduates seeking employment, they argue that globalization and, in particular, the footloose activities of transnational corporations has led to a global restructuring of the labour market. A 'global auction for jobs' has emerged, not only in low-skill employment, but also in high skill employment, and which is beginning to 'squeeze' (graduate) job opportunities and incomes, particularly in Western economies. Moreover, this is combined with a restratification of knowledge based (graduate) work, which is generating wider income dispersions between new (chosen) elites and other graduates (many of whom are employed in 'non-graduate' work). In this regard, the challenge is to move away from traditional (neoclassical) human capital approaches and for industrial policy to help facilitate a greater supply of graduate type jobs.

In Chapter (12), Tim Page and Janet Williamson explore UK corporate governance and put forward the case for greater worker representation (voice) on UK corporate boards. Unlike other countries, notably Germany, UK workers are typically excluded when corporations take strategic decisions (such as the relocation of production or in takeover decisions) that affect the orientation of the company (and the livelihoods of the workforce). Moreover, a prevailing feature of UK corporate governance is a high volatility in shareholdings (and ownership) with transient shareholder interests typically focused upon maximizing short-term profits (and share price) at the expense of long-term business success. Indeed, 'short-termism' has long been recognized as an endemic problem in UK business, which results in relatively lower investments in R&D, training, and other long-term investment strategies compared with other European-based companies. The authors argue that greater worker representation on corporate boards is thus an important adjunct for industrial policy, since it may act as a constraint upon corporate power (and 'short-termist' strategies). Indeed, they point to a variety of evidence from other countries where worker representation and labour-management partnerships have enhanced long-term company productivity and performance, with firms generally pursuing a much broader (and long-term) company strategy with a greater focus upon innovation-led, higher value added activities. The chapter concludes by (briefly) exploring some of the different models of worker representation on corporate boards, and sets out a tentative set of proposals for reforming UK corporate governance.

Promoting a greater consensus between business and employee interests is also the focus of Paul Latreille and Richard Saundry's chapter (13), which explores the case of employment rights within a new industrial policy framework. The chapter considers the recent reforms to employment law and practice, providing a critical assessment of recent policies that are based on the (unfounded) notion that (further) deregulation is likely to raise business competitiveness by reducing employment costs (such as those arising from (unfounded) litigation claims and employment tribunals). The chapter argues that while such policies are typically predicated on a 'race to the bottom', the weakening of employment rights can actually be counter-productive, since it can lead to 'lower employee commitment, more perfunctory performance, and high rates of employee turnover', thus adversely impacting upon company performance. Latreille and Saundry argue there is a need to recognize the long-term mutual interests between

employers and employees, and resolve conflicts possibly through greater internal mediation and workplace institutions. The chapter concludes that a 'high road' industrial
strategy might therefore be enhanced by promoting a greater balance in the respective
interests and rights of employers and employees which, in turn, is likely to foster greater
trust, engagement, and mutual productivity gains within UK companies.

1.2.4 Part 4: Industrial Policy and Regional Development

Part 4 considers the role of industrial policy in regional development. Regions offer the
potential for dynamic agglomeration and sources of growth; the challenge for industrial policy is to nurture the conditions to facilitate this agglomeration and dynamism.
It is within this context that David Bailey, Keith Cowling, and Philip Tomlinson
(Chapter 14) explore the potential for industrial policy to rejuvenate UK cities. The
chapter draws inspiration from the earlier work of Jane Jacobs, who saw cities as centres
of creativity and experimentation. The chapter argues that while agglomeration (of activity) is necessary, it is not sufficient to generate the Jacobian externalities to facilitate
innovation and sustainable development. The authors argue cities require a diverse
economic base to generate serendipitous cross-sector spillovers, and this springs from
a relatively diffuse economic governance structure. Unfortunately, many UK cities
(outside London and the Greater South East) have struggled to maintain their earlier
economic dynamism and are largely 'locked in' to mono-sectoral profiles, which reflect
a long-standing over-reliance (for investment and employment opportunities) upon
corporate entities. The chapter concludes by suggesting that much can be learned from
the experience of industrial districts in generating a new dynamic within UK cities,
with new districts—with coherence in a city environment—possibly forming the basis
for UK industrial strategy.

Complementing this, in Chapter 15, David Bailey, Paul Hildreth, and Lisa De Propris
attempt to address the question: What would a genuinely 'place-based' strategy mean
for industrial and regional policy in England? It draws on the international literature to
outline the basic foundations of 'place-based' policy approaches, drawing out two key
features, particularly as they relate to 'institutions' and to 'knowledge'. After examining
key concepts in the 'place-based' policy literature, such as 'communities of interest' and
'capital city and local elites', they show how such concepts might be interpreted in a UK
(or English) policy context. The chapter then discusses a 'place-based' approach towards
an understanding of the role of knowledge, linked to debates around 'smart specialization' and contemporary industrial policy. In doing so it shows why there is an important
'missing space' in *local growth* between the 'national' and the 'local' and how that space
might be filled through appropriate institutions and policy responses. Overall, the
chapter outlines what a 'place-based' approach might mean in particular for Whitehall,
in changing its approach towards sub-national places and for local places, in seeking to
realize their own potential. Furthermore, it outlines what the 'missing space' is and how

it might be filled, and therefore what a 'place-based' sub-national economic strategy might address.

1.2.5 Part 5: Regulation, FDI, and Industrial Policy

In Part 5, the book explores issues relating to regulation, FDI, and industrial policy. Privatization led to a major restructuring of the UK industrial economy, and while one of the aims of the process was to introduce greater competition, it also saw the introduction of new regulatory bodies to curb the abuse of monopoly power. In this regard, regulation can be an efficacious industrial policy instrument. In Chapter 16, Michael Waterson provides a considered evaluation of the regulatory regimes and ensuing competition within several UK utility industries, which had been privatized. One of the salient points emerging from his analysis is for policy-makers to exercise greater care (and attention) in implementing policy which alters industrial structures since such changes are often very difficult to reverse (in the event of policy mistakes). Moreover, policy should also be aware that firms will act strategically in reaction to new regulations and incentives, which in itself can compromise policy objectives. This is, of course, a wider lesson for industrial policy per se.

The issue of foreign direct investment is considered by Nigel Driffield, Sandra Lancheros, and Yama Temouri (Chapter 17). Since the 1980s, UK policy has tended to regard inward FDI largely as a de facto regional policy, in generating (and maintaining) employment in declining UK regions, although there has been relatively less attention to the potential benefits of inward FDI for technology transfer (and generating spillover effects). Indeed, to some extent, the authors argue these goals are mutually exclusive. The chapter evaluates policy towards inward FDI and argues for a more nuanced approach, with policy (and policy instruments) being applied more discriminately on a case by case basis. The chapter also concludes by suggesting policy should facilitate a closer alignment between the strategic priorities of (UK) regions and the strategic interests of inward investors.

In Chapter (18), Ajit Singh, Gurjmail Singh, David Bailey, and Helena Lenihan provide an overview of the literature on the market for corporate control and nature of takeovers before offering some suggestions as to how takeover policy might be developed in the UK context. The chapter first examines the dynamics of takeovers and mergers by charting six great historical takeover 'waves'. It examines why takeover waves exist, and why they rise and fall. It then examines the market for corporate control in civil law and non-civil law countries before discussing the determinant of share prices, the market for corporate control and nature of the takeover mechanism. It finishes by examining the recent debates on takeover policy stimulated by the Cadbury and AstraZeneca cases before offering some suggestions as to how takeover policy might be developed in the UK context, for example through 'throwing some sand' in the wheels of the takeover machine and through the adoption of a new 'Public Interest Test'.

1.2.6 Part 6: Industrial Policy and Sustainable Development

One potentially ripe area for industrial policy is to promote green technology. This is not only attractive to generate employment and rebalanced growth, but is also essential for sustainable socio-economic development. This is the main thrust of Karl Aiginger's chapter (19), which begins with reviewing the premise for industrial policy to revive European manufacturing. In doing so, there is a critical appraisal of 'old industrial policies' through which he makes the case for a new coordinated approach that essentially focuses upon 'high road' strategies and competitiveness. For Aiginger, a critical adjunct is for a more holistic approach to assessing progress measures which go 'beyond GDP', so as to better account for wider social welfare, such as the environment, in policy. Within this framework, there is significant scope for industrial policy to develop new green technologies, while simultaneously achieving wider societal goals on climate change. Aiginger argues these challenges might be met by setting incentives, particularly those impacting on technical progress (for example, to make it less labour-saving and more energy-saving) and through the role of governments in the education and research sectors in promoting greater public awareness especially with regard to socio-ecological transition within the economy.

The final chapter (20) by Dan Coffey and Carole Thornley also explores the prospects for aligning industrial policy with the green agenda. Their analysis, however, highlights significant difficulties in shifting industrial policy from being largely 'horizontal' in terms of supporting a broad range of sectors to one which is targeted upon specific sectors, where there is a concomitant aim of reducing carbon emissions. By considering recent policy initiatives in the UK, they argue that beyond the rhetoric of promoting low carbon industrial development, political and economic constraints often undermine sustainable economic development. As the chapter highlights, significant stresses arise in matching traditional industrial policy goals (such improvements to the balance of trade, employment, and growth) with sustainability outcomes. Indeed, Coffey and Thornley warn that, while there are potential gains in a policy emphasis upon sustainability, in seeking to supplement a 'horizontal' framework there is a risk policy outcomes will critically ignore important cross-sector linkages and as such, 'a preoccupation with industrial growth will trump sustainability'. The chapter illustrates these contradictions through a careful policy review of the UK car industry, which is branch-arm of a global industry and a major source of carbon emissions, and where sustainability is a major theme. The authors conclude by noting the recent UN Environmental Programme (UNEP) initiative on new business models (and product service systems), and they call for further research on market redesign for sustainability.

References

Aiginger, K. (2007). 'Industrial Policy: A Dying Breed or a Re-emerging Phoenix', *Journal of Industry, Competition and Trade* 7(3/4), 297–323.

Bailey, D., Lenihan, H., and Arouzo-Carod, J.-M. (eds). (2012). *Industrial Policy after the Crisis: Regional, National and International Perspectives*. London: Routledge.

Bianchi, P., Cowling, K., and Sugden, R. (eds). (1990). *Europe's Economic Challenge: Analyses of Industrial Strategy and Agenda for the 1990s*. London: Routledge.

Chang, H.-J. (2002). *Kicking Away the Ladder: Development Strategy in Historical Perspective: Policies and Institutions for Economic Development in Historical Perspective*. London: Anthem Press.

Cimoli, M., Dosi, G., and Stiglitz, J. E. (2009). *Industrial Policy and Development: The Political Economy of Capabilities Accumulation*. Oxford: Oxford University Press.

Cowling, K. (ed.). (2000). *Practical Proposals for Industrial Policy in Europe*. London: Routledge.

Cowling, K., Dunn, S., and Tomlinson, P. R. (2011). 'Global Imbalances, the Present Crisis and Modern Capitalism: A Structural Approach', *Journal of Post Keynesian Economics* 33(4), 575–600.

Cowling, K. and Tomlinson, P. R. (2011). 'Post the Washington Consensus: Economic Governance and Industrial Strategies for the 21st Century', *Cambridge Journal of Economics* 35(5), 831–52.

European Commission. (2010). *An Integrated Industrial Policy for the Globalisation Era Putting Competitiveness and Sustainability at Centre Stage*, Communication from the Commission to the European Parliament, the Council, the European Economic and Social Committee, and the Committee of the Regions, Brussels, COM (2010) 614.

European Commission. (2014). *For a European Industrial Renaissance*, Communication from the Commission to the European Parliament, the Council, the European Economic and Social Committee, and the Committee of the Regions, Brussels, COM (2014) 014final.

Heseltine, M. (2012). 'No Stone Unturned: In Pursuit of Growth', <https://www.gov.uk/government/publications/no-stone-unturned-in-pursuit-of-growth>.

Hutton, W. and Lee, N. (2012). 'The City and the Cities: Ownership, Finance and the Geography of Recovery', *Cambridge Journal of Regions, Economy and Society* 5, 325–37.

Irwin, Douglas A. (2004). 'The Aftermath of Hamilton's "Report on Manufactures"', *The Journal of Economic History* 64(3), 800–21.

List, F. (1841[1904]). *The National System of Political Economy*, tr. S. S. Lloyd. London: Longmans.

Rodrik, D. (2009). *One Economics, Many Recipes: Globalization, Institutions, and Economic Growth*. Princeton, NJ: Princeton University Press.

Sugden, R. (ed.). (1993). *Industrial Economic Regulation: A Framework and Exploration*. London: Routledge.

Wade, R. (2009). 'From Global Imbalances to Global Reorganisations', *Cambridge Journal of Economics* 33, 539–62.

Wright, M. (2014). 'Making the UK a Globally Competitive Investment Environment. The Wright Review of Advanced Manufacturing in the UK and its Supply Chain', <http://thewrightreport.net/report.html>.

PART I

PERSPECTIVES
ON INDUSTRIAL
POLICY

CHAPTER 2

....

DIP-LY SPEAKING

Debunking Ten Myths, and a Business Strategy-Informed Developmental Industrial Policy

....

CHRISTOS PITELIS

2.1 INTRODUCTION

....

THE current financial, sovereign debt, economic, and indeed moral, crisis, alongside the success of countries such as the BRICs (Brazil, Russia, India, and China), which have relied on 'state capitalism', has helped contribute to the renewed interest in the role of the state and developmental industrial policy (DIP) in economic development.[1] Following years of ill repute, industrial policy (IP) is no longer seen as a 'dirty word': it is quite openly entertained in fora such as *The Economist* and *Time* magazine. In the latter, for instance, Zakaria (2012) observed that IP is so clearly successful in so many countries, that perhaps we should employ it, despite the fact that we lack a supporting theory.[2] While useful in recognizing the need for microeconomic industrial policy to counterbalance the almost exclusive focus of the policy debate today on macroeconomic policy—notably monetary policy—such statements fail to acknowledge that there is a body of theoretical/conceptual ideas behind DIP—it is just not the neoclassical economics one.

This chapter has four interrelated aims. First, we critically assess extant perspectives and principles of DIPs, in their relationship to international trade policies (ITPs). Second, we aim to debunk ten myths in the DIPs–ITPs debate and propose integrative and/or novel principles instead. Third, we draw upon business strategy in order to

---

[1] See for example, EC (2010, 2011); Aghion et al. (2011); McFadden (2012); *The Economist*, 5 May 2012, 'Going for growth, but how?', 12 May 2012, 'Ode to Growth', and 21 September 'The new intervention'; Warwick (2013).

[2] See F. Zakaria's article in *TIME* magazine, 'The case for making it in the USA', 6 February 2012.

propose a DIP in line with our proposed principles that aims to marry the pursuit of sustainable competitive advantage (SCA) to economic sustainability. Finally, we discuss the very challenging requisite conditions for economic sustainability to ensue under the extant political and governance structures.

2.2 PERSPECTIVES ON DIPS IN THEIR LINK TO INTERNATIONAL TRADE POLICIES (ITPs)

2.2.1 Extant Perspectives on DIPs

The precise definition of industrial policy (IP) has been and remains a matter of dispute (Pitelis, 1994; Warwick, 2013). Generically speaking, IP refers to a set of measures taken by a government that aim to influence the performance of firms, sectors, industries, and clusters towards a desired objective, as well as the financial, human and organizational resources, and organizational and contingency arrangements made in order to implement this objective. IP originally referred to manufacturing, but this has gradually shifted, not least because of the increasing interdependence between manufacturing and services, and even agriculture (Rodrik, 2004). For instance, today firms such as IBM, Rolls-Royce, and Xerox rely on their manufacturing expertise in order to provide specialist services. A number of agro-business clusters involve the co-location and complementarity of agricultural and manufacturing activities (Galvez-Nogales, 2010).

In this context, we can define IP as public policy measures aiming to have an appreciable effect on the performance of manufacturing, directly and/or through impacting on supporting and complementary activities and sectors. In this context, DIP, also referred to as Industrial Strategy (IS), goes beyond IP, in that it involves purposive strategic intent, planning, and actions by the public sector to shape, extend, create, and co-create markets and ecosystems, as opposed to merely setting the 'rules of the game' (institutional framework), or focusing on solving 'market failures'. DIPs can even often help to create 'market failures', so as to foster a wider developmental perspective (Pitelis, 1994; Cowling and Tomlinson, 2011a).

Anti-trust in the USA, or competition policies (CPs), in the above context, refers to the stance governments adopt towards competition and cooperation between firms in sectors and clusters. The boundaries between industrial/competition-anti-trust, and other types of public policies such as trade, technology, innovation, regional, structural, competitiveness, and even macroeconomic, are not always obvious. The closest one can get to a demarcation line is arguably by referring to a government's own perception of what it aims its IP, or DIP and supporting CP to be, alongside the underlying conceptual framework, purportedly informing this perception. This is usually hard to decipher, as it depends on the degree of sophistication, desired involvement, and clarity of the under-lying theory and proposed measures.

In mainstream 'neoclassical' economics, the government's objective is assumed to be the improvement of the welfare of its citizens, which is achieved when scarce resources are allocated efficiently (typically via the price mechanism). Classical and post-Keynes-ian economists instead paid attention to the objective of resource and wealth creation. In their view, efficient resource allocation can lead to wealth creation, but this is neither a necessary nor a sufficient condition. For example, wealth creation can also be achieved by different means, such as through innovation and market extension and creation (Kaldor, 1970)—aspects downplayed by the neoclassical school.[3] On the other hand, a country can manage to allocate its scarce resources efficiently but fail to create new resources through innovation at the same pace as another country, which is not as good in resource allocation, but fares better in resource/wealth creation.

Manufacturing is widely believed to be an important contributor to wealth creation, for reasons such as the high degree of tradability of its products, its positive link with technology, innovation, and productivity growth, and even the close links between manufacturing and services (Kaldor, 1972; Amsden, 2008).

The dominant perspective on IP and anti-trust-CP among economists arguably (and rather inexplicably) still remains the neoclassical IO-based one. In its context, competi-tion is seen as a type of industry structure, which can be perfect (or contestable, Baumol, 1982), or imperfect. 'Perfection' and 'contestability' are defined in terms of price-taking behaviour; hence zero excess profits (Augier and Teece, 2009). According to this view, monopolistic restrictions lead to a misallocation of resources through structural market failures, and engender 'welfare losses' due to monopoly, which need to be removed through CP. This focus on resource misallocation and static 'welfare losses' fails to ac-count for differences in efficiency, such as resources and capabilities, between firms. Such differences can involve differential innovations, the ability to reduce transaction costs, and dynamic capabilities (Teece, 2007). In reality, it is recognized that it is unlikely that markets will be perfectly competitive or contestable (Dixit, 1982). Moreover, the as-sumption that technology, innovation, and capabilities are constant, or simply linked to the type of market structure (Scherer and Ross, 1990), is a major limitation that has been well rehearsed in literature and will not detain us further here (see Pitelis, 1991; Jorde and Teece, 1992).

The dominance of the neoclassical view on CP and IP is currently under question, in part as a result of the emergence and current popularity of the evolutionary, resource, capabilities, knowledge, and systems-based views. This encompasses the diverse group of contributions, all of which share the view that competition should not be seen as a type of market structure, but rather as a process of rivalry, sometimes combined with collusive behaviour (Cowling, 1982) and often characterized by 'creative destruction'

---

[3] For alternative theories of the state, see Pitelis (1994) and North et al. (2006).

(Schumpeter, 1942). Moreover, proponents of this perspective share the view that the classical focus on value and wealth creation, realization, and distribution are important objectives of economics, and that these cannot be achieved merely through efficiency in resource allocation (Pitelis, 2009b). There is also a widespread belief that firms are important contributors to value and wealth creation, that each firm is an individual entity, which differs from other firms in terms of its distinct resources, capabilities, knowledge, and learning potential, and that big business competition can help foster resource, value, and wealth creation (Cimoli et al., 2009).

The lineage of this perspective includes classical and post-Keynesian economists, as well as scholars such as Joseph Schumpeter (1942), and more recently Edith Penrose (1959), George Richardson (1972), and Richard R. Nelson and Sidney G. Winter (1982). Its focus on evolution, knowledge, and innovation, and institutions, as well as its 'systemic' (as opposed to market failure alone), are arguably fashioning a major shift in CP and IP in some policy circles, notably the European (Nubler, 2011) and also the Organisation for Economic Co-operation and Development (OECD) countries (Warwick, 2013) and recently Great Britain (Foresight, 2013).

Implications of the evolutionary, resource, and systems-based perspective for CP and DIP include the need for a broader welfare criterion than maximization of consumer surplus (Mahoney et al., 2009), and that superior capabilities can provide another efficiency-based reason for industrial concentration/consolidation and large firm size. In addition, viewing competition as a dynamic process of creative (or less creative) destruction through innovation implies the need to account for the determinants of innovation, when considering the effects of 'monopoly'. Last, but not least, competition with cooperation (or 'co-opetition'), as in Richardson (1972), implies the need to account for the potential productivity benefits of co-opetition when devising anti-trust policy (Jorde and Teece, 1992).

While engaging more with the neoclassical perspective, and without much recognition of the literature summarized above, more recent work by more eclectic scholars, such as Rodrik (2009), Hausmann et al. (2011), and Aghion et al. (2011), also emphasizes the need for IP, when there exist information asymmetries, missing inputs and coordination failures—which means virtually always! In this context, Stiglitz (2011) pointed to a need to promote learning across the board, thereby creating a learning-based economy. This supports earlier ideas by Cambridge school scholars, such as Luigi Pasinetti (see Pasinetti 2009; Pitelis, 2012c). More recently Warwick (2013) proposed moving beyond earlier approaches to IP towards one that aims to help build systems, networks, and institutions, as well as to align strategic priorities. All these point to an emerging consensus that DIPs matter much more than originally acknowledged by neoclassical theory. As the conservative British Prime Minister David Cameron has put it, government is involved with industry anyway, so we had better focus on how to improve this involvement (Pitelis, 2011), rather than keep debating its existence. Foresight (2013) has since moved in this direction.

2.2.2 DIP-ly Linked International Trade Policies

As we have already noted, DIP is closely linked to other public policies. From these, ITPs have become virtually inseparable from DIPs. This is because DIPs are linked more often than not to the target of improved export performance-current account balances. In this context it is important to discuss perspectives and principles of ITP as they relate to DIPs. In brief, one can distinguish two major economics-based approaches on ITPs: the neoclassical economic theory-based-Washington consensus and the Japanese/East Asian consensus, an apparently more practice-based approach with the more recently discussed 'Beijing Consensus'. A third perspective with important implications on DIPs is the 'systems of innovation'/'varieties of capitalism' perspective. So far this has not been linked to an approach to ITP, but we suggest below that it could be. We start with the first two.

The neoclassical theory focuses first on nationwide growth fostered by appropriate international trade. 'Growth theory' goes back to the landmark contribution of Solow (1956), in which capital and labour could be argued to explain circa 30 per cent of growth, with circa 70 per cent attributed to 'exogenous' technological change. More recently, the 'endogenous growth' theory, with important contributions by Lucas (1988) and Romer (1986, 1990), aimed to capture the endogenous role of 'technical change', human capital, and 'increasing returns'; see Fine (2000) and Solow (2000) for critical assessments. Suffice it to note that neither Solow (from a mainstream neoclassical), nor Fine (from a heterodox) perspective, respectively, is impressed with the conceptual, empirical, and policy implications of the new theory.

In international trade, neoclassical theory built on the idea of Ricardo (1817) that free trade, based on comparative productivity-related advantages, can benefit all nations. The Heckscher, Ohlin, Samuelson (HES) model relied on comparative advantage (abundance) in factor endowments, and supported the Ricardian prescription for free trade, under conditions of non-increasing returns; see Samuelson (1962). More recently, 'new trade' theorists, such as Krugman (1987, 1989), questioned the predictions of the HES model, for situations involving imperfect competition, increasing returns, spillover effects, and first-mover advantages. In such cases, Krugman showed that strategic trade policies in support of some sectors and firms could favour a nation that employs them (Krugman, 1992). On the other hand, however, such policies were said to be prone to conflicts over the division of benefits, and plagued by the possibility of 'government failures' (in identifying the right sectors/firms), as well as retaliations by other nations-trade wars. These could lead to lose-lose situations (Boltho and Allsopp, 1987).[4]

The 'endogenous growth' and 'new trade' theories reinvented ideas from post-Keynesian scholars, such as Kaldor (1970), Pasinetti (1974, 2009), Robinson (1977), and earlier List (1841); see Freeman (2004), Pitelis (2012b). Unlike these last mentioned authors, however, the theories of their modern counterparts are arguably quite static,

---

[4] In the case of high adjustment costs, characterizing the case of inter-industry trade, these problems could be accentuated; see Krugman (1989, 1992), Deraniyagala and Fine (2001).

hence ill-equipped to deal with the creative role of markets (as opposed to their alloca-tive functions, once they exist), and with resource creation, not just through efficient al-location of 'scarce' resources (Pasinetti, 2009; Pitelis, 2012c). For Stiglitz (2001), this approach to development 'misunderstands the nature of the transformation itself—a transformation of society, not just of the economy' (p. xiv). This weakens their useful-ness in providing policy prescriptions; see Kaldor (1972), Audretsch (1989), North (1994), Amsden (1997), Nelson and Winter (2002), Freeman (2004), Rodrik (2005), and more recently Coase (2012). The policy prescriptions for catching up countries, deriving from the conceptual foundations of the neoclassical economics perspective, have been encapsulated in variants of the so-called Washington and post-Washington Consensus. These emphasize the role of free markets, free trade, privatization, and deregulation; see Williamson (1990). Their record has been questionable; see Stiglitz (2001), Rodrik (2005), Serra and Stiglitz (2008), Cowling and Tomlinson (2011a).

A second approach on ITP is that adopted by the Japanese government during the post-Second World War reconstruction, by the 'tiger' economies of East Asia, and more recently by China. Hence the approach can be defined as the 'Japanese/East Asian' (Pite-lis, 2007). An important characteristic of the Japanese/East Asian approach, was the DIP of the state in partnership with business, and with the explicit aim to restructure the economy and create competitive advantages, as opposed to solely leveraging existing comparative ones (Lin and Chang, 2009). Elements of the industrial competitiveness strategies of Japan, devised and implemented by the Ministry of Economy, Trade and Industry (METI, formerly known as Ministry of International Trade and Industry—MITI), included the targeting and support of specific firms and sectors, perceived to be important in terms of high value-added, high income elasticity of demand, and oligo-polistic structures with high profit margins. These were protected from international competition through managed-trade policies. Intra-sector competition was managed too, in that in each sector the major players should be not too many in order to allow for critical mass and reduce resource dissipation, but not too few either, so as to avoid collu-sive practices and engender workable competition. In effect, that was managed, locally based big-business competition. To ensure the flow of technology in the absence of for-eign direct investment (FDI), which was discouraged, MITI pursued a policy of buying licenses from foreign firms. To foster competition for big players, hence a more level-playing field, MITI required that firms purchasing licences would make them accessible to smaller players; see Johnson (1982), Best (1990), Pitelis (1994, 1998), Cowling and Tomlinson, (2000, 2011b), and Freeman (2004).

In addition to the above state-orchestrated policies, Japanese firms pursued a strategy of growth and market share acquisition, not short-term profit/'shareholder value' maxi-mization, in the expectation that through scale, learning, and increasing returns, they could eventually outperform their western 'rivals' (Best, 1990). Additional characteris-tics of this approach included innovative business practices, for example just-in-time, life time employment, worker participation, and total quality management. These have been widely discussed in literature and were felt by many scholars to have contributed to the remarkable performance of the Japanese economy, up to the late 1980s, when it was leading global markets in sectors such as electronics, semiconductors, and automotives; see Amsden (1989), Aoki (1990), Shapiro and Taylor (1990), Wade (1990), Grabowski (1994); Freeman (2004).[5] Variants of the Japanese approach were adopted by countries such as South Korea, Taiwan, and Singapore, and, more recently, by China (Chang, 1994; Nolan, 2001; Lin, 2011), as well as newer 'tigers', such as Thailand, Malaysia, Indonesia (Jomo et al., 1997), and Vietnam (Chesier and Penrose, 2007). As compared with the Japanese approach, smaller economies, including Taiwan, Singapore, and Malaysia, chose to encourage FDI, as much as practicable and in a way that was perceived to be aligned to the overall international competitiveness strategy (Pitelis, 1994; Jomo et al., 1997).[6]

The Chinese DIP arguably represents a synthesis and enrichment of previous experiences with the ubiquitous 'Chinese characteristics'. For Rodrik (2005) this included institutional innovations that were seen as fit for purpose and worked up to a point (such as Town and Villages Enterprises), while for Lin (2011) it was the gradualist comparative advantage-friendly approach that did the trick. No one questioned the use of DIPs by China, or its leveraging of 'state capitalism', and its economic growth record, unprecedented in human history. This is despite different views as to the extent to which the policy was comparative advantage-following or defying (Lin and Chang, 2009), and of course on whether it was sustainable.

The apparent economic success of the Chinese approach, and its more recent influence in other emerging economies, notably in African countries, has led to talk of a 'Beijing Consensus', which is meant to be more pragmatic, experimental, business-like, and arm's length (for example, without the 'conditionality' imposed by Western countries and institutions). Despite important criticisms, not least on issues relating to environmental, social, and eventually economic sustainability, commentators across the board now widely recognize that the Chinese economic miracle is unlikely to have been effected without state capitalism and DIPs (Lin and Chang, 2009; Rodrik, 2009; Cowling and Tomlinson, 2011a).

A third approach with application to DIPs and ITPs includes contributions under the evolutionary, resource-capabilities, and systems-based banners. Much of this has been encapsulated in the 'systems of innovation', agglomeration and clusters, and 'varieties of capitalism'-related literature; see Lundvall (1988), Krugman (1991a, b), Freeman (1995, 2004), Nelson (1995), de la Mothe and Paquet (1997), Fagerberg et al. (2005), Jackson and Deeg (2006), Lundvall (2007), Cimoli et al. (2009), Pitelis (2009b). A characteristic of the evolutionary and systems-based views is a focus on intertemporal efficiency through innovation, alongside a belief that the latter is best promoted through big-business competition and systems-wide linkages and interactions (Freeman, 1995;

---

[5] For a critique of the Japanese model of industrial organization, see Coffey and Tomlinson (2003a and b).

[6] For a more detailed/nuanced account of similarities and differences between the various East Asian countries, see Shapiro and Taylor (1990) and Rodrik (2005). For differences between older and newer 'tigers', see Jomo et al. (1997).

Deeg, 2007). The strength, or otherwise, of the innovation system depends on system-wide linkages and on government policies and institutions. Markets are but a part of the system. They need not be 'perfectly competitive'—indeed, big business competition may well have innovation-promoting advantages; see Nelson (1995), Nelson and Winter (2002). In addition, the existence and promotion of agglomeration and clusters by small and medium-sized enterprises (SMEs) is seen as a potent means to promote linkages, diversity, and innovation (Metcalfe 2003; Wignaraja, 2003; Fagerberg et al., 2005; Cowling and Tomlinson, 2011a; Pitelis, 2012a).

In the above context, the systems view is more in line with the constructed or competitive advantage-based export-oriented approach to international trade. While the 'systems perspective' departs from neoclassical economics in that it focuses on the supply-side, production side of the economy and on microeconomic policies, it shares with neoclassical economic theory a focus on value creation through efficiency, at the expense of value realization, and appropriation/capture. Hence, it fails to pay attention to the possibility that the potential benefits from innovation, efficiency, and value creation need not always be realized in the market place due to lack of effective demand, and/or that any realized benefits may not be captured by the innovators themselves (Teece, 1986, 2006; Pitelis, 2009b). To varying degrees, all three approaches discussed so far fail to deal adequately with the issue of the potential impact of value capture strategies by nations on system-wide sustainability, and hence eventually the sustainability of any competitive advantages enjoyed by the nations in question. We turn to this issue in Section 2.3.

2.3 TEN MYTHS OF DIPs-ITPs AND A BUSINESS STRATEGY-INFORMED DIP FOR SCA

2.3.1 Debunking Ten Myths of DIPs-ITPs

In this section we aim to identify and debunk ten myths in DIPs and ITPs literature and propose integrated and/or alternative principles of DIPs and ITPs, as well as a business strategy-informed DIP that relies on these and aims to marry the acquisition of sustainable competitive advantage (SCA) to economic sustainability.

The literature on DIPs-industrial and business strategy rarely cross. Porter's (1990) Competitive Advantage of Nations 'Diamond', which draws on business strategy and goes on to effectively promote a cluster-based DIP, is an exception. Given that the underlying perspectives on strategy are likely to be of relevance to both types of strategies, private and public, the cross-fertilization of the two types of enquiry may well be advisable. In business strategy, firms are said to aim to obtain SCA, namely the capability to capture created and co-created value in a sustainable way (Pitelis and Teece, 2010). We submit that much of the debate on DIPs and ITPs shares the same objective, albeit under the often-disputed term of 'international competitiveness' (Krugman, 1994). In this context, a focus on SCA is arguably less controversial and in line with the DIPs-ITPs debate on comparative versus competitive advantages. Importantly, SCA includes the word 'sustainable', which is often ignored in extant debates on DIPs-ITPs. Our definition of SCA involves the words 'creation' and 'co-creation' of value, 'capture' of value, and 'sustainability'. As we have noted, extant literature has failed to explore the relationship between value capture and value creation, and co-creation. Hence the focus here will be on value co-creation, value capture, and sustainability. In discussing these, we will also aim to debunk ten myths/principles of engagement in DIPs-ITPs.

We start with the emphasis placed in the 1990s, notably in Europe, on 'horizontal measures' (Pitelis, 1994). These are measures that cover the economy as a whole, that is without a sectoral dimension, such as education, innovation, hard and soft infrastructure (such as efficiency of public sector and institutions), anti-trust and competition-regulation policies, and so on.

Horizontal measures are very important and can afford a huge space for the public sector. When done effectively, they help co-create value with the private sector. This is not merely because of 'market failure', as suggested by IO-based neoclassical economics, but also because of a division of labour based on differential resources, skills, and capabilities. The private sector does not normally run a police and army service, nor does it have the legitimacy to legislate and tax. Calling 'legitimacy'—and 'democracy' for that matter—an outcome of 'market failure' would be rather far-fetched. Hence we submit that both market (and government) failures and differential capabilities can help explain the division of labour and value co-creation between the two (Klein et al., 2013).

Many of the aforementioned functions of the state are recognized as legitimate by free market champions such as Hayek (1944), who added the delineation and protection of rights, defence against foreign armies, and even anti-trust policies based on the notion of 'planning for competition'. A critical question is whether DIPs can go further than that, in a way that it is likely to enhance the capture of co-created value in a sustainable way, whereby the satisfaction of an objective in the short run does not prejudice the achievement of the same objective in the longer run. This presupposes economic sustainability, which at its most basic level is the avoidance of destructive economic crises (Pitelis, 2013). In order to do this, we first try to go beyond a number of apparently contradictory principles of DIPs and ITPs. We claim that these involve false dichotomies and that an integrated view on these apparent dilemmas can afford the basis for a theory-founded, 'efficiency-compatible' DIP that goes beyond Hayek's proposed legitimate scope for public policy. On this basis, we then draw on business strategy's analysis of SCA, in order to propose four specific ingredients of such a DIP that are in line with our proposed synthesis and foster nationwide SCA.

The first apparent contradiction/'myth' is that of market failure versus market guidance by developmental states, which are themselves subject to 'government failures'. We propose that this dichotomy is false and that 'market-guided market guidance' is likely to be a better basis for public policy. That would involve taking into account/'reading' market signals and help build on them whenever desirable. Moreover, when markets are absent, 'market creation and co-creation', sometimes including 'market failure creation and co-creation' (e.g. national champions policies), can be a legitimate function of public policy by imperfect governments aiming to acquire SCA.

Another false dichotomy is that of comparative versus competitive advantages. This is because the very process of economic development by definition involves the upgrading and/or development of new comparative advantages. Hence, while at any given point in time countries can be said to trade based on their CAs, over time their CAs shift, for various reasons, including chance, design, and serendipity. In this context, the more relevant question is whether the evolution of CAs should be CA-friendly or CA-defying. Since development involves the eventual defying of CAs by definition, it is arguable that the best way to defy one's CAs is in a CA-friendly way. This way one builds on extant strength. Of course, this will not always be possible or desirable. In cases such as the emergence of mobile banking in Kenya, the CA was not there—if anything, it was the lack of a CA that triggered a radically new business model that changed fundamentally the face of banking in that country and more widely. Accordingly, while our proposed 'CA-friendly CA defiance' is likely to be advisable at most times, pure CA defiance can both work and be best in certain cases.

Concerning the long-standing debate on DIP on manufacturing versus services (Pitelis, 1994), it is arguable that manufacturing-based services (and sometimes the opposite) are likely to lead to more sustainable advantages, in that they are harder to imitate. This calls for economic diversification (and in the context of its absence in countries such as Great Britain, rebalancing) based on strength and manufacturing-services bridging business model innovations. For example, in the case of the British manufacturer Rolls-Royce, over 50 per cent of its revenues are now accounted for by their servicing of aircraft engines, while engines themselves are sold at near cost, to create lock-in and quasi-captive service recipients-customers.[7] Important in such cases is that servicing requires manufacturing skills, knowledge, and capabilities to start with—this renders the two inseparable in a fundamental, even definitional, manner, hence the emergence of terms such as 'manuservices'.

Concerning the other long-standing debate on large-size and big business competition (advocated by the systems view), in order to gain economies of size/create resources, versus perfect competition advocated (half-heartedly) by the neoclassical perspective in order to achieve efficient resource allocation, it is arguable that efficient resource allocation-respecting resource creation through large and smaller firms and clusters can help marry the advantages of both, as well as the benefits resulting from diversity.

Concerning the debate on the degree of targeting of specific policies, we submit that the horizontal/vertical policies dichotomy is also a false one. In most countries (especially in smaller ones) there is a limited number of sectors that exhibit CAs. Any horizontal measure helps these disproportionally; hence, it involves a vertical dimension, we can call these 'horizontical'. In this context, some outright vertical policies may well help

---

[7] See 'Forging ahead', *The Economist*, 21 April 2012. See also McFadden (2012).

level the playing field, hence be more horizontally friendly than the horizontal ones. This is in line with the recognition by the EU that horizontal policies should target particular sectors (EC, 2010a, 2010b, 2011), but goes further in recognising that extant non-vertically oriented policies may well have undesirable vertical dimensions that need to be considered.

The next apparent dichotomy is that of competition and cooperation, both between firms (and nations) and between the public and the private within or between nations. Here again, involved to varying degrees is *co-opetition*. In particular, the public and the private sectors within an economy can both be arm's length, and even compete (e.g. for the part of profit that goes to taxation), as well as cooperate, for example in the promotion of exports. In this context the issue becomes the identification of the scope for co-opetitive policies that leverage the comparative advantages towards the achievement of a mutually satisfying objective. The public sector, for example, can be best for the provision of 'general purpose technologies', 'public goods', and legitimacy, the creation of laws, institutions and regulation. Private entrepreneurs can be best in commercialization and value capture. Moreover, the often ignored 'third sector' (here the 'polity'), can help provide 'social capital' and cohesion, and foster sustainability (Putnam, 1993; Moran and Ghoshal, 1999; Branston et al., 2006). This questions the private–public dichotomy and calls for *public-private-polity-based partnerships (PPPPs)* (Pitelis, 2013).

Another well-known dichotomy concerns the global/local contradiction. This, too, is false today, in that local advantages help foster global success while with increasing globalization the leveraging of globally based advantages and opportunities is often a prerequisite for local presence and even survival. Hence the issue becomes the identification of the 'optimal mix' between global and local, or *glocal*.

The final dichotomy/myth we deal with concerns the debate on bottom-up versus top-down approach to DIP. We propose *top-down-bottom-up* as a better principle. This is because strategy is set at the top, and the scope for bottom-up is severely limited by co-ordination and incentive, as well as power and capability-related challenges. On the other hand, without the knowledge, involvement and support/guidance by the 'bottom', no top-down strategy is likely to succeed. This is evidence by the theory and evidence on business strategy and strategic entrepreneurship (Klein et al., 2013).

It is worth noting that some of the dichotomies/myths purportedly debunked here and our proposed alternatives, such as co-opetition, glocal, manuservices, and PPPP, are now extant in much of literature. However, our other identified dichotomies/myths are still widely persistent, and in our view quite damaging for taking the debate further, hence our contribution in this direction. Based on this, below we draw on business strategy in order to propose a business strategy-informed DIP for SCA.

2.3.2 A Business Strategy-Informed DIP-IS for SCA

Having tried to debunk the ten dichotomies/myths, we claim below that four proposed ingredients of a business strategy-informed DIP can foster SCA, in a way that goes beyond Hayek's proposed legitimate scope for state intervention, while observing our proposed solutions to the apparent contradictions above. These are the following: first, the identification of extant and potential comparative advantages; second, the adoption of a 'positioning strategy'; third, the use of 'vehicles', such as regional or innovation clusters, and/with appropriate inward FDI; fourth, the identification and development of 'bottleneck' assets and capabilities in the context of specialization within global and local value chains. We develop these ideas below.

Much like private firms, regions and countries need to diagnose their evolving comparative advantages, and decide on whether they wish to 'compete' on their basis or to try to develop new advantages in activities, where they perceive future returns are likely to be more lucrative and/or sustainable. The latter can be defined as constructed, or 'competitive advantages'. Differently put, countries, too, may wish to diagnose what Penrose (1959) called 'productive opportunity'—the dynamic interaction between their internal resources and competencies and the external opportunities and threats. Sometimes, potential future advantages are latent and hard to identify, in some cases they exist only in the minds of some entrepreneur, or even bureaucrat. Take, for example, the case of Mr Toyoda (the founder of the Toyota company), who diversified from textiles to cars, despite the lack of any obvious link between the two, thereby laying the foundations of the Japanese miracle. The desired mix of comparative and competitive advantages for each country requires in-depth investigation and cannot be decided on a priori grounds and without analysis on the ground. Our argument is that this process of CA defiance should be as much CA-friendly as possible, while the resultant market guidance should be market guided. It can often involve market creation and co-creation. The informational and capability requirements for the private sector alone (especially the smaller firms) can be far too high for it to deal with this without government collaboration, hence the CA-friendly defiance of extant CAs through market-guided market guidance and co-creation, is a legitimate function of government and indeed of polity (the 'third sector'), given its local knowledge on the ground.

Once the comparative or competitive advantages have been diagnosed, selected, and (in the case of competitive ones) co-constructed, another decision can involve the country's 'positioning' (Pitelis, 2009b). Countries, like firms, could aim to position themselves along a relative to other countries cost-relative differentiation ('image') spectrum. These can be high or low. The best position to be in is low relative cost/high relative differentiation-'image'. This is normally the case of countries with a high innovation culture and performance—with strong 'systems of innovation', so to speak. This allows them to simultaneously reduce costs (through organizational and institutional innovation), and produce products, services and an 'image' (country differentiation-branding) of a leader, an innovator, a 'quality' player. Small Scandinavian European players, such as Sweden and Denmark, are cases in point; see Freeman (1995) and Fagerberg et al. (2005).

Countries with high relative costs and low differentiation produce expensive goods and services, and the image of the country is of low quality. High relative costs can be due to low innovative capability, poor infrastructure, lack of increasing returns, and/or a weak organizational and institutional configuration. Greece in the 1990s is such an example. Despite Greece's apparent 'competitiveness' in terms of growth rates of GDP being well in excess of other European countries, that performance was not built on supply-side foundations, and was not sustainable (Pitelis, 2012b).

Countries with high costs and high differentiation are likely to be developed, with high technical and operational competencies, but without a strong innovation system. They can have relatively high labour costs, as a result of distributional and welfare policies. The lack of innovative capabilities can be an outcome of organizational and institutional sclerosis, and path dependence—doing already proven things in proven ways. The lack of curiosity and innovation could result in a 'stuck in the middle'/question-mark position. It is likely to characterize developed economies that have relinquished their incentive and capability to innovate. Germany in the 1990s was a case in point.[8] Low relative cost/low relative differentiation countries are also 'stuck in the middle', but are likely to be at an earlier stage of their development—perhaps these are transition or emerging economies. Here, unit costs can be low because of very cheap labour and resource costs, but there is also a lack of differentiation/comparative or competitive advantages, that places them in that category. Eastern European transition economies are an example (Cowling and Tomlinson, 2011a).

The relative costs/differentiation framework can help countries identify ways to improve their competitiveness by reducing unit costs, improving differentiation, and strengthening their innovation capabilities. A small country, for instance, with good climate, low costs of labour, and limited manufacturing capabilities, can aim to achieve high country differentiation (for instance, in specialized, quality tourism), with good service (which need not require much higher costs, if brought about through culture and education), and low costs. Countries with human resources that possess ample time to spare due to lack of employment opportunities, could aim to achieve differentiation through emphasizing service provision—call centres, IT services, and so on. These are 'niche-differentiation' strategies, more appropriate for countries that cannot pursue an across-the-board differentiation strategy (Shapiro and Taylor, 1990).

The idea of positioning comes from Michael Porter (1985) and was originally applied to the case of firms. When applied to the case of nations, positioning involves naturally market-guided market guidance, CA-friendly CA defiance and PPPP-based co-opetition, not least because the informational, capability, and incentive-related requirements for the market or private sector alone to achieve, or even aim for, this, are simply not there. Simply put, nationwide positioning requires institutional and regulatory structures that are without the brief of markets and/or firms but are within the brief of the public, sometimes the polity, and hence of PPPP-based DIPs.

A third ingredient of a business strategy-informed DIP-IS involves 'vehicles', through which supply-side structural international competitiveness can be improved. By 'vehicles' we refer mainly to the inward FDI, and agglomerations of firms and related

---

[8] See interview of G. Schröder by R. Zhong, *Wall Street Journal*, 9 July 2012, titled 'The man who rescued the German economy'.

organisations such as clusters, business ecosystems, and special economic zones (EZs). Independently, and when pursued together, these can foster productivity and SCA (Porter, 1990; Pitelis, 2009a). The sustainability of such competitiveness requires embeddedness. This means that countries should aim to create linkages between a local production base, and FDI, so that FDI does not 'fly' when conditions change, e.g. costs increase.

Besides positioning and branding, it is important for business, regions, and nations to specialize within the emergent global value chains-production systems and/or create (segments of) their own locally based ones to the extent possible, in a way that places them in the position of 'bottleneck' players/assets. These are the players/assets whose contribution to the final product is most critical), so that they can capture the biggest part possible of the globally co-created pie (UNCTAD, 2012). For example, despite her recent success in luxury cars, Britain still only captures a small part of the value added, as a result of 'bottleneck' inputs, which she buys in.[9] Identifying this challenge and helping to address it by bringing into the country the production of such parts can be one solution. Once again, the institutional, regulatory, incentive and resource-capability bases of the market and (even very big) firms are not normally available, and/or within their remit, hence public policy and PPPPs of the type we advocated here can be of help.

The four ingredients should be considered simultaneously. Competitive advantages could be linked to the positioning, clusters and business ecosystems should be diagnosed and upgraded and FDI attracted, in a way that is in line with advantages and supports the pursued positioning. Bottleneck assets and capabilities should be identified and leveraged in the context of specialization within advantages-compatible segments of global value chains.[10] What is advantages-compatible is often beyond the capabilities and resources, even the radar, of many firms, especially SMEs. The public sector can therefore be critical in funding the requisite research and disseminating the information and knowledge to whoever can benefit from it. It can act as a 'public entrepreneur' (Klein et al., 2010, 2013).

Concerning adaptation, advantages and positioning should be reviewed regularly to ensure consistency with evolving circumstances/stages of development. For example, in order to attract high knowledge-intensive FDI, it may be useful to discourage some FDI, for instance by rendering such FDI expensive to firms, through a high-wage policy—as pursued by Singapore (Pitelis, 1994; Lall, 2000). Care should be taken to achieve a coincidence between what multinational enterprises (MNEs) require in their quest to leverage locational advantages, and what the country considers consistent with its advantages/positioning strategy. Such policies may become important in an era of 'fragmentation' (Venables, 1999), where MNEs can slice the value chain and choose 'optimal'

---

[9] John Leech, 'The motor industry: Taking the high-road', *The Economist*, 17 November 2012.

[10] The requisite conditions for achieving these are not easy, and are arguably becoming more stringent for developing countries, (Boltho and Allsopp, 1987; Stiglitz, 2001; Fagerberg and Verspagen, 2002). At the same time, specialization in segments of global value chains, can to provide some scope for smart, agile and effective DIPs (UNCTAD, 2012).

locations for each part of their production process. SMEs can, in this context, aim to specialize in 'bottleneck' parts, which are outside the radar or interest of the 'giants', but of importance to their own objectives. Germany's 'Mittelstand' (its highly specialized advanced manufacturing SMEs), and more recently Britain's aptly named 'Middland-stand', are cases in point. Such moves often require public–private collaboration, hence DIPs, at the very least through the provision of intelligence and advice by the government. This is now recognized widely, even enthusiastically embraced. *The Economist* (21 September 2013) recently cited the case of the 'high-value manufacturing catapult' outside Coventry as a case of public-private-polity (university, in this case) collaboration, championed by the coalition government in the UK, alongside a series of other interventionist measures; see also Foresight (2013).

In summary, our analysis so far suggests that a business strategy-informed IS-DIP for sustainable rejuvenation and CA should leverage nationwide capabilities to create and co-create global value, and to capture as high a share of this as possible. This can be achieved through the adoption of the four ingredients discussed in the sections above. Capturing co-created value in a sustainable way, through the co-creation of sustainable clusters and business ecosystems, and the adoption of requisite positioning and specialization in global and local value chains strategies can be seen as a new rationale for DIPs-IS. In this context, nations could aim to position themselves as 'regions' characterized by 'value for money' products and services ('relatively high quality'—'relatively low costs') that specialize in bottleneck assets, such as advanced manufacturing products and services.

Our proposed IS-DIP requires re-industrialization and locally based manufacturing. Innovations take place in R&D labs, but mostly on the ground, and thanks to people who do things. Practice makes perfect, and this induces innovation. The loss of production capabilities, eventually, can also mean loss of innovation capabilities (Pisano and Shih, 2009). Information and support by the state can involve possible advantages-compatible segments of global and local value chains, bottleneck assets/parts, and the targeting of diversification to new markets, such as the BRICs. A re-industrialization strategy, additionally, requires supporting demand. This comes from consumption, investment, public deficits, and exports. In today's era of deficits, debts, and austerity, exports are the main route to sustaining demand. In this context, nations such as the UK need to target the emerging world markets and help to co-develop them. Productivity can increase when output goes up, or when employment goes down! Unemployment is arguably Europe's most pressing challenge, especially in the south and among the young, where 50 per cent figures no longer raise eyebrows (Pitelis, 2012b). A knowledge-based economy need not generate sufficient numbers of new jobs. For example, in 2010 in the US, Apple, Microsoft, Facebook, Cisco, Google, and Amazon created fewer jobs than the mid-size Kroger supermarkets. In the past fifty years, while labour productivity increased fourfold, the productivity of materials increased twofold, and the productivity of energy increased by only 20 per cent (Milberg, 2012). This does not bode well for employment prospects. Jobless competitiveness, however, is Hamlet without the Prince of Denmark—it is short term and undermines future SCA through the dissipation of skills

and capabilities, as well as organizational knowledge and the ability to learn. Active labour market policies by the government in collaboration with intra-firm apprentices (as
in Germany), can be of the essence. A cultural mindset that promotes entrepreneurship
among the youth is important. This needs education, institutions, and the right culture,
as well as incentive structure and enabling policies—hence, DIP.

It is important to state that our suggested DIP is not about 'picking winners'. It is about
co-creating the conditions that facilitate the emergence of winners, but also their challengers, competitors, complementors, suppliers, and consumers. Policies that appropriate co-created value in a sustainable way also help to increase global value added.
Appropriating as much of the co-created value, as possible, in this context, is not at the
expense of other nations. These can pursue similar policies, thereby fostering further
global value added. The important proviso is that value appropriation is not achieved by
restraining competition, through monopolistic practices and/or protectionist policies.
When this is the case, the 'game' becomes zero- or even negative-sum. Sustainability,
moreover, requires respecting the sources of future growth—the new generations and
the environment. This calls for the mitigation of negative externalities and the promotion of positive ones, in a way that acknowledges the importance of transaction costs
(Coase, 1960), but also the productivity advantages of innovative forms of societal
cooperation (Ostrom, 1990).

The mitigation of negative externalities and the promotion of positive ones, in turn,
pose the challenge of free-riding (Olson, 1971). Sustainable value co-creation requires
the minimization of shirking, which can be fostered by concentrated, embedded power
structures and relations between economic agents, such as firms, governments, and
sometimes NGOs. While there is no fool proof solution to this problem, it is at least arguable that diversity and pluralism can foster mutual monitoring and help mitigate it, at
least in part.

Implementing our proposed strategy requires requisite infrastructure, institutions
and authorities, governance structures, attitudes, values, ideology, and culture (North,
1981). This is a major challenge and a critical foundation for successful DIPs (Pitelis,
2014).

Despite challenges, such 'top-down/bottom-up strategies' are feasible and have been
implemented in Europe and elsewhere. A case in point are the policies adopted by the
German government in the early 1990s under the leadership of Gerhard Schröder,
which involved centrally coordinated, yet in agreement with the trade unions, re-
strained wage rate increases, alongside apprenticeships. These were anticipatory and
proactive, and aimed to address emerging competitiveness challenges. Quite independently of their scope and possible ideological objections, they help highlight the feasibility of a DIP for SCA for other nations, too.

Our proposed DIP goes beyond extant approaches and could foster worldwide wealth
creation. However, 'globalization' and an emergent 'winner takes all' ideology and practice can prejudice its potential success. These have now facilitated an unprecedented income redistribution in favour of the well-off within nations, placing pressure on demand
and undermining the abilities of governments to balance their books (Atkinson and

Morelli, 2011). For the first time in the history of capitalism, the top 0.01 per cent of the population appropriates circa 5 per cent of global co-created value.[11]

The emergent concentration and embeddedness of such power structures help to foster overly cosy relations between business, governments, and media that help to take challenging issues off the agenda. Disenfranchised groups abstain from the political arena, helping lead to parliamentary democracies that are thinly veiled oligarchies. All these have led to, and are being exacerbated by, the current crisis. The sustainability of the system is now under question. Major investors, including Warren Buffet, call for capitalism to be saved from (greedy) banks and capitalists, asking for them to be taxed, as US President Obama put it, as much as their secretaries! As Zingales (2011) observes, meritocracy and social mobility are retreating in the US and everywhere. The coincidence of personal and corporate corruption renders the problems of many countries virtually insurmountable (Pitelis, 2012a). Neoclassical economic theory is of little, if any, help here. Ronald Coase has recently echoed Keynes's plea to save capitalism from capitalists, with a new call to save Economics from the economists (Coase, 2012). Our proposed DIP offers little relief to such challenges. What we propose is necessary and possible, but requires no less than a revamp of the system, a reinvention and rejuvenation of 'old Europe' and of capitalism, as a whole. This is beyond our scope here, but see Cowling and Tomlinson (2011a) and Pitelis (2013), for some thoughts.

In the above context, it is also beyond the scope of this paper, and the space available, to discuss further precise policy measures. These should be based, as a minimum, on the public policies acknowledged as necessary by Hayek (who has yet to be accused to be a pro-interventionist), and draw on our principles, focus, and business strategy-informed suggested actions and vehicles, based on a detailed analysis on the ground and in collaboration with those closer to the action, in the context of the overall strategic framework provided here.

2.4 SUMMARY, CONCLUSIONS, LIMITATIONS

We claimed that national SCA could be achieved through a DIP that learns from business strategy and involves a value capture and a value co- creation aspect, usually lacking in the predominantly macroeconomic approaches. The conceptual basis behind such a DIP involve an integration of some commonly perceived 'dichotomies', notably market failure versus guidance, CA defiance versus CA-following, manufacturing versus services, horizontal versus vertical policies, competition versus cooperation, global versus local, and a top-down versus bottom-up approach. We argued for a 'top-down/bottom up' approach that involves market-guided market guidance, creation and co-creation, CA-friendly CA defiance, with 'horizontical' measures that involve co-opetition and manuservices in the context of glocal value chains and production systems.

---

[11] See the special report by Z. M. Beddoes, 'For richer, for poorer', *The Economist*, 13 October 2012.

Within this general context, ingredients of such a DIP include the diagnosis of comparative and the co-construction of competitive advantages, the adoption of positioning strategies, the co-creation of clusters, markets and business ecosystems, the specialization in global value chains and the creation and specialization in local production systems/value chains through the acquisition and adoption of bottleneck positions in such systems/chains. These can be achieved by leveraging the comparative advantages and capabilities of the public, private, and 'third' sectors (polity). It requires appropriate implementation and co-ordination mechanisms, which is a challenge.

Another important challenge relates to the impact of power structures on policies for sustainable global value creation. While early advocates of free markets, such as Hayek, were pro-competition, free-market advocates have gradually moved towards becoming pro-market and eventually pro-business. However, in the long run, it is pro-competition that fosters sustainable business and markets, hence it is pro-business and pro-market. In this context, anti-trust and regulation policies should seek to enhance competition through innovation by thwarting anti-competitive practices and fostering new firm creation and growth, as well as new market and business ecosystem creation and co-creation. States (especially the more developed ones) should refrain from 'strategic trade' policies. Pluralism and diversity, through the creation and growth of the 'polity', should be encouraged, in order to engender mutual stewardship and monitoring. This, in practical terms, aims to eliminate 'regulatory capture', rent-seeking, and corruption by all, especially by the more powerful constituents.

Our proposed IS-DIP could help foster SCA. Its scope for implementation and success, however, depends on wider challenges and constraints. These require a wider debate on the future of capitalism, as a whole. This is beyond the scope of this chapter. It shouldn't be!

ACKNOWLEDGEMENTS

I am grateful for comments and discussion on earlier drafts to numerous colleagues, notably Keith Cowling, Roger Sudgen, Liudmyla Svystunova, David Teece, and Philip Tomlinson. The usual disclaimer applies.

REFERENCES

Aghion, P., Boulanger, J., and Cohen, E. (2011). 'Rethinking Industrial Policy', *Bruegel Policy Brief* 04/2011.

Amsden, A. H. (1989). *Asia's Next Giant: South Korea and Late Industrialization*. Oxford: Oxford University Press.

Amsden, A. H. (1997). 'Korea: Entrepreneurial Groups and Enterprising Government', in A. D. Chandler, F. Amatori, and T. Hikino (eds), *Big Business and the Wealth of Nations*, pp. 336–67. Cambridge: Cambridge University Press.

Amsden, A. H. (2008). 'The Wild Ones: Industrial Policies in the Developing World', in N. Serra and J. Stiglitz (eds), *The Washington Consensus Reconsidered: Towards a New Global Governance*, pp. 95–119. Oxford: Oxford University Press.

Aoki, M. (1990). 'Toward an Economic Model of the Japanese Firm', *Journal of Economic Literature* 28, 1–27.

Atkinson, A. B. and Morelli, S. (2011). *Economic Crises and Inequality*. Human Development Research Paper No. 2011/06. Research Background Paper for the Human Development Report 2011, UNDP, UN, 1–70.

Audretsch, D. B. (1989). *The Market and the State*. London: Harvester-Wheatsheaf.

Augier, M. and Teece, D. J. (2009). 'Dynamic Capabilities and the Role of Managers in Business Strategy and Economic Performance', *Organization Science* 20(2), 410–21.

Baumol, W. J. (1982). 'Contestable Markets: An Uprising in the Theory of Industry Structure', *The American Economic Review* 72(1), 1–15.

Best, M. (1990). *The New Competition: Institutions for Industrial Restructuring*. Oxford: Polity Press.

Boltho, A. and Allsopp, C. J. (1987). 'The Assessment: Trade and Trade Policy', *Oxford Review of Economic Policy* 3, 1–19.

Branston, J. R., Cowling, K., and Sugden, R. (2006). 'Corporate Governance and the Public Interest', *International Review of Applied Economics* 20, 189–212.

Chang, H. J. (1994). *The Political Economy of Industrial Policy*. New York: St. Martin's Press.

Chesier, S. and Penrose, J. (2007). *Top 200 Industrial Strategies of Viet Nam's Largest Firms*. Vietnam: United Nations Development Programme.

Cimoli, M., Dosi, G., and Stiglitz, J. (eds). (2009). *Industrial Policy and Development: The Political Economy of Capabilities Accumulation*. Oxford: Oxford University Press.

Coase, R. H. (1960). 'The Problem of Social Cost', *Journal of Law and Economics* 3, 1–44.

Coase, R. H. (2012). 'Saving Economics from the Economists', *Harvard Business Review* <http://hbr.org/2012/12/saving-economics-from-the-economists>.

Coffey, D. and Tomlinson, P. R. (2003a). Globalisation, Vertical Relations and the J-mode Firm', *Journal of Post Keynesian Economics* 26(1), 117–44.

Coffey, D. and Tomlinson, P. R. (2003b). 'Co-ordination and Hierarchy in the Japanese Firm: The Strategic Decision Making Approach vs Aoki', in M. Waterson, (ed.), *Competition, Monopoly and Corporate Governance: Essays in Honour of Keith Cowling*, pp. 3-19. Cheltenham: Edward Elgar.

Cowling, K. (1982). *Monopoly Capitalism*. London: Macmillan.

Cowling, K. and Tomlinson, P. R. (2000). 'The Japanese Crisis: A Case of Strategic Failure?', *The Economic Journal* 110(464), F358–81.

Cowling, K. and Tomlinson, P. R. (2011a). 'Post the "Washington Consensus": Economic Governance and Industrial Strategies for the Twenty-First Century', *Cambridge Journal of Economics* 35, 831–52.

Cowling, K. and Tomlinson, P. R. (2011b). 'The Japanese Model in Retrospective: Industrial Strategies, Corporate Japan and the "Hollowing out" of Japanese Industry', *Policy Studies* 32(6), 569–83.

Deeg, R. (2007). 'Complementarity and Institutional Change in Capitalist Systems', *Journal of European Public Policy* 14(4), 611–30.

De La Mothe, J. and Paquet, G. (1997). *Evolutionary Economics and the New International Political Economy*. London: Pinter.

Deraniyagala, S. and Fine, B. (2001). 'New Trade Theory Versus Old Trade Policy: A Continuing Enigma', *Cambridge Journal of Economics* 25, 809–25.

Dixit, A. (1982). 'Recent Developments in Oligopoly Theory', *The American Economic Review* 72, 12–17.

EC (European Commission). (2010a). *An Integrated Industrial Policy for the Globalisation Era: Putting Competitiveness and Sustainability at Centre Stage.* Brussels: Commission of the European Communities.

EC (European Commission). (2010b). *EUROPE 2020: A Strategy for Smart, Sustainable and Inclusive Growth.* Brussels: Commission of the European Communities.

EC (European Commission). (2011). *Industrial Policy: Reinforcing Competitiveness.* Brussels: Commission of the European Communities.

Fagerberg, J., Mowery, D., and Nelson, R. R. (2005). *The Oxford Handbook of Innovation.* Oxford: Oxford University Press.

Fagerberg, J. and Verspagen, B. (2002). 'Technology-Gaps, Innovation-Diffusion and Transformation: An Evolutionary Interpretation', *Research Policy* 31, 1291–304.

Fine, B. (2000). 'Endogenous Growth Theory: A Critical Assessment', *Cambridge Journal of Economics* 24(2), 245–65.

Foresight (2013). *The Future of Manufacturing: A New Era of Opportunity and Challenge for the UK.* London: The Government Office for Science.

Freeman, C. (1995). 'The "National System of Innovation" in Historical Perspective', *Cambridge Journal of Economics* 19, 5–24.

Freeman, C. (2004). 'Technological Infrastructure and International Competitiveness', *Industrial and Corporate Change* 13(3), 541–69.

Galvez-Nogales, E. (2010). Agro-Based Clusters in Developing Countries: Staying Competitive in a Globalized Economy. Food and Agriculture Organization (FAO), United Nations, Agricultural Management, Marketing, and Finance Occasional Paper.

Grabowski, R. (1994). 'The Successful Developmental State: Where Does It Come From?', *World Development* 22(3), 413–22.

Hausmann, R., Hidalgo, C., Bustos, S., Coscia, M., Chung S., Jimenez, J., Simoes, A., and Yildirim, M. (2011). *The Atlas of Economic Complexity: Mapping Paths to Prosperity.* Boston; Harvard Center for International Development and MIT, <http://atlas.media.mit.edu/>.

Hayek, F. A. (1944). *The Road to Serfdom.* Chicago: The University of Chicago Press.

Jackson, G. and Deeg, R. (2006). *How Many Varieties of Capitalism?*, Max Planck Institute, Cologne, MPIfG Discussion Paper No. 06/2.

Johnson, C. (1982). *MITI and the Japanese Miracle: The Growth of Industrial Policy, 1925–1975,* Stanford: CA, Stanford University Press.

Jomo, K. S., Chung, C. Y., Folk, B. C., Ul-Haque, I., Phongpaichit, P., Simatupang, B., and Tateishi M. (1997). *Southeast Asia's Misunderstood Miracle: Industrial Policy and Economic Development in Thailand, Malaysia and Indonesia.* Oxford: Westview Press.

Jorde, T. M. and Teece, D. J. (1992). *Antitrust, Innovation and Competitiveness.* Oxford: Oxford University Press.

Kaldor, N. (1970). 'The Case for Regional Policies', *Scottish Journal of Political Economy* 17(3), 337–48.

Kaldor, N. (1972). 'The Irrelevance of Equilibrium Economics', *The Economic Journal* 82(328), 1237–55.

Klein, P. G., Mahoney, J. T., McGahan, A. M., and Pitelis, C. N. (2010). 'Toward a Theory of Public Entrepreneurship', *European Management Review* 7(1), 1–15.

Klein, P. G., Mahoney, J. T., McGahan, A. M., and Pitelis, C. (2013). 'Capabilities and Strategic Entrepreneurship in Public Organizations', *Strategic Entrepreneurship Journal* 7(1), 70–91.

Krugman, P. R. (1987). 'Is Free Trade Passe?', *Journal of Economic Perspective*. 1(2), 131–44.

Krugman, P. R. (1989). 'Economic Integration in Europe: Some Conceptual Issues', in A. Jacquemin and A. Sapir (eds.), *The European Internal Market*, pp. 357–80. Oxford: Oxford University Press.

Krugman, P. R. (1991a). *Geography and Trade*. Massachusetts: MIT Press.

Krugman, P. R. (1991b). 'Increasing Returns and Economic Geography', *Journal of Political Economy* 99, 183–99.

Krugman, P. R. (1992). 'Does the New Trade Theory Require a New Trade Policy?', *The World Economy* 15(4), 423–42.

Krugman, P. R. (1994). 'Competitiveness: A Dangerous Obsession', *Foreign Affairs* 73(2), 28–44.

Lall, S. (2000). 'Technological Change and Industrialization in the Asian Newly Industrialising Economies: Achievements and Challenges', in L. Kim and R. Nelson (eds), *Learning and Innovation: Experiences of Newly Industrialising Economies*, pp. 13–69. Cambridge: Cambridge University Press.

Lin, J. and Chang, H.-J. (2009). 'DRP Debate: Should Industrial Policy in Developing Countries Conform to Comparative Advantage or Defy It? A Debate between Justin Lin and Ha-Joon Chang', *Development Policy Review* 27(5), 483–502.

Lin, J. (2011). *Demystifying the Chinese Economy*. Cambridge: Cambridge University Press.

List, F. (1841 [1904]). *The National System of Political Economy*, tr. S. S. Lloyd. London: Longmans.

Lucas, R. E. (1988). 'On the Mechanics of Economic Development', *Journal of Monetary Economics* 22(1), 3–42.

Lundvall, B. A. (1988). 'Innovation as an Interactive Process from User-Producer Interaction to the National System of Innovation', in G. Dosi, C. Freeman, R. R. Nelson, G. Silverberg, and L. L. G. Soete (eds), *Technical Change and Economic Theory*, pp. 349–69. London: Pinter.

Lundvall, B. A. (2007). 'National Innovation Systems: Analytical Concept and Development Tool', *Industry and Innovation* 14(1), 95–119.

Mahoney, J. T., McGahan, A., and Pitelis, C. N. (2009). 'The Interdependence of Private and Public Interests', *Organization Science* 20(6), 1034–52.

McFadden, P. (2012). Making Things: A Reassessment of British Manufacturing. Policy Network Paper, May.

Metcalfe, S. (2003). 'Science, Technology and Innovation Policy', in G. Wignaraja (ed.), *Competitiveness Strategy in Developing Countries: A Manual for Policy Analysis*, pp. 65–130. London: Routledge.

Milberg, W. (2012). Industrial Policy in the Era of Vertical Specialized Industrialization, Working Paper Presented at the UNCTAD/ILO Workshop on Growth, Productive Transformation, and Employment: New Perspectives on the Industrial Policy Debate, 16–17 February, Geneva.

Moran, P. and Ghoshal, S. (1999). 'Markets, Firms, and the Process of Economic Development', *Academy of Management Review* 24(3), 390–412.

Nelson, R. R. (1995). 'Coevolution of Industry Structure, Technology and Supporting Institutions, and the Making of Comparative Advantage', *International Journal of the Economics of the Business* 2, 171–84.

Nelson, R. R. and Winter, S. G. (1982). *An Evolutionary Theory of Economic Change*. Massachusetts: Harvard University Press.

Nelson, R. R. and Winter, S. G. (2002). 'Evolutionary Theorizing in Economics', *Journal of Economic Perspectives* 16(2), 23–46.

Nolan, P. (2001). *China and the Global Economy*. London: Palgrave.

North, D. C. (1981). *Structure and Change in Economic History*. New York: Norton.

North, D. C. (1994). 'Economic Performance through Time', *The American Economic Review* 84(3), 359–68.

North, D. C., Wallis, J. J., and Weingast, B. R. (2006). *A Conceptual Framework for Interpreting Recorded Human History*. National Bureau of Economic Research, Massachusetts NBER Working Papers No. 12795.

Nubler, I. (2011). *Industrial Policies and Capabilities for Catching-Up: Framework and Paradigms*, International Labour Office, Geneva, Employment Working Paper No.77.

Olson, M. (1971). *The Logic of Collective Action*. Massachusetts: Harvard University Press.

Ostrom, E. (1990). *Governing the Commons: The Evolution of Institutions for Collective Action*. Cambridge: Cambridge University Press.

Pasinetti, L. (1974). *Growth and Income Distribution: Essays in Economic Theory*. Cambridge: Cambridge University Press.

Pasinetti, L. (2009). *Keynes and the Cambridge Keynesians: A 'Revolution in Economics' to be Accomplished*. Cambridge: Cambridge University Press.

Penrose, E. (1959). *The Theory of the Growth of the Firm*. Oxford: Basil Blackwell.

Pisano, G. and Shih, W. (2009). Restoring American Competitiveness, *Harvard Business Review* July–August, 114–25.

Pitelis, C. N. (1991). *Market and Non-Market Hierarchies*. Oxford: Basil Blackwell.

Pitelis, C. N. (1994). 'Industrial Strategy: For Britain, in Europe and the World', *Journal of Economic Studies* 21(5), 2–92.

Pitelis, C. N. (1998). 'Productivity, Competitiveness and Convergence in the European Economy', *Contributions to Political Economy* 17, 1–20.

Pitelis, C. N. (2007). 'European Industrial and Competition Policy', *Policy Studies* 28(4), 365–81.

Pitelis, C. N. (2009a). 'The Sustainable Competitive Advantage and Catching-Up of Nations: FDI, Clusters and Liability (Asset) of Smallness', *Management International Review* 49(1), 95–120.

Pitelis, C. N. (2009b). 'The Co-Evolution of Organizational Value Capture, Value Creation and Sustainable Advantage', *Organization Studies* 30(10), 1115–39.

Pitelis, C. N. (2011). 'Cameron Recovers Keynes from Mrs Thatcher's Dustbin', *Parliamentary Brief* March, 17–18.

Pitelis, C. N. (2012a). 'Clusters, Entrepreneurial Ecosystem Co-Creation, and Appropriability: A Conceptual Framework', *Industrial and Corporate Change* 21(6), 1359–88.

Pitelis, C. N. (2012b). 'On PIIGS, GAFFS, and BRICS: An Insider-Outsider's Perspective on Structural and Institutional Foundations of the Greek Crisis', *Contributions to Political Economy* 31(1), 11–89.

Pitelis, C. N. (2012c). 'Innovation, Resource Creation, Learning and Catching-up: Building on Pasinetti to Revitalize Cambridge Economics', <http://ssrn.com/abstract=2155692> or <http://dx.doi.org/10.2139/ssrn.2155692>.

Pitelis, C. N. (2013). 'Towards a More "Ethically Correct" Governance for Economic Sustainability', *Journal of Business Ethics* 118(3), 655–65.

Pitelis, C. N. (2014). 'Rejuvenating "Old" Europe: A Strategy for Sustainable International Competitiveness', *Contributions to Political Economy*, 33(1), 69–98.

Pitelis, C. N. and Teece, D. (2010). 'Cross-Border Market Co-Creation, Dynamic Capabilities and the Entrepreneurial Theory of the Multinational Enterprise', *Industrial and Corporate Change* 19(4), 1247–70.

Porter, M. E. (1985). *Competitive Advantage: Creating and Sustaining Superior Performance*. New York: The Free Press.

Porter, M. E. (1990). *The Competitive Advantage of Nations*. Basingstoke: Macmillan.

Putnam, R. D. (1993). *Making Democracy Work: Civic Traditions in Modern Italy*. Princeton, NJ: Princeton University Press.

Ricardo, D. (1817). *The Principles of Political Economy and Taxation*. London: John Murray, (reprinted by Dent Dutton, 1973).

Richardson, G. B. (1972). 'The Organisation of Industry', *Economic Journal* 82(327), 883–96.

Robinson, J. (1977). 'What are the Questions?', *Journal of Economic Literature* 15(4), 1318–39.

Rodrik, D. (2004). *Industrial Policy for the Twenty-First Century*. Cambridge, MA: Harvard University.

Rodrik, D. (2005). 'Growth Strategies', in P. Aghion and S. Durlauf (eds), *Handbook of Economic Growth*, pp. 968–1014. Amsterdam, Elsevier B.V.

Rodrik, D. (2009). *One Economics, Many Recipes: Globalization, Institutions, and Economic Growth*. Princeton, NJ: Princeton University Press.

Romer, P. M. (1986). 'Increasing Returns and Long-Run Growth', *Journal of Political Economy* 94(5), 1002–37.

Romer, P. M. (1990). 'Endogenous Technological Change', *Journal of Political Economy* 98, 71–101.

Samuelson, P. A. (1962). 'The Gains from International Trade Once Again', *The Economic Journal* 72(288), 820–9.

Scherer, F. M. and Ross, D. (1990). *Industrial Market Structure and Economic Performance*. 3rd edition. Boston: Houghton Mifflin.

Schumpeter, J. (1942). *Capitalism, Socialism and Democracy*. London: Unwin Hyman.

Serra, N. and Stiglitz, J. (2008). *The Washington Consensus Reconsidered: Towards a New Global Governance*. Oxford: Oxford University Press.

Shapiro, H. and Taylor, L. (1990). 'The State and Industrial Strategy', *World Development* 18(6), 861–78.

Solow, M. R. (1956). 'A Contribution to the Theory of Economic Growth', *Quarterly Journal of Economics* 70, 65–94.

Solow, M. R. (2000). *Growth Theory: An Exposition*. Oxford: Oxford University Press.

Stiglitz, J. (2001). 'Foreword', in K. Polanyi (ed.), *The Great Transformation: The Political and Economic Origins of Our Time*, pp. vii–xvii. Boston: Beacon Press.

Stiglitz, J. (2011). 'Rethinking Development Economics', *The World Bank Research Observer* 26(2), 230–6.

Teece, D. J. (1986). 'Profiting from Technological Innovation: Implications for Integration, Collaboration, Licensing and Public Policy', *Research Policy* 15(6), 285–305.

Teece, D. J. (2006). 'Reflections on "profiting from innovation"', *Research Policy* 35(8), 1131–46.

Teece, D. J. (2007). 'Explicating Dynamic Capabilities: The Nature and Microfoundations of (Sustainable) Enterprise Performance', *Strategic Management Journal* 28(13), 1319–50.

UNCTAD (United Nations Conference On Trade And Development) (2012). *World Investment Report: Towards a Generation of Investment Policies*. New York and Geneva: United Nations.

Venables, A. J. (1999). 'Fragmentation and Multinational Production', *European Economic Review* 43(4), 935–45.

Wade, R. (1990). *Governing the Market: Economic Theory and the Role of Government in East Asian Industrialization*. Princeton, NJ: Princeton University Press.

Warwick, K. (2013). *Beyond Industrial Policy: Emerging Issues and New Trends*, OECD Publishing Technology and Industry Policy Papers, No. 2.

Wignaraja, G. (ed.). (2003). *Competitiveness Strategy and Industrial Performance in Developing Countries: A Manual Policy Analysis*. London: Routledge.

Williamson, J. (1990). 'What Washington Means By Policy Reform', in J. Williamson (ed.), *Latin American Adjustment: How Much Has Happened?*, pp.8–17. Washington: Washington, Institute for International Economics.

Zakaria, F. (2012). 'The Case for Making It in the USA'. *TIME*, 6 February, 19.

Zingales, L. (2011). *A Capitalism for the People: Recapturing the Lost Genius of American Prosperity*. New York: Basic Books.

....

CHAPTER 3

INDUSTRIAL POLICY
International Experiences

....

DAVID COATES

BEFORE we can report on the character and use of industrial policy in modern advanced economies we need some conceptual precision on both dimensions of the term. We need to be clear about what we mean by 'industry' and then what we mean by 'policy'. In both academic scholarship and policy design, a high degree of conceptual clarity is always important; but it is doubly so here because of the important ways in which the meaning of both terms, and the content of both entities, have changed over time. Indeed it is that change—change in both the nature of modern industry and in the role of policy towards it—that holds one important key to a full understanding of the record and potential of industrial policy in the modern-day UK.

3.1 Defining and Placing Industrial Policy

....

The focus on industrial policy can be set narrowly or widely, depending on how the term *industry* is understood (Coates, 1996, pp. 16–19). Conceived very narrowly, industrial policy is simply a set of initiatives designed to strengthen the economic viability of locally based manufacturing firms—that is, it is policy focused on the health of economic units which produce tangible commodities and employ local labour to do so. Conceived narrowly, therefore, industrial policy is not concerned with the similar viability of other sectors of the economy. It is not concerned with agriculture. It is not concerned with energy production or distribution. It is not concerned with transport, or with service provision in sectors like retailing and hospitality. Nor is it concerned with the economic viability of the financial sector. There may be agriculture policy, energy policy, or policy regulating financial institutions—indeed there invariably is—but such policy is qualitatively different from industrial policy narrowly understood. Conceived more widely, however, industrial policy is exactly the reverse of that. It is policy concerned with the economic viability of all those sectors, and with the relative weight of each deemed appropriate in the economy to which the policy is applied. Conceived narrowly, industrial policy is concerned with the economic health of firms that make things. Conceived widely, industrial policy is concerned with the health of any firm employing local sources of labour. The story we will tell here is essentially one of the movement over time, among governing circles in advanced economies, from industrial policy narrowly focused on the development of locally based manufacturing industry to one whose focus is more diffuse.

Our understanding of industrial policy can also be framed narrowly or widely on the policy side (Coates, 1996, pp. 20–6). In one sense, since everything governments do impacts the conditions under which individual firms operate, on the widest definition of industrial policy all governments inevitably have one whether they realize it or not. But things that are ubiquitous are best understood by the components from which they are constructed, and here some of the components of overall government policies impact firms directly and some do not. There is analytical mileage to be gained, therefore, by distinguishing between policies that indirectly and eventually affect firms from those whose impact is more immediate and targeted; and by restricting our understanding of industrial policy initially to the latter. Among the range of government policies affecting firms indirectly are fiscal and monetary policy, trade and competition policy, policy on education and welfare rights, and policy on infrastructure spending and consumer demand. Among the range of policies more directly impacting firms are such things as investment assistance, publicly funded training programmes, export promotion, regional location grants, infant industry protection, and labour codes. Within that more focused set of policies, it is then possible to establish a continuum of instruments available for their implementation—one stretching in this instance from public ownership and extensive subsidization, through direct administrative guidance and planning agreements, to privatization and deregulation. Some of these policy instruments increase the exposure of firms to market competition, some lessen that exposure, and some remove that exposure altogether (Coates, 1996, pp. 27–9). The general story to be told here will be one of a general move over time from direct to indirect forms of industrial policy, from the deployment of a wide range of policy instruments to the deployment of a more restricted set, and from policy designed to manage markets to policy designed to increase exposure to unregulated market forces.

Two other sets of distinctions need to be in play, too, before the detail of this analysis can begin. One is a distinction between policy goals. Industrial policy can be deployed to protect the scale and distribution of local employment. It can be deployed to increase international competitiveness. It can be deployed to strengthen national security; and sometimes it can be deployed for all three purposes simultaneously. Put broadly, the story to be told here will be one of shifting goals, with employment concerns giving way over time to concerns about international competitiveness and national security. But it will also be a story of difference (in goals, policy ranges, and definitions of industry) between various kinds of national capitalism. Since 1945 at least, the governing circles of the leading capitalist economies have all faced a broadly similar set of choices in relation to the development and deployment of industrial policy, but they have not been thereby compelled always to make the same choices of policy. On the contrary and as we will now see, since the Second World War differing national models of capitalism can be broadly distinguished by the scale and character of industrial policy persisting within them. The general centre of gravity of industrial policy has shifted over time in all leading capitalist economies, but even now that trajectory remains differently positioned in liberal market capitalisms than it is in more coordinated forms of capitalism.

3.2 The Rise of Industrial Policy

The heyday of narrowly defined industrial policy was definitely the decades immediately following the end of the Second World War. Wartime damage made economic regeneration a vital prerequisite for electoral survival for governments of both the left and the right in each of the major industrial economies, and the development of semi-automated methods of production during the war itself gave the manufacturing sector of each of those economies the capacity to raise living standards significantly if conversion from military to civilian production could be achieved with speed and effectiveness. Each major economy entered the post-war period having experienced full government oversight over economic activity. The question in each was how far that control would be retained, and in what form. The answers varied from economy to economy, but close government involvement in industrial regeneration remained common to all.

The 'victors' in the Second World War found themselves with either new (as in the case of the US) or renewed (as in the case of the UK) global responsibilities and capacities. The US in particular found itself militarily deployed in both Europe and Asia, and the effective head of an international group of capitalist economies increasingly closed off from their wartime communist allies. Governments in both countries were in no position, and in no mood, to retreat from global leadership, so both settled into a form of industrial policy characterized later by David Edgerton as 'liberal militarism'. The term 'liberal' here is being used in its European rather than in its American sense, as reflecting a preference in public policy for the freeing of private enterprise and market competition, rather than for (as a modern American would understand the term 'liberal') a capitalism managed by public bodies in the interests of social reform. Industrial policy in both the US and the UK in the post-war period was initially directed to the creation of a globally dominant military industrial complex, while over time removing wartime controls over the activities and commercial decisions of firms producing manufactured goods for general civilian use. The clearest examples of that preoccupation with military-industrial issues in the UK were the decisions by the Attlee Government to develop the atomic bomb, and the speed with which the later Macmillan Government moved to restructure the UK aircraft-building capacity when that industry came under growing competitive challenge in the late 1950s (Lee, 1996, pp. 39–42). The UK's Ministry of Defence never developed the key leadership role in the UK manufac-

turing sector that the Pentagon effected in the US, but in both economies industrial production for military purposes initially established to defeat fascism was continued after
the Second World War to sustain positions of global dominance left in place by the
defeat of Germany and Japan.

Governing circles in those two latter economies found themselves faced with problems of economic reconstruction not dissimilar to that faced by the UK, but constrained
by military defeat and subsequent Allied occupation from following a similar focus on
the maintenance of military greatness. Allied policy towards both economies immediately after the war favoured state-initiated de-industrialization—particularly in relation
to Japan; but once the Cold War was in place and with each former enemy now situated
as a front-line state in a world divided between capitalist and communist military
camps, new imperatives came into play. It became a vital US (and to a lesser degree, UK)
interest to see West Germany prosper under Allied rule—to the degree indeed that as
government regulation of domestic car industries was wound down back home, planners in the allied zones of occupation actively restructured the German civilian car
industry (Reich, 1990, pp. 172–84). Likewise, the need to see Japanese capitalism flourish
in an Asia threatened by Chinese communism led Allied commanders there to withdraw their initial support for independent trade union action, and to support the
McCarthyite weakening of the Japanese Left. Cold War exigencies led the US in particular to tolerate and encourage the emergence in Germany and in Japan of forms of
organized capitalism more reminiscent of the New Deal economy of the 1930s from
which by then the US itself was in full retreat.

The result was a definite variation in the degree and kind of industrial policy prevalent in each major industrial capitalist economy in the years preceding the collapse of
the Cold War. The US established itself in those years as a successful *liberal* capitalism.
Germany and Japan established themselves as successful *coordinated* capitalisms,
though the form of coordination varied in each; and the UK struggled as a hybrid
between these forms—initially liberal, increasingly coordinated—as the cost of maintaining its global empire drained it of the capacity to compete economically with the
societies it had helped militarily to defeat in the years before 1945. Industrial policy
varied in consequence.

3.3 INDUSTRIAL POLICY IN PRACTICE

In the *United States*, the immediate post-war years saw the consolidation of what
Michael Bingham later called 'industrial policy, American-style' (Bingham, 1998).
Behind a political rhetoric of free-market capitalism, post-war US governments at the
federal level—and critically, also at the level of the individual states (Eisinger, 1990)—
provided more direct assistance to US-based industrial producers than the rhetoric
implied. Industrial policy was not so much missing as hidden, carrying on a discrete
pattern of publicly funded support for home-based producers that stretched back to at

least Alexander Hamilton's initially rejected *Report on the Subject of Manufactures* of 1791, and to the post-Civil War maintenance of a protective tariff high enough to meet Hamilton's requirements. The entrepreneurial activities of the late nineteenth-century American state have been extensively documented elsewhere (Kozul-Wright, 1995; Bingham, 1998). For those years at least, as Di Tommaso and Schweitzer (2013, p. 46) have noted, 'American Governments and presidencies…, with a surprising degree of continuity, guided industrial development from the take-off years, through the catching-up decades, to the global leadership times.' Post-1945, in addition to funding heavily the development of the inter-state road system that progressively turned the US from a rail-based transport system to a vehicular one, administrations of both parties oversaw direct subsidies to American farmers and US oil producers; regulated airlines, drug manufacturers, and food suppliers; established tight rules on the banking industry to prevent any repetition of the financial crisis of 1929; and funded an enormous weapons-producing set of engineering industries. Public policy here was a complex mixture of 'subsidy, tax exemption, direct loans, insurance, government contracts…and the promotion of research' (Bingham, 1998, p. 23).

The key federal public agency in play in the post-war US was not, however, some department of industry—there was none, just federal departments of commerce, energy, transport, and agriculture. The key agency was the Pentagon, whose procurement division—DARPA (Grant, 1989, pp. 122–8)—played a role in the development of the US military-industrial complex not entirely dissimilar to the impact of MITI on the Japanese civilian export sector in the same period (Coates, 2000, p. 204). The justificatory structures were different—the purpose of Pentagon economic intervention was and remains national security, not international economic competitiveness—but the results of defence spending and the American space programme have been similar: giving the US in the Cold War years 'important competitive advantages in a wide variety of high-technology sectors' (Vogel, 1987, p. 94). The positive impact of Pentagon funding and procurement policies on the competitiveness of key sectors of US manufacturing industry in the 1950s and 1960s is hard to exaggerate (Di Tommaso and Schweitzer, 2013, pp. 50–4) since these sectors include such world-leaders as 'high-definition television, superconductors, and other advanced electronic technologies' (Graham, 1992, p. 228).

Other important sectors of the US civilian industrial economy were left largely untouched, however, by direct policy for most of post-war capitalism's golden years. Indeed the flow of skilled labour away from these sectors towards those favoured by the military did have a long-term negative impact on overall US global competiveness, particularly since any compensating industrial policy at the level of individual US states was largely concerned with the 'capturing' of US-based plant and equipment for one state from another—industrial policy, that, whose effect was to move industrial firms around *within* the US rather than to strengthen their collective competitiveness globally. But when that period of sustained private-sector growth stalled in the oil crisis and stagflation of the 1970s, even Republican administrations experimented with price controls and Democratic ones with corporate bailouts (from Lockheed in 1971 to Chrysler in 1979)—more visible examples of industrial policy instruments more readily deployed elsewhere in the global system. The Carter Administration even began, late in its tenure, an internal review of industrial policy that stretched out to consider the picking of winners, the restructuring of less efficient industries and the funding of industrial reconstruction. It was a review that ultimately came to nothing, however, because of internal divisions within the Administration itself (Bingham, 1998, pp. 11–12).

What served to obscure this underlying but very definite willingness of sections of the federal government to, as David Vogel (1987, p. 92) put it, 'target winners, and encourage the movement of capital and labor away from losers', were ultimately two things. One was the governing preoccupation of US Administrations with global issues. The other was the governing philosophy of classically liberal anti-statism that both parties came increasingly to share—a philosophy that, for example, directly precluded US governments at both federal and state level from taking any major industry or firm directly into public ownership. Indeed, US Administrations prior to 1980 were as likely to encourage American capital to move abroad as to stay at home, if moving abroad would reinforce US national security concerns in an era of intense Cold War rivalry with the communist bloc. The fact that so much of US industrial policy in the years after the Second World War remained hidden from public view was to prove ultimately its most serious weakness: since 'de facto industrial policy' of that kind, 'once discovered, had no defenders' (Bingham, 1998, p. 6). But in the golden years of capitalist growth between 1948 and 1973, this weakness was obscured by the United States' continuing superiority as the 'free world's' leading economic power.

In *Japan*, by contrast, industrial policy was consciously and publicly pursued in the post-war years as a deliberate tool of national economic reconstruction. From very early in the post-occupation period, Japanese governments took it upon themselves to reset the economy's growth trajectory in a series of ways: by creating state-owned financial institutions linking individual savers to industries short of capital, by deciding which industries should receive privileged access to that capital, and by using 'administrative guidance' to ensure that access to that capital was granted only in return for long-term improvements in export performance. Post-war Japanese governments inherited from the pre-war state and economy a planning ministry (MITI) equipped with skilled personnel able to play that role (Krauss, 1992; Matsumoto, 1992; Bingham, 1998, pp. 171–96) and a structure of networked companies (*zaibatsu* reconfigured post-1945 as *keiretsu*) able quickly and effectively to deploy investment and labour resources as agreed. And using these institutions and networks, successive Japanese governments (all LDP-controlled) moved the entire centre of gravity of the Japanese economy first out of agriculture and textiles into steel, chemicals, machinery, and other heavy industries, then later (after the 1973 oil crisis) out of those into transport and electrical goods (cars, motor bikes, televisions, videos, calculators, and the like) and, later still, into a range of high-technology products (Coates, 2000, p. 215). In doing so, the Japanese state deployed and developed a model of state-directed economic growth ('embedded mercantilism' in T. J. Pempel's telling phrase) that was later replicated in South Korea—industrial policy designed to place a whole economy on a higher growth path than that guaranteed by the simple interplay of free-market forces (Amsden, 1989), one using the threat and reality of the withdrawal of state support to head off any rent-seeking tendencies associated with protected markets and managed competition. This was not expensive industrial policy—the US government spent a much higher percentage of GDP supporting private sector R&D than MITI ever did (Kitschelt, 1991, pp. 389–90)—but it was highly effective industrial policy nonetheless.

To create comparative advantage in industries in which it initially had none, MITI encouraged the systematic import of foreign technology while maintaining high tariff protection around infant industries. As that strategy succeeded, the Japanese state shifted its priority from generalized development and reverse engineering to the pursuit of strength in key export sectors: initially in medium-technology sectors like automobiles, later in more technologically sophisticated consumer products. To that end, MITI encouraged 'structural rationalization' (i.e. mergers) in key industries like steel and automobiles, increasingly prioritized the nurturing of indigenous R&D capacity, and oversaw the rundown and relocation of what it termed 'structurally depressed' industries. There were initially eleven of these, including textiles, sugar-refining, shipbuilding, aluminum refining, and the production of chemical fertilizers (Coates, 2000, p. 217). The policy tools deployed to shape the Japanese economy in ways congruent with the state planners' vision included 'bank financed and directed credit, import controls and protection, restrictions on entry and exits of firms in the domestic market, control over foreign exchange, and not least, controlled importation of foreign technology' (Singh, 1993, p. 281). Japanese state planners could not use military procurement as the Americans did, and made little use of direct public ownership in the manner of the French and the British. They preferred instead to rely on the many faces of their much vaunted 'administrative guidance'—including 'preferential financing, tax-breaks and import controls to protect and develop targeted industries, and orchestrated cartels and bank-based industrial groupings to trigger competitiveness' (Coates, 2000, pp. 218–19).

The character of industrial policy in post-war continental Europe was different again. In *West Germany*, industrial policy was set in a post-war configuration of institutions and networks unlike those prevalent in either the US or Japan. In contrast to Japan, the West German state was federal rather than unitary, lacked an institution of central state planning of the MITI variety, faced an already strong and cartelized engineering sector, and was surrounded by large universal banks long used to a close investment relationship with both large and medium-size German firms. West Germany, that is, emerged from the Second World War, as Nazi Germany went into it, as an 'organized capitalism' (Lash and Urry, 1987). Unlike the US, West Germany emerged from the war with a revitalized labour movement, an active Christian Democratic commitment to the creation of a strong welfare state, and newly reconfigured industrial trade unions keen to prevent any West German slippage back into fascism. In such a social market economy, with a world-class industrial base now denied permission to produce weapons of war, the main thrust of federal policy was to maintain the health of the social partners and to facilitate dialogue between them. The need for and scope of industrial policy narrowly defined was itself narrow; but that did not preclude more targeted policy initiatives designed initially to facilitate post-war reconstruction and to strengthen market competition

(Smith, 1994, pp. 427–47), and later to enhance the competitiveness of locally based manufacturing industry. Indeed, as Andrew Shonfield (1965, p. 296) later noted, in the first two decades after the Second World War, in West Germany 'subsidies, cheap loans provided by the state, and above all, discriminating tax allowances which supported favored activities, [were] used with an abandon that could only be acceptable in a society where the average citizen expects the state to choose its favorites and to intervene on their behalf'. The result, in Wolfgang Streeck's telling phrase, was the post-war emergence of a West German state that was 'neither *laissez-faire* nor *étatiste*' but rather 'enabling' (Streeck, 1997, p. 38).

As such, the post-war West German state was initially willing to give substantial tax advantages to basic industries like coal and steel (Shonfield, 1965, p. 282), to protect its textile and agrarian sectors, and to encourage exports by providing both tax advantages and subsidized rail shipping rates to firms in its export sector. But as the 'economic miracle' kicked in during the 1950s, the need for much of that fell away, though federal support remained in place for the next three decades to manage the social consequences of declining industries (mainly via the use of temporary subsidies and protection). Policy to protect German agriculture, mining, iron, and steel was increasingly passed up the line, over time, to EC institutions—though as late as 1994 German 'coal, iron and steel number[ed] among the most heavily subsidized industries in the world' (Feldenkirchen, 1999, p. 110). Even so, from the 1960s the 'new industrial policy' adopted by successive West German governments privileged support for industries able to establish competitive advantage in the global economy, and worked to strengthen the innovative capacity of German-based engineering. To that end, 'in 1962 the government established the Ministry for Scientific Research, which was transformed into the Federal Ministry for Research and Technology in 1972,' charged above all with 'the promotion of microelectronics as well as the aerospace industry through direct and indirect support measures'. Those direct measures included public funding for basic research. The indirect methods involved 'tax relief for enterprises by improved depreciation possibilities and lower trade taxes', and the heavy use of regional aid (Feldenkirchen, 1999, pp. 102–3). What the German model added to both the American and the Japanese equivalents was heavy federal and state support for skill training. The quality of German labour was an important concern of industrial policy in the Federal Republic of Germany (FRG) from the outset in ways that lacked parallels elsewhere in the industrial world.

3.4 Industrial Policy at its Peak

'By the end of the 1970s, the high tide of interventionism…in most of Western Europe, electricity, gas, coal, airlines, and steel were likely to be owned by the state' (Foreman-Peck and Federico, 1999, p. 441). The heyday of narrowly focused industrial policy in major capitalist economies in Western Europe occurred in the years either side of 1980, and was most developed in two of those economies: one to be expected, one rather less so.

The one to be expected was *France*, because post-war French governments could and did draw on a strong tradition of powerful state leadership stretching back to Napoleon, and because they had at their disposal in consequence a highly centralized governmental and administrative system concentrated in Paris. French governments also faced an economy damaged by war, weakened by post-war colonialism, and still burdened by a larger than average military-industrial complex built up in the period of French colonial expansion. Add to that the relatively late emergence—certainly late relative to the UK—of a coherent socialist political formation, and a politically much wider sense of the importance of French autonomy (both against Germany and against the US), and the ingredients were all in place for the emergence of a set of policies specifically designed to strengthen the global competitiveness of major French-owned and French-based manufacturing companies. Such policies 'enjoy nearly unanimous support in France', Bernard Vernier-Palliez told the Brookings Institute in 1986 (Adams and Stoffaës, 1986, p. 1); and certainly there were lots of them to support. The initial driving force of industrial policy was post-war reconstruction and modernization. By the 1960s it was a growing awareness of a technology gap opening up between French industry and its competitors. By 1981, after France's brief Thatcherite moment under the Presidency of Giscard d'Estaing, the driving force was the Left—supplementing policy long guided from the Treasury Department of the Ministry of Finance with policy from Ministries of Industry, Research and Development, International Trade and Planning. But even prior to 1981, post-war France showed a penchant for industrial policy that was more extensive and consistent than elsewhere in Western Europe. Peter Hall described it as an approach to state-led economic growth 'characterized by expansion of the nationalized sector, a highly interventionist industrial policy towards the private sector, the extensive use of diplomatic pressure in support of exports, and the development of a system of national planning' (Hall, 1986, p. 140). There were nine such plans between 1946 and 1968.

When first elected in 1981, the Mitterrand Government favoured the strengthening of industry vertically—by industry-specific planning and state intervention at every stage of the production process. In consequence, 'individual companies were asked to merge, increase spending on research and development, increase production and employment, increase ratios of exports to production, or modify product lines' (Aujac, 1986, p. 18). In return, the French state offered investment aid, public funding of labour training, enhanced government purchases of those companies' products, and encouragement of private sector purchasing of things produced by co-operative companies. Particular industries were targeted for development and support—including machine tools, steel, aerospace, nuclear energy—and the mix of policy tools included financial aid (grants and loans), tax concessions, planning agreements, industrial subsidies, regional aid, and preferential purchasing policies. The subsidies used were often company-specific rather than industry-wide, and they were dispensed from a multiplicity of ministries. Many of them had been well in place since at least 1970, and cumulatively they had come to constitute approximately 20 per cent of all gross fixed capital formation in French industry as a whole even before the Mitterrand experiment began (Aujac, 1986, p. 22; Hall, 1986, pp. 189–90). What the Mitterrand Government then added to the mix was a new round of public ownership—in 1982 five of France's largest industrial enterprises were nationalized—additions to an economy in which the scale of public ownership was already extensive (Hall, 1986, p. 203). French governments in power immediately after the Second World War had already nationalized the transport and energy industries (coal, gas, and electricity), the main commercial banks and insurance companies, and even several manufacturing firms (including the car-maker Renault). De Gaulle in the 1960s had then added government enterprises to a set of new industries (oil, aerospace, nuclear materials, and informational processing) so that at the height of the Mitterrand experiment, the public sector took in 25 per cent of manufacturing industry and about 50 per cent of large-scale industry (Stoffaës, 1986, p. 42). The French state, of course, also controlled the flow of credit to private-sector firms through the nationalized banks and the Bank of France. In an economy with only a modest stock market, the leverage given to state planners by this degree of direct and indirect financial control was significant.

The unexpected latecomer to this European explosion of narrowly focused industrial policy was the *United Kingdom* under what is now labelled as Old Labour but at the time presented itself as anything but old—the Labour Party led between 1963 and 1979 first by Harold Wilson and then by James Callaghan. That second post-war generation of Labour politicians actually offered themselves as something new and modernizing. They quietly sustained the UK's global partnership with the US whenever they could—their non-participation in the Vietnam War being a major but rare exception to their ongoing commitment to the American alliance; but they combined that commitment with a growing sense that previous governments had neglected the competitiveness of UK-based manufacturing industries for too long (Lee, 1996, p. 45). Keen to catch up on more successful economies abroad (America always, but increasingly West Germany too) and conscious of the growing effectiveness of the Japanese economy under clear state administrative guidance, the first Wilson Government (1964-70) set out to strengthen the UK economy in a tripartite partnership with organized business and labour, while the second Wilson/Callaghan government (1974–9) went even further, developing a series of agencies and policies designed to give the British state a leadership role in the modernization of its economy. The model for the first Wilson government was definitely French indicative planning (Hall, 1986: 87). The model for the second was more properly Japanese administrative guidance.

The first Wilson Government created the Ministry of Technology, charged to strengthen the technological edge of the UK's new industries, from electronics and air-craft production to computers and machine tools (Coates, 1975, pp. 117–18). Closed down by the intervening Conservative Government of Edward Heath, MinTech was resurrected by the second Wilson Government as the Department of Industry, and given the widest of briefs on industrial modernization: effectively 'to implement government policy on job creation, new investment, technological innovation, price restraint, export promotion, import substitution, and industrial democracy' (Coates, 1980, p. 88). Labour in power after 1974 took a number of firms into public ownership, including British Leyland and British Aerospace, adding to a list that had begun under the Heath Government (including partial state ownership of Ferranti and full ownership of Rolls-Royce). It created a state holding company, the National Enterprise Board, to supervise the running of those firms and industries. It created tripartite sectoral working parties for each major UK industry. It signed planning agreements with at least two major economic players—Chrysler and the National Coal Board—and intended to sign more. It even toyed with the introduction of a degree of industrial democracy. It provided 'massive subsidies to British Leyland, Chrysler, Rolls-Royce, Alfred Herbert, Ferranti and a variety of other firms' (Hall, 1986, p. 90) and it did so in three broad ways. It devised aid schemes for sixteen separate industrial sectors (from machine tools to slaughterhouses). It devised general schemes to encourage new industrial investment, particularly schemes to offset recession and to encourage firms to bring forward already planned investment projects; and it used public funds to rescue particular firms, not least British Leyland and Chrysler. Significant sums of public money were involved throughout: at 1979 prices £1,350 million in 1974–5, £1,500 million in 1975–6 and £1,040 million in 1976–7 (Grant, 1982, pp. 51–3).

But for all these desperate attempts to catch up on the UK's more successful industrial competitors, the second Wilson Government's deployment of large-scale specifically focused industrial policy ultimately failed. It failed in part because of resistance to its presence and control from sections of UK industry—even the planning agreement it signed with Chrysler turned out to be entirely hollow (Chrysler quietly sold its UK division off to Peugeot-Citroën in 1979 without even telling the Government ahead of time); and big multinationals like the Ford Motor Company simply refused to subordinate their global corporate strategy to the requirements of one national government, even one as globally significant as the UK government then still was. The strategy failed too because of internal divisions within the Government itself—once the EC referendum had gone the way Wilson wanted and his left-wing critics did not—a reshuffle of ministerial portfolios reduced the importance and potency of the Industry Ministry that Tony Benn had previously led. But the strategy ultimately failed because it came too little and too late—too late to prevent a balance of payments crisis and International Monetary Fund (IMF) bailout in 1976 that had strong neo-liberal conditions attached; and too little to generate the economic growth and rising living standards vital to the maintenance of trade union support for large-scale industrial restructuring. Industrial policy under the second Wilson Government was accompanied by years of high inflation and falling real wages—a conundrum that industrial policy could not immediately resolve, and one that triggered the 1978–9 'winter of discontent' which destroyed Labour's electoral credibility and let a revitalized Conservative Party back into power under its new leader, the as yet untested Margaret Thatcher.

The Mitterrand experiment in large-scale focused industrial policy was similarly unsuccessful and even more quickly brought to heel by the market power of international capital. By 1981 the external constraints on the French economy, not least its 80 per cent dependency on foreign sources of energy, were putting heavy pressure on the franc as France's balance of payments went heavily into deficit; so that just one year in office, the government had to reverse course, devaluing the franc and deflating the internal economy. Cutbacks in industrial subsidies to key industries then followed: to coal, to steel, to shipbuilding, even to Renault and the French car industry (Adams and Stoffaës, 1986, p. 206), so that by the later 1990s 'the proportion of capital injections from the public purse had fallen under 10%' and 'the old arsenal of subsidized loans, equity capital and insurance provision managed by the state' (Dormois, 1999, p. 92) had given way to a higher reliance, even by state-owned enterprises, on private sources for their investment funds. As Peter Hall wrote at the time:

> 'The Mitterrand years revealed the extent to which even a Socialist regime with a firm mandate is constrained by the international economy and the existing organization of society. As the Government ran up against economic constraints that derived from its insertion into world markets, it faced the difficult choice of adapting its strategy to the operation of market forces or of moving down a more radical path than anticipated. In this unenviable position, it chose the former'. (Hall, 1986, p. 225)

Both the French and UK experiments in high-volume industrial policy are ultimately best understood as both a response to, and a casualty of, the stagflation crisis of the 1970s. Behind the policy changes fundamental processes were at work in the wider economy and society. A generation of economic growth built on the enhanced productivity of Fordist production methods had by then run into its own limits: limits of productivity growth generated by the extensive application of those methods (so that no new sectors could easily absorb them and continue the productivity surge); and limits set by the changing balance of class power produced by the full employment that Fordism sustained (Coates, 1995, pp. 97–103). By the late 1970s, with the business cycles of each major economy increasingly interconnected with the cycles of the rest because of the growth of trade and capital flows between them all, the space for any one leading economy to alter its relationship to the rest was increasingly squeezed. The French and British pursued industrial policy with the vigour they did precisely because their economies had slipped behind the best of the rest during the years of the Fordist boom, but each was by then working against the tide of increasingly powerful international integration. It was an integration that required a fundamental resetting of overall economic policy—either a systematic retreat from globalized competition as many on the radical left were by then advocating, or a total immersion within it, as right-wing critics of Keynesianism and corporatism advocated. By 1979/80 both the US and the UK were at a clear economic watershed, and the active pursuit of focused industrial policy was an early casualty of the way in which that watershed was resolved politically.

3.5 THE RETREAT FROM INDUSTRIAL POLICY

The resulting retreat from large-scale specifically focused industrial policy, when it came, was both sudden and dramatic. The legacy of the Wilson/Callaghan Government's attempt directly to stimulate rapid economic growth was a 'paradigm shift'

(Matthijs, 2011, p. 121) now widely labelled as Thatcherism. Her conservative Government entered power armed with a renewed faith in the growth-generating capacity of unregulated markets and in the inflation-killing capacity of monetarist macroeconomic policy. Accordingly the Thatcher Government immediately removed controls on the free movement of capital, began a prolonged series of privatizations that pushed the boundaries between the public and private sectors firmly in the private sector direction, introduced market-based modes of resource allocation into whatever remained as publicly provided and owned (not least, health care), cut public spending and slashed subsidies to struggling UK industries, and concentrated its European policy on the completion of a single market (Lee, 1996, pp. 54–7). The Thatcher governments did one other important thing as they reset industrial policy. Through both a series of legislative initiatives packaged as 'trade union reform' and a year-long resistance to striking miners they entirely broke the power of organized labour in the UK economy, leaving managers in the private sector free to manage their businesses constrained by only a minimum sets of labour rights for those they chose to hire and fire.

The story in the US was ultimately the same, though with less privatization (because of previously less public provision at either federal/state level) and with less focus on trade union power (because, particularly in the wake of President Reagan's defeat of the air traffic controllers, union membership in the US remained low and continued to decline). But the Reagan Administration was as committed as was Margaret Thatcher's to the establishment of a new policy paradigm for industrial competitiveness and economic growth: one built around the deregulation of industry and finance, the weakening of labour rights and the toleration (indeed encouragement) of high earnings for those successful in business. Trickle-down economics became the conventional wisdom of the day. Tax incentives and deregulated markets became the dominant answer to all economic problems. The prioritizing of industrial employment characteristic of the New Deal years was abandoned in favour of the growth of the service sector and the hegemony of financial institutions. Foreign Direct Investment was privileged as a source of private sector capital growth, and state spending (both on investment goods and social welfare) was heavily curtailed. It became axiomatic in both the US and the UK that governments could not pick winners, and so should not try. It also became axiomatic that given the new and enhanced degree of globalization associated with the end of the Cold War, national economies could only flourish by making themselves attractive to foreign investors rather than by building up a series of state-sponsored national champions. In the process, the economic debate shifted from one between Keynesians and monetarists to one between neoclassical economists and post-neoclassical endogenous growth theorists. Centre-left theorists and politicians initially toyed with more radical ideas and theories—the Alternative Economic Strategy pursued by the Labour Left in the UK until Labour's crushing electoral defeat in 1983 (Wickham-Jones, 1996), and in the US the Democratic Party's industrial policy debate ahead of the defeat of the Mondale presidential bid in 1984 (Johnson, 1984; Cohen and Zysman, 1987; Thompson, 1989, pp. 23–45)—but thereafter it was 'morning again in America' (and in the UK) for economic thought and policy of a self-confidently neo-liberal kind.

The new neo-liberal economic orthodoxy of the Thatcher/Reagan years was institutionalized within the European Union in the detail of the Maastricht Treaty signed in 1992. Though ironically, 'under the Maastricht Treaty for the first time the European Union was granted industrial policy powers,' in practice, as the OECD noted, since the 1980s industrial policy 'gradually moved from…measures in support of industries in decline or aiming at stimulating promising activities by "picking the winners" to… measures which did not interfere with the market process directly and instead attempted to improve its mechanism' (Federico and Foreman-Peck, 1999, pp. 1 and 6). The Maastricht Treaty set limits on the permissible proportion of GPD that could be absorbed by public sector debt, and set Europe on track for a single currency that would require European-wide monetary policy privileging low inflation over full employment. The European Commission, for its part, continued to press through the 1980s and beyond the need for greater competition, more deregulation, and the full exploitation of the Single European Market by the removal of the last barriers to cross-border trade and the encouragement of transnational networks of private companies.

That is not to say, of course, that more specifically focused industrial policy vanished from the agendas of governments in leading industrial economies. It did not. It simply went underground, and in the US case, also relocated itself at the level of individual states. In the Reagan years, 'every state in the Union provide[d] some kind of fiscal and investment incentive for business, to try to attract them into its area' (Thompson, 1989, p. 53) and at the federal level, policy continued to privilege certain sectors over others in the distribution of industrial support. Agriculture remained heavily subsidized. So too did the energy sector. Basic research in pharmaceuticals remained heavily government-dependent; and the entire military-industrial complex continued to flourish under Pentagon leadership. In fact, for all the political rhetoric about setting the private sector free from government interference, 'the federal government spent $92 billion in direct and indirect subsidies to businesses and private-sector corporate entities' (Slivinski, 2007, p. 1) in 2006, and the US federal government still currently funds 'a quarter of R&D and nearly 60 per cent of basic research' (Wolf, 2013, p. 1). That R&D support is not randomly distributed across the American economy as a whole. On the contrary, in 2004 'the two agencies with the largest R&D programmes—the Department of Defense and the National Institutes of Health—together accounted for 73 percent of federal R&D outlays' while 'the agencies that focus on the physical sciences and engineering – the National Science Foundation, NASA and the Department of Energy – accounted for 19 percent' (CBO, 2007, p. ix). But what is most striking about the scale and impact of this 'hidden' industrial policy, and of the gap between claim and reality in Reaganomics, is the degree to which the economic sectors most favoured by federal tax relief, research-assistance and direct purchasing power continue to outperform—in terms of long-term profitability and growth—those that are not so favoured. As Clyde Prestowitz—himself a one-time member of the Reagan Administration's economic team—reminds us, the Reagan Administration certainly had an industrial policy. It was just one that he, Clyde Prestowitz, found to be short-sighted and inadequate. It was 'to over-consume, and to promote weapons production, financial services, con-struction, medical research and services, agriculture, and oil and gas consumption and production. Further, it [was] both to offshore production and provision of all tradable manufacturing and services as well as, increasingly high-technology R&D, and to expand the domestic retail, food service, and personal medical services industries. At the macro-level, the strategy [was] to run up massive debt and to borrow as much and as long as possible.' (Prestowitz, 2010, pp. 270–1)

This was not simply a US subterfuge. Behind the political rhetoric of free markets and deregulation, UK governments too continued to selectively fund 'schemes assisting re-search and development in microelectronics, fibre optics, information technology and outer space' (Hall, 1986, p. 113). That was under Thatcher: under her successor John Major and at the behest of his much more interventionist deputy, Michael Heseltine, a retooled Department of Trade and Industry quietly returned to many of the practices associated with industrial policy in the later Wilson years, including the orchestration of private-public investment partnerships. For their part, German governments continued to subsidize declining industries—particularly coal—with state rather than federal agencies playing the major role, and continued to pursue regional policy designed to re-duce imbalances between Germany's various constituent states, not least that between the old East Germany and the rest (Feldenkirchen, 1999, p. 112). Indeed, and for this reason, 'Germany was one of the few European Union nations with an increase in total public industry support' between 1985 and 2000, 'from about €36,000 million in 1985 (West Germany only) to about €60,000 million in 2000 (reunified Germany)' (Buigues and Sekkat, 2009, p. 115). Japan likewise maintained the total of its industrial support through the last two decades of the century, focusing most on locally provided aid to small and medium-size enterprises, on R&D support and on export-insurance (Buigues and Sekkat, 2009, p. 184). EU competition rules did not prevent the continued heavy subsidization of European agriculture, and countries continued to compete for foreign direct investment (FDI) by multinational firms by offering tax concessions, infrastruc-ture support and modest labour laws. The UK was particularly adept at the latter. The subsidization of R&D continued unabated at the national level across the European Union, and cross-European subsidization of key new industries and products continued in spite of both the rhetoric of neo-liberalism and the pressure of American trade nego-tiators. Continuing European steel subsidies, for example, provoked a tariff response from the US as late as 1993, and transatlantic tension continued thereafter as European subsidies flowed to the private consortium that jointly produced the Airbus.

Where neo-liberal orthodoxies took deepest hold, levels of negative de-indus-trialization were particularly pronounced by the turn of the new millennium. By then, both the US and UK were running major trade deficits, particularly with an emerging China. In both, wage rates and job security were eroded (US) or threatened (UK) by significant degrees of corporate outsourcing; and rising living standards were maintained in the context of wage stagnation only by the accumulation of ever greater levels of private debt. Financial institutions flourished particularly well in this new climate (Greenwood and Scharfstein, 2013), effectively lending future wages to

existing wage earners in return for generous fees; and in their increasingly deregulated condition, moving away from safe banking practices to more lucrative speculative ones. By 2007 even governments of the centre-left, not least that in the UK, had
become enthusiastic advocates of light-touch regulation and the retreat from active
and focused industrial policy. Indeed that retreat had been central to New Labour's
understanding of why it was new and why it was successful. It was new because it
didn't do industrial policy the Old Labour way, and it was successful because, in a globalized economy, old industrial policy (and tax and spend politics) could only drive
foreign direct investment away. Gordon Brown, in his last major budget statement as
Chancellor of the Exchequer, even went so far as to claim he had tamed the business
cycle. But then Lehman Brothers collapsed in 2008, and the business cycle returned
with a vengeance.

3.5.1 The Re-Emergence of Industrial Policy

The financial crisis of 2008 brought to an abrupt halt a period of generalized economic
growth based on the premises of neo-liberalism, and there is currently no way back to
sustained growth and full employment without a re-examination of those premises.
That re-examination is now well under way in both academic and policymaking circles.

Academically, voices once drowned by the weight of neo-liberal orthodoxy and the
persistence of economic growth based on rising levels of private debt are drowned no
more. The case for state intervention as part of a successful development strategy is
being made again (Weiss, 2013). The role of the state in stimulating private sector innovation is once more being established (Mazzucato, 2013 and Chapter 9 in this volume).
The case for a re-stimulation of consumer demand on classical Keynesian lines is no
longer academic heresy (Krugman, 2013) and both in academia and related policy circles arguments now abound that the recent rapid growth in financial institutions has
damaged rather than strengthened overall economic performance. As Adair Turner put
it 'there is no clear evidence that the growth in the scale and complexity of the financial
system in the rich developed world over the last twenty to thirty years has driven
increased growth or stability' (Bartlett, 2013, p. 2).

Even in the heartland of Anglo-American orthodoxy, there seems to be a growing
recognition in certain policymaking circles of the need to rebalance economies too
structured—in the Reagan/Thatcher years—towards service employment and unregulated financial markets. At the core of that rebalancing is a strengthening of locally
based manufacturing industry, and the development of industrial policy designed for
exactly that purpose. The Republican Party in the US may still have not got the mes-
sage, but the US President certainly has. He is on record as seeking that rebalancing. So
too is the British Prime Minister, his Industry Secretary Vince Cable, and a still active
and unrepentant Michael Heseltine (Heseltine, 2012). To quote Vince Cable, 'market
forces are insufficient for creating the long term industrial capabilities that we need,'
which is why—in his view—'government must show more leadership in identifying
and supporting key technologies....; be willing to identify...and get behind success

stories….; and identify some loosely defined sectors which merit close attention and backing' (Cable, 2012). Likewise, Barack Obama:

> The first cornerstone of a strong and growing middle class has to be an economy that generates more good jobs in durable, growing industries. Over the past four years, for the first time since the 1990s, the number of American manufacturing jobs hasn't gone down; they've gone up. But we can do more. So I'll push new initiatives to help more manufacturers bring more good jobs back to America. We'll continue to focus on strategies to create good jobs in wind, solar and natural gas that are lowering energy costs and dangerous carbon pollution. And I'll push to open more manufacturing innovation institutes that turn regions left behind by global competition into global centers of cutting-edge jobs. Let's tell the world that America is open for business. (Goldfarb, 2013)

It is really like old times. As Yogi Berra would have it, it is '*déjà vu* all over again.' For rebalancing is no longer simply an argument and aspiration of the European and North American centre-left. As an aspiration, it is now more mainstream that that. More focused industrial policy is back in vogue. But what is less clear is exactly what form that more focused industrial policy can and should take: hence this particular volume.

References

Adams, J. and Stoffaës, C. (eds). (1986). *French Industrial Policy.* Washington DC: The Brookings Institution.

Amsden, A. (1989). *Asia's Next Giant: South Korea and Late Industrialization.* Oxford: Oxford University Press.

Aujac, H. (1986). 'An Introduction to French Industrial Policy', in J. Adams and C. Stoffaës (eds), *French Industrial Policy*, pp. 13–35. Washington DC: The Brookings Institution.

Bartlett, B. (2013). '"Financialization" as a Cause of Economic Malaise,' *Economix* 11 June, <http://economix.blogs.nytimes.com/2013/06/11/financialization-as-a-cause-of-economic -malaise/?_r=0>.

Bingham, M. (1998). *Industrial Policy American Style.* Armonk, New York: M. E. Sharpe.

Buigues, P.-A. and Sekkat, K. (2009). *Industrial Policy in Europe, Japan and the USA.* Basingstoke: Palgrave Macmillan.

Cable, V. (2012). *Industry Policy.* London: Department for Business Innovation and Skills.

Coates, D. (1975). *The Labour Party and the Struggle for Socialism.* Cambridge: Cambridge University Press.

Coates, D. (1980). *Labour in Power? A Study of the Labour Government 1974–79.* London: Longman.

Coates, D. (1991 [1995]). *Running the Country.* London: Hodder & Stoughton.

Coates, D. (1996). 'Introduction,' in D. Coates (ed.), *Industrial Policy in Britain*, pp. 3–29. Basingstoke: Macmillan.

Coates, D. (2000). *Models of Capitalism: Growth and Stagnation in the Modern Era.* Cambridge: Polity Press.

Cohen, S. and Zysman, J. (1987). *Manufacturing Matters: The Myth of the Post-Industrial Economy.* New York: Basic Books.

Congressional Budget Office (2007). *Federal Support for Research and Development*. Washington DC: Congress of the United States.

Di Tommaso, M. and Schweitzer, S. (2013). *Industrial Policy in America: Breaking the Taboo*. Cheltenham: Edward Elgar.

Dormois, J.-P. (1999). 'France: The Idiosyncracies of *Volontarisme*', in J. Foreman-Peck and G. Federico (eds), *European Industrial Policy: The Twentieth Century Experience*, pp. 58–97. Oxford: Oxford University Press.

Eisinger, P. (1990). 'Do the American States Do Industrial Policy?', *British Journal of Political Science* 20(4), 509–35.

Federico, G. and Foreman-Peck, J. (1999). 'Industrial Policies in Europe: Introduction', in J. Foreman-Peck and G. Federico (eds), *European Industrial Policy: The Twentieth Century Experience*, pp. 1–17. Oxford: Oxford University Press.

Feldenkirchen, W. (1999). 'Germany: The Invention of Interventionism', in J. Foreman-Peck and G. Federico (eds), *European Industrial Policy: The Twentieth Century Experience*, pp. 98–123. Oxford: Oxford University Press.

Foreman-Peck, J. and Federico, G. (1999). 'European Industrial Policy: An Overview', in J. Foreman-Peck and G. Federico (eds), *European Industrial Policy: The Twentieth Century Experience* pp. 426–60. Oxford: Oxford University Press.

Goldfarb, Z. (2013). 'READ: Obama's Big Speech on the Economy', *The Washington Post* July 24, <http://www.washingtonpost.com/blogs/wonkblog/wp/2013/07/24/obamas-speech-on-the-economy/>.

Graham, O. (1992). *Losing Time: The Industrial Policy Debate*. Cambridge MA, Harvard University Press.

Grant, W. (1982). *The Political Economy of Industrial Policy*. London: Butterworths.

Grant, W. (1989). *Government and Industry*. Aldershot: Edward Elgar.

Greenwood, R. and Scharfstein, D. (2013). 'The Growth of Finance', *Journal of Economic Perspectives*, 27(2), 3–28.

Hall, P. (1986). *Governing the Economy*. New York: Oxford University Press.

Heseltine, M. (2012). *No Stone Unturned: In Pursuit of Growth*. London: HMSO.

Johnson, C. (ed.). (1984). *The Industrial Policy Debate*. San Francisco: ICS Press.

Kitschelt, H. (1991). 'Industrial Governance Structures, Innovation Strategies, and the Case of Japan: Sectoral or Cross-National Comparative Analysis?', in W. Grant (ed.), *Industrial Policy*, pp. 367–407. Aldershot: Edward Elgar.

Kozul-Wright, R. (1995). 'The Myth of Anglo-Saxon Capitalism: Reconstructing the History of the American State', in H.-J. Chang and R. Rowthorn (eds), *The Role of the State in Economic Change*, pp. 81–113. Oxford: Oxford University Press.

Krauss, Ellis S. (1992). 'Political Economy: Policymaking and Industrial Policy in Japan', *Political Science & Politics* 35(1), 44–57.

Krugman, P. (2013). *End This Depression Now!*. New York: W. W. Norton.

Lash, S. and Urry, J. (1987). *The End of Organized Capitalism*. Cambridge: Polity.

Lee, S. (1996). 'Manufacturing', in D. Coates (ed.), *Industrial Policy in Britain*, pp. 33–61. Basingstoke: Macmillan.

Matsumoto, G. (1992). 'The Work of the Ministry of International Trade and Industry', in K. Cowling and R. Sugden (eds), *Current Issues in Industrial Economic Strategy*, pp. 145–62. Manchester: Manchester University Press.

Matthijs, M. (2011). *Ideas and Economic Crises in Britain from Attlee to Blair (1945–2005)*. London: Routledge.

Mazzucato, M. (2013). *The Entrepreneurial State: Debunking Public and Private Sector Myths.* London: Anthem Press.

Prestowitz, C. (2010). *The Betrayal of American Prosperity.* New York: Free Press.

Reich, S. (1990). *The Fruits of Fascism: Postwar Prosperity in Historical Perspective.* Ithaca: Cornell University Press.

Shonfield, A. (1965). *Modern Capitalism.* Oxford: RIIA/Oxford University Press.

Singh, A. (1993), 'Asian economic success and Latin American failure in the 1980s: new analyses and future policy implications', *International Review of Applied Economics*, 7(3), 267–89.

Slivinski, S. (2007). *The Corporate Welfare State: How the Federal Government Subsidizes U.S. Businesses.* Washington DC: The Cato Institute.

Smith, E. O. (1994). *The German Economy.* London: Routledge.

Stoffaës, C. (1986). 'Industrial Policy in the High Technology Industries,' in J. Adams and C. Stoffaës (eds), *French Industrial Policy*, pp. 36–62. Washington DC: The Brookings Institution.

Streeck, W. (1997). 'German Capitalism: Does It Exist? Can It Survive?', in C. Crouch and W. Streeck (eds), *Political Economy of Modern Capitalism*, pp. 33–54. London: Sage.

Thompson, G. (ed.). (1989). *Industrial Policy: USA and UK Debates.* London: Routledge.

Vogel, D. (1987). 'Government-Industry Relations in the United States: An Overview', in S. Wilks and M. Wright (eds), *Comparative Government-Industry Relations: Western Europe, the United States and Japan*, pp. 91–116. Oxford: The Clarendon Press.

Weiss, L. (2013). 'The Myth of Free-Market Capitalism Versus the Rest,' *Comment*, the blog site of SPERI (Sheffield Political Economy Research Institute), January 15, <http://speri.dept. shef.ac.uk/2013/01/15/myth-free-market-capitalism-rest/>.

Wickham-Jones, M. (1996). *Economic Strategy and the Labour Party: Politics and Policy-Making 1970–83.* New York: Macmillan.

Wolf, M. (2013). 'A Much-Maligned Engine of Innovation,' *The Financial Times* August 4.

CHAPTER 4

REFRAMING INDUSTRIAL POLICY

ANDREW BOWMAN, JULIE FROUD, SUKHDEV JOHAL, ADAM LEAVER, AND KAREL WILLIAMS

> Our economy has become more and more unbalanced, with our fortunes hitched to a few industries in one corner of the country, while we let other sectors like manufacturing slide.
>
> (David Cameron, UK Prime Minister, 2010)

4.1 INTRODUCTION

MOST economists would regard industrial policy, or indeed most other policy issues, as a matter of technical choice within an accepted framework, so that the issue is one of choosing appropriate and adequately resourced policies to attain a given object. This chapter takes a rather different approach: the recent (re)discovery of industrial policy is a politically sponsored development resulting from confused concern about an 'unbalanced economy', signalled by David Cameron's hand-wringing in the first speech he made on the economy after becoming prime minister. The chapter argues that the intellectual framework and the object of industrial policy both need to be rethought before an industrial policy relevant to British specifics can be formulated.

To begin with some context, Britain is a country in secular decline whose post-war economic history is dominated by two thirty-year policy experiments. The post-war settlement combined social security through insurance with a state-led economy of nationalized utilities and social housing, with health and education services free at point of use. As the antidote to a discredited settlement, the Thatcher–Blair experiment in competition and enterprise after 1979 put its faith *inter alia* in flexible labour markets, lower direct taxes, privatization-plus-regulation, and asset sales. Both experiments came apart on their own contradictions. The overhead cost of the post-war settlement was unsustainable given the feeble performance of tradable goods and privately owned manufacturing. The Thatcher–Blair economy was destabilized by the unproductive dynamic of housing equity withdrawal which was larger than nominal GDP growth under both premiers; more broadly, the deregulation of credit also produced a bloated financial sector, which first privatized gains and then socialized losses on its huge liabilities.

When policy experiments do not deliver on their promise, the classic mainstream response is to add *bolt-ons*—auxiliary policies which promise to improve outcomes. Bolt-ons leave the fundamental policy framework unchallenged and (partly for that reason) are likely to fail because they leave conjunctural problems ill-defined and alternative possibilities unexplored. So it was in the 1960s and 1970s under the Wilson, Heath, and Callaghan governments, which discovered indicative planning, and prices and incomes policy as part of the primitive form of corporatism that Thatcher swept away. There have been similar recent developments under the Brown and the Coalition Governments. The financial bolt-on since 2008 is a modest increase in capital requirements and ring-fencing of retail banking in the hope of protecting citizens from a financial sector with liabilities four times as large as GDP. The productive bolt-on is industrial policy which, in the mainstream version, aims to revive manufacturing. Industrial decline has been 'problematized' since 2010 as part of an 'unbalanced economy' which is London-centred, over-dependent on finance, and regionally divided with the North and West sustained by public expenditure (see Chapter 14 by Bailey, Cowling, and Tomlinson in this volume).

Before or after 1979, the economic policy debate in the UK has also often defaulted onto generic positions for and against state and market. For some, the recent interest in industrial policy bolt-ons is therefore a welcome development. The Westminster political classes and Whitehall civil service, who had for thirty years caricatured 1970s industrial policy as 'picking winners', are now increasingly positive about a new industrial strategy of targeting high-tech sectors. But, few have asked or adequately answered the hard questions about what this kind of new industrial strategy can achieve in the specific circumstances of Britain in the 2010s. These hard questions can, however, be explored by shifting away from generics about the role of the state in the capitalist economy and by engaging with the specifics of what's left in the British economy after fifty years of continuing manufacturing decline. Structural change has removed the giant British-owned diversified conglomerates like GEC and ICI but increasing reliance on foreign-owned branches of firms like Siemens and Honda has not solved the tradable goods problem.

The record of British manufacturing performance and accumulating problems over the past forty years can be summarized as follows (Froud et al., 2011).

- In the aggregate, British manufacturing output has fluctuated cyclically in a damaging way; there has been no sustained growth in the real value of manufacturing output since the 1970s.

- Since the 1950s, manufacturing imports have grown consistently faster than exports; unsteady currency depreciation has becomes less effective at stimulating British manufacturing since 2008.
- Manufacturing investment has recently broken from its long run pattern of cyclical fluctuation with output. Since the early 2000s, investment has flat-lined at record low levels; in 2010 the Office for Budget Responsibility predicted an investment and export-led recovery from recession which has not materialized.

Behind these deteriorating aggregates, there are problems of broken supply chains across many sectors. These are now structurally embedded through lost domestic capabilities, predatory supply chain behaviour and foreign ownership. For example, the back hoe loaders produced by an exemplary firm like JCB were 96 per cent British by value in 1979 but, by 2010, this proportion had fallen to 36 per cent, largely because of collapsed domestic supply chains. The process of deterioration continues today in the UK's largest manufacturing sector, food processing, because buyer-led supermarkets use their predatory power against domestic suppliers (Bowman et al., 2012). More generally, the factory sector which directly produces exports is now dominated by foreign-owned branch assemblers with a high propensity to import components: this problem is more acute in the UK where 50 per cent of intermediate purchases in UK mechanical vehicles and engineering are imported, compared with 30 per cent in Germany.

A manufacturing sector with these characteristics is beyond the fixes on offer from the Department for Business, Innovation and Skills (BIS) which now preaches the gospel of supply chain cooperation (see, for example, Department for Business, Innovation and Skills, 2014). Arguably, a substantial increase in output, investment, and employment in British manufacturing in the 2010s requires a miracle worker who could achieve something like the raising of Lazarus. Hence the need to start rethinking what has been economically taken-for-granted and to start reframing the issue of industrial policy.

The chapter does this in four sections. Section 4.2 considers the mainstream definition of the policy field and argues that new industrial strategy and its competitor policies share a framework whereby all are concerned with identifying the element that drives innovation (which in turn delivers productivity and GDP growth within a dynamic economy); their differences are then about the identity of that element. Section 4.3 argues that this model is of little relevance to the British economy, firstly because of the lack of policy levers which can secure major change, and secondly because the model does not take account of how post-1979 increases in GDP are unequally divided between social groups and regions. Section 4.4 proposes a new framing which would refocus industrial policy on what we call the UK's 'foundational economy' which produces everyday goods and services and is distributed according to population. The final section (4.5) then argues the case for the new policy instrument of social licensing applied to the foundational economy.

4.2 The Policy Field: New Industrial Strategy, Competitor Policies, and Shared Framing

> Industrial Policy is an attempt by a government to encourage resources
> to move into particular sectors that the government views as important
> to future economic growth.
>
> (Krugman and Obstfeld, 2003)

Recent official enthusiasm for a new industrial strategy is a British development which exists within a broader national and international field. This field is one of lively debate between overlapping and competing positions on industrial policy instruments and objectives, with two classical and competing positions represented in the UK by Mariana Mazzucato (see her Chapter 9 in this volume) from economics of innovation and by Max Nathan and Henry Overman from economic geography. But the different positions of these authors, and of British civil servants at BIS, are unified by a shared framing so that all agree that the ultimate objective is GDP growth, as identified by Krugman and Obstfeld in the quotation above. Within this frame, the mainstream policy maker's task is to identify the dynamic element which drives the intermediate objectives of technical innovation and higher productivity, which are the preconditions of higher output per capita and GDP growth. From this point of view, the unified field is structured around a series of primary differences about whether the dynamic elements are activity-based or place-based, sectors or locations; and then around a series of secondary differences about the role of drivers like research and development (R&D), or about the appropriate forms of policy intervention.

After 2010 in the UK, we see growing and broad-based enthusiasm for a sectorally focused programme of industrial policy as a bolt-on whose time has come: there is no fundamental mainstream rethinking of the ends and means of macro-policy, which is about more or less austerity (Bentham, Bowman, and Froud et al., 2013). Under Vince Cable, BIS has produced a series of reports about industrial strategy, promoting and reporting general and sector-specific documents (see, for example, Department for Business, Innovation and Skills, 2012, 2013; HM Government, 2013a). Employers, organized labour, and think tanks, notably including those on the centre right, have made similar arguments. Supporters of industrial policy include the Confederation of British Industry (CBI) and the Engineering Employers Federation (EEF). The Trades Union Congress (TUC), in line with its long-established enthusiasm for stakeholder capitalism, points to lessons from Germany (TUC, 2012a) but at the same time is attempting to build cross-party support for 'industrial policy activism' (TUC, 2012b).[1] Think tanks

---

[1] See also Chapter 12 in this volume.

of the centre right have joined in. For example, Policy Exchange (headed by Universities' Minister, David Willets) backs interventions that support 'science' and has 'Industrial Policy' as one of its projects (Policy Exchange, 2013; Willets, 2013). In 2013 Civitas argued for a 'proactive export policy' and also published a volume that explores the role for industrial policy in a rebalanced economy (Hunt, 2013; Pourvand, 2013).

From the chorus of official and quasi-official voices it is possible to discern two common motifs about the object and instruments of policy. The emphasis is on the need to *pick sectors* (rather than winning firms) in high-technology manufacturing, where Britain can be a world leader in the global race and achieve export success to eliminate the deficit in tradable goods. This means pharmaceuticals, aerospace, and automobiles, where there is a claim to already be among the 'world leaders', alongside green technology, information technology, and precision engineering, where there is an aspiration to join the leading group. The usual recommendation then is for government intervention in the form of targeted subsidies to overcome market failure in these key sectors, specifically in technological 'risk-taking' and innovation. The place of government intervention is at the embryonic stage of industries of the future, with the task to link cutting-edge university R&D to industry supply chains. More generally, manufacturers' access to credit needs to be improved through new (state) lending institutions, such as the Green Investment Bank or a version of German regional banks.

Thus, official British advocates of new industrial strategy have a wish list about the desirability of new technology sectors and some ideas about how to add innovation. Their ideas overlap with the more academic arguments made by Mariana Mazzucato from an economics of innovation perspective. Mazzucato focuses on the driving role of R&D expenditure as the precondition of innovation; and then adds some incisive criticism of financialized capitalist firms which prefer to distribute to shareholders or buy-back shares rather than spend on R&D. In adding a criticism of the financialized corporation, Mazzucato provides a necessary corrective to the official visions of new industrial strategy in which an essentially virtuous manufacturing sector is held back by early stage failures and external funding constraints. This argument rests on a model of economic growth where the state must lead as 'risk taker' in modern capitalism because the private sector is not willing to take on risk when it cannot capture the majority of the value created (2013, pp. 193–5). The policy implication is that the state—in the US, Southern Europe, or anywhere in between—should set up a central government agency which uses taxpayer funds to boost the stock of knowledge through 'investment in research and human capital formation that produce innovation' (p. 41). Interestingly, this is already echoed within government by 'enthusiasm for eight great technologies' (HM Government, 2013b; Willets, 2013) and funding for 'catapult centres' where state money is used to underpin commercialization of innovation in high value manufacturing and other sectors (Technology Strategy Board, 2013a, b).

While Mazzucato's model highlights the role of the state, it fails to note the most striking peculiarity of the UK's new industrial strategy, which is the absence of geography in BIS documents and in many of the other quasi-official visions of 'how the UK can win'. New industrial strategy policy proposals are for the UK economy as a national entity and the focus has been on activity-based, technology-intensive sectors, producing tradable and exportable goods and services with potential for enhancing national competitiveness. There is an unwillingness to explain how these policies relate to the differing needs and capabilities of the UK's regions; or, more specifically, on how and why individual areas might win or lose. This neglect of geography in national policy is immediately surprising given that regional specialization figures very prominently in current EU versions of industrial policy. For example, regions benefiting from EU structural funds must now have a 'smart specialization strategy' which shows how they plan to build competitive advantage on their existing strengths and capabilities (McCann and Ortega-Argiles, 2013). Furthermore, in many established theories of innovation including those of Michael Porter (1990), location is crucial because the focus is on regional activity clusters or urban agglomerations as the drivers of innovation.

Within economic geography, in recent years the emphasis has increasingly been on importing mainstream economic methods, arguments, and assumptions. In British geographical debate, the leading exponent of economics argument and place-based industrial policy is Henry Overman who argues against activity cluster-based approaches and for the importance of urban agglomeration. This static urban economics argument is that spatial concentration boosts productivity because a great city like London brings together a dense network of capability in workers, infrastructure, and suppliers. This provides learning opportunities which are reinforced by dynamic effects and increasing returns from selection and exit, as firms prefer to locate in larger markets (Nathan and Overman, 2013, pp. 384–7). This opens up a quite different perspective on industrial policy because, from Nathan and Overman's point of view, most of Britain's provincial cities are simply too small and the aim of industrial policy should be to 'increase the benefits of urban location' through policies for better transport and up-skilling the workforce (p. 399).

There is an obvious gap between Mazzucato's criticism of extractive financialized capitalist firms and Nathan and Overman's argument that agglomeration principles explain London's brilliant success. These academic arguments are much less bland than the official versions of new industrial strategy, but, Mazzucato, Nathan and Overman, and BIS's new industrial strategy represent variants on the dynamic economy framing. All provide different answers to the same question: What drives the technical innovation and higher productivity that will result in increased GDP at the national economy level? This national economy is, of course, uneven, in terms of regional character and sectoral distribution; but it is, in effect, treated as singular because everything that matters is encapsulated in GDP growth as the superordinate goal and measure of success for industrial policy.

4.3 THE LIMITS OF CONVENTIONAL FRAMING: POLICY LEVERS AND OUTCOMES

It's the same the whole world over,
It's the poor what gets the blame,
It's the rich what gets the pleasure,
Isn't it a bleeding shame.

(Billy Bennett, English comedian 1887–1942)

An intellectual framing (as in the case of the singular, dynamic economy) is about selection and sense-making, and has to meet some basic criteria of distinctiveness and internal coherence to differentiate it from other framings. This kind of frame only becomes policy-relevant if it meets certain further criteria and identifies policy levers that produce meaningful changes of the desired kind in the objects it constructs. And this immediately brings us to problems with the singular dynamic economy framing. The first most obvious point is that versions of the frame envisage various interventions, from boosting R&D to improving infrastructure, but none of them seem likely to have strong leverage on GDP. The second, subtler point is about GDP growth, which remains the ultimate policy goal for all major actors. The problem is that growth no longer has the same meaning since 1979. In earlier periods, this policy objective was defensible insofar as any increase in GDP was reasonably broadly distributed across all income groups and regions. But, as we shall see in this section, this assumption is no longer empirically justified because the trickle-down from GDP growth is meagre.

The immediate leverage problem for official policy is that it concentrates on technology-intensive sectors which are relatively small. In the UK, the R&D-intensive sectors account for 1.76 per cent of GDP and, although manufacturing employs more than 2 million, much of that is in mundane activities like food manufacture which is, by employment, the largest manufacturing sector. Food production, processing, distribution and retail employ twice as many as in all the favoured manufacturing sectors together (such as automotive, aerospace, pharma, and IT) combined. A quantum leap in the competitive performance and size of the technology intensive sectors is necessary before they would have any large impact on UK GDP. It could be argued that something like IT is a sector of the future whose current size in the 2010s is no more an indicator of its future growth and transformative potential than car assembly was in the 1910s. This future possibility cannot be completely discounted but it rests on an historical analogy which has been greeted sceptically by Robert Gordon (2012), who has repeatedly questioned whether digital technologies are as transformative in the present day as were universal electrification and the internal combustion engine in an earlier era. The cautious wait-and-see verdict would be that digitally led transformation requires a top-to-bottom reformatting of the economy which is the work of more than a generation and limits early pay-offs.

Meanwhile, structural transformation of the national economy and an improvement in British competitive performance is unlikely to be delivered by the kind of stepping up of R&D that Mazzucato recommends (2013, pp. 41, 52). The problem is not that the story about the US before 1979 is wrong but that it generalizes the special case. Against a background of cold war hysteria and sustained economic growth, it was politically possible for US military and civil agencies to funnel huge investments into basic research in technologies whose subsequent commercialization produced global leaders which included many American companies that, initially at least, sited much activity in the US. But none of these special case conditions applies currently in the UK or in South European countries, like Italy, Greece, or Portugal. The fundamental problem in the UK case is structural and organizational. A new material like graphene may be invented at Manchester University but, as Jones (2013) argues, the UK no longer has large corporates with research labs that can undertake the next stage of commercialization. Nor is there a market large enough to sustain profitable production of the commercialized innovations. The contrast with the earlier stored programme computer is quite telling: sixty years ago, the world's first stored programme computer, 'the Baby' was invented at Manchester University and then moved a couple of miles across the city to Ferranti, which turned it into a commercially available machine whose lineal descendants were predictably beaten in the market place by IBM which had a huge base in American military and civil demand. The only plausible way back into high-tech manufacturing for the British would be through cooperative multinational projects on the Airbus model. However, such projects are not on the British government's agenda and would require broader political commitment and economic co-operation amongst EU members. Thus, while R&D may be a sensible option for winners, the British economy is not organized to capture the benefits of state-funded innovation, nor is it economically performing so as to generate a politically available surplus for high-tech investment.

Beyond the problem of absent levers, there is that of unwelcome outcomes. When GDP growth and job creation were enshrined as the joint objectives of new kinds of macroeconomic policy in the post-1945 period it was assumed that GDP growth would be broadly distributed within and across the national territory and that jobs would be well enough paid to allow one full-time wage earner to support a family. Now, although macro-policymakers have not fully registered the implications, neither jobs nor GDP growth have the same meaning. The data presented in this section illustrate the division of the gains from income and output growth in the UK between different income groups and regions since 1979.

The story on the division of gains from growth between different income groups shows the limits of trickle-down and the extent of gains by upper income groups. The income measure is the primary flow into economically active households, i.e. the incomes received by working households before taxes and benefits complicate the outcome. The result is startling: as Figure 4.1 shows, the top decile of active households captured 40 per cent of all income gains since 1979 and the top quintile captured 60 per cent; in contrast, the bottom 30 per cent made no gains since 1979 and the bottom half

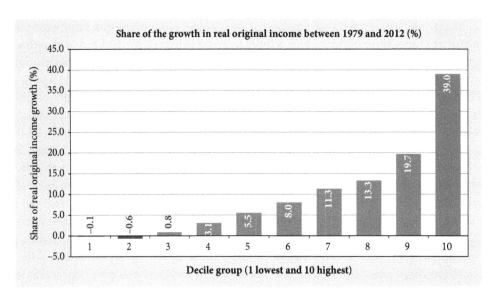

FIGURE 4.1 Share of the Growth (%) in Real Original Income between 1979 and 2012 in Economically Active Households.

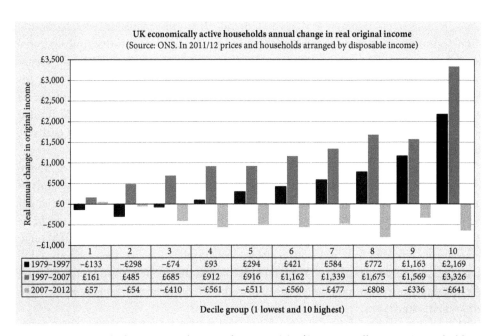

FIGURE 4.2 Annual Change in Real Original Income (£) of Economically Active Households.

claimed only 10 per cent of the gains in original income. The patterns are different by sub-periods, as Figure 4.2 shows. All active groups (except for the lowest decile on or near the minimum wage) lost income after the 2008 downturn and the absolute losses were largest in the upper income groups (such groups have more income to lose). But this was little more than a pause after thirty years of sustained, spectacular gains for the top decile; it did not change the long run pattern which is that the bottom half of active households have no claim on increasing income.

The pattern of regional gains from growth is very similar, with gains concentrated in London and the inner South East, while regions with collapsed industrial bases gain little and fall further behind. Again our measure is a primary one and the obvious choice here is gross value added (GVA) which measures the value of goods and services produced in each region (minus intermediate consumption) over a given period. The spatial pattern of inequality is different because this intensifies in the most recent period, as Figure 4.3 shows. Over the years 2007–12, London and the South East with around 25 per cent of population claimed more than 50 per cent of the increase in output; whereas a peripheral region like Wales with around 5 per cent of the population claimed no more than 2.5 per cent of GVA growth. The share of output growth in London and the South East in the previous twenty years had been lower, and all regions make some claim on increases in the value of GVA (partly as a result of New Labour spending on health and education). Some trickle-down is taking place but not enough to halt steady deterioration in the relative position of peripheral regions like the North East, the West Midlands, or Wales, where GVA per capita relative to London has fallen from 54 to 43 per cent over the twenty years from 1989 to 2009, as Figure 4.4 indicates.

This markedly spatial evidence about growing inequality provides a point of entrance for economic geographers. In the case of Nathan and Overman (2013), the influence of mainstream economics is such that there is little in their policy thinking that challenges established mainstream post-1979 policy ideas. Their argument on disadvantaged regions endorses up-skilling and infrastructural improvements to make the market work better and updates that, as many now do, with recommendations that city regions should have more political power and economic resource to do these things for themselves. With or without devolution, there is dispute about whether such improvements always or usually benefit disadvantaged regions: thus, Tomaney and Marques (2013), after reviewing the international evidence, suggest that high-speed rail will not benefit

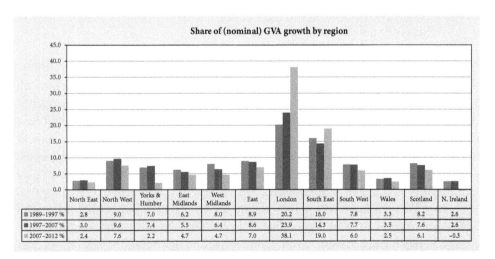

FIGURE 4.3 Share of Nominal GVA Growth (%) by Region.

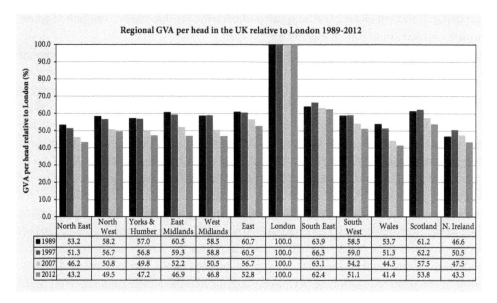

FIGURE 4.4 Regional GVA as a Percentage of London's GVA, 1989–2012.

the North. While better transport can transform a locality through disenclavement, it is less likely that such processes can quickly transform the performance of a region. Such complexities mean that it is easier to diagnose problems than to prescribe effective solutions that can tackle entrenched and growing inequalities. In this respect, it is useful to move away from a singular economy and frame issues in a different way.

4.4 A Different Framing: Heterogeneity, Specifics, and the Foundational

> There were not one but several economies.
>
> (Braudel, *The Structures of Everyday Life*, 1981)

The idea of the singular, dynamic economy is an invention of recent date. It owes much to the mid-twentieth-century rise of national income accounting and the associated idea that all output can be aggregated into the one measure of GDP; and it is reinforced by medical metaphors about the body economic which is in 'recovery' from recession or at risk of 'contagion'. If we wish to unsettle this framing, we can turn to Fernand Braudel who recognized multiple economies as part of his challenge to historians preoccupied with dynamic commerce and innovation that would in due course deliver industrial revolution, Western imperialism and much else. Against this, in his *Civilization and Capitalism* volumes Braudel argued that from the fifteenth to the eighteenth century there were two further economic zones, one above and one below the market. Most of the world's population lived in a quite different, mundane and slow-moving *infra economy* of 'material life'. This was organized around immediate production and consumption rather than exchange. At the same time, above the market was a *supra economy* of a few insiders engaged in long-distance trade and speculation as they managed exchange under the aegis of the state (1981, p. 23). Braudel's three-level scheme is specific to the early modern period, but his strategy of recognizing multiplicity in a multi-zonal economy applies just as well to the present day.

Mainstream discussion of industrial policy is preoccupied with what happens in the zone of competition where goods are tradable and firms are mobile; and the idea of the singular economy then encourages the notion that we all (must) live in a zone where competition is universalized by globalization in the product market and financialization in the capital market. But there is another zone, a largely sheltered infra economy in what we call the foundational economy. We define this as the economic zone that produces mostly mundane and sometimes taken-for-granted goods and services that have three interrelated characteristics: first, they are necessary to everyday life; second, they are consumed by all citizens regardless of income; and third, they are therefore distributed according to population through branches and networks. The list of such activities includes: the privatized pipe and cable utilities together with transport; some traditionally private activities such as retail banking, supermarket food retailing and food processing; and some traditionally state-provided activities including health, education, and welfare or social care, which are now increasingly outsourced.

The idea of the multi-zone economy is subversive because it changes the field of the visible and opens new possibilities. The formal difference between singularity and multiplicity is important for policy. The logic of singularity is a preference for generic policy prescriptions, whether for better transport or more R&D: in this frame, policy is about identifying and pressing a model of economic intervention which engages with the singular logic of a world disclosed through a preferred GDP growth model. The radical heterogeneity of the activities in the foundational economy list immediately suggests the limits of generic policy and, by implication, the limits of any one kind of privileged economic intervention in a world where one size cannot fit all. But, before turning to policy in the next section, it is useful to provide a brief description of the foundational economy and some analysis of its pervasive and multifaceted problems which complicate the task of policy.

Using the definition above, the foundational economy is relatively large whether we consider production or consumption measures (Bentham, Bowman, and de la Cuesta et al., 2013).

- Employment data shows that at least one third of the UK's workforce is employed in the foundational economy, with nearly 10 per cent in private and privatized activities and twice that number in state-provided and state-funded activities. The number working in capital-intensive pipe and cable utilities is small, but retailing remains labour-intensive with some 440,000 employed in retail banking, 1 million in supermarkets and some 323,000 in food processing. But by far the largest number of foundational workers are to be found in the state or para-state sectors of health, education and welfare/social care which in total employ some 4.5 million. In the UK, such services were traditionally delivered locally by the state; but they are now increasingly delivered by the para-state (including private sector firms, charities and social enterprises), with some or all of the funding coming from government. With outsourcing, the number employed in the para-state sector has already grown to one third of those directly employed by the British state.

- Taking consumption measures, the figures are equally striking. The foundational economy is partly financed indirectly by tax revenues and partly by direct house-hold expenditure. The latter can be tracked from household expenditure data which shows how foundational activity reaches into every household in the country. In 2011, £141 or nearly 30 per cent of all household expenditure went on foundational activities with the big ticket items being £55 on groceries (excluding alcoholic drink), £42 on pipe and cable utilities and £34 mainly on car fuel. The other notable point is that, although expenditure on these objects varies with income, all house-holds are foundational consumers. So, for instance, food and non-alcoholic drink accounts for 15.9 per cent of total expenditure in the poorest quintile (Q1) of house-holds and 9 per cent in the richest quintile (Q5) of households.

For thirty years or more, politicians have generally assumed that in these founda-tional activities private ownership can supply capital which the state cannot provide while private management will drive badly need efficiency gains. But, on closer inspec-tion, the private and privatized activities are not being managed in ways that meet broad social objectives or even private efficiency standards along the supply chain; this is usu-ally because private corporate players are dedicated to realizing value at a point regard-less of consequences for other stakeholders. A series of CRESC public interest reports on railways and meat supply have presented a distinctive *follow the money* sectoral ana-lysis and described dysfunctionality in some detail (Bowman et al., 2012, 2013). This ac-count is reinforced by three new case study reports on telecoms, dairy and retail banking in a follow-up book, *The End of the Experiment?* (Bowman et al., 2014). Here are evi-denced accounts about how investment-averse firms exercise predatory supply chain power and use confusion marketing so as to make consumer price comparisons more difficult. The behaviours detailed in these sectoral case studies have more to do with cost-avoidance and risk-passing by firms who have urgent financial return motives and limited organizational capabilities, than they do with efficiency. The dysfunction is clearest in analysis of supermarkets and meat supply where buyer-led supermarkets like Tesco are passing up opportunities to profit from integrated meat processing on the Morrisons model because they lack manufacturing capability (Bowman et al., 2012).

In the privatized utilities, the problem is that financialized motives inhibit essential investment in network upgrading and construction whose cost then falls on the state amidst increasing confusion and opacity. The industry structures and problems in rail and telecoms are apparently very different but the outcome is the same. In telecoms the one ex-state utility has turned into a sector-dominating giant BT, which has turnover of

£18 million. But BT will not invest in a nationwide and future-proof fast broadband network which takes fibre to the premises; and, without generous state incentives for rural provision, BT's fibre to the cabinet network will be confined to the two-thirds or so of population in the urban areas where BT can construct a business case (Bowman et al., 2014). In rail, a multiplicity of franchise operators want an option on profit with no downside risk and have dodged any requirement to contribute to investment in network upgrading (Bowman et al., 2013). All franchisees have benefited financially from artificially low track access charges which meant that the infrastructure company Network Rail had to finance infrastructure improvement by issuing £30 billion of government bonds which have now been taken onto the government's books as a liability. Worse still, the franchisees are allowed to make back-loaded premium bids which create distributable profits in the early years and then allow the franchisees to walk away with token penalties when they wish to avoid onerous premium payments in the later years of the franchise. Much the same point about uncontrolled opportunism could be made about BT's unwillingness to disclose costs and margins on its state-subsidized rural broadband contracts.

In many other, traditionally private, foundational activities the rather different problem is that corporate players with supply chain power use it against other stakeholders so as to maintain their margins at others' expense. It is ironic that, from a customer service point of view, many commentators contrast 'good' supermarkets with 'bad' retail banks. In both activities, the big chains are using power to defend their margins at the expense of another stakeholder. The only difference is that the chain damage which supermarkets do is partly hidden from view because the injured stakeholder is a supplier not a customer. In supermarkets and dairy there is a supply chain involving farmers and processors in liquid milk and cheese. Dairy farmers have long complained about oppressive conduct by the supermarkets but our financial analysis highlights the plight of the processors (especially in liquid milk) which have become the squeezed middle of the chain: the processors' share of the price of a litre of milk fell from 35 per cent to 19 per cent over the decade after 2001. They are silent victims because processors do not have the cultural capital of the farmers and are inhibited from speaking out by their direct dependence on supermarket orders. In banks, it is the customers and direct employees that are obviously squeezed. In the absence of a supply chain, the retail banks have hit on customers and use their branches for pressure selling of fee-earning products. The result has been repeated scandals about mis-selling, most recently through staff incentives to sell highly profitable protection products like PPI and interest rate swaps.

The business model is often not examined because it is supposed that many of the problems with private business have exogenous causes; and confusion is then compounded by the general assumption that (more) competition will fix outstanding sectoral problems. In mainstream new industrial strategy, it is often assumed that the private sector would deliver more if it were not held back by external restraints such as access to finance, decrepit infrastructure, lack of government R&D support, or too few engineering graduates. Many are reluctant to accept that, for example, problems may be inherent in embedded forms of private sector supply chain behaviour. There is now some official effort to (re)build supply chains by encouraging cooperative activity in sectors like automotive; but this is largely disconnected from analysis of business models, ownership constraints and shareholder value requirements which combine to drive supply chain behaviours. The many economists, who are rightly sceptical about the conduct of private business, are distracted by the idea that competition or the simulation of competition by utility regulators, can keep firms virtuous. The limits of this approach are clearest in the case of supermarkets which have survived successive competition inquiries quite unscathed because they can show they are not colluding. More competition is the invariable prescription when problems cannot be denied in the privatized utilities or retail oligopolies where five or six giant firms take more than 80 per cent of the market. But little may be achieved by breaking up chains like Lloyds and RBS in retail banking and encouraging challengers like TSB, if the challengers have the same business model as the incumbents. It is the standardized business model which needs changing not the amount of competition which needs increasing.

4.5 Social Licensing: The Foundational as an Object of Policy

> I here suggest that big business, in the American system, exists and derives its right to exist under, and only under, a tacit social contract. This social contract requires management of big business to assume certain responsibilities. Assumption and fulfillment of them entitles big business to the privileges it receives from the State, and to acquiescence in their existence by the economic community they affect and serve.
>
> (Berle, 1962)

Within the new industrial strategy consensus, industrial policy is about building something new—specifically, high-tech sectors of the future—through which the UK will find the export success that has eluded it for the past fifty years and more. We would not argue against this aim but have cautioned about limited policy leverage and unwelcome outcomes. If so, why not shift the focus of industrial policy to make better use of what exists in the foundational economy which, as we have argued, is relatively large and in many ways mismanaged by the private sector because public policy does not engage and challenge the business models that undermine social objectives like national network coverage and supply chain security. Given the increasing disconnect between growth and wages/living standards for one third or more of the working population, the foundational sectors offer greater potential opportunities to improve equity and welfare, though maybe without increments to GDP.

However, the foundational economy only becomes an object of policy if we can identify levers and instruments which are more likely to be effective than those favoured by mainstream industrial policy-makers. Here the news is mixed. It is relatively easy to come up with economic instruments, like the social licensing described below, that do have leverage over a population of immobile firms, but it is not clear that centralized government has the political will or economic knowledge to implement social licensing policies because it has shifted far from the kind of liberal collectivism that Berle supported. The preconditions of serious industrial policy are therefore political because they require substantial decentralization and devolution to regional and local government. Hence the relevance of liberal collectivist figures from the 1930s like Berle, because devolution will only take a turn towards social licensing of firms if it is legitimated by ideas of the social contract between business and community, and if we set ideas of 'innovation' in a new socio-economic context.

The notion of 'social licence' is most familiar in the mining industry, particularly in the developing world. Here it takes the form of a formal or informal agreement between an investor seeking to extract natural resources, and the community affected by these activities. It can cover labour conditions, environmental standards, the sharing of economic benefits and other locally important concerns such as the protection of sacred sites (Socialicense, n.d.; miningfacts.org, n.d., etc.). Our suggestion is that something comparable to the more formal version of mining social license might be applied to firms and sectors in the foundational economy. Here we are working by analogy. The extractive industries seek immobile natural resources, but so too do private sector operators in the foundational economy which tap the household spend and taxes of an immobile population. In mining, as in the foundational economy, a limited number of operators are granted the right to extract. The fundamental rationale is thus the same. In the foundational economy, as in countries sitting on large mineral deposits, businesses need to earn the right to extract cash from a territory rather than expect sweeteners to operate locally.

How might social licensing work in the foundational economy? Our suggestions which are tentative and for discussion are as follows.

- Licensing would be an explicit arrangement that gave contracting enterprises or sectors privileges and rights to trade whilst placing them under reciprocal obligations to offer social returns: a formal licensing system would make the right to trade dependent on providing a service that meets relevant criteria of community responsibility on issues such as sourcing, training or payment of living wages. This is not just because being 'socially responsible' is a good in itself or burnishes corporate reputation, but also because these issues are important for promoting the sustainability of services—economic and social—of good quality and that are widely accessible over the longer term.
- The scale and scope of licensing agreements would vary. They might be with whole sectors, including all the firms above a certain size threshold. In other cases, where firm size and market position varied greatly within a sector, it might be more appropriate to have separate firm agreements. For example, the sourcing obligations on the big four supermarket chains would probably be different from those placed on a smaller chain like Waitrose or Booths. Note, as a part of this, that the 'community'

is not a natural domain but a variable political and economic unit, influenced for example by local and regional government forms and boundaries. Agreements, with rewards and sanctions such as variation in corporate tax rates, would clearly need to work round relevant national and EU legislation at the same time as putting the appropriateness of such rules into question.

The rationale for such agreements is socio-political. Foundational enterprises have direct and mutually dependent relations with communities or user-groups. As we have seen, they often benefit from limited competition and sheltered streams of revenue as they draw their customers and profits from communities in specific catchment areas. The argument is that in return for their sheltered existence they owe something to those communities or groups, and therefore should be brought within a new kind of regime. To reframe the foundational economy as a matter of social license is thus to insist that the foundational is not simply about point-value economic transactions, but also about reciprocal social relations within local, regional, and national spaces. The provision of mundane goods and services in the foundational economy is intertwined with the multiple identities of people as consumers, workers, and local residents so that prices, wages and quality of life would need to be triangulated across politically negotiated spaces. The aim would be a new world of social licensing where it was no longer so easy for councils to collude with payment of below minimum wages, or for supermarkets to ignore local concerns about sourcing.

The proposal is thus for an extension of government which would take the burden of expectation from (corporate) governance as we presently understand it. Corporate governance, or the rearrangement of stakeholder claims around the individual firm, is not able to police behaviour and consequences in a way that would allow us to curb irresponsible business models. Instead, government would need to consider licensing arrangements whereby firms and sectors trade only if they make a return (economic and otherwise): to the localities in which they operate; to their employees; to their consumers; to their supply chains; and to the broader social and natural environment. Any such strategy will require knowledge of sectors and of regional and local circumstances which central government departments do not have. The central state would have to loosen its grip so that social licensing can take various forms in different places: we will need to move from abstraction—from the idea that one size fits all in economic policy—to the kind of multiplicity pointed to by Braudel.

From this point of view, in the present conjuncture at the point when the Thatcher/Blair experiment is exhausted, the political precondition for a serious industrial policy is a decentralization of the British state. The centralized political machine delivered a real transformation in the conditions of everyday life after 1945, but in the UK in the 2010s after thirty years of dogmatic, centralized experiment, devolution is the more sensible proposition. In principle, devolved governments and regions are in a position to ask territorially relevant questions precisely because they are different industrially, historically, politically, and culturally. Further political devolution would allow industrial experiments to take different local or regional forms and government to explore different forms of social licensing. Such devolution is needed at this juncture, if we are to turn the state back into an experimental apparatus capable of learning from its failures rather than simply repeating them. So a truly experimental form of social licensing will need powerful and substantially autonomous elected authorities.

REFERENCES

Bentham, J., Bowman, A., de la Cuesta, M., Engelen, E., Froud, J., Johal, S., Law, J., Leaver, A., Moran, M., and Williams, K. (2013). *A Manifesto for the Foundational Economy*, University of Manchester/Open University, CRESC Working Paper No. 131.

Bentham, J., Bowman, A., Froud, J., Johal, S., Leaver, A., and Williams, K. (2013). *Against New Industrial Strategy: Framing, Motifs and Absences*, University of Manchester, CRESC Working Paper No. 126.

Berle, A. (1962). 'A New Look at Management Responsibility', Lecture to the Bureau of Industrial Relations, University of Michigan, 9 April, <http://3197d6d14b5f19f2f440-5e13d29c4c-016cf96cbbfd197c579b45.r81.cf1.rackcdn.com/collection/papers/1960/1962_0409_ManagementBerleT.pdf>.

Bowman, A., Froud, J., Johal, S., Law, J., Leaver, A., and Williams, K. (2012). *Bringing Home the Bacon: From Trader Mentalities to Industrial Policy.* University of Manchester/Open University: CRESC.

Bowman, A., Folkman, P., Froud, J., Johal, S., Law, J., Leaver, A., Moran, M., and Williams, K. (2013). *The Great Train Robbery: The Economic and Political Consequences of Rail Privatisation.* Manchester and Milton Keynes: CRESC.

Bowman, A., Erturk, I., Froud, J., Johal, S., Law, J., Leaver, A., Moran, M., and Williams, K. (2014). *The End of the Experiment?.* Manchester: Manchester University Press.

Braudel, F. (1981). *The Structures of Everyday Life: Civilization and Capitalism*, vol. 1, tr. S. Renolds. New York: Harper and Row.

Cameron, D. (2010). 'Transforming the British Economy. Coalition Strategy for Economic Growth', Speech, 28 May, <https://www.gov.uk/government/speeches/transforming-the-british-economy-coalition-strategy-for-economic-growth>.

Department for Business, Innovation and Skills (2012). *Industrial Strategy: UK Sector Analysis*, BIS Economics Paper No. 18, September, <https://www.gov.uk/government/uploads/system/uploads/attachment_data/file/34607/12-1140-industrial-strategy-uk-sector-analysis.pdf>.

Department for Business, Innovation and Skills (2013). *Industrial Strategy Conference 2013: Securing Jobs and a Stronger Economy*, BIS Analysis Paper No. 1,<https://www.gov.uk/government/uploads/system/uploads/attachment_data/file/237323/bis-13-1165-securing-jobs-and-a-stronger-economy-analytical-insights.pdf>.

Department for Business, Innovation and Skills (2014). 'Strengthening UK Supply Chains. Good Practice from Industry and Government', <https://www.gov.uk/government/uploads/system/uploads/attachment_data/file/278211/bis-14-515-strengthening-uk-supply-chains-good-practice-from-industry-and-government.pdf>.

Froud, J., Johal, S., Law, J., Leaver, A., and Williams, K. (2011). *Rebalancing the Economy (Or Buyers' Remorse)*, University of Manchester/Open University, CRESC Working Paper No. 87.

Gordon, R. J. (2012). *Is US Economic Growth Over? Faltering Innovation Confronts the Six Headwinds*, National Bureau of Economic Research, Cambridge, MA, NBER Working Paper No. 18315.

HM Government (2013a). 'Lifting Off: Implementing the Strategic Vision for UK Aerospace', <https://www.gov.uk/government/uploads/system/uploads/attachment_data/file/142625/Lifting_off_implementing_the_strategic_vision_for_UK_aerospace.pdf>.

HM Government (2013b). 'Industrial strategy', <https://www.gov.uk/government/uploads/system/uploads/attachment_data/file/278324/industrial_strategy_booklet.pdf>.

Hunt, T. (ed.). (2013). *Rebalancing the British Economy*. London: Civitas, <http://www.civitas.org.uk/pdf/RebalancingtheEconomyAPPG.pdf>.

Jones, R. (2013). *The UK's Innovation Deficit and How to Repair It*, University of Sheffield, SPERI Working Paper No. 6.

Krugman, P. and Obstfeld, M. (2003). *International Economics: Theory and Policy*. Boston, MA: Addison-Wesley.

Mazzucato, M. (2013). *The Entrepreneurial State*. London: Anthem Press.

McCann, P. and Ortega-Argiles, R. (2013). 'Modern Regional Innovation Policy', *Cambridge Journal of Regions, Economy and Society* 6(2), 179–86 (Advanced open access).

Miningfacts.org (n.d.). 'What is the Social License to Operate (SLO)?', <http://www.miningfacts.org/Communities/What-is-the-social-licence-to-operate/>.

Nathan, M. and Overman, H. (2013). 'Agglomeration, Clusters and Industrial Policy', *Oxford Review of Economic Policy* 29(2), 383–404.

Policy Exchange (2013). 'Industrial Policy', <http://www.policyexchange.org.uk/advanced-modules/industrial-policy>.

Porter, M. (1990). *The Competitive Advantage of Nations*. New York: Free Press.

Pourvand, K. (2013). 'Developing a Proactive Export Policy', *Civitas Ideas for Economic Growth* 4, <http://www.civitas.org.uk/economy/IdeasForEconomicGrowth4.pdf>.

Socialicense (n.d.). 'The Social License to Operate', <http://socialicense.com/>.

Technology Strategy Board (2013a). 'About Catapult Centres', <https://www.catapult.org.uk/about-us>.

Technology Strategy Board (2013b). 'What is a Catapult?', <https://www.catapult.org.uk/documents/2155693/2268412/What+is+a+Catapult/e68c7c90-39e0-45b7-be4b-9ba1e1c51232?version=1.2 >.

Tomaney, J. and Marques, P. (2013). 'Evidence, Policy and the Politics of Regional Development: The Case of High-Speed Rail in the United Kingdom', *Environment and Planning C* 31, 414–27.

TUC (2012a). *Lessons from Germany. Developing Industrial Policy in the UK*, <http://www.tuc.org.uk/industrial-issues/manufacturing/german-lessons-developing-industrial-policy-uk>.

TUC (2012b). 'Building a Secure Future: A New Industrial Policy', <http://www.afterausterity.org.uk/2012/building-a-secure-future-a-new-industrial-policy/>.

Willets, D. (2013). *Eight Great Technologies*. London: Policy Exchange, <http://www.policyexchange.org.uk/images/publications/eight%20great%20technologies.pdf>.

CHAPTER 5

··

THE ROLE OF INDUSTRIAL POLICY

Lessons from Asia

··

MUSHTAQ KHAN

5.1 INTRODUCTION

IN the second half of the twentieth century, a number of Asian countries achieved significant growth accelerations and began to rapidly catch up with advanced countries. Their success was based on their vigorous participation and competition in global markets, but it is now widely recognized that they were so successful in developing their competitiveness because of equally vigorous state support and industrial policies. Their experience demonstrated that competitiveness was not always exogenously determined by 'comparative advantage'. Competitiveness could be developed and changed by deliberate policies, though obviously within limits set by what could feasibly be achieved given the initial conditions of different countries. While these successful Asian countries were rapidly industrializing, the emergence of a new market fundamentalism in advanced countries, and particularly in the UK and the US, led to an unconditional acceptance of an accelerated de-industrialization in these countries as a normal consequence of changing comparative advantage. Over the longer term, the important lesson from the East Asian success stories is surely that comparative advantage is not a 'given' and policy can influence comparative advantage within broad limits. The policy question facing Britain is whether de-industrialization has proceeded too far and what if anything can be done about it.

The Asian experience is important for a number of reasons beyond establishing the importance of industrial policies. The Asian experience also shows that industrial policy was not uniformly successful. Many countries, including those in the Indian subcontinent, achieved much poorer results with their industrial policies in the 1960s and 1970s. These countries ended up protecting and subsidizing many infant industries that refused to become competitive despite decades of support. However, South Asia went through a realignment of its industrial policies in the 1980s and achieved much greater success as a result, with some of their most important competitive sectors emerging through new versions of industrial policies in a number of these countries. While Asian countries are still far away from European ones in terms of their levels of development, and therefore in the types of industrial policy challenges that they face, there are a number of general lessons from some of the diverse Asian experiences that could be relevant for policy discussions in the UK.

For an advanced country like the UK, industrial policy clearly has to support both innovation and the development of competitive production capabilities that can convert ideas and knowledge into marketable products. There is no question therefore that industrial policy must have a focus on supporting innovation and the development of new knowledge. This involves investment in public bodies such as universities as well as in networks linking public and private players engaged in innovation. Countries such as the UK still have a lead over most emerging Asian countries in the organization of innovation, though there may be particular strategies of financing or organizing innovation that may be worth looking at. However, the second plank of any effective industrial policy has to be the development of competitive manufacturing capabilities so that good ideas and technologies can be converted into competitive products. Here the UK can learn a lot about the types of problems countries can face when they try to acquire (or, in the case of the UK, re-acquire) firm-level competitive capabilities. Britain's gradual loss of manufacturing competitiveness after the Second World War was exacerbated after the 1980s in the context of its rapid de-industrialization. The country lost much of the tacit knowledge embedded in the organizational routines of manufacturing firms, and as a result fell even further behind in terms of its capacity to regain a broad base of competitive firms. The experience of Asian industrial policy shows that the achievement of competitiveness in new sectors and technologies can be a difficult problem to crack. The two planks of industrial policy are closely connected because without a broad base of firms that can organize production competitively, a successful innovation strategy will simply result in the offshoring of manufacturing somewhere else.

The rest of this chapter is organized as follows. Section 5.2 outlines a number of different dimensions of the industrial policy debate using the Asian experience as the backdrop. Industrial policies face a dual challenge: they have to identify and target the most important constraints facing a particular country, and they also have to address these problems in ways that can be implemented and enforced in the contexts of particular political and institutional contexts. The experience of success and failure in Asia shows the importance of designing policy so that it satisfies both these requirements. The implication of the second requirement in particular is that industrial policies have a high degree of country specificity and instruments that have been effective in one context will not necessarily work in others. Section 5.3 outlines the range of different contracting failures that can constrain the emergence of a broad-based and competitive manufacturing sector. There are obviously a number of different theoretically plausible problems that can constrain the emergence of a diversified and competitive industrial sector.

However, the most fundamental requirement of success is that emerging firms can acquire the *organizational and technological capabilities* to become competitive. If this problem is not effectively addressed, solving other constraints blocking the emergence of competitive firms is unlikely to deliver sustainable results. While the absence of a sufficient base of firm-level organizational capabilities used to be a problem primarily affecting developing countries, this is now just as likely to be a major constraint in advanced countries that have experienced rapid de-industrialization. Finally, Section 5.4 outlines the problem of designing policy solutions that are consistent with the enforcement capacities of the state, which in turn depends on national institutions and politics operating within the confines of global rules and power structures. It is therefore not only important to identify the relevant contracting failures and constraints correctly, it is equally important to design responses to these problems that will work given local implementation and enforcement capabilities. The comparative Asian experience shows that industrial policies can fail for either reason. An appropriate methodology of policy analysis can reduce the dangers of mistakes in policy design but a viable industrial policy strategy should also be 'experimentalist', so that different policy instruments can be trialled and policies redesigned and reformed in the light of experience. This too is an important lesson from the Asian experience.

5.2 Dimensions of Industrial Policy

Industrial policy in the broadest sense describes policies that aim to support the development and adoption of technologies and capabilities that raise social productivity. Industrial policies (or technology policies as they are sometimes referred to) are required when private contracting fails to organize potentially gainful investments that achieve these outcomes. The problems that could prevent organizations independently contracting to arrange these investments are variants of contracting failures that emerge because of high transacting and contracting costs. The most important variants of contracting problems that industrial policies have to address will be discussed briefly later. It is conceptually possible to distinguish investments in innovation that result in the generation of new technologies and products from investments in firm-level capability development that enable these technologies to be used to produce competitive products. The distinction can often be difficult to make in practice as firms are often simultaneously engaged in innovating and changing their production processes and internal management systems. But the conceptual distinction is easy to see when a country or a firm is attempting to competitively produce a product that is already being produced by some other firm. The latter is not necessarily an easier problem to solve; indeed it is probably the bigger challenge for an economy such as the UK as it attempts to re-enter the processes of manufacturing to a significant extent.

Industrial policy defined in this way is not necessarily restricted to the promotion of the industrial sector alone, though some proponents of industrial policy do indeed interpret it in the narrower sense on the grounds that technological progress and social productivity are likely to rise faster if the industrial sector is prioritized (Greenwald and Stiglitz, 2006). In this chapter, industrial policy will be used in the broader sense to refer to technology policies generally, though the examples of applications that we look at primarily involve manufacturing. Industrial policies can be 'horizontal', if they seek to improve the general efficiency of markets and the provision of broadly defined public goods to facilitate greater private investment in innovation and capability development. Industrial policy can also be 'vertical' or targeted if it focuses on solving *particular* contracting failures affecting investments relevant for particular sectors or technologies (Khan and Blankenburg, 2009). There is greater political and policy resistance to targeted policies because they are seen as discriminatory as well as involving judgements about 'picking winners'. In fact, the distinction between the two types of policies is not very sharp, and the real distinction is about effectiveness and relevance for solving particular problems.

In reality, policies always discriminate between individuals, sectors, or firms in some way or another. For instance, apparently non-discriminatory policies may be discriminatory in reality if firms or sectors face very different constraints, and horizontal policy ignores these differences. A policy that fails to recognize differences in the types and intensities of problems across sectors effectively discriminates against sectors with more severe problems. Conversely, policy that does identify priorities across sectors, regions, and so on, and then sequentially addresses them, may help to create a more level playing field over time. Obviously not all problems, whether they are general or particular, can be feasibly addressed by policy. The real question is whether the priorities identified by the policy are politically acceptable and whether the policy is effective in the sense of achieving the outcomes that are desired. It is true that highly targeted policy responses that create rents and opportunities for a relatively small number of firms can be more susceptible to capture by sectional interests. Policy design has to ensure that the policy does not end up protecting uncompetitive activities and monopolistic privileges. That would indeed be a discriminatory outcome. The way to avoid such outcomes is through better policy design, and by avoiding policies that are more susceptible to this danger. The relevant point is that we do not necessarily achieve better outcomes by always selecting 'horizontal' policies that appear not to be targeting specific problems or sectors. The most neutral policies in these terms may sustain a very undesirable status quo.

The Asian experience suggests that the choice between horizontal and vertical industrial policies should be interpreted differently. Clearly some policies are more horizontal in the distribution of benefits across firms and sectors and others are more targeted. Truly horizontal policies that do not discriminate between firms and sectors in any way are unlikely to exist, and highly targeted strategies that benefit a very few firms are very likely to be captured and may in any case be strongly opposed by other interests in society. The relevant choices are always likely to be between policies located in the middle of the horizontal–vertical spectrum. When we look at this range, there are no compelling theoretical reasons why policies that are somewhat more horizontal will necessarily perform better in terms of social objectives. The Asian experience supports this expectation because the most successful high-impact strategies generally targeted specific technologies, regions, and contracting problems that were inevitably of greater interest and benefit to some sectors and firms in the first instance. These policies ranged from the sectorally targeted industrial policy instruments of South Korea and Taiwan in the 1960s and 1970s, to the region-specific incentives and provincial competition in China in the 1980s and beyond (Wade, 1988; Amsden, 1989; Wade, 1990; World Bank, 1993; Qian and Weingast, 1997; Qian, 2003). The distinguishing characteristic of more successful policies was that they identified and targeted the most important problems, *and* the policy solutions were implementable and enforceable in particular political and institutional contexts.

The last sentence describes a combination of characteristics that is often not properly understood by policy-makers. Moreover, many widely shared interpretations of what is required for a successful industrial policy are actually misleading. An example is the common perception both amongst supporters and opponents of industrial policies that success requires a state with the vision and the capacity for 'picking winners'. This metaphor is very unfortunate because it implies that successful industrial policy countries had wise bureaucrats whose vision of the future was particularly prescient. The implication is that if bureaucrats and politicians display few signs of such innate abilities, industrial policies of the Asian type are best avoided. The reality in Asia was very different. East Asian countries did not initially differ from South Asian ones (in the 1950s and 1960s) in the quality let alone the prescience of their bureaucrats. The difference was rather that the policy instruments that emerged in East Asia could be enforced or altered in their political contexts. But the South Asian industrial policy instruments, though they were very similar to the East Asian ones, were rapidly captured by powerful interests. With the benefit of hindsight, these instruments were inappropriate for the South Asian political settlements. The initial policy instruments emerged rather serendipitously in all these countries, but in East Asia the instruments created benefit streams (or rents) that could be effectively monitored and withdrawn, and their conditions of allocation changed in the light of the results achieved. In South Asia the same rents could not be easily withdrawn or altered once they had been introduced. This was not at all a characteristic of the quality or capacities of the state but rather of the configuration of power between state agencies and rent-receiving firms given the types of rents that these policies created. What emerges as important is the 'fit' of particular policies within particular 'political settlements', defined as the distribution of organizational power in a society, which determined whether appropriate conditions could be defined and enforced for these policies.

The ability or otherwise of particular bureaucrats or politicians to pick the right winners *ex ante* obfuscates these issues. In fact, East Asian industrial policies frequently targeted the wrong firms and sectors to begin with. The difference was that mistakes were quickly corrected and policy design and sectoral choices evolved rapidly in the light of experience. Far from any mysterious capacity of some policy-makers to pick winners *ex ante*, industrial policy was successful here because the fit between initial policy design and the political and institutional conditions of the country allowed incremental policy evolution through the correction of mistakes. In contrast, in less successful countries such as those in South Asia, the initial policy design was inappropriate given the political settlement, and benefits were created for powerful organizations which had the ability to capture and protect their policy-induced rents regardless of performance. The result was policy stagnation and the failure to correct mistakes years or decades after it had become obvious to everyone that the wrong firms or sectors had been 'picked'. The difference in outcomes had almost nothing to do with any capacity for 'picking winners' and a lot more to do with the complex mix of policy, institutional, and political characteristics that added up to a capacity for 'dropping losers'. But even this phrase can be misleading because it does not capture the complex set of conditions we want to highlight. The interdependence of policy design, political settlements, and implementation success is unfortunately not widely understood, even within Asian countries with their different experiences with industrial policy.

The implementation issue is at the heart of industrial policy success or failure. But it is obviously not the only factor determining the success of industrial policy. The significance of the implementation and enforcement issues can be better understood by separating them from other types of problems. First, industrial policies can fail simply because policy-makers have multiple objectives and are attempting to achieve too many goals with a limited set of instruments. For instance, a policy that aims to achieve productivity growth can be diluted and distorted if policy-makers also want to protect employment in the firms and sectors being targeted. Multiple objectives require packages of policies targeting different problems because of these types of trade-offs.

A second and more important problem emerges when a policy targets a discrete problem but the diagnosis of the problem is wrong. Many different types of contracting failures can constrain investments in innovation and learning, and policies that may have been appropriate if the problem was due to one set of problems may be insufficient or inappropriate if the real problem was something else. For instance, policies relevant for solving a problem of insufficient investments in skills may be irrelevant and wasteful in a context where the main problem was that firms lacked the organizational capability to achieve competitiveness. To make matters worse, if low capability firms are surveyed, their managers are very likely to attribute their low competitiveness to poor worker skills or other constraints. But if low organizational capabilities were the more important problem, an expenditure of public resources in skills training may end up creating an additional problem of unemployed skilled labour on top of the already existing problem of uncompetitive firms. Policy-makers clearly need to have a careful analysis of the causes of low competitiveness, low investment or whatever the proximate problem appears to be, because superficial assessments and survey evidence may be misleading.

Finally, industrial policies can also fail even if the problems have been correctly identified because the particular instruments chosen to address these turn out to be ineffective in that political and social context. This problem has resulted in many failures in Asian industrial policy. A society always has a specific economic and political structure that can be described by the capabilities and the distribution of power across different types of organizations. The relative bargaining power of different types of firms, government agencies, and other stakeholders can vary greatly across countries given their initial conditions. We describe this distribution of organizational power as the political settlement within the country (Khan, 1995, 2010). Features of the political settlement matter for the enforcement of industrial policy because the latter typically provides explicit or implicit policy support (rents) to particular firms or sectors conditional on the achievement of desired outcomes. The results of industrial policy (or indeed of any policy in general) depends critically on how effectively the state can monitor the outcome that is desired, and change the allocation and terms of support in the light of emerging results. The historical evidence shows that the effectiveness of monitoring and enforcement depends only partly on the technical and bureaucratic capabilities of state agencies and quite a bit on the political settlement defining the relative bargaining power of the different types of organizations receiving and managing these rents.

When policy-induced rents are captured without delivering results, the outcome is often referred to as a government or state failure. Conservative political economists have argued that intervention should in general be avoided because the costs of government failure are very often more significant than those of the market failures the policy attempted to address (Krueger, 1990). This debate is important because the causes of success or failure are usually not properly understood. The defeatism of conservative political economists is often countered by a 'possibilistic' progressive optimism based on an equally selective choice of examples. But just as conservative pessimism cannot explain the successes that were sometimes achieved through industrial policy, the optimism of progressives does not explain why there were frequent failures, and what needs to be done to avoid more failures in the future. The possibility of failure certainly does not imply that non-intervention or horizontal policies are the best response. Rather, the evidence from Asia shows that policy design that improves the compatibility of the policy's enforcement requirements with the enforcement conditions possible under the prevailing political settlement can significantly reduce the chances of failure.

The challenge for policy-makers at the design stage is that they have to be able to imagine whether a particular policy, with feasible improvements in governance capabilities, can be well enough enforced in the existing political settlement to yield useful results. It is at this stage that an analysis of the policy-induced incentives and compulsions facing different types of actors and their likely responses given their bargaining power can help to reduce the chances of a failure in policy design. Analysis of the likely contracting failures that are constraining policy and of international experiences in different contexts can contribute to this policy discussion. This thought process does not guarantee success, but it can reduce the chances of failure. The final component of the policy process is therefore an explicit commitment to experimentation. Here too, policy design is relevant, so that policies are constructed keeping in mind that they may need to be reversed or modified as evidence about outcomes comes in.

5.3 THE FUNDAMENTAL CONSTRAINT OF ORGANIZATIONAL CAPABILITIES

One of the long-term effects of the rapid de-industrialization in advanced countries has been the loss of organizational capabilities as manufacturing firms were shut down. Their internal routines and the knowledge of how to organize production on which their competitiveness had been based in the past were in many cases entirely lost. This was an important contributor to the long-term hysteresis of the manufacturing sector in many advanced countries. As wages and exchange rates continue to rise in China, it may become increasingly viable to bring some outsourced manufacturing back to the UK. But the loss of firms with productive organizational capabilities means that this shift in production is no longer likely to happen without policy support, even in sectors that could be potentially competitive. The 'knowledge' on which firm competitiveness is based includes the internal routines and systems that sustain high levels of productivity, high standards in quality control, efficiency in inventory management, low levels of input wastage and downtime, and so on. This is largely tacit knowledge that is essential for achieving competitiveness, and is often embedded in the routines of how things are done by different members of a complex team. The requisite tacit knowledge can be 'learnt' through a process of learning-by-doing, but the investments that enable learning-by-doing are also subject to significant contracting failures. This is therefore an important area of concern for industrial policy strategies.

Given the missing capabilities in manufacturing, it would be insufficient for an industrial policy programme in Britain just to support innovation. Industrial policy does of course have an important role in supporting innovation and that is well understood. There is a large literature, for instance, on the role of patent policy and the direct public funding of research. These policies create technology rents and their effectiveness raises issues such as the management of the length of protection and the conditions attached to patents, the institutional organization of the public funding of research, the structure of public-private networks, the competitiveness of the markets in which innovating firms operate, and so on (Dosi, 1988; Pelikan, 1988; Stiglitz, 1995; Khan, 2000a; Aghion et al., 2002; Stiglitz, 2007). As the importance of innovation is not in question in an advanced country, and as the Asian experience is more useful for understanding the second plank of industrial policy, we will focus on the policy support required to develop a broad base of competitive firms. Domestic innovation would be much more likely to translate into domestic production if many competitive firms already existed in the UK manufacturing sector. Otherwise, innovation would most likely find its way to production in some other country. Here there are important lessons to learn from the Asian experience of developing firm-level competitiveness. In the rest of this section we will discuss the important contracting failures that can affect the development of competitiveness and the policy responses that are called for. This will take us to the next section where we discuss the problem of effectiveness of enforcement and implementation, which depends on the interface of policy solutions with the political settlement.

The common feature of all policies addressing contracting failures is that they create different types of rents for the supported firms and organizations. However, an accurate diagnosis of the underlying problem is important otherwise support may be provided for the wrong problem. Since production is normally carried out by organized groups of people, the capacity to organize a production team in an effective and efficient way is a necessary condition for the success of any productive enterprise. If there are contracting failures preventing the development of these missing organizational capabilities, then policies that only solve other problems are not likely to help the emergence of a productive sector. The empirical evidence shows that policy-induced rents can support learning-by-doing but only if very specific conditions are set for rent recipients to induce high levels of effort in experimentation and learning. Not surprisingly, policies that simply provide rents to firms facing a variety of contracting failures rarely achieve good results. In many cases, unconditional rent allocation to 'infant industries' can simply create perverse incentives and incentives to engage in rent-seeking activities to protect these rents. Thus, in the typical case where multiple problems exist, policy has to address each separately, but in most cases, the problem of missing organizational capabilities is the most basic constraint that has to be addressed.

The contracting problems that can constrain the development of firm-level competitiveness can include externality problems affecting investments in improving workforce skills, externalities facing first-mover investors in sectors that may or may not turn out to be competitive, a variety of coordination problems affecting investments across interdependent sectors, and, most importantly for us, the principal-agent problems facing investors investing in learning-by-doing processes (Khan, 2013a). If private contracting fails to find appropriate solutions to these and other problems, policy interventions are required. But policy is only likely to be effective if it targets the most relevant problem.

Developing countries have used a variety of instruments to address this mix of problems, but very often the design of the instruments was not differentiated enough to identify the most appropriate conditions to impose on supported sectors to ensure that particular problems were addressed. The rents created were usually broadly defined with loose conditions, and it is not surprising that in many cases the results achieved were not very dramatic. Results were only dramatic in contexts where the power relationships between rent-creating agencies and the rent-receiving firms allowed an evolution of the conditions attached to rents in the light of the results achieved. When this happened, policy rapidly evolved to define conditions for rent allocation that solved particular problems, and in these cases there were often very dramatic results. The challenge is to understand the mix of conditions that created these good results so that what happened serendipitously and over relatively long periods in a few countries can inform deliberate policy design more generally. The early instruments of industrial policy often created rents for targeted firms without too many conditions or with conditions that were not very carefully thought through. Rent-creating policy instruments included the protection of domestic markets for infant industries, subsidizing technology acquisition through implicit or explicit subsidies such as low interest credit, and export subsidies and tax breaks for investing in new machinery. Each of these instruments provided rents which could in principle have addressed specific contracting failures but only if the rents were granted with the right performance conditions.

For instance, positive externalities can constrain investments in training because investors may fear a loss of their investment if trained workers leave to work in other firms or sectors. One policy response to positive externality problems is to reduce the risk and cost for firms investing in training by providing subsidies for these firms or to the workers undergoing training. But clearly, the subsidy would be insufficient on its own in many cases without arrangements for monitoring the content and quality of the training achieved. So the terms of the rent allocation would have to include credible withdrawal and penalty arrangements and the monitoring of training quality (Dosi, 1988; Khan, 2000a). In the same way, the externality problem associated with first-mover investments can also be dealt with using a subsidy, but now very different conditions need to be identified and enforced. The problem here refers to the possibility that the first investors in a sector have additional costs that later investors can free-ride on. An example is the possibility discussed by Hausmann and Rodrik (2003) that first movers may have to invest a lot in discovering areas in which a country has comparative advantage. As first movers may fail to capture sufficient returns on their investments, for instance because subsequent entry into the sector can reduce their profits by raising wages and input prices, investments in discovery and other first-mover investments may be constrained. Unlike new innovations, discovery cannot be patented, and therefore the solution to this contracting failure may require temporary subsidies that encourage trials in new sectors. These rents need their own set of effective conditions: they have to be available for short periods, they should only be given for investments in 'new' sectors, and for no longer than is needed to set up the trials and discover the presence or absence of comparative advantage.

Coordination of investments across sectors may be important because of both demand and supply side complementarities. High transaction costs, information asymmetries, and the possibility of opportunistic behaviour by second movers may preclude private contracting solutions to solve coordination problems (Rosenstein-Rodan, 1943; Nurkse, 1953; Scitovsky, 1954; Williamson, 1985; Murphy et al., 1989). Government agencies charged with the implementation of coordination policies are in a position to provide rents to firms in promoted clusters. But here a complex set of conditions has to be enforced to ensure that the desired coordination comes about. The identification of the clusters to be supported and the complementary investments that private investors have to provide have to be agreed upon, monitored, and enforced. Coordination is a part of industrial policy that finds a lot of support amongst economists advising governments, largely because writing complex plans creates significant job opportunities. However, few countries have made significant progress in industrialization because of the quality of their coordinated planning. This is largely because the implementation of coordinated national investment plans faces significant enforcement problems. There can, however, be payoffs for the proper coordination of investments in industrial clusters, but this too requires high levels of capacity and the appropriate design of incentives, as the Chinese experience has shown. It is at this level that attention on coordination should initially be focused.

But the solutions to all these contracting failures assume that a more fundamental contracting failure has been addressed. Many countries find it difficult to absorb and use existing technologies even when their wages are low enough compared to their competitors and they have sufficient workers with the appropriate formal skills. The missing factor is often the *organizational capability* of the production team. Owners, managers, and supervisors often do not know how best to set up the factory, align the machinery, set up systems for quality control, reduce input wastage and product rejection, manage inventories, match order flows with production cycles, maintain after sales services, and approach a host of other internal team coordination and management issues that are essential for achieving competitiveness. Differences in these capabilities can result in very significant differences in labour, input, and capital productivity across countries (Khan, 2009, 2013a). As a result, a firm that is able to buy the same machinery as its competitors at international prices, and employ workers and managers at the same or lower wages than the most competitive country, may yet be unable to achieve competitiveness. This is a problem that developing countries face all the time, but is likely to be just as relevant for advanced countries that have de-industrialized.

Organizational capabilities of the type that we are discussing can only be learnt to a limited extent as *codified knowledge* or formal knowledge that can potentially be provided by training institutes. Organizational capabilities are largely based on *tacit knowledge* that is acquired through learning-by-doing, and moreover, it involves experimentation with and restructuring of the organization of a production team. The knowledge gained through this learning-by-doing is thus embedded in the routines and practices of the team. To make matters more complicated, the most effective organization for the same production process can vary from country to country depending on the work patterns and habits of the workforce (Whitley, 1992). Once an effective organizational structure emerges for a particular sector in a country, it can be copied by other firms, but a new team will also require some time to experiment and come up with its own modifications and details to produce similar results. Firm organization can vary from firm to firm, but the closer the existing routines of a production team are to the routines and processes it is trying to emulate, the faster the learning-by-doing is likely to be. By definition, learning-by-doing requires opportunities for *doing*, and this requires periods of loss-financing when the firm is engaged in production but is unable to make sufficient or any profits. One of the classical justifications for infant industry protection was to allow infants to grow up in precisely this sense. However, here too, rents have to be delivered with appropriate conditions. Here 'learning rents' provide the opportunity for a production team to engage in production, but it also has to be under pressure to continuously experiment with new internal organizational arrangements to achieve the increases in productivity that justify the investment in learning (Khan, 2000a). Thus, the 'doing' is necessary but does not guarantee 'learning', unless there is some compulsion on the owners, managers, and supervisors to put in high levels of *effort* in the learning process (Khan, 2013a).

In theory, complex contingency contracts between the private parties involved could address these investment requirements. Essentially, private investors putting in their money in building firm-level competitiveness would need to have credible ways of penalizing non-performance and extracting their capital if the project fails. These contracts are difficult to write and enforce, and the returns are not that high if the firm is attempting to achieve competitiveness in competitive sectors. The problem is that innovative sectors where there are high returns due to technology rents require underlying productive capacities that would also have been able to produce competitive products competitively. Otherwise, the production of even high rent products will migrate to countries where firm-level organizational capabilities are higher. A necessary condition for achieving the goal of organizational capability development is that conditions of rent allocation and withdrawal have to be clearly set out so that owners, managers, supervisors, and others feel the compulsion to put a high level of *effort* into the learning process. This problem usually cannot be solved by announcing the time period for support in advance. Unlike a trial that is supposed to *discover* comparative advantage (where reasonable time periods for trials can be pre-specified), here comparative advantage is being *created* through learning and the development of organizational capabilities. The creation of comparative advantage can take periods of time that differ from country to country, sector to sector, and perhaps even firm to firm. More complex monitoring and incentives are required here to induce the right kinds of effort.

Why is it necessary to impose conditions on firms to ensure that they put the requisite effort into the learning process? It may appear that the rational strategy for the leadership of a firm would be to ensure a high learning effort anyway. The prize for the firm would be to achieve competitiveness and became self-sustaining. This motivation can sometimes work, but the evidence suggests that this can by no means be taken for granted. Indeed, there are good reasons why this is not necessarily the only rational strategy for key stakeholders in the firm. Learning and experimentation are costly exercises. Internal distributive conflicts have to be managed as hierarchies and responsibilities may have to be restructured frequently. In addition, the prize is not necessarily very attractive. The firm that puts a lot of effort into raising its productivity and achieves competitiveness through organizational learning is rewarded by losing its rent and the security that comes with it. In exchange it gains the dubious privilege of sinking or swimming in a competitive market. Without some degree of compulsion to do otherwise, the rational behaviour of many firm managers may well be to 'satisfice', in the sense described by Herbert Simon (1956, 1983), and put more effort into the political activity that preserves their rents.

Given these examples of very different problems that may constrain competitiveness, industrial policies clearly have to be formulated to address specific problems and issues. If an industrial policy strategy fails to identify the most important problems relevant for the sector or country, strategies of supporting emerging firms are likely to fail. In some countries, famously the East Asian ones, ambitious technology policies that provided support simultaneously for many firms and sectors resulted in accelerated technology acquisition and development. But when we look at these examples in detail, it was because very specific and unusual configurations of bargaining power allowed the development of policy conditions and targets in a pragmatic way. In many other countries, policies with a similar level of ambition resulted in the proliferation of subsidies to protected industries that refused to grow up. Subsidies kept growing and could not be withdrawn, despite the poor performance of the supported firms and sectors. Similarly, in some countries development banks played a dynamic role, while in others their low interest loans were not repaid and development banks eventually went bankrupt. In these less dynamic cases, consumers and taxpayers often ended up paying the price for these failing policies till they were finally abandoned.

The identification of the most relevant contracting failures is therefore the necessary first stage of developing effective industrial policy solutions. The second stage is to investigate whether a policy with the requisite characteristics can be enforced given the configuration of power and capabilities across the organizations affected by the policy. Policy responses that worked in one country may not be implementable in another. On the other hand, there are typically multiple solutions to the same problem, and each solution implies a different allocation of rents and a somewhat different set of conditions for achieving desirable outcomes. This makes it more likely that effective solutions can be found despite differences in political settlements, as long as the relevant features of the political settlement are understood.

5.4 The Political Economy of Rent Management

There are in principle *many* ways in which a particular contracting failure can be addressed. Each solution involves different distributions of costs and benefits and requires different sets of conditions to be enforced on different organizations. Given the relative power and capability of different types of organizations in that society, some solutions may be more feasible to implement than others. Some theoretically feasible solutions may not be feasible in practice if their implementation requires the enforcement of conditions on very powerful or well-connected organizations. The attempt to enforce these policies may then result in 'government failures' as the policy gets distorted by the rent-seeking activities of powerful organizations. This does not necessarily mean that this contracting problem cannot or should not be addressed. A different approach addressing the problem using different instruments or targeting different types of firms and technologies may enjoy greater success. Paradoxically, a second-best strategy that starts by assisting smaller firms or firms using less-developed technologies may be better in developing organizational capabilities or solving other contracting problems in political settlements where the bargaining power of the best firms is likely to result in unconditional rent capture. The political economy of enforcing a policy thus depends on three factors. First, it depends on the design of the policy that determines who gets the rents and the conditions that need to be imposed on the rent recipients to address the particular problem. Second, the outcome depends on the governance, monitoring, and enforcement capacities of the government agencies involved in monitoring the policy and its conditions. And last but not least, the outcome depends on the political settlement that describes the relative bargaining power of the different organizations affected by the policy. Clearly, the design of any policy is less likely to be wrong if it explicitly identifies the rent allocation conditions required to solve the problem in the different variants of policy design that are possible, and then selects the variant that is most likely to be implemented given the existing political settlement and feasible improvements in governance capacities.

The relevance of policy design can be illustrated with reference to the somewhat simpler contracting failures that can result in environmental externalities. Policy can respond to an externality problem using different instruments, including regulation, taxation, or subsidization. If we ignore the 'transaction costs' of monitoring and enforcement, all these instruments are theoretically equivalent. But in reality, the effectiveness of these policy instruments can vary greatly because the costs of monitoring and enforcement are *not* the same given differences in the organizational structures of countries. For instance, if polluters are relatively weak and can be effectively monitored and taxed, the tax solution may work better than a subsidy solution as the latter typically faces greater problems of financing and monitoring. But if polluting firms are powerful and can successfully obstruct monitoring and enforcement, a tax solution may fail to achieve much, and regulatory or subsidy solutions may work *relatively* better in that context. This is in general why policies that work in one country can often perform much less well or fail entirely in others.

The dramatic success of industrial policies in East Asia largely reflected the ability of these countries to incrementally modify the design of their ambitious policy instruments in the light of experience. None of these countries began with a complete map of what needed to be done. Rather, trial and error resulted in the refinement of rent allocation conditions to achieve productivity-enhancing outcomes because these conditions proved to be implementable and provided greater and greater economic and political benefits to the top leadership. The emergence of effective conditions being imposed on broadly based industrial policy strategies reflected very specific political settlements in these countries, which were fairly untypical in the broader Asian context. The favourable configuration of holding power between the top political leadership, political groups, and factions at the intermediate levels of society and the emerging business sector allowed the evolution and enforcement of tough conditions on domestic firms receiving support (Khan, 2009; Khan and Blankenburg, 2009). The financing provided in South Korea to the *chaebol* through low interest loans, protected domestic markets, and export subsidies was increasingly made conditional on the achievement of particular outcomes, for instance meeting export targets. These conditions ensured high levels of effort because the enforcement of the conditions proved to be credible. The state could not only withdraw subsidies from particular *chaebol*; it could also reallocate entire plants from one *chaebol* to another if performance was poor. Not surprisingly, the imposition of these conditions on the *chaebol* created strong compulsions on them to accelerate their productivity growth through the rapid learning of organizational skills and technical capabilities.

Political settlements are effectively exogenous in the short term and cannot easily be changed through policy choices. The favourable political settlements in East Asia were clearly not the result of policy choices of the South Korean or Taiwanese states. Rather, these states inherited favourable configurations of relative power, which were outcomes of their histories and in particular of the social engineering carried out by the Japanese when they occupied these territories in the early part of the twentieth century. However, policy choices did play a role in East Asia. The choices of the East Asian state leaderships that mattered were the introduction of ambitious industrial policies, followed by their discovery that it was relatively easy to modify and refine the conditions associated with rent allocations to achieve productivity-enhancing outcomes.

The South Asian countries also introduced ambitious industrial policies in the 1950s but in the context of very different political settlements. In these conditions it proved to be virtually impossible for policy to evolve in the direction of imposing appropriate conditions on the rent-receiving firms. In the typical South Asian country power within the ruling coalition was much more fragmented, again because of long historical processes including the nature of the colonial impact in these countries. As a result there were many powerful political organizations at the intermediate levels of society that were competing to capture rents, and these organizations could not always be overridden by the top leadership. When ambitious industrial policies began to create large rents for emerging business organizations, satisficing strategies for protecting rents could be easily implemented because there were many political organizations that could protect the rents of particular businesses in exchange for kickbacks. The result was that here policy could not plausibly evolve in the direction of imposing stricter conditions on rent-receiving firms or threaten to withdraw rents from non-performing firms (Khan, 2000b).

The failure of policy to evolve in these obvious directions in South Asia cannot be explained by the ignorance of bureaucrats and politicians in these countries. This was not just an oversight. The political and bureaucratic elites in these countries were perfectly aware of the problem at a very early stage, but they also knew that policy evolution in the direction of greater effectiveness and the withdrawal of rents from non-performers would not be enforceable. As long ago as the mid-1960s, the Dutt Committee set up by the government of India recognized that the licensing regime that was directing rents to infant industries was primarily helping a small group of large firms who were capturing these rents on their own terms (Government of India, 1969). But the politics of responding to this effectively was not simple. To the extent that responses were attempted, they were often blunt and counterproductive. Thus, in India, one response was Indira Gandhi's Monopolies and Restrictive Trade Practices Act (MRTP) of 1969, which set asset limits on the holdings of large business houses that were thought to have unduly prospered under the licensing regime. The new act was largely punitive, was not properly enforced, and had little effect on actual levels of concentration. Significantly, it did not seek to address the problem of rent management to achieve better outcomes. The state did not try to set new conditions for achieving competitiveness by changing the broad contours of the policy, including the choice of supported sectors and firms, even though the necessity of such changes was explicitly recognized by the Dutt Committee. In other words, the failure to move in the direction of better rent management, at least in India in the 1960s, cannot be attributed to ignorance. However, there may have been missed opportunities of a more complex sort. The political settlement could not be easily changed but policies could have been radically redesigned to be more credible in this context. The problem was that a policy design that allocated significant learning rents *ex ante* to broadly defined sectors made it difficult to exclude large business houses from these capturing rents.

A general feature of the policies that both East Asian and South Asian countries were attempting in the 1960s and 1970s was that much of their rents for learning were allocated *ex ante*, before the firms in question had established their competitive organizational capabilities. These *ex ante* rents were also significant in their scope (in terms of the numbers of sectors and firms supported). Enforcing effective conditions on these financing instruments was clearly beyond the political capacity of the Indian state, and it did not even attempt to move in that direction. However, other financing instruments may have been more successful, and some insights into what may have worked became clearer with the experiences of the 1980s. A change in the design of the financing instrument could in principle ensure high levels of effort in learning even in countries where the political settlements precluded the enforcement of tough conditions on *ex ante* rent recipients. Monitoring requirements could be very different if the rent was promised to the learning firm *ex post*, and delivered after success was established. The typical patent-based technology rent that creates incentives for innovation becomes available to successful innovators *ex post*. For rents allocated *ex post*, the public monitoring requirements are less demanding and the institutional requirement is mainly to determine the period of *ex post* rent protection, which primarily determines the magnitude of the prize allocated to successful innovators (Khan, 2000a). If rents are only available *ex post*, they can still help to make the financing of innovation or learning more viable, because innovators or firms engaged in learning can offer investors higher returns in the future, thereby getting access to longer periods of financing at a lower up-front cost.

In contrast to Schumpeterian rents, learning rents are typically provided *ex ante* (for instance through tariffs on imports or the provision of low cost credit). Unfortunately, as we have seen, there are demanding monitoring and enforcement requirements with *ex ante* rents if high-effort learning is to be achieved. If instead, the policy instrument allocated some of the rent *ex ante* but reserved significant rents as a prize *ex post*, conditional on the achievement of competitive success, these conditions can help to self-select firms that believed they could make the learning jump as well as creating strong compulsions and incentives for high levels of effort in learning. This is because these firms would be initially investing in the learning itself, in anticipation of a prize *ex post*. In addition, if the *ex post* rents were sufficiently large and credible, firms engaged in learning could also raise financing on viable terms from investors in the same way as innovators aiming for innovation rents can raise money for financing innovations.

In the 1980s a number of sectors in South Asian countries made significant progress in technology adoption and in developing organizational capabilities for competitive production by (serendipitously) adopting *ex post* rent allocation strategies. This period of rapid learning is often mistakenly attributed to 'liberalization', even though it is widely recognized in the South Asian literature that liberalization did not happen in any significant way until a decade later. Given their political settlements, the enforcement conditions were now a lot better for these types of strategies, and the results achieved were correspondingly dramatic. Examples include the financing of learning in the Indian automobile and pharmaceutical industries and the Bangladeshi garments and textiles industry (Khan, 2009, 2013a, 2013b). These examples differ significantly in the details of the financing strategies, but a brief look at the Indian automobile industry can provide a broad outline of the very different monitoring and enforcement requirements here.

In the 1980s India's automobile industry was transformed from a protected sector with limited global competitiveness to a globally competitive sector that made the country one of the leading global automobile exporters in a very short span of time. The transformation began with a partnership between a public sector enterprise and the Japanese company Suzuki, which participated in a joint venture agreement signed in 1982. Suzuki was effectively offered an *ex post* learning rent in the form of access to the protected Indian automobile market, which still had tariffs in the region of 85 per cent. But to be able to sell in this protected market, Suzuki first had to make the Maruti-Suzuki car, which would have to have a high enough quality to carry the Suzuki name and reputation, and it would have to achieve a 60 per cent domestic content within five years. This combination of rewards and conditions meant Suzuki had to make a significant investment in improving the organizational capabilities of an entire swathe of Indian Tier 1 and Tier 2 component producers to meet the domestic content target and yet produce a car that would be of a quality that could justify the Suzuki brand name. The design of the financing helped to address the contracting failure that would have otherwise constrained investment in learning. It provided Suzuki with significant additional incentives for financing the organizational learning of Indian producers. The significance of the policy design here was that Suzuki's effort no longer had to be monitored by the Indian state, as strong incentives were created for Suzuki to monitor itself and its Tier 1 and 2 partners, simply because it was investing first. The recovery of this investment and of the additional rent required rapid success in building not only the organizational capabilities in its own plant but also in the plants of its supplier chain. The achievement of global organizational capabilities and competitiveness in Indian-owned Tier 1 and 2 companies began in this way, and the Suzuki deal was replicated with other foreign automobile companies throughout the 1980s and 1990s. The result was a rapid growth in the capabilities and competitiveness of these suppliers, which eventually allowed the development of a diversified Indian automobile industry producing globally competitive Indian-branded cars.

Features of the political settlement in India are important for understanding the enforceability of the conditions associated with this industrial policy package. Suzuki as a Japanese company operating in India did not have the political links to renegotiate its contract if it failed to achieve the domestic content requirements that it had signed up to deliver. This was important for imposing credible compulsions on the company to achieve the domestic content agreed upon. The Indian Tier 1 and 2 companies that were getting assistance from Suzuki to build their organizational capabilities were not getting public funds, and these investments (which were effectively rents for learning for the supplier firms) could not be protected indefinitely through any rent-seeking activities of these firms. The only rational strategy for the supplier firms was to cooperate with Suzuki in a high-effort strategy to raise their competitiveness, as that was the only mechanism available for increasing their incomes over time. Thus, an examination of the terms and conditions of the financing strategy, keeping in mind the learning problem that had to be solved and the political context in which the conditions had to be enforced, shows that the unexpectedly rapid success that was achieved was not really surprising after all. While the other sectoral stories that we have referred to are different in detail, in every case these strategies offered part of the rent *ex post* with a combination of financing conditions that generated high effort in the learning process in the context of the political settlements of these countries.

These examples provide important methodological insights, even though the substantive details of how learning was financed and the conditions that were effective are not replicable. Even in India, the precise mechanisms are no longer available because after India joined the WTO, levels of tariff protection became much lower on average and domestic content requirements can no longer be imposed on foreign investors. The point, however, is not about the precise mechanisms of funding and the conditions that were used, but the more general one about the sequence of financing, the allocation of rents, and the credibility or otherwise of the conditions required for high-effort learning given the political settlement. The financing methods and conditions that may be appropriate for financing organizational capability development in British manufacturing are likely to be different from both the East Asian and South Asian examples. However, the examples of successful and less successful industrial policy strategies demonstrate the importance of thinking through the rent allocation conditions and the feasibility of their enforcement in the relevant political settlement.

The policy discussion about industrial policy options for Britain could usefully look at some aspects of the Asian experience. The issues discussed here pointed to the importance of identifying the most important contracting failures that warrant industrial policy interventions. Surprising as it may seem, this is often not done, and all types of problems are sometimes jointly addressed with the same package of rents and conditions, which then achieves very little. The issue of organizational capability development is particularly important and is likely to be an important constraint for the UK. Addressing this problem requires very specific forms of assistance, with credible conditions that compel high levels of effort. We saw how instruments that were very similar to East Asian ones failed to create broad-based competitive sectors in South Asia but new types of financing instruments were more effective in the 1980s. The *ex post* rents that were used are particularly interesting to examine in detail, though the precise instruments are likely to be different in an advanced country context. However, to be effective, policies aiming to develop the competitiveness of firms will in general have to satisfy the dual requirement of creating an opportunity for companies to engage in learning-by-doing as well as creating credible compulsions for high levels of effort in learning organizational capabilities. This requires thinking through mechanisms of financing organizational learning and conditions attached to that financing that are credible in the context of the contemporary British political settlement.

REFERENCES

Aghion, P., Bloom, N., Blundell, R., Griffith, R., and Howitt, P. (2002). *Competition and Innovation: An Inverted U Relationship*, The Institute for Fiscal Studies Working Paper No. WP02/04.

Amsden, A. (1989). *Asia's Next Giant: South Korea and Late Industrialization*. Oxford: Oxford University Press.

Dosi, G. (1988). 'The Nature of the Innovative Process', in G. Dosi, C. Freeman, R. R. Nelson, G. Silverberg, and L. Soete (eds), *Technical Change and Economic Theory*, pp. 221–38. London: Pinter Publishers.

Government of India (1969). *Report of the Industrial Licensing Policy Inquiry Committee (Main Report)*. (Chairman Shri Subimal Dutt). Ministry of Industrial Development: New Delhi.

Greenwald, B. and Stiglitz, J. E. (2006). 'Helping Infant Economies Grow: Foundations of Trade Policies for Developing Countries', *American Economic Review* 96(2), 141–6.

Hausmann, R. and Rodrik, D. (2003). 'Economic Development as Self Discovery', *Journal of Development Economics* 72(2), 603–33.

Khan, M. H. (1995). 'State Failure in Weak States: A Critique of New Institutionalist Explanations', in J. Harriss, J. Hunter, and C. M. Lewis (eds), *The New Institutional Economics and Third World Development*, pp. 71–86. London: Routledge.

Khan, M. H. (2000a). 'Rents, Efficiency and Growth', in M. H. Khan and K. S. Jomo (eds), *Rents, Rent-Seeking and Economic Development: Theory and Evidence in Asia*, pp. 21–69. Cambridge: Cambridge University Press.

Khan, M. H. (2000b). 'Rent-Seeking as Process', in M. H. Khan and K. S. Jomo (eds), *Rents, Rent-Seeking and Economic Development: Theory and Evidence in Asia*, pp. 70–144. Cambridge: Cambridge University Press.

Khan, M. H. (2009). *Learning, Technology Acquisition and Governance Challenges in Developing Countries*. Research Paper Series on Governance for Growth. School of Oriental and African Studies, University of London: London, <https://eprints.soas.ac.uk/9967/1/Learning_and_Technology_Acquisition_internet.pdf>.

Khan, M. H. (2010). *Political Settlements and the Governance of Growth-Enhancing Institutions*. Research Paper Series on Governance for Growth. School of Oriental and African Studies, University of London: London, <http://eprints.soas.ac.uk/9968/1/Political_Settlements_internet.pdf>.

Khan, M. H. (2013a). 'Technology Policies and Learning with Imperfect Governance', in J. Stiglitz and J. Y. Lin (eds), *The Industrial Policy Revolution I: The Role of Government Beyond Ideology*, pp. 79–115. London: Palgrave.

Khan, M. H. (2013b). *The Political Settlement, Growth and Technical Progress in Bangladesh*, Danish Institute for International Studies, Copenhagen, DIIS Working Paper No. 2013:01, <http://eprints.soas.ac.uk/id/eprint/13049>.

Khan, M. H. and Blankenburg, S. (2009). 'The Political Economy of Industrial Policy in Asia and Latin America', in G. Dosi, M. Cimoli, and J. E. Stiglitz (eds), *Industrial Policy and Development: The Political Economy of Capabilities Accumulation*, pp. 336–77. Oxford: Oxford University Press.

Krueger, A. O. (1990). 'Government Failures in Development', *Journal of Economic Perspectives* 4(3), 9–23.

Murphy, K. M., Shleifer, A., and Vishny, R. W. (1989). 'Industrialization and the Big Push', *Journal of Political Economy* 97(5), 1003–26.

Nurkse, R. (1953). *Problems of Capital Formation in Underdeveloped Countries*. Oxford: Oxford University Press.

Pelikan, P. (1988). 'Can the Innovation System of Capitalism be Outperformed?', in G. Dosi, C. Freeman, R. R. Nelson, G. Silverberg, and L. Soete (eds), *Technical Change and Economic Theory*, pp. 370–97. London: Pinter Publishers.

Qian, Y. (2003). 'How Reform Worked in China', in D. Rodrik (ed.), *In Search of Prosperity: Analytical Narratives on Economic Growth*, pp. 297–333. Princeton NJ: Princeton University Press.

Qian, Y. and Weingast, B. R. (1997). 'Institutions, State Activism, and Economic Development: A Comparison of State-Owned and Township-Village Enterprises in China', in M. Aoki, H.-K. Kim, and M. Okuno-Fujiwara (eds), *The Role of Government in East Asian Economic Development: Comparative Institutional Analysis*, pp. 254–75. Oxford: Clarendon Press.

Rosenstein-Rodan, P. N. (1943). 'Problems of Industrialisation of Eastern and South-Eastern Europe', *The Economic Journal* 53(210/211), 202–11.

Scitovsky, T. (1954). 'Two Concepts of External Economies', *Journal of Political Economy* 62(2), 143–51.

Simon, H. (1956). 'Rational Choice and the Structure of the Environment', *Psychological Review* 63(2), 129–38.

Simon, H. (1983). *Reason in Human Affairs*. Oxford: Basil Blackwell.

Stiglitz, J. E. (1995). 'Social Absorption Capability and Innovation', in B. H. Koo and D. H. Perkins (eds), *Social Capability and Long-Term Economic Growth*, pp. 48–81. London: Macmillan St. Martin's Press.

Stiglitz, J. E. (2007). *Making Globalization Work*. London: Penguin.

Wade, R. (1988). 'The Role of Government in Overcoming Market Failure: Taiwan, Republic of Korea and Japan', in H. Hughes (ed.), *Achieving Industrialization in East Asia*, pp. 129–63. Cambridge: Cambridge University Press.

Wade, R. (1990). *Governing the Market: Economic Theory and the Role of Government in East Asian Industrialization*. Princeton: Princeton University Press.

Whitley, R. (1992). *Business Systems in East Asia: Firms, Markets and Societies*. London: Sage.

Williamson, O. E. (1985). *The Economic Institutions of Capitalism*. New York: Free Press.

World Bank (1993). *The East Asian Miracle: Economic Growth and Public Policy*. Oxford University Press: Oxford.

PART 2

FINANCE FOR INDUSTRY, ENTREPRENEURSHIP, AND INNOVATION

CHAPTER 6

....

FINANCE AND INDUSTRIAL STRATEGY

....

MALCOLM SAWYER[1]

6.1 INTRODUCTION

....

AN industrial strategy involves the government adopting a broad view of the future development of the economy in terms of which sectors are to be built up and developed. It
also involves perceptions of which types of firms are in need of support (often this is
viewed in terms of small and medium-sized enterprises or the role of foreign direct investment [FDI]). The implementation of an industrial strategy requires the funding of
investment in ways which are consistent with the overall strategy. This is to state the obvious, but it does have important ramifications. It first raises the question of whether
there is sufficient funding available. The answer which we give to that is, in broad terms,
that there is. The second relates to the direction of funds; that is, does the funding flow
into those sectors which are to be developed? If the financial sector allocated funds in an
efficient manner and in the required direction, there would be little requirement for the
direction of funding.

The relationship between finance and industry is a long-standing issue. Collins
(1991), for example, in a survey book on industry and finance in UK in the period
1800–1939, opens with, 'Have the banks failed industry? In Britain there has long been
a sizeable body of opinion that believes so. Throughout this century [that is the twen-
tieth] economists and other commenters have expressed doubts about the role placed
by British monetary institutions in providing the financial services—especially the
provision of long-term finance—essential for nourishing a modern, competitive in-

[1] This chapter draws on long-standing interests in industrial policy and strategy. It also draws on
work undertaken for the EU-funded project Financialisation Economy Society and Sustainable
Development (website: fessud.eu) project number 266800, for which I am the principal investigator.
The views expressed in this chapter are my own, and should not be taken to reflect either the views of
the EU or partners in the FESSUD project.

dustrial sector' (p. 9). The structures and activities of the financial sector have changed since those debates on banks and industry. There have been processes of financialization. By financialization at a general level we mean 'the increasing role of financial motives, financial markets, financial actors and financial institutions in the operation of the domestic and international economies' (Epstein, 2005, p. 3). It is the forms which financialization in the UK has taken over the past 30 to 40 years which attracts our particular attention.[2] These include the continuing growth of the financial sector particularly in terms of 'value added'[3] albeit with relatively little growth of employment, growth of activities focused in the creation of and trading in derivatives, securitization, the pyramid of assets and liabilities, the growth of consumer debt, the tendency for shifts in the direction of flow of funds with corporations becoming net savers, and shifts to deregulation and 'light touch' regulation.[4] There has been the further emphasis on 'shareholder value', which many have argued pushes in the direction of lower investment. For example, 'regarding investment in capital stock, financialization has been associated with increasing shareholder power vis-à-vis management and labourers, an increasing rate of return on equity and bonds held by rentiers, and decreasing managements' animal spirits with respect to real investment, which each have partially negative effects on firms real investment' (Hein, 2012).

There have been many changes in the relationships between the financial sector and industry (as well as with households). The focus of our attention here is how well the financial sector operates to serve industry in terms of the provision of financial services and specifically the financing and funding of investment. Two aspects of recent financialization which are particularly relevant for what follows are the forms in which the financial sector has grown and the higher levels of savings by corporations.[5] The first means that the activities of the financial sector (and the resources deployed there) are increasingly concerned with transactions in 'existing pieces of paper', with profits from such transactions arising when asset prices are rising and through arbitrage opportunities. The other side of this is that activities become less focused on the funding of investment. The second has involved corporations having savings in excess of their investment (in capital formation), as will be evidenced below; and the counterpart of that is corporations seek to find outlets for their savings in the form of financing consumer debt and the purchase of financial assets. It also means that as far as

[2] The precise dating is not crucial here. However, note that financialization is often associated with the period since *circa* 1980. For the UK the liberalization represented by the Competition and Credit Control in 1971, the instability of the financial system evidenced by the house price boom, credit explosion (following Competition and Credit Control), and the near-collapse of the banking in 1973.

[3] This is value added as reported in the national income accounts: it should not be taken to imply that the financial sector generates value (however value may be considered).

[4] See Shabani et al. (2014) for a detailed story.

[5] This should not be read as saying the other features are unimportant for a general consideration of the role of the financial sector and financialization.

corporations are concerned there is not a shortage of funds; indeed it is rather that there is an excess.

There has been a long-standing literature which has been concerned with 'economic development and financial development' (which I have recently reviewed in Sawyer, 2014a), which has generally found a positive relationship between the two, though without determining the direction of causation. However, more recent work has cast doubt on the sign and strength of the financial sector, and hence whether recent developments in the financial sector, notably the growth of securitization, have detracted from the role of the banking system in the allocation of savings. It should also be noted that financial development has generally been measured by variables such as bank deposits relative to gross domestic product (GDP) and market valuation to GDP, whereas the growth of the financial sector in the past few decades has been particularly focused on securitization. These types of development are not conducive to the role of the financial sector in linking savings with investment and with the financing of investment. Epstein and Crotty (2013) extend this argument when they write that they derive a 'very preliminary range of estimates' which 'suggests that the financial sector in the United States is extracting 2–4 times as much income relative to the services it provides to the real sector in the decade of the 2000's as it did during the high growth period of the 1960s. This suggests that the financial sector may need to be only one-half to one-quarter as large as it is currently to serve the existing needs of the real sector' (p. 13). Although this is specific to the US, many similar factors would be at work in the UK.

One aspect of that is the financial industry (and particularly if a broad FIRE (finance, insurance, and real estate) definition is used) has become a significant industry in its own right. Whereas the relationship between finance and industry was viewed in terms of the degree to which finance went to domestic industry and to the foreign sector in earlier times, it would also now be viewed in terms of its contribution to employment, output, and more so to the current account position. In former times, the financial sector and the exchange rate would be considered in terms of the interests of the City for a stable high exchange rate; now it could be viewed in terms of the impact which financial sector activities have on the exchange rate in a floating exchange rate world, and thereby the impact on other exporting sectors. Thus with regard to industrial strategy, that should now include a strategy for the financial sector, as well as a strategy which enables the financial sector to serve industry in general. It is to state the obvious that any industrial strategy involves investment (broadly interpreted), and that such investments have in some way to be funded. As such, there are always issues of the quantity of funds and the direction of the funds. In other words will there be sufficient funds for the levels of investment required for a successful industry strategy, and will the funds available be channelled in the relevant directions.

The chapter begins with a consideration of the roles of the financial sector and relationships with the industrial sector. There have been long-standing debates going back more than a century about the failures of the financial sector vis-à-vis the industrial sector. The processes of financialization over the past three decades have involved developments of the financial sector which have been to the detriment of the industrial sector. The key roles of the financial sector should be the financing (through bank loans) of and the longer term funding of investment, and the need to reconstruct the financial sector to focus on those roles. There is then a need to refocus the financial sector away from the development of 'exotic' financial products (derivatives) which do little for savings and investment, and which absorb resources: a financial transactions tax could be one element of that refocusing and provide funds for industrial development. The thrust of this introduction will be the argument that the financial sector has to serve industrial development (and economic performance more generally) rather than its own interests and the extraction of rent from the rest of the economy.

The banking system has a particular crucial role to play here. One feature of banks (narrowly defined) is that their liabilities are means of payment; that is, treated as money. The undertaking of investment ahead of savings requires that banks provide loans to firms, which not only creates money (in the form of bank deposits) but enables the investment to be financed and to take place. In turn, the investment stimulates savings. At the end of the circuit, when the savings have been generated, there is the flow of funds to the firms. The first key role of banks is then the provision of loans, which can initiate investment ahead of savings. But to state the obvious this relies on the willingness of banks to provide loans and firms to acquire the loans. The second key role of the financial sector as a whole is the reallocation of the funds which have been generated.

A pervasive feature of finance is that there will be forms of credit rationing—by which we mean that the cost of finance will reflect the provider perception of the risks attached, notably the likelihood of default (partial or total).[6] The higher the perceived risk of default and the higher the perceived costs of default (e.g. what proportion of the loan would be recoverable in the event of default as it is secured against other property), the higher will be the cost of finance; and a higher cost of finance may itself shift the risk of default. In a world of uncertainty where the risks of default are not known, it is the perceptions of the borrowers of the risks which are relevant. Further, the risk of default depends on the actions of the borrower in a range of ways; and hence the perceived risk will also have to take into account the possible actions of the borrower. The assessed risk of default may be sufficiently high that the cost of borrowing becomes very high and in practice there would not be lending. The perceptions of lenders on risk will be strongly influenced by a wide range of social and economic factors: some groups (e.g. ethnic, gender) may be systematically judged high risk and face high costs of borrowing. In the context of industrial strategy the significant question is the allocation of funds to specific sectors such as small and medium-sized enterprises, and environmentally friendly investment.

---

[6] See Sawyer (2014b) for a detailed survey of the relationships between finance and industry with a particular focus on the roles of credit rationing.

6.2 INVESTMENT AND SAVINGS

It is argued that there is an 'over-savings' issue in the UK economy and not a shortage of funds (and this is reflected in the budget deficit when it is recalled that from national accounts budget deficit = private savings minus private investment plus capital account surplus). There has been a long-standing imbalance between private savings and private investment (which is detailed below for the past decade), which has shown up in consumer debt, budget deficits, and financial investment by corporations. It is argued that an industrial policy would not involve a higher level of investment (as compared with the level prior to the financial crisis) but a restructuring of investment which is more environmentally friendly. Thus it is not a matter of a general insufficient funding for investment, but rather the need to ensure that finance is forthcoming from banks and that funding is channelled in the socially desired directions.

Some broad sweep statistics on investment in the UK are given in Table 6.1, covering the period 2004–12. In the period of the mid 2000s prior to the financial crisis, gross investment relative to GDP averaged 19.02 per cent, of which 17.40 per cent of GDP was private investment and 1.62 per cent public investment. The figures presented in Table 6.1 suggest that the savings made by non-financial corporations substantially exceed the investment which they undertook, and similarly for financial corporations. Savings undertaken by households (which in this context would also include unincorporated firms) had low savings prior to the financial crisis,[7] aligned with the rising debt of many households on the back of rising house prices. Combined with an inflow of capital from the rest of the world (the counterpart to the current account deficit), a government budget deficit is an inevitable feature which is in effect required to absorb the excessive savings.

It is a well-known feature of many industrialized economies that the general shift away from wages and towards profits has not been associated with a comparable rise in investment. Related to that, and as is apparent from Table 6.1, the savings out of profits by corporations exceed the investments of corporations, leaving the corporations with a surplus of funds which have to be lent out, directly or indirectly, to others, notably to government (thereby help to fund the budget deficit) and to households (which may show up in the extension of credit to the household sector). From 1990 to 2007 growth of GDP averaged 2.4 per cent per annum with infamously 63 successive quarters of output expansion; in the words of the then governor of the Bank of England Mervyn King this was the 'nice' period—non-inflationary continuous expansion.[8] We postulate that the rate of investment was broadly consistent with the economic growth achieved (that is,

---

[7] In the years 2004–8, savings as percent of disposable income for households averaged 2.6 per cent; for the years 2009–12, they averaged 6.9 per cent. However, in the years 2004–8 household expenditure and gross disposable income were virtually equal, and the savings of households were largely accounted for by 'the change in net equity of households in pension funds'. Source: National Income Accounts, 2013, Table 6.1.6.

[8] Excluding the recession years of the early 1990s, the average for 1993–2007 is just under 3 per cent per annum.

Table 6.1 Savings and Investment in the UK

		2004	2005	2006	2007	2008	2009	2010	2011	2012
Private savings as % GDP		17.30	19.15	17.70	20.55	23.18	25.15	24.71	24.89	19.36
of which	Non-financial corporations	12.45	13.94	13.07	13.94	14.13	13.40	14.69	15.36	13.72
	Financial corporations	2.01	2.73	1.86	4.54	6.80	5.40	3.10	3.18	−0.83
	Households	2.83	2.48	2.77	2.07	2.26	6.35	6.92	6.35	6.48
Private investment as % GDP		15.61	17.35	17.59	19.41	17.95	13.37	15.48	16.39	16.35
of which	Non-financial corporations	9.60	10.98	10.05	11.24	11.44	8.79	9.98	10.61	10.48
	Financial corporations	0.46	0.62	0.54	0.63	0.65	0.45	0.56	0.63	0.60
	Households	5.55	5.74	7.00	7.53	5.86	4.14	4.94	5.14	5.27
Public investment as % of GDP		1.73	0.70	1.98	2.05	2.71	3.05	2.93	2.62	2.67

Source: Calculated from *National Income Accounts*, 2013

there was not a major rise or fall in the capital–output ratio). An investment ratio in the upper teens appears to be consistent with the type of growth rate that was experienced in the 1990s and 2000s. We further postulate that a growth rate in per capita terms of the order of 2.5 per cent appears to be the ceiling on the growth of the UK economy, and further that the future growth rate is likely to be slower rather than faster than that for two essential reasons. The first relates to environmental considerations and whether the planet is capable of withstanding continuing growth at the rates experienced over the last few decades. The second is the perception that growth rate of productivity has slowed: in the UK productivity has declined in the years since 2008, and this may portend slower productivity growth in the future. From these considerations we postulate the requirements for investment funds are not going to be substantially higher than they were in the first part of the 2000s. However, there will be requirements on the direction of funding—particularly in the environmentally friendly direction. Further, consideration must be given to the ways in which the savings of corporations ahead of their investment requirements are utilized.

6.3 Financial Sector and Industrial Strategy

The financial industries are industries, and as such would come under the general rubric of industrial policy. Indeed industrial policy in the UK could be characterized by 'defend' the City of London, a notable example being the responses to proposals from the EU over financial transactions taxes.

There has been much talk of the rebalancing of the UK economy—with precious little indication of what that means and little movement in the direction of rebalancing. An industrial strategy is at heart a strategy for the rebalancing of the economy. By rebalancing we mean securing a macroeconomic balance at a high level of employment which does not rely on a series of 'unsustainable processes' (Godley, 1999). The 'boom' of the mid-2000s was heavily reliant on consumer debt fuelled by rising house prices—both of which have strong elements of unsustainability (and also the profits of the financial sector). The excess of savings over investment in the corporate sector as revealed in Table 6.1 could be similarly seen as a source of imbalance—the consequence of such an excess is that the corporate sector is a lender—whether to the household sector (consumer debt) or to government (budget deficit). The further requirement is for changes in the industrial structure which are more compatible with the sustainable growth of the UK economy.

The financial sector has been compared by some, notably Shaxson and Christensen (2013), to a 'finance curse' which echoes the arguments of a 'resource curse' which can afflict countries with large natural resources. There is not space here to fully develop the argument, but let us consider some of the possible effects. The real exchange rate is higher than it would be otherwise. This, of course, can be viewed as a benefit since imports become cheaper to the benefit of consumers. But, as is well known from the North Sea oil experience, a high exchange rate operates to the detriment of other industries. This could mean a reallocation of resources, though the financial sector is in general not as employment-intensive as other industries. The authors argue that the finance curse involves "'country capture'—where an oversized financial sector comes to control the politics of a finance-dependent country and to dominate and hollow out its economy".

The underlying points being made here are twofold. The first is that the policies towards the financial sector should be viewed within the context of an overall industrial strategy. This involves debates over the future role of the financial sector as employer and whether it should continue to receive the support of recent years. The second is that the key role of the financial sector should be to facilitate sustainable development in the real economy. The financial sector should then be viewed in terms of the services it provides to support industry and its development (though not limited to that).

6.4 INSTITUTIONAL ARRANGEMENTS

The underlying assumptions here are that there is not a shortage of potential savings which would fund investment, and that the major issue is the direction of funds rather than the quantity.[9] In this respect, let us note that a higher level of investment would generate a higher level of savings through an expansion of the economy (and also a higher level of tax revenue and imports). It is also taken that the major role of the financial sector should be the financing of investment and the channelling of savings into investment.

In light of the financial crisis, its long-lasting impacts on economic prosperity and employment, and the costs of that crisis (in terms of 'bail-outs' and of lost output), there has been much discussion of reforms of the financial system and its regulation. Although there has, in general, not been much discussion of the links between industrial strategy and reforms of the financial sector, those discussions can be drawn on here. The purposes of such reforms of the financial system would be to construct a financial system less prone to instability and crisis. If reforms were carried through, and their purposes achieved, that would be above all beneficial for economic performance. But how far would it aid industrial development and strategy? Here we argue for four 're-forms' of the financial sector which would aid industrial strategy (and economic performance more generally). We would argue that these reforms would also facilitate a less unstable financial system.

---

[9] The stress should be on *potential* savings, as savings can only be realized if there is prior investment, government net spending, and net exports.

6.4.1 The Role of Financial Transactions Taxes

The key role of the financial sector (alongside provision of a transactions technology) is the provision of bank loans to finance investment and linking savings and investment. The trading of existing financial assets, the growth of 'fictitious capital', and the rise of assets and liabilities (relative to GDP) contribute little to that key role. A particular recent example has been the development of high frequency trading (HFT), which relies on computer algorithms in the context of trading strategies carried out by computers to move in and out of positions in seconds or fractions of a second. 'As of 2009, studies suggested HFT firms accounted for 60–73% of all US equity trading volume, with that number falling to approximately 50% in 2012.'[10] 'Financial markets have undergone a dramatic transformation. Traders no longer sit in trading pits buying and selling stocks with hand signals, today these transactions are executed electronically by computer algorithms. Stock exchanges 'becoming fully automated ... increased the number of transactions a market executes and this enabled intermediaries to expand their own use of technology. Increased automation reduced the role for traditional human market makers and led to the rise of a new type of electronic intermediary (market maker or specialist), typically referred to as high frequency traders (HFTs)' (Brogaard et al., 2013).

The rise in the frequency of trading in equity, and the development of derivatives and high volume trading raise a range of interesting issues for industrial policy.[11] The growth of high frequency trading raises issues of corporate governance: someone who is the (proud) owner of equity in a company for a second cannot exercise much influence on the corporate governance of that company! Further, when price movements are in effect following a random walk, then high frequency trading is akin to playing the casino. High frequency trading exacerbates the issues raised by Keynes in the 1930s when he wrote that 'Speculators may do no harm as bubbles on a steady stream of enterprise. But the position is serious when enterprise becomes the bubble on a whirlpool of speculation. When the capital development of a country becomes a by-product of the activities of a casino, the job is likely to be ill-done ... The introduction of a substantial government transfer tax on all transactions might prove the most serviceable reform available, with a view to mitigating the predominance of speculation over enterprise in the United States' (Keynes, 1936, pp. 159 and 160). The casino analogy should also be viewed in terms of who profits from HFT—in the case of the casino we know it is the 'bank': for HFT those operating the system appear to find it highly profitable, but at whose expense?

The essential rationale for a financial transactions tax remains and is indeed reinforced by financialization, by which we mean the growth of the financial sector in its economic activities, power, and influence, and the specific direction which financialization has taken in the past three decades with the growth of securitization and

---

[10] <http://en.wikipedia.org/wiki/High-frequency_trading> (accessed March 2014).
[11] See Gower (2010) for advocacy of financial transaction tax in the context of the growth of high frequency trading.

derivatives. The advocacy of a financial transactions tax is not to preclude other taxes on the financial sector such as financial activity taxes. The advantages of a financial transaction tax would not only dampen down the resources deployed in the buying and selling of existing financial assets which are of little social benefit, but also serve as a source of tax revenues which can be deployed for the funding of public investment.

6.4.2 Separation and Ring Fencing

There has been substantial discussion of the separation of 'narrow banking' from 'casino banking'; less pejoratively expressed as separation between commercial banks and investment banking/securities trading. Such a separation was embodied in the American Glass–Steagall Act, the final repeal of which in the 1999 Gramm–Leach–Bliley Act has been attributed a role in the generation of the financial crisis of 2007–9. The response of the UK Independent Commission on Banking (2011) was 'ring fencing'—that is, while a financial institution could engage in both commercial banking and investment banking there would be internal separation between the activities, with the intention of 'insulating UK retail banking from external shocks and of diminishing problems (including for resolvability) of financial interconnectedness'. They proposed that a 'wide range of services should *not be permitted* in the ring-fence'. The 'activities [which] should not be carried on inside the ring-fence: services to non-EEA customers, services (other than payments services) resulting in exposure to financial customers, "trading book" activities, services relating to secondary markets activity (including the purchases of loans or securities), and derivatives trading (except as necessary for the retail bank prudently to manage its own risk)' (Executive summary Independent Commission on Banking, 2011, p. 11).

The essential arguments for 'ring fencing' relate to the stability of the financial system. The concern here is somewhat different, namely for the focus of the financial sector on the savings—investment linkages, and not on trading in existing assets.

6.4.3 Structure of the Banking Sector

The structure of the banking sector can be viewed in terms of what would be conducive for financial stability, and indeed much of the discussion about the structure and regulation of the banking sector has focused on that issue. The focus here is somewhat different, being directly on the structure of the banking system which would aid industrial policy and strategy, though financial stability would generally aid industrial development.

The Independent Commission on Banking (2011) viewed its recommendations as aiming to 'create a more stable and competitive basis for UK banking in the longer term', which 'means much more than greater resilience against future financial crises and removing risks from banks to the public finances. It also means a banking system that is effective and efficient at providing the basic banking services of safeguarding retail deposits,

operating secure payments systems, efficiently channelling savings to productive investments, and managing financial risk' (p. 7). The British banking sector is highly concentrated, as has been the case for the last century. The proposals here would run along three
lines. The first comes from banks concentrating on 'channelling savings to productive investment', to which we would add the role of the initial provisions of loans for investment.
The other side of that is the discouragement of dealings in derivatives and other financial
assets. This can come from the 'legally enforceable separation between retail and speculative banking. This would help to contain the toxic effects of future crises. However, merely
separating the banking arms is not enough because speculators would continue to be
funded by monies from savers, pension funds and insurance companies to finance their
gambling habits' (Sikka, 2014, pp. 21–2). Policies such as this are generally proposed with
regard to lessening financial fragility and proneness to credit bubbles. From the perspective here they are viewed in terms of the linkages of savings and investment.

The second is diversity of the banking system (see the chapter by Michie in this
volume). Although building societies were technically not banks for many years, and
their key function was the provision of housing funding and a vehicle for household savings, they were mutual organizations providing specialized services. The German
banking system stands in some contrast to the UK system with a range of different ownership forms (private, public, and mutual) and the local and regional focus of much of
the banking system with landesbanken, savings, and co-operative banks.[12] Without
eulogizing the German system it does seem to have been rather more adept at funding
small and medium-sized enterprises and less prone to financial instability.

'All of this suggests that government can and should play a central role in structuring
the financial system to achieve sustainable long-term economic growth. And in contrast
to the current system, which centralizes power in mega-firms and directs capital in just a
handful of channels, an ideal system would be more decentralized and create more
diverse channels for capital investment' (Block, 2014, p. 12). 'This kind of automation is a
particular problem with small-business lending. Since failure rates of small business
loans are high, the computerized algorithms tend to limit credit to firms that have
already proven themselves or to firms that have collateral in the form of real property.
This tends to bias credit availability toward real estate development and away from other
endeavours. The best way to overcome this dynamic is to introduce significant competition from financial intermediaries who are not seeking to generate profits. These could
take the form of credit unions, community banks, nonprofit loan funds, or banks that
are owned by government entities; but the key is that their mission is defined as facilitating economic development in a particular geographical area. With this mission, they
have a reason to employ loan officers who develop the skill set needed to provide credit
to individuals and firms who fall outside the parameters of the standard lending algorithms' (Block, 2014, p. 16).

The third is to reduce the degree of concentration in the banking sector, some of
which could be achieved through more diverse organizations, and the application of

---

[12] See Detzer et al. (2013) for a detailed survey of the German financial system.

competition policy more stringently to the financial sector. The reduction of concentration could go alongside a more regionally based banking system. But this raises the losses of economies of scale. 'However, these industry studies rely primarily on case studies and anecdotal evidence to support their claims. The majority of academic studies, on the other hand, do not find positive evidence for economies of scale and scope beyond a relatively small size. For instance, Saunders (1996) surveys at least 20 empirical studies and finds little evidence of scale economies for banks with assets greater than $5 billion. Similarly, in a survey of more than 50 studies by Amel et al. (2004), the minimum efficient scale in retail commercial banking appears to be somewhere below $10 billion in assets, depending on the sample, country and time period. Applying these findings to the global population of banks in 2008 would suggest that several hundred are above the threshold at which no positive evidence for economies of scale could be found. Beyond a certain size there may even be diseconomies of scale, possibly due to the complexity of managing large institutions (Haldane, 2010). While some recent studies are more supportive of the existence of scale economies in banking, including a review of studies of mergers and acquisitions in banking by DeYoung et al. (2009), taken together the bulk of the empirical literature to date has failed to identify material economies of scale in commercial banking beyond a relatively modest size' (Davies et al., 2010, p. 325).

However, in a more recent paper it has been argued that 'from a standard model of bank production that does not control for any TBTF [too big to fail] funding cost advantage, we find evidence that scale economies exist for our international sample of large banks. These results are similar to recent findings in the literature' (Davies and Tracey, 2014, p. 243). But, and most significantly, 'from both methods that attempt to uncover the production technology for banks that is unaffected by TBTF, we no longer find evidence of scale economies for our sample of large banks. These results imply that estimated scale economies for large banks are affected by TBTF factors' (Davies and Tracey, 2014, pp. 243–4).

6.4.4 Guided Lending

An important element of an industrial strategy is to seek to ensure that funds flow in the direction which is compatible with that strategy. This can involve some degree of guided lending for banks—that is, requirements that a specified proportion of their lending are to those sectors identified for development and growth. In the current circumstances, we would advocate that the key focus here should be on green and environmentally friendly investment. This could draw on the US experience of the Community Reinvestment Act (CRA), introduced in 1977 and revised in 1995, whereby banks and other financial institutions are legally required to direct a portion of funds to lending to the local community. 'The Community Reinvestment Act is intended to encourage depository institutions to help meet the credit needs of the communities in which they operate, including low- and moderate-income neighborhoods, consistent with safe and sound operations. The CRA requires that each depository institution's record in helping meet the credit needs of its entire community be evaluated by the appropriate Federal financial supervisory agency periodically. Members of the public may submit comments on a bank's performance. Comments will be taken into consideration during the next CRA examination. A bank's CRA performance record is taken into account in considering an institution's application for deposit facilities' (http://www.federalreserve.gov/communitydev/cra_about.htm, accessed March 2014). Dayson et al. (2013) explore the use of a Banking Disclosure Act as 'it is believed that disclosure could support research into the determinants of underinvestment and lending, which in turn would aid by enhancing our understanding of financial exclusion and under-investment. In particular, it would help identify groups and areas less likely to access financial services'.

The underlying philosophy is that banks are making credit allocation decisions all the time, and the decisions which come out are not necessarily socially desirable. The purpose here would be to seek to ensure that sufficient credit is channelled in the directions consistent with the overall industrial strategy. The local aspect of this is stressed by Sikka when he writes that 'banks should be part of local communities. They should not be permitted to up sticks and leave local communities in the lurch. Maintaining a socially desirable network of branches should be a necessary quid pro quo for a deposit-taking licence and the state's deposit protection guarantee. Each branch closure must be sanctioned by the regulator, and banks must be required to demonstrate that after closure, the local community's access to banking services will not suffer' (Sikka, 2014, p. 24). An alternative view on this is that 'government has an active role to play in allocating credit to finance productive economic activity, and it should use a full range of policy tools including interest rate subsidies, loan guarantee programs, and tax incentives to assure that capital flows in the most productive directions' (Block, 2014, p. 13).

6.4.5 Development Banks

A further arm in policies designed to strengthen an industrial strategy which has to be put on the table is the establishment of a state-sponsored development bank along the lines of the European Investment Bank to generate funds in the financial markets for onward lending to enterprises including small and medium-sized enterprises. The UK Green Investment Bank could be one arm of this.

Insofar as a state-sponsored development bank was drawing on government funds (as the Green Investment Bank does), it would run into the objection that it adds to budget deficit and to the public debt. Our response to that would be that borrowing for investment also adds to the assets of the public sector (whether through infrastructure investment or through onward lending to the private sector), and that the concern should be that the funds are well used, adding to the desired direction of investment, and aiding the achievement of full employment. There is no 'tipping point' for the national debt to GDP ratio which threatens growth.[13] But also note that as with the European Investment Bank any lending by governments can be leveraged through direct borrowing by the development bank, and that such borrowing (as is the case with the European Investment Bank) does not appear on the balance sheets of any national or EU organization.

6.5 CONCLUDING COMMENTS

One theme underlying this chapter is that the financial sector has to serve the economy and industry, rather than vice versa. It has been argued that an industrial strategy would contribute to a rebalancing of the economy (a significant element of which would be an improvement in net exports).[14] It has been asserted that there is not an essential lack of savings in the UK economy, and that the focus needs in the short run to be on raising investment levels back to around the pre-crisis level, and in the longer term to channelling savings and investment into areas of development and sustainability. Although it has not featured in this piece, much of that focus has to be on 'green investment' and environmentally sustainable investments. The financial sector should be restructured in ways which are conducive to sustainable development. This would involve focusing activities of the financial sector on commercial banking, promotion of a financial sector less prone to financial instability, and direction of funds. A well-designed financial transaction tax along with other taxes on the financial sector would aid focusing the financial sector onto commercial banking activities. The promotion of a more diverse (e.g. in forms of ownership) and regionally based banking system could contribute to stability. Specifically in terms of industrial strategy and development, we advocate a combination of 'directed lending' with requirements that a stated proportion of bank lending be directed towards specified areas such as 'green investment', small and medium-sized enterprises, and the birth of a state development bank.

REFERENCES

Amel, D., Barnes, C., Panetta, F., and Salleo, C. (2004). 'Consolidation and Efficiency in the Financial Sector: A Review of the International Evidence', *Journal of Banking and Finance* 28(10), 2, 493–519.

Arestis, P. and Sawyer, M. (2014). 'On the Sustainability of Budget Deficits and Public Debts with Reference to the UK', in P. Arestis and M. Sawyer (eds), *Fiscal and Debt Policies for the Future*, pp. 38–75. Basingstoke: Palgrave Macmillan.

[13] See Herndon et al. (2014) for critical assessment of work which purported to show that there was a 'tipping point'. Arestis and Sawyer (2014) provide an extensive discussion of the points mentioned in the text.

[14] It should be noted that some combination of a rise in net exports and reduction in net savings (savings minus investment) has to accompany a reduction in the budget deficit as a matter of national income accounting.

Block, F. (2014). 'Democratizing Finance', *Politics & Society* 42(1), 3–28.

Brogaard, J., Hendershott, T., and Riordan, R. (2013). *High Frequency Trading and Price Discovery*, European Central Bank Working Paper Series No. 1602.

Collins, M. (1991). *Banks and Industrial Finance in Britain 1800–1939*. London: Macmillan.

Davies, R., Richardson, P., Katinaite, V., and Manning, M. (2010). 'Evolution of the UK Banking System', *Bank of England Quarterly Bulletin* Q4, 321–32.

Davies, R. and Tracey, B. (2014). 'Too Big to Be Efficient? The Impact of Implicit Subsidies on Estimates of Scale Economies for Banks', *Journal of Money, Credit and Banking* 46 (Supplement/1), 219–53.

Dayson, K., Vik, P., Rand, D., and Smith, G. (2013). *A UK Banking Disclosure Act: From Theory to Practice*. Dorking: Friends Provident Foundation.

Detzer, D., Dodig, N., Evans, T., Hein, E., and Herr, H. (2013). *The German Financial System*, FESSUD Studies in Financial Systems No. 3.

DeYoung, R., Evanoff, D. D., and Molyneux, P. (2009). 'Mergers and Acquisitions of Financial Institutions: A Review of the Post-2000 Literature', *Journal of Financial Services Research* 36, 87–110.

Epstein, G. (2005). 'Introduction: Financialization and the World Economy', in G. Epstein (ed.) *Financialization and the World Economy*, pp. 1–13. Cheltenham and Northampton: Edward Elgar.

Epstein, G. and Crotty, J. (2013). 'How Big Is Too Big? On the Social Efficiency of the Financial Sector in the United States', PERI Working Paper Series No. 313.

Godley, W. (1999). 'Seven Unsustainable Processes: Medium-Term Prospects and Policies for the United States and the World', Levy Institute Special Report, <http://www.levyinstitute.org/pubs/sr/sevenproc.pdf>.

Gower, R. (2010). Financial Crisis 2: The Rise of the Machines, *The Robin Hood Tax*, <http://robinhoodtax.org.uk/sites/default/files/Rise%20of%20the%20Machines_1.pdf>.

Haldane, A. G. (2010). 'The $100 Billion Question', <http://www.bankofengland.co.uk/archive/Documents/historicpubs/speeches/2010/speech433.pdf>.

Hein, E. (2012). *The Macroeconomics of Finance-Dominated Capitalism—and Its Crisis*. Cheltenham: Edward Elgar.

Herndon, T., Ash, M., and Pollin, R. (2014). 'Does High Public Debt Consistently Stifle Economic Growth? A Critique of Reinhart and Rogoff', *Cambridge Journal of Economics* 38, 257–79.

Independent Commission on Banking (2011). *Final Report Recommendations*, <http://bankingcommission.independent.gov.uk/>.

Keynes, J. M. (1936). *The General Theory of Employment, Interest and Money*, London: Macmillan.

Saunders, A. (1996). *Financial Institutions Management: A Modern Perspective*. Burr Ridge, IL: Irwin Professional Publishing.

Sawyer, M. (2014a). *Financial Development, Financialisation and Economic Growth*, FESSUD Working Paper No. 21, <http://www.fessud.eu>.

Sawyer, M. (2014b). The Effects of Finance on Industry under Different Financial Systems. FESSUD Working Paper, <http://www.fessud.eu>.

Shabani, M., Tyson, J., Toporowski, J., and McKinley, T. (2014). *UK Country Report*, FESSUD Studies in Financial Systems No. 13, <http://www.fessud.eu>.

Shaxson, N. and Christensen, J. (2013). *The Finance Curse: How Oversized Financial Centres Attack Democracy and Corrupt Economies*. Margate: Commonwealth Publishing.

Sikka, P. (2014). Banking in the Public Interest: Progressive Reform of the Financial Sector. February CLASS Policy Paper.

CHAPTER 7

....

FINANCIAL ARCHITECTURE AND INDUSTRIAL POLICY

*Alternative Ownership Structures
and the Role of Mutuals*

....

JONATHAN MICHIE

7.1 INTRODUCTION

....

AT the end of the nineteenth century, Britain was the world's leading industrial and economic power. The international financial system was based on the gold standard underpinned by the pound sterling. The 'long' twentieth century, from that era to the present
day, has seen a continual, gradual, relative decline in the UK economy, most particularly
in manufacturing and industry, but also in the economy more generally. There is a large
literature on the causes of this decline; or rather, various and several large literatures
around different aspects. Three interlinked themes are firstly, the dominance of the 'City
of London', and the UK's financial interests over and above its industrial and economic
interests more widely; secondly, the prioritization of overseas interests against domestic;
and thirdly, the relative dominance of the UK economy by large companies, often multinational, and usually owned by shareholders with their shares traded on the stock
exchange, owned by individuals and institutions quite external to the company.

One of the more recent contributions to this extensive literature was the Report from
the Ownership Commission (2012), which lamented the lack of corporate diversity
within the UK economy, and called on government to take action to promote a more
corporately diverse economy, including through the promotion of 'mutuals', broadly
defined—that is, companies owned not by private individuals nor families and nor by
external shareholders, but by their members, where these will be their customers, their
employees, or other groups such as producers or the local community—or indeed
by some combination of such stakeholders. The UK's 2010–15 Coalition Agreement

committed the government to bringing about a more corporately diverse financial services sector, including through promoting mutuals, and to responding to the 2007–8 international financial crisis and the subsequent global recession of 2009 by rebalancing the economy, with the Chancellor heralding the 'march of the makers' as manufacturing, investment, and exports would be promoted, rather than financial innovation and speculation.

The reality has been disappointing. The financial services sector is no more corporately diverse than when the Coalition government made its pledges, in the *Coalition Agreement* of 2010. Quite the contrary: the situation has actually become worse rather than better; as reported below, new research demonstrates that the financial services sector is even less corporately diverse in 2014 than when the government pledged to deliver diversity. The Co-operative Bank's withdrawal from attempting to buy bank branches from Lloyds, and the subsequent transfer of 80 per cent of the Co-operative Bank's shares out of the Co-operative Group has made matters worse. The previous government had boasted of 'light touch' regulation, and while the 2007–8 international financial crisis demonstrated the reckless folly of such an abdication of power to the free market, this was reinforced by the evidence of the Financial Services Authority having approved as Chairman of the Co-operative Bank an individual who was patently unqualified and unfit for such a role.

But even before the problems of the Co-operative Bank, the Coalition government had reneged on their commitment to promote corporate diversity in the financial services market including by promoting mutual, through their refusal to return Northern Rock—which had been a successful mutual prior to demutualizing, and which then failed as a private bank—to the mutual sector. The disposal of Northern Rock was generally reported as having been a sale to Richard Branson, but in reality 44 per cent went to the American leveraged buyout investor Wilbur Ross—and all at a loss to the taxpayer.[1]

Alongside the failure to have tackled the long-standing dominance of the UK's financial services sector by large shareholder-owned banks, the Coalition government have also failed to diversify the economy more generally. Manufacturing remains weak, and itself relatively dominated by large shareholder-owned firms, lacking the family owned, public sector, and mutual presence that characterize the manufacturing sectors in other European economies. Alongside this imbalanced industrial and economic structure, the UK has continued to suffer from regional imbalances; and the failure to tackle the economic imbalances are perpetuating these regional imbalances (see Hutton and Lee, 2012; Bailey, Cowling, and Tomlinson in this volume). At the time of writing, the recovery from the 2009 recession is relying in part at least on reflating the housing

---

[1] For a detailed analysis of Northern Rock, and the potential to have returned it to the mutual sector, see Michie and Llewellyn (2010). Branston et al. (2012, 2015 forthcoming) also make the case for a return to mutuality for Northern Rock and the other 'failed' banks; in doing so, these authors also suggest reforms to governance structures to address the problems of 'elite capture' and monopolistic practices that afflicted some mutuals in the 1970s and 1980s (see Barnes, 1984).

bubble, through the government's 'help to buy' scheme, which is further exacerbating the country's regional imbalances.

And the increase in inequality which was created from the 1980s onwards remains, with both incomes and wealth far more skewed than in the more economically successful decades before the 1980s era of Thatcher and Reagan. This inequality contributed to the global financial crisis of 2007–8, and threatens to stall and undermine any sustained recovery (see Stiglitz, 2013). The poverty at the bottom is a drag on consumer demand, and encourages the growth of credit-fuelled consumer debt, such as that which led to the sub-prime crisis in the US, which was one of the contributory factors in causing the 2007–8 financial crisis. Conversely, the huge wealth at the top fuels the search for new financial products for financial speculation; this is analysed by, for example, Goda and Lysandrou (2014) who summarize recent evidence about the negative impact of investor demand on US bond yields in the pre-crisis period, and present new evidence regarding the specific contribution of high-net-worth individuals to this negative impact. Having helped to cause the yield problem in the major US debt markets, high-net-worth individuals (via hedge funds) continued to be a major source of the pressure on US banks to resolve this yield problem through the mass production of collateralized debt obligation (CDO) 'products'.

7.2 THE IMPORTANCE OF OWNERSHIP

The ownership of productive assets plays a crucial role in the functioning of any economy, and also has profound implications for other aspects of social life, such as the degree of wealth and income inequality, the quality of working life, and the functioning of democracy. The rise of capitalism historically was based originally upon private (and family) ownership of productive assets, and then led to the development of 'limited liability', which facilitated the creation and growth of shareholder-owned companies.

This private ownership of the nation's productive resources—the factories, farms, mills, mines, railroads, and so forth—placed great economic power in the hands of the new class of owners, which in turn tended to bestow upon them political power and social influence. The resulting inequality of income, harsh working conditions, and economic instability—where economic downturns left the unemployed with no means to support themselves—led to various alternative visions for a non-capitalist society, where wealth and power would be more evenly distributed, crucially through some alternative to private ownership of the 'means of production'. For Robert Owen this would be based on co-operative and mutual principles; for Marx it would be through the 'appropriation of the appropriators', with the means of production owned collectively by society—operating in the first instance through the state.

These alternatives to capitalist ownership led in the centrally planned economies to state ownership and planning, and across most Western European economies to the 'commanding heights of the economy' being government owned and controlled—the utilities (gas, electricity, and water), major infrastructure industries (railways, post, tele-communications), and other large scale enterprises such as coalmining and steel. To these would be added companies and even whole industries that were seen to be failing in private hands, which needed to be nationalized in order to keep them operating—such as, in different countries at different times, shipbuilding and car production. Alongside these forms of state ownership, co-operative and mutual ownership flourished to varying degrees—in the UK the co-op held a major market share in food retail up until the 1960s, before gradually losing out to the large supermarket chains (see Burt and Sparks, 2003).

From the early 1980s, Thatcherism in the UK led to privatization, and this concept was subsequently exported globally. With the collapse of the Soviet Union, the whole historical era of public ownership and regulation was pushed back significantly. There followed an era of 'capitalism unleashed' (Glyn, 2006), with a shift back to private ownership (by individuals and shareholders) of companies, away from public and state ownership; a rolling back of public regulation of industries and sectors; a financial-ization of society, where ever-more relations became marketized, with fewer and fewer free and subsidized goods; and with a resultant increase in inequality of wealth and income in almost every country across the world (Stiglitz, 2006, 2013).[2] This new era of laissez-faire capitalism led to the global financial crisis of 2007–8, which in turn created the first global recession—with world output and income levels actually declining (ra-ther than just the rate of growth declining, as had happened during the downturns during the 'golden age of capitalism' of the 1950s and 1960s)—since the 1930s, in 2009 (see Stiglitz, 2010). Five years on, in 2014, the global economy had still not fully recovered, and the UK's levels of output and income are still lower than they had been five years previously—an almost unprecedented poor economic performance and out-come (and with the UK balance of payments position in a worse state than ever).

Yet despite this major failure of free market capitalism, there have been no major al-ternatives gaining widespread support along the lines of the above-described planned economies, or social democratic control of the 'commanding heights' of the economy. Neither has there been a generally accepted alternative to the failed ideology and theory of neoclassical economics and laissez-faire capitalism which justified and promoted the era of capitalism unleashed, as had occurred in the 1930s with Keynes's *General Theory of Employment, Interest and Money*, which helped support the shift in thinking away from the old orthodox 'Treasury' view of the economy and economics, towards a recog-nition of the need for policy activism, including public works and spending, in the face of economic recession.

It is true that Fukuyama's (1992) claims of 'an end of history' have been generally de-rided—most clinically and successfully by Milne (2012), whose aptly named *Revenge of History* documents in detail the failings of this 'end of history' analysis and the associ-ated policy agenda of Bush and Blair. As Milne (2012) documents, there have been

---

[2] Many of these neo-liberal policies were widely advocated by the major Washington institutions such as the International Monetary Fund and the World Bank. They became associated with the term 'Washington Consensus' (Williamson, 1990).

socialist and social democratic governments elected across South America, and also in some European countries and even US cities. But in general, outside South America, whichever political party was in office at the time of the global financial crisis has tended to suffer the political backlash. There has been no new global consensus to replace the free-market model of 'capitalism unleashed'.

This chapter thus considers what this sort of alternative might look like—for the UK and globally, in the short term and longer term. Just as the rise of capitalism led to the co-operative, Marxian, and other critiques, and just as the crisis of the 1930s led to Keynesianism and social democracy across much of Western Europe and a new international order as fashioned at Bretton Woods, so the failure of capitalism unleashed needs to herald a new era of global development based on new analysis and a new policy agenda.

7.3 PERIODIZATION OF CAPITALISM

The history of capitalism can be seen as having developed through distinct phases. While these various phases will have lasted for different lengths, and will have varied across the globe, one might consider the following thirty-year eras, generally with five-year interregnums between the long swings:

i. *1840–70*: the rise of capitalism, with the industrial revolution generally considered to have been completed by 1840, the UK became the world's leading industrial power and trading nation, establishing the gold standard based on the pound sterling; but with the rise and establishment of capitalism came the 1848 revolutions, the concomitant birth of Marxism (the *Communist Manifesto* also being published in 1848), and the development of organized labour.

ii. *1875–1905*: the development of limited liability and joint stock companies, with the UK having established herself as the leading economic (and military) power globally, but with increased inter-imperialist rivalry between the emerging capitalist economies, most notably the US and Germany (whilst the year 1905 witnessed the first Russian Revolution).

iii. *1910–40*: An interregnum: the First World War, the Russian Revolution, the 'Roaring 20s' leading to the 1929 Wall Street Crash, the rise of fascism and Hitler, the Great Depression and the New Deal, and the Second World War; the UK's economic dominance had started to wane, leaving it incapable of maintaining the gold standard after the Chancellor of the Exchequer, Winston Churchill, had re-established it at the pre-First World War level (despite warnings from Keynes—on which see Kitson and Michie, 2000).

iv. *1945–75*: the Golden Age of Capitalism—social democracy and centrally planned economies, Keynesianism, and international economic institutions that generally delivered full employment (usually defined in Beveridge terms as around 3 per cent to account for labour market frictions) and sustained economic growth that had not been witnessed previously and has not been achieved since (on which, see Marglin and Schor, 1992).

   v. *1980–2010*: capitalism unleashed: the Washington Consensus, an era of privatization, deregulation, demutualization, and financialization, with a concomitant rise in inequality; slower economic growth than in the previous—Keynesian—era, although with rapid expansion during credit-fuelled bubbles, culminating in the 2007–8 international financial crisis and concomitant global economic recession

   vi. *2015–45*: a new model is required, to provide global economic growth that is sustainable economically, socially, and environmentally; this calls for the promotion of corporate diversity, with a proper mix of public, private, and mutual ownership, underpinned by a global green new deal

We should therefore be approaching the end of the 2010–15 interregnum, with a new era of global development ahead of us. There probably is a fair degree of consensus globally about what a new progressive era would look like, although making progress in the face of vested interests is always difficult, and there is not the head of steam necessary as there was, say, following the global defeat of fascism in 1945. The challenge is thus political as well as ideological and economic.

We need to try to ensure that the forthcoming era, of 2015–45, is driven by a global Green New Deal, with a return to global economic co-operation, along the lines of the new international economic order that was being pressed for before the collapse of the Golden Age of Capitalism. Wealth and income inequality should be tackled, to create the economic basis for sustainable growth. Ecological outcomes should be at the forefront of public policy and private industry. This requires not just 'carbon credits' and other such market schemes, but rather a deep understanding of what drives corporate and managerial decision-making—which is lacking from neoclassical economics—so that these decision-makers and decisions can be targeted through appropriate polices (on which see Michie and Oughton, 2011; and Foxon et al., 2013). Privately and shareholder-owned companies should be encouraged to take long-term investment decisions and to behave responsibly, via new requirements on corporate governance, a new ethos and ideology across society, and via competition from the public sector—with public ownership at national, regional, and local levels offering a ready alternative to private ownership where this is seen to be failing.

Ownership is thus a key issue.[3] A new era of global economic development needs to be underpinned by public ownership of major economic sectors. Alongside this, a dynamic and entrepreneurial co-operative and mutual sector could deliver social as well as economic benefits. Private ownership should increasingly be seen as the exception, where there is an obvious justification—otherwise co-operative, mutual, and public ownership should become natural alternatives to shareholder-owned models. And the

---

[3] Though the wider concept of economic governance is also critical to development (see for instance Cowling and Tomlinson (2011).

privately owned sector itself needs to be encouraged—and if necessarily forced—to act responsibly, taking a long-term view, and seeking to deliver on the corporate purpose of the organization, as set out in the company's Articles of Association, rather than private firms being seen simply as a vehicle for personal enrichment. Increased corporate diversity is needed not only to provide competition to the shareholder-owned firms from other business models, but also to provide greater competition within the shareholder- (and privately) owned sector itself—most importantly in the financial services sector, to tackle the 'Too Big to Fail' problem. As argued by, for example, Arestis and Karakitsos (2013), this would be assisted through the splitting of commercial banks from investment banks, whereby those participating in casino activities could be allowed to lose their money when their gambles had failed—without this causing wider economic damage, and hence leaving governments to bail out the banks or otherwise clear up the mess using taxpayers' money.

7.4 THE MICHIE-OUGHTON INDEX OF CORPORATE DIVERSITY

Capitalism unleashed tended to prioritize profit-making through the financial markets, which alongside the bonus culture that encouraged speculative behaviour, and the lack of strong public ownership and regulation, led to the global financial crash and world economic recession. Hence the calls to 'rebalance the economy', with more emphasis upon the real economic activity of providing goods and services, and investment and exporting—as opposed to the financial speculation of the banking sector, much of which has little economic or social use (or purpose), and on the contrary can prove quite costly in both economic and social terms; when the speculation fails, the economy suffers, and the public sector and taxpayer are generally left to clear up the mess and pay the bills.

The UK economy has suffered more than most countries from this dominance of the 'City of London', and from the resulting short-termism (on which see Fine and Harris, 1985; and Kitson and Michie, 1996). Hence Winston Churchill's desire to see manufacturing more successful and the financial sector 'less proud', and Keynes's critique of market contagion and economic stagnation. Ed Miliband (2011) is thus absolutely correct to identify predatory capitalism as one of the major problems for the UK economy. This needs to be tackled by productive firms being promoted, including through public and co-operative ownership. As for encouraging shareholder-owned companies to take the productive rather than the predatory road, the use of 'wage-earner' funds to enable the employees to have a stake in the business, as proposed in Sweden in the 1980s, would be worth revisiting and encouraging.

We need a more corporately diverse economy, including a more corporately diverse financial services sector. The UK economy is peculiar not only in having a relatively dominant financial services sector and a correspondingly weak industrial sector, but also in having such a lack of corporate diversity within the financial services sector itself.[4] In other countries there is generally a strong co-operative and mutual sector, whereas in the UK that sector was hugely damaged by the 'demutualization' of the member-owned building societies, which were turned into private sector banks following the UK Building Societies Act 1986—thus weakening the mutual sector, and reducing the degree of corporate diversity. It was argued that becoming shareholder-owned banks would strengthen these companies. Yet not one of them has survived as a separate company. Every one either failed or was taken over by a larger private bank—thus reducing corporate diversity even at the level of number of competitors, let alone the more fundamental aspect of having competition from alternative corporate forms.[5]

The Coalition government of 2010–15 pledged to bring about a greater degree of corporate diversity within the financial services sector:

> We want the banking system to serve business, not the other way round. We will bring forward detailed proposals to foster diversity in financial services, promote mutuals and create a more competitive banking industry. (HM Government, 2010, p. 9)

But even had they been serious, how would the electorate or anyone else know whether they had succeeded in meeting this goal, when they did nothing to measure the degree of corporate diversity within the financial services sector?

The failure of government to measure corporate diversity within the financial services sector led to the Oxford Centre for Mutual & Employee-owned Business undertaking this task itself. The 2007–8 global financial crisis did focus attention on the issue of corporate diversity—most obviously with the problem of the 'Too Big to Fail' banks that had been allowed to emerge, with insufficient regulation or planning as to what would be done should they fail. It seemed to be implicitly assumed that they would not fail—or at least, not all at once. The phenomenon of bank runs seemed to have been a thing of the past, with minimum reserve requirements and other mechanisms in place to ensure sufficient liquidity. That complacency was exposed with the world's media carrying pictures of the customers of Northern Rock queuing all night to wait for the bank to open, so they could take out their money. This run on the bank caused it to collapse, just as in the good old pre-regulation days. Of course, central banks are there to act as the banker of last resort, and to deal with failing banks. But once the banks began failing, it became apparent that the Bank of England had no department to deal with this eventuality—an indication that they had been rather complacent about the need to regulate

---

[4] Indeed, in what now seems like a prescient warning, Llewellyn and Holmes (1991) argued before the large demutualizations of the 1990s, that a wider variety of financial institutions provides greater stability (and reduces systemic risk) in the overall financial architecture vis-à-vis a concentration of similar types of institutions. Since mutual (building) societies are not prone to (short-term) shareholder pressure, they are less likely to undertake risky projects; a balance of different ownership types forms thus plays a role in limiting (overall) instability in the event of a banking crisis.

[5] On the need for a more corporately diverse economy, and in particular a more corporately diverse financial services sector, see Michie (2011).

the financial sector, clearly assuming that generally banks wouldn't fail—or at least not all at once. The Bank of England thus had to establish a Special Resolutions Unit to deal with the new scenario.

In order to be able to see whether the government's commitment to making the financial services sector more diverse was being achieved over time, we developed an index of diversity in financial services—the 'Michie-Oughton index'—which we constructed from creating four sub-indicators or indices, which measured in turn: ownership diversity; competitiveness; balance sheet structure/resilience; and geographic spread (as described, discussed, and reported on in detail in Michie and Oughton, 2013):

i. A key distinction is between the shareholder-owned banks on the one hand, and the mutual and co-operative banks on the other. These different categories of institutions have different ownership structures, business models, and modes of behaviour (as reported by, for example, Heffernan, 2005; Hesse and Cihak, 2007; and Ayadi et al., 2009, 2010). The first of these sub-indicators thus created a new measure of ownership diversity, which we based on the Berry index of diversification and the Gini-Simpson index of bio-diversity. It measures the extent of diversity in ownership types—banks, mutuals, and the government-owned NS&I—where each of these types has discernibly different objectives so that there is diversity in behaviour.

ii. There has been a long-standing recognition that the UK's banking sector has been peculiarly dominated by a few large banks (see Baer and Mote, 1985; Beck, 2008; De Jonghe, 2010; Independent Commission on Banking, 2011; OECD, 2011; Vives, 2011; HM Treasury, 2012; and Vallascas and Keasey, 2012, 2013). This has been a concern because of a lack of competition, including over the servicing of particular markets, such as long-term financing for small and medium-sized enterprises. In addition, this concentration has led to the 'Too Big to Fail' problem, of large banks that can speculate on the markets, where success feeds straight through into increased bonuses, but failure will likely be met with taxpayer-funded bailouts. Our second indicator is thus designed to capture the extent of competition and is based on the inverse of the Hirshmann-Herfindahl index of concentration.

iii. In the years preceding the 2007–8 international financial crisis, there had been a degree of convergence in the funding models used by financial institutions, with banks shifting their funding models from retail deposits to wholesale funding. This trend was noticeable across several countries, including the UK, the US, and Germany. It has been identified as a major contributory factor towards the international financial crisis—on which see Bologna (2011) for an analysis of US bank failures, Norden and Weber (2010) for an earlier review of funding models used by German banks, and Le Leslé (2012) for an analysis of the European bank funding models. Our third indicator was thus designed to measure diversity in balance sheet structures, and resilience across the sector.

iv. The geographical concentration of financial services can have both direct and indirect effects on the performance of an economy. Direct effects are related to the employment and income generated in the sector and its geographical spread or concentration. Indirect effects spring from the pivotal role that the financial services sector plays in providing finance to industry and consumers, which in turn has a significant impact on the development of the non-financial sector and the housing market. Our fourth indicator thus seeks to capture the extent of geographic spread and the regional concentration of financial services.[6]

These indicators are combined into a single index—the Michie-Oughton 'D' index—that measures diversity in financial services. Michie and Oughton (2013) report the movement in this index from the years 2000 through to 2011. The index shows a marked decline in the run-up to the 2007–8 international financial crisis, followed by more significant falls during both 2008 and 2009. Since then the index has remained more or less flat. As a result, we are no closer to creating the conditions—of diversity—that have been identified as constituting an important component of avoiding a repeat of the international financial crisis. The Michie-Oughton index provides for the first time a measure of corporate diversity in the financial services sector, and offers policy-makers a means of tracking movements in the degree of corporate diversity in the financial services sector.

What is needed is for government to take their commitments seriously, so when the 2010 Coalition Agreement commits to creating a more corporately diverse financial services sector, the degree of diversity needs to be measured and reported, so that government—and the electorate—know whether or not they have delivered on this commitment. Thus, the Office for National Statistics should be charged with calculating and reporting this index of diversity over time. While this is a particular need for the UK economy, given the glaring lack of corporate diversity in the UK's financial services sector, and given the specific commitment of the UK government, the need for corporate diversity in the financial services sector applies globally. Certainly, other countries are generally in a better position than the UK in this regard. But there is no room for complacency. There is always the danger that the 'Too Big to Fail' banks will take over others, thus reducing the degree of diversity over time. Thus there is a need for the diversity index to be reported in other countries too.[7]

In addition to promoting greater corporate diversity, the economy—domestically and globally—needs the sort of co-ordinated push that was given by governments across the world in 2008 and 2009 to try to prevent the global economy sliding into another 1930s-style depression. But that sort of co-ordinated action needs to be sustained. It requires a global Green New Deal along the lines of the New Deal in 1930s America, with

---

[6] For an analysis and discussion of the regional imbalances in the UK economy, most especially in the financial services sector, see Gardiner et al. (2012).
[7] We are currently working with colleagues in the US to produce an analogous index for the US.

major public works on infrastructure, energy, and housing.[8] The current economic and social needs—nationally and globally—are certainly large enough to require and enable a major programme of investment and development to continue year on year for a generation or more. This would not be a matter of requiring borrowing and debt finance to pay for it. When the economy is in recession there are good Keynesian reasons for deliberately paying for such works through borrowing, in order to boost demand and to help pull the economy out of recession—as argued in detail by, for example, Krugman (2009). But once the economy has recovered, such works can be paid for through taxation and through the economic activity itself generating a return. Thus, houses can be rented out or sold, in either case repaying the costs of their construction. Electricity from renewable energy projects can be sold to consumers, and so on. Indeed, the more that such a sustained push for economic development can create work for firms and their employees, the more tax revenue will be received by government in the form of VAT, income tax, corporation tax, and so forth. It is this tax revenue, from successful economic activity, that can underpin and pay for the programme, which may thus require no additional taxation revenue at all, once it is properly underway.

7.5 CONCLUSION

The British economy needs to be rebalanced away from the 'City of London', towards the creation of goods and services across the breadth of the country, with companies operating on a basis of long-term and sustainable decision-making—socially, environmentally, and economically sustainable. A Green New Deal needs to be at the heart of this—for the next thirty-year generational epoch.

Such developments are needed globally just as they are in individual countries. Global financial speculation needs to be reigned in with a 'new Bretton Woods' era of responsible economic and financial institutions on an international scale, which prioritize stability and sustainability. A Tobin Tax on currency speculation (sometimes referred to as a 'Robin Hood' Tax) could contribute positively to tackling the damaging degrees of financial speculation. Arestis and Sawyer (2013) examine the potential of a large number of such financial transaction taxes, and conclude that 'A range of financial transaction taxes would be a route to addressing the relative undertaxing of the financial sector and its activities. Such taxes can be designed in a way that stimulates the economy, depending upon how the taxes are structured, how the overall tax revenue is affected, and the uses to which the funds raised by financial transactions taxes are put' (Arestis and Sawyer, 2013, p. 115).

---

[8] For an analysis of the New Deal in the 1930s, see for example Perry and Vernengo (2014) who argue that active fiscal policy played an important role in the success of the New Deal in delivering policies that contributed to the recovery.

Greater corporate diversity is needed domestically and globally, with stronger public and mutual ownership, operating at local, regional, national, and international levels. Governments and other public organizations do need to target this as a policy goal—as the UK's Coalition government of 2010–15 claimed it would. But to target corporate diversity requires that it be measured. Thus, the Michie-Oughton diversity index needs to be calculated and reported periodically over time by the National Statistical Office, so an improvement in the index can be an explicit goal of policy, for which there should be cross-party support, and with all public institutions, such as the Bank of England, and local authorities, encouraged or if possible required to assist in delivering on this goal of enhancing the degree of corporate diversity.

Moreover, privately owned companies need to focus on their corporate purpose, creating and providing goods and services, rather than just being the vehicle for private speculation and personal enrichment. Wage-earner funds could assist with this—or more generally, any actions to enable and facilitate the employees to have a collective, long-term stake in the organization.[9] This sort of economic alternative is viable and quite possible, domestically for the UK and globally. It would be the natural next era in global economic development. If pursued consciously, it could lead to further eras of progress subsequently, rather than another lurch back to capitalism unleashed. As the golden age of capitalism was running out of steam in the early 1970s, alternatives were being promoted domestically and globally to take forward the social democratic project to a new era, in more far-reaching ways, from the 'wage-earner funds' in Sweden—which could have increasingly moved the bulk of the economy beyond a narrow capitalist outlook, with corporate ownership being increasingly collective, held on behalf of employees jointly—to the demands for a new international economic order that would have delivered fair prices to producers, in the same way as the Fair Trade Movement has succeeded in doing to some extent.

The economy needs this type of active industrial policy, bolstered by a generation-long commitment to renewable energy and sustainability in production (see Chapter 20 by Coffey and Thornley in this volume). That sustainability needs to incorporate social sustainability and economic sustainability, as well as environmental sustainability. Thus, it needs to include urban development. Indeed, a major programme of sustainable urban development, in the UK and globally, could be an important driver of global economic development (see Chapter 14, by Bailey, Cowling, and Tomlinson). It would bring together the economic, social, and political; it could provide a massive and continuous programme of house building and infrastructure provision; and the public, private, and mutual sectors could combine as appropriate to focus on real outputs and sustainable development, rather than short-term speculation and profiteering. That is an economic agenda that would suit countries across the globe. The urbanization of the world's population is a major phenomenon, requiring new towns and cities to be constructed to house the shifting populations. The failure to date to have prevented climate change will

---

[9] On the benefits of employee engagement for promoting organizational performance and innovation, see for example Michie and Sheehan (1999).

only add to these population shifts, as areas of the globe become uninhabitable, whether from drought or from rising sea-levels.

This is therefore a policy agenda that speaks to the needs of individual countries, most certainly the UK, but also globally. It could thus form the basis of a renewed international economic order, of the sort that was created in the late 1940s out of the destruction of war, with a commitment of 'no return to the 1930s'—the era of mass unemployment which had given rise to fascism and war, and which was to be replaced by government commitments to full employment, health, education, housing; and to economic development domestically and globally. This is another such point in history, calling out for a new path of sustainable development domestically and globally.

References

Arestis, P. and Karakitsos, E. (2013). *Financial Stability in the Aftermath of the 'Great Recession'*. Basingstoke: Palgrave Macmillan.

Arestis, P. and Sawyer, M. (2013). 'The Potential of Financial Transactions Taxes', in P. Arestis and M. Sawyer (eds), *Economic Policies, Governance and the New Economics*, pp. 87–121. Basingstoke: Palgrave Macmillan.

Ayadi, R., Arbak, E., Carbo Valverde, S., Rodriguez Fernandez, F., and Schmidt, R. H. (2009). *Investigating Diversity in the Banking Sector in Europe: The Performance and Role of Savings Banks*. Brussels: Centre for European Policy Studies.

Ayadi, R., Llewellyn, D. T., Schmidt, R. H., Arbak, E., and De Groen, W. P. (2010). *Investigating Diversity in the Banking Sector in Europe: Key Developments, Performance and Role of Co-operative Banks*. Brussels: Centre for European Policy Studies.

Baer, H. and Mote, L. R. (1985). 'The Effects of Nationwide Banking on Concentration: Evidence from Abroad', *Federal Reserve Bank of Chicago: Economic Perspectives* 1, 3–17.

Barnes, P. (1984). *Building Societies: The Myth of Mutuality*. London: Pluto Press.

Beck, T. (2008). *Bank Competition and Financial Stability: Friends or Foes?*, World Bank, Washington, DC, Policy Research Working Paper Series No. 4656.

Bologna, P. (2011). *Is There a Role for Funding in Explain Recent US Bank Failures?*, Banca D'Italia Eurosistema, Occasional Papers No. 103.

Branston, J. R., Cowling, K. G., Tomlinson, P. R., and Wilson, J. R. (2015 forthcoming). 'Addressing Strategic Failures: Widening the Public Interest in the UK Financial and Energy Sectors', in D. Coffey, C. Thornley, and J. Begley (eds), *Global Economic Crisis and Local Economic Development: International Cases and Policy Responses*', London: Routledge.

Branston, J. R., Tomlinson, P. R., and Wilson, J. R. (2012). '"Strategic Failure" in the Financial Sector: A Policy View', *International Journal of the Economics of Business* 19(2), 169–89.

Burt, S. L. and Sparks, L. (2003). 'Power and Competition in the UK Retail Grocery Market', *British Journal of Management* 14(3), 237–54.

Cowling, K. and Tomlinson, P. R. (2011). 'Post the Washington Consensus: Economic Governance and Industrial Strategies for the 21st Century', *Cambridge Journal of Economics* 35(5), 831–52.

De Jonghe, O. (2010). 'Back to the Basics in Banking? A Micro-Analysis of Banking System Stability', *Journal of Financial Intermediation* 19(3), 387–417.

Fine, B. and Harris, L. (1985). *Peculiarities of the British Economy*. London: Laurence & Wishart.

Foxon, T. J., Kőhler, J., Michie, J., and Oughton, C. (2013). 'Towards a New Complexity Economics for Sustainability', *Cambridge Journal of Economics* 37(1), 187–208.

Fukuyama, F. (1992). *The End of History and the Last Man*. New York: Free Press.

Gardiner, B., Martin, R., and Tyler, P. (2012). Spatially Unbalanced Growth in the British Economy. Paper Presented at the Regional Studies European Conference, Delft University of Technology, Netherlands, 13–16 May.

Glyn, A. (2006). *Capitalism Unleashed: Finance, Globalisation and Welfare*. Oxford: Oxford University Press.

Goda, T. and Lysandrou, P. (2014). 'The Contribution of Wealth Concentration to the Subprime Crisis: A Quantitative Estimation', *Cambridge Journal of Economics* 38(2), 301–27.

Heffernan, S. (2005). 'The Effect of UK Building Society Conversion on Pricing Behaviour', *Journal of Banking and Finance* 29(3), 779–97.

Hesse, H. and Cihak, M. (2007). *Co-operative Banks and Financial Stability*, IMF Working Paper No. WP/07/02.

HM Government (2010). *The Coalition: Our Programme for Government*. London: Cabinet Office.

HM Treasury (2012). *The Future of Building Societies*. London: HM Treasury, <http://www.hm-treasury.gov.uk/d/condoc_future_building_societies.pdf>.

Hutton, W. and Lee, N. (2012). 'The City and the Cities: Ownership, Finance and the Geography of Recovery', *Cambridge Journal of Regions, Economy and Society* 5, 325–37.

Independent Commission on Banking (2011). Final Report and Recommendations, September, ICB, London, <http://bankingcommission.independent.gov.uk>.

Kitson, M. and Michie, J. (1996). Britain's Industrial Performance Since 1960: Underinvestment and Relative Decline', *The Economic Journal* 106(434), 196–212.

Kitson, M. and Michie, J. (2000). 'The Tale of Two Recessions: 1929 and the Gold Standard, 1992 and the ERM', in M. Kitson and J. Michie (eds), *The Political Economy of Competitiveness: Essays on Employment, Public Policy and Corporate Performance*, pp. 90–108. London and New York: Routledge.

Krugman, P. (2009). *The Return of Depression Economics and the Crisis of 2008*. New York and London: W.W. Norton.

Le Leslé, V. (2012). *Bank Debt in Europe: Are Funding Models Broken?*, International Monetary Fund Working Paper No. WP/12/299.

Llewellyn, D. T. and Holmes, M. J. (1991). 'In Defence of Mutuality: A Redress to an Emerging Conventional Wisdom', *Annals of Public and Co-operative Economics* 62, 319–54.

Marglin, S. A. and Schor, J. B. (eds). (1992). *The Golden Age of Capitalism: Reinterpreting the Postwar Experience*. Oxford: Clarendon Press.

Michie, J. (2011). 'Promoting Corporate Diversity in the Financial Services Sector', *Policy Studies* 32(4), 309–23.

Michie, J. and Llewellyn, D. T. (2010). 'Converting Failed Financial Institutions into Mutual Organisations', *Journal of Social Entrepreneurship* 1(1), 146–70.

Michie, J. and Oughton, C. (2011). 'Managerial, Institutional and Evolutionary Approaches to Environmental Economics: Theoretical and Policy Implications', in S. Dietz, J. Michie, and C. Oughton (eds), *The Political Economy of the Environment: An Interdisciplinary Approach*, pp. 44–73. Abingdon: Routledge.

Michie, J. and Oughton, C. (2013). *Measuring Diversity in Financial Services Markets: A Diversity Index*, SOAS, London, Centre for Financial & Management Economics Discussion Paper No. 113.

Michie, J. and Sheehan, M. (1999). 'No Innovation without Representation? An Analysis of Participation, Representation, R&D and Innovation', *Economic Analysis* 2(2), 85–97.

Miliband, E. (2011). Speech to the Social Market Foundation, 17 November, London.

Milne, S. (2012). *The Revenge of History: The Battle for the 21st Century*. London: Verso.

Norden, L. and Weber, M. (2010). 'Funding Modes of German Banks: Structural Changes and their Implications', *Journal of Financial Services Research* 38(2–3), 69–93.

OECD (2011). *Bank Competition and Financial Stability*. Paris: OECD.

Ownership Commission (2012). *Plurality, Stewardship and Engagement: The Report from the Commission on Ownership*. London: Mutuo.

Perry, N. and Vernengo, M. (2014). 'What Ended the Great Depression? Re-Evaluating the Role of Fiscal Policy', *Cambridge Journal of Economics* 38(2), 349–67.

Stiglitz, J. (2006). *Making Globalisation Work*. London: Penguin Books.

Stiglitz, J. (2010). *Freefall: The Fall of Free-Markets and the Sinking of the Global Economy*. New York: Penguin Books.

Stiglitz, J. (2013). *The Price of Inequality*. New York: Penguin Books.

Vallascas, F. and Keasey, K. (2012). 'Bank Resilience to Shocks and the Stability of Banking Systems: Small is Beautiful', *Journal of International Money and Finance* 31(6), 1745–76.

Vallascas, F. and Keasey, K. (2013). 'Banking Volatility Across Europe: A Twenty Year Study', *Journal of Financial Services Research* 43(1), 37–68.

Vives, X. (2011). 'Competition Policy in Banking', *Oxford Review of Economic Policy* 27(3), 479–97.

Williamson, J. (1990). *The Progress of Policy Reform in Latin America*. Washington, DC: Institute for International Economics.

CHAPTER 8

··

HARNESSING THE PRIVATE SECTOR TO ENHANCE INDUSTRIAL INNOVATION

··

GORDON MURRAY, WEIXI LIU, AND
MARC COWLING

8.1 INTRODUCTION

IT is widely recognized that small and medium-sized enterprises (SMEs), especially in high-tech and 'new knowledge'-based sectors, can have an important effect on job creation, innovation, and economic growth (Timmons and Bygrave, 1986; Lerner, 1999, 2002a; Davila et al., 2003; Acs and Storey, 2004; Audretsch and Keilbach, 2004a, 2004b; Alemany and Martí, 2005; Wong et al., 2005; and Audretsch et al., 2008). However, such firms and the dynamic and volatile environments in which they are born and operate present manifold challenges to investors. The complexity of the innovation process in young firms (Acs and Gifford, 1996) means that there is often an asymmetry of information to the investors' disadvantage. Adverse selection is common in SME capital markets (Hyytinen and Väänänen, 2006; Cowling, 2010). The immaturity of rapidly evolving, and highly contested, markets means that there can be little guarantee of the success of one single firm. Further, given the difficulty of monopolizing the rents of an innovation, private investors are likely to invest below a level that would realize the full social returns from the new innovation (Stiglitz and Weiss, 1981; Berger and Udell, 1998; Audretsch and Keilbach, 2004a; Dimov and Murray, 2008). Accordingly, venture capitalists (VCs) are often reluctant to invest in these high potential firms despite being viewed as the most appropriate source of external finance for these companies (Maier and Walker, 1987; Gompers and Lerner, 1999, 2001a, 2001b; Keuschnigg and Nielsen, 2003, 2004).

Over the last two decades, policy-makers around the world have become increasingly concerned at the lack of risk capital available to new and early-stage entrepreneurial ventures (Bank of England, 1996; Commonwealth of Australia, 1997, 2001; OECD 1997, 2004, 2006; Nightingale et al., 2009; Pierrakis, 2010). As a public response to this perceived 'financing gap', several governments have set up programmes to channel equity finance to capital constrained but high potential, young enterprises through private sector VC firms (Jääskeläinen et al., 2007; Brander et al., 2010). These vehicles are termed 'hybrid schemes' given that they involve a significant participation by the state as a 'special' limited partner (LP) in the total funds raised and invested.[1] Critically, the state delegates full operational autonomy of the jointly financed fund to a commercial general partner (GP). Management is incentivized to achieve commercially attractive returns to the LPs.

This chapter investigates one particular government-sponsored hybrid scheme: the Australian Innovation Investment Fund (IIF). The establishment of the IIF programme in 1997 was predicated on a perceived failure in the Australian market in the supply of risk capital for investment in early-stage ventures (Murray, 1996). The IIF programme was designed to improve the commercialization of Australian R&D through the provision of venture capital to young technology companies in their pre-seed, seed, start-up, and early-expansion stages. The programme has been responsible for the raising of a total amount of AUD524 million of which AUD224 million was committed by private investors (LPs).[2] These monies were allocated to the thirteen[3] IIF VC funds that have participated via the three consecutive financing rounds of the programme to date.

Using secondary data already collected by the programme's managers from the supported VC funds and their portfolio companies, this study sought to determine the quantitative impact of the IIF programme on the young firms in receipt of this 'risk capital'. By 2009, we have been able to gain access to the data on two completed IIF investment Rounds. Accordingly, we can better address the effectiveness of the IIF programme on the Australian venture capital market. Our study looks specifically at the types of firms which are selected via the programme; the scale of the support they received; the result of this support on firm performance; and the subsequent outcomes from supported firms to the Australian economy. Our analysis is comparative and references IIF-assisted firms to comparable young enterprises supported by independently financed VC firms. This analysis is used to arrive at a set of largely positive but not uncritical conclusions as to the impact to date of the three rounds of investment on the eleven investigated VC funds and 102 recipient portfolio firms financed by the IIF programme. Our findings are referenced to the four published objectives set for the IIF programme at the time of its inception by the sponsoring Department of Innovation, Industry, Science and Research (DIISR). We conclude the paper by looking at the IIF programme and its ambitions in the wider context of international measures to support the financing of

---

[1] The state assumes the same legal responsibilities as other LPs. However, it may choose to distribute a part of its returns to the other LPs in order to strengthen their incentive to engage in VC finance.

[2] The figure is the maximum amount that can be raised. The total capital committed up till 2009 (Round 3, Tranche 2) is AUD484 million.

[3] Nine funds from Rounds 1 and 2, four funds from Round 3 (NB we have data on only eleven funds).

entrepreneurial and high potential young firms via the vehicle of publicly supported hybrid VC schemes.

In particular, we use data provided by the Australian Venture Capital Association (AVCAL) and DIISR. This consists, respectively, of data on 201 entrepreneurial firms financed by private VC funds and data on a further 102 firms financed by the hybrid VC funds of the IIF programme. The independent VC funds to which IIF funds were compared included IIF affiliate investors.[4] We find that IIF funds are:

- significantly more likely to provide initial and follow-on funding to capital constrained businesses;
- heavily concentrated on 'new knowledge' industry sectors;
- more likely to make smaller sized investments;
- more likely to exit via an IPO but also more likely to be liquidated.

We also find that non-Australian investors do not appear to support very early-stage investments in Australian companies, and the recent economic downturn has had significant effects on the effectiveness of the IIF programme. Our results show some improvements of the programme over time regarding its operational efficiency especially in terms of better targeted markets and successful exits. Further, we are able to establish that IIF portfolio companies are smaller than non-IIF fund investments, and are more likely exit via an IPO or a liquidation. They are, however, also less likely to be acquired.

The chapter is structured as follows. Section 8.2 discusses the rationale and international experience of government interventions in VC markets. Section 8.3 introduces details of the IIF programme and presents some preliminary analysis of the Australian venture capital market. Section 8.4 explains the evaluation criteria we use to measure the effectiveness of the IIF programme. Section 8.5 presents the empirical methodologies and summary statistics for the sample selected. Section 8.6 reports the empirical results on the investigation of evaluation criteria. Section 8.7 discusses the limitations of this study and suggests future research directions. Finally, Section 8.8 provides policy recommendations based on our analyses and concludes the chapter.

8.2 Government Intervention in Venture Capital Markets

There continues to be a considerable debate among academics and practitioners on the degree to which young and technology-based small firms are faced with severe constraints, or 'financing gaps', arising from imperfections in capital markets allocations

---

[4] An IIF Affiliate Fund was defined as a private VC fund which was managed by a general partnership which was also responsible for managing an IIF fund in any of the three rounds of the programme.

(Westhead and Storey, 1997; Cressy 2002; Auerswald and Branscomb, 2003; European Commission, 2003; HM Treasury/Small Business Service, 2003; Revest and Sapio, 2010). In the context of SME finance, a market failure occurs when the market mechanism fails to provide sufficient finance to meet the demands of young firms regardless of their willingness to pay the price of capital required. Since the severe contraction in the capital markets' interest in technology focused, early-stage VC investment post the first quarter Year 2000, there has been a protracted (albeit erratic) long run decline in commitments from institutional investors in allocating finance to venture capital as an 'alternative asset class' (Sohl, 2003; HM Treasury and BIS, 2010; Pierrakis, 2010). The 'classic' venture capital industry has largely metamorphosed into a Private Equity/Management Buy-Out activity (Dimov and Murray, 2008) in advanced Western economies. Early-stage VC investing has become a small and imperilled activity in many national markets for entrepreneurial finance.

As a response to this underinvestment in early-stage venture capital markets, several government bodies have set up intervention schemes in order to provide risk capital to young and technology-based ventures (Lerner, 1999, 2002b; Keuschnigg and Nielsen, 2004; Da Rin et al., 2006; Murray, 2007).[5] Direct interventions by governments acting as venture capitalists have largely proved to be inappropriate[6] (Maula and Murray, 2003). First, direct involvement in new venture investments by government agencies carries a material risk of market disruption through the potential misallocation of capital and the possible 'crowding out' of private investors (Leleux and Surlemont, 2003; Armour and Cumming, 2006). Second, the market may be further distorted because of the different return requirements from public and purely commercial, private investors (OECD, 1997; Manigart et al., 2002; Armour and Cumming, 2006). As an alternative, several governments have adopted an approach where government *co-invests* as a 'special' limited partner in a limited liability VC partnership which is run by a professional and commercially incentivized management team (Murray, 2007; Murray et al., 2009). In effect, the venture capital firm or general partner is acting as an 'agent' for a group of principals (LPs) one of which is the state providing its contribution to the fund from public monies (Sahlman, 1990).

Such hybrid VC structures of intervention are seen as an element of 'best practice' (OECD, 1997, 2004; European Commission and United States Department of Commerce, 2005). The Australian IIF programme is an important and early example of this

---

[5] Another form of government intervention is through indirect influence in the form of, for example, the institutional legal and fiscal frameworks (Fenn et al., 1995; La Porta et al., 1997, 1998), and the incentive structure of personal and corporate tax systems (Poterba, 1989a, 1989b; Gompers and Lerner, 1998; Jeng and Wells, 2000; Cumming et al., 2006). These schemes are beyond the scope of discussion here.

[6] It is important that government programmes are evaluated with full information given that they can change materially over their life-cycle. For example, the direct government VC programmes Finnish Industry Investment and the Danish *Vækstfonden* programme have both changed significant elements of their focus and operations since their genesis. Both programmes currently include a considerable element of co-investment with private VCs.

model of public and private co-financing. However, there are several challenges in evaluating the effectiveness of hybrid funds. First, governments should only intervene in financial markets if there is clear evidence of market failure leading to a serious mis-allocation of resources (Maula and Murray, 2003; Murray, 2007). Just because some firms have difficulty finding funding does not mean that a market failure *automatically* exists or that government policy interventions would improve the situation (Nightingale et al., 2009). Informed investors refusing to invest in firms that are not commercially attractive and consequently reducing the supply of finance may actually be a rational decision indicating an efficient market. Thus governments' willingness to override market decisions may be counterproductive in the absence of other material spill-overs or positive externalities from the investment.

Second, the problem of entrepreneurial finance needs to be viewed holistically. A firm could experience multiple financing gaps as it grows and its capital needs change. Thus, the need for growth capital is by no means a single or short-term requirement. The development of a flourishing national VC industry is seen as one component of an effective 'funding escalator' whereby appropriate funding resources are available at the different stages of a young firm's growth trajectory (Murray et al., 2009; Nightingale et al., 2009).

Third, the performance of early-stage VC funds is positively associated with the scale of the investments (Murray and Marriott, 1998; Dimov and Murray, 2008; Kaplan and Lerner, 2010). Specialist early-stage funds, which are often created or supported with public finance, are more likely to be measured in tens of millions rather than the hundreds of millions of dollars under management common in Silicon Valley. The small scale of such funds presents an immediate and major problem for the operational efficacy of such entities. Firstly, venture capital activity requires significant start up and fixed costs such as 'due diligence' and the recruitment of professional investment executives in a highly competitive market. In addition, a small level of finances under management also means that the fund itself is constrained in the number of deals that can be financed, as well as the number of rounds of subsequent financing that can be allocated to any one investee firm. Small investors without the resources either to diversify or follow on in successive rounds invariably face greater risks. These outcomes have direct and negative implications for the fund's performance.

Last but not least, a hybrid structure where public and private investors share returns under identical terms (*pari passu*) is not likely to attract private investors to areas of perceived market failure.[7] In order to incentivize the general and limited partners to be prepared to engage in a fund that includes public welfare goals as part of its *raison d'être*, many hybrid schemes have adopted the Small Business Investment Corporation (SBIC) model of 'equity enhancement' (Lerner, 2002b; Jääskeläinen et al., 2007; Murray, 2007). As a special LP, and usually the largest single investor in the fund, the government can

---

[7] A *pari passu* structure is only likely to enhance the fund returns to a limited extent as a result of the scale effect discussed above. It is the asymmetric return distribution that really benefits the LPs. However, this 'leveraging' comes at the cost of the fund having to limit its investments to areas of policy concern; for example, the financing of young new knowledge businesses (Jääskeläinen et al., 2007).

choose to use its financial leverage to the direct benefit of other investors in the fund rather than maximizing its own financial returns. Government can also craft 'asymmetric' return distributions to further incentivize general and limited partners at the cost of returns received by the state. All these measures can help to skew the return distributions to private limited partners' advantage albeit at a direct cost to the public investor (Jääskeläinen et al., 2007).

An implicit assumption by most free market proponents is that government intervention in enterprise finance is a 'second best' option. The government advised by its civil servants is seen as a less experienced investor which is also challenged by having multiple (and often conflicting) objectives (Lerner, 2002b). It is only a desired LP if a fully commercial investor cannot be found and there is a financing shortfall. Lerner (2002b) stresses the needs for government to better understand the VC industry and to appreciate that ultimately VC investment is about realizing *commercial* goals. This scepticism is supported by Brander et al. (2010), who find that beyond a total funding share of approximately 30 per cent, public finance appears to have a negative effect on the probability of a successful exit. This would suggest that government funding is most effective as a minority co-investor with private and fully commercial funds. Such an arrangement is often attempted in hybrid VC structures.

The IIF programme is a typical example of a hybrid scheme broadly based on the SBIC programme devised in 1958 by the Small Business Administration in the US. It is therefore legitimate to compare hybrid schemes between countries where they are based on risk capital investments directly from VC funds to portfolio companies and where the government and private investors' joint participation in the fund is allocated by professional VC agents. However, it should be noted that although the GP has exclusive operating control, it is on an investment strategy that has first to be accepted by all the LPs including government.

A number of national public schemes are immediately relevant to the IIF programme including, for example, the UK's Enterprise Capital Funds (ECFs) and Regional Venture Capital Funds (RVCFs), the Dutch TechnoPartners Fund, the Israeli Yozma programme and German High-tech Gründerfonds. Thus, the question becomes how should the operation of the IIF programme be seen in the light of these or other programmes which are each seeking to achieve the same broad policy goals? In answering this question, we can look at the sectors supported, the addition of any geographic conditions of investment, the maximum level of finance per investee firm, and/or the remuneration and incentives given to the VC fund's general and limited partners (other than government as the special LP). However, we can summarize by saying that the IIF appears to exhibit no operational or structural characteristics that are exceptionally different from the generic hybrid model. The limitations on the maximum investment per portfolio company, the constraint of fee income to between 2.5 and 3 per cent (of funds managed) per annum, an industry standard 'carried interest' of 20 per cent of net capital gain, and the sharing between government and other LPs in the ratio of 10:90 after the original investment has been returned, all appear to conform broadly with international practice (Jääskeläinen et al., 2007).

8.3 IIF AND THE AUSTRALIAN VENTURE CAPITAL MARKET

The IIF programme was established in 1997 and was aimed at assisting innovative, high-potential young firms in the early stages of commercialization. The IIF programme was one of a number of public enterprise finance initiatives in Australia which included the Pooled Development Fund (PDF), Venture Capital Limited Partnerships (VCLP), and Early-stage Venture Capital Limited Partnerships (ESVCLP). The focus of this paper is exclusively on the Innovation Investment Fund programme.

As a response to the perceived 'market gap' in Australia (National Investment Council, 1995), the first round of the IIF programme was announced in March 1997, with five IIF funds licensed and the first investment in portfolio companies made in 1998. The total capital commitment for IIF Round 1 was AUD196.5 million with the Commonwealth government contributing AUD130 million and the private sector providing AUD66.5 million. The desire of the government to attract private LPs was evidenced in the agreement to fund the first round of the programme on the basis of a 2:1 public/private ratio. The government has since launched two further rounds of the IIF programme. Round 2 was announced in 2000 and commenced operations in 2001. Four funds were licensed, with funding from both the government and private sector totalling AUD156.6 million (government providing AUD90.7 million and private sector AUD65.9 million). Round 3 was announced in 2006, with funding commencing in 2007. Under Round 3 up to ten fund managers will eventually be licensed in five tranches with total government and private funding of at least AUD400 million. In Round 3, the government intends to cap its contribution at 50 per cent of the total programme funding, AUD200 million. The total committed capital of the overall programme as of May 2010 amounts to AUD524 million with the public contribution being AUD300.7 million.

The IIF programme is designed to accelerate and increase the commercialization of Australian research through the provision of venture capital to small companies in their pre-seed, seed, start-up, and early-expansion stages. The objectives of the IIF programme were announced as (DIST, 1997):

1. by addressing capital and management constraints, to encourage the development of new-technology companies which are commercializing research and development
2. to develop a self-sustaining Australian early-stage, technology-based venture capital industry
3. to establish in the medium term a 'revolving' or self-funding scheme
4. to develop fund managers with experience in the early-stage venture capital industry.

The objectives are not given in any order of priority and are all treated with equal weight. For Round 3, however, the references to the development of *new-technology companies* and a *technology-based venture capital industry* have been removed. This signals that companies commercializing innovative services, products, and processes are all within the ambit of the programme. Our econometric analysis mainly addresses the effectiveness of the IIF programme against Objective 1 but we do comment on the other objectives.

Over time, improvements have been made in the IIF programme to reflect contemporary economic conditions and the growing maturity of the Australian VC market. For example, the annual management fee arrangements of the IIF programme have been reduced over the three tranches from 3 per cent to 2.25 per cent. Similarly, management 'success fees' on investment exits have metamorphosed into an industry standard 'carried interest' of 20 per cent. This reflects the government's effort to reduce the fixed costs of fund managers and to align GPs' compensations more closely to the net performance of the VC fund (Amit et al., 1998; Bergemann and Hege, 1998; Gompers and Lerner, 1999). Such measures also help to reduce the agency costs associated with fixed fees.

As discussed in the previous sections, the severe contraction in the capital market's interest in technology focused, early-stage VC investment over the last decade has reduced early-stage VC activities. This is a direct consequence of the poor investment performance of extant funds. Figure 8.1 illustrates the changing share of VC investments as a percentage of total PE/VC investments for the US, UK, and Australia. An upturn in the US trend since 2008 reflects both a recent decline in PE activity[8] and the simultaneous burgeoning of 'clean tech' investment activities by VC investors keen to be at the forefront of the next, potentially disruptive, technology wave.[9]

This persistent pattern of a modest commitment to early-stage investment by Australian investors is more evident when looking at the annual investment activity in the early-stage market (Figure 8.2). As reported by AVCAL, both the amount of investment and the number of investee companies have experienced either declining or static trends. It is important to note that the temporary increases in Australian early-stage investments (around 2000–1 and 2006–7) are broadly coincident with the commencement of IIF Rounds 1, 2, and 3, which started in 1999–2000, 2000–1, and 2006–7, respectively.

One consequence of the contemporary unattractiveness of venture capital returns is that the number of specialist early-stage VC funds prepared to undertake the highly speculative first stages of investment including seed capital, start-up, and early development finance has continued to remain limited. The modest proportion of investments in early-stage firms (see Figure 8.3) indicates that Australian PE/VC investors have also tilted strongly towards a preference for later-stage and larger investee companies (AVCAL, 2009). The current global economic difficulties may further exacerbate this trend as investors seek greater security for large amounts of private savings. Independent data from the Australian Bureau of Statistics given to the authors confirms that

---

[8] A decline in PE has in part been due to a decline in the availability of debt with which to fund the leverage of large PE acquisitions.

[9] According to the 2008/9 MoneyTree Report by PricewaterhouseCoopers and the National Venture Capital Association, total 'clean-tech' investments in the US has increased by more than ten times from $0.4 billion 2004 to over $4 billion in 2008.

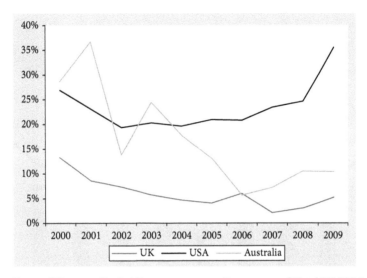

FIGURE 8.1 Share of Venture Capital Investments as a Percentage of Total PE/VC Investments for US, UK, and Australia.

Source: NVCA, BVCA, and AVCAL

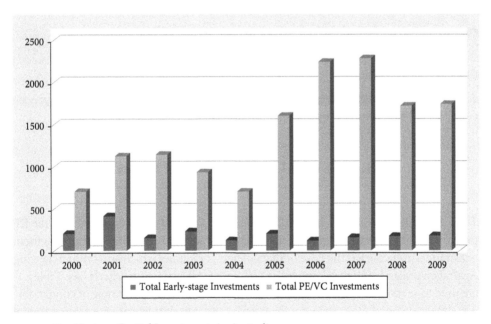

FIGURE 8.2 Venture Capital Investments in Australia.

Source: AVCAL (2009), Australian Private Equity and Venture Capital Activity Report/Thompson Venture Economics ®

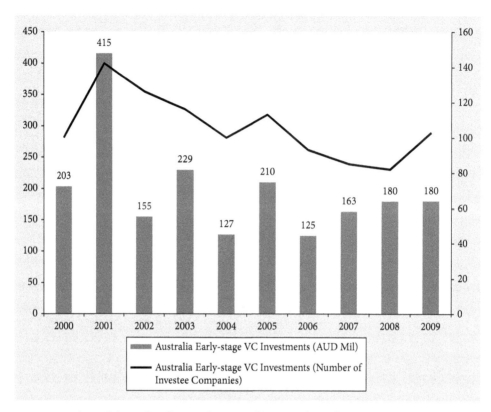

FIGURE 8.3 Annual Australian Private Equity and Venture Capital Investments.

Source: AVCAL (2009), Australian Private Equity and Venture Capital Activity
Report/Thompson Venture Economics ©

early-stage venture capital has remained flat since 2004–5, while later-stage and private equity investment levels have grown.[10]

8.4 EVALUATION CRITERIA

This section discusses the evaluation criteria used to quantify the effectiveness of the IIF programme given its declared objective, that is 'by addressing capital and management constraints, to encourage the development of new companies which are commercializing Australian research and development' (DIST, 1997). All evaluation criteria (see Table 8.1) are used to measure the effectiveness of IIF investments against a sample of comparable investments in portfolio companies financed by either exclusively private venture capital firms (including bank, corporate, and foreign investors) or from IIF 'affiliate funds'.

[10] ABS trend data is available from the authors on request but is not included here because of space limitations.

Table 8.1 IIF Programme Effectiveness

Evaluation Criteria*	
Early-stage investments	Negative
'New-knowledge' investments	Positive
More staged investments	Positive
Likelihood of IPO	Positive
Likelihood of acquisition	Negative
Likelihood of liquidation	Positive
Smaller deal size	Positive

*Based on econometric analysis and as compared to IIF affiliate and non-IIF private VC funds.

8.4.1 Supply of Multiple Funding Rounds

A healthy and active VC market is not merely concerned with firm survival. More importantly, it is about success as measured both in the quality of the entrepreneurial firms supported and the attractiveness of net returns to investors. Separate policies and programmes that focus myopically on resolving one single 'funding gap' with the assistance of public money can be counterproductive by creating artificial barriers between successive rounds of funding (Nightingale et al., 2009). Thus, an effective intervention needs to address holistically the long-term, multiple-round, financing requirements of the investee company (see Table 8.2).

8.4.2 Early-Stage Focus of Investments

Start-up and early-stage investments are vulnerable to serious information asymmetry problems as most investors lack comparable experience and expertise to the entrepreneurial recipients of risk capital finance (Stiglitz and Weiss, 1981; Myers, 1984; Myers and Majluf, 1984; Bester and Hellwig, 1989; Hillier and Ibrahimo, 1993). This agency problem, and the associated adverse selection, is particularly evident in high-tech and new knowledge-based firms where an 'information gap' between principals (investors) and agents (entrepreneurs) can occur (Lerner 2002a, 2002b; Kaplan and Strömberg, 2004). Such information disparities can lead to an underinvestment in early-stage enterprises by risk-averse investors (Audretsch and Keilbach, 2004a; Dimov and Murray, 2008), and to more strict credit rationing by debt providers (Berger and Udell, 1995, 1998; Cowling, 2010).

8.4.3 Amount of Investment in Individual Business

Given the relatively high risks and extended periods before positive cash flows (Meyer and Mathonet, 2005), the finance constraints of new knowledge-based firms cannot

Table 8.2 Operating Characteristics of Hybrid VC Funds

Programme Name	Size of the Fund	Deal Size	Public/Private Share	Share of Profit	Management Fees	Carried Interest
Innovation Investment Fund	528 Mil, spread evenly between 13 IIF funds	Average size 2.75 Mil	Up to 2:1 (Round 1 and 2) or 1:1 (Round 3)	10:90 between Government and private LPs	Round 1: 3% Round 2 & 3: 2.5% to 2.8%	20% or market standard
Pre-Seed Fund (PSF)	104.1 Mil for 4 funds. No upper limit for fund size.	Up to 1 Mil with extension up to 500,000.	Up to 3:1	Government: capital + interest; further amounts share between private LPs/GPs	3% to 3.5%	Market standard
New Zealand Venture Investment Fund	NZD323 Mil committed (NZD220 Mil invested) in 6 funds. Maximum fund size: NZD25 Mil.	NZD2 Mil and must not exceed the percentage limit for public investments.	On average 1:2, the maximum match is 1:1 and minimum 1:5.	50:50	Between 2–3%	–
Regional Venture Capital Funds	GBP250 Mil in 9 regional funds.	Up GBP660,000.	Up to 1:1	Cap on public return	–	–
Enterprise Capital Fund	Funds total size GBP250 Mil in 10 ECFs No upper limit for a single fund.	Up to GBP2 Mil.	Up to 2:1	Public return capped at 4.5% (the current government loan rate)	As specified in applicant's bid, market standard	As specified in applicant's bid, market standard
KfW Venture Capital Programme	–	Up to EUR5 Mil	Up to 1:1	Loan guarantee	–	–
High-tech Gründerfonds	EUR272 Mil budget, total investment EUR65 Mil.	Up to EUR1 Mil	Public investment currently at 88%	Distribution to public and private LPs pro rata	–	–
Technostarters	EUR 150 Mil in 22 funds.	EUR 100.000 to EUR 2.5 Mil.	Up to 1:1	20:80 between Government and private LPs	–	–

Source: Authors' own summary from the public information for each scheme

easily be addressed by debt. Financial demands are commonly above the range of family and friends as 'informal investors'. This equity financing gap within early-stage entrepreneurial firms was first identified by the Macmillan Committee on Finance and Industry in 1931 and continues to remain relevant (Bolton, 1971; Cressy, 2002; Mason and Harrison, 2003; Denis, 2004; OECD, 2006). More recent studies have focused on estimating the size of the gap. However, the results are at best inconclusive (Cressy and Olofsson, 1997; Egeln et al., 1997; HM Treasury and Small Business Service, 2003; Library House, 2006). There is a growing recognition that there may be multiple gaps (Murray, 1994), as seen in the recent popularity of the term 'finance *escalator*'.

The scale and commercial terms of public programmes to address financial constraints is important. Critically, public interventions should not crowd out private sector investment activities given that this could lead to a reduction in the aggregate pool of venture capital (Cumming, 2009). However, more often public VC interventions are ineffectively modest rather than over generous (Murray and Marriott, 1998; Nightingale et al., 2009).

8.4.4 'New Knowledge' Industry Investments

Underinvestment at the pre-start (seed), start-up, and early-growth stages is especially prominent in costly new knowledge and technology-based industries such as biotechnology. However, these high-tech investments can produce significantly positive externalities in the form of major technology innovations. Thus, the social rate of return is often greater than the private rate of return received by VC investors (Timmons and Bygrave, 1986; Lerner, 1999, 2002a; Davila et al., 2003; Acs and Storey, 2004; Audretsch and Keilbach, 2004a, 2004b; Alemany and Martí, 2005; Wong et al., 2005; Audretsch et al., 2008). For the government, the aggregate social and economic return from a supported hybrid VC fund is of greater interest than the commercial return to its own committed finance once government's cost of borrowing is met. One logic of hybrid VC programmes with their asymmetric rewards structure is to reduce the disparity between social and private returns in the private investors' direction. By such means, it is hoped that *effective* public interventions could encourage the participation of more skilled and experienced entrepreneurs and investors in key technology sectors (Armour and Cumming, 2006; Da Rin et al., 2006).

8.4.5 Exit Opportunities and Routes

Exit performance is another important criterion to assess the entrepreneurial firm performance and the success of its venture capital financiers. An initial public offering (IPO) is generally regarded as the best exit outcome for VC investors. An IPO exit signals the degree of support from venture capitalists in start-up or early-stage enterprises (Gompers and Lerner, 1999; Cumming and MacIntosh, 2006; Lerner, 2009). IPOs are also seen as more favourable than other forms of exit, such as trade sales, because the firm often continues to be managed by the successful entrepreneur after the IPO event (Black and Gilson, 1998). Importantly, a robust market for public offerings is a critical driver of the venture capital cycle (Jeng and Wells, 2000; Lerner, 2009). Lastly, IPOs are an effective way of addressing the financing constrains for the growth of young and especially high-tech firms, as an IPO is usually accompanied by a major increase in firm size (Carpenter and Petersen, 2002). However, as noted by Cumming (2007), an active IPO market should not automatically be associated with better firm performance after the exit (Gompers and Lerner, 1999, 2001a, 2001b; Florin, 2005).

8.5 METHODOLOGY AND DATA DESCRIPTION

This section first discusses the empirical methodology for the econometric analyses of the IIF programme. Descriptive statistics are provided for our sample. A total of 102 Australian businesses assisted by the IIF programme between 1997 and 2009 were included in this assessment, in addition to 106 businesses funded solely by private sector VC firms. A further 95 businesses which received equity investments through an IIF affiliate fund (see definition in footnote 4) were also included in the appraisal. It should be noted that the most serious limitations to the depth of our quantitative analysis are as a result of the lack of comprehensive time series data available from either the participating VC funds, the sponsoring department (DIISR) managing the IIF programme, or from the investee firms which have been in receipt of IIF finance. For example, there are thirteen IIF funds (nine in Rounds 1 and 2, and four in Round 3) in the programme. However, we have only been able to access information for eleven funds, with data from two funds in Round 3 remaining unavailable. The majority of VC funds in Rounds 1 and 2 still have portfolio firms that have not yet exited and which might still produce valuable uplifts to the funds' terminal performances. Further, given the immaturity of the Round 3 funds' investment activities, we are not able to make any substantive comment on their performance. Despite this important caveat, the analyses produced have allowed us to come to largely unequivocal conclusions as to the effectiveness of the IIF programme.

8.5.1 Methodology

Our analysis seeks to compare the consequences of the programme on recipient firms. These portfolio firms, which have been funded by IIF VC funds across the three rounds of investment of the programme, are compared to an equivalent set of firms which have received venture capital financing from exclusively private sources of capital (including bank, corporate, and foreign investors) or from IIF affiliate funds. Our dependent variables include the value, frequency, and stage(s) of investments made; the characteristics of the portfolio firms chosen, including age and sector; and the business outcomes, including IPO, acquisition, trade sale, and failure. The choice of dependent variables reflects the evaluation criteria and programme objectives discussed in the previous sections. Because we employ different econometric approaches for individual evaluation criteria, the detailed methodology for each criterion assessment is discussed in the following empirical results section.

8.5.2 Data Sources and Summary Statistics

This study uses data from two independent sources. The data on non-IIF and IIF affiliate investee firms is provided by AVCAL and consists of 201 entrepreneurial firms. For the eleven IIF funds, the data on their investment in 102 entrepreneurial firms was provided by the DIISR. Both data sets include information about:

- Company demographics: company founded year, investment and divestment year (where applicable);
- Investor type: either IIF, IIF affiliate, or other non-IIF funds;
- Investment characteristics: total investments, number of co-investors, and the number of investment made per round;
- Investee firm characteristics: stage of development, industry/sector classification, exit status.

In addition, market data (e.g. stock market index return) are sourced from MSCI (Morgan Stanley Capital International Index). Table 8.3 provides variable definitions.

Table 8.4 summarizes the descriptive statistics for the three categories of compared investors by key variables, including major investee firm demographics and evaluation criteria. The last three columns of Table 8.4 report the significance level of univariate comparison tests for variable means between IIF, IIF affiliate, and non-IIF investee firms.[11] (Note that in case of a dummy variable, the mean of the variable is equivalent to the percentage of observations where the dummy variable takes a value of 1.)

The median value of an IIF investment was AUD2.9 million. IIF investee firms receive significantly smaller financings when compared to AUD11.5 million for IIF affiliate investments and AUD4.0 million for private VC investments. The IIF programme appears to be tightly focused on those nascent firms which are least likely to be able to access commercial sources of equity because of their small size, commercial immaturity, and (as yet) speculative nature. The programme is clearly separated from alternative commercial investment as seen by the core range (i.e. 25th to 75th percentile) of the deal sizes

---

[11] Test results should be viewed with caution because the effects of other relevant variables are not 'controlled for', and this is especially problematic if the evaluation criteria are correlated with variables other than the types of investment funds (e.g. stock market returns).

Table 8.3 Variable Definitions

Variable Name	Variable Definition
Portfolio companies	
Investment Year	The first year the firm receives any form of VC investment.
Age	The firm's life horizon (number of years from firm establishment to divestment or Q1 2009 if not divested).
Years To Investment	Number of years since firm establishment to the year the firm received its first equity investment.
Fund type indicator variables	
IIF	A dummy variable equal to one for an IIF fund investment and zero otherwise.
IIF Affiliate	A dummy variable equal to one for an affiliated IIF fund investment and zero otherwise. An affiliated IIF fund is one which is part of a VC organization that has a companion fund that is an IIF fund, but the particular fund investing is not the companion IIF fund, but rather the companion fund.
IIF Round1	A dummy variable equal to one for an IIF fund investment for IIFs awarded in 1997 and zero otherwise.
IIF Round 2	A dummy variable equal to one for an IIF fund investment for IIFs awarded in 2001 and zero otherwise.
IIF Round 3	A dummy variable equal to one for an IIF fund investment for IIFs awarded in 2007 and zero otherwise.
Corporate	A dummy variable equal to one for a corporate fund investment and zero otherwise.
Bank	A dummy variable equal to one for an investment bank investment and zero otherwise.
Overseas	A dummy variable equal to one for an investment funded by non-Australian firms and zero otherwise.
Evaluation Criteria	
Biotechnology	A dummy variable equal to one for an investee in the biotechnology industry and zero otherwise.
ITT	A dummy variable equal to one for an investee in the information, technology, and telecommunications industry and zero otherwise.
Industrial/Energy	A dummy variable equal to one for an investee in the industrial and/or energy industries and zero otherwise.
Internet	A dummy variable equal to one for an investee in the internet related industry and zero otherwise.
Medical	A dummy variable equal to one for an investee in the medical industry and zero otherwise.
Staging	The number of staged investment Rounds in which VCs financed the company.
IPO	A dummy variable equal to one for an IPO exit and zero otherwise.
Acquisition	A dummy variable equal to one for an acquisition exit and zero otherwise.
Liquidation	A dummy variable equal to one for a write-off exit and zero otherwise.
Investee characteristics	
Total investment	Total AUS$ (millions) equity investment per company.
Crisis	A dummy variable equal to one for a first Round investment in or after 2007 and zero otherwise.

Table 8.4 Summary Statistics for Australian Risk Capital Investment by Type of VC Provider

Variables	(1) IIF investment					(2) IIF affiliate investment					(3) Private VC investment					(1) vs. (2) Mean	(1) vs. (3) Mean	(2) vs. (3) Mean
	Investees	Mean	Median	Min	Max	Investees	Mean	Median	Min	Max	Investees	Mean	Median	Min	Max			
Total Investment (Million AUD)	102	2.75	2.89	0.2	5.99	91	21.47	11.54	0.06	143.35	103	18.24	4.03	0.03	320.05	***	***	
Years To Investment	80	3.91	2	0	60	73	5.41	1	0	56	73	3.59	2	0	21			
Age	80	11.29	9	2	70	73	11.10	8	0	62	73	9.33	8	1	25			
Staging	102	4.84	4	1	15	95	4.31	3	1	13	106	3.27	2	1	17	***	***	**
Corporate	102	0	0	0	0	95	0.08	0	0	1	106	0.11	0	0	1	***	***	
Overseas	102	0	0	0	0	95	0.31	0	0	1	106	0.25	0	0	1	***	***	
Bank	102	0	0	0	0	95	0.05	0	0	1	106	0.07	0	0	1	**	**	
Biotechnology	102	0.35	0	0	1	95	0.17	0	0	1	106	0.10	0	0	1	***	***	
ITT	102	0.21	0	0	1	95	0.22	0	0	1	106	0.39	0	0	1		***	***
Industrial/Energy	102	0.09	0	0	1	95	0.12	0	0	1	106	0.05	0	0	1			*
Internet	102	0.22	0	0	1	95	0.09	0	0	1	106	0.17	0	0	1	**		
Medical	102	0.05	0	0	1	95	0.19	0	0	1	106	0.14	0	0	1	***	**	
IPO	102	0.17	0	0	1	95	0.06	0	0	1	106	0.07	0	0	1	**	**	
Acquisition	102	0.02	0	0	1	95	0.13	0	0	1	106	0.16	0	0	1	***	***	
Active	102	0.43	0	0	1	95	0.71	1	0	1	106	0.68	1	0	1	***	***	
Liquidation	102	0.25	0	0	1	95	0.04	0	0	1	106	0.09	0	0	1	***	***	

Notes: The last three columns report the results of univariate comparison tests for variable means between IIF, IIF affiliated, and non-IIF investee firms. *** indicates significant at the 1% level, ** at the 5% level, and * at the 10% level.

Table 8.5 Stage of Investment for IIF Supported Businesses

Stage of Investment	Number of Firms
Seed and Pre-seed	22
Start-up	43
Early-expansion	38
Total	103

Source: DIISR data

for three investor types.[12] Accordingly, the IIF programme is precisely and properly focused on the specified target firms. It is therefore unlikely to crowd out or compete with existing commercial providers of equity finance to small or, more accurately, medium-sized enterprises.

IIF portfolio firms are likely to be genuinely early-stage (see Table 8.5) as seen from data provided by the DIISR. Two-thirds of our sample (i.e. 65 portfolio firms) are at pre-seed, seed, and start-up stages when they first receive finance from IIF funds. IIF is clearly targeting nascent and young firms. As such, IIF firms sometimes receive external finance later than IIF affiliate or Private VC investments. This is likely to be because very young firms need to reach a certain level of maturity before the need for external equity finance can be properly assessed. Encouragingly, both IIF and IIF affiliate investee firms receive more rounds of finance, indicating the existence of a continuity of funding to meet the portfolio firm's growing need for follow-on finance; that is, the escalator model. IIF and IIF affiliate firms are also more concentrated in the biotechnology, industrial energy, and internet sectors. This is a result of the IIF investment strategies reflecting the programme's priorities. However, it could also imply that IIF funds are targeting at firms in high-tech, knowledge-based industries which are most likely to experience capital constraints. With respect to exit routes, significantly more IIF invested firms exit via an IPO than firms financed by the non-IIF funds. However, the percentage of liquidation exits (i.e. failures) is also significantly higher for IIF firms, indicating the programme's focus on high risk/high potential young firms.

Another way to investigate the relationship between investor types and the effectiveness of the investment in addressing IIF policy objectives is to look at the pair-wise correlation coefficients between variables (Table 8.6). The correlation coefficients review the 'direction' of the performance sensitivities of fund type indicators, that is, the value-added effects provided by IIFs in investee firms as reflected in the evaluation criteria. Correlations analysis allows us a useful but limited view of the data. (The coefficients fail to control for the effects of other variables nor do they address the magnitude of the sensitivities of independent variables.) It can be seen that the presence of IIF is positively related to the number of staged investments (Staging) in investee firms.

---

[12] The core ranges are AUD1.83 million to 3.6 million, AUD4.29 million to 28.89 million, AUD0.81 million to 17.85 million for IIF, IIF affiliate, and private VC investors, respectively. Results are available upon request.

Table 8.6 Pair-Wise Correlations between Variables

	Staging	Years to Investment	Total Investment	Biotech	ITT	Industrial/ Energy	Internet	Medical	Active	Acquisition	IPO	Liquidation
Staging	1.000											
Years to Investment	-0.151	1.000										
Total Investment	0.447		1.000									
Biotechnology				1.000								
ITT				-0.315	1.000							
Industrial/ Energy			0.144	-0.154	-0.184	1.000						
Internet				-0.225	-0.270	-0.132	1.000					
Medical				-0.194	-0.233	-0.114	-0.166	1.000				
Active								0.144	1.000			
Acquisition			0.167	0.211	0.159				-0.417	1.000		
IPO					-0.129				-0.274		1.000	
Liquidation			-0.117	0.255				-0.116	-0.251	-0.130	-0.127	1.000
IIF	0.151		-0.278	0.117			0.165	-0.164	-0.214	-0.194	0.161	0.248
IIF1			-0.183	0.185				-0.127	-0.143	-0.131	0.188	0.305
IIF2			-0.151									
IIF3						0.193						
IIFaffiliate			0.174	0.135			-0.123	0.131				-0.175
Corporate	0.288		0.268							0.237		
Overseas	0.326	-0.145	0.539							0.155		
Bank	0.117		0.304									

This table reports the pair-wise correlation coefficient for major variables used in the empirical analysis. Only coefficients with significance level greater than 95% are presented. The correlation between the last eight variables (i.e. between fund types) is not reported to save space.

However, corporate and overseas investments are also likely to be positively related to staging and the coefficient is larger than the value of 0.15 for IIF firms. In terms of the duration of time between firm foundation and its first equity investment (Years to Investment), which proxies the stage focus of investment funds, both IIF and IIF affiliate funds do not appear to invest earlier than their private sector peers. This may reflect the greater 'investment readiness' of larger and older portfolio firms.

With regard to industry choices, IIF funds are more likely to invest in high-tech sectors. More specifically, IIF Round 2 investments have a higher propensity towards biotechnology firms, whilst IIF Round 3 funds are more likely to invest in the industrial/energy sector. No such sector propensity is evident in non-IIF firms. The total amount of investment is negatively related to IIF firms and positively related to non-IIF or IIF affiliate firms. This implies that IIF funds are more likely to address firms' smaller (and often earlier) financial development needs compared to other more 'traditional' VC funds. This finding again reflects the realization of the IIF programme's remit to address a shortfall in the supply of early-stage risk capital.

With respect to exit outcomes, the company operating status as being active (Active) is negatively correlated with IIF investments (correlation coefficient of −2.5). However, IIF firms are more likely to achieve successful IPOs, albeit at the cost of a higher probability of non-survival. This statistic is likely to indicate the greater intrinsic riskiness of IIF investee firms. In contrast, successful non-IIF firms are more likely to exit via acquisition. The recent economic crisis (Crisis) has impacted directly on the VC industry by lowering the number of staged investments and successful exits (see Figure 8.4). The

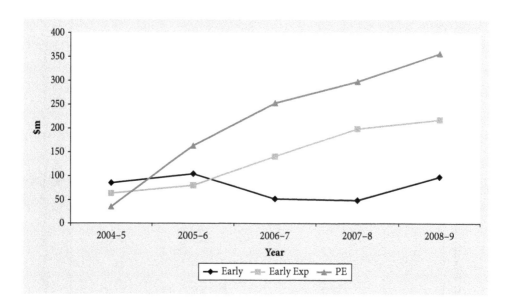

FIGURE 8.4 Australian Follow-On Venture Capital Investments by Stage.

Source: ABS data

positive correlation between IIF Round 3 investments and the financial crisis may be a result of either the timing of the fund establishment (2006–7), or its focus on less favourable investments during the economic downturn. The positive effects of the IIF programme on the Australia early-stage VC market are presently most clearly captured by IIF Rounds 1 and 2 investments. This does not mean IIF Round 3 investments are less effective. Rather, it remains too early to ascribe significant benefits to Round 3 investment activity given the immaturity of the portfolios.

IPO share price performance is an objective measure of entrepreneurial firm performance and the effectiveness of venture capitalist support (Barry et al., 1990; Gompers and Lerner, 1999; Chang, 2004). However, with only DIISR being prepared to provide us with the IPO share price data on IIF investee firms, we were not able to compare the effectiveness of the IIF programme with other private VC funds. Nonetheless, some preliminary analysis using the data available allows us to shed some tentative light on the IPO performance (see Figure 8.5).

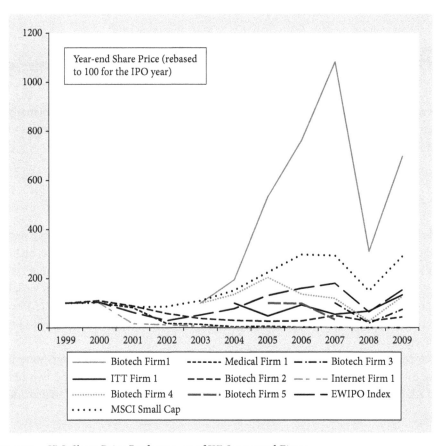

FIGURE 8.5 IPO Share Price Performance of IIF Supported Firms.

Source: IIF investee firm data as of 30 June 2009 (DIISR)

The nine IIF financed companies that had completed an initial public offering (IPO), and for which we have data,[13] were tracked on a yearly basis against the MSCI small cap index for all Australian stocks. IIF financed companies appeared—on the very limited information available—to have underperformed an index of publicly listed small firms in their post IPO behaviour with the exception of one biotech outlier. Figure 8.5 demonstrates the time-series returns of the nine IPO companies from the IIF programme using an equal weighted return index of these companies against the MSCI small cap index.

It can be seen that the equal-weighted index appears to track the MSCI market index closely. This is consistent with the finding by Cumming (2007) that market conditions are the most important determinant of share price returns. When we compare the IPO performance with the market return, a one-tail t-test comparing the means of the IPO index and the market index (MSCI) indicates that the IPO index underperforms the market at a 1 per cent significance level with or without the inclusion of the outlier. Our data lends support to the 'overpriced' IPO theory (Gompers and Lerner, 1999; Ritter and Welch, 2002), where 'information advantaged' VCs tend to take their portfolio firms public when they are overvalued.

8.6 EMPIRICAL RESULTS

This section provides a more rigorous multivariate analysis to investigate formally the effectiveness of the IIF programme against the five evaluation criteria discussed in Section 8.4.

8.6.1 Supply of Multiple Funding Rounds

Table 8.7 reports the regression results for the number of staged investments (*Staging*) for the sample firms. As the dependent variable is not a continuous variable, ordinary least squares (OLS) is not an appropriate methodology. Here the Poisson model is employed as the appropriate discretionary choice model for count dependent variables. Explanatory variables used are fund indicator variables (*IIF, IIF Affiliate,* etc.) as well as variables to control for the development stage of the sample firms (*Years to Investment, Age*).

Our results show clearly at the 1 per cent significance level that IIF funds were more likely to provide follow-on finance to portfolio firms than either of the two benchmarked, private sector equity providers. On average, IIF funds are likely to provide 0.6

---

[13] Seventeen firms from the IIF programme exited via an IPO. However, we have only been able to get data on IPO share prices (given by DIISR) and share price information from IPO on nine such companies.

Table 8.7 Poisson Regression: Number of Staged Investments

Specifications	Number of Staged Investment	
	(1)	(2)
IIF	1.64***	
IIF Round1		1.58***
IIF Round2		1.87***
IIF Round3		1.10
IIF Affiliate	1.29***	1.30***
Corporate	1.33***	1.34***
Overseas	1.83***	1.83***
Bank	0.84	0.84
Biotech	0.70***	0.71***
ITT	0.89	0.88
Industrial/Energy	1.14	1.17
Internet	0.91	0.91
Medical	0.81	0.83
Crisis	0.69***	0.75***
Years To Investment	0.92***	0.92***
Age	1.07***	1.07***
Number of Observations	221	221
Log likelihood	−495.66	−493.78
χ^2	231.93	235.68
Pseudo R^2	0.19	0.19

This table reports the Poisson regression results for the staging of sample firms. The dependent variable is the number of staged investment rounds in which VCs financed the company. Explanatory variables include fund and sector indicator dummies, as well as fund characteristic variables to control for the stage of development for the sample firms. The dummy variable for private funds (*Non-IIF* funds) is excluded to avoid collinearity, so that the basis of comparison is against the private funds. Similarly, two dummy variables are excluded for private fund types and sector choices as appropriate. The coefficient estimates are transformed (as the exponential of the original logarithm coefficient estimates) to show the marginal effects of independent variables (i.e. relative risk ratios). This transformation does not alter the statistical inference or the estimation method of the model. Model diagnostics include the log likelihood, chi-squared statistic and pseudo R-square of the regression. *, **, *** stand for 10%, 5%, and 1% significance levels, respectively.

times more funding rounds than private sector investors.[14] This public provision helps support a credible 'funding escalator' and allows growth-oriented, young businesses access to development capital. Similarly, IIF affiliate funds also provide 0.3 times more funding rounds than private investors. This result could be interpreted that the IIF programme has provided relevant experience to fund managers over time so that they are also more confident to invest in capital constrained businesses from other (non-IIF) funds under their management.

[14] The number is calculated as the exponential of the original coefficient estimate. It measures the relative value of the probabilities of staging conditioned on different funding types and this ratio is called the relative risk ratio.

Similar to the findings by Hill et al. (2009), corporate venture capital funds are also more likely to make follow-on investments, as are non-Australian funds. They provide 0.3 and 0.8 times more funding rounds, respectively. However, in both cases, this greater funding activity is because these VC funds are targeting more developed, later-stage firms which provide less risky follow-on finance opportunities. Note that biotechnology businesses were *less* likely to receive follow-on investment funding. They receive on average 0.3 times fewer funding rounds than other firms. This dearth of follow-on finance may reflect the inability of biotechnology entrepreneurs to generate commercially attractive deals. In periods of severe economic recession, follow-on funding typically declines across the VC industry. The latest international financial crisis has reduced the number of funding rounds for all firms by a factor of 0.7. This reflects a contemporary environment characterized by shortages of investment capital, higher market risk, and lower investment returns. In such circumstances, VC managers (GPs) often eschew new deals and concentrate on their existing portfolio firms in order to conserve capital.

Staging is also significantly related to the entrepreneurial development status of a firm. Using the number of years from firm foundation until its first investment (*Years to Investment*) as an indicator for the development stage of an entrepreneurial firm, the negative coefficient estimate implies that the earlier the firm receives its first equity investment the more funding rounds the firm will receive (see Table 8.8). It is difficult to confirm a reasonable explanation for this finding. It might suggest (implausibly) that the earliest investors are making better decisions regarding portfolio firm selection. Conversely, we might deduce that as investment managers have gained greater experience over time they become less optimistic about the future success of portfolio firms.

The same model is applied to firms differentiated by the three IIF investment rounds, i.e. Specification (2). VC fund managers from IIF Rounds 1 and 2 are providing 0.6 and 0.9 times more financing rounds. For Round 3, the small number of investment (seven financings) and the immaturity of investee firms do not yet allow any substantive comment to be made.

8.6.2 Early-Stage Focus

Providing more funding rounds does not necessarily indicate that the IIF is targeting areas of capital rationing to young firms. As discussed in Section 8.4, underinvestment is most likely to appear in start-up and early-stage enterprises. Therefore, in order to meet its public sponsors' objectives, the IIF programme should also have a specific focus on early-stage SMEs. The obvious empirical approach would be to investigate the propensity of different types of VC funds to invest in firms of different stages of development (i.e. seed, start-up, early stages, and later stages). However, we only had access to information on the development stages of IIF-supported firms. We are therefore unable to assess the stage focus of the benchmarked, non-IIF investee firms using stage indicators as in Cumming (2007). To address this data deficiency, we use the number of year

Table 8.8 OLS Regression: Years to Investment and Total Equity Investment

Specifications	Ln (Years to Investment)			Total Investment		
	(1)	(2)	(3)	(4)	(5)	(6)
IIF	0.44**		-0.07	-9.27**		-14.46***
IIF Round1		0.31	0.19		-12.43**	
IIF Round2		0.56**			-5.20	
IIF Round3		0.54			-12.84	
IIF Affiliate	-0.04	-0.04		-1.00	-1.03	-4.06
Corporate	-0.21	-0.21		3.24	3.12	4.03
Overseas	-0.44**	-0.44**		32.89***	32.76***	24.69***
Bank	0.36	0.35		22.33***	21.78***	26.39***
Biotech	-0.77***	-0.76***	-1.07**	-2.31	-2.12	-0.97
ITT	-0.65***	-0.65***	-0.25	-7.05	-6.83	-7.05
Industrial/Energy	-0.72**	-0.72**	-0.28	13.40**	14.20**	13.14**
Internet	-0.61**	-0.60**	-0.85**	-9.59*	-9.29*	-7.45
Medical	-0.68**	-0.68**	-0.39	-5.85	-5.33	-7.25
Crisis	0.20	0.17	0.21	9.26*	10.90**	5.21
Biotech * IIF			1.13			
ITT * IIF			-0.15			
Internet * IIF			1.13*			
Medical * IIF			0.16			
Biotech * IIF Affiliate			0.21			
ITT * IIF Affiliate			-0.66			
Industrial/Energy * IIF Affiliate			-0.47			
Internet * IIF Affiliate			0.61			
Medical * IIF Affilate			-0.45			
Investment Year				-2.16***	-2.42***	
Staging						3.42***
Number of Observations	197	197	197	288	288	288
F-statistic	3.15	2.71	2.41	14.85	12.87	20.78
Adjusted R^2	0.11	0.10	0.13	0.37	0.37	0.45

This table reports the OLS regression results for the timing of investments (Specifications 1 to 3) and total equity investments (Specifications 4 to 6). The dependent variables are the number of years from firm establishment and first equity investments, and the sum of equity investments an investee firm receives. Explanatory variables include fund and sector indicator dummies, controlling fund characteristic variables (*Investment Year* and *Staging* in Specifications 4 to 6), as well as interactive terms between fund type and sector choice (Specifications 1 to 3). The dummy variable for private funds (*Non-IIF* funds) is excluded to avoid collinearity, so that the basis of comparison is against the private funds. For the same reason, two dummy variables are excluded for private fund types and sector choices as appropriate. Model diagnostics include the F-statistic and adjusted R-square of the regression. *, **, *** stand for 10%, 5%, and 1% significance levels, respectively.

from firm establishment to its first equity investment (*Years to Investment*) as a proxy for the stage of an entrepreneurial firm's development.

Specifications (1) to (3) in Table 8.8 report the results for OLS regressions of ln(*Years to Investment*). The independent variables used are fund indicator and sector dummies, as well as a variable controlling for the general economic conditions (*Crisis*).

Specification (1) provides results for the overall IIF programme and Specification (2) segregates into the three financing rounds. It is found that IIF investments are typically made eighteen months *later* in the life cycle of a business than private sector equity investments.[15] This counter-intuitive finding may reflect the fact that IIF-affiliated funds are largely investing in later-stage businesses, many of which will have been created (as a 'newco' vehicle) specifically for the investment activity. Private investments also include some very early seed investments from corporate and foreign investors. In both cases, non-IIF funds will be able to invest earlier than IIF investors, who have to wait for the start-up enterprise to be of a sufficient size and development before external finance can be introduced effectively. Evidence from Specification (2) reveals that the later-stage focus of IIF investments is mainly captured by IIF Round 2 funds.

Ranked in order of investment timing with the earliest sector first, biotechnology businesses typically receive the earliest stage of investment, followed by industrial energy, medical, ITT, and internet. In order to test the sensitivity of different investor types on sector levels, Specification (3) in Table 8.8 introduces nine interactive terms between fund types and sector indicators, calculated as the product of fund type dummies (*IIF, IIF Affiliate*) and five sector dummies.[16] It can be seen that the effect on investment timing is influenced by sector and not by type of investors. The only exception is IIF investments in the internet sector, which is only marginally significant at the 10 per cent level.

For private sector investors, Australian funds also tended to make their first investments eighteen months earlier than non-Australian funds. This may reflect national differences in investors' willingness to take risks and/or the effect of proximity on the composition of the deal flow. Foreign funds may also wish to invest larger amounts of finance in more established businesses. This is possibly because of their information disadvantage compared to domestic investors, which is likely most evident at the earliest stages of a new enterprise. Finally, selection may also be influenced by the higher transaction costs for an overseas investor when making small investments in young businesses.

8.6.3 Investment Size

Specifications (4) to (6) of Table 8.8 report the OLS regression results for the sum of equity investments for each VC portfolio firm. As discussed earlier, deal size is a critical indicator of whether the IIF scheme is actually targeted at the perceived 'equity gap' and does not crowd out private investments in the VC market. Evidence from our descriptive statistics suggests that IIF is filling an important market gap in the provision of smaller scale investment demand and that the public sector does not compete

---

[15] The number is calculated as the exponential of the original coefficient estimate. It measures the relative value of the probabilities of staging conditioned on different funding types. In Specification (1) this figure is first given as an exponential value (0.44) and is then expressed in months.

[16] The term *Industrial/Energy * IIF* is dropped for statistical reasons so there are in total nine interactive terms.

directly with private capital providers. This finding is further confirmed by the multi-variate analysis.

From Specification (4) it can be seen that IIF investments in each investee firm are on average AUD9.3 million *smaller* than investments by private investors. The three types of non-IIF funds are more likely to concentrate on larger investments, especially for firms funded by either banks or non-Australian investors. Average total investment for non-Australian funds was AUD32.9 million greater than Australian funds. As noted, this preference for scale might reflect the lack of willingness to take risks in younger and smaller companies by the managers (GPs) of non-Australian funds as well as the higher costs of investment appraisal associated with distance and a lack of local knowledge. This means that early-stage investments will largely remain the responsibility of Australian private and, particularly, public funds. Similar findings were apparent for investment bank funds which, on average, made total investments in the region of AUD22.3 million *larger* than other funds. Again, this suggests a preference for fewer, lower risk but larger scale investments. Importantly, as reported in Specification (6), firms that receive more follow-on finance are also more likely to receive larger-scale investments. These firms are seen as more likely to succeed. Accordingly, such firms are also able to attract additional private investors with greater capital resources.

We can conclude that the IIF programme increases the supply of risk capital at the pre-start (seed), start-up, and early-growth phases of investment. This is a focus where private sector equity investors are much less willing to operate. For GPs managing both IIF and other funds, their experience of IIF may also have increased their confidence in making other early-stage investments. However, this effect is not statistically prominent. When separating IIF investments into 3 rounds (Specification 5), IIF Round 1 funds are found to perform the best in addressing the finance gap. Their investments are on average AUD12.4 million smaller than private sector investments. However, in contrast, there is no statistically significant difference in investment values between IIF and private VC funds in Rounds 2 and 3. A possible explanation is that these rounds were invested at a time of economic downturn. Accordingly, pragmatic short-run financial considerations had overridden long run public policy objectives. Thus, contemporary investments have moved towards larger scale, less risky activities—even in publicly supported VC funds. Later-stage deals appear more attractive than 'classic' venture capital investment for all but the most committed technology specialist—and thus risk-accepting—investors.

8.6.4 'New Knowledge' Industry Investments

The direction of causality between fund type and sector choice is worthy of note. We believe that it is firms with unmet financing needs which seek additional investors. Their sector is a 'given' and growing firms do not change sector to attract more capital. This is because of the very high levels of specialist, and specific, human capital required to enter and compete in any advanced knowledge-based sector. Therefore, we believe that industry sector will determine investor source.

Table 8.9 Multinomial Logistic Regression: Probability of IIF/IIF Affiliate Investment

| Specifications | Probability of IIF/IIF Affiliate Investment | | | |
| | (1) | | (2) | |
	IIF	IIF Affiliate	IIF	IIF Affiliate
Biotech	49.37***	1.13	51.51***	1.12
ITT	7.43*	0.39**	7.39*	0.39**
Industrial/Energy	32.53***	1.87	34.19***	1.87
Internet	17.31***	0.38*	14.85**	0.40*
Medical	5.90	1.01	6.66*	1.00
Crisis	0.38**	0.65	0.20***	0.69
MSCI Investment Year			0.13***	1.54
Number of Observations	295		295	
Log likelihood	−289.49		−281.89	
χ^2	68.32		83.51	
Pseudo R²	0.11		0.13	

This table reports the multinomial logit regression results for the probability of an investee firm being an IIF/IIF affiliate investment. Explanatory variables include sector indicator dummies and a control variable for market conditions. MSCI Investment Year is the Morgan Stanley Capital International Index (MSCI) returns for the Australian small cap market. The dummy variable for private funds (Non-IIF funds) is used as the benchmark outcome for comparison. One dummy variable (the 'other' sectors) are excluded sector choices to avoid collinearity. The coefficient estimates are transformed (as the exponential of the original logarithm coefficient estimates) to show the marginal effects of independent variables (i.e. relative risk ratios). This transformation does not alter the statistical inference or the estimation method of the model. Model diagnostics include the log likelihood, chi-squared statistic and pseudo R-square of the regression. *, **, *** stand for 10%, 5%, and 1% significance levels, respectively.

Table 8.9 reports the results of the multinomial logistic regression on the probability of an investment being IIF/IIF affiliate. The multinomial logit model is an appropriate choice when the dependent variable has more than two outcomes. In the context of the IIF evaluation, a firm can be invested by an IIF or IIF affiliate fund as well as a private VC not related to the IIF programme (a non-IIF fund). Here the non-IIF category is used as the benchmark outcome for comparison in the interpretation of coefficient estimates.

Interpreted in 'relative risk ratios' (i.e. the exponential of the original coefficient estimates), the results from our analysis show that IIF investments are nearly fifty times more likely to be made in the biotech sector than for non-IIF funds. IIF funds are also significantly more likely to invest in industrial energy and internet sectors. The effects on ITT and medical sectors are less pronounced. Conversely, IIF investments are very unlikely to be made in communications or consumer related sectors.[17] IIF affiliate funds

---

[17] Work by the authors on the rapidly internationalizing of new technology based firms (Bürgel et al., 2004) confirms that young high-tech enterprises based on consumer related products are less likely to internationalize and in consequence grow more rapidly than firms serving industrial customers.

are not found to be significantly more likely to invest in these 'new knowledge' industries than purely private funds. In fact, IIF affiliate investments are less likely to be made in the ITT and internet sectors. Economic conditions are also likely to influence the investment decisions made by IIF/IIF affiliate funds. It can be seen that IIF funds are 0.6 times less likely than private investors to invest during periods of severe economic downturn. Moreover, IIF managers appear to track the broader market as they are also less likely to invest when the market return is low (Specification 2). This suggests that they are as sensitive as their private VC peers to the constraints of difficult investment environments.

8.6.5 Exit Opportunities and Routes

Nearly half (44 per cent) of IIF supported businesses have changed their trading status. They are 16 per cent less likely to remain trading today in their original form when compared to IIF affiliate and private VC supported businesses. For IIF affiliate and non-IIF investments, the probabilities of change are 23 and 32 per cent, respectively. These changes are a result of both beneficial (IPO) and adverse (liquidation) outcomes. An acquisition by a third party firm can be a success for investors in a highly attractive company. It can also be the 'least worst' exit choice for investors in a weakened or non-performing portfolio company (aka 'the living dead') with attractive assets. Located at the earliest and most speculative stages of a firm's life cycle, IIF supported businesses are more volatile than their peers. At the sector level, businesses in communications and consumer related industries are between 18 and 20 per cent less likely to remain trading in their original form than businesses in biotechnology, ITT, industrial energy, internet, and medical sectors. This pattern may reflect sector specific trading conditions and the more proprietary nature of IP intensive businesses. As each year elapses since the original equity investment, the probability that a business will not be trading in its original form increases by 6 per cent. Table 8.10 quantifies the above observations using probit models for each of the three major exit routes (IPO, acquisition, and liquidation).

Unlike the earlier evaluation of IIF by Cumming (2007), we have found significant difference between IIF investee firms and benchmarked private VC backed firms regarding exit outcomes. We first investigate the probability of an IPO in Specifications (1) to (4). We find that IIF supported businesses are 9 per cent more likely to have gone to market via an IPO than IIF affiliated or private VC backed businesses. Although including IIF affiliate investment in the regression (Specification 2) reduces the statistical significance of IIF investments, they are still 8 per cent more likely to achieve an IPO exit. Medical businesses were 15 per cent more likely to have floated than businesses in any other sectors. In periods of severe economic downturn, the probability of an IPO event occurring declines by 9 per cent. This likely reflects supply-side reductions in the availability of investment capital to finance new market entry and demand-side effects from businesses unwilling to hazard the vagaries of a market flotation when share prices are falling. We further include fund characteristic controls on follow-on finance and the

Table 8.10 Probit Regressions: Exit Outcomes

Specifications	Probability of IPO				Probability of Acquisition			Probability of Liquidation		
	(1)	(2)	(3)	(4)	(5)	(6)	(7)	(8)	(9)	(10)
IIF	0.094**	0.078*	0.086*		−0.070**	−0.105**		0.096**	0.142**	
IIF Round1				0.143**			−0.065*			0.123**
IIF Round2				0.031			−0.046			0.031
IIF Affiliate		−0.022		−0.021	−0.020	−0.020	−0.019	−0.052	−0.044	−0.062
Corporate					−0.037	−0.033	−0.038	0.114	0.185	0.116
Overseas					0.109**	0.075	0.111**	−0.051	−0.027	−0.057
Bank					0.119	0.131	0.120	−0.021	−0.004	−0.024
Biotech	0.074	0.072	0.136	0.070	−0.071**	−0.042	−0.074**	−0.065	−0.107*	−0.060
ITT	−0.056	−0.061	−0.054	−0.065	−0.018	0.003	−0.018	−0.034	−0.034	−0.033
Industrial/Energy					−0.035	0.025	−0.036	0.004	0.043	0.003
Internet	−0.026	−0.030	−0.037	−0.038	−0.048	−0.028	−0.048	0.033	−0.006	0.033
Medical	0.154*	0.150*	0.178*	0.143†	−0.076**	−0.066	−0.077***	−0.074		−0.072
Crisis	−0.087**	−0.088***	−0.073	−0.081†	−0.077***	−0.071*	−0.073**	−0.090*	−0.114*	−0.083**
Staging			0.006			0.004			−0.014*	
Years To Investment			0.003*			0.002			−0.000	
Number of Observations	270	270	204	270	295	221	295	295	193	295
Log likelihood	−79.65	−79.50	−59.01	−77.98	−78.31	−60.15	−78.23	−91.74	−64.35	−91.64
χ^2	29.07	29.37	29.77	32.41	41.69	35.72	41.84	35.39	23.86	35.58
Pseudo R^2	0.15	0.16	0.20	0.17	0.21	0.23	0.21	0.16	0.16	0.16

This table reports the probit regression results for the exit comes of sample firms. The dependent variables are the probabilities of IPO, acquisition and liquidation. Explanatory variables include fund and sector indicator dummies, as well as fund characteristic variables to control for the stage of development for the sample firms. The dummy variable for private funds (*Non-IIF funds*) is excluded to avoid collinearity, so that the basis of comparison is against the private funds. Similarly, two dummy variables are excluded for private fund types and sector choices as appropriate. IIF Round 3 investments are excluded from the regression as they are too early to evaluate. The coefficient estimates are reported as marginal effects to illustrate the direct effect of explanatory variables on the dependent variables. This does not alter the statistical inference or the estimation method of the model. Model diagnostics include the log likelihood, chi-squared statistic, and pseudo R-square of the regression. *, **, *** stand for 10%, 5%, and 1% significance levels, respectively.

entrepreneurial stage of a firm in Specification (3). We find that firms at later stages of development (high values of the *Years to Investment* variable) are marginally more likely to exit via IPOs. This is not surprising as firms receiving their first investments at later stages of development are likely to be more mature and more 'investment ready'. As such they are more likely candidates for a successful exit.

IIF investments are found to be less likely to exit through the 'second best' route of an acquisition, as seen in Specifications (5) to (7). Biotech and medical firms are both around 7 per cent less likely to be acquired than businesses in all other sectors. Interestingly, businesses supported by non-Australian funds were 11 per cent more likely to be acquired by another business. This may reflect the imperative of finding an exit for overseas investors after a broadly proscribed tenure of investment. In periods of severe economic downturn, acquisitions reduced by 7 per cent. This illustrates the curtailing of investment activity in the corporate sector or general difficulties in finding a successful exit for entrepreneurial firms when the economic climate is unfavourable. Unlike the results for IPOs, investee characteristics are found to be irrelevant to the probability of acquisitions.

The last three specifications in Table 8.10 investigate the probability of liquidation, i.e. business termination, for sample firms. IIF supported businesses were 10 per cent more likely to terminate via liquidation. This 'double edged' outcome of both greater opportunity and greater risk faced by high potential young firms further supports the logic of government intervention to improve the risk/reward balance for investors. An interesting finding was that in periods of severe economic downturn the probability of liquidation fell by 9 per cent. On first reading this is counter-intuitive. However, it is common to see business failure rising in the immediate aftermath of a recession rather than during the recession itself. This is attributed to creditors delaying foreclosure until asset prices have recovered, thereby reducing their debt exposure. Again, we take firm characteristics into consideration and it is found (in Specification (9)) that firms with one additional round of finance are on average 1.4 per cent less likely to fail. This is an important finding which indicates that the creation of a funding escalator forms a critical driver for entrepreneurial firms towards a successful market exit.

In all three models, we investigated the effect of three separate IIF rounds on the exit outcomes of portfolio firms. We excluded firms receiving IIF Round 3 finance as most of these later funds were not fully invested. This could bias our results.[18] IIF Round 1 investments are 16 per cent more likely to achieve an IPO exit and 7 per cent less likely to be acquired than other investments. This result is reasonable given that IIF Round 1 funds are more mature. Further, IIF Round 1 was launched in a period (1997–2000) of considerable bullishness for technology stocks, many of which floated. However, it is also true that IIF Round 1 funds are more likely (12 per cent) to be liquidated. With their relatively greater probability of an IPO exit, IIF Round 1 investments have been the most effective in improving the attractiveness of the investee firms to private investors.

---

[18] As a robustness check, we include IIF Round 3 samples into all three models. They have been dropped from the regressions as they predicted overall survival perfectly. This has not altered our empirical results significantly but has reduced the sample size for the analysis.

8.7 RESEARCH LIMITATIONS

As noted in the previous sections, data issues are the primary reasons that limited the depth of our quantitative analysis. DIISR, as a government funding agency, provided us with the information on IIF fund investments. However, the comparative information on IIF affiliate and non-IIF investments provided by AVCAL was less comprehensive. Thus, we cannot guarantee the similar distributions of firm characteristics such as age and size for IIF-invested and privately invested firms. Biases may arise from this 'unmatched' control group of private firms. Second, our analysis suffers the similar limitation as found by Cumming (2007), where details on portfolio firms' performance metrics—including employment, sales, profits, cash flow, and other relevant accounting data—are either incomplete or not publicly available. The absence of time-series data on investee firm performance meant that the authors were not able to assess the investment performance of government supported VC funds over time, nor the wider economic effectiveness, or value for money, of the IIF programme. Given the above limitations, future evaluation of this important programme is warranted using a 'matched-sample' time-series analysis and a more comprehensive set of data.

8.8 DISCUSSIONS AND CONCLUSION

A self-sustaining, profitable, and growing venture capital industry—with positive effects on employment, innovation, and economic growth—has been the common objective of government policy-makers in several nations. But early-stage venture capital investment activity has been static or in long run decline from 2001. Given governments' widely held belief in the importance of early-stage risk capital to a nation's innovation capability, this trend has resulted in several supply-side responses from government. The hybrid public-private model of intervention whereby the state uses professional VC 'agents' (GPs) to manage commercial funds in which the government becomes an important investor alongside private investors (LPs) has become a popular instrument of government intervention in entrepreneurial finance.

Despite the importance of such models and the substantial public funds committed, there has been very little academic scrutiny of hybrid VC programmes. This paper investigates one large and established government-sponsored hybrid VC fund, the Australian IIF programme. Our analysis follows on from the first independent and rigorous analysis of the IIF programme by Cumming (2007). We seek to assess the IIF's effectiveness in providing finance to attractive but capital constrained, new technology-based enterprises. Using data on eleven IIF funds and their investment in 102 entrepreneurial firms, alongside comparative data on 201 entrepreneurial firms financed by private VC investors, we are able to quantify and discuss the relative effectiveness and the performance of the IIF programme over an eleven-year period with direct reference of the programme's stated policy objectives.

We find that the programme is well focused and has provided material and relevant support to a significant number of early-stage enterprises from Australia's science and technology base. IIF supported portfolio firms are more likely to be early-stage and 'new knowledge' industry investments; to have attracted follow-on finance; and to achieve a successful exit than comparable firms financed by other private VC investors. However, these IIF supported firms are also more likely to fail than comparator firms. This is a reasonable outcome in part because the programme focuses on genuinely early-stage and therefore highly risky firms. Thus, we conclude that the programme has been effectively targeted to provide early-stage, risk capital for young and new knowledge-based firms. There is no evidence that public funds 'crowd out' private providers. IIF operates at funding levels and the early stages of young firms largely ignored by private VC investors in Australia. It is probable that these portfolio firms would have remained capital rationed in the absence of the IIF programme. Moreover, using more contemporary data on two completed IIF investment rounds, our results have evidenced improvements of the programme over time. Younger and smaller firms have been better targeted by IIF funds than private investors, and the number of successful exits has increased.

Second, the advent of the IIF programme has allowed a cadre of professional early-stage VC fund managers to be created, trained, and become able to operate specifically within an Australian context. This is evident, although to a limited extent, of additional complementarities. Organizations or fund managers that run both IIF funds and IIF affiliate funds are found to be more likely to invest in high-tech firms and to provide additional follow-on finance from their private funds. While these VC managers are unlikely to have the depth of skills or experience of the best of their US or European peers, the IIF initiative has produced a material improvement in the innovation finance infrastructure in Australia.

Third, without detailed cash flow data, we are not able to test whether or not the IIF programme could eventually become 'self-funding'. To gain investors' approval, a revolving or 'evergreen' fund requires a consistent level of success as measured by the risk adjusted, annualized returns to its investors (LPs). Such funds are a rarity in the VC industry where a ten-year closed-end fund structure is the industry norm. The creation of a revolving or self-funding (i.e. profitable or, at a minimum, cost neutral) programme is the goal of any public intervention designed to act as a catalyst and provide short/medium term incentives. However, the reality is that there is little evidence of this being the case in any country that has supported a public or hybrid VC programme.[19] The drift from early-stage VC to development capital and increasingly PE activity (e.g. management buy-outs) is a trend that appears inevitable given both the historically higher returns,[20] the velocity with which PE investments can be made and then successfully

---

[19] Israel's Yozma would be a notable and well-known exception.

[20] Some top quartile VC funds in the US have consistently outperformed PE funds, but the opposite is consistently true in Europe and elsewhere.

exited, and the considerably larger sums of institutional finance including leveraged debt that can be invested in later-stage deals. What government can do through properly targeted support is to ameliorate the worse societal consequences of this drift by ensuring that the most proficient VC firms and innovative entrepreneurs continue to have access to risk capital (equity) and professional investor guidance.

A preliminary analysis of IPO share prices for floated IIF investee firms demonstrates that their performance is no different from, or even underperforms, their private sector counterparts. It is unlikely that such average performances are, or will become, attractive to professional investors (other than the government). So far, we are obliged to conclude that the goal of a self-sustaining and privately financed early-stage VC activity based on the present scale and performance of the IIF programme is very unlikely to be realized. In the absence of such a goal, it is probable that government will be required to continue to be a major supporter and funder of innovative young companies via hybrid forms of VC activity and other funding initiatives. The state has no choice if it wishes to harvest the long run returns from public financed R&D and other public investments in the nation's knowledge infrastructure and assets.

We conclude that the IIF programme is an important and valuable building block in Australia's entrepreneurial and innovation infrastructure. Nonetheless, we do not ignore the very high investment skills from general partners that such public VC programmes require in order to be successful. Further, it would be unwise to assume that this single public policy in isolation can realize material and lasting benefits to a nation's innovative and entrepreneurial activities. The IIF can sensibly be seen as a part of Australia's policy arsenal but it should only remain one element of a necessarily diverse entrepreneurial and innovation policy and programme structure.

ACKNOWLEDGEMENTS

We would like to thank the staff of the Innovation Policy Branch in the Australian Department of Innovation, Industry, Science and Research for their considerable support and guidance. We are also indebted to the Australian Venture Capital Association for their assistance.

REFERENCES

Acs, Z. J. and Gifford, S. (1996). 'Innovation of Entrepreneurial Firms', *Small Business Economics* 8, 203–18.

Acs, Z. J. and Storey, D. (2004). 'Introduction: Entrepreneurship and Economic Development', *Regional Studies* 38, 871–7.

Alemany, L. and Martí, I. (2005). Unbiased Estimation of Economic Impact of Venture Capital Backed Firms. Paper Presented at the European Financial Management Association Annual Meetings, 28 June–1 July 2006. Madrid, Spain.

Amit, R., Brander, J., and Zott, C. (1998). 'Why Do Venture Capital Firms Exist? Theory and Canadian Evidence', *Journal of Business Venturing* 13(6), 441–66.

Armour, J. and Cumming, D. J. (2006). 'The Legislative Road to Silicon Valley', *Oxford Economic Papers* 58(4), 596–635.

Audretsch, D. B., Bönte, W., and Keilbach, M. (2008). 'Entrepreneurship Capital and its Impact on Knowledge Diffusion and Economic Performance', *Journal of Business Venturing* 23, 687–98.

Audretsch, D. B. and Keilbach, M. (2004a). 'Does Entrepreneurship Capital Matter?', *Entrepreneurship Theory and Practice* 28(5), 419–29.

Audretsch, D. B. and Keilbach, M. (2004b). 'Entrepreneurship Capital and Economic Performance', *Regional Studies* 38, 949–59.

Auerswald, P. E. and Branscomb, L. M. (2003). 'Valleys of Death and Darwinian Seas: Financing the Invention to Innovation Transition in the United States', *Journal of Technology Transfer* 28(3–4), 227–39.

AusIndustry (2008*). Innovation Investment Fund: Fact Sheet*. Canberra: AusIndustry.

AVCAL (2009). *Yearbook. Australian Private Equity and Venture Capital Activity Report: November 2009.* Sydney: AVCAL.

Bank of England (1996). *The Financing of Technology Based Small Firms*. London: Bank of England.

Barry, C., Muscarella, C., Peavy, J., and Vetsuypens, M. R. (1990). 'The Role of Venture Capital in the Creation of Public Companies: Evidence from the Going Public Process', *Journal of Financial Economics* 27(2), 447–71.

Bergemann, D. and Hege, U. (1998). 'Venture Capital Financing, Moral Hazard, and Learning', *Journal of Banking & Finance* 22(6–8), 703–35.

Berger, A. N. and Udell, G. F. (1995). 'Relationship Lending and Lines of Credit in Small Firm Finance', *Journal of Business* (68), 351–82.

Berger, A. N. and Udell, G. F. (1998). 'The Economics of Small Business Finance: The Roles of Private Equity and Debt Markets in the Financial Growth Cycle', *Journal of Banking & Finance* 22(6), 613–73.

Bester, H. and Hellwig, M. (1989). 'Moral Hazard in Credit Markets: Some Recent Developments', in G. Bamberg and K. Spremann (eds), *Agency Theory, Information and Incentives*, , pp. 135–66. New York: Springer Verlag.

Black, B. S. and Gilson, R. J. (1998). 'Venture Capital and the Structure of Capital Markets: Banks Versus Stock Markets', *Journal of Financial Economics* 47(3), 243–77.

Bolton, J. E. (1971). *Report on the Committee of Enquiry into Small Firms. Cmnd 4811.* London: HMSO.

Brander, J., Du, Q., and Hellmann, T. (2010). 'Effects of Government-Sponsored Venture Capital: International Evidence', Working Paper 16521. National Bureau of Economic Research. Cambridge MA: NBER.

Bürgel, O., Fier, O., Licht, G., and Murray, G. C. (2004). *The Internationalization of Young High-Tech Firms: An Empirical Analysis in Germany and the United Kingdom.* ZEW Economic Studies 22. Heidelberg: Physica-Verlag.

Carpenter, R. E. and Petersen, B. C. (2002). 'Capital Market Imperfections, High-Tech Investment, and New Equity Financing', *The Economic Journal* 112, F54–F72.

Chang, S. J. (2004). 'Venture Capital Financing, Strategic Alliances, and the Initial Public Offerings of Internet Startups', *Journal of Business Venturing* 19(5), 721–41.

Commonwealth of Australia (1997). *Investing for Growth.* Canberra: Department of Industry Science and Tourism.

Commonwealth of Australia (2001). *Backing Australia's Ability.* Canberra: Department of Industry Science and Resources.

Cowling, M. (2007). *The Role of Loan Commitments in Credit Allocation on the UK Small Firms Loan Guarantee Scheme*. Sussex, United Kingdom: Institute for Employment Studies.

Cowling, M. (2010). The role of loan guarantee schemes in alleviating credit rationing in the UK. *Journal of Financial Stability* 6(1), 36–44.

Cressy, R. (2002). 'Funding Gaps: A Symposium', *The Economic Journal* 112, F1–F16.

Cressy, R. and Olofsson, C. (1997). 'European SME Financing: An Overview', *Small Business Economics* 9, 87–96.

Cumming, D. J. (2007). Government policy towards entrepreneurial finance: Innovation investment funds. *Journal of Business Venturing* 22, 193–235.

Cumming, D. J. (2009). 'Pre-Seed Government Venture Capital Funds', *Journal of International Entrepreneurship* 7(1), 26–56.

Cumming, D. J., Fleming, G., and Schwienbacher, A. (2006). 'Legality and Venture Capital Exits', *Journal of Corporate Finance* 12, 214–45.

Cumming, D. J., and MacIntosh, J. G. (2006). 'Crowding Out Private Equity: Canadian Evidence', *Journal of Business Venturing*, 21(5), 569–609.

Da Rin, M., Nicodano, G., and Sembenelli, A. (2006). 'Public Policy and the Creation of Active Venture Capital Markets', *Journal of Public Economics* 90(8–9), 1699–723.

Davila, A., Foster, G., and Gupta, M. (2003). 'Venture Capital Financing and the Growth of Startup Firms', *Journal of Business Venturing* 18(6), 689–708.

Denis, D. J. (2004). 'Entrepreneurial Finance: An Overview of the Issues and Evidence', *Journal of Corporate Finance* 10(2), 301–26.

Dimov, D. and Murray, G. C. (2008). 'Determinants of the Incidence and Scale of Seed Capital Investments by Venture Capital Firms', *Small Business Economics* 30(2), 127–52.

DIST (1997). *R&D Start Program: Policies and Practices of the IR&D Board in Relation to the Innovation Investment Fund (IIF) Program Direction No. 1 of 1997*. Canberra: Department of Industry, Science and Tourism.

Egeln, J., Licht, G., and Steil, F. (1997). 'Firm Foundations and the Role of Financing Constraints', *Small Business Economics* 9, 137–50.

European Commission (2003). *Green Paper: Entrepreneurship in Europe*. Brussels: Directorate General for Enterprise and Industry, European Commission.

European Commission, United States Department of Commerce (2005). *Working Group on Venture Capital: Final Report*. Brussels: European Commission.

Fenn, G., Liang, N., and Prowse, S. (1995). *The Economics of the Private Equity Market*. Washington, DC: Board of Governors of the Federal Reserve System.

Florin, J. (2005). 'Is Venture Capital Worth It? Effects on Firm Performance and Founder Returns', *Journal of Business Venturing* 20(1), 113–35.

Gompers, P. A. and Lerner J. (1998). 'What Drives Venture Fundraising?', *Brookings Papers on Economic Activity—Microeconomics* 33, 149–92.

Gompers, P. A. and Lerner, J. (1999). *The Venture Capital Cycle*. Cambridge, MA: The MIT Press.

Gompers, P. A. and Lerner, J. (2001a). *The Money of Invention: How Venture Capital Creates New Wealth*. Boston, MA: Harvard Business School Press

Gompers, P. A. and Lerner, J. (2001b). 'The Venture Capital Revolution', *Journal of Economic Perspectives* 15, 145–68.

Hill, S., Birkinshaw, J., Maula, M., and Murray, G. C. (2009). 'Transferability of the Venture Capital Model to the Corporate Context: Implications for the Performance of Corporate Venture Units', *Strategic Entrepreneurship Journal* 3, 3–27.

Hillier, B. and Ibrahimo, W. (1993). 'Asymmetric Information and Models of Credit Rationing', *Bulletin of Economic Research* 45, 271–304.

HM Treasury, BIS (2010). *The Path to Strong, Sustainable and Balanced Growth.* London: Department of Business Innovation and Skills.

HM Treasury, Small Business Service (2003). *Bridging the Finance Gap: Next Steps in Improving Access to Growth Capital for Small Businesses.* London: HM Treasury and SBS.

Hyytinen, A. and Väänänen, L. (2006). 'Where Do Financial Constraints Originate From? An Empirical Analysis of Adverse Selection and Moral Hazard in Capital Markets', *Small Business Economics* 27, 323–48.

Jääskeläinen, M., Maula, M., and Murray, G. C. (2007). 'Performance of Incentive Structures in Publicly and Privately Funded Hybrid Venture Capital Funds', *Research Policy* 36(7), 913–29.

Jeng, L. and Wells, P. (2000). 'The Determinants of Venture Capital Funding: Evidence across Countries', *Journal of Corporate Finance* 6, 241–89.

Kaplan, S. N. and Lerner J. (2010). 'It Ain't Broke: The Past, Present, and Future of Venture Capital', *Journal of Applied Corporate Finance* 22(2), 36–47.

Kaplan, S. N. and Strömberg, P. (2004). 'Characteristics, Contracts, and Actions: Evidence from Venture Capitalist Analyses', *Journal of Finance* 59(5), 2177–210.

Keuschnigg, C. and Nielsen, S. B. (2003). 'Tax Policy, Venture Capital, and Entrepreneurship', *Journal of Public Economics* 87(1), 175–203.

Keuschnigg, C. and Nielsen, S. B. (2004). 'Taxation and Venture Capital Backed Entrepreneurship', *International Tax and Public Finance* 11(4), 369–90.

La Porta, R., Lopez-de-Silanes, F., Shleifer, A., and Vishny, R. W. (1997). 'Legal Determinants of External Finance', *Journal of Finance* 52(3), 1131–150.

La Porta, R., Lopez-de-Silanes, F., and Shleifer, A. (1998). 'Law and Finance', *Journal of Political Economy* 106(6), 1113–55.

Leleux, B. and Surlemont, B. (2003). 'Public Versus Private Venture Capital: Seeding or Crowding Out? A Pan-European Analysis', *Journal of Business Venturing* 18(1), 81–104.

Lerner, J. (1999). 'The Government as Venture Capitalist: The Long-Run Impact of the SBIR Program', *Journal of Business* 72(3), 285–318.

Lerner, J. (2002a). 'Boom and Bust in the Venture Capital Industry and the Impact on Innovation', *Federal Reserve Bank of Atlanta Economic Review* 4, 25–39.

Lerner, J. (2002b). 'When Bureaucrats Meet Entrepreneurs: The Design of Effective 'Public Venture Capital', *Programs Economic Journal, Royal Economic Society* 112(477), F73–F84.

Lerner, J. (2009). *Boulevard of Broken Dreams.* Princeton, NJ: Princeton University Press.

Library House (2006). *Beyond the Chasm: The Venture-Backed Report—UK—2006.* Cambridge: Library House.

Maier, J. B., II, and Walker, D. A. (1987). 'The Role of Venture Capital in Financing Small Business', *Journal of Business Venturing* 2(3), 207–14.

Manigart, S., De Waele, K., Wright, M., Robbie, K., Sapienza, H., Desbrières, P., and Beekman, A. (2002). 'Determinants of Required Return in Venture Capital Investments: A Five Country Study', *Journal of Business Venturing* 17(4), 291–312.

Mason, C. and Harrison, R. (2003). 'Closing the Regional Equity Gap? A Critique of the Department of Trade and Industry's Regional Venture Capital Funds Initiative', *Regional Studies* 37(8), 855–68.

Maula, M. and Murray, G. C. (2003). *Finnish Industry Investment Ltd: An International Evaluation.* Helsinki: Ministry of Trade and Industry.

Meyer, T. and Mathonet, P. Y. (2005). *Beyond the J-Curve: Managing a Portfolio of Venture Capital and Private Equity Funds*. Chichester: Wiley Finance.

Murray, G. C. (1994). 'The Second Equity Gap: Exit Problems for Seed and Early-Stage Venture Capitalists and Their Investee Companies', *International Small Business Journal* 12(4), 59–76.

Murray, G. C. (1996). The Relevance of 'New Technology Based Firms' and Related Support Mechanisms to the Commercialisation of Australia's Federal Research & Development Activities. Report to the Industrial Research & Development Board, Department of Industry Science and Technology, Canberra.

Murray, G. C. (2007). 'Venture Capital and Government Policy', in H. Landström (ed.), *Handbook of Research on Venture Capital*, pp. 113–51. Cheltenham: Edward Elgar.

Murray, G. C., Hyytinen, A., and Maula, M. (2009). 'Growth Entrepreneurship and Finance', in *Evaluation of the Finnish National Innovation System*, pp. 147–202. Helsinki: Ministry of Education & Ministry of Employment and the Economy.

Murray, G. C. and Marriott, R. (1998). 'Why has the Investment Performance of Technology-Specialist, European Venture Capital Funds been so Poor?', *Research Policy* 27(9), 947–76.

Myers, S. C. (1984). 'The Capital Structure Puzzle', *Journal of Finance* 39, 575–92.

Myers, S. C. and Majluf, N. (1984). 'Corporate Financing and Investment Decisions When Firms Have Information Investors Do Not Have', *Journal of Financial Economics* 13, 187–221.

National Investment Council (1995). *Financing Growth*. Canberra: National Investment Council.

Nightingale, P., Baden-Fuller, C., Cowling, M., Dannreuther, C., Hopkins, M., Mason, C., Murray, G. C., and Siepel, J. (2009). *From Funding Gaps to Thin Markets: The UK Support for Early-Stage Venture Capital in the 21st Century*. London: BVCA and NESTA.

OECD (1997). *Government Venture Capital for Technology-Based Firms: OCDE/GD (97) 201*. Paris: Organization for Economic Co-operation and Development.

OECD (2004). *Venture Capital: Trends and Policy Recommendations*. Paris: Science Technology Industry, Organization for Economic Co-operation and Development.

OECD (2006). *The SME Financing Gap: Theory and Evidence*. Paris: Organization for Economic Co-operation and Development.

Pierrakis, Y. (2010). *Venture Capital: Now and After the Dotcom Crash*. London: NESTA.

Poterba, J. M. (1989a). 'Tax Reform and the Market for Tax-Exempt Debt', *Regional Science and Urban Economics* 19(3), 537–62.

Poterba, J. M. (1989b). 'Lifetime Incidence and the Distributional Burden of Excise Taxes', *American Economic Review* 79(2), 325–30.

Revest, V. and Sapio, A. (2010). 'Financing Technology-Based Small Firms in Europe: What Do We Know?', *Small Business Economics* 35, 1–27.

Ritter, J. R. and Welch, I. (2002). 'A Review of IPO Activity, Pricing, and Allocations', *Journal of Finance* 57(4), 1795–828.

Sahlman, W. A. (1990). 'The Structure and Governance of Venture Capital Organizations', *Journal of Financial Economics* 27, 473–521.

Sohl, J. E. (2003). 'The Private Equity Market in the USA: Lessons from Volatility', *Venture Capital: An International Journal of Entrepreneurial Finance* 5(1), 29–46.

Stiglitz, J. E. and Weiss, A. (1981). 'Credit Rationing in Markets with Imperfect Information', *American Economic Review* 71(3), 393–410.

Timmons, J. A. and Bygrave, W. D. (1986). 'Venture Capital's Role in Financing Innovation for Economic Growth', *Journal of Business Venturing* 1(2), 161–76.

Westhead, P. and Storey, D. J. (1997). 'Financial Constraints on the Growth of High Technology Small Firms in the United Kingdom', *Applied Financial Economics* 7, 197–201.

Wong, P., Yuen, P., and Autio, E. (2005). 'Entrepreneurship, Innovation and Economic Growth: Evidence from GEM Data', *Small Business Economics* 24, 335–46.

CHAPTER 9

....

HOW TO MAKE 'SMART' INNOVATION-LED GROWTH ALSO 'INCLUSIVE' GROWTH

....

MARIANA MAZZUCATO

9.1 INTRODUCTION

....

FOR an 'innovation union' to emerge, 'systems' of innovation are needed so that new knowledge and innovation can diffuse throughout the European economy. *Systems* and eco-systems of innovation (sectoral, regional, and national) require the presence of dynamic links between the different *actors* and institutions (such as firms, financial institutions, research/education, public sector funds, and other intermediary institutions) as well as horizontal links *within* organizations and institutions (Freeman, 1995). What, however, has not been given enough attention in the debate about the different actors and institutions required for innovation-led growth is the exact role that each actor in the system plays along the 'bumpy' and complex *risk landscape* (Mazzucato, 2013a). Considering these roles more explicitly allows us to reflect on the degree to which the division of labour in risk-taking is matched by a division of rewards, which one would expect if there is a *risk-return* relationship. Such analysis of roles also helps us to better understand whether the eco-system is creating the right incentives. Is it the case that because some actors are putting in a lot, other actors have been given fewer incentives to do their share?

Market failure theory discusses 'risk' in terms of the 'wedge' between private and social returns, which may arise from the 'public' nature of goods (which limits the ability of private actors to appropriate returns), and different types of externalities (Laffont, 2008). This is the classical argument that justifies state spending on basic research (Nelson, 1959; Arrow, 1962). However, *mission oriented* investments, which make up about 75 per cent of public sector investments in innovation in many advanced economies, cannot be understood within the market failure perspective. Missions, from putting a man on the moon to developing the internet (which was done in DARPA, an agency of the US Department of Defense), involve both basic and applied research, and are driven not by the dynamics of the private/social 'wedge' but by direct objectives of the government (Foray et al., 2012). Indeed, the very heavy funding of the US pharmaceutical industry arises from the US government mission, through its National Institutes of Health (NIH), to 'seek fundamental knowledge about the nature and behaviour of living systems and the application of that knowledge to enhance health, lengthen life, and reduce the burdens of illness and disability' (NIH, 2014: online). The budget of the NIH has reached $400 billion over the last decade, with $31 billion in 2012 (see Figure 9.1).

At a more micro level, Block and Keller (2011a) find that between 1971 and 2006, 77 out of the most *important* 88 innovations (rated by *R&D Magazine*'s annual awards) were fully dependent on federal support, especially, but not only, in the early phases. Moreover, all major 'general purpose technologies', from aviation to the internet, owe their core funding to the public sector (Ruttan, 2006). Far from the often-heard criticisms of the state potentially 'crowding out' private investments, such bold 'mission oriented' public investments (amongst a network of decentralized actors) created new opportunities, which were then seized by private initiative (Mazzucato, 2013a).

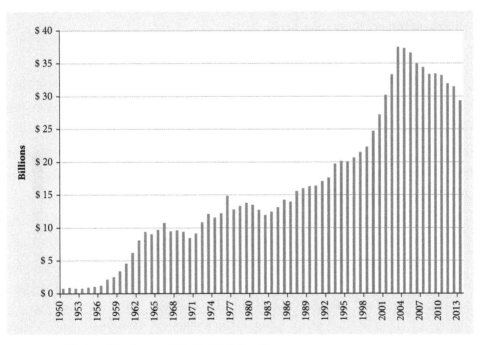

FIGURE 9.1 National Institutes of Health R&D Funding.
Source: <http://officeofbudget.od.nih.gov/approp_hist.html> (courtesy of William Lazonick)

These examples are important because it is often argued that what is missing in Europe is the availability of *private* finance willing to fund the radical technologies, as well as the specific phases in which risk is highest, such as the 'death valley' stage of the innovation cycle. Yet what is not said is that private finance works especially well when it rides the wave of state investments, as it has done in the US. All the major technologies that make the iPhone so 'smart' have been funded by public sector organizations: GPS, the internet, touch screen display, and even the latest voice activated personal assistant 'SIRI'—all owe their funding to the state (Mazzucato, 2013a). 'Geniuses' like Steve Jobs, and the presence of private VC, are fundamental, but without state funding of (or guaranteeing early demand for) both basic and applied research in the core radical technologies, it is not clear whether the VC model would work at all, and whether individuals like Jobs would have much to add their 'design' talent to.

And it is not only about research. While many associate risk-capital with either business angels or VC, in reality in many countries, including in the US's Silicon Valley, it has been public not private funds that have filled the high-risk funding gap. In the US, the SBIR programme, which began in 1982, provides almost $2.5 billion annually to small firms. It is administered by eleven government agencies and divided between phase 1 ($150,000) and 2 ($1 million). And as VC has become increasingly short-termist, pursuing returns in a three- to five-year period, the SBIR programme has had to step up and fund firms that VC is too risk averse for (Figure 9.2) (Block and Keller, 2011a). Pisano (2006) has argued that the short-termism of venture capital makes it an inappropriate model to drive innovation in science-based sectors, such as biotech, nanotech, and today's clean-tech, which require much longer time horizons.

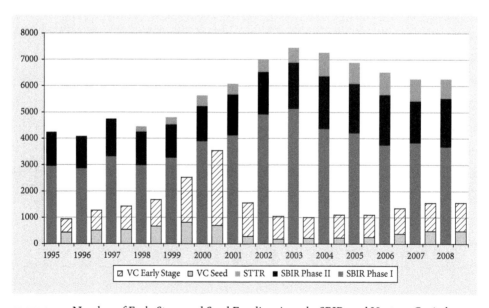

FIGURE 9.2 Number of Early Stage and Seed Funding Awards, SBIR, and Venture Capital.

Source: Keller and Block, 2013

9.2 A DYSFUNCTIONAL ECO-SYSTEM: SOCIALIZED RISK, PRIVATIZED REWARDS?

Interestingly, one of the results of this eco-system in which the state plays a leading role beyond that which has been attributed to it by either the market failure perspective or the national systems of innovation perspective (which focuses on 'system failures') has been a fall in the investments actually made by private firms in the innovation process. As argued by Angell (2005), the NIH has been much more 'risk-taking' than private large pharmaceutical companies, with up to 75 per cent of the most radical new drugs (new molecular entities with 'priority' rating) emerging from public, not private, labs. Yet, as the NIH has been spending more and more on the knowledge base that underpins the biotech and pharmaceutical industry, the large pharma companies themselves have been spending an increasing amount on repurchasing their own stock. In 2011, along with $6.2 billion in dividends, Pfizer repurchased $9 billion in stock, equivalent to 90 per cent of its net income and 99 per cent of its R&D expenditures. Amgen, the largest dedicated biopharma company, has repurchased stock in every year since 1992, for a total of $42.2 billion up to 2011, including $8.3 billion in 2011 alone. Since 2002 the cost of Amgen's stock repurchases has surpassed the company's R&D expenditure in every year except 2004, and for the period 1992–2011 was equal to fully 115 per cent of R&D outlays and 113 per cent of net income (Lazonick and Tulum, 2011).

The problem is widely diffused: in the last decade, Fortune 500 companies have spent $3 billion in share buybacks (Lazonick and Mazzucato, 2013). While they claim that this is due to the lack of new opportunities, the reality is that the most expensive (e.g. capital intensive) investments in new opportunities (with high market and technological risk) are being made by the public sector. In this sense, the problem is not one of 'crowding out' as is sometimes argued—because in fact the state is investing in areas that the private sector has chosen not to invest in.

Unfortunately the same problem seems to be appearing now in the emerging clean-technology sector (Mazzucato, 2013a). On the one hand, in 2010, the US American Energy Innovation Council (AEIC) asked the US government to increase its spending on clean technology threefold to $16 billion annually, with an additional $1 billion given to the Advanced Research Projects Agency for Energy (ARPA-E). On the other hand, they have together spent $237 billion on stock repurchases between 2001 and 2010 (Hopkins and Lazonick, 2012: 44). What is required today for the 'green' revolution to occur, is for more symbiotic public private partnerships: where, in the energy sector, are the equivalent of the Xerox Parcs and Bell Labs, which in the 1960s co-invested with the state in the difficult but exciting 'missions' of the future?

But the question arises whether this heavy funding has allowed big corporations to think they can earn the same or even higher profits while themselves putting in fewer resources into innovation. Pharmaceutical companies have publicly announced their rethinking of whether they need to be doing basic research at all, given that most of their knowledge comes from either small biotech or publicly funded labs (or publicly funded research in private/public universities). And they react with their feet, with companies like Pfizer closing down labs in countries where there is less public R&D (e.g. the UK, where the R&D/GDP ratio is low), going to countries where there is more (US, with a 2.7 per cent R&D/GDP and heavy NIH funding).

The widespread myth that the private sector (markets) is both more efficient than the state and the key source of innovation-led growth results in a system where the risks of investing in innovation are socialized but the rewards are privatized. In this system, 'smart growth' does not result in 'inclusive growth': indeed, the long-term trend in modern capitalism has been one of increasing inequality between people, countries, and regions, with deleterious consequences to societal welfare and environmental sustainability (Wilkinson and Pickett, 2009; Piketty, 2014). Some authors (e.g. Acemoglu, 2002) argue that the issue is that technological change is 'skill biased', so that skilled personnel are rewarded above unskilled labour, which in the extreme is excluded from the system. What the 'skill-biased technological change' perspective fails to explain is where skills come from: in this theory, 'skill' is an exogenous factor. Other authors (Hacker and Pierson, 2011) analysed the politics of 'winners take all', in which policies (e.g. capital tax breaks) make the rich richer, while squeezing the middle and labour classes. In Lazonick and Mazzucato (2013) we go one step further and identify the mechanisms behind 'winners take all' policies, providing an alternative explanation that takes into account the generation of skills and knowledge. We argue that the uncertain, cumulative, and collective characteristics of the innovation process (which generates skills, knowledge, and technical change) make possible a disconnection between risks and rewards. Often, actors (such as private venture capital funds and business managers) that contribute less than others (such as the state and workers) to the innovation process are able to reap a return on their investments that is higher than the risk they assumed. This leads to increasing inequality between different actors involved in the innovation process, because certain actors manage to position themselves at the point where the innovative enterprise generates financial returns (e.g. close to the final product market or to the financial market) (Lazonick and Mazzucato, 2013: 1105–17).

Correcting this dysfunctional system is essential if we want to prevent happening in greentech the same dynamic that has characterized areas like biotech. The biotechnology industry is one where most of the VC backed companies remain productless yet make much money for the venture capitalists when they exit via an IPO. So if the state is very important for funding high risk investments in innovation, and, given the commonly accepted relationship between risks and returns in finance, it could be argued that more thinking is required on whether and how the state should earn back a more direct return on its risky investments. That is, rather than worrying so much about the *picking winners* problem (whether the state is able or not to pick successful technologies, firms, and sectors), more thinking is needed about how to reward the winning investments so they can cover some of the eventual losses—which are inevitable as innovation is so deeply uncertain, in the Knightian sense (Knight, 1921). Put provocatively, had the state earned even just 1 per cent from the investments it made in the internet, there would be much more today to invest in greentech (Mazzucato, 2013a). Or put another way, is it right that the National Science Foundation, which funded the algorithm behind Google, received nothing back when Google made billions (Block and Keller, 2011b)?

Many argue that it is inappropriate to consider direct returns to the state because the state already indirectly earns on its investments via the taxation system. There are three arguments against this reasoning: (1) tax evasion (legal and illegal) is common and realistically will not disappear; (2) corporate income tax and capital gains tax have been falling as a proportion of income; (3) global movements of capital mean that the particular region (which could also include the European Union) funding the innovation might not reap the benefits in terms of local job creation, so that the taxation question remains an open question (see the case of Apple discussed in the next paragraph); and (4) investments in innovation are different from spending, on say education. The former embody a great degree of risk, similar to that experienced by private venture capital, with one in ten investments earning a return. If the state is being asked to make such investments (which it undoubtedly has been making and increasingly so), it is necessary for it to cover its inevitable losses when those arise.

The case of Apple Inc. is a case in point. Apple received its early stage funding from the US government's SBIR programme, and, as pointed out before, all the technologies which make the iPhone 'smart' are also state funded (Mazzucato, 2013a: 165–78). Yet Apple has employed commonly used accounting practices, which have resulted in a much lower tax bill for the US government. According to Duhigg and Kocieniewski (2012), in order to avoid taxes, Apple formed a subsidiary in Reno, Nevada, where there is no corporate income or capital gain tax. Creatively naming the company Braeburn Capital, Apple used it to channel a portion of its US sales instead of including them in the revenues it reported in California, where its headquarters are located. Apple reportedly saved $2.5-billion in taxes with this scheme—a very large amount, particularly if compared to the $9.2 billion state deficit California experienced in 2009. In other words, the entire state budget deficit would have been significantly reduced (by more than 25 per cent) if Apple had fully reported its US revenues in the state where a significant portion of its value (discovery, design, sales, marketing, etc.) was created and achieved (Duhigg and Kocieniewski, 2012).

This story is not about bashing Apple or to argue that what it does with the technologies funded by the state is trivial—in fact, the kinds of *architectural* innovations that Apple continuously develops is one of the most radical types of innovation, as it departs from established technologies and systems of production, and creates new linkages to markets and users, which in turn defines the technical and marketing agenda that guides subsequent product development (Abernathy and Clark, 1985). The story is about highlighting the fact that the tax system is currently not working for recouping investments, in this case both by the state of California and the Federal government, in risky and uncertain innovation. And the problem is structural: as argued by Lazonick et al. (2013), avoiding taxes or promoting share-buybacks programmes (as announced by Apple in April 2013) are the symptoms of Apple's embracing shareholder-value ideology, which resulted in the adoption of a new financialized business model.

Reinforcing or reforming the tax system is therefore a red herring. The real problem is the financialization of the real sector (Krippner, 2005; Dore, 2008). In this sense, financial reform proposals need to include considerations as to how to de-financialize real economy companies, in order to reward value creation activities over value extraction activities (Mazzucato and Shipman, 2014). Such reform entails creating new financial structures that support the capital development of the economy (i.e. long-term committed financial capital), and also penalizing speculative practices that simply extract value and causes innovation-led growth to lead to a less equitable and highly unstable economy (Mazzucato, 2013b). And it is crucial to remember that even if companies were paying their fair share of tax, tax rates themselves have been falling, often from pressure of the ' innovators'. From 1976 to 1981 alone, after heavy lobbying from the Natural Venture Capital Association, the capital gains tax rate in the United States fell from 40 per cent to 20 per cent. And in the name of bringing Silicon Valley's dynamism to the United Kingdom, in 2001, the government of British Prime Minister Tony Blair reduced the time that private-equity funds have to be invested to be eligible for tax reductions from ten years to two years. It is only by rethinking the more collective contributions made by different actors—public and private—that such lobbying can be diminished, and the tax system itself become a better mechanism for receiving returns for public investment.

9.3 Reaping a (Direct) Return

Where technological breakthroughs have occurred as a result of targeted state interventions, there is potential for the state, over time, to reap some of the financial rewards by retaining ownership over a small proportion of the intellectual property created. This is not to say the state should ever have exclusive licence or hold a large enough proportion of the value of an innovation that it deters a wider spread of its application (and this has never been the case)—the role of government is not to run commercial enterprises but to spark innovation elsewhere. But government should explore whether it is possible to own a slither of the value it has created, which over time could generate significantly higher value and then be reinvested into growth generating investments.

For example, as discussed briefly above, in the US three-quarters of the new molecular bio-pharmaceutical entities owe their creation to publicly funded laboratories. Yet in the past ten years, the top ten companies in this industry have made more in profits than the rest of the Fortune 500 companies combined. The industry also enjoys great tax advantages: its R&D costs are deductible, and so are many of its massive marketing expenses, some of which are counted as R&D (Angell, 2005). After taking on most of the R&D bill, the state often gives away the outputs at a rock bottom rate. For instance, Taxol, the cancer drug discovered by the NIH, is sold by Bristol-Myers Squibb for $20,000 per year's dose, 20 times (!) the manufacturing cost. Yet the company agreed to pay the NIH only 0.5 per cent in royalties for the drug.

Similarly, where an applied technological breakthrough is directly financed by the government, it should in return be able to extract a small royalty from its application.

Again, this should not be sufficient for prohibiting its dissemination throughout the economy, or to disincentivize the innovators from taking the risk in the first place. Instead, it makes the policy of spending taxpayers' money to light the innovative spark more sustainable, by enabling part of the financial gains from so doing to be recycled directly back into the programme over time.

There are various possibilities for considering a direct return to the state for its investments in innovation. One is to make sure loans and guarantees that are handed out by the state to business do not come without strings attached. Loans and grants could have conditions, like income contingent loans, similar to that of *student loans*. If and when a company makes profits above a certain threshold, after it has received a loan/grant from the state, it should be required to pay back a portion. This is of course not rocket science but it goes against some deep-seated assumptions. And currently, with budget deficits under so much pressure, it is no longer possible to ignore the issue.

Another possibility for obtaining a direct return is the state retaining equity in the companies that it supports. This does in fact occur in some countries, such as Finland, where SITRA, one of Finland's public funding agencies, retained equity in its early stage investments in Nokia. These are exactly the type of early stage investments that VC has increasingly shied away from. But state equity in private companies is feared in countries such as the US and the UK (and other countries copying the Anglo-Saxon model) for fear that the next step is communism. Yet the most successful capitalist economies have had active states, making such risky investments, and we have been too quick to criticize them when things go wrong (e.g. Concorde) and too slow to reward them when things go right (e.g. the internet).

Other than income contingent loans, and retained equity, there is of course a more direct tool—a state investment bank. Indeed, while many have argued the importance of a state investment bank for the needs of counter-cyclical lending (Skidelsky et al., 2011), another reason why they are important is precisely to reap a return in order to fund future investments. In 2012 KfW, the German state investment bank, reported €2.2 billion in profits (KfW, 2013), while most private banks are in the red, with many experiencing falling profits. And, if/when the state institution is run by people who not only believe in the power of the state but also have the expertise around innovation, then the result produces a high reward. An interesting example is the Brazilian national development bank BNDES, which has been actively investing in innovation in both cleantech and biotechnology, while making hefty profits from its investments. In 2010 it made 21 per cent return on equity (ROE) (which accrued also from investments in other sectors than cleantech and biotech), most of which was reinvested by the treasury into the economy (e.g. in health and education). A percentage retained by BNDES goes to a technology fund to be reinvested in key new sectors, focusing, for example, on the Death Valley stage of biotechnology in which private VC is markedly absent.

Thus rather than worrying so much about the *picking winners* problem, more thinking is needed about how to reward the winning investments so they can both cover some of the eventual losses (which are inevitable in the innovation game) and also raise funds for future investments. Going hand in hand with this consideration is the need to rethink how public investments are accounted for in national income accounting. Investments in innovation are different from administrative expenditures: the latter does not add to balance-sheet assets; the former does and is potentially productive investment in the sense that it creates new value (Mazzucato and Shipman, 2014). When setting limits to fiscal deficits, it is therefore necessary to distinguish public debt contracted for investment in R&D and infrastructure (value-creating investments) from public debt contract for (public or private) consumption. In this sense, financial and accounting reforms should be regarded as an essential prerequisite for any successful smart and inclusive growth plan. Indeed, these reforms and innovation policy must be thought through together, something that is not done in most Western countries (Mazzucato, 2013b).

9.4 Conclusion

Understanding the state as lead risk-taker opens the question about how such risk-taking can reap a return. While many commentators and analysts have been quick to blame the government when it fails to 'pick winners', the same people have been much less quick to praise it when it succeeds. It is argued here that a framework is required both for understanding the risk-taking (beyond the risk-averseness argument in the market failure approach) and for understanding how the collective system of innovation (emphasized by the national systems of innovation approach) maps into a system of rewards. More research should be devoted to examining how to reward upstream and downstream public investments in the innovation chain, as such policies need to take into consideration the 'market shaping and creating' function of public investments, which will inevitably result in many failures due to the inherent uncertainty in the innovation process. Reaping a reward on the upside, to cover downside losses, needs to be adapted to idiosyncratic geographic, historical, and cultural conditions. The importance of establishing a system of rewards to state investments is also to legitimize before the public the visible hand of the state in the innovation process. Consequently, getting the balance right between risks and rewards will make the objective of smart and inclusive growth less about spin and more about concrete mechanisms.

References

Abernathy, W. J. and Clark, K. B. (1985). 'Innovation: Mapping the winds of creative destruction', *Research Policy*, 14(1), 3–22.

Acemoglu, D. (2002). 'Technical Change, Inequality, and the Labor Market', *Journal of Economic Literature* 40(1), 7–72.

Angell, M. (2005). *The Truth About The Drug Companies: How They Deceive Us and What To Do About It.* New York: Random House.

Arrow, K. (1962). 'Economic Welfare and the Allocation of Resources for Invention', in R. R. Nelson (ed.), *The Rate and Direction of Inventive Activity*, pp. 609–26. Princeton, NJ: Princeton University Press.

Block, F. and Keller, M. R. (2011a). *Where do Innovations Come From? Transformations in the US Economy, 1970–2006*. TUT Ragnar Nurkse School of Innovation and Governance, Technology Governance and Economic Dynamics Working Papers No. 35.

Block, F. L. and Keller, M. R. (2011b). *State of Innovation: The US Government's Role in Technology Development*. Boulder, CO: Paradigm Publishers.

Dore, R. (2008). 'Financialization of the Global Economy', *Industrial and Corporate Change* 17(6), 1097–112.

Duhigg, C. and Kocieniewski, D. (2012). 'How Apple Sidesteps Billions in Taxes', *The New York Times iEconomy Series*, 28 April.

Foray, D., Mowery, D., and Nelson, R. R. (2012). 'Public R&D and Social Challenges: What Lessons From Mission R&D Programs?', *Research Policy* 41(10), 1697–902.

Freeman, C. (1995). 'The "National System of Innovation" in Historical Perspective', *Cambridge Journal of Economics* 19(1), 5–24.

Hacker, J. S. and Pierson, P. (2011). *Winner-Take-All Politics: How Washington Made the Rich Richer—and Turned Its Back on the Middle Class*. New York: Simon and Schuster.

Hopkins, M. and Lazonick, W. (2012). 'Soaking Up the Sun and Blowing in the Wind: Renewable Energy Needs Patient Capital'. *Ford Foundation Conference on Finance, Business Models, and Sustainable Prosperity*. New York: Ford Foundation.

Keller, M. R. and Block, F. (2013). Explaining the Transformation in the US Innovation System: The Impact of a Small Government Program. *Socio-Economic Review* 11(4), 629–56.

KfW. (2013). *Annual Report 2012*. Frankfurt am Main: KfW Bankengruppe.

Knight, F. H. (1921). *Risk, Uncertainty and Profit*. New York: Augustus M. Kelley.

Krippner, G. R. (2005). 'The Financialization of the American Economy', *Socio-Economic Review* 3(2), 173–208.

Laffont, J.-J. (2008). 'Externalities', in S. N. Durlauf and L. E. Blume (eds) *The New Palgrave Dictionary of Economics Online*, 2nd edn. New York: Palgrave Macmillan.

Lazonick, W. and Mazzucato, M. (2013). 'The Risk-Reward Nexus in the Innovation-Inequality Relationship: Who Takes the Risks? Who Gets the Rewards?', *Industrial and Corporate Change* 22(4), 1093–128.

Lazonick, W., Mazzucato, M., and Tulum, Ö. (2013). 'Apple's Changing Business Model: What Should the World's Richest Company Do With All Those Profits?', *Accounting Forum* 37(4), 249–67.

Lazonick, W. and Tulum, Ö. (2011). 'US Biopharmaceutical Finance and the Sustainability of the Biotech Business Model', *Research Policy* 40(9), 1170–87.

Mazzucato, M. (2013a). *The Entrepreneurial State: Debunking the Public vs. Private Myth in Risk and Innovation*. London: Anthem Press.

Mazzucato, M. (2013b). 'Financing Innovation: Creative Destruction vs. Destructive Creation', *Industrial and Corporate Change* 22(4), 851–67.

Mazzucato, M. and Shipman, A. (2014). 'Accounting for Productive Investment and Value Creation', *Industrial and Corporate Change* 23(4), 1059–85.

Nelson, R. (1959). 'The Simple Economics of Basic Scientific Research', *The Journal of Political Economy*, 67(3), 297–306.

NIH. 2014. *Mission*. <http://www.nih.gov/about/mission.htm>.

Piketty, T. (2014). *Capital in the Twenty-First Century*. Cambridge, MA: Harvard University Press.

Pisano, G. P. (2006). 'Can Science Be a Business? Lessons from Biotech', *Harvard Business Review* October, 114–25.

Ruttan, V. (2006). *Is War Necessary for Economic Growth? Military Procurement and Technology Development*. Minnesota: University of Minnesota, Department of Applied Economics.

Skidelsky, R., Martin, F., and Wigstrom, C. W. (2011). *Blueprint for a British Investment Bank*. London: Centre for Global Studies.

Wilkinson, R. G., and Pickett, K. (2009). *The Spirit Level: Why Greater Equality Makes Societies Stronger*. New York: Bloomsbury.

PART 3

....

EMPLOYMENT ISSUES AND INDUSTRIAL POLICY

....

SKILLS AND TRAINING FOR A MORE INNOVATION-INTENSIVE ECONOMY

FRANCIS GREEN AND GEOFF MASON

10.1 INTRODUCTION: THE NEED FOR A SKILLS STRATEGY

A successful system for skills development and utilization is a basic ingredient for economies and nations to grow and maintain the competitiveness of their workplaces. It is also crucial for the cohesion of societies, including the limitation of income inequalities and social exclusion. The need for a strategy arises because the skill needs of modern societies are changing and education systems are expanding. The pace of these changes implies that piecemeal, ad hoc adjustments to vocational education and training systems, and normal business evolutions, risk the creation of skills mismatches and inefficiencies in the system that can be greatly detrimental to economic and social well-being. In this chapter we argue that, when introducing a progressive industrial strategy, the need for an effective skills strategy is especially pressing.

Among the principal aims of a new industrial policy will be a rebalancing between manufacturing and service sectors and a shift towards higher value added activities in both old and new industries. New product and process innovations will be central to any such shifts in production structure. Industrial policy design in the UK needs to confront a level of research and innovation activity which appears to be markedly lower than in many other countries which the UK is urged to emulate (Hughes and Mina, 2012). The relatively low proportion of firms with innovative capacity in the UK has hampered efforts to emulate successful foreign programmes of support and restricts the potential to operate successful home-grown programmes such as SMART (formerly Grants for Research and Development) and Knowledge Transfer Partnerships (KTPs) on a larger scale than has been achieved so far (Mason and Nathan, 2014). The premise of this chapter is that a new industrial policy, if it is to be effective in improving UK economic performance, needs to encourage higher levels of innovation by firms. In particular, the policy must encourage a sizeable number of firms who do not currently engage in innovation to start doing so.

In this chapter we focus on what skills such firms need if they are to become more innovative, and we discuss what changes in training policy and institutions might help develop those skills.[1] The chapter proceeds as follows. In Section 10.2 we identify in general terms the skills needed to improve innovative performance. We proceed in Section 10.3 with a picture of skills and training trends in the UK, in which we identify the core of the problem facing British workplaces to be a 'skills deficit'—a relatively low level of employer demand for skills as well as relatively low levels of skills supply—that might be expected in an economy with relatively low levels of innovation and investment. Section 10.4 then presents an approach to skills policymaking that would be more appropriate for an economy with an innovation-orientated industrial strategy.

10.2 THE SKILLS NEEDED FOR IMPROVED INNOVATION PERFORMANCE

We use the term 'innovation' in a broad sense, conceived to include research and development (R&D) activities, the introduction of new products and processes, marketing methods, business practices, workplace organization or external relations—any such thing which is new to the firm (OECD/Eurostat, 2005, p. 46). Estimates derived from the UK Innovation Survey 2011 suggest that, between 2008 and 2010, only 39 per cent of UK firms were engaged in any innovative activity (BIS, 2013a). In total, just under one in five firms had introduced new products, and one in ten firms had implemented new or significantly improved processes.

What influence do skills have on innovative performance? In recent reviews, the Organisation for Economic Co-operation and Development (OECD) (2011a) find evidence of positive associations between firms' involvement in innovation and proxy measures of skill such as workforce qualifications while Jones and Grimshaw (2012) find similar positive links between innovative performance and expenditures on training. Skilled people are likely to be well placed to generate new ideas and knowledge relevant to innovation, make improvements to existing products and processes, and adapt to changing circumstances. However, skills and training are not sufficient in themselves to enhance innovative performance. Rather, they may contribute positively to innovation when they are combined with other important production inputs such as investments in

---

[1] We use 'skills' in a broad sense, covering all levels and types (including knowledge), defined as personal characteristics that add value and can themselves be invested in (Green, 2013, ch. 2).

physical capital (e.g. machinery and equipment), in capacity for research, design and development, and in organizational capital (e.g. improvements in work organization and other business practices and processes).

Many of the key mechanisms by which skills influence innovative performance are connected with new technologies. US evidence suggests that skills play a key role in facilitating the effective utilization of Information and Communication Technologies (ICTs) and that there has been a complementarity over several decades between ICTs and the educated labour required to perform non-routine tasks (Bresnahan et al., 2002; Autor et al., 2003). A number of studies in European countries have also found evidence of a positive relationship between workforce skills and the adoption of ICTs (for example, Hollenstein, 2004; Bayo-Moriones and Lera-López, 2007; Green, 2012). The principal mechanisms involved are that high skilled workers can contribute more than low skilled workers to the selection, installation, operation, and maintenance of ICTs and also to the adaptation of ICTs to firm-specific requirements.

Other important mechanisms by which skills may affect innovative performance include knowledge transfer processes (Lundvall, 1992), the mobility of highly qualified engineers and scientists between firms (Saxenian, 1994; Mason et al., 2004), and foreign direct investment (FDI). These processes are often self-reinforcing: for example, FDI is attracted to economies with a high skills base while simultaneously bringing with it new technologies and knowledge which augment the skills base of host countries (Barrell and Pain, 1997; Blomstrom and Kokko, 2003).

Skills are an essential ingredient of firms' 'absorptive capacity'—their ability to identify and make effective use of knowledge, ideas and technologies that are generated outside each firm (Cohen and Levinthal, 1989). The impact of multinational enterprises on host-country innovation is reduced if host-country firms lack such capacity. As suggested by Zahra and George (2002), it is useful to distinguish between potential absorptive capacity (the ability to acquire and assimilate external knowledge) and realized absorptive capacity (the ability to transform and apply acquired knowledge within organizations). At each stage of this process—recognizing useful external knowledge, seeing how it might be applied, and then successfully making use of it within firms—workforce skills have a key role to play. Furthermore, supply chains involving foreign investors have greater prospects of becoming 'developmental' in nature (with close collaborative relationships between supply chain partners) rather than 'dependent' (with suppliers being used primarily to cut costs) if prospective host-country suppliers are well endowed with skills.[2]

In some industries such as auto and aerospace manufacturing, the lead customers in supply chains now seek to speed up new product development times and reduce costs by requiring first-tier and second-tier suppliers to produce goods to meet performance specifications rather than to conform with blueprints (Brown, 1998; Petersen et al., 2003). This obliges suppliers to develop their own design capabilities and, for those firms

[2] For more discussion of this distinction between developmental and dependent supply chains, see Turok (1993) and Brown (2000).

with the skills base to succeed in doing so, future growth prospects may be enhanced by increased knowledge spillovers within those supply chains. Brown (2000) shows how supplier linkages of this kind contributed to rapid employment growth in high-tech firms supplying specialized services to aerospace customers in West Sweden.

Much of this evidence on the positive relationship between skills and innovation emphasizes the role of high-level skills (e.g. university graduates) rather than intermediate-level skills (e.g. technicians, craft workers and other employees with qualifications below university graduate level). However, there are a number of ways in which the skills of non-graduate workers can also contribute to innovation. For example, Toner (2011) notes that incremental innovations in products, services, processes, and modes of work organization rely heavily on workers in direct production, marketing, finance, and human resources departments who have developed new ideas through learning-by-doing in the course of their work. In countries such as Germany with well-established apprenticeship training systems, intermediate-skilled workers are particularly well equipped to make modifications and improvements to production processes and assist with bringing complex new products into commercial-scale production (Prais, 1995; Mason and Wagner, 2005).

While highly skilled employees such as professional engineers and scientists contribute disproportionately to potential absorptive capacity, through the identification and acquisition of useful external knowledge, firms' ability to apply this knowledge will depend in many ways on intermediate-skilled employees as well as on high-skilled employees. For example, there are many key support roles for technicians in product design and development areas and for craft-skilled workers in improving production processes.

In addition to assessing the mix of skill *levels* required for successful innovation, we also need to consider available evidence on the different *types* of skill which are most relevant to innovation. In general, this evidence points to a wide diversity in skill needs, reflecting the several different types of innovation which are relevant to economic performance (including, as noted above, marketing and organizational innovations as well as product and process innovations). Across different workplaces, industries, and countries, the range of skill requirements for innovation encompasses technical and practical skills, generic skills (such as communication and problem-solving skills), and managerial and entrepreneurial skills (OECD, 2011a).

Some indirect light on the different types of skill that are most likely to be in demand by firms engaging in innovation emanates from research on the labour market returns to different types of skill. In some European countries employer surveys of pay data suggest that employers place a high value on practical skills and experience which are best acquired through employment-based training such as apprenticeships (Winkelmann, 1996; Gangl, 2000; Mason, 2001; Fersterer and Winter-Ebmer, 2003). However, other researchers suggest that the innovation and performance benefits of vocational education and training (VET) may be less than those deriving from general education. For example, Krueger and Kumar (2004) develop a model of technology adoption and economic growth which suggests that specialized vocational education in some Continental European countries may be less well suited to developing the skills needed to adapt to fast-changing technologies than general or academic education which is more common in the US. In the UK this judgement is supported by evidence of a large positive wage premium attached to having studied mathematics during post-compulsory secondary education. Dolton and Vignoles (2002) argue that mathematics study at this intermediate level of education helps to develop generic skills such as logical thinking and problem-solving which are closely matched to many employers' skill requirements.

In common with the US, the use of high-level skills in the UK has been reinforced by the growth of mass higher education since the late 1980s. According to estimates derived from the Labour Force Survey, the proportion of graduates among UK persons in employment rose steadily from 14 per cent in 1993 to 31 per cent in 2013, while the proportions with intermediate-level qualifications (both vocational and general in nature) remained fairly steady.[3] In general, the fact that average returns to graduate education have held up fairly well since the early 1990s suggests that demand for graduate-level skills has largely matched the growth in graduate supply (Machin, 2003; Walker and Zhu, 2008), even though there has been some widening in the dispersion of returns to university education and there are concerns about under-utilization of some graduates' skills (Green and Zhu, 2010).

Overall, the highest salary returns to educational qualifications derive from a standard academic route through GCSEs and A levels (or their equivalents in Scotland) to Bachelor and higher degrees (McIntosh, 2006; Powdthavee and Vignoles, 2006). In the case of intermediate vocational qualifications, average returns are positive at NVQ Levels 3 and 4 even though they are not as high as returns to academic or general qualifications at the same levels. At Level 3 and above, intermediate vocational qualifications are most rewarding to people who left school without any qualifications at all. But at Level 2 returns to vocational qualifications are often very low or even zero.

However, qualifications are imperfect measures of skill. Direct evidence from other indicators shows that a more innovation-intensive economy is likely to need a wide range of types and levels of skill. In the 2013 UK Commission's Employer Skills Survey (UKCESS), as many as 71 per cent of UK establishments reported that some of their employees needed to acquire new skills or knowledge, with many of these new skill requirements deriving from innovation-related factors such as the introduction of new goods or services and new work practices and new technologies (Winterbotham et al., 2014). These skill updating needs, which were also evident for employees deemed competent to perform current tasks (i.e. most employees), were reported across a wide range of occupations but applied particularly to professionals, personal service workers, managers, and skilled trades workers (see Table 10.1). Across all occupations the main types of skill in need of improvement included technical and practical skills, planning and organizing skills, and problem-solving skills. Other priority skill updating needs included advanced IT/software skills for managers, professionals, associate professionals, and

---

[3] Population-weighted estimates derived from Labour Force Survey (Spring Quarters), 1993 and 2013.

Table 10.1 Single Occupation Most Affected by Skill Updating Needs, UK Commission's Employers Skills Survey, 2013

	Percent of establishments which employ staff in each occupation	n =
Managers	32	44,018
Professional occupations	40	8739
Associate professional and technical occupations	29	6268
Administrative and clerical occupations	12	26,945
Skilled trades occupations	31	11,811
Personal service occupations	37	6973
Sales and customer service occupations	29	13,690
Process, plant and machine operatives	21	7002
Elementary occupations	14	16,100

Source: Derived from Winterbotham et al., 2014, Figure 3.3
Base: All establishments which employ staff in each occupation

administrative and clerical workers and customer handling skills for workers in sales and elementary occupations (Winterbotham et al., 2014, Table A.3.8). In analysis of similar survey findings for 2009, the highest levels of employer demand for skills improvement and updating among existing staff were found in firms which were seeking to implement high value added product strategies (Mason, 2011).

Overall the evidence reviewed in this section implies that an industrial strategy that promotes innovation in previously non-innovative firms will entail an increased demand for skills of several types and at both intermediate and upper levels. The supply of skills will therefore need to be enhanced. In the next section, we consider to what extent the current skills system in the UK is already set on an expansionary path.

10.3 EXISTING SKILLS AND TRAINING IN THE UK: OUTCOMES AND PROBLEMS

A traditional response to the long-standing productivity problems of the British economy has been to attribute the problems to skill shortages and to an education system said to prepare students poorly for the world of work. Despite much evidence to the contrary, this misleading diagnosis recurs in modern discourse, not least because it deflects from the need to address with employers the problem of skill development at work. In reality, the issue for policy-makers is the UK's 'skills deficit', the relatively low level (by international standards) of *both* supply and demand for skills in many parts of the British economy. Correspondingly, there is also a 'training deficit', that is, a relatively low level of training supply and demand.

Conceptual clarity is important at this point. A 'skills deficit' describes where the skills being used are below the optimum, that is, the level consistent with a growing, sustainable economy at the technological frontier. A skills deficit can be indicated by comparison with good practice and outcomes observed in other, more productive, economies, though international comparisons must be interpreted with care. A 'training deficit' is where the level and quality of training are sub-optimal, defined and indicated similarly. 'Skills shortage', by contrast, is a disequilibrium concept, capturing the difference between market demand and supply. It is indicated by evidence of recruitment difficulty, where the reason for the difficulty is insufficient job applicants with the required skills. A parallel disequilibrium concept for firms' existing workforces is internal 'skills gap', where incumbent workers lack adequate skills to perform their jobs competently. It is typically indicated by managers' evaluations. The opposite of skills shortage is skilled worker unemployment, while the opposite of skills gap is employees' perceptions of skills under-utilization. Finally, there can also be a mismatch or disequilibrium in the training market, of which the most likely is a 'training barrier', whereby workers (or employers) have an unmet demand for training (Green, 2013, chs 2–4).

The conclusion that the UK has a skills deficit relative to other industrial nations—and a corresponding training deficit—derives, not from any single decisive observation, but from a patchwork of evidence drawn from a variety of sources. One source is cross-country comparisons of Human Resources in Science and Technology (HRST) which are defined broadly as 'persons having graduated at the tertiary level of education or employed in a science and technology occupation for which a high qualification is normally required and the innovation potential is high' (OECD, 2013a, p. 92). Table 10.2 focuses on professional and technician-level (associate professional) occupations and shows that HRST accounted for 37 per cent of total UK employment in 2012, below several high-innovation countries such as the US, Denmark, Sweden, Switzerland, the Netherlands, and Germany. Countries below the UK on this measure included several low-innovation Southern European nations. Another distinctive feature of HRST stocks in the UK by this measure is the relatively low share of intermediate-skilled technicians compared to that of professionals (typically university graduates).

Rising education levels in the UK in recent decades signal a lasting social change whose wider significance remains to be fully assessed. Yet education levels rose faster in many comparator economies. Moreover, forecasts of future education levels—typically based on comparisons between the education levels of younger and older cohorts—suggest that the average educational level continues to grow less rapidly than in the majority of other countries. By 2009 some 82 per cent of those aged 25-34 had attained at least upper secondary education levels, but this proportion was exceeded by 25 other countries (OECD, 2011b).

At the same time, there is evidence from the OECD's Survey of Adult Skills (SAS) in 2012 of a relatively low demand by UK employers for their employees to have educational qualifications: the proportion of jobs in England and Northern Ireland where tertiary

Table 10.2 Human Resources in Science and Technology (HRST) as a Percentage of Total Employment, 2012

	Professionals (ISCO 2)	Technicians and associate professionals (ISCO 3)	Total
Denmark	26	17	43
Sweden	25	17	42
Switzerland	24	18	42
United States	23	18	41
Norway	24	17	41
Finland	23	18	40
Netherlands	23	16	40
Germany	18	21	39
France	17	20	37
United Kingdom	24	13	37
Belgium	22	15	37
Austria	15	19	34
Ireland	22	11	34
Italy	14	17	31
Spain	17	11	28
Greece	19	8	27
Portugal	15	10	25

Source: OECD, Science, Technology, and Industry Scoreboard 2013
Note: ISCO = International Standard Classification of Occupations, 2008

qualifications are required for entry is among the lowest in the OECD. The proportion of over-qualified workers—those whose qualification level exceeds the level required for someone to be recruited to their job—is the second highest (OECD, 2013b, pp. 168–71). This comparative finding reflects the trend towards increasing over-qualification in the UK as a whole between 1986 and 2006, and which was only reversed slightly between 2006 and 2012 (Felstead et al., 2013).

This macro-level evidence is complemented by detailed sectoral studies that typically indicate relatively low levels of skills use in British industry. In this vein, a particularly influential genre was the matched-plant study: using the methodology of qualitative comparison in matched plants in comparator countries, several studies found evidence of low use and low stocks of intermediate skills in British plants (Prais, 1995). Typically, these studies also found a link between skills and productivity differences.

SAS also provides some direct evidence of relatively low skills supply which complement comparisons based solely on formal qualifications. In England and Northern Ireland numeracy proficiency is significantly below the OECD average, while literacy proficiency is close to the average. What bodes least well is that the average proficiencies of the population aged 16–24 are among the lowest of all countries. Moreover, high levels of inequality characterize the skills of the younger population in England and Northern Ireland, as well as relatively high 'social gradients' (the link between skill and parental background—an inverse indicator of social mobility) (BIS, 2013b; OECD, 2013b; Green, A. et al., 2014).

As well as an overall skill deficit, there is a deficit of management skills in Britain. Studies have shown that, on average, British managers lag behind many foreign counterparts in implementation of practices known to enhance productivity (covering four domains: operations management, performance monitoring, target setting, and talent management) (Bloom and Van Reenen, 2010; Bloom et al., 2011; BIS, 2012a, pp. 20–1). The UK average management score for use of eighteen management practices trailed behind the North American and most Northern European countries, while exceeding those in Southern European countries and a number of developing countries. Moreover, practices were found to vary substantially within the same industry and country, and there is a relatively long tail of poorly managed firms in the UK. The achieved education level of managers, in particular, was found to be a significant determinant of whether managers adopted effective practices. Many British managers were found to lack key skills, to fail to use their skills strategically, and to receive inadequate training provision. Specific problems included gaps in managers' awareness of the value of management skills or of management training, their ability to self-assess their capacities, and their knowledge of many good management practices.

While skills are on average relatively low in the UK compared with more innovative economies, there is little evidence that this takes the form of systematic skill shortages or internal skills gaps. In 2013 only 4 per cent of UK firms reported vacancies that were hard to fill for skills reasons, while only 15 per cent of firms reported internal skill gaps. Overall, internal skill gaps concerned only an estimated 5 per cent of the total UK workforce (Winterbotham et al., 2014). Both these disequilibrium measures are partly linked to the large proportion of UK firms that do not have high skill requirements because, as noted in Section 10.2, they tend to be engaged in low-skill low-innovation activities. Thus, the real skill problems for the UK concern the overall skills deficit relative to other more productive and innovative nations.

How far does employer-provided training in the UK go towards rectifying this overall skills deficit? Much of the criticism of existing employer training provision over recent decades has focused on apprenticeships and training for intermediate skill levels. Successive governments have made attempts to revive apprenticeships as a mode of skills development, following its decline in the 1970s and early 1980s. Apprenticeships compete as a lifecourse choice with going to university, however, and the decision to favour the expansion of higher education in the late 1980s and early 1990s was never going to encourage the apprenticeship route. After higher education became relatively more expensive renewed attempts were made to encourage apprenticeships. However, while the rhetoric typically refers to the problem of persuading bright young people to choose the vocational route, in reality the constraint is on the demand side with applicant numbers for good-quality apprenticeships far exceeding the number of trainee places.[4] 'Good' apprenticeships are those providing a substantive training of two years or more and leading to a recognized membership of, and identification with, an occupation.

The picture of training in the workforce as a whole is also not encouraging. In the 1990s and up to the early 2000s there was a rising trend in the participation rate in job-related training in the UK, reaching a peak of 15 per cent of employees in 2001. The subsequent decade saw a reversal, with participation falling to 13 per cent. Moreover, there was also an ongoing substantial decline since at least the mid-1990s in the duration of training episodes. In the mid-1990s about a third of all training episodes lasted less than a week; by 2012 this proportion had risen to one half. The net effect is that the average volume of training—in terms of days per employee—is estimated to have fallen by about a half between the mid-1990s and 2012 (Green et al., 2013). This decline took place across the board, but was most marked for those in younger age groups, those at lower levels of prior education, and those living in Northern Ireland. Relative to comparator countries in the OECD, the short duration of training is also in evidence: the volume of non-formal training per employee is middling, with several countries providing substantially more training, including notably the United States, Spain, the Netherlands, Denmark, and Japan (Green, A. et al., 2014).

The falling training volumes in Britain do not derive from training barriers. For example, successive Employer Skill Surveys have found that where firms do report doing less training than they would have preferred, the main reasons for this shortfall tend to be internal to firms (such as a perceived lack of funding and time) rather than external barriers such as insufficient suitable training providers (Hillage et al., 2002; Winterbotham et al., 2014). Thus, one can conclude that that there has been a decline in employer demand for the skills which can be developed through training (even if some firms have been increasing the efficiency of their training, by targeting their expenditures more narrowly to their skills needs (Felstead et al., 2012). To some extent firms may have been able to deliver skills development through careful organization of work patterns to ensure transfer of technical skills and knowledge; there is indirect evidence of small increases in the extent to which jobs are requiring workers to 'learn new things' in the course of their work (Green et al., 2013). Nevertheless, it is hard to avoid the conclusion that the magnitude of the fall in employer willingness to provide training—especially long-duration training—is a symptom of an economy on a relatively low-skill/low-innovation trajectory.

Low levels of training are sometimes attributed to the deterrent effect from the risk of employees quitting, taking with them the transferable skills they have acquired for the benefit of another employer. But for many UK managers low training is embedded in a productive model that lacks innovative ambition; in addition, managers with a short-termist perspective are thought to prefer to train less when faced with uncertainty about

---

[4] For information on highly regarded apprenticeship schemes having to turn away large numbers of applicants for training places, see <http://www.telegraph.co.uk/finance/jobs/8710305/School-leavers-scramble-for-apprenticeships.html> (accessed 17 November 2014).

the effectiveness and value of training investments, in effect making sub-optimal choices (Green, 2013, chs 5 and 6). It is likely that this 'management failure' is itself linked to the deficit in management skills noted above, though there have been no formal studies to date that have investigated the association. In the late 2000s, UK managers' skills in managing human capital were substantially exceeded in Sweden, the United States, Japan, and Germany, roughly equivalent to those in France, and in excess of those in Italy, Poland, Portugal, Ireland, and China.[5] It is unlikely to be a coincidence that the countries with high managerial skills for managing human capital also score highly in international comparisons of formal and informal training.

10.4 A New Approach to Skills Policy Development

In part as a consequence of the neo-liberal approach to policymaking which has eschewed most forms of intervention in employer decision-making, the skills policies of the last twenty-five years have very largely been focused on the supply side. If the main UK skills problem is a skills deficit, however, it follows that policies designed to stimulate the supply of skills risk disappointment if they are not accompanied by a strategy to stimulate the demand for skills. Without such a strategy, employers may tend to use whatever social support is offered inefficiently or channel it into their existing training plans ('deadweight loss'); individuals may become disillusioned if they do not get to use the skills they have acquired.

Yet the introduction of an innovation-oriented industrial strategy would directly address the issue of demand, and with it immediately raise the stakes for skills strategy. Policy must indeed address the new demands that will follow for innovation-relevant skills. A supply-side failure, in this scenario, would be manifested in rising skill shortages and skill gaps, which if sufficiently dire would lead to the collapse of the industrial strategy. What is needed is for a skills strategy and an industrial strategy to be conceived together as mutually reinforcing, ideally as an integrated whole. Policy development and support for training and education should go hand in hand with the emergence of the new industrial policy.

The basis for a new approach to skills policy goes beyond the traditional case derived from conventional economics. The latter, conventional, philosophy advocates that employers should be left, in negotiation with their employees, to manage their employees' skills development, except where there is 'market failure'. The latter arises where, owing to rigidities and imperfections, other employers are able to benefit from the skills training an employer provides. When there are market imperfections—including mobility

---

[5] Authors' calculation from Management Practices Survey data, at <http://worldmanagementsurvey. org/?page_id=183> (accessed 17 November 2014).

restrictions, and institutional constraints on wages—employers and employees are together incentivized to pay for the development of transferable skills, but not enough. Thus conventional economics yields a case for social intervention to support skills development in workplaces. But the case is limited because, in practice, economists have found it hard to estimate the extent of market failures: the 'training externality' is a valid theoretical construct but not something that has been quantified and found particularly useful in driving training policy (Keep, 2006; Green, 2013, pp. 143–5). Meanwhile, scarcity of evidence about the externalities from higher education may have contributed to acceptance of the case for shifting the cost to students.

The case for social intervention in workplace skill formation is, however, supplemented by management theory, which recognizes the agency of managers, and the salience of culture and strategy in determining employer behaviour in an uncertain economic environment. In this approach, the conventional economist's assumption that firms are at their 'production possibility frontiers' (where no output can be augmented without extra cost or the loss of some other valued outcome) is jettisoned, and it is recognized that there is a spectrum of firms with differing overall strategies, heterogeneous management skills, and accordingly differing approaches to skills development (Green, 2013).

This broader intellectual underpinning for an expanded skills policy is also consistent with the need for skills and industrial policies to be integrated. Thus, as we have argued above, the skills policy should be focused on expanding the capacity of firms to be innovative. The strategy will, in effect, be addressing simultaneously the supply and demand for skills, attempting to coordinate the two through a series of market-supplementing interventions.

New policies should not be conceived outside of the historical conjuncture in which they are to be applied. To what extent could a new strategy build on the skills policies of the Coalition government and its 'new Labour' predecessors? Could an extension of such policies stimulate a higher level of employer demand for skills?

The existing strategy has been dominated by support for the expansion of higher education in all parts of the UK, with higher education participation rates in England, for example, rising to approximately 38 per cent of the 17–20 year-old age group in 2011–12.[6] Two strands of higher education policy have sought to influence the development of innovation-relevant skills:

(1) efforts to enhance the provision of courses in Science, Technology, Engineering and Mathematics (STEM) subjects;
(2) initiatives designed to enhance the teaching of 'employability skills' such as communication, numeracy, information technology, problem-solving, and teamworking skills.

Partly in response to some employers' claims about STEM skill shortages, some STEM subjects were classified as 'strategically important and vulnerable' subjects by the

---

[6] Source: Statistical First Release on Higher Education, 24 April 2013, Department of Business, Innovation and Skills (provisional estimates).

Higher Education Funding Council for England (HEFCE) and given extra funding support.[7] Part of the perceived problem is that a large and apparently growing proportion of STEM graduates work in non-STEM jobs and industries (Bosworth et al., 2013). However, from the perspective of innovation-related skill requirements across the UK economy, this can be seen as diffusing graduates who, by dint of their studies in STEM subjects, are widely seen as possessing desirable skills in mathematics and in 'logical approach[es] to solving problems' (BIS, 2011, p. 7). If such skills are in short supply among the wider graduate pool, this partly reflects the fact that STEM subjects absorb a high proportion of those entrants to UK universities who have studied maths beyond the age of 16. Indeed, England in particular is conspicuous by international standards for the relatively large proportion of school pupils who abandon maths study at that age (Hodgen et al., 2013).

Employability skills in higher education are also considered to be highly relevant to innovation. However, empirical evidence on the effectiveness of different kinds of employability skills initiatives in higher education suggests that structured work experience is more likely to have positive effects on graduates' employment prospects than is the case for university departments' efforts to develop employability skills in classroom settings (Mason et al., 2009).

Such findings serve as a reminder that many relevant employability skills are best learned in workplaces rather than through full-time education courses. This point is also relevant to the development of innovation-relevant skills at intermediate level. A defining characteristic of 'apprenticeship training' is that it combines employment-based training with part-time attendance in vocational education classes or workshops related to the field of training. Under both the Coalition and preceding Labour governments, apprentice training levels were growing. In 2012–13 some 510,220 people started apprentice training in England, up threefold in ten years (Table 10.3). As in Wales,[8] the majority of English apprentice trainees aim for NVQ Level 2, in contrast to Scotland, where most people starting on the Modern Apprenticeship programme have been aiming for Level 3 qualifications.[9] Apprenticeship completion rates have also risen substantially, and the proportion of trainees aged 19 or older has grown. As shown in Table 10.3, much of the growth in apprentice training in England has occurred in service sectors such as information and communication technology, health, public administration and care and business, administration, and law, which had little or no previous tradition of apprenticeship training.

Thus, by some criteria—especially growth in numbers and the extension to non-traditional sectors—the apprentice training system has flourished. Nevertheless, apprentices remain a much smaller proportion of employees in the UK than in many

---

[7] For details of HEFCE support for subjects deemed to be strategically important and vulnerable, see <http://www.hefce.ac.uk/whatwedo/crosscutting/sivs/> (accessed 21 November 2014).

[8] <http://wales.gov.uk/docs/statistics/2011/110427sdr682011en.pdf> (Table 4) (accessed 21 November 2014).

[9] <http://www.skillsdevelopmentscotland.co.uk/media/1121561/modern_apprenticeships__early_publication__quarter_4_2013-14.pdf> (accessed 21 November 2014).

Table 10.3 Apprenticeship Programme Starts, England, 2012–13, Analyzed by Sector Subject Area and Rate of Growth Since 2002–3

Sector subject area	Total	Percent of total	Percent change since 2002–3
Agriculture, Horticulture and Animal Care	7,090	1	106
Arts, Media and Publishing	1,120	0.2	833
Business, Administration and Law	160,410	31	335
Construction, Planning and the Built Environment	13,730	3	-13
Education and Training	8,050	2	na
Engineering and Manufacturing Technologies	66,410	13	118
Health, Public Services and Care	123,370	24	562
Information and Communication Technology	14,120	3	193
Leisure, Travel and Tourism	14,360	3	100
Retail and Commercial Enterprise	101,240	20	105
Science and Mathematics	320	0.1	na
Total	*510,220*	*100*	*204*

Source: https://www.gov.uk/government/statistical-data-sets/fe-data-library-apprenticeships, (Apprenticeships by sector subject area, age, and level 2002/03 to 2013/14) (accessed 21 November 2014)

Continental European countries (Steedman, 2010). Moreover, many of the apprenticeships at NVQ Level 2 would not be classified as apprentices in Continental Europe. Only about a third of Level 2 Apprentices subsequently progress to Level 3 training (Skills Commission, 2009). Furthermore, in the absence of statutory regulation of training content, there are marked variations between different sectors in the amount of on- and off-the-job training and related vocational education that apprentices receive, with particular concerns that some training under the 'apprenticeship' heading for older workers in their existing jobs has amounted to little more than short-duration skills updating or accreditation of existing skills (Richard, 2012).

Yet in general, the limited employer commitment to apprentice training has reflected relatively low levels of employer demand for the types of skills that are developed through long-duration employment-based training and related college studies. Thus we return to our assessment of relatively weak employer demand for innovation-relevant skills in the UK which in turn reflects the business strategies deployed by many British firms, which do not engage in innovation and have no plans to do so. This is the root source of many UK employers' reliance on short periods of continuing training and their reluctance to invest in apprenticeships or any other form of long-duration education and training.

In a 2013 review of training policy, plans were announced to reduce variation in the quality and value of different apprenticeships and ensure that apprentices reach minimum standards in generic subject areas such as English and maths, thus recognizing some of the criticisms of the recent expansion of UK apprentice training made by independent observers (e.g. Fuller and Unwin, 2008, 2010; Richard, 2012). There was also to be a renewed emphasis on 'employer demand', but the interpretation of this phrase requires unpacking: it appears to have two meanings, which one can call 'Respect' and 'Stimulate'. On the one hand, the intention is to *respect* employers' needs by giving them better control of the training market, for example through increased employer flexibility in setting apprentice training standards and choice of training providers (DfE/BIS, 2013). On the face of things, this emphasis on employer flexibility seems to accept current levels of employer demand for skills without recognizing the problems created by the relatively low level of that demand in the majority of UK firms.

On the other hand, some elements of the review could be seen as supporting the principle of trying to *stimulate* employer demand for skilled labour. It gave support for funding of a new round of Employer Ownership Pilots (EOPs) which will cohere with plans announced in 2012 for a somewhat more active approach by government to industrial policy. Among other things, it was proposed to develop collaborative strategic partnerships with key sectors that are identified as having good prospects for increasing innovation, productivity and employment in the future (BIS, 2012b).[10] This EOP funding is expected to include:

> large cross-sector and supply chain collaborations to tackle emerging skills needs in industrial strategy sectors; and innovative new approaches to addressing SME needs in localities ... [There will be] a focus on collaborative projects, including promoting industrial partnerships, which will be new employer-led groupings that will take end-to-end ownership of the skills agenda in their sectors. We are particularly keen to see these partnerships forming in sectors which are priorities for the industrial strategy. (DFE/BIS, 2013, pp. 35–6)

These were ambitious objectives but welcome in principle. An integrated skills and (expanded) industrial strategy could build on these already-existing foundations. In further developing policy to achieve the twin objectives of expanding skills demand and supply, three balances will need to be respected: between technical and generic skills, between graduate and intermediate skills, and between initial and continuing training.

10.4.1 The Mix of Technical and Generic Skills

Public debates surrounding the skills needed for innovation typically emphasize technical skills and knowledge in key areas of science and technology. However, the evidence reviewed in Section 10.2 shows that, in addition to technical and practical skills, a wide range of generic skills such as mathematical, communication, problem-solving, and managerial skills are needed to support innovation in different industries. In the

---

[10] Specifically, the 'key sectors' identified in BIS (2012b) are automotive; aerospace; life science (health/agri-tech); offshore wind; oil and gas; nuclear; construction; education; professional business services; and information economy. See also Vince Cable, Speech at Imperial College, 11 September 2012, 'Industrial Strategy—Cable outlines vision for future of British industry', <https://www.gov.uk/government/speeches/industrial-strategy-cable-outlines-vision-for-future-of-british-industry> (accessed 21 November 2014).

British context one particularly important precondition for higher levels of innovation is likely to be improvements in mathematical skills among many different sections of the workforce. It seems likely that employer demand for mathematical skills will increase still further if industrial policy is successful in stimulating higher levels of innovation. Accordingly, renewed attention needs to be paid to improving mathematical skills at all levels, including steps to prevent school and college students from abandoning maths study at the relatively early age of 16. Similarly, attention needs to be paid to redressing Britain's long tail of poor management skills.

10.4.2 The Mix of Graduate and Intermediate Skills

While it is typically maintained that Britain is well placed with leading global universities, there is need for an appropriate balance between graduate and intermediate skills. In a number of industries the graduate share of employment has increased sharply and yet employer demand for associate or 'para' professional and technician-level skills remains strong, for example, health services, financial services and some branches of advanced manufacturing such as aerospace and innovative areas of electronics and chemicals (SEMTA 2009; Skills for Health et al., 2010). There is a need, even at relatively high skill levels, for the mix of skills to include practical skills developed through employment-based training as well as skills and knowledge acquired in classroom settings. To get this balance right, UK policy can usefully draw on international experience of the ways that other countries address the need for upper-level skills.

For instance, in Germany, Switzerland, and Denmark, there are long-established graduate-level courses of a practical or occupation-specific nature which have few parallels among British university courses. In Germany graduates from *Fachhochschulen* ('universities of applied sciences') represent between 40 and 50 per cent of all graduates. In Switzerland *Fachhochschulen* accounted for 35 per cent of students in higher education in 2009. In Denmark holders of 'professional Bachelor's degrees' from colleges offering 'medium-cycle' higher education represent more than 60 per cent of all graduates.[11]

An alternative approach is found in France where two-year higher education courses lead to technician-level qualifications such as the BTS (*Brevet de technicien supérieur*, Advanced Technician Certificate) and the DUT (*Diplôme universitaire de technologie*, University Technical Diploma). These provide clear pathways so that students completing those courses can choose between entering employment as technicians or going on to study for Bachelor or higher degrees. Taken together, enrolments

---

[11] Estimates of the mix of graduates in Germany derived from Mikrozensus, 2004; estimates of Swiss student numbers in 2009 derived from Office fédéral de la statistique (<http://www.bfs.admin.ch>, accessed 21 November 2014); Danish estimates of graduate shares derived from Statbank Denmark database for 2008.

on these courses account for about 15 per cent of all higher education enrolments.[12] Similarly, in the United States two-year higher education qualifications (Associates degrees) are potential routes to either intermediate-skilled employment or to further study to Bachelor degree level. By 2000 an estimated one in five people holding Bachelor degrees had started as students in community colleges and other 'two-year institutions' (Bailey et al., 2004). In 2005 about 40 per cent of all students enrolled in post-high school education in the US were at colleges of this kind, up from 27 per cent in 1970 (Marcotte, 2006).

Because Foundation degree and Higher National courses (typically requiring two years of study) are already in place in Britain, it is the French and US models of intermediate qualifications serving as stepping-stones towards Bachelor degrees which perhaps provide most food for thought for policy-makers. Although Foundation degree student numbers in England rose steadily from 2002 they peaked in 2009/2010 and declined to only 13,000 in 2012/2013 (HEFCE, 2014), representing about 3 per cent of all higher education enrolments in the UK. Higher National Certificate or Diploma enrolments represent only 2 per cent of total higher education enrolments (Mason, 2010), and these also have been in decline. Any expansion of course provision at this level could usefully be integrated with Higher Apprenticeships, and support for progression to higher education (Kewin et al., 2011).

10.4.3 The Balance between Initial and Continuing Training

Another balance at issue concerns the extent of support for initial training and ongoing training throughout a working career. A case might be made that, with either a sufficiently transformed apprenticeship training or a training through higher education, the large majority of employees can be equipped to learn further and develop their skills through experience in their workplaces. In Germany, with a well-developed apprenticeship system, ongoing training through the lifecourse is not especially high, arguably because the need is lower. The case would be further enhanced if accompanied by progress in enhancing the quality of learning environments, not least by the promotion of more participative work practices. In parallel, to enable higher education to take place alongside work, we also join with others in advocating that part-time study should be made more attractive. However, given the relatively large proportion of the 2030 workforce which is already in employment, it would not be advisable to rely mostly on reforms to initial training and education reforms. Policies need to pay at least equal attention to the continuing training needs of adult workers already in employment.

A number of policies for promoting continuing training have been under consideration by the UK Commission for Employment and Skills, some of which would be of value in a training policy for an innovative industrial strategy (Cox et al., 2009;

---

[12] <http://www.education.gouv.fr/pid316/reperes-references-statistiques.html> (accessed 21 November 2014).

Stanfield et al., 2009; Forth et al., 2011; Gospel, 2012; Cox et al., 2013; Tamkin et al., 2013; UKCES, 2013). One set of potential policies is designed to make skills development and utilization more cost-effective, such as inter-employer networks (e.g. group training associations), government subsidies or tax breaks for training, or improvements in the design of public training programmes. To achieve the latter, the method has been to put the employer in the driving seat (promoted as championing employer demand). But as we have noted, it will not be sufficient to rely on existing levels of employer demand for skills. Instead, additional policies are needed which help to raise employer demand for skills and training. These include both policies on advice and support, and policies which involve placing regulatory requirements on employer decision-making, such as enacting employee rights to training time, industry levy systems, occupational licensing and public procurement policies, and industry-level statutory regulation.

In selecting the mix of such policies, an important factor should be the extent to which the policy fosters employer learning and awareness of the benefits of skills development. Another factor should be the extent to which each policy can be embedded in the emerging industrial strategy. For example, most firms with innovative potential but little or no prior track record in innovation will need external advice and support if they are to stand a chance of succeeding in new and unfamiliar markets. Well-funded regional agencies would be best placed to identify firms with such potential and help broker relationships between these firms and research and technology organizations and universities, with the aim of helping firms fill gaps in their skills and knowledge. We advocate that training support policies should be integrated where feasible with new regional development policies of this kind.

10.5 CONCLUSION: THE NEED TO EMBED SKILLS IN AN INDUSTRIAL STRATEGY

There is a tendency for researchers and policy advisers in the world of skills to become so totally committed to their object of study that skills come to be regarded as a panacea for economic and social problems. Among the training and higher education community, debate becomes centred on supply-side skills issues, ignoring the problem of low demand for skills. Issues such as rising over-education, or relatively low productivity, do not form part of the conversation. Meanwhile, for businesses and for researchers and policy-makers in other fields studying research and innovation, the problem of skills hides down the agenda as a minor and easily resolved problem. We think that both are wrong. In this chapter we have argued that:

- Innovation should be an essential part of any new industrial strategy, and there should be particular emphasis on policies designed to identify and support firms which currently do not engage very much in innovation but have the potential to do so.

- Innovation requires skills, as evidenced by survey work and estimates of returns to skills investments, and of the links between firms' innovation and workforce skills. While higher-level skills figure in most discussions of innovation, intermediate-level skills are also going to be important. No single type of skill is required: rather, innovation calls for a wide range of skill types.
- The UK is suffering from a skills deficit, with relatively low levels of skills demand and supply, which will need to be addressed as an integral part of the new industrial strategy. Increasing skills, in the absence of policies to raise skills demand, is a limited strategy.
- However, an expansionary skills strategy becomes especially important when an industrial strategy is in place. It should build on elements of existing policy which emphasize engagement with, and support for, that section of employers who have the potential and market incentives to become innovative. The policy needs to be balanced in three dimensions: between technical and generic skills, between higher and intermediate skills, and between initial and continuing education and training.
- A culture of evaluation and of selected policy-learning from other countries should prevail. While it is not necessary to invent new policies for training, an imaginative selection of policies can be used, drawing on existing and prospective studies. Wherever feasible a training strategy should be embedded in innovation support and regional development policies.

References

Autor, D., Levy, F., and Murnane, R. (2003).'The Skill Content of Recent Technological Change: An Empirical Explanation', *Quarterly Journal of Economics* 118(4), 1279–333.

Bailey, T., Kienzl, G., and Marcotte, D. (2004). The Return to a Sub-Baccalaureate Education: The Effects of Schooling, Credentials and Program of Study on Economic Outcomes. Report to National Assessment of Vocational Education, US Department of Education.

Barrell, R. and Pain, N. (1997).'Foreign Direct Investment, Technological Change, and Economic Growth within Europe', *Economic Journal* 107, 1770–6.

Bayo-Moriones, A. and Lera-López, F. (2007). 'A Firm-Level Analysis of Determinants of ICT Adoption in Spain', *Technovation* 27, 352–66.

BIS (2011). *STEM Graduates in Non-STEM Jobs: Executive Summary*, Department for Business, Innovation and Skills, London, Research Paper No. 31.

BIS (2012a). *Leadership & Management in the UK: The Key to Sustainable Growth*. London: Department for Business, Innovation and Skills.

BIS (2012b). *Industrial Strategy: UK Sector Analysis*, Department for Business, Innovation and Skills, London, BIS Economics Paper No. 18.

BIS (2013a). *First Findings from the UK Innovation Survey 2011 (Revised)*. London: Department for Business, Innovation and Skills.

BIS (2013b). *The International Survey of Adult Skills 2012: Adult Literacy, Numeracy and Problem Solving Skills in England*, London, BIS Research Paper No. 139.

Blomstrom, M. and Kokko, A. (2003). *Human Capital and Inward FDI*, Centre of Economic Policy Research, London, Discussion Paper No. 3762.

Bloom, N. and Van Reenen, J. (2010). 'Why Do Management Practices Differ across Firms and Countries?', *Journal of Economic Perspectives* 24(1), 203–24.

Bloom, N., Van Reenen, J., Lemos, R., Sadun, R., and Qi, M. (2011). *Constraints on Developing UK Management Practices*, Department for Business, Innovation and Skills, London, BIS Research Paper No. 58.

Bosworth, D., Lyonette, C., Wilson, R., Bayliss, M., and Fathers, S. (2013), *The Supply of and Demand for High-Level STEM Skills*, UK Commission for Employment and Skills, London, Evidence Report No. 77.

Bresnahan, T. F., Brynjolfsson, E., and Hitt, L. M. (2002). 'Information Technology, Workplace Organization, and the Demand for Skilled Labor: Firm-Level Evidence', *Quarterly Journal of Economics* 117(1), 339–76.

Brown, R. (1998). 'Electronics Foreign Direct Investment in Singapore: A Study of Local Linkages in Winchester City', *European Business Review* 98(4), 196–210.

Brown, R. (2000). 'Clusters, Supply Chains and Local Embeddedness in Frystad', *European Urban and Regional Studies* 7(4), 291–305.

Cohen, W. and Levinthal, D. (1989). 'Innovation and Learning: Two Faces of R&D', *Economic Journal* 107, 139–49.

Cox, A., Higgins, T., Marangozov, R., Breuer, Z., and Garrett, R. (2013). *Understanding Employer Networks*, UK Commission for Employment and Skills, London, Evidence Report No. 66.

Cox, A., Sumpton, F., Hillage, J., and Sloan, J. (2009). *Review of Employer Collective Measures: Policy Review*, UK Commission for Employment and Skills, London, Evidence Report No. 8.

DFE/BIS (2013). *Rigour and Responsiveness in Skills.* London: Department for Education and Department for Business, Innovation and Skills.

Dolton, P. and Vignoles, A. (2002). 'The Return on Post-Compulsory School Mathematics Study', *Economica* 69(273), 113–42.

Felstead, A., Gallie, D., Green, F., and Inanc, H. (2013). *Skills at Work in Britain.* London: Centre for Learning and Life Chances in Knowledge Economies and Societies, Institute of Education.

Felstead, A., Green, F., and Jewson, N. (2012). 'An Analysis of the Impact of the 2008–09 Recession on the Provision of Training in the UK', *Work, Employment and Society* 26(6), 968–86.

Fersterer, J. and Winter-Ebmer, R. (2003). 'Are Austrian Returns to Education Falling Over Time?', *Labour Economics* 10, 73–89.

Forth, J., Bryson, A., Humphris, A., Koumenta, M., and Kleiner, M. (2011). *A Review of Occupational Regulation and its Impact*, UK Commission for Employment and Skills, London, Evidence Report No. 40.

Fuller, A. and Unwin, L. (2008). *Towards Expansive Apprenticeships: A Commentary for the ESRC's Teaching and Learning Research Programme.* London: Institute of Education.

Fuller, A. and Unwin, L. (2010). 'Change and Continuity in Apprenticeship: The Resilience of a Model of Learning', *Journal of Education and Work* 25(5), 405–16.

Gangl, M. (2000). *Changing Labour Markets and Early Career Outcomes: Labour Market Entry in Europe Over the Past Decade*, Arbeitspapiere—Mannheimer Zentrum für Europäische Sozialforschung, Working Paper No. 26.

Gospel, H. (2012). *Understanding Training Levies*, UK Commission for Employment and Skills, London, Evidence Report No. 47.

Green, A., Green, F., and Pensiero, N. (2014). *Why are Literacy and Numeracy Skills in England so Unequal?*, Centre for Learning and Life Chances in Knowledge Economies and Societies, LLAKES Research Paper No. 47.

Green, F. (2012). 'Employee Involvement, Technology and Evolution in Job Skills: A Task-Based Analysis,' *Industrial & Labor Relations Review* 65(1), 35–66.

Green, F. (2013). *Skills and Skilled Work. An Economic and Social Analysis.* Oxford: Oxford University Press.

Green, F., Felstead, A., Gallie, D., Inanc, H., and Jewson, N. (2013). *What Has Been Happening to the Training of Workers in Britain?*, Institute of Education, Centre for Learning and Life Chances in Knowledge Economies and Societies (LLAKES), Research Paper No. 43.

Green, F. and Zhu, Y. (2010). 'Overqualification, Job Dissatisfaction, and Increasing Dispersion in the Returns to Graduate Education,' *Oxford Economic Papers* 62(2), 740–63.

HEFCE (2014). 'Higher Education in England 2014. Analysis of Latest Shifts and Trends', <http://www.hefce.ac.uk/heinengland/2014/>.

Hillage, J., Regan, J., Dickson, J., and McLoughlin, K. (2002). *Employers Skill Survey 2002*, Department for Education and Skills, London, Research Report No. RR372.

Hodgen, J., Marks, M., and Pepper, D. (2013). *Towards Universal Participation in Post-16 Mathematics: Lessons from High-Performing Countries.* London: Nuffield Foundation.

Hollenstein, H. (2004). 'Determinants of the Adoption of ICT: An Empirical Analysis Based on Firm-Level Data for the Swiss Business Sector', *Structural Change and Economic Dynamics* 15, 315–42.

Hughes, A. and Mina, A. (2012). *The UK R&D Landscape.* London: Council for Industry and Higher Education and UK-Innovation Research Centre (revised edition).

Jones, B. and Grimshaw, D. (2012). *The Effects of Policies for Training and Skills on Improving Innovation Capabilities in Firms*, National Endowment for Science, Technology and the Arts (NESTA), London, Working Paper No. 12/08.

Keep, E. (2006). *Market Failure In Skills*, Sector Skills Development Agency, Wath-Upon-Dearne, SSDA Catalyst Series No. 1.

Kewin, J., Hughes, T., Fletcher, T., and Sheen, J. (2011). *The Road Less Travelled: Experiences of Employers that Support the Progression of Advanced Apprentices to Higher Education.* Leicester: CFE.

Krueger, D. and Kumar, K. (2004). 'Skill-Specific rather than General Education: A Reason for US-Europe Growth Differences?', *Journal of Economic Growth* 9, 167–208.

Lundvall, B-A. (1992). *National Systems of Innovation: Towards a Theory of Innovation and Interactive Learning.* London: Pinter Publishers.

Machin, S. (2003). 'Wage Inequality Since 1975', in R. Dickens, P. Gregg, and J. Wadsworth (eds), *The Labour Market under New Labour*, pp. 191–200. Basingstoke: Palgrave Macmillan.

Marcotte, D. (2006). *The Earnings Effect of Education at Community Colleges*, Institute for the Study of Labor (IZA), Bonn, Discussion Paper No. 2334.

Mason, G. (2001). 'The Mix of Graduate and Intermediate-Level Skills in Britain: What Should the Balance Be?', *Journal of Education and Work* 14(1), 5–27.

Mason, G. (2010). *Part-Time Higher Education Students in the UK: Statistical Review.* Manchester: Higher Education Careers Services Unit (HECSU).

Mason, G. (2011). *Product Strategies, Skills Shortages and Skill Updating Needs in England: New Evidence from the National Employer Skills Survey, 2009, Evidence Report 30.* London: UK Commission for Employment and Skills.

Mason, G., Beltramo, J-P., and Paul, J-J. (2004). 'External Knowledge Sourcing in Different National Settings: A Comparison of Electronics Establishments in Britain and France', *Research Policy* 33(1), 53–72.

Mason, G. and Nathan, M. (2014). Rethinking Industrial Policy Design in the UK: Foreign Ideas and Lessons, Home-Grown Programmes and Institutions. Centre for Learning and Life Chances in Knowledge Economies and Societies (LLAKES) Research Paper.

Mason, G. and Wagner, K. (2005). 'Restructuring of Automotive Supply chains: The Role of Workforce Skills in Germany and Britain', *International Journal of Automotive Technology and Management* 5(4), 387–410.

Mason, G., Williams, G., and Cranmer, S. (2009). 'Employability Skills Initiatives in Higher Education: What Effects Do They Have On Graduate Labour Market Outcomes', *Education Economics* 17(1), 1–30.

McIntosh, S. (2006). 'Further Analysis of the Returns to Academic and Vocational Qualifications', *Oxford Bulletin of Economics and Statistics* 68(2), 225–51.

OECD (2011a). *Skills for Innovation and Research*. Paris: Organisation for Economic Co-operation and Development.

OECD (2011b). *Education at a Glance 2011: Highlights*. Paris: OECD Publishing.

OECD (2013a). *Science, Technology and Industry Scoreboard 2013*. Paris: Organisation for Economic Co-operation and Development.

OECD (2013b). *OECD Skills Outlook 2013: First Results from the Survey of Adult Skills*. Paris: OECD Publishing.

OECD/Eurostat (2005). *Oslo Manual: Guidelines for Collecting and Interpreting Innovation Data*. Paris: Organisation for Economic Co-operation and Development and Statistical Office of the European Communities.

Petersen, K., Handfield, R., and Ragatz, G. (2003). 'A Model of Supplier Integration into New Product Development', *Journal of Product Innovation Management* 20(4), 284–99.

Powdthavee, N. and Vignoles, A. (2006). *Using Rate of Return Analyses to Understand Sector Skill Needs*, Centre for the Economics of Education, London, Discussion Paper No. 70.

Prais, S. (1995). *Productivity, Education and Training*. Cambridge: Cambridge University Press.

Richard, D. (2012). *The Richard Review of Apprenticeships*. London: Department for Business, Innovation and Skills.

Saxenian, A. (1994). *Regional Advantage: Culture and Competition in Silicon Valley and Route 128*. Cambridge, MA: Harvard University Press.

SEMTA (2009). *Skills and the Future of Advanced Manufacturing: A Summary Skills Assessment for the SSC Advanced Manufacturing Cluster*. Watford: Sector Skills Council for Science, Engineering and Manufacturing Technologies.

Skills Commission (2009). *Progression Through Apprenticeships: The Final Report of the Skills Commission's Inquiry Into Apprenticeships*. London: The Skills Commission.

Skills for Health, SEMTA and Cogent (2010). Life Sciences and Pharmaceuticals: A Future Skills Review with Recommendations to Sustain Growth in Emerging Technologies, <http://www.cogent-ssc.com/research/Publications/LSPReport.pdf>.

Stanfield, C., Cox, A., and Stone, I. (2009). *Review of Employer Collective Measures: Final Report*, UK Commission for Employment and Skills, London, Evidence Report No. 10.

Steedman, H. (2010). *The State of Apprenticeship in 2010*. London: Centre for Economic Performance, London School of Economics.

Tamkin, P., Miller, L., and Williams, J. (2013). *Understanding Occupational Regulation*, UK Commission for Employment and Skills, London, Evidence Report No. 67.

Toner, P. (2011). *Workforce Skills and Innovation: An Overview of Major Themes in the Literature*. Paris: Organisation for Economic Co-operation and Development.

Turok, I. (1993). 'Inward Investment and Local Linkages: How Deeply Embedded is Silicon Glen?', *Regional Studies* 27(5), 401–17.

UKCES (2013). *Employer Ownership of Skills: Building the Momentum*. London: UK Commission for Employment and Skills.

Walker, I. and Zhu, Y. (2008). 'The College Wage Premium and the Expansion of Higher Education in the UK', *Scandinavian Journal of Economics* 110, 695–709.

Winkelmann, R. (1996). 'Training, Earnings and Mobility in Germany', *Konjunkturpolitik* 42, 275–98.

Winterbotham, M., Vivian, D., Shury, J., and Davies, B. (2014). *UK Commission's Employer Skills Survey 2013: UK Results*. London: UK Commission for Employment and Skills.

Zahra, S. A. and George, G. (2002). 'Absorptive Capacity: A Review, Reconceptualisation, and Extension', *The Academy of Management Review* 27(2), 185–203.

CHAPTER 11

....

BEYOND A HUMAN CAPITAL APPROACH TO EDUCATION AND THE LABOUR MARKET

The Case for Industrial Policy

....

PHILLIP BROWN, SIN YI CHEUNG, AND HUGH LAUDER

11.1 INTRODUCTION

....

HUMAN capital approaches remain at the heart of education and economic policy. In the developed economies investments in education and marketable skills continue to be viewed as holding the key to innovation and social justice in a knowledge-based society. In developing economies they are touted as the best way of entering the global economy, especially through attracting inward investment from transnational companies (TNCs).

The neo-liberal orthodoxy, encompassing most of the neoclassical tenets of human capital, declares that investments in human capital can only be captured in returns to individuals and nations when markets are 'flexible' and 'free' from state intervention. As Gary Becker (1985), the doyen of human capital theorists, has argued, 'The best industrial policy is none at all' (p. 3). Governments should therefore limit themselves to addressing 'market failure', especially underinvestment in education and training, leaving market forces to enable employers to respond to the greater productive potential of educated workers. With respect to developing economies, human capital theorists have avoided asking the difficult questions concerning economic strategy by pointing to a strong correlation between levels of education and per capita income, which they derive from supply side policies (Hanushek and Woessmann, 2007; Hanushek et al., 2013).

The global financial crisis and subsequent Great Recession within Western economies has so far led to a limited re-examination of human capital assumptions: human capital continues to be viewed in many policy circles as a vital source of enterprise and innovation as economies in Europe and North America seek a return to economic growth and individual prosperity. Nowhere is this clearer than in government responses to the various OECD reports on education and skills (Meyer and Benavot, 2013).

This chapter will outline a different approach and argue that there will be no return to 'business as usual' because we are witnessing a fundamental structural shift in the relationship between education and the labour market. This conclusion is based on over a decade's worth of comparative research in both developed and emerging economies, including those of China and India (Brown et al., 2011). Our studies identify a number of interrelated trends contributing to a 'global auction' for jobs (GAJ),[1] no longer limited to low-skilled employment in factories and call centres, but including many of the jobs that require significant investments in education and training. From the perspective of developed economies, the foundations of middle-class employment are under threat as many of those who previously traded on investments in their education and training find themselves in a reverse auction for cut-price brainpower. At the same time elites continue to benefit from a Sotheby-type progressive auction where the value of their knowledge has continued to rise. From the perspective of emerging economies, the global auction looks rather different as it represents an opportunity for rapid economic development by 'leapfrogging' decades of industrial development to enter the competition for high-skilled work. However, both developed and emerging economies confront a formidable challenge of job creation, job quality, and social inclusion. The market cannot deliver this alone no matter how well educated a nation's workforce. Therefore, we will argue that the labour market needs to take centre stage in state-led industrial activism.

11.2 HUMAN CAPITAL THEORY

Human capital theory makes a series of inferences about the relationship between education, productivity, and income. The insight of the early human capital theorists was that a significant element of economic growth, that had hitherto been unexplained, could be accounted for by education (Schultz, 1961). With the rise of technology it was assumed that more educated workers were needed to service the economy. These educated workers were considered more productive than those with only basic education because

---

[1] It does not assume that all jobs are becoming subject to global competition, as this is obviously wrong. But the impact of globalization is not only direct as more areas of the economy become tradable, jobs are offshored, or workers migrate in search of employment; its impact is also indirect in spreading best practice and technological change such as through the use of digital software, and the spread of foreign ownership, global value chains whose impact on jobs may be less apparent.

they could put their knowledge to good use in servicing and developing technology. It was further assumed that employers would, over time, always choose educated workers because they would raise productivity and hence profits.

Human capital theory was developed within neoclassical economics, which employed the idea that as more educated workers came into the labour market, so a new equilibrium would be established whereby educated workers would receive higher returns for their productive potential. In essence, this account rests on the idea of a constant upward adjustment of equilibria as employers reap the benefits of greater productivity and reward their educated workers accordingly. It is precisely the promise of greater reward that is believed to drive individuals to invest in themselves through education, based on the neoclassical view that students act according to the tenets of *homo economicus*.

Human capital theorists have also claimed that the 'economic view' (Becker, 1992) has universal application. It is assumed that the regularities they identify between education, work, and income hold true irrespective of time and place (see e.g. Hanushek and Woessmann, 2007; Hanushek et al., 2013). Such claims often related to the idea that returns to human capital approximate a universal model as labour markets come closer to being perfectly competitive, leading to an upward movement towards new equilibria.

On this account, it is possible to see why the demand for graduates would rise as economies emerge from recession. If we assume that technology will continue to develop and that graduates will be more productive, then we might expect the demand for graduates to continue to increase. As Becker (2006, p. 292) has argued, 'Technology may be the driver of the modern economy, especially in the hi-tech sector, but human capital is certainly the fuel'. There may be time lags between the demand for graduates and the supply; however, in the long run it could be expected that new equilibria will be achieved.

From the earliest days of human capital theory there were cogent criticisms of its tenets. In particular, it failed to take into account that wages do not reflect productivity as assumed by human capital theory (see e.g. Bluestone, 1972; Thurow, 1972; Carter and Carnoy, 1974). Indeed, contemporary analyses of wages and productivity show a sharp divergence between productivity and the median wage (Mishel, 2012). Other factors, apart from education and skill, also determine wages (Doeringer and Piore, 1971; Gordon, 1971). These include unionization, the minimum wage, and traditions of status and exploitation that continue to affect male and female wages, as well as those of people of different races. Critics of human capital argue that we can only understand wage-setting by reference to a range of national institutions and power relations. Such a view is explicit in the seminal paper by Finegold and Soskice (1988) in which they argued that Britain had a dual equilibrium economy based on high and low skills respectively. In other words, far from being able to make universal claims, the relationship between education, productivity, and income will always be contingent upon specific institutions and contexts.

These criticisms remain valid but we need to link them to an analysis of structural changes in economy and society which add to existing limitations of the human capital account of education, productivity, and income. Here there are three major considerations: firstly, human capital theory is wedded to a relatively static equilibrium model of the labour market and therefore cannot account for the impact of global labour markets for college and university graduates, except in the most superficial way. Secondly, although some human capital theorists claim that its tenets are universal, it rests on a model of methodological nationalism (Wimmer et al., 2002). Thirdly, human capital theory typically assumes a race between education and technology (Goldin and Katz, 2008), given that technological change is skill biased, increasing the demand for higher skilled workers. But such a view fails to understand the realities of global knowledge capitalism (Brown et al., 2011). Our analysis of the global auction for jobs points to fundamental changes in the relationship between education, employment, and incomes causing major structural changes in the graduate labour market. It follows that in today's global economy, human capital theory does not provide reliable policy prescriptions, which, after all, was what neoclassical economists claimed as its outstanding achievement (Clarke, 1982).

We will outline four related trends that are reshaping productive forces and creating a global auction for jobs:

11.3 THE GLOBALIZATION OF HIGH SKILLS

There has not only been a 'great doubling' in the size of the global workforce, but a 'great doubling' of university enrolments around the world, reaching close to 140 million by 2007. This has led to a massive increase in the global supply of highly qualified workers, able to compete on price as well as knowledge. China now has many more students in higher education than the United States and is currently pursuing a 'talent strategy' with a target of increasing the number of graduates entering the labour market by an additional 10 million per annum between 2010 and 2020.

Although the quality of education will vary in countries experiencing rapid expansion in educational provision, it is nevertheless the case that Asia is also producing more engineers and physical scientists than Europe and North America combined. In both Britain and the United States, home students make up less than half of those undertaking postgraduate degrees in some key STEM subjects.

11.4 THE QUALITY–COST REVOLUTION

If the barriers to higher education that previously protected Western middle classes from price competition are collapsing, it remains less of a problem if emerging economies are unable to achieve the quality standards required to deliver high quality goods and services, including research and development. However, today's competition is based on quality *and* cost, as business organization is being turned 'inside out'. If companies have access to decent infrastructure (roads, communications) and a supply of well-educated and motivated workers, they are able to set up 'oasis operations'—high-tech factories, offices, and research facilities—in low-spec locations.

This has led to a narrowing in productivity standards between operations in different parts of the world. Consequently, the wage rates and working conditions of Western employees are no longer the global benchmark. This benchmark has gravitated towards high-skilled but lower-waged economies rather than those in Western Europe and North America. These cost pressures are being driven not only by Western companies but by those companies from emerging economies with global ambitions.

11.5 THE RISE OF DIGITAL TAYLORISM

While the policy spotlight has been on the creation of new ideas, products, and services, the ability of companies to leverage new technologies to globally align and coordinate business activities has also brought to the fore a different agenda involving the standardization of functions and jobs within the service sector, including an increasing proportion of technical, managerial, and professional roles.[2] Today, advances in communication technologies, including the capacity for digital processing and internet capability, have created the realistic possibility of developing global standards that reduce technical complexity and diversity. A building block or 'Lego' approach using platform architectures and reusable IT components is now seen by some companies as a more efficient way of making organizations adaptable to change, applied to systems, processes, and people.

Terms such as 'financial services factory' and 'industrialization' are used by leading consultancy companies to describe this transformation of the service sector. Accenture Consulting is a proponent of 'the concept of industrialization – breaking down processes and products into constituent components that can be recombined in a tailored, automated fashion – to non-manufacturing settings' (Brown, Lauder, and Ashton, 2011:76). This process is exemplified by a business relations manager working for a leading British bank. He told us how his discretion over the amount of money he could lend to his clients had been removed. The bank previously respected his expertise and judgement in making decisions, but loans are now authorized by a credit controller. This credit controller is a software package that automatically assesses a loan application according to standard criteria. Only in appealing against the controller's judgement does the manager now have a role, but even in these cases he is often overruled. From a position of authority and respect, he described himself as a salesperson, armed with a series of software manuals instructing him how to sell particular kinds of products, which means that 'a junior with a ready smile could now do my job'. In a follow-up study, we undertook an interview with an Indian HR manager for an American transnational company, who commented that:

---

[2] Digital Taylorism addresses the problem of the cost disease as identified by Baumol (1993).

The presence of Digital Taylorism can't be overstated because it is happening everywhere. All your call centre jobs or your business processing that happens, it's typically Taylorism in a more digitalized world, because there are only five or six things you have to answer and they're on your system and you don't customize anything...this is true of all kinds of jobs today in India...much of the work is very much like an assembly line.

This suggests that if the twentieth century brought what can be described as mechanical Taylorism characterized by the Fordist production line, where the knowledge of craft workers was captured by management, codified and re-engineered in the shape of the moving assembly line, the twenty-first century is the age of digital Taylorism. This involves translating *knowledge work* into *working knowledge* through the extraction, codification, and digitalization of knowledge into software prescripts that can be transmitted and manipulated by others regardless of location (Brown et al., 2011).

11.6 THE GLOBAL 'WAR FOR TALENT'

In America and Britain the expansion of higher education has been associated with an increase in wage differentials. This is not only between university graduates and non-graduates but within the graduate workforce itself. Frank and Cook argue that income inequalities are not the result of changes in the distribution of human capital—that some have invested more in their education and training than others—but due to the changing structure of the job market. Even within occupations requiring a college education, those at the top of the occupational pyramid receive a disproportionate share of rewards, in what Frank and Cook call 'winner-takes-all markets'. They argue that changes in domestic and global competition make 'the most productive individuals more valuable'.[3] This argument is consistent with that of consultants from McKinsey who popularized the idea of a 'war for talent',[4] but whatever the merits of this argument, virtually all the TNCs we interviewed believed they were in a war for talent which was increasingly global.

It is assumed that the best people gravitate towards elite universities. This view is actively promoted by leading universities given that higher education has become a global business. The branding of universities and faculty members is integral to the organization of academic enquiry. Claims to world-class standards depend on attracting 'the best' academics and forming alliances with elite universities elsewhere in the world, while recruiting the 'right' kinds of students. Universities play the same reputational games as companies, because it is a logical consequence of market competition. In short, almost without exception, companies were not only 'segmenting' their educated

[3] Robert H. Frank and Philip J. Cook, *The Winner-Takes-All-Society* (New York: Penguin, 1995), p. 6.

[4] Ed Michaels, Helen Handfield-Jones, and Beth Axelrod, *The War for Talent* (Boston, MA: Harvard Business School Press, 2001).

workforce based on skills, credentials, or expertise but also on 'performance' driven by an attempt to reduce the cost of knowledge work, while retaining what they perceived as top talent.

11.7 The Great Recession and the Stratification of Knowledge Work: Severing the Ties between Human Capital, Jobs, and Incomes

There are two arguments that emerge from the GAJ: the first is that when we consider these factors together, they suggest that 'graduate' jobs and incomes will be squeezed in countries like the UK and US due to increasing global cost competition. The quality–cost revolution is consistent with a high-skilled, low-wage workforce from which Western workers are not exempt. Secondly, as digital Taylorism advances up the skills ladder, various aspects of technical, managerial, or professional work will be standardized or substituted by technology. This analysis challenges the idea of a linear progression towards more of the workforce being employed in knowledge-intensive occupations. It points towards a global dual auction (Brown et al., 2011) in which some with a graduate education will continue to be well rewarded for their 'investments' in higher education while many others, with the same credentials, will struggle to gain much by way of a 'graduate premium'. This dual auction is symptomatic of the global restructuring of the division of labour and the (re)stratification of knowledge work, where those defined as 'talent' are fast-tracked into senior management positions and given 'permission to think'. Below them there will be 'developer' roles executing the strategies of the talented, while below them are those that operate digitalized routines. This stratification will be reflected in the dispersion of income for graduate work.

Overall, this suggests that new forms of work organization are being used to reduce the costs of graduate workers. But these new forms of work organization may equally apply to non-graduate work. Therefore, the increased supply of graduates may not be utilized in the way that human capital theorists predicted. In the UK, there is evidence of substantial graduate underemployment (ONS, 2013). Recent research also shows that graduates in non-graduate work are paid more than those without a bachelor's degree (Purcell et al., 2013). Brynin (2002) has suggested that such workers are being employed because they are more flexible than their non-graduate counterparts, which could account for the higher wages they attract. But their wages, skills, and occupational autonomy are less than if they could gain 'graduate' work.[5]

---

[5] The notion of 'graduate work' is not unproblematic. There may be significant differences in what constitutes a graduate degree, largely because universities are stratified in terms of reputation and possibly

Policy-makers have consistently drawn attention to the graduate premium, in which a degree is seen to give an overall financial advantage to graduates as opposed to non-graduates. In the UK, estimates as to the nature of this advantage have varied, with the current figure being some £100,000 over a lifetime (Purcell et al., 2013). But in the light of the GAJ, we would predict that the restructuring of graduate work will result in increasing income dispersion in the returns to a degree. Evidence from the UK Labour Force Survey is presented below.

These data show that the notion of the graduate premium, as a measure of wage advantage over non-graduates, needs to be treated sceptically. What we see is the increasing dispersion of graduate incomes across age groups and major differences in income between men and women. What is striking about graduate returns in the twenty-first century, is that they have changed little and the dispersion of graduate incomes clearly preceded the Great Recession (Brown et al., 2011; Mishel et al., 2012). Moreover, when we look at the incomes of top A-level students it is also clear that they confound human capital assumptions. We would expect that the more highly skilled a worker is the more they will earn. If we assume that graduates will be more highly skilled than non-graduates then this does not conform to the mantra of 'learning equals earning'.

Moreover, Mincer (1958) and others argued that human capital theory should take account of differences in work experience alongside education and training. Work experience is used to explain why incomes may increase with age, especially for those in more highly skilled occupations as their contribution becomes more valuable over time. There has also been a long-standing assumption in much of the policy literature on graduate incomes that they are characterized by incremental progression. However, Figures 11.1–11.4 below show that most graduates' incomes do not increase in line with acquired skills and experience as human capital theorists hypothesized. This suggests that the basis for remuneration has now changed significantly and that these data can be explained by flatter work organizations, the increasing supply of graduates entering the labour market, and changing wage structures, including performance- rather than seniority-based pay based on annual salary increments. That said, there is clearly more work to be done on how we are to understand the restructuring of knowledge work and its effects on graduate demand.

---

in terms of pedagogy and learning (Naidoo and Jamieson, 2006). Operationally, there are at least three ways of defining graduate work. The first is to ask graduates whether they are utilizing the knowledge, skills, and dispositions related to their degree. Most of the research in this area has adopted such an approach. The second is that employers are asked whether they have recruited graduates to undertake graduate level work, or whether they have employed them for other reasons to do with their social skills, reliability, punctuality, etc. The third way is to take an 'objective' view by a priori classification of graduate and non-graduate occupations and then estimating whether graduates are in graduate or non-graduate occupations. It is significant that estimates of underemployment are typically higher when objective measures are used rather than subjective measures related to graduates' judgements. An inference to be drawn is that the subjective measures reflect judgements relative to the type of university education respondents received.

That said, without a concept like that of 'graduate work' it is difficult to benchmark concepts like underemployment, under- and over-qualification. One way out of this conundrum might be that adopted by the OECD (2013).

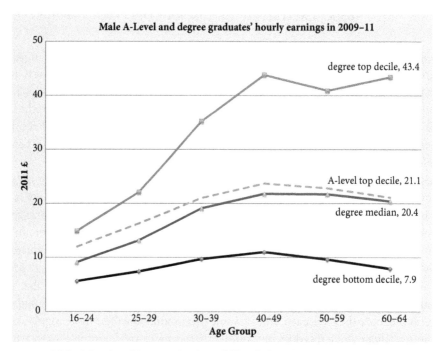

FIGURE 11.1 Male A-level and Degree Graduates' Hourly Earnings 2009–11.

Source: Labour Force Survey 2009–11 pooled samples. Data weighted by piwt10 and CPI adjusted to 2011 £

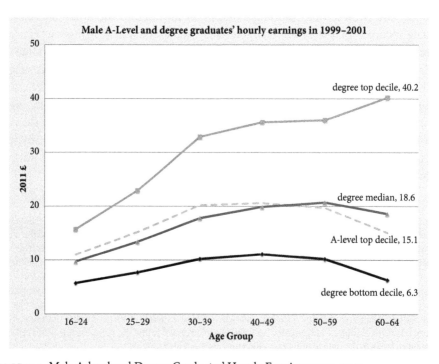

FIGURE 11.2 Male A-level and Degree Graduates' Hourly Earnings 1999–2001.

Source: Labour Force Survey 1999–2001 pooled samples. Data weighted by piwt10 and CPI adjusted to 2011 £

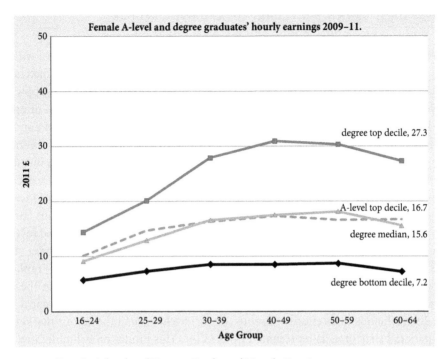

FIGURE 11.3 Female A-level and Degree Graduates' Hourly Earnings 2009–11.

Source: Labour Force Survey 2009–11 pooled samples. Data weighted by piwt10 and CPI adjusted to 2011 £

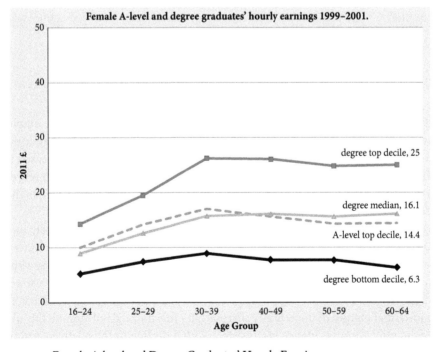

FIGURE 11.4 Female A-level and Degree Graduates' Hourly Earnings 1999–2001.

Source: Labour Force Survey 1999–2001 pooled samples. Data weighted by piwt10 and CPI adjusted to 2011 £

While we have argued that the dispersion of graduate incomes is consistent with the GAJ, it can also be interpreted as consistent with the notion of skills mismatches in human capital theory. The latter sees skills mismatches as a function of the supply side in two standard ways. The first is vertical mismatches in which there is an over- or under-supply of skills, precisely the point at issue in this discussion. The second concerns horizontal mismatches in which the skills supplied do not match demand. There is a considerable literature on both vertical and horizontal mismatches and it is inevitable that there will always be some mismatch of this kind given the dynamic nature of capitalism. The question is whether a skills mismatch can explain the dispersion of incomes in the above figures, or indeed the dispersion of incomes within occupations (Brown et al., 2011). Human capital theory rarely takes into account the dispersion of incomes within occupations, which we would argue reflects changes in labour market structures rather than simply a mismatch between skill supply and demand (Frank and Cook, 1995; Newfield, 2012). As such, human capital theory cannot explain the relationship between graduate skills and income given its reliance on methodological individualism which is theoretically blind to the major changes in the labour market and occupational structure, as represented by the GAJ. This limitation is highlighted by a consideration of the 'over-qualification' of graduates which has been heightened by the Great Recession.

We now turn to what can be taken as the effects of the Great Recession on graduate jobs and wages.

11.8 EARLY CAREER GRADUATES AND THE GREAT RECESSION

According to the ONS (2013) the percentage of recent graduates who were employed in non-graduate roles has risen from 37 per cent in 2001 to 47 per cent in 2013. Much of this rise is explained by the recession in 2008/09, when the percentage increased from 40 per cent to 47 per cent in the five years following 2008. Similar trends with respect to both returns to a degree and the type of work undertaken can also be observed in the US as a consequence of the Great Recession (Vedder et al., 2013).

It would follow that the mean income of underemployed graduates is likely to have declined relative to those who are in 'graduate' jobs. But recent evidence also shows this to be true for those who found 'graduate' jobs. The UK Futuretrack study (Purcell et al., 2013) calculates an average 21.9 per cent decline in wages relative to average weekly earnings between 1999 and 2009/10. However, the principal authors caution that 'there is a substantial margin of uncertainty surrounding this finding' but 'despite this uncertainty the most recent evidence is consistent with a decline in the relative earnings of newly qualified graduates' (Elias and Purcell, 2013, p. 1). These findings raise questions about the returns to graduates and also about the cost in tuition fees as part of the investment in becoming a graduate. There is now a debate developing about the sustainability of tripling the cost of current fee levels introduced by the UK Coalition government and these data clearly speak to this debate.[6]

Arguably, these trends have been exacerbated by the recession rather than caused by it.[7] Given market failure prior to the Great Recession (Stiglitz, 2012), it is clear that the demand for graduate work has not matched the rhetoric associated with the graduate premium or with the theoretical assumptions of human capital theory. Our analysis suggests that the relationship between education, jobs, and incomes has become increasingly 'disorganized'. As such, there is a need for the development of industrial strategies to re-engineer the links between skills, jobs, and incomes. The alternative to human capital theory is to develop industrial policies that work with the market to raise the demand for graduate jobs and narrow income inequalities. This is not an easy task. If we are to understand the challenge that is presented for industrial policy we need to identify the tensions within current policies that have adopted a human capital approach. We then outline the formidable challenge in developing industrial policy in the light of the GAJ.

11.9 INDUSTRIAL POLICY AND THE TENSIONS WITHIN HUMAN CAPITAL PRESCRIPTIONS

There are three issues that relate to human capital theory which cast doubt on its policy prescriptions. Firstly, policy-makers who follow the precepts of human capital theory assume that there is a coincidence of interests between workers, the nation state, and TNCs. But TNCs now have more options to play national education and training systems off against each other, as they internationalize their sourcing options or indeed substitute skilled labour with technology through the increasing use of digital Taylorism (Brown et al., 2011; Brynjolfsson and McAfee, 2011). The key point is that while nations see upgrading their skills as crucial to raising individual and national income, transnational companies have found new ways of sourcing high skills at lower cost. This suggests that industrial policy should not conflate national with corporate economic interests, although these can converge in certain circumstances. Putting business at the centre of industrial policy makes sense; putting business at the heart of government decision-making does not. To achieve 'embedded autonomy' (Evans, 1995) in today's world economy requires leading civil servants and policy-makers to be, as we were told in Singapore, 'smarter than the smartest captains of industry'.

---

[6] See the reports in the *Guardian*, Saturday 22 March 2014.

[7] It is not only transnational corporations that seek to reduce costs by offshoring but also the state. While figures on the offshoring of state jobs are difficult to ascertain, there has been a major corporate effort to encourage the state to reduce costs in this way.

Secondly, as the Great Recession has demonstrated, markets do not always allocate resources efficiently. Re-engineering the link between education, jobs, and incomes cannot be achieved simply by investing in more skills even if they are of a better quality, or by improved productivity, because countries—including the US—have found that productivity gains have been captured by corporate executives and shareholders rather than employees (Piketty, 2014). In turn, this raises fundamental questions about the links between productivity and rewards. The key point here for industrial policy is to make it possible for education, productivity, and rewards to be more closely aligned.

Thirdly, the nature of education and skills and their relationship to productivity constitutes an elephant in the theoretical room of human capital theory, despite being crucial to understanding the possibilities for economic development. Human capital theorists assume that the nature and quality of education can be accurately reflected in international test scores (e.g. PISA, TIMMS), yet these scores tell us very little about the different national forms of pedagogy, curricula, and assessment. We might expect that different educational systems will construct future workers in quite different ways with respect to their views of knowledge and learning. It is perhaps for this reason that East Asian countries have had a fundamental concern with what they perceive to be the failure of their education systems to produce creative workers. In turn, this issue suggests that education may have an important role to play in economic development but that it is far more complex than that suggested by human capital theorists (Lauder et al., 2012) and those policy-makers who believe that repeated academic testing is the route to higher educational standards and economic success.

11.10 The GAJ and the Restructuring of the Global Labour Market

11.10.1 Supply Issues

Investment in education and skills remains an essential part of any national strategy for emerging economies to enter the global economy and for developed economies to remain competitive.[8] This remains true even with trends towards the globalization of high skills that reduce the value of human capital as a source of national competitive advantage. A key policy challenge is to identify what learning, knowledge, and employability skills could continue to offer a competitive advantage even if there is less to be gained from simply investing in the generic expansion of college or university education.

---

[8] That said, the changing fortunes of Nokia in Finland provides something of a test case, since Finland has one of the world's best-educated workforces. But given the fate of Nokia, the question remains as to whether Finland can recover from the 'hit' its economy has taken as a result of the decline of Nokia.

Countries such as China have shown that it is possible to expand higher education on a massive scale in a relatively short period of time, but along with many emerging and developed economies they confront an endemic problem of over-qualification and graduate underemployment and unemployment. This is closely related to an issue that governments need to recognize in developing supply-side strategies that often expose a fault line between the perceived demands of global competition and commitment to educational opportunity and social inclusion. In attempting to create 'world-class' schools, colleges and universities, national hierarchies can also be transformed. This is exemplified by reforms in German higher education. The German system was previously based on 'parity of esteem' between research universities. There has been little difference in the market value of a degree from one German university rather than another. The introduction of 'excellence' reforms threatens to change this as more resources have been targeted at a small number of universities, creating an elite in an attempt to lift the profile of German higher education within global rankings of leading universities (Kupfer, 2011).

Therefore, abandoning a national commitment to educational opportunities based on a 'level playing field' has the (un)intended consequence of creating educational elites which transforms the positional relationship between students from different universities. In an attempt to recruit the 'best' and to be seen to do so, leading companies will target these elite groups, assuming that the most talented students will go to these universities because they are the most selective. Hence, the idea of a war for talent in Germany is real in its consequences. The result may be growing inequalities in income and life chances between German graduates (Kupfer, 2011).

The final point to make in respect to supply-side issues is that investments in human capital are a 'complementary condition' for a viable industrial strategy. It is to how the supply-side complements other aspects of a nation's industrial strategy, including labour demand, that we now turn.

11.10.2 Demand Issues

In constructing industrial policy to raise the demand for graduate work, the approach we've developed in respect to the GAJ emphasizes two key issues. TNCs are now as agile as they are restless, as Marx and Schumpeter have famously described. The result is that TNCs can react more quickly to new market opportunities, undermining national strategies to meet the 'needs' of industry. The 'inside-out' model of production, noted above, creates a significant temporal issue at the heart of national skill formation. So long as corporations have a supply of skilled labour and basic infrastructure they can set up more or less anywhere and decamp when they see cost advantages elsewhere (see also Coffey and Tomlinson, 2006). Moreover, Wade (2012) has suggested that FDI by itself does not necessarily produce gains for a nation; rather, the key is to create the spillovers that can benefit national development.

In thinking through these issues, it is clear that there are opportunities for industrial policy which do not need to rely on top-down decision-making. There are other ways of raising graduate demand. In Germany, for example, there is a clear recognition that its success has rested on engineering high quality products and incremental innovation. Now they are seeking to develop firms that will be world leaders in what they view as the knowledge-driven global economy. In an interview with a senior policy-maker who played a leading role in developing a national 'cluster competition', he asserted, 'we don't trust the market, we pick winners'. The cluster competition is based on different consortia or networks of SMEs and larger national firms and universities entering the competition for federal funds based on specific ways in which they can demonstrate the potential for high level innovation.

Here the role of industrial policy does not stop with investments from a TNC or in facilitating international market access for local companies. Underlying the cluster concept is the imperative to work with companies, universities, and training systems to improve productivity and quality. Under these conditions successful companies are less likely to relocate overseas if they are in receipt of public investment for skills training and business innovation. However, any state support for skills training or building productive capability needs to be linked to employee incomes. Any improvement in productivity resulting from public investment must be shared with employees rather than wholly captured by employers and shareholders, which often happens when it is left to the market to decide who gets what, given significant differences in labour market power. In this respect the cluster competition is not the only viable form of industrial policy; however, it does attempt to address the challenges that we have outlined.

11.10.3 Returns (Who Gets What)

In human capital theory, the returns to education are calculated as individual wages and then, as in the case of Hanushek and Woessmann (2007), aggregated to the national level. However, from the perspective of the GAJ model, calculations of this kind are problematic for at least two reasons. Firstly, they assume a form of inductive reasoning from which the future can be extrapolated from the past, a point that we would challenge. What such a method ignores is precisely Schumpeter's insight about the fundamental changes that capitalism can create, such that assumptions of 'business as usual' assumed by inductivist methods no longer apply. Secondly, in the account of the GAJ that we have given, it is not at all clear where the benefits to education will be captured. One of the key points here is that incomes within occupations are polarizing (Brown et al., 2011). The rates of return to employees with the same level of education and skills are far removed from the equation of 'learning equals earning'. While skill bias theories (Goldin and Katz, 2008) posit unobserved skills to explain this phenomenon, our account of the GAJ provides an alternative 'grounded' approach that highlights a number of interrelated factors including the restructuring of the global labour market. Newfield

(2012) has noted with respect to engineers in the United States that an explanation for the disparity in their incomes stems not from a shortage of engineers but from a glut in supply. This has enabled leading firms like Microsoft and Apple to differentiate a few core or 'insider' workers from those hired on a project-by-project basis, leaving many well-qualified people with little option other than to 'pitch' for project work from these companies. This project-based competition can now be extended globally through, for example, crowd sourcing. At the same time as we are seeing these disparities in incomes within the same occupations, the benefits of producing goods like an iPhone accrue largely to the executives and core workers in Seattle despite the supply chain stretching across the Pacific to China and South Korea (Dedrick et al., 2009).

Our research shows that the assumption that hi-tech economic development depends on social sophistication in the form of democratic politics, skill formation, and welfare provision fails to capture the extreme forms of uneven development, especially in emerging economies (Brown et al., 2011) as the case of the inside-out model of production demonstrates.

Hence, governing the market (Wade, 1992) through judicious industrial policies must address income inequalities and the distribution of returns from gains in productivity. To say this much is to articulate an aspiration. But in the context of the GAJ, what we are most likely to confront is the spread of high-skills, low-cost models in developed as well as emerging economies. While this poses a threat to the livelihoods of college-educated workers in the West, it also represent a significant policy challenge to emerging economies for the simple reason that the high-skills, low-cost model has been used as a source of competitive advantage. Therefore, emerging economies have compelling reasons to maintain this cost advantage by restricting the speed and scale of wage hikes that may ultimately impact on their cost advantage. National governments and corporations in emerging economies, including China and India, therefore confront a major challenge in managing the salary and social expectations of a rising middle class, and at the same time lift more of the population out of poverty.

11.11 CONCLUSION

At the most abstract level, human capital theorists could claim that these structural changes are entirely consistent with their theory; instead of viewing the theory within national contexts, we should apply it to global labour markets. If there is an oversupply of graduates and they are appreciably cheaper in some places than others, then it might be claimed that our account is consistent with theirs. This is a pyrrhic victory. It fails in both explanatory power and the ability to make plausible policy prescriptions. As regards explanatory power, it fails in its own terms since a new global equilibrium is not likely, except in the very long term, and it lacks the explanatory power of the GAJ account on which to make policy. For example, the transformation of the global division of labour and the integration of production by transnational corporations through global value chains means that the focus on labour supply and flexible labour markets cannot be left to resolve the issues of labour demand.

Given these points, the idea that the Great Recession represents little more than a hiccup along the evolutionary path of human capital development is, at best, doubtful. Indeed, the data we have presented show that many of the key trends, with respect to graduate incomes, were in train well before the Great Recession. If the structural changes that we have outlined provide a better understanding of why there will be no return to 'business as usual' as predicted by human capital theory, it follows the nation state must play a key facilitating role, requiring a different way of thinking about the market. Creating quality jobs that offer decent wages cannot be achieved by neo-liberal market policies. We are, however, also aware that there is much more work to be done to develop a better understanding of the structural hypotheses that we have developed in this paper. Developing new theories of globalization, new technologies, and the labour market constitutes a key building block from which to start the arduous task of developing viable industrial policy. The stakes could not be higher as the quality of a nation's industrial policy will determine its global competitiveness and its ability to address issue of social cohesion and justice.

REFERENCES

Baumol, W. (1993). 'Health Care, Education and the Cost Disease: A Looming Crisis for Public Choice', *Public Choice* 77, 17–28.

Becker, G. (1985). 'The Best Industrial Policy is None At All', *Business Week* August, 25.

Becker, G. (1992). *The Economic Way of Looking at Life*, Nobel Prize Lecture, Stockholm.

Becker, G. (2006). 'The Age of Human Capital', in H. Lauder, P. Brown, J. A. Dillabough, and A. H. Halsey (eds), *Education, Globalization and Social Change*. Oxford: Oxford University Press.

Bluestone, B. (1972). 'Economic Theory and the Fate of the Poor', *Social Policy* 2, 30–1 and 46–8.

Brown, P., Lauder, H., and Ashton, D. (2011). *The Global Auction: The Broken Promises of Education, Jobs and Incomes*. New York: Oxford University Press.

Brynin, M. (2002). 'Graduate Density, Gender and Employment', *The British Journal of Sociology* 53(3), 363–81.

Brynjolfsson, E. and McAfee, A. (2011). *Race Against the Machine*. Digital Frontier Press.

Carter, M. and Carnoy, M. (1974). Theories of Labour Markets and Worker Productivity, Centre for Economic Studies, Palo Alto California, Discussion Paper.

Coffey, D. and Tomlinson, P. R. (2006). 'Multiple Facilities, Strategic Splitting and Vertical Structures: Stability, Growth and Distribution Reconsidered', *The Manchester School* 74(5), 558–76.

Clarke, S. (1982). *Marx, Marginalism and Modern Sociology*. London and New York: Macmillan.

Dedrick, J., Kraemer, K. L., and Linden, G. (2009). Who Profits from Innovation in Global Value Chains?, Industry Studies Association, Working Paper WP-2008-15.

Doeringer, P. and Piore, M. (1971). *Internal Labour Markets and Manpower Analysis*. Lexington, MA: DC Heath.

Elias, P. and Purcell, K. (2013). *The Earnings of Graduates: Reviewing the Evidence from Futuretrack*, Institute for Employment Studies, Warwick University, Working Paper No. 6.

Evans, P. (1995). *Embedded Autonomy: States and Industrial Transformation*. Princeton, NJ: Princeton University Press.

Finegold, D. and Soskice, D. (1988). 'The Failure of Training in Britain: Analysis and Prescription', *Oxford Review of Economic Policy* 15(1), 60–81.

Frank, R. and Cook, P. (1995). *Winner Take All Society*. New York: The Free Press.

Goldin, C. and Katz., L. (2008). *The Race between Education and Technology*. Cambridge, MA: Harvard University Press.

Gordon, D. (1971). *Theories of Poverty and Underemployment*. Lexington, MA: DC Heath.

Hanushek, E. and Woessmann, L. (2007). *Education, Quality and Economic Growth*. Washington DC: World Bank.

Hanushek, E., Schwerdt, G., Wiederhold, S., and Woessmann, L. (2013). *Returns to Skills around the World: Evidence from PIAAC*, OECD Education Working Papers No. 101, <http://dx.doi.org/10.1787/5k3tsjqmvtq2-en>.

Kupfer, A. (2011). 'Towards a Theoretical Framework for the Comparative Understanding of Globalisation, Higher Education, the Labour Market', *Journal of Education and Work* 24(1–2), 185–208.

Lauder, H., Brown, P., and Tholen, G. (2012). 'The Global Auction Model, Skill Bias Theory and Graduate Incomes: Reflections on Methodology', in H. Lauder, M. Young, H. Daniels, M. Balarin, and J. Lowe (eds), *Educating for the Knowledge Economy?: Critical Perspectives*, pp. 43–65. Abingdon: Routledge.

Meyer, D. and Benavot, A. (2013). *Pisa, Power and Policy*. Oxford: Symposium Books.

Michaels, E., Handfield-Jones, H., and Axelrod, B. (2001). *The War For Talent*. Boston, Mass: Harvard Business School Press.

Mincer, J. (1958). 'Investment in Human Capital and Personal Income Distribution', *Journal of Political Economy* 66, 281–302.

Mishel, L. (2012). *The Wedges Between Productivity and Median Compensation Growth*, Economic Policy Institute, Issue Brief No. 330.

Mishel, L., Bivens, J., Gould, E., and Sherholz, H. (2012). *The State of Working America*. Ithaca: Cornell University.

Naidoo, R. and Jamieson, I. (2006). 'Empowering Participants or Corroding Learning? Towards a Research Agenda on the Impact of Consumerism in Higher Education', in H. Lauder, P. Brown, J.-A. Dillabough and A. H. Halsey (eds), *Education, Globalization and Social Change*, pp. 875–84. Oxford: Oxford University Press.

Newfield, C. (2012). 'The Structure and Silence of the Cognotariat', in A. Kupfer (ed.), *Globalisation, Higher Education, the Labour Market and Inequality*, pp. 163–78. Abingdon: Routledge.

OECD (Organisation for Economic Co-operation and Development) (2013). *Skills Outlook 2013: First Results from the Survey of Adult Skills*. Paris: OECD.

ONS (Office for National Statistics) (2013). *Graduates in the Labour Market*. London: ONS.

Piketty, T. (2014). *Capital in the Twenty-First Century*. Harvard, MA: The Belknap Press.

Purcell, K., Elias, P., Atfield, G., and Ritva, H. Futuretrack Stage 4 Report (2013). Transitions into Employment, Further Study and other Outcomes.

Schultz, T. (1961). 'Investment in Human Capital', *American Economic Review* 51(1), 1–17.

Stiglitz, J. (2012). *The Price of Inequality*. New York: W. W. Norton.

Thurow, L. (1972). 'Education and Economic Equality', *The Public Interest* 28, 66–81.

Vedder, R., Denhart, C., and Robe, J. (2013). *Why Are Recent College Graduates Underemployed?* Centre for College Affordability and Productivity.

Wade, R. (1992). *Governing the Market: Economic Theory and the Role of Government in East Asian Industrialization.* Princeton, NJ: Princeton University Press.

Wade, R. (2012). 'Return of Industrial Policy?', *International Review of Applied Economics* 26(2), 223–39.

Wimmer, A. and Glick Schiller, N. (2002). 'Methodological Nationalism and Beyond: Nation-State Building, Migration and the Social Sciences', *Global Networks* 2(4), 301–34.

CHAPTER 12

WORKERS' VOICE
IN COMPANY
DECISION-MAKING

JANET WILLIAMSON AND TIM PAGE

12.1 INTRODUCTION

IT is an important principle of natural justice and of democracy that those affected by decisions should have some say in the making of those decisions. Not a veto, but a voice. In many areas of our lives, this basic principle is taken for granted. From it stems our right to elect people to represent us in local, national, and European government. It is reflected in the governance arrangements of many institutions, including schools, where it is well established that teachers and parents should be represented on governing bodies, and pupils selected by their peers feed in views through school councils.

However, on entering the workplace, this basic tenet of democracy is left at the door. Despite the fact that those in full-time employment spend a significant proportion of their daily lives at work, workers have no automatic right to influence the decisions that are taken there. In the UK, many workers are not even informed and consulted in advance about changes to workplace strategy or organization. Under the Information and Consultation of Employees Regulations 2005 (ICE Regs), employers are only required to inform and consult their workers if such rights have been 'triggered' by a request from at least 10 per cent of the workforce—which in non-unionized workplaces is a pretty high barrier to what should be a basic right for all.

This is in stark contrast to the situation in much of Continental Europe. Many European countries have well-developed structures that combine strong union representation with works councils and worker representation on boards, creating a system where the voice of workers is captured by different means and at different levels within the organization. Some of these will be explored in more detail below.

This chapter argues for workers' voice to become part of the architecture of corporate governance in the UK. A definition of workers' voice clearly needs to be established.

In our view, mechanisms for workers' voice should allow a say for workers in the way the company is managed and in its strategic objectives. Crucially, workers' voice would allow the input of workers to be heard when major changes are occurring within the company. Workers are not, of course, the only company stakeholders, but they are a major stakeholder.[1] In addition, steps must be taken to ensure that workers' voice is independent of management and that workers are able to speak collectively in order to ensure that worker representatives can engage with management on a legitimate basis. In many cases, this is likely to mean that workers' voice should come via an independent trade union.

There is a strong argument for strengthening provisions for workers' voice in UK companies based on the case for natural justice and rights to a voice. However, as we shall see, the value of workers' voice goes beyond that. There is convincing evidence that strengthening workers' voice would make an important contribution to addressing the problems of low productivity and low investment that have dogged British industry over recent decades.

12.2 CORPORATE GOVERNANCE IN THE UK (AND THE WEAKNESS OF SHAREHOLDER PRIMACY)

An important part of the reason for the lack of provision for workers' voice in the private sector in the UK lies in the UK's corporate governance system, which is based on what can be called 'shareholder primacy'. Under UK corporate governance, shareholders are the only stakeholder group with significant rights in relation to how companies are run. For example, shareholders, and shareholders alone, elect company directors, now annually in the FTSE 350, at company AGMs. Shareholders have had an advisory vote on company remuneration reports since 2003, and a binding shareholder vote on some aspects of executive remuneration was introduced in October 2013. Shareholders can propose resolutions at company AGMs and can vote on all resolutions. They can convene EGMs. Shareholder representatives can and do engage regularly with company boards, using meetings, letters and phone calls to make their views known. This engagement is seen as exerting a discipline on company boards which makes it an essential part of our corporate governance system; thus a common response from Government and others in response to corporate misdemeanours is that 'it's a matter for the company and its shareholders'.

In the market for corporate control, shareholders again hold all the cards. Despite the major impacts that mergers and takeovers can have on all stakeholder groups, in

---

[1] On exercising 'voice' and widening participation in strategic decision-making processes (in corporations and society more widely), see also Branston et al. (2006, 2015, forthcoming). On the general concept of 'voice', see Hirschman (1970).

particular workers, and indeed the company itself, the decision as to whether a merger or takeover goes ahead rests with shareholders alone. However, the most fundamental right that shareholders enjoy is that under UK company law, directors' duties require them to promote the success of the company for the benefit of its shareholders as their primary aim. In so doing, directors are required to have regard to the long-term consequences of their decisions, the interests of employees, supplier and customer relationships, and community, environmental, and reputational impacts. However, these factors are to be considered insofar as they contribute to shareholder interests, rather than in their own right.

The changing patterns of share ownership in recent years present a major challenge to the reliance on shareholder engagement within the UK's corporate governance system. In the 1960s, the majority of shares in UK companies were owned by individuals, many of whom took a reasonable level of interest in the companies whose shares they owned. By the 1980s, the majority of shares were owned by UK institutional investors such as pension funds and insurance companies. Today, this has changed again. The most recent figures from the Office for National Statistics show that by the end of 2012, UK pension funds and insurance companies held just 4.7 per cent and 6.2 per cent of UK equities respectively, the lowest percentages since the survey started in 1963, sharply down from a combined total of 43 per cent in 1998 and 26 per cent in 2008. In contrast, while individuals held 10.7 per cent, over half of UK listed shares—53.2 per cent—were owned by investors from outside the UK (data from ONS, 2013).

It will by definition be harder for investors from outside the UK to develop the kind of engaged relationships with UK companies that are required if the UK's corporate governance system is to work as intended. Language, culture, proximity, and availability of information all make engagement much more straightforward within a national context in comparison with engaging with companies abroad. However, engagement between UK investors and companies is also problematic. In contrast to individual domestic shareholders, who tend to hold shares in a limited number of companies in which they take a strong interest, institutional investors generally hold highly diversified portfolios. This means that for institutional investors, the sheer number of companies whose shares they own presents considerable practical obstacles to the quality and quantity of their engagement. The Investment Association (previously The Investment Management Association) says that on average its members hold shares in around 450 different companies, and for many it will be in the thousands. The other side of this coin is that the shareholders of a large listed company will number in the thousands if not the tens of thousands. Bizarrely, given the central role of shareholders in corporate governance, it can be difficult for a company even to get full information on who holds their shares. This fragmentation is in contrast to many Continental European countries, where more concentrated shareholdings are the norm. Systems that support concentrated shareholdings are often viewed unfavourably by UK investors, the argument being that the existence of a dominant shareholder will weaken the influence of other shareholders. However, in countries where such patterns are more common, concentrated shareholdings facilitate engaged and long-term relationships between companies and investors far better than the fragmented and diversified pattern of UK shareholding.

Directors' duties were codified for the first time in the Companies Act 2006. The justification for requiring directors to prioritize the interests of shareholders was that in the long term the interests of shareholders converge with those of other stakeholders. According to this argument, long-term shareholder interests are best served by companies that develop a long-term strategic approach to company success, which will benefit all stakeholders and the wider economy (The Company Law Review Steering Group, *Modern Company Law for a Competitive Economy: Developing the Framework* (2000)).

However, this convergence of interests between shareholders, the company, and other stakeholders only holds true if shareholders are long-term investors whose economic interest in a company is in receiving dividend payments over a significant period of time. If, on the other hand, the shareholder is a short-term share trader whose economic interest is in selling the company's shares for more than they bought them for, their interest will be in short-term strategies to boost the company's share price, regardless of the impact on long-term, organic company growth (see Sawyer, Chapter 6, this volume). In this case, the investor's interests will not coincide with those of other company stakeholders, nor, crucially, with the long-term interests of the company itself. If the investor is shorting the stock, their interests will actually be diametrically opposed to those of other company stakeholders, including long-term shareholders, and indeed the company, as they will stand to gain if the company's share price falls. In this scenario, it is impossible to justify why shareholders are the group whose interests companies are required to promote, and why shareholders have the ultimate say over how companies are run.

Increasingly, even so-called long-term investors rely on strategies based on share trading, rather than long-term shareholding, to generate income from share ownership. Share trading is essentially a zero-sum game in terms of overall economic gain, as for each beneficiary of a transaction there will also be a loser. However, unless substantial reform of the way in which asset managers operate takes place, including in the area of contracts and incentives for individual fund managers, the likelihood of fund managers adopting longer-term approaches to share ownership appears remote.

Investors' increasingly short-term approach to their shareholdings and reliance on strategies based on share trading rather than long-term share ownership cuts a deep hole in the UK's corporate governance system and leaves the arguments for shareholder primacy in tatters. Worryingly, there is evidence that directors tend to regard their legal duty as being to maximize short-term shareholder interests, rather than to promote long-term company success. For example, a study carried out for the Association of Chartered Certified Accountants found that executives generally regarded their duty as being to maximize their company's share price over the short term (Collison et al., 2011).

In contrast to short-term shareholders, the interests of workers are well correlated with those of the company they work for. As any union representative knows, the best employment security for their members is long-term company success, so effective mechanisms for workers' voice can help companies to prioritize long-term, organic growth over short-term financial engineering. While short-term share traders may favour using company profits to finance share buybacks to boost the company's share price, the interests of workers—and those of other long-term stakeholders and indeed the company itself—will be served by using company profits to finance R&D, training, and other long-term investment strategies. Thus policies to facilitate workers' voice can help to boost levels of company investment (as illustrated by the comparative international evidence in Section 12.3.2 below). The UK has a historic problem of low business investment that predated the financial crisis and subsequent recession, which makes the search for policies that would encourage higher rates of business investment increasingly urgent.

One of the justifications sometimes offered for the priority given to shareholder interests in corporate governance is that shareholders carry the greatest risk in relation to companies. However, this is contradicted by reality, whereby institutional shareholders hold large portfolios of shares precisely to spread their risk. Workers, on the other hand, invest their labour, skills, and commitment in the company they work for and cannot diversify this risk. If this investment goes wrong, for any reason, they and their families pay a heavy price—the loss of employment and loss of income, skills opportunities, and often health that this can bring. If carrying risk gives rights to representation and protection of interests, this supports the case for workers' voice in corporate governance.

There is no logical reason why our corporate governance should prioritize the interests of share traders over those of other stakeholders, nor why share traders should occupy such a privileged position in terms of their rights in relation to companies. The UK system of corporate governance should be reformed to make good the aim of representing the interests of a wider group of stakeholders. We will return to this in our recommendations and conclusions.

12.3 Economic Benefits of Facilitating Workers' Voice

There is clear evidence that shows that allowing the views of the workforce to be heard and taken into account can promote company success. As well as encouraging companies to take a long-term approach to strategy and investment, effective channels for workers' voice can also boost productivity.

12.3.1 Productivity

There is a great deal of evidence that shows a productivity benefit in allowing 'voice' for the workforce. A move towards workers' voice would therefore be particularly timely, as the UK needs to address the so-called 'productivity puzzle' that has existed since the 2008 economic downturn. Output per hour fell by almost 5 per cent in the five years after the crash; it remained below its 2008 levels, while employment levels (and hours worked) have both reached new highs.

The productivity puzzle remains unexplained, but at least part of the explanation is likely to be that there has been some sort of change in the composition of the labour market (which is likely to be at least partially reversed as demand in the economy grows). This compositional change may have accompanied a decline of high productivity sectors, with poor access to capital and weak investment contributing to exceptionally weak productivity performance.

The obvious next question is: What will happen to productivity going forward? With the return of economic growth, it seems likely that some productivity improvements should emerge, as increased demand boosts output, which should start to rise more quickly than hours worked. But the risk also remains that after such a long period of recession and economic stagnation, permanent damage has been done to the UK's productive potential, and that challenges we faced before the financial crash have been exacerbated since.

If this scenario is to be avoided there must be a serious focus on targeted action to address low productivity. In the absence of such action, there is a very real risk that the UK is now heading down the path towards becoming an even lower-productivity, lower-waged economy. Tackling Britain's long-running problems of underinvestment, short-termism, and powerful property-related business cycles is part of the solution. Harnessing the full contribution of employers is another part.

Strengthening workers' voice could play a vital role in tackling the UK's productivity deficit. Applebaum et al. (2011) summarize the evidence of a link between workers' voice and productivity. The authors note the Obama Administration's plan for supporting long-term, sustainable growth, which requires significant investments in various industries. However, according to the authors, a large body of evidence demonstrates that achieving a return on these investments requires a matching workforce development and workplace innovation strategy. In short, companies should adopt high performance work practices.

According to the authors, high performance work practices work in three different ways:

- They foster development in human capital, including increased employee skill development;
- They enhance the motivation and commitment of employees;
- They build organizational social capital, which facilitates knowledge sharing and the coordination of work.

The authors go on to say that labour–management partnerships based on mutual respect for worker, union, and employer rights and responsibilities have been shown to achieve high performance by facilitating employee participation and related high performance work practices and by creating social networks within and across organizations. Applebaum et al. go on to say: 'In particular, the presence of a union is positively associated with a greater number and greater effectiveness of high performance work practices.'

Tüselmann et al. (2007) studied worker representation, employee participation, and employment relations in German subsidiaries in the UK and their associated impact on firm performance. They found that German subsidiaries are more likely than their US counterparts to use participative systems that afford independent worker structures, taking the form of trade unions in the UK, a role in the decision-making in the introduction and operation of comprehensive direct employee participation schemes. Tüselmann et al. argue that this is because a majority of German multinational companies use a German works council model, which alongside sectoral collective bargaining promotes trust, cooperation, and long-term perspective in management–works council relations in Germany. They find that German subsidiaries with trade union recognition exhibit above-average productivity performance while experiencing no negative effect on their financial performance.

More recently, Bevan (2012) noted that the Swedish Metalworkers Union, about whom we will discuss more below, launched 'good work' as a generic policy concept in the mid-1980s. This concept had nine dimensions, of which worker co-determination was one. Bevan cites evidence to show that certain national institutional arrangements exacerbate the problem of shifting from low- to high-road strategies of work organization and quality. He argues that in the UK and the US, many businesses are forced to follow low value added, low skills and low innovation strategies by a combination of unregulated labour markets, weak trade unions, and pressure on companies to maximize short-term shareholder returns. This, he argues, is an example of the inherent tensions between the European social model and the so-called Anglo Saxon model which favours deregulation of labour markets.

12.3.2 The European Participation Index

Table 12.1 compares countries with high standards of workers' participation—meaning widespread rights and practices on board representation, workplace representation, and collective bargaining—with countries with comparatively lower standards. It shows that those countries with stronger participation rights score highly across a range of important measures, including R&D expenditure, employment rates, educational participation among young people, and educational achievement among older workers. What is more, these countries achieve both stronger economic success and a more equitable economic settlement: poverty and inequality rates are both lower than in countries with weaker workers' participation rights.

While correlations do not in themselves prove causality, the evidence on the productivity benefits of workers' voice and other clear evidence illustrating the positive impact of employee engagement supports the supposition that the link illustrated by the Participation Index is not just coincidental (see also Vitols, 2010).[2]

---

[2] See for example evidence in Macleod and Clarke (2009).

Table 12.1 The European Participation Index (2008–9 Data)

Europe 2020 headline indicator	Group 1 countries with stronger participation rights*	Group 2 countries with weaker participation rights*
Employment rate by gender, age group 20–64 (2009)	72.1	67.4
Gross domestic expenditure on R&D (GERD) (2008)	2.2	1.4
Share of renewables in gross final energy consumption (2008)	12.3	6.1
Energy intensity of the economy (2008)	171.2	181.7
Early leavers from education and training (2009)	14.0	16.1
Tertiary educational attainment by gender, age group 30–34 (2009)	36.6	31.1
Population at risk of poverty or exclusion (2008)	19.1	25.4

* Group I countries: Austria, Denmark, Finland, France, Germany, Greece, Luxembourg, the Netherlands, and Sweden.
** Group II countries: Belgium, Bulgaria, Cyprus, the Czech Republic, Estonia, Hungary, Ireland, Italy, Lithuania, Latvia, Malta, Poland, Portugal, Romania, Slovakia, Slovenia, Estonia, and the UK.

12.4 Workers' Representation on Company Boards in Europe

In the majority of Continental European countries, workers have a voice in corporate governance.[3] In France, Norway, Sweden, and Romania, workers have the right to attend and speak at company AGMs. In Slovenia, Germany, and Poland, the workforce is entitled to elect or appoint a member of the management team in certain cases. In France, Sweden, Bulgaria, Hungary, and the Netherlands, workers are entitled to attend and/or submit a resolution to the company AGM. However, by far the most common mechanism for workers' voice in corporate governance in Europe is for workers to be represented on company boards. Sometimes workers' rights to board representation exist alongside other corporate governance rights as outlined above.

In fourteen of the EU Member States plus Norway (i.e. 14 out of 29) workers have significant rights to be represented on company boards. These countries are Austria, Croatia, the Czech Republic, Germany, Denmark, Finland, France, Hungary, Luxembourg, the

---

[3] This section draws extensively on a TUC report written by Aline Conchon, Workers' voice in corporate governance: a European perspective, Conchon (2013).

Netherlands, Norway, Sweden, Slovenia, and Slovakia. In addition, there are five countries in which workers have more limited rights to board representation, mainly in state-owned or privatized companies. These are Greece, Ireland, Poland, Portugal, and Spain.

This means that 19 of the EU Member States plus Norway (i.e. 19 out of 29) have some provision for workers' representation on company boards. If the analysis is narrowed to the European Union, 18 out of 28 Member States have some form of provision for worker representation on company boards. In the other ten countries there are no provisions for workers' representation on company boards. In addition to the UK, these are Belgium, Bulgaria, Cyprus, Estonia, Italy, Latvia, Lithuania, Malta, and Romania. However, it is worth noting that in two of these countries, Bulgaria and Romania, there are other provisions for workers' voice in corporate governance.

There is no one model of workers' representation on boards across Europe, and the way in which workers' participation rights operate varies from country to country. These variations include:

- how worker representatives are nominated and elected;
- who is eligible to become a worker board representative;
- which companies are covered by requirements on workers' board participation;
- the proportion or number of worker representatives required per board; and
- the board structure (unitary or two-tier) to which workers' participation rights apply.

In nearly all the countries, candidates are elected by the workforce, but there are also a few countries where the appointment is at the company AGM (for example, the Netherlands and Hungary). In a majority of countries unions have nomination rights or are involved in the nomination of candidates in some way. There are also examples of works councils having nomination rights (sometimes alongside union nomination rights).

In terms of eligibility, a majority of countries stipulate that worker representatives must be company employees. However, there are variations, and Austria restricts eligibility to works council members and a number of countries have no restrictions on eligibility. In Germany and Luxembourg, eligibility varies according to sector and is restricted to trade union representatives in some sectors, while in others it is restricted to company employees. The Netherlands is a distinct case in which the representative cannot be a company employee nor a trade union representative. The role is therefore carried out by people sympathetic to the labour movement but one step removed from it, such as academics.

The scope of requirements on workers' participation varies greatly. In most countries the rights apply to both private and listed companies, but four countries restrict rights to plcs (the Czech Republic, France, Luxembourg, and Slovakia). As has already been mentioned, there are five countries where workers' participation rights are restricted to state-owned or privatized enterprises. The size of company covered by workers' participation rights varies significantly from country to country, and also in some cases within countries according to sector. In eight countries, workers' participation rights apply at state-owned enterprises regardless of company size. There are also two countries—Austria and Croatia—in which workers' participation rights apply to all plcs regardless of size.

However, most countries do apply a minimum size threshold for the application of workers' participation rights, especially for their private sector companies. These vary from 25 to 50 employees in six countries, to 50 to 500 employees in seven countries and 1,000 employees in Luxembourg. The highest threshold is found in France, which in May 2013 adopted a law extending mandatory worker representation on boards to plcs with at least 5,000 employees in France or 10,000 employees worldwide.

In terms of the number or proportion of worker representatives, again there are significant variations. The most common provision is that worker representatives should make up one-third of the board. There are four countries where worker representatives make up half the board in some cases (Germany in companies with over 2,000 employees and the Czech Republic, Slovenia, and Slovakia where allowed for in company articles). However, even in these cases, workers cannot exert a blocking or binding vote against the whole of the rest of the board; in Germany and Slovenia the chair, who always comes from the 'shareholder side', has a casting vote in the case of a tie.

It is important to note that workers' rights to representation on boards apply in countries that operate with a unitary board structure (like the UK) as well as in countries that operate with a two-tier or supervisory board structure. This has particular relevance in the context of the UK corporate governance debate, where hostility is often expressed towards dual or two-tier boards systems. Five countries—Sweden, Norway, Spain, Greece, and Ireland—combine a unitary board structure with established worker participation rights. There are also nine countries where the unitary and two-tier board systems operate alongside each other and companies can choose which they adopt, and in these countries workers' participation rights generally apply regardless of whether the company has a unitary or two-tier board.

Importantly, in all the countries where it exists, workers' representation on boards operates alongside unions carrying out their traditional role of directly representing their members' interests through collective bargaining (although, as discussed above, in many countries where workforce representatives must be company employees, it is very common for those employees to be union representatives or at least union members).

Overall, while worker representation on boards is very much the norm across Europe as a whole, there is considerable diversity in the way it operates and the form it takes. Workers' participation can operate in a variety of ways, and works well across a wide range of very different corporate governance systems. In considering possible options for workers' board participation in the UK, there is much to learn from the existing systems across different countries, but it is clear that this is not something that lends itself to 'one size fits all'. There may nonetheless be elements from particular systems that could work well in the UK. It would be entirely possible to combine elements from different existing systems with new provisions to create a workers' participation framework uniquely suited to the UK context.

The value of worker board representatives is recognized by company representatives and other board members. For example, a survey of Swedish companies showed that 61 per cent of managing directors found the impact of worker board representation at their company positive, with just 9 per cent finding it negative. Company chairpersons had a still more positive view, with 69 per cent describing the impact on their company as positive and just 5 per cent finding it negative. In the same survey, 64 per cent of managing directors and 61 per cent of company chairpersons thought that employee board representatives contributed to a 'positive cooperative climate'. Only a tiny minority (7 per cent of managing directors and 6 per cent of company chairpersons) thought that it created a risk of conflict between board members and only a minority thought it led to an increased risk of information leakage (which is often cited by detractors as an argument against introducing worker board representation) (see Levinson, 2001).

Gold's (2011) recent study based on interviews with worker board representatives in thirteen countries presents a picture of worker representatives making a genuine difference to the way in which decisions are made. Examples of their influence included cases where the worker representatives had recognized the risks of a merger and combined with some of the shareholder representatives to reject the plans; the rejection of plans for a new office on the grounds of cost; and a situation where a worker representative had argued against plans for outsourcing using arguments about exchange rates and other market factors that turned out to be right and convinced shareholder board representatives to reject the plans. The author concludes that 'employee representation contributes towards a more broadly based corporate strategy by ensuring that it takes into account at an early stage the views and interests of organised labour'.

The argument that worker representatives contribute towards a broadly based corporate strategy is also supported by a Danish study which found that worker representatives were more likely than shareholder representatives to take into account broader stakeholder interests, including community interests and environmental impacts (Rose, 2005). Closer to home, the Irish Think-tank for Action on Social Change (TASC) published a report on worker board participation in Ireland in 2012 based on interviews and discussions with worker board representatives, other board members, company executives, and independent experts. It concluded that 'worker directors were felt to be loyal to the company, trustworthy and diligent in their duties; their contribution was viewed as positive and unique by over three-quarters of respondents; in particular, their intimate operational knowledge of the enterprise was highlighted by respondents. Almost all respondents stated that they had never heard of a breach of confidentiality or conflict of interest in relation to worker directors'. In addition, over half the interviewees mentioned the importance of having a contrary voice on the board in order to avoid group-think and promote diversity (TASC, 2012).

Still closer to home is the experience of FirstGroup, which has had an employee director since the company was created in 1992. Employee representation exists at different levels of the company: each division elects an employee representative to sit on their divisional board. The employee director for the main board is elected by this group of divisional employee representatives from their ranks. The company also recognizes trade unions, and the current employee board director is a union member.

Martin Gilbert, outgoing chair of FirstGroup, described the company's experience in the following terms: 'The presence of employee directors on the FirstGroup board is invaluable. The few drawbacks are greatly outweighed by the benefits and having this two-way channel of communication has positively impacted on the running of FirstGroup.'[4]

12.5 WORKERS' VOICE BELOW BOARD LEVEL

Workers' representation at board level is generally part of a wider structure for workers' voice at other levels of the company. Here we will look briefly at the systems in place in Sweden, Germany, and France for workers' voice below board level.

In Sweden, the system of employee engagement stipulates a role only for trade unions; the workers' representative is the trade union with a collective agreement with the employer. Employee involvement is defined as any mechanism, including information, consultation, and participation, through which employees' representatives may exercise influence on decisions to be taken within the company. Under the Swedish system, the trade union with collective agreement may also demand consultations with the employer on other issues that concern a member. There are no thresholds as to when the legislation is applicable; in other words, the union need have only one member. In companies with more than 25 employees the trade union with collective agreement may, if they wish, appoint members of the board.

Sweden's system of employee engagement operates in a context of high trade union membership, high employer organization, and a high level of collective agreement coverage, in the private as well as public sectors. The trade union density is 71 per cent and collective agreement coverage is about 90 per cent. Indeed, the law prevents information and consultation in the absence of trade unions. Collective agreements can build on the provisions of Swedish labour law if management and union wish to do so.

Supporters of the Anglo-Saxon model of employee relations, where a union role is minimal and where employers are seen as the wealth creators of the economy, may recoil at the Swedish system, yet in Sweden it works well. In an interview with the TUC, Roger Nilsson, of the Swedish metalworkers union, IF Metall, said:

> I think (when I speak with managers), what's the main question? The labour cost in every business is the highest cost you have as a company and you're not interested to discuss matters of interest within your company and your workers? And so far I haven't seen so many denying that and saying, 'I'm not interested'... they have to be in all other decisions they are making. So almost all managers are very keen to have a good relationship with their workforce.... Me, as a trade unionist, I want to have a good performance within the company and also a good work environment. And I need my salary every month, but for having that I need also to have a developing company and a good performance. I also need that my supervisor and middle management give some respect for me in my position as a worker, because I have my

---

[4] Speaking on 13 June 2013 at a PIRC seminar, Employees in Corporate Governance.

skills, they have their skills, and we work together. So that's the main core in the information and consultation.

Similarly, a greater role for unions does not result in unions blocking change. Instead, they use their influence constructively. Conny Holm, the workers representative on the board of directors at SAAB AB, in the Swedish city of Jönköping, told the TUC:

> the Swedish union has never been against the rationalisation of the company. We never say no. Even if they say we want to do this and that will mean that twenty per cent of the people have to leave, we were never against that. We know that if we [refuse to agree], we are in a bad situation because of [the need to be competitive], it's not so good.... But then we have an agreement to help these people get a new job.

A similar situation exists in Germany, where culturally employers have a responsibility to a wider group of stakeholders than merely shareholders.

Germany defines itself as a social market economy, meaning, according to the German Embassy in London: 'The state guarantees the free play of entrepreneurial forces, while at the same time endeavouring to maintain the balance'.[5] In addition to their right to be represented on supervisory boards, German workers elect representatives to sit alongside employer representatives on company-level works councils. Works councils have responsibility for decisions on a wide range of issues concerning work organization and other areas. This sits alongside strong collective bargaining coverage: according to the European Trade Union Institute, 61 per cent of employees in the former West Germany and 49 per cent of employees in the former East Germany are covered by such agreements, while half of all companies not covered say they take account of these agreements in determining their own pay.[6]

If German trade unions value this situation, employers are just as enthusiastic. Interviewed for the TUC's 'German Lessons' report, Thymian Bussemer of Volkswagen's industrial relations department at its factory in Wolfsburg said of the social market economy:

> This is very strong in Germany, which means that there is a very close interaction between enterprise, especially big ones, the welfare state, the unions. We saw that in the [economic] crisis. The main contribution to the German state is to provide stable industrial relations and to provide the welfare state which linked up with the companies.

Volkswagen's human resources manager, Martin Rosik, confirmed the view of the Swedish trade unionists quoted above, that employee engagement and workers' voice allows meaningful dialogue that is of value to management:

> If you have a conversation on a matter of importance, and you have a partner and you discuss this with your partner, if he only gives you the answers you expect to hear, you wouldn't ask him anymore.

---

[5] See <http://www.tatsachen-ueber-deutschland.de/en/economy/main-content-06/successful-social-market-economy-model.html>.

[6] See <http://www.worker-participation.eu/National-Industrial-Relations/Countries/Germany/Collective-Bargaining>.

Rosik paints a picture of well-informed, responsible trade unionists:

> Labour representatives expect the company to be competitive, they force the company
> to be competitive, and they take care of the interests of their members.

France, like Germany, has strong systems for workers' voice despite low levels of union
density (about 8 per cent of French employees are trade union members, compared with
about 18 per cent in Germany and about 26 per cent in the UK[7]). In France, the right to
information and consultation is enshrined in law for every company that employs more
than 50 people. Like in Germany, works council members may or may not be trade union
members (although they usually are, in practice). Five French trade union confeder-
ations are sanctioned to reach sectoral collective agreements with employers; agreements
reached become the collective agreement for the sector, so long as at least 30 per cent of
those voting support the agreement in so-called 'social elections'.

David Tournadre, senior vice president of human resources at Thales, the French
engineering firm, believes the system works well. Tournadre told the TUC:

> Once a collective agreement has been sanctioned by 30 per cent of the company's
> workforce, it is applicable to all the workers in the sector. It is a positive aspect. It
> works well because it helps to defend high standards.

Describing his company's attitude towards information and consultation as 'something
strategic', David Tournadre agreed that it works when managers and unions approach it
positively:

> it is not because you've got a legal framework that it leads straight to an improvement
> of your internal dialogue. It also has to come from a general will from both parties
> to make it successful.

Tournadre adds:

> The legal framework allows you to do a lot of things but at the end of the day it is
> how you implement it within an organisation that will make it successful or not.

12.6 CONCLUSION AND RECOMMENDATIONS

The situation in the UK provides a stark contrast with the picture of more inclusive
company decision-making painted above. Workers in the UK do not have the right to
be represented on company boards, nor do they have an automatic right to be informed
and consulted about workplace developments; and company directors are required to
promote the interests of shareholders, even when these shareholders are short-term
share traders, over those of other stakeholders, even where such stakeholders have a
long-term stake in the company.

---

[7] See <http://www.worker-participation.eu/National-Industrial-Relations/Across-Europe/
Trade-Unions2>.

Reform of corporate governance alongside strengthened workforce rights to consultation and information are required to facilitate workers' voice in company decision-making. We propose the following reforms.

- A mandatory system for workers' representation on boards should be established. This does not need to be a replica of one of the existing European systems, but can draw on different experiences as well as existing UK traditions to create a system of workers' representation on boards that is best suited to the UK.
- Workers should have the right to regular information and collective consultation on matters that affect their workplace. One way of achieving this would be to reform the Information and Consultation of Employees Regulations 2005 to remove the 'trigger', so that rights to information and consultation apply automatically and do not have to be established only following a request from 10 per cent of the workforce.
- Directors' duties should be reformed so that directors' primary duty is to promote the long-term success of their company rather than prioritizing shareholders' interests as at present.
- Shareholder voting rights should be dependent on a minimum period of shareholding of at least two years.

Establishing effective systems for workers' voice in companies could deliver not only better outcomes for workers but also more sustainable and productive companies. We believe it should become a key focus of industrial and corporate governance policy in the months and years ahead.

References

Appelbaum, E., Hoffer-Gittell, J., and Leana, C. (2011). 'High-Performance Work Practices and Sustainable Economic Growth', <http://www.isn.ethz.ch/Digital-Library/Publications/Detail/?ots591=0c54e3b3-1e9c-be1e-2c24-a6a8c7060233&lng=en&id=128703>.

Bevan, S. (2012). 'Good Work, High Performance and Productivity', Centre for Workforce Effectiveness at the Work Foundation, May, <http://www.theworkfoundation.com/Reports/316/High-performance-good-work-and-productivity>.

Branston, J. R., Cowling, K., and Sugden, R. (2006). 'Corporate Governance and the Public Interest', *International Review of Applied Economics* 20(2), 189–212.

Branston, J. R., Cowling, K. G., Tomlinson, P. R., and Wilson, J. R. (2015, forthcoming). 'Addressing Strategic Failures: Widening the Public Interest in the UK Financial and Energy Sectors', in D. Coffey, C. Thornley, and J. Begley (eds), *Global Economic Crisis and Local Economic Development: International Cases and Policy Responses*. London: Routledge.

Collison, D., Cross, S., Ferguson, J., Power, D., and Stevenson, L. et al. (2011). *Shareholder Primacy in UK Corporate Law: An Explanation of the Rationale and Evidence*, ACCA Research Report No. 125, <http://www.accaglobal.com/content/dam/acca/global/PDF-technical/business-law/rr-125-001.pdf> Certified Accountants Educational Trust (London).

Conchon, A. (2013). *Workers' Voice in Corporate Governance: A European Perspective*. Congress House, London: TUC.

Gold, M. (2011). 'Taken On Board: An Evaluation of the Influence of Employee Board-Level Representatives in Company Decision-Making Across Europe', *European Journal of Industrial Relations* 17(1), 41–56.

Hirschman, A. O. (1970). *Exit, Voice and Loyalty: Responses to Decline in Firms, Organizations and States*. Cambridge, MA: Harvard University Press.

Levinson, K. (2001). 'Employee Representatives on Company Boards in Sweden', *Industrial Relations Journal* 32(3), <http://www.seeurope-network.org/homepages/seeurope/file_uploads/sweden_levinsonartikelirj.pdf>.

Macleod, D. and Clarke, N. (2009). 'Engaging for Success: Enhancing Performance Through Employee Engagement, A Report to Government', Department of Business Innovation and Skills, <http://www.engageforsuccess.org/wp-content/uploads/2012/09/file52215.pdf>.

Office for National Statistics (2013). *Statistical Bulletin, Ownership of UK Quoted Shares 2012*. London: ONS.

Rose, C. (2005). 'Medarbejdervalgte bestrelsesmedlemmer I danske virksomheder', in *Tidsskrift for Arbejdsliv*, <http://www.rosalux.de/fileadmin/rls_uploads/pdfs/Themen/Europa/>.

TASC (2012). *Good for Business? Worker Participation on Boards*, July, <http://www.tasc.ie/publications/good-for-business-worker-participation-on-boards/>.

The Company Law Review Steering Group (2000). 'Modern Company Law for a Competitive Economy: Developing the Framework', Department of Trade and Industry, <http://webarchive.nationalarchives.gov.uk/> and <http://www.berr.gov.uk/files/file23245.pdf>.

Tüselmann, H. F., McDonald, F., Heise, A., Allen, M., and Voronkova, S. (2007). *Employee Relations in Foreign-Owned Subsidiaries: German Multinational Companies in the UK*. London: Palgrave Macmillan.

Vitols, S. (2010). 'The European Participation Index (EPI): A Tool for Cross-National Quantitative Comparison', European Trade Union Institute, <http://www.worker-participation.eu/About-WP/European-Participation-Index-EPI>.

CHAPTER 13

··

EMPLOYMENT RIGHTS AND INDUSTRIAL POLICY

··

PAUL L. LATREILLE AND RICHARD SAUNDRY

13.1 Introduction and Context

··

THERE has been considerable debate in the UK since the election of the Coalition government in 2010 concerning employment protection, with liberal policy-makers calling for (and implementing) various amendments to employment laws so as to promote economic activity and job creation. Underpinning these changes has been a perception that the risk of litigation subjects employers to an excessive cost burden (Saundry et al., 2014). The acme or nadir of this debate, depending on one's perspective, was perhaps the *Beecroft Report*, which asserted that 'much of employment law and regulation impedes the search for efficiency and competitiveness... [and] deters small businesses in particular from wanting to take on more employees' (Beecroft, 2011, p. 2).

While not all of Beecroft's proposals have been implemented, the government has enacted various deregulatory measures such as an increased qualifying period for unfair dismissal from 12 months to two years and the introduction of fees for claimants taking cases to the Employment Tribunal (ET). The basis of decision-making has also been challenged, with the role of non-legal (lay) members further reduced in both first instance and appellate tribunals, leading some to question their legitimacy and argue that these bodies have become increasingly like civil courts (Corby and Latreille, 2012a, b).

Arguably these reforms represent *in toto* as substantial a shifting of the individual employment rights landscape as occurred for collective rights in the 1980s, reflecting a similar ideological stance concerning the appropriate operation and (de-)regulation of the labour market (Hepple, 2013). While a continuation of the previous New Labour administration's policy of 'regulating for competitiveness' (Hepple, 2013), that is 'the use of law as a tool for economic stimulation rather than a source of rights protection' (Mangan, 2013, p. 409), it differs substantially in degree, language, and, arguably, partiality.

This chapter explores these changes, beginning with a brief history and overview of more recent reforms, before considering some of the evidence around employment protection and its impact, and hence the claims made for the reforms in relation to performance. This is followed by a broader consideration of conflict at work and its costs, and a reframing of the debate to propose a set of alternative policy measures. These seek to rebalance the interests of employers and employees while also being more in keeping with the spirit of the *Donovan Report* that resolving problems at work should be 'easily accessible, informal, speedy and inexpensive' (Royal Commission on Trade Unions and Employers' Associations, 1968, p. 156).

13.2 RECENT HISTORY AND POLICY

That recent years have been challenging times under what has become known as the Great Recession is easily illustrated by various macroeconomic indicators (see Figure 13.1 panels (a)–(c)). This prompted the Coalition government to introduce a series of austerity measures involving substantial cuts to public budgets and, ultimately, jobs. The impact continues to be especially pronounced in the public sector (Figure 13.1 panel (d)). While much of the workforce reduction there occurred as a result of freezes on vacant posts and voluntary rather than compulsory redundancies, together with reduced use of agency or temporary staff and other changes in work organization (van Wanrooy et al., 2013), those employees that remain have seen the intensification (and often extensification) of work, with corresponding increases in both stress and pressure on relationships at work (CIPD, 2012).

The Coalition government's response to this has been multifaceted, including significant changes in the employment rights arena, adding to an already large volume of legislation in recent years, with something of a pendulum effect under regimes of differing political colours. Successive Labour governments from 1997 to 2010, and critically the signing of the Social Chapter, saw the extension of workers' rights, primarily through the introduction of new jurisdictions (types of claim) at ETs, including protections from discrimination on the grounds of age, sexual orientation, and religious belief. The qualifying period for unfair dismissal claims was reduced from two years to one, while the upper limit on unfair dismissal awards was increased from £12,000 to £50,000. Such changes were accompanied by other important reforms including the introduction of a National Minimum Wage and implementation of the European Working Time Directive.

Given these changes, and in particular the increased number of jurisdictions, it is perhaps unsurprising that the number of claims to Employment Tribunals has risen markedly over time, from around 30–40,000 per year in the late 1980s to a peak of 236,000 in 2009/10, before falling back below 200,000 in 2011/12 and 2012/13. Much of the variation over time has arisen from claims involving multiple claimants, the number of single claimant cases having been relatively stable and actually having fallen slightly

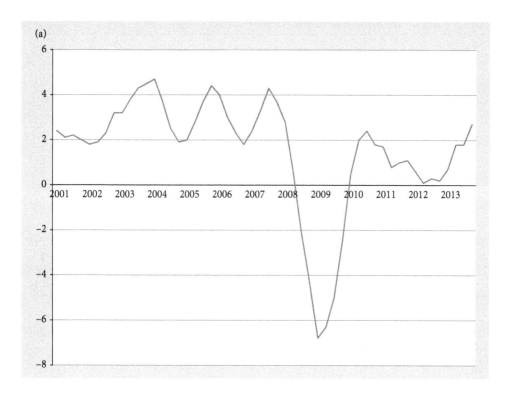

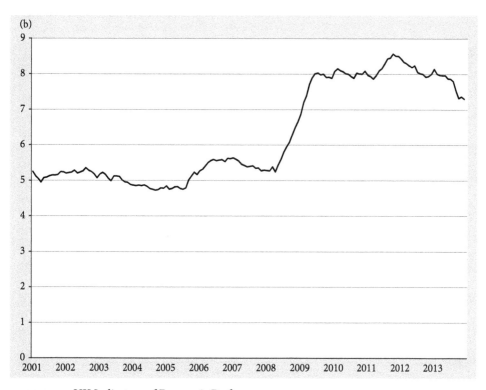

FIGURE 13.1 UK Indicators of Economic Performance 2001–13.

Panel a—GDP, % change on 1 year ago Panel b—Unemployment rate

Panel c—Real wages, % change on 1 year ago Panel d—Public–private sector employment

Source: Office for National Statistics (various). Panel d, left-hand scale relates to public sector, right-hand scale to private sector

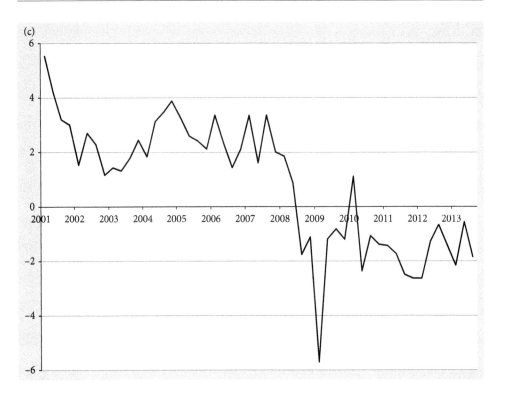

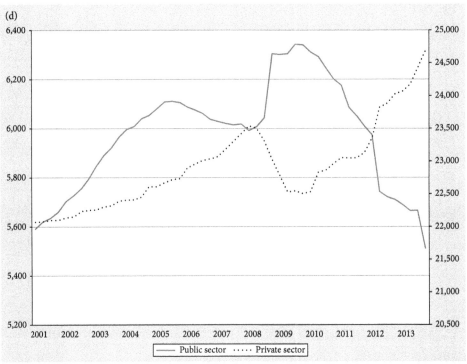

FIGURE 13.1 Continued

since 2009/10 (HMCTS, 2014a, b). Some commentators have suggested ETs now represent a means for unions to pursue grievances that would previously have been pursued by collective means, in essence amounting to a class action (Shackleton, 2002). Moreover, evidence suggests that the erosion of trade union organization is positively associated with the rise in employment tribunal applications (Burgess et al., 2000).

This long-term upwards trend in numbers of claims (see Dix et al., 2009) has led policy-makers to consider various efforts at promoting early resolution of work-related problems—both prior to and following a claim—so as to reduce pressure on the system. Much of this has focused on services provided by the Advisory, Conciliation and Arbitration Service (Acas) which has a statutory duty to conciliate in most Employment Tribunal cases (BIS, 2013) and which resolves around four out of every ten cases (Peters et al. 2010), thereby avoiding the need for a full hearing.

A response to the growing juridification of employment relations and the rising tide of tribunal applications was the introduction, by Acas, of an independent, voluntary arbitration scheme for unfair dismissal (and subsequently flexible working) cases under the Employment Rights (Dispute Resolution) Act 1998. This provided for decisions to be made by an independent arbitrator drawn from an Acas panel. Little used (Dickens, 2012), the scheme has largely fallen into abeyance, although it remains extant.

Major changes were introduced under the Employment Act (2002) and associated Dispute Resolution Regulations (2004). These attempted to effect resolution at the workplace under a three-step process required prior to a claim, in which grievance and dismissal issues had to be set out in writing; there had to be a meeting between the parties to discuss these; and the employee had the right of appeal. In essence, the idea was that some disputes might be avoided if parties were required to communicate earlier in a dispute, with a potential financial penalty at the tribunal depending on which party was responsible for non-compliance. At the same time the value of deposits that could be ordered was increased, along with the maximum size of any potential costs award (Dickens, 2002).[1] For cases entering the system, fixed periods for Acas individual conciliation were introduced for claims other than those involving discrimination, in an attempt to focus parties' minds by bringing 'deadline effect' pressure to bear.

In some respects, these reforms illustrated the uneasy (and some might say contradictory) regulatory balance that the New Labour government attempted to strike. On one hand, the introduction of statutory procedures (for the first time) sought to establish minimum standards and was particularly targeted at safeguarding workers in smaller organizations. On the other, the fact that most organizations had more extensive procedures arguably produced a 'levelling down' of regulation. This, combined with the introduction of new hurdles for employees bringing employment tribunal claims, led some to claim that the overall effect of the measures was to undermine protection for employees (Hepple and Morris, 2002; Sanders, 2009).

---

[1] Typically parties pay their own costs, but these may be awarded against the losing party in certain circumstances, including actions resulting in postponement of a hearing, failure to comply with an order, or the conduct of that party or their representative.

Following the Gibbons Review (Gibbons, 2007), the statutory three-step discipline and grievance resolution regulations were repealed by the Employment Act (2008), having come 'to be seen as the first step in the ET process itself rather than as an opportunity for the parties to resolve their differences and hence circumvent it' (Latreille, 2009, p. 1). Instead, they became part of a revised, principles-based Acas *Code of Practice on Disciplinary and Grievance Procedures* in 2009, although at Gibbon's recommendation, incentives for compliance were provided in the form of increased or decreased compensatory awards at tribunal. However, it could be argued that this reflected an acceptance by government of employers' calls for greater freedom in the way that workplace disputes were managed, and part of a fundamental shift in the state's approach to employment regulation to what (in the context of EU social policy) has been termed 'neo-voluntarism' (Streeck, 1995).

A further strand of the UK government's reform of workplace dispute resolution has been the enthusiastic promotion of the use of Alternative Dispute Resolution (ADR). Acas's long-standing conciliation function for ET claims is one such form (see Latreille et al., 2007), along with its pre-claim conciliation (PCC) offering where litigation was considered likely (now supplanted by Early Conciliation). A particular focus has been on the use of mediation, following a strong espousal of its merits in Gibbons. One noteworthy government initiative in this regard is the judicial mediation scheme. Initially piloted in Newcastle, Central London and Birmingham in 2006–7, the scheme involves judges undertaking mediation with parties in discrimination cases in an attempt to avoid the need for a hearing. The results were disappointing, with judicial mediation failing to 'have a discernible, statistically significant impact on rates of early resolution or satisfaction when compared to a matched control group, while provision of the service also involves a large net cost to the taxpayer' (Urwin and Latreille, 2014, p. 332). Surprisingly then, the scheme was rolled out nationwide in January 2009, albeit with the emphasis shifting from time/cost reduction to party satisfaction (Urwin and Latreille, 2014).

The Coalition government has continued to pursue this agenda, introducing a requirement to notify Acas and to consider Early Conciliation prior to lodging an ET claim. Workplace mediation, encouraged via inclusion in the Foreword and Guidance to the Acas *Code*, is gaining increasing traction, particularly in the public sector (Latreille, 2011; Saundry et al., 2014). However, beyond exhortation and the demonstration effect of its own use of mediation under the ADR Pledge launched in 2001 (now replaced by the Dispute Resolution Commitment), relationship-preserving mediation has received only limited tangible support from policy-makers.

While some would argue that such processes are consistent with a consensual and collaborative approach to employment relations, others have suggested that the extension of workplace mediation represents the privatization of dispute resolution, transferring the responsibility for the settlement of employment disputes from the state (through the ET system) to the organization (Colling, 2004). Importantly, given the weakness of internal workplace institutions of employment regulation such as collective bargaining and trade union organization, Colling argues that this will only undermine the ability of workers to enforce their rights and 'entrench managerial prerogative' (Colling, 2004, p. 576).

The promotion of ADR has run in parallel with a series of deregulatory reforms informed by a philosophy which characterizes claimants (and their representatives/lawyers) 'as potential abusers of the system' (Mangan, 2013, p. 417).[2] Among other measures, the Coalition government has introduced fees for both the bringing and hearing of claims, as well as for any subsequent appeal to the Employment Appeal Tribunal (EAT). The longer, two-year qualifying period for claims of unfair dismissal has been reinstated, while compensatory awards for same have been capped. There has also been a curtailing of the consultation period for collective redundancies from 90 to 45 days, reforms that remove what has been described as the 'gold plating' of Transfer of Undertakings (Protection of Employment) (TUPE) Regulations and, despite tepid employer reception, the introduction of a new 'employee shareholder' status under which employees can choose to forego certain employment rights—most notably in relation to unfair dismissal—in return for a minimum of £2,000 of shares in the company (see Prassl, 2013). Hepple (2013, p. 206) notes other changes including the abolition of the Agricultural Wages Board for England and Wales, reversal of '[t]he presumption that there is a right to civil action against employers for breach of strict statutory safety and health obligations', and repeals to various equality provisions.

Arguably the most significant of the above measures has been the introduction of fees. These vary according to the nature of the claim and number of claimants involved. For single claimants the 'issue fee' is either £160 for simpler, Type A claims, or £250 for more complex, Type B claims. Proceeding to the hearing requires payment of a further fee of £230 or £950 respectively, bringing the total for most claims, including unfair dismissal and all discrimination heads, to £1,200. A remission scheme based on that operating in the civil courts was intended to ensure potential claimants were not discouraged from pursuing a case for purely financial reasons. However, in the first full quarter since the fees were introduced (October–December 2013), the number of claims received was reported to have fallen by 79 per cent compared with the same quarter in the previous year. While these figures may be affected by delays in recording due to the need to process fees and any application for remission, subsequent data shown in Figure 13.2 suggest the numbers have not recovered in any noticeable fashion (HMCTS, 2014a). Strikingly, provisional data suggest around three-quarters of the 2,500 remission applications received in the first five months of the new fees regime were rejected (Hansard 12 May 2014: Column 418W).

Another change—albeit one whose impact is harder to predict—is what amounts to the removal of lay (non-legal) members from first instance hearings for unfair dismissal, and also from the EAT, although employment judges retain the discretion to sit with members where the circumstances of a particular case make this desirable. Over time, a range of jurisdictions has been added to the list of those where employment judges can

---

[2] Similar arguments have been part of the public debate in New Zealand (see Walker and Hamilton, 2011).

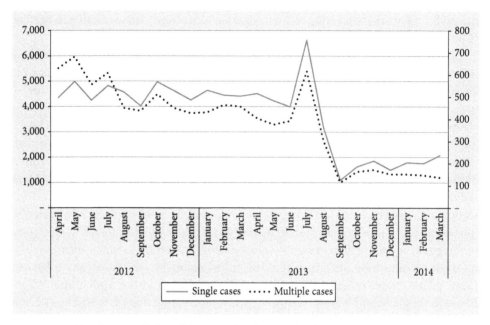

FIGURE 13.2 Employment Tribunal Receipts April 2012–March 2014.

sit alone. And while the result of this in terms of party success rates may be a priori unclear, it arguably represents a further and important step towards the institutional isomorphism described by Corby and Latreille (2012a). It also raises important questions of legitimacy (Corby and Latreille, 2012b), not least where decisions hinge on tests of actions falling within a range of reasonable responses, where the industrial experience of lay members plays an important role in augmenting the legal expertise of judges.

13.3 Business and the Regulatory 'Burden'

While there have been policy changes that have extended employment rights, most notably in relation to family-friendly provisions (Hepple, 2013, p. 205), the overall direction of travel of regulatory reform has clearly altered the balance in favour of employers. In short, the opportunity for employees to enforce their rights has been substantially curtailed. However, these changes to 'external' regulation have important consequences *within* the organization, as mechanisms of 'internal' regulation such as grievance and disciplinary procedures have historically been a reaction to the threat of litigation (Edwards, 1995). This is likely to be amplified in the context of weak trade union organization, particularly in the private sector (van Wanrooy et al., 2013).

For employers, reducing the risk of litigation provides greater space and freedom in which to manage. This search for 'maximum flexibility', exemplified by some of

Beecroft's recommendations, remains ongoing as part of a Department for Business, Innovation and Skills (BIS) Employment Law Review. As Mangan (2013) argues, 'costs have been confirmed as a paramount concern' (p. 410), with changes 'premised on cost certainty for employers' (p. 417), and flexibility essentially being 'about meeting business needs' and the ability to effect workforce reductions if necessary (p. 418). Furthermore, the changes to the framework of employment protection are rooted in a broad assertion that greater freedom to end the employment relationship will also liberate employers from the anxiety of hiring staff.

However, the evidence to support this is inconclusive. For example, Skedinger (2010) reviews over a hundred empirical studies of the effects of employment protection legislation, concluding that the evidence from these is generally mixed. However, Lindbeck (2011) has suggested the balance is probably negative in the sense that more studies find negative effects than positive. Nonetheless, this remains very much a contested area.

Moreover, research commissioned by the Coalition government into the (perceived) impact of employment regulation on businesses casts doubt on whether reforms will change employer behaviour. Jordan et al. (2013) highlight an important distinction between survey and more qualitative data. The former includes a range of data collected by or on behalf of government departments and business organizations, but 'support the general finding that regulation can be burdensome for employers' (Jordan et al., 2013, p. 12). However, an important caveat from their more qualitative evidence is that the inhibiting effects of employment regulation are much less commonly mentioned unless prompted, suggesting that 'the perception of legislative burden may be more indicative of employers' anxiety than the actual impact of regulation on running a business' (Jordan et al., 2013, p. 44), arising from the long-standing 'anti-legislation discourse' (see Clifton and Tatton-Brown, 1979) rather than genuine effects.[3]

This view is given further credence by the UK's position in international league tables. Although there are variations according to the measure chosen (see OECD, 2013), the UK consistently ranks among the economies offering the lowest levels of protection against (especially) individual dismissal (see for example Figure 2.6 in OECD, 2013). It is far from clear that from this initial position, further deregulation would necessarily offer substantial benefits (Jordan et al., 2013), nor that movement in the other direction would result in major damage. Indeed, it might be argued that stricter standards could have the benefit of incentivizing employers to exercise greater care in recruitment, leading to higher-quality matches and longer-term attachments with benefits in terms of lower future separation and replacement costs.

As Saundry et al. (2014, p. 6) note, however, there remains 'significant anxiety and uncertainty over the potential for, and implications of, employment litigation', especially given its increasing complexity and legalistic and adversarial nature (Corby and Latreille, 2012a, b). This can make the process especially daunting for those seeking to

---

[3] One effect, albeit difficult to measure, is that 'increasing proceduralisation... [may be] detrimental to the informality and flexibility viewed as essential to effective working relationships in the smaller enterprise' Harris (2002, p. 296).

navigate it without legal advice/representation (on which, see Urwin et al., 2014), and lead employers to adopt risk-averse approaches to conflict management (Jones and Saundry, 2012). The irony is that such approaches may undermine the use of alternative approaches to conflict, channelling issues instead into the formalized and legalistic processes that are the subject of such concern.

13.4 REFRAMING THE POLICY DEBATE

The Coalition government's emphasis on the end of the employment relationship that has been central to much of the recent policy debate is, however, ultimately likely to be unhelpful for long-term economic success. Instead, as Lord Mandelson argued in the Foreword to MacLeod and Clarke's *Engaging for Success* report (2009), 'Britain's economic recovery and its competitive strengths in a global economy will be built on strong, innovative companies and confident employees, [so] there has never been a more important time to think about employee engagement in Britain'. There is a need to recognize that, while sometimes opposed, there is far greater mutuality of interests between employers and employees than the current discourse allows, and thus that their respective interests and rights need to be more appropriately balanced.

The current government's approach is arguably schizophrenic, with exhortations to informal resolution on the one hand, yet incentives that, perversely, actually undermine that on the other. Worse than that: the approach as a whole is one that might be described as 'beggar-thy-neighbour', risking a 'race to the bottom' by governments seeking to leverage competitive advantage and to attract mobile international capital, mirroring in the context what has previously been described in financial services as 'competitive deregulation' (see for example Bradley, 1991).

However, the relationship between employee engagement and the way that employment disputes are handled is notably absent from managerial discourses in the UK (Saundry et al., 2014). This is partly due to the focus on ETs which are very much the most conspicuous form of conflict for senior managers. This creates an emphasis on legal compliance and arguably elevates the risks associated with litigation. It also tends to draw attention away from the scale of workplace conflict. One estimate reported employees in the UK spending 1.8 hours each week on average dealing with conflict, or some 370 million working days (OPP, 2008). Such costs dwarf those arising from ETs, with consequences for the functioning of teams (Latreille and Saundry, forthcoming), performance, health (primarily stress), and employee welfare (De Dreu, 2008). Moreover, there is some evidence that fear and anxiety over the prospect of dismissal, discrimination, and victimization has increased in the last ten years (Gallie et al., 2013), particularly among public sector workers.

While the thrust of current policy is to suppress discontent through restricting channels of enforcement, it can be argued that there needs to be 'a greater emphasis on what happens in the workplace and on ways in which employment relationships can be salvaged'

(Saundry et al., 2014, p. 13). In short, conflict is an inevitable part of organizational life, and a proactive approach to its management can underpin employee commitment. Research has shown that organizational support is a fundamental strut of employee engagement (Saks, 2006). Both have the potential for beneficial effects on organizational performance (Dromey, 2014). Furthermore, as Purcell (2012) has suggested, this is underpinned by perceptions of fairness, justice, and trust.

In addition, the fixation of policy with external regulation has drawn attention away from the decline of internal workplace institutions and networks of social relationships that have traditionally regulated employment and underpinned effective dispute resolution. The decline of trade union organization, the increased centralization of the HR function, and the devolution of people management responsibility to a cadre of front-line managers who lack the necessary confidence and expertise to address difficult issues has been argued to create a 'resolution gap' (Saundry and Dix, 2014; Saundry et al., 2014). It is this, rather than the chimera of employment litigation, that needs to be the focus of policy.

What follows sets out an alternative view of employment conflict resolution which encompasses the full panoply of problems, both justiciable and interpersonal, in recognition of the substantial costs associated with both. In doing so, it reflects the spirit of Donovan's vision of dispute resolution that is 'easily accessible, informal, speedy and inexpensive, and which gives... [parties] the best possible opportunities of arriving at an amicable settlement of their differences' (Royal Commission on Trade Unions and Employers' Associations, 1968, p. 156). The costs of discipline and grievance handling, as well as of dealing with the personality clashes that are often the single most common source of conflict (see for example Latreille and Saundry, forthcoming), suggest those same principles apply equally to resolution within the organization as to those dealt with via legal redress.

There are three strands to this: first, a renewed and more ambitious programme to improve conflict management at the workplace; second, augmenting and enhancing resolution processes for issues that require handling by the ET system; and third, changes to the operation of tribunals themselves, reorienting them towards practice enhancement and the setting of standards rather than a narrower focus on adjudication. These essentially seek to address three dimensions of the 'resolution gap' articulated in the previous section.

13.4.1 Internal Resolution

In relation to the first of these, an obvious place to begin is to identify the potential to deal with issues more effectively in the workplace. To some extent, the measures needed to close the 'resolution gap' rely on managerial action to rebuild conflict management capacity. This is not straightforward. As noted above, there is limited evidence of organizations adopting proactive and/or strategic approaches to dispute resolution. Nonetheless, government can provide a framework which supports and incentivizes such developments. For example, given the lack of conflict competence among front-line managers, the government could take steps 'to embed the importance of conflict resolution within its skills strategy' (Saundry et al., 2014, p. 14), working in partnership with employer organizations to address the managerial skills deficit it is widely recognized exists. This might include more direct involvement in the line manager training on dealing with employment issues that some have argued elsewhere is needed (Purcell, 2012).

Furthermore, effective structures of employee representation are vital in establishing social processes of resolution in the workplace. Here, the international evidence suggests that there is little alternative to statutory intervention (see Bryson et al., 2012). In the UK, this has revolved around the introduction of the Information and Consultation of Employees (ICE) Regulations. However, the wide discretion and flexibility provided to employers has led to a lack of enthusiasm from trade unions and limited uptake. It could be argued that a strengthening of the regulations, for example by providing clear rights to representatives for time off to carry out their duties, could increase their impact (Purcell and Hall, 2012). There is also evidence that UK trade unions, in the face of the continuing erosion of collective bargaining, may now see the ICE regulations as a way of beginning to rebuild their influence.

However, the political obstacles to such government action should not be underestimated. There is no support for state intervention to stimulate the creation of representative mechanisms within the Coalition government. Perhaps more surprisingly, there is no clear indication that this is among the priorities for a putative Labour administration. In this context we would argue that the development of workplace mediation could play a role in regenerating workplace conflict resolution processes.

This clearly runs counter to the persuasive arguments of those that portray mediation as a privatized source of managerial control (Colling, 2004). In this context, government claims that its increased use 'has the potential to lead to a major and dramatic shift in the culture of employment relations' (BIS, 2011, p. 13) may simply seem like the sugaring of a 'deregulatory pill'. However, there is tentative evidence to suggest that mediation can both help to develop conflict handling skills and also underpin the rebuilding of social processes of dispute resolution (see Latreille and Saundry, 2014 and the references there).

In terms of the former, a wide range of evidence from both the UK and the US suggests that participation in mediation and/or mediation training can improve the ability of managers to handle workplace conflict (Bingham, 2003, 2004; Latreille, 2011; Saundry, Bennett et al., 2013). Moreover, a longitudinal study of the US Postal Service's REDRESS initiative found that the introduction of mediation improved the organizational climate, reducing the number of formal discrimination complaints and stimulating early resolution. In the UK, Saundry, McArdle et al. (2013) have argued that the introduction of mediation can build high-trust relationships between managers and trade union representatives.

Despite extolling its virtues, however, only modest effort has been expended by policy-makers to promote its use. Implicitly, policy-makers seem to think this is ultimately an area where the business case will be axiomatic; that is far from being true for many organizations, where the focus may be on cost reduction (Saundry et al., 2014). Such evidence as exists suggests usage remains relatively low, particularly among SMEs (Williams, 2011; Wood et al., 2014). More significant efforts are clearly required in this regard.

The extension of mediation faces a number of challenges. These include limited resilience of outcomes, a tendency for it to be deployed as a last resort, and resistance from managers who see mediation as potentially undermining their authority or being an admission of failure. It may also be reputationally 'fragile' where mediation 'fails' (Latreille, 2010). Nonetheless, organizations that have used mediation are typically very positive about the experience (Latreille, 2010, 2011), so an important part of driving its wider adoption is stimulating initial use.

There are a number of ways in which this might be achieved. For example, there is evidence that its limited mention in the 2009 Acas Code of Practice on Disciplinary and Grievance Procedures was influential on uptake (Rahim et al., 2011), so the fore-grounding of mediation (and other forms of ADR) in a revised Code would likely be helpful, although issues of power and justice—distributional, procedural, and inter-actional—need to be part of the debate (see Dolder, 2004).

Because relationships in SMEs are closer, more informal, and personal, problems can often undermine trust and cause irreparable damage to the employment relationship. However, mediation has the potential to salvage potentially productive relationships. There is evidence of latent demand for mediation among SMEs (Seargeant, 2005; Williams, 2011; Latreille et al., 2012), but the cost of hiring a mediator looms large for smaller organizations, especially in the context of an uncertain prospect of success (Latreille et al., 2012). However, the introduction of mediation schemes across much of the public sector provides a potential pool of trained mediators who could offer support to local SMEs. This would facilitate earlier intervention when there is a greater prospect of saving the relationship, with the costs to the public purse being both the direct savings of administering any ET claim and also the job displacement of the individual concerned (see Drinkwater et al., 2011).

Other possibilities that policy-makers might consider include exploring with the insurance industry the potential for mediation/ADR cover to become part of policies, for example those offering cover for legal expenses. To the extent that SMEs may use accounting services for advice/guidance on a range of issues including HR, it may be that they could be targeted for mediation awareness-raising, perhaps via professional accrediting bodies such as ACCA or CIMA. Similarly, the government might work with key employer and employee representative organizations to provide support and resources for the development of mediation capacity in the form of a pool of shared mediators.

If the government is to secure the transformation of employment relations, it will need to encourage a more strategic approach to conflict handling. The literature in the US suggests the notion of Integrated Conflict Management Systems (or ICMSs) has gained some traction, including among household names such as Coca Cola and General Electric (Lipsky, 2012). Indeed, in the US, recent survey evidence suggests around a third of organizations in the Fortune 1000 had adopted features consistent with CMS (Lipsky et al., 2012)—mediation and arbitration being the most common, but early case assessment and peer review also having emerged. Interestingly, such adoption was mainly in 'high road' organizations, suggesting it is complementary to other good practices.

Defining such systems is problematic (Roche and Teague, 2014), but broadly they can be described as 'a comprehensive, systems approach to the prevention, management and resolution of conflict...changing the philosophy (and, in many cases the terminology) of organizational life' (Lynch, 2001, pp. 207, 208). In theory, ICMSs share a number of key characteristics (Lynch, 2001; see also Roche and Teague, 2014): they are 'all-encompassing' in scope; focus on developing a 'conflict competent culture' in which issues are surfaced and conflict is recognized as having potentially positive (functional) as well as negative (dysfunctional) effects (Pondy, 1967); contain 'multiple access points' with the option to switch between processes; provide options and choice, including both rights and interest-based methods; and also enabling structures. The last includes such features as high level leadership and support; training of managers and possibly other employees (including awareness-raising as well as a basic understanding of the tools and language of mediation); incentives for conflict management, etc.; and might include conflict competencies as part of selection, promotion, and training, rather than the narrow technical skills that have typically been the focus of such processes.

In essence, one can conceive of an ICMS as encompassing prevention, early intervention, management, and resolution, recognizing that dealing with conflict effectively is a key driver for employee health and well-being and ultimately performance. And while there is some debate about the adoption of ICMSs on this side of the Atlantic, and for the claims made concerning their impact/efficacy (Roche and Teague, 2012[4]), the four key elements above would seem appropriate even in their absence. Notable too is that 'proactive line management and supervisory engagement in conflict resolution as a key dimension of conflict management systems is found to be positively associated with a range of organizational outcomes' (Roche and Teague, 2012, p. 231).

13.4.2 External Resolution

For conflict which escapes the organization, the recently introduced requirement to notify Acas prior to bringing an ET claim and thus to be offered the chance for Early Conciliation appears to be a positive initiative. This builds on the demonstrable success of PCC which, despite its relative lack of success in preserving relationships (Acas and Infogroup/ORC International, 2010; TNS-BMRB, 2013), resulted in fewer than one-third of cases referred proceeding to ET in 2012/13 (Acas, 2013). Importantly, it was found to be especially heavily used by smaller employers and by unrepresented claimants.

---

[4] It should be noted, however, that their modelling is essentially of the options and their interaction rather than a 'system', including, in particular, changes in culture/language.

The judicial mediation scheme described above, while innovative, is demanding of resource and could be argued to represent a misallocation of same. While it may give parties a sense of 'having their day in court', the facilitative model of mediation used by judges is similar in many regards to Acas conciliation, albeit typically conducted in person rather than by telephone. However, as Urwin and Latreille (2014, p. 334) document using survey data from the pilot, 'the comments from a number of claimants and employers suggest that they would have perhaps preferred a more evaluative or directive approach'. Similarly, several participants in an earlier Acas SME pilot project indicated a preference for an investigative process (Seargeant, 2005). Resources currently used to offer facilitative judicial mediation could instead therefore be used to support a more directive process, for example an early neutral evaluation (ENE) scheme, utilizing judges' legal expertise and experience to provide an objective assessment of the strengths and weaknesses of cases.

As noted above, the Acas arbitration scheme, introduced under powers in the Employment Rights (Dispute Resolution) Act 1998 and described in language strongly reminiscent of Donovan, was subject to very low uptake. As Dickens (2012) notes, this likely arose from its narrow jurisdictional coverage and lack of incentives. Perhaps the time is ripe to revisit the 'arbitration alternative' (Dickens, 2012, p. 32) with wider scope and encouragement.

13.4.3 Adjudication

Of course, some issues will require judicial decisions for the reasons set out in Genn (2012). Mediation and other forms of ADR should not be seen as 'cheap' or 'privatized' justice, but rather options in a range of responses that includes both rights and interest-based approaches whose fitness for purpose will depend on circumstance. Nor should other more radical options that question the underlying process itself be ruled out (see Dickens, 2012).

One key reform is that fees should be abolished or reduced to a purely notional administrative level; the evidence is unambiguous that they have deterred claims and so denied potentially legitimate complaints from receiving the attention they deserve. If, as the Coalition has claimed, ill-conceived and speculative claims are problematic—and the evidence for this is very much contested (Dickens, 2012)—this could be addressed both through enhancing the case management process and in applying the long-standing provisions for the award of costs (something that occurs in only a tiny minority of cases).

A second key change would be to reinstate lay members in unfair dismissal claims, where their workplace experience is essential in providing the context for the application of the 'range of reasonable responses test'. Notwithstanding judges' legal expertise, van Dijk et al. (2012) suggest improved decision quality with multiple judges (in criminal cases), despite the potential time costs involved. Latreille and Corby (2011) provide survey evidence that many judges often prefer to sit with lay members, identifying important contributions from their presence and participation. While the argument for their reinstatement may be more marginal at the EAT, where decisions are made on legal points only, there is nonetheless potential value in terms of regime legitimacy (Corby and Latreille, 2012a, b), especially when set against the almost negligible costs of their presence (£90,000–£120,000 and £120,000–£130,000 per annum at the ET and EAT respectively, according to the Impact Assessment).

Finally, reflecting Genn's (2012, p. 7) observation (ironically) in the civil court context that 'the justice system has both dispute resolution and behaviour modification functions', the move to withdraw the ability to make wider recommendations in discrimination claims should be abandoned and such powers instituted more broadly. This would enable tribunals to play a greater role in norm-setting rather than being largely norm-reflecting, again drawing on the valuable workplace experience of lay members.

13.5 Conclusions

Employment rights policy under the Coalition government has been largely predicated on the basis that it represents an avoidable and substantial cost for business arising from largely unfounded claims that employers are obliged to defend. However, as the shift of issues from collective to more individualized expressions of conflict evidences, the upshot may be for problems to manifest in other ways, such as lower commitment, more perfunctory performance, and high rates of turnover and so forth, with potentially adverse effects on performance (see Purcell, 2012).

Crucially, the UK obsession with external regulation in terms of ET and rights enforcement has neglected the importance of internal workplace institutions which not only act as important initial screening and resolution devices but also have the potential, as part of a wider 'high road' strategy, to foster greater trust, engagement, and mutual gains. In encouraging such change, the interrelationship between internal and external regulation is critical. Current policy provides a disincentive to adopt new innovations such as mediation and ICMSs.

To this end, the current neo-voluntaristic regime adopted by the Coalition government threatens to promote an illusion of industrial harmony and consequently a sense of complacency among employers. Thus, effective regulation and mechanisms of rights enforcement are essential drivers for managerial innovation. At the same time, a return to a less adversarial system of adjudication arguably offers both employees and employers access to justice.

References

Acas (2013). *Annual Report and Accounts, 2012–2013.* London: Acas.
Acas and Infogroup/ORC International (2010). *Evaluation of the First Year of Acas' Pre-Claim Conciliation Service,* Acas Research Paper No. 08/10.

Beecroft, A. (2011). *Report on Employment Law*, London: BIS, <http://www.bis.gov.uk/assets/biscore/employment-matters/docs/r/12-825-report-on-employment-law-beecroft.pdf>

Bingham, L. B. (2003). *Mediation at Work: Transforming Workplace Conflict at the United States Postal Service*. Arlington, VA: IBM Center for the Business of Government.

Bingham, L. B. (2004). 'Employment Dispute Resolution: The Case for Mediation', *Conflict Resolution Quarterly*, 22, 145–74.

BIS (2011). 'Resolving Workplace Disputes: A Consultation', London: BIS, <http://www.bis.gov.uk/assets/biscore/employment-matters/docs/r/11-511-resolving-workplace-disputes-consultation.pdf>.

BIS (2013). 'Triennial Review of the Advisory, Conciliation and Arbitration Service (Acas)', London: BIS, <https://www.gov.uk/government/uploads/system/uploads/attachment_data/file/252571/bis-13-p191-triennial-review-of-acas-REVISED-2.pdf>.

Bradley, C. (1991). 'Competitive Deregulation of Financial Services Activity in Europe after 1992', *Oxford Journal of Legal Studies* 11(4), 545–58.

Bryson, A., Forth, J., and George, A. (2012). 'Workplace Social Dialogue in Europe: An Analysis of the European Company Survey 2009', EUROFOUND, <http://www.eurofound.europa.eu/pubdocs/2012/14/en/2/EF1214EN.pdf>.

Burgess, S., Propper, C., and Wilson, D. (2000). *Explaining the Growth in the Number of Applications to Industrial Tribunals 1972–1997*, Department of Trade and Industry, London, Employment Relations Research Series, No. 10.

CIPD (2012). *Employee Outlook: Spring 2012*. London: CIPD.

Clifton, R. and Tatton-Brown, C. (1979). *Impact of Employment Legislation on Small Firms*, Department of Employment Research Paper No. 6.

Colling, T. (2004). 'No Claim, No Pain? The Privatization of Dispute Resolution in Britain', *Economic and Industrial Democracy* 25(4), 555–79.

Corby, S. and Latreille, P. (2012a). 'Employment and the Civil Courts: Isomorphism Exemplified', *Industrial Law Journal* 41(4), 387–406.

Corby, S. and Latreille, P. (2012b). 'Tripartite Adjudication: An Endangered Species', *Industrial Relations Journal* 43(2), 94–109.

De Dreu, C. (2008). 'The Virtue and Vice of Workplace Conflict: Food for (Pessimistic) Thought', *Journal of Organisational Behaviour* 29, 5–18.

Dickens, L. (2002). 'Individual Statutory Employment Rights Since 1997: Constrained Expansion', *Employee Relations* 24(6), 619–37.

Dickens, L. (2012). 'Employment Tribunals and Alternative Dispute Resolution', in L. Dickens, (ed.), *Making Employment Rights Effective: Issues of Enforcement and Compliance*, pp. 29–48. Oxford: Hart Publishing.

Dix, G., Sisson, K., and Forth, J. (2009). 'Conflict at Work: The Changing Pattern of Disputes', in W. Brown, A. Bryson, J. Forth, and K. Whitfield (eds), *The Evolution of the Modern Workplace*, pp. 176–200. Cambridge: Cambridge University Press.

Dolder, C. (2004). 'The Contribution of Mediation to Workplace Justice', *Industrial Law Journal* 33, 320–42.

Drinkwater, S., Latreille, P. L., and Knight, K. G. (2011). 'The Post-Application Labour Market Consequences of Employment Tribunal Claims', *Human Resource Management Journal* 21(2), 171–89.

Dromey, J. (2014). *MacLeod and Clarke's Concept of Employee Engagement: An Analysis based on the Workplace Employment Relations Study*, Acas Research Paper No. 08/14.

Edwards, P. K. (1995). 'Human Resource Management, Union Voice and the Use Of Discipline: An Analysis of WIRS3', *Industrial Relations Journal* 26(3), 204–20.

Gallie, D., Felstead, A., Green, F., and Inanc, H. (2013). 'Fear at Work in Britain: First Findings from the Skills and Employment Survey, 2012', <http://www.cardiff.ac.uk/socsi/ses2012/[hidden]resources/4.%20Fear%20at%20Work%20Minireport.pdf>.

Genn, H. (2012). 'Why the Privatisation of Civil Justice Is A Rule of Law Issue', 36th F. A. Mann Lecture, <http://www.ucl.ac.uk/laws/academics/profiles/docs/Hazel/36th%20F%20A%20Mann%20Lecture%20Website.pdf>.

Gibbons, M. (2007). *Better Dispute Resolution: A Review of Employment Dispute Resolution in Great Britain*. London: DTI.

Harris, L. (2002). 'Small Firm Responses to Employment Regulation', *Journal of Small Business and Enterprise Development* 9(3), 296–306.

Hepple, B. (2013). 'Back to the Future: Employment Law under the Coalition Government', *Industrial Law Journal* 42(3), 203–23.

Hepple, B. and Morris, G. (2002). 'The Employment Act 2002 and The Crisis of Individual Employment Rights', *Industrial Law Journal* 31(30), 245–69.

HMCTS (2014a). 'Tribunal Statistics: January to March 2014', <https://www.gov.uk/government/uploads/system/uploads/attachment_data/file/319488/tribunal-statistics-quarterly-january-march-2014.pdf>.

HMCTS (2014b). 'Tribunal Statistics: January to March 2014: Tables', <https://www.gov.uk/government/uploads/system/uploads/attachment_data/file/320226/tribunal-statistics-january-march-2014-tables.xls>.

Jones, C. and Saundry, R. (2012). 'The Practice of Discipline: Evaluating the Roles and Relationship between Managers and HR Professionals', *Human Resource Management Journal* 22(3), 252–66.

Jordan, E., Thomas, A., Kitching, J., and Blackburn, R. (2013). *Employment Regulation – Part A: Employer Perceptions and the Impact of Employment Regulation*, Department for Business, Innovation and Skills Employment Relations Research Series, No. 123.

Latreille, P., Buscha, F., and Conte, A. (2012). 'Are You Experienced? SME Use of and Attitudes Towards Workplace Mediation', *International Journal of Human Resource Management* 23(3), 590–606.

Latreille, P. and Saundry, R. (2014). 'Workplace Mediation', in W. K. Roche, P. Teague, and A. Colvin (eds), *Oxford Handbook of Conflict Management in Organizations*, 190–209. Oxford: Oxford University Press.

Latreille, P. and Saundry, R. (forthcoming). Towards a System of Conflict Management? An Evaluation of the Impact of Workplace Mediation at [currently anonymised] NHS Trust. Acas Research Paper.

Latreille, P. L. (2009). *Characteristics of Rejected Employment Tribunal Claims*, Department for Business, Innovation and Skills Employment Relations Research Series, No. 96.

Latreille, P. L. (2010). *Mediating at Work: Of Success, Failure and Fragility*, Acas Research Paper No. 06/10.

Latreille, P. L. (2011). *Workplace Mediation: A Thematic Review of the Acas/CIPD Evidence*, Acas Research Paper No. 13/11.

Latreille, P. L. and Corby, S. (2011). 'The Role of Lay Members in Employment Rights Cases: Survey Evidence', <http://www2.gre.ac.uk/__data/assets/pdf_file/0012/611202/Survey-of-ET-and-EAT-judges-and-lay-members.pdf>.

Latreille, P. L., Latreille, J. A., and Knight, K. G. (2007). 'Employment Tribunals and Acas: Evidence from a Survey of Representatives', *Industrial Relations Journal* 38(2), 136–54.

Lindbeck, A. (2011). 'Comment on Skedinger: Employment Consequences of Employment Protection Legislation', *Nordic Economic Policy Review* 1, 85–90.

Lipsky, D. (2012). 'How Corporate America Uses Conflict Management: The Evidence from a New Survey of the Fortune 1000', *Alternatives* 30(7), 139–42.

Lipsky, D. B., Avgar, A. C., Lamare, J. R., and Gupta, A. (2012). The Antecedents of Workplace Conflict Management Systems in US Corporations: Evidence from a New Survey of Fortune 1000 Companies. mimeo.

Lynch, J. F. (2001). 'Beyond ADR: A Systems Approach to Conflict Management', *Negotiation Journal* 17(3), 207–16.

MacLeod, D. and Clarke, N. (2009). *Engaging for Success: Enhancing Performance through Employee Engagement. A Report to Government*. London: Department for Business, Innovation and Skills.

Mangan, D. (2013). 'Employment Tribunal Reforms to Boost the Economy', *Industrial Law Journal* 42(4), 409–21.

OECD (2013). *OECD Employment Outlook 2013*. Paris: OECD Publishing.

OPP (2008). *Fight, Flight or Face It: Celebrating the Effective Management of Conflict at Work*. Oxford: OPP.

Peters, M., Seeds, K., Harding, C., and Garnett, E. (2010). *Findings from the Survey of Employment Tribunal Applications 2008*, Department of Business, Innovation and Skills Employment Relations Research Series, No. 107.

Pondy, L. R. (1967). 'Organizational Conflict: Concepts and Models', *Administrative Science Quarterly* 12, 296–320.

Prassl, J. (2013). 'Employee Shareholder "Status": Dismantling the Contract of Employment', *Industrial Law Journal* 42(4), 307–37.

Purcell, J. (2012). 'Management and Employment Rights', in L. Dickens (ed.), *Making Employment Rights Effective: Issues of Enforcement and Compliance*, pp. 159–82. Oxford: Hart Publishing.

Purcell, J. and Hall, M. (2012). *Voice and Participation in the Modern Workplace: Challenges and Prospects*, Acas Future of Workplace Relations Discussion Paper Series, No. XX.

Rahim, N., Brown, A., and Graham, J. (2011). *Evaluation of the Acas Code of Practice on Disciplinary and Grievance Procedures*, Acas Research Paper No. 06/11.

Roche, W. and Teague, P. (2012). 'Do Conflict Systems Matter', *Human Resource Management* 51(2), 231–58.

Roche, W. K. and Teague, P. (2014). 'Conflict Management Systems', in W. K. Roche, P. Teague, and A. Colvin (eds), *Oxford Handbook of Conflict Management in Organizations*, pp. 250–72. Oxford: Oxford University Press.

Royal Commission on Trade Unions and Employers' Associations (1968). *Report*, HMSO, London, Cmnd No. 3623.

Saks, A. (2006). 'Antecedents and Consequences of Engagement', *Journal of Managerial Psychology* 21(7), 600–19.

Sanders, A. (2009). 'Part One of the Employment Act 2008: "Better" Dispute Resolution', *Industrial Law Journal* 38(1): 30–49.

Saundry, R., Bennett, T., and Wibberley, G. (2013). *Workplace Mediation: The Participant Experience*, Acas Research Paper No. 02/13.

Saundry, R. and Dix, G. (2014). 'Conflict Resolution in the UK', in W. K. Roche, P. Teague, and A. Colvin (eds), *Oxford Handbook of Conflict Management in Organizations*, pp. 475–93. Oxford: Oxford University Press.

Saundry, R., Latreille, P., Dickens, L., Irvine, C., Teague, P., Urwin, P., and Wibberley, G. (2014). *Reframing Resolution: Managing Conflict and Resolving Individual Employment Disputes in the Contemporary Workplace*. Acas Policy Discussion Paper.

Saundry, R., McArdle, L., and Thomas, P. (2013). 'Reframing Workplace Relations? Conflict Resolution and Mediation in a Primary Care Trust', *Work, Employment and Society* 27(2), 212–31.

Seargeant, J. (2005). *The Acas Small Firms Mediation Pilot: Research to Explore Parties' Experiences and Views on the Value of Mediation*, Acas Research Paper No. 04/05.

Shackleton, J. R. (2002). *Employment Tribunals: Their Growth and the Case for Radical Reform*. London: Institute for Employment Affairs.

Skedinger, P. (2010). *Employment Protection Legislation: Evolution, Effects, Winners and Losers*. Northampton, MA: Edward Elgar.

Streeck, W. (1995). 'Neo-Voluntarism: A New European Social Policy Regime?', *European Law Journal* 1(1), 31–59.

TNS-BMRB (2013). *Evaluation of Acas' Pre-Claim Conciliation Service 2012*, Acas Research Paper No. 06/13.

Urwin, P., Buscha, F., and Latreille, P. (2014). 'Representation in UK Employment Tribunals: Analysis of the 2003 and 2008 Surveys of Employment Tribunal Applications (SETA)', *British Journal of Industrial Relations*, 52(1), 158–84.

Urwin, P. and Latreille, P. (2014). 'Experiences of Judicial Mediation in Employment Tribunals', in W. K. Roche, P. Teague, and A. Colvin (eds), *Oxford Handbook of Conflict Management in Organizations*, pp. 333–52. Oxford: Oxford University Press.

van Dijk, F., Sonnemans, J., and Bauw, E. (2012). *Judicial Error by Groups and Individuals*, Tinbergen Institute Discussion Paper No. TI 2012-029/1.

van Wanrooy, B., Bewley, H., Bryson, A., Forth, J., Freeth, S., Stokes, L., and Wood, S. (2013). *Employment Relations in the Shadow of Recession: Findings from the 2011 Workplace Employment Relations Study*. Basingstoke: Palgrave Macmillan.

Walker, B. and Hamilton, R. T. (2011). 'The Effectiveness of Grievance Processes in New Zealand: A Fair Way to Go?', *Journal of Industrial Relations* 53(1), 103–21.

Williams, M. (2011). *Workplace Conflict Management: Awareness and Use of the Acas Code of Practice and Workplace Mediation: A Poll of Business*, Acas Research Paper No. 08/11.

Wood, S., Saundry, R., and Latreille, P. (2014). *Analysis of the Nature, Extent and Impact of Grievance and Disciplinary Procedures and Workplace Mediation using WERS 2011*, Acas Research Paper.

PART 4

INDUSTRIAL
POLICY AND
REGIONAL
DEVELOPMENT

CHAPTER 14

....

AN INDUSTRIAL STRATEGY FOR UK CITIES

....

DAVID BAILEY, KEITH COWLING,
AND PHILIP R. TOMLINSON

14.1 INTRODUCTION

....

CITIES are increasingly recognized as a potential environment for creativity and generating dynamic agglomeration, and thus acting as a driver of economic growth (ODPM, 2006; Glaeser, 2010). Yet while London has become a 'global city', many UK cities, particularly 'older' industrial cities in the North and the Midlands, have lost their former vitality, with their socio-economic landscapes and trajectories being transformed over decades by the forces of globalization, technological change, de-industrialization, and tertiarization (Sassen 2006; MacKinnon et al., 2008). Many of these cities have for too long been over-dependent upon corporate entities (in particular transnational corporations) and have become mired in mono-structures; these cities' lack of economic diversity has inhibited their socio-economic development (see Bailey and Cowling, 2011). Moreover, the recent Great Recession (2008–13) appears to have extenuated the widening schism between a dynamic London and a sluggish periphery of (in particular) Northern and Midlands provincial UK cities (see Hutton and Lee, 2012). These widening disparities and, more generally, the underperformance of many UK cities represent an unfulfilled potential within the UK economy.

Across the political divide, politicians and policy-makers are beginning to recognize that not only are regional imbalances inequitable, but they need to be re-addressed if the UK economy is to enjoy a sustainable economic recovery. Indeed, revitalizing UK cities was a focus of the Conservative Lord Heseltine's (2012) recent report ('No Stone Unturned') on promoting economic growth, while the Labour Party Opposition Leader, Ed Miliband, has recently invoked the nineteenth-century Conservative Prime Minister, Benjamin Disraeli, in calling for a return to 'one nation' politics (which hints at more balanced growth across the UK).[1] Given the potential rewards associated with the creativity of the city as a source of dynamic growth, we also argue that cities should be a key facet for a new UK industrial strategy and that policies should especially be geared towards unlocking the capabilities of the country's stagnating older cities—thus unleashing their potential. Unfortunately, previous UK policy responses towards reviving cities are not encouraging. They have often been based around attracting (transnational) mobile investment to enhance 'competitiveness', with disappointing results. Indeed, such policies have often exacerbated the vulnerabilities of cities to the vagaries of corporate interests; many of the observed mono-economic structures in UK cities reflect the strategic interests of the corporate sector. In advocating a more place-based industrial strategy, we will argue that restructuring UK cities will require not only a more diverse economic base, but also reform of their underlying economic governance (Cowling and Tomlinson, 2011).

The chapter is set out as follows. In Section 14.2, we consider the theoretical issues relating to city dynamics. Rooted in the work of Jane Jacobs (1961, 1969, 1984), we argue agglomeration is necessary but not sufficient for the development of cities. Rather, it is economic diversity that is essential in generating Jacobian externalities to facilitate innovation and long-run growth, and this thrives in cities (and regions) with relatively diffuse economic governance structures. In Section 14.3, we assess the actual dynamics of UK cities, and in so doing highlight some of the evidence—in relation to business dynamics—on the so-called North–South divide. We find that many provincial UK cities (outside London and the Greater South East) have struggled to maintain their earlier dynamism, largely because they have been over-reliant upon corporate entities (for investment and employment) and have lost their economic diversity; many have become 'locked in' to mono-sectoral profiles. In Section 14.4, we deliberate upon how a new industrial strategy might help to revitalize UK cities and suggest that much can be learned from the experience of industrial districts in generating a new dynamic within cities; we suggest new districts, with coherence in a city environment, might be the basis for a UK industrial strategy. Finally, Section 14.5 concludes.

14.2 THEORETICAL CONSIDERATIONS

14.2.1 Jacobian Economies: The Importance of Diversity

Our view that reviving cities should be a key facet in a new industrial strategy is very much influenced by the work of the prominent US journalist, author, and urban activist Jane

---

[1] In a recent speech to the New Local Government Network Conference, Jon Cruddas (2014)—Labour MP and Party Policy Coordinator—called for greater powers to be devolved to UK cities and for policies to reduce regional imbalances (see <http://www.joncruddas.org.uk/sites/joncruddas.org.uk/files/power%201%20%282%29.pdf>).

Jacobs (1961, 1969, 1984). For Jacobs, cities are hubs of vitality which open up possibilities for the emergence of new ideas, experimentation, and innovation. These possibilities arise from the intensity of interactions between actors within the close physical proximity of the city, which in turn provides the impetus for knowledge spillovers to flow and creative talents to surface.

These external economies support the agglomeration of activities within cities, underpinning their (dynamic) growth and developing cumulative competences, often in specific industrial and/or commercial specialisms. Of course, since Marshall (1919), agglomeration has been foremost in the lexicon of the competitive advantage of places, and since the early 1990s the concept has gained much wider attention as economists and other social scientists have sought to understand regional dynamics (see for instance Camagni, 1991; Cooke and Morgan, 1994, 1998; Maillat, 1995; Porter, 1998). A key issue, however, is whether agglomeration economies can be sustained over time, and it is now increasingly recognized that this depends upon the diversity of a city's (or region's) economic base (Jacobs, 1969; Menzel and Fornahl, 2010; Martin and Sunley, 2011).

Diversity is important in a number of ways. Jacobs (1969) regarded diversity as the source of a city's innovative capability since it provides greater opportunities for actors to engage in a wider set of criss-crossing relationships, possibly facilitating serendipitous cross-sector spillovers (see also De Propris and Cooke, 2011). For Jacobs (1969, 1984), the inhabitants' diversity and their own (spontaneous) ideas were seen as essential for a city's future growth and prosperity since they lessened the dangers of becoming locked into particular specialisms.[2] Indeed, Glaeser (1994, p. 9) noted that while physical proximity facilitates the flow of ideas, 'the urban environment can foster the unexpected combination of seemingly unrelated ideas that may provide the most important forward leaps of knowledge'. More recently, the evolutionary (economic) geography literature has emphasized the importance of diversity in rejuvenating regions (including cities), while also acting as an important buffer to external (exogenous) shocks. This is because a city with a wider set of skills, knowledge, and competences is better equipped to adapt, absorb, and respond to external shocks, since it can recombine and reintegrate such attributes in different ways to meet changing (market) environments. Frenken et al. (2007) refer to this as exploiting 'related variety', whereby a city (or region) utilizes its existing expertise and specialisms and fuses these with newer, complementary ideas and technologies in (typically) adjacent (and related) sectors.[3] In turn, this may encourage

---

[2] Some validation for Jacobs's argument came from Glaeser et al. (1992) in their econometric analysis of panel data for large cities, and industries in large cities, in the United States for the period 1956 to 1987: local employment growth was aided by city industrial diversity and competition within industries for those cities.

[3] Or as Jacobs (1969, p. 122) noted in observing that a generation of new firms and industries emerge (within cities) through 'new work being added to old work'. Swann and Prevezer (1996) provide an example of exploiting 'related variety' when they highlight how US and UK software firms typically established themselves in declining clusters of computer hardware manufacture to take advantage of redundant engineers and expertise. Klepper (1997) also describes how clusters of US radio producers shifted into producing television.

new entry (of firms) and opens up the possibility of cities (or regions) moving onto new and possibly more dynamic trajectories (see also Swann et al., 1998; Menzel and Fornahl, 2010; Asheim et al., 2011; Neffke et al., 2011).

The prerequisite for these new development paths is diversity, or (in a narrower technological sense) what Menzel and Fornahl (2010) refer to as the degree of 'technological heterogeneity', that is, the breadth of technological (and knowledge) capabilities within the city (or region). Where cities can maintain sufficient breadth in technological capabilities, the prospects for long-run dynamic growth are brighter. For instance, at the regional level, Asheim et al. (2011, p. 895) note how several new and distinct industries emerged (post-Second World War) within Emilia-Romagna, which originated from its wide knowledge base in engineering (see also Grabher and Stark, 1997). On the other hand, decline is evident where diversity is not maintained. Here cities (and regions) can become 'locked in' to particular specialisms and mono-structures in relation to technology, networks, and policy (see Grabher, 1993). The negative lock-in effects can be stifling, with such cities prone to a lack of dynamism, inertia, and slow adaptation to change (see also Hill et al., 2008; Pike et al., 2010). Birmingham (UK) and Detroit (US) may be cases in point, their precipitate (and relative) decline connected with a mono-sectoral profile, with a heavy concentration on the automotive industry in both cases, while Krasnoiarsk-26 would be perhaps a more extreme case of a highly mono-sectoral city from a so-called planned economy.[4]

14.2.2 The Importance of Economic Governance

An important adjunct (to diversity) in promoting dynamic growth within cities is the economic governance structure. Economic governance essentially relates to the nature of socio-economic relationships within the city, specifically between firms, institutions, and other actors.[5] Firms play a prominent role in this respect since, as Coase (1937) first

---

[4] It is worth noting that whereas Detroit and Birmingham have not received the core investment in the industry necessary to secure its long-term dynamism, German and French auto firms—with government support—have essentially been able to maintain this. While they have moved some assembly activity offshore, they have maintained a strong engineering, research and development, design, and marketing base in their home cities of Stuttgart, Munich, and Paris, and such countries and regions have also attracted high-level activities from foreign auto transnationals in search of highly skilled workforces (e.g. the Korean auto firm Kia locating a design and development base in Frankfurt). In relation to Krasnoiarsk-26, Glazyrina (2000) notes the city had a golden age from 1958 to the early 1980s as a centre for Soviet nuclear weapons production, but could 'not adapt to changed circumstances and operate in conditions of a market economy' (Glazyrina, 2000, p. 200). It is seen as a 'City without a Future', despite possessing 'significant scientific potential'.

[5] According to Le Gales and Voelzkow (2001, pp. 6–7), governance 'refers to the entirety of institutions which co-ordinate or regulate action or transactions among subjects within a system'. These authors then identify the main components of a governance system as the market, the (business) organization or firm, the state, the community, and associations of shared interests (such as local business consortia or trade unions). Our specific focus is upon economic governance structures of cities, which although more specific in its focus, essentially embodies these elements.

identified, they are 'islands of planning', that is, they plan and organize economic activity. For Zeitlin (1974), this involves a firm having the ability to take and pursue strategic decisions in determining its own orientation (such as decisions relating to investment, employment, and location) and such decisions can impact on other interested parties (see Cowling and Sugden, 1998). A key issue is thus the distribution of economic power within a city and, related to this, where such power (ultimately) resides, since strategic decisions (on economic variables) will largely affect the direction of a locality's trajectory (see Sacchetti and Tomlinson, 2009). Indeed, where strategic decision-making processes are concentrated within, say, a corporate hierarchy, there is a danger of misalignment in the strategic interests of a few actors and those of the wider locality (or public interest); we refer to this as a 'strategic failure' (Cowling and Sugden, 1998).[6]

Asymmetries in economic power and governance processes can have significant implications for the development of cities and localities. In exploring the implications of the distribution of economic power within cities, it is useful to consider Sacchetti and Sugden's (2003) polarity between 'networks of direction' and 'networks of mutual dependence'. Networks are important since firms and other actors are often connected in some way, either through vertical supply chains or horizontal cooperative linkages and/or industry institutions. At one end of the spectrum, networks of firms are directed by the strategic decisions (and economic planning) of a few core firms. These networks (of direction) are hierarchical, with core firms independently pursuing their own strategic objectives with little consultation with their (trading) partners and/or other stakeholders in the locality. Smaller partners, often with deep roots in the city, play a largely subservient role and are often required to deliver upon targets to lower production costs and meet tight (output) efficiency criteria. The (local) production system is geared towards serving the flexibility requirements of the main beneficiaries, the core firms (see De Propris, 2001). The danger of such (local) production systems is they become mono-directional and overly vulnerable to economic factors affecting the core firm; this raises the risk of technological isomorphism, as the degree of diversity within a city is curtailed (see Section 14.2.1, this chapter; Bailey, 2003).

Moreover, in most cases the core firms are transnational corporations, often with headquarters elsewhere in the global economy, and they will have limited loyalty and responsibilities to the cities in which they operate. Yet many cities have become overly dependent upon transnational corporations to steer their own development path. The difficulty for local development is that externally determined corporate strategies will be pursued at the expense of 'community' strategies and the interests of a wider set of local actors, thus raising the spectre of 'strategic failure' (see Sugden and Wilson, 2002). For instance, with their global orientation, transnational corporations are increasingly and strategically 'footloose' in their operations; a strategic decision (or even a threat) by a domiciled transnational to relocate production to another (usually overseas) location

---

[6] We have previously documented several cases of 'strategic failure' across the globe (see for instance Cowling and Tomlinson, 2000, 2005, 2011; Branston et al., 2012).

can thus have significant repercussions for a city's development. Such a strategic decision creates widespread instability, since it adversely affects not only the firm's (local) workforce, but also the city's skills base and local small firms and suppliers dependent upon the transnational's (local) sourcing arrangements. There is now substantive evidence that transnational firms are actively engaging in such activities often to secure more favourable terms (such as lower labour costs/regulations) and (via what is referred to as a 'divide and rule' strategy) playing cities, regions, and workforces off against each other to attain them (see Peoples and Sugden, 2001; Coffey and Tomlinson, 2006; Christopherson and Clark, 2007). Thus transnational corporations have the power to determine the global distribution of economic activity, and at one and the same time to de-industrialize some regions (and cities therein) and industrialize 'new' regions (see also Dicken, 2010).

In contrast, in cities (and regions) where networks of mutual dependence are more prevalent, relations between firms and actors are relatively 'flat' or 'heterarchical', 'diffuse', and 'pluralistic' (Sacchetti and Sugden, 2003).[7] This type of network was an enduring feature of the post-Second World War vitality and (ongoing) renewal of the Italian industrial districts. These (mature) districts embodied numerous crisscrossing 'heterarchical' and collaborative relations consisting of local firms and actors, which were often described as 'reciprocal' and 'flexible' and involved 'joint actions' in productive activities (such as the co-sharing of information and technology). This engineered a dynamic climate of coopetition, which allowed such districts and their indigenous firms to compete in global markets (often successfully vis-à-vis large transnational corporations) during the turbulent economic period of the 1970s and 1980s (Brusco, 1982; Piore and Sabel, 1984; Becattini, 1990; Best, 1990; Porter, 1998). In addition, local institutions such as trade associations and municipal governments were often the conduits for promoting these types of dyads, and crucially also in reinvigorating old(er) networks with new partners to prevent them from becoming staid and over-embedded (see Bellandi, 2003, 2011). Critically, from a wider governance perspective, Brusco (1982) described the typical Italian districts as not having a centre for strategic decision-making, since no one firm was dominant. Becattini (1990) later noted how the socio-economic development of the Italian districts moved together in an integrated and inclusive process.

Of course nurturing, managing, and sustaining heterarchical relations can be difficult; as networks grow and/or are renewed, coordinating resources and ensuring compliance (and negating 'free-riding') among actors can be problematic. In addition, an over-emphasis upon cooperation and consensus-building within cities can occasionally impede the emergence of creative tensions and constrain crisis resolution, which can be particularly problematic in times of economic turbulence, when quick and immediate solutions may be required (see Jessop, 1998). Resolving such dilemmas will depend upon the nature of the dyad between firms, the extent of their mutual interdependence,

---

[7] In such networks, firms recognize their mutual interdependencies and engage in mutually reinforcing activities (see Powell, 1990; Jessop, 1998; Sacchetti and Sugden, 2003).

and their joint commitment and determination in reaching solutions that are inclusive. This might suggest an important role for local government and other institutions as mediators of dyads and as facilitators of renewing (dynamic) networks. Returning to Jacobs, it is worth recalling that she also envisaged a largely diffuse system of production, with a recurring theme in her work being 'the need of cities for a most intricate and close-grained diversity of uses that give each other constant mutual support, both economically and socially, and city planning and design must become the science and art of catalysing and nourishing these close-grained relationships' (Jacobs, 1984, p. 24). She saw cities evolving without any central direction from either the government or the corporate sector, celebrating the grass roots with the successful city being an embodiment of the culture, interests, and participation (in (strategic) decision-making) of its population.

14.3   Cities: Engines of Growth or Submerged in Crisis?

14.3.1   Global Cities and the Periphery

In the early twenty-first century, there are several notable examples of dynamic, cosmopolitan cities thriving in the global economy; some of these have been termed 'global cities' (e.g. London, Paris, New York, Tokyo, and the emerging Shanghai and Mumbai) and are internationally renowned (as hierarchical centres of finance and trade) since they have developed global socio-economic (and political) linkages which have a direct and tangible effect upon global affairs (see Sassen, 1991). The emergence of global cities was foreseen by Stephen Hymer (1972), who raised concerns that other cities and regions (across the globe) would be consigned to a peripheral status. He saw this arising directly from the activities of transnational corporations, who would base their corporate headquarters in a few of the large cities of the world (predominantly concentrated in the global cities listed) and from which they would centralize their strategic decision-making, while lower-level activities such as the management and operation of individual production units would be located elsewhere around the globe. As discussed in Section 14.2.2, the strategic decisions of these transnationals would have a direct impact upon these 'lesser' localities, and Hymer (1972, p. 114) was concerned this would lead to a 'new imperial system' with 'a tendency (of the system) to produce poverty as well as wealth, underdevelopment as well as development'.

Hymer was largely distinguishing between cities in the core 'developed' OECD economies and the 'undeveloped' periphery elsewhere in the world. However, while this is true at the global level, we would argue a *double dualism* exists, as within the 'developed' world a similar gap has arisen. Indeed, while 'global cities' thrive, many cities within the 'developed' economies are submerged in crisis, characterized by sluggish and stagnant growth, and mired with social problems.[8] Moreover, this polarization—between dynamic and sluggish cities—is often observed between cities within the same country, of which the UK is a prime example with a long-standing divergence in the performance of London (and the Greater South East) and cities outside this metropolis (see Section 14.3.2 and Table 14.1). As a global city, London has gained from centripetal developments, such as employment in (transnational) corporate headquarters and business services related to headquarters' functions. In addition, it has also benefited from employment multipliers of the (sometimes huge) salaries and bonuses received within corporate headquarters, which are spent locally on services (e.g. medical, education, recreation, entertainment, and culture). In contrast, many of the 'older industrial cities' have declined as their over-reliance upon transnational corporations has been exposed; these corporations have increasingly switched their operations to localities with significantly lower costs, whether they be in lower-cost locations within trade blocs such as the EU (such as central Europe) or in 'developing' countries. Thus, within Hymer's core nations there is another core–periphery, and the question of inequalities across locations has taken on not only an international dimension but also an intra-national one (and, perhaps, increasingly so). The centrifugal and centripetal tendencies connected with this new globalism, with production leaving the old manufacturing cities of the core (nations) for the low wages of the periphery, and control over this process being concentrated within the core, provide the backdrop for the decaying old manufacturing cities unambiguously damaged by this process.

14.3.2 Two Nations in the UK: North and South?

Like in other cities across the globe, much of the socio-economic landscape of UK cities has been transformed in recent decades by the processes of globalization, technological change, de-industrialization, and tertiarization (Sassen, 2006; MacKinnon et al., 2008). This transformation predates the recent Great Recession (and its aftermath), although this has further exposed the deep-seated structural and strategic issues facing UK cities. Indeed, the growing gap between London (and the Greater South East) and other UK cities has long been referred to as the UK's North–South divide (Martin, 1988).

In an enlightening account of the UK's evolving economic geography, Martin (1988) documents the growing gap between London (and the South East) and the UK's Northern and Midlands cities, tracing it to at least the 1850s.[9] The historical reasons for

---

[8] This is not to dismiss the socio-economic problems and wide income inequalities existing within 'global cities'. Indeed, the prosperity of these cities lies alongside the poverty of significant minorities, especially male manual workers or former workers, largely untouched by the wealth generated within. For instance, we have seen the resentment built up by the juxtaposition of this rising local inequality in the riots within the *banlieue* of Paris, and more positively in the campaign for a living wage in cities such as London (Wills, 2009; see also Bailey and Cowling, 2011).

[9] The conventional view is that following the Industrial Revolution and until 1914, the UK's industrial heartlands (the North and the Midlands) were the most dynamic and among the most

this (widening) divide are varied and a full discussion is beyond the scope of this chapter, although Martin (1988) provides a useful summary up to the 1980s (see also note 9). In short, the divide between North and South continued into the twentieth century, growing wider particularly during the inter-war years. The so-called 'Golden Age' after the Second World War did little to narrow the gap; indeed it again (albeit marginally) widened and by the mid-1960s, the South East became 'the country's major geographical concentration of manufacturing (and services)' (Martin, 1988, p. 395, our words in parentheses). The breakdown of the Keynesian consensus in the mid-1970s and the shift towards neo-liberal economic policies further exposed the North to the vagaries of the market.

Interestingly (and writing in the 1980s), Martin (1988) saliently noted the impact of de-industrialization being most acute in UK regions which were overly reliant upon a specialized industrial base (mainly the North, Wales, and regions of Scotland, but also the major conurbations (including parts of London) and the core region of the West Midlands), whereas other regions which were more economically diverse (and had established research and development facilities) were not only less vulnerable (to de-industrialization) but were also able to grow into the new high-technology and service industries. This is particularly pertinent given our earlier remarks in relation to the importance of diversity to stimulate Jacobian externalities and generate dynamic growth and agglomeration; this seems to have occurred within London and several cities in the Greater South East. We might argue the mono-sectoral profiles of the UK's older industrial cities, in the North and Midlands, largely reflect the prominence of resident transnationals and these cities' dependence upon them; the adherence to specific sectors (to suit the strategic interests of transnationals) narrows these cities' economic bases.

Table 14.1 provides a contemporary picture of UK cities, with some comparative data (2012–13) on the stock of businesses, business start-ups and closures, innovation (as measured by patents), and employment and skills within the UK's 35 largest cities (largely

prosperous parts of the country, with the South East (outside London and its finance and service economy) being predominantly an agriculture-based economy that generally 'lagged behind'. The transformation and the rise of the North–South 'regional problem' occurred following the First World War, as the decline of the British Empire and the rise of new international competition, combined with the deflationary policies of the inter-war years, imposed severe shocks on traditional UK manufacturing industries (shipbuilding, engineering, coal mining, and textiles), predominantly based in the North. At the same time (in the 1930s), new growth manufacturing industries such as light engineering and consumer goods began to cluster in the South East and (to a lesser extent) in the Midlands (Massey, 1979, 1984, 1986). While accepting much of this analysis, Martin (1988, pp. 391–5) seeks to correct several historical inaccuracies, namely the notion that in the nineteenth century, the North enjoyed an economic advantage over the South. He shows that even in the second half of the nineteenth century, growth in the North and the industrial periphery lagged behind the South East and other regions in terms of manufacturing employment growth and per capita income. Moreover, at this time, the 'South East region ranked alongside the North West as a major spatial concentration of manufacturing activity; in fact London was the single largest centre of manufacturing in the country' (Martin, 1988, p. 392). For Martin (1988, p. 394), the dualism that existed in the UK was 'between a "north" based primarily on industrial growth and exports, and the metropolitan South East specialised in commerce, banking, finance and government. In terms of wealth, the South East was clearly the leading region.'

Table 14.1 The UK's Largest Cities: A Comparative Economic Picture

City	City Status (Year)	Population (2012 est.)	Region	Business Stock (per 10,000 population)	Business Start-ups (per 10,000 population)	Business Closures (per 10,000 population)	Business Churn Rate (start-ups less closures/ business stock)	Patents Granted (per 100,000 population)	Employment Rate (%)	% Working Population with NVQ Level 4 +	Workplace Weekly Earnings (2013)
Brighton	2000	337,700	Gt South East	403.46	54.49	48.12	1.58	4.15	71.89	42.36	501.11
Cambridge	1951	125,200	Gt South East	345.45	43.13	36.74	1.85	68.69	76.79	65.88	556.20
London	AD 47	9,629,600	Gt South East	463.30	75.51	60.44	3.25	4.74	70.59	46.54	634.14
Norwich	AD 450	259,500	Gt South East	312.33	32.76	36.42	-1.17	5.39	74.18	35.83	444.73
Peterborough	1541	186,400	Gt South East	272.30	36.48	33.80	0.98	2.68	70.81	26.09	464.50
Oxford	1542	152,500	Gt South East	276.39	33.11	26.89	2.25	5.25	71.54	62.30	493.20
Portsmouth	1926	524,200	Gt South East	264.78	33.19	31.57	0.61	4.20	74.12	28.88	470.58
Southampton	1964	366,200	Gt South East	270.75	33.45	34.13	-0.25	6.28	72.59	31.14	465.02
Birmingham	1889	2,439,600	Midlands	252.85	33.49	33.02	0.19	3.28	63.41	26.14	450.94
Coventry	1043	323,100	Midlands	240.33	33.74	31.10	1.09	5.26	64.13	26.84	462.80
Derby	1977	250,600	Midlands	243.62	33.32	32.72	0.25	2.79	71.06	28.02	482.20
Leicester	1919	482,300	Midlands	282.29	38.57	36.39	0.77	3.32	65.98	27.86	428.56
Nottingham	1897	646,300	Midlands	250.58	29.78	30.87	-0.43	3.56	65.85	30.54	462.15
Stoke-on-Trent	1925	374,100	Midlands	224.54	24.46	26.33	-0.83	2.67	70.03	22.95	422.39
Bradford	1897	524,600	North	250.19	31.93	33.36	-0.57	2.67	65.62	24.73	426.40
Hull	1897	257,200	North	208.40	26.83	25.86	0.47	1.91	61.87	22.92	373.10
Leeds	1893	757,700	North	295.04	39.20	36.23	1.01	2.38	68.81	35.09	473.60
Newcastle	1882	832,500	North	218.50	30.03	28.11	0.88	2.04	64.97	30.86	455.11
Sheffield	1893	815,700	North	235.50	28.69	30.16	-0.62	4.05	67.51	29.98	430.42
Sunderland	1992	275,700	North	175.73	22.49	23.94	-0.83	0.36	65.77	21.85	413.60

Wakefield	1888	327,600	North	236.11	27.93	27.47	0.19	2.14	70.47	20.23	430.00
York	AD 71	200,000	North	297.50	36.00	32.00	1.34	3.50	73.60	41.34	480.20
Liverpool	1880	791,700	North	209.99	30.06	28.36	0.81	1.52	63.19	23.21	443.39
Manchester	1853	1,892,500	North	304.41	43.70	41.29	0.79	4.49	67.65	33.38	462.07
Belfast	1888	673,800	Northern Ireland	257.35	21.74	26.94	−2.02	1.19	67.75	32.82	452.90
Aberdeen	1891	225,000	Scotland	373.11	57.11	39.56	4.71	10.67	75.60	41.01	532.90
Dundee	1889	147,800	Scotland	199.93	27.06	25.03	1.02	1.35	64.30	37.50	435.50
Edinburgh	1329	482,600	Scotland	323.77	44.45	39.37	1.57	12.23	73.08	56.13	559.30
Glasgow	1492	1,056,600	Scotland	246.21	34.31	37.24	−1.19	2.18	64.77	41.11	501.94
Bristol	1542	698,600	South West	329.59	44.09	37.36	2.04	8.30	73.43	38.61	476.15
Gloucester	1541	123,400	South West	250.81	32.01	32.82	−0.32	8.91	77.79	30.20	436.30
Plymouth	1928	258,000	South West	203.29	27.52	26.94	0.29	2.71	70.35	29.14	415.00
Cardiff	1905	348,500	Wales	263.13	34.15	31.85	0.87	4.88	64.81	38.19	480.80
Newport	2002	146,100	Wales	222.79	28.06	32.51	−2.00	4.79	68.05	30.70	464.40
Swansea	1969	239,600	Wales	229.34	25.25	30.68	−2.37	2.09	65.07	32.80	436.00
UK Average (all cities)	–	63,705,000	–	332.50	42.30	40.00	0.70	4.60	71.00	34.20	502.20

Source: Centre for Cities (Cities Outlook: <http://www.citiesoutlook.org/>); Office of National Statistics 2013 for English Cities

City boundaries are defined as 'Primary Urban Areas', which measures the built-up areas of a city, as opposed to local authority districts. For Welsh and Scottish cities, local authority data is used, except for Glasgow, where the city was defined as an aggregate of five local authorities. A similar methodology was applied to Belfast (See Centre for Cities, 2014: 11).

defined by 'Primary Urban Areas'). The data was collated by the Centre for Cities (2014), although it was sourced from Office for National Statistics publications. For our analysis, we have also grouped the city data into (wider) regions (See Table 14.1), thus facilitating comparison and highlighting the schism between London (and the Greater South East) and the rest of the country. The business indicators in particular demonstrate substantive differences in dynamism across UK cities. For instance, in 2012, London (the top city) has 2.6 times more businesses per capita than Sunderland (the bottom city), while Manchester is the only northern English city in the top ten for business stock (see Column 5). Indeed, London accounts for 21 per cent of all businesses registered in the UK (Centre for Cities, City Outlook, 2014). Business start-ups and closures per capita are also key indicators, with the difference between them (as a proportion of business stock) being the churn rate. This data captures a city's entrepreneurial capability to nurture and attract new firms while simultaneously abandoning redundant activities (via firm closures); they are generally a sign of vibrancy in the local economy. London again records by far the highest number of business start-ups per capita, 32 per cent higher than Aberdeen (in second place) and over twice that of the UK's second city (by population), Birmingham, and over one and a half times that of Manchester. Indeed, many UK cities, particularly in the Midlands and the North, fall below the national average for new business creation. Finally, registered patents are included to proxy innovation across cities.[10] Cambridge records by far the largest number of patents per capita, though one firm accounted for 30 per cent of all patents granted (Centre for Cities, 2014). Nevertheless, its world-class university has long-established links with industry, notably in the software and biotechnology industries, and this has facilitated a unique dynamism in the city.

Finally, two Scottish cities, specifically Edinburgh and Aberdeen, are noteworthy exceptions to the North–South divide. These cities in particular score well across the range of indicators. Scottish devolution and comparatively generous funding from the Barnett formula has provided the country with a wider degree of political and economic autonomy to steer local economies. Moreover, Edinburgh can exploit its political status as a provincial capital and as a hub of arts and culture alongside a thriving finance centre, while Aberdeen is very much an oil-based economy. However, Scotland's largest city, Glasgow, lags significantly behind the UK national averages and has a similarly dismal performance to many other Northern English cities (see Table 14.1).

14.3.3 A Tale of Two Cities: The Jobs Deficit

The labour market has long been a particularly important socio-economic indicator of the UK's North–South divide. For instance, Martin (1988) provides substantive evidence

---

[10] Patents should be interpreted carefully in measuring innovative activity. This is because patents are usually lodged by large firms, often as a means of strategic entry deterrence, while small and medium-sized firms generally do not patent. In addition, patents are typically recorded in relation to more technical (product) innovations, with process innovations and innovations in the service sector excluded (see Tomlinson, 2010).

of the 'jobs gap' and regional unemployment disparities for the 1980s, while during the 1990s, the larger industrial conurbations in the UK were again the worst performers (in terms of unemployment and also labour market inactivity), with Glasgow, Coventry, and Merseyside (excluding Liverpool) being particularly hard hit (Webster, 1999).[11] This decline in job prospects was associated with lower life expectancy—with an increasing gap between the industrial cities and less urban areas, with no (former) industrial cities featuring among the areas with highest life expectancy (Office of National Statistics, 2004). Recent data has again highlighted these cities' poor record on job creation and worklessness. The Centre for Cities (2009), for example, estimated the scale of the 'jobs deficit' facing England's cities, and suggested that even *before* the Great Recession unfolded, over 500,000 more jobs would have been needed simply to raise such cities' employment levels to the national average; their recent report (2014) suggests this figure has now grown to 560,000.

In fact, UK job creation displays severe regional as well as intra-urban imbalances, with a skew in high-skill/high-wage jobs towards London and the South East, with far smaller 'islands' of prosperity in cities elsewhere (Glasmeier et al., 2008). And within cities, urban regeneration favouring high-skill service sector jobs has primarily occurred in city centres, especially in those cities seen globally as service 'poles' or 'nodes', such as London (or more widely Seattle, Hong Kong, Barcelona, or Milan (van Winden, 2008; Gospodini, 2009)). In contrast, 'regeneration' in the suburban centres of UK cities has often amounted to little more than the building of supermarkets and its association with low-wage, part-time (and increasingly zero-contract), low-skill jobs (Nolan, 2004), where policy-makers have championed the 'importance of retail as a creator of jobs' in a wider context of declining manufacturing (Dixon, 2005: 171). In such cases, efforts at 'regeneration' may actually serve to widen inequalities (Young et al., 2006). Many lesser-skilled workers leaving declining industries—largely concentrated in outer suburban areas—have therefore been at risk of long-term unemployment, underemployment, or of leaving the workforce entirely. More broadly, as Turok (2010) notes, people who have re-entered work have struggled to find permanent and/or rewarding jobs, being 'trapped in low-paid jobs or forced to move in and out of successive temporary posts' (Turok, 2010, p. 43). This is evident in Birmingham, for example, where after the collapse of MG Rover and the 'lift and shift' of production to China, the city's former car workers experienced lower pay and satisfaction levels as they found themselves in a more precarious labour market (Bailey et al., 2008, 2010).

---

[11] Labour market inactivity provides a wider measure of employment opportunities, since the decline in jobs (in UK cities) is not entirely represented in the growth of urban unemployment. This is because, since the early 1980s, there has been substantial growth in the economically inactive (largely male) population in British cities. For instance, even before the Great Recession (2008–13) which had such profound effects, one in six working-age households had no adult in paid employment (Kemp et al., 2004). More broadly, and in a telling example of the depth of the urban problem in the UK, Turok and Edge (1999) calculated that between 1981 and 1996, the twenty major cities in Britain lost half a million jobs, equivalent to about 25% of their male labour force, compared to a net gain of 1.7 million elsewhere, with such cities transformed from being major centres of employment to centres of *non*-employment, *under*-employment, and social crisis.

Ironically, given the concentration of financial services in London (and the South East), the impact of the financial crisis of 2008 and the ensuing Great Recession has further extenuated the North–South divide. Hutton and Lee (2012), for instance, note London experienced relatively low increases in unemployment, while cities further away from the capital were more severely hit (particularly cities in the West Midlands, North East and Wales) (see also Clayton, 2011). Using a wider measure of joblessness (defined as the officially unemployed plus hidden unemployed such as discouraged job-seekers), Fothergill (2009) has also highlighted how the recession has again impacted most on the old industrial areas such as Birmingham, Wolverhampton, and Sandwell, where the real *joblessness* rate was by 2009 well above 15 per cent. Table 14.1 provides some recent employment data on the functioning of UK regional labour markets. While high employment rates indicate high levels of demand for employees, the data does not distinguish between types of employment (full/part-time and/or temporary/zero-hours contract). Nevertheless, the majority of cities recording higher employment rates are in the South, with many in the North and Midlands recording rates significantly lower than the national average. Indeed, it is estimated Birmingham would require 112,300 residents to acquire (some form of) employment to raise its participation rate to the UK average (Centre for Cities, 2014).

A similar story arises with regard to labour skills, measured here in relation to the proportion of working-age residents with qualifications equivalent to NVQ level 4 (equivalent to a Certificate in Higher Education (or BTEC)) and above. Skill sets are important since they are a key facet of pecuniary external economies and wider ag-glomeration effects that attract and retain firms in cities (see also Green and Mason, Chapter 10, this volume). Again, the majority of Northern and Midlands cities lag be-hind the national average in recognized skill sets, which is indicative of their wider relative decline. These lower skill sets are often reflected in fewer high value-added job opportunities and lower wage rates in |English regions outside the Greater South East. As Hutton and Lee (2012) note, the most severely hit cities (from the Great Recession) shared common characteristics; 'they tended to have poorly skilled populations...and the paucity of their business bases made them reliant upon the public sector as major employer and (thus) more vulnerable to public spending cuts'. They conclude, 'in short the recession exacerbated structural change in the economy and furthered the bias to-wards cities with high skills (in the South East)' (Hutton and Lee, 2012, pp. 4–5, our words in parentheses).

14.4 An Industrial Strategy for UK Cities

Given the preceding analysis, it is hard not to concur with the Centre for Cities (2014) verdict that many UK cities, in particular the UK's so-called second tier cities Bir-mingham and Manchester, are 'punching below their weight'. Previous policies towards regeneration have varied, although they have often involved measures for 'reimaging' cities and attracting and subsidizing investment (including offering lucrative land sites and supporting infrastructure) by transnational corporations or at the other end of the spectrum for small firms. However, too often transnationals extricate public resources and relocate when it becomes attractive to do so,[12] while small firms often have very low survival rates, especially in hostile environments where they are subservient to dominant corporate players (see also Christopherson and Clark, 2007).[13] Moreover, small firms in the UK have often been crowded out (by corporate firms) in publicly funded university knowledge transfer initiatives (see Huggins et al., 2008).[14]

We are thus confronted in the UK—but also in other Western economies—with decaying or decayed manufacturing cities as well as decaying areas in the so-called 'command' or global cities; these are different but connected problems which we have argued have their roots in the *strategic failure* related to the dominance of major corporations in the economy. In many respects, *strategic failure* is systemic and this has stifled the dynamism of UK cities. A potential way forward is to explore possibilities of nurturing city development paths that negate such failures. Fundamentally, this would require—in parallel with industrial and regional policy—the reform of underlying economic governance structures. Such a project would be long term, exploratory, and highly political and involve exploring avenues for more diffuse structures which facilitate wider involvement (and influence) of local actors in strategic decision-making processes that affect their city. In part this would require more democratic frameworks to include wider 'public interests' within the hierarchical structures of large corporate firms; this in itself would require a degree of monitoring to ensure compliance (see Branston et al., 2006; Bailey and de Ruyter, 2007). A further dimension of policy would be the nurturing of alternative production structures characterized by largely symmetrical, heterarchical relations and based predominantly upon small and medium-sized firms rooted within the locality. Such a structure might offer an antidote to the hierarchical corporate structures that currently dominate city trajectories (see discussion in Section (14.2.2)).

By itself, the presence of small firms is no guarantee of socially optimal outcomes. Yet intuitively local economies predominantly comprised of small and medium-sized firms might facilitate more diffuse governance structures and wider community involvement in determining (local) trajectories. This is very much the story behind the earlier success of the Italian districts discussed in Section 14.2.2. Furthermore, groupings of small and medium-sized firms in these districts were able to lead on technology sharing and innovation, and this was historically achieved without a concentration of production within a large-scale hierarchical organization (see Becattini et al., 2003, 2009).

---

[12] Dell's assembly operations in (or rather now out of) Limerick are a recent example (see Lenihan and Bailey, 2009).

[13] Occasionally we see small firms succeeding but they are typically acquired by their larger rivals and become, often unsuccessful, divisions of these corporate giants; see Ravenscraft and Scherer (1989).

[14] Huggins et al. (2008) find that UK universities are less inclined to engage in knowledge transfer activities with the small firm community unless they receive a market return (or state subsidy); they note that small firms are often regarded as 'inferior and less lucrative collaborators and partners in comparison to larger and more internationally focused firms'(Huggins et al., 2008, p. 333).

In recent years, the Italian districts have faced significant challenges relating to global-ization and the emergence of new competition (Becattini et al., 2009). This may reflect the emergence of more hierarchical structures and a consolidation of production within some districts, as smaller firms shelter under the umbrella of their lead partners' brand identities (see Sacchetti and Tomlinson, 2009). Indeed, the recent trend towards large leader firms in these districts has led to a marked deterioration in the innovative capacity of inter-firm networks in the region (Boschma and Lambooy, 2002). It is likely these changing governance structures have led to over-specialization and narrowed the dis-tricts' technological path. Moreover, this may be a deterministic feature of district evolu-tion and is associated with the so-called 'cluster paradox'. This arises as a district matures and there is a 'shake out' of inferior technologies. Consequently, producer concentration rises and the district adopts (and becomes reliant upon) dominant technologies, and while this process initially facilitates synergies (and agglomeration) among firms (since it reduces technological uncertainty), it ultimately diminishes economic diversity and gen-erates negative 'lock-in' effects (see Swann et al., 1998; Menzel and Fornahl, 2010).

Thus, agglomeration alone is not sufficient to maintain growth and development (see also Polese, 2005); rather, as Jacobs (1969, 1984) argued, maintaining economic diversity is necessary and this springs from a diffuse (and democratic) industrial base (whereas mono-structures tend to (re-)arise as a result of corporate dominance; see Sections 14.2.1 and 14.2.2).[15] Indeed, faced with repeated exogenous shocks, cities need to adapt their industrial structures to different market conditions and a diversified industrial base offers the best opportunity to exploit Jacobian economies (and thrive) via the cross-fertilization of ideas (see also De Propris and Cooke, 2011). The challenge for in-dustrial strategy in regenerating older cities (and their industrial bases) lies in widening their economic diversity, possibly through unlocking their existing expertise, compe-tencies, and knowledge bases and combining them with new, complementary ideas and technologies in adjacent (and related) sectors (see Frenken et al., 2007). This is particu-larly relevant for the UK's 'old' industrial cities where there is considerable potential for 'phoenix' industries to emerge from the ashes of old manufacturing industries. More-over, as Christopherson notes (2010, p. 79), the evidence suggests these possibilities are greater where there is not one dominant employer, but rather many small and medium-sized firms (i.e. a diversity of firm sizes as well as sectors). These often produce sophisti-cated components sold on to equipment manufacturers in fields as diverse as defence and health, and are often seen as 'enabling industries' given their cross-sectoral linkages. For phoenix industry start-ups, 'the incubator is not a technology park; it is the whole urban region' (Christopherson, 2010)—again suggesting the need for diversity and cross-sector fertilization within the city.[16]

---

[15] Recent life cycle cluster models, in the evolutionary geography literature, suggest localities can renew themselves along their existing path or transform themselves into different fields only by widening their economic base (or technological heterogeneity) (see Menzel and Fornahl, 2010; Martin and Sunley, 2011).

[16] Tomlinson and Branston (2014) have documented how the ceramics city of Stoke-on-Trent is beginning to avert its long decline by widening its industrial base in the field of 'material

It would seem constructive, therefore, to consider the possibility of establishing city structures which are largely reminiscent of industrial districts; less specialized in the traditional sense, but having coherence within the city and yet mingling many different aspects of the city to facilitate cross-fertilization and in doing so, nurturing new industries for the city's future. We would envisage production structures of intersecting webs of small and medium-sized firms and related actors, including different areas of activity which have elements of complementarity; for example, the digital technology platform with its links into design, media, IT, telecommunications, and so on. These could comprise a large group of production units which individually are quite small but, taken as a group, constitute a production process on a large(r) scale. The aim would be for units to cooperate or network through reciprocity and mutual support in an evolving process which also promotes the emergence of new and rival production units. To achieve this will require policy operating with a light touch, eschewing monopoly positions, and maintaining open access to knowledge and critical financial support especially for micro-firms, allowing for constant change. For instance, financial support would not imply subsidies for the large and dominant, but credit at critical times for the evolution of the small and new (perhaps along the lines of the Grameen bank tailored to the needs of the European city).

Over the long run, the city needs to adapt and change in response to the inevitable multitude of exogenous shocks it will face: a diverse industrial structure can act as a buffer and an opportunity for renewal. Yet as noted in the cluster life cycle literature, there may be a tendency for cities (and clusters) to become more specialized over time, which combined with political pressures to retain past structures can reinforce negative 'lock-in' effects (Menzel and Fornahl, 2010; see also Bailey, 2003). Thus an industrial strategy (for cities) should be orientated towards fostering and maintaining diversity, and this might be achieved through ongoing investment in public research such as joint research institutes (which act as technological gatekeepers and can initiate new knowledge), support for private research and development (R&D) (to facilitate adoption of new technologies across the district), and, critically, the renewal of networks (to overcome problems of over-embeddedness and 'lock-in').[17] Ultimately, success will depend upon the capabilities of local firms and actors to (over time) absorb new ideas and adapt to new challenges, with more resilient cities typically being those that can attract new firms, develop new skill sets, and embrace new technologies, thus enhancing innovative endeavour (see also Pike et al., 2010).

transformation' and 'advanced materials research and production'. For instance, ceramics-based technology is being used in a range of other sectors, from bio-inserts to mobile phone transmitters, while other advanced materials include the use of lightweight, recycled metals (with anti-corrosive properties) in vehicles. In addition, the city recently won £31 million of government funding to nurture a new geothermal energy industry based upon converting water to electricity, while there are also proposals for the (non-fracking) extraction of methane gas from the region's dormant coalfields for more efficient energy use.

[17] Brenner and Schlump (2011) argue the efficacy of policy will depend upon employing appropriate measures in specific phases of a cluster's (or city's) trajectory. Their simulations suggest the measures mentioned here are particularly potent in clusters (cities) seeking to avert decline.

These types of policies link closely with the notion of nurturing self-sustaining high-skill ecosystems, which are based upon a supportive host and thrive on a high degree of interdependence among actors (see Finegold, 1999; Alcorso and Windsor, 2008). Interestingly, Finegold (1999) saw the UK as possessing many of the ingredients (good universities, telecoms, science parks, culture) but also some weaknesses (outflows of scientific stars, limited seed corn funds, and poor links between firms and universities). Obviously, creating successful high-skill ecosystems will not solve the low-skill equilibrium problems of UK provincial cities.[18] Indeed, fifteen years on from Finegold's observations, there has been little progress, although the recent creation of seven Catapult Innovation Centres by the UK Technology Strategy Board might act as a catalyst (though five of these centres are based in the South East, thus extenuating the North–South divide). These 'physical' centres are geared to bring together business and specialists from science and engineering to develop late-stage R&D and transform potential ideas into new products.[19]

Finally, while being critical of the current globalization process and the global concentration of economic power, we *do not* advocate a narrow, national or intra-national approach to industrial strategy. Rather, a critical function of policy will be to explore the possibility of fostering greater multinational cooperation between cities. Many European cities face similar problems but have similar opportunities (e.g. Edinburgh/Dublin; Glasgow/Hamburg; London/Berlin; Paris/Milan). Cooperation, perhaps through multinational webs of firms and other actors, might facilitate the sharing of ideas and technology and joint problem-solving and help to reshape the economic basis for cities (and offer new opportunities). We envisage such relationships as being largely non-hierarchical and inclusive, allowing cities (and societies) to realize their full potential (Cowling and Sugden, 1999; Sugden and Wilson, 2002). There have already been some EU initiatives in this regard. The EU-funded (2008–11) Urban Network for Innovation in Ceramic Cities (UNIC) established a network of nine European (ceramics-focused) cities (including Stoke-on-Trent), which brought together ceramics industrialists, policy-makers, and other stakeholders from across Europe in a series of workshops and exchange visits to share ideas and discuss policy initiatives to revitalize and promote growth within these cities. Although the EU funding has ended, the links between these localities remain.[20] More widely, and returning to the phoenix industries example, multinational cooperation between cities and regions would seem critical; as phoenix industry regions do not compete in the way that regions do when dominated by large firms, so they can benefit from strategic alliances. Christopherson (2010) gives the example of potential

---

[18] Finegold argues policy should try to improve educational levels so as to provide wider opportunities for participation in such systems (see also Green and Mason, Chapter 10, this volume).

[19] See <https://www.catapult.org.uk/>.

[20] For further details, see <http://urbact.eu/en/projects/innovation-creativity/unic/homepage/>. One proposal is to establish a world heritage route (or at least European) of ceramics cities to promote tourism, similar to the way Santiago de Compostela promotes religious tourism. On this see <http://ec.europa.eu/enterprise/sectors/tourism/sustainable-tourism/documents/cera_dest_en.pdf>.

cooperation between Rochester in the US (with its expertise in lasers) and Sheffield in the UK (with its expertise in cutting technologies and steels), with the potential for fostering innovation and developing new markets; through such alliances the 'cross-fertilisation of regionally based technical expertise may be possible' (Christopherson, 2010, p. 85).

14.5 CONCLUDING COMMENTS

In this chapter, we have argued that while cities can be an engine for growth and creativity, many old industrial cities in the UK are glued to mono-structures and mired in the 'slow lane'. This largely reflects these cities historic over-reliance upon corporate and transnational firms (for investment and employment), which have pursued their own strategic interests and, in doing so, have shaped city trajectories. This has raised the spectre of *strategic failure*, with UK cities (particularly outside London and the South East) suffering from a chronic lack of economic diversity which has inhibited socio-economic development. The key to reversing this decline and unlocking the potential of UK cites lies in altering the very industrial, organizational, and economic structures of the city. This requires releasing cities from the dominion of corporate control, but also that of central government; UK cities have significantly less autonomy in terms of fiscal and other economic levers to tailor (public) resources to local requirements compared to other cities within the OECD (Blöchliger and Petzold, 2009).[21]

Industrial strategy should be geared not only towards promoting agglomeration within cities but also, critically, in widening the economic base, which is best maintained through more diffuse governance structures. As Jacobs (1969, 1984) first identified, cities with more diverse economic bases tend to be more innovative and dynamic, since they facilitate the cross-fertilization of ideas. They also tend to be more resilient cities and are better able to absorb and adapt to exogenous shocks. Through supporting a variety of industrial processes, policy will not only serve to support an array of talents but will also be more inclusive and diffuse.[22] By nurturing cities along the lines of new industrial districts, such cities can become less reliant upon corporate finance (and authority) and act as havens for experimentation, the germination of new ideas, and innovation. Such ingredients are critical for cities to succeed in the global economy of the twenty-first century. Moving forward, an industrial strategy requires a set of coordinated initiatives pursued at city, regional, national, and pan-European levels. Democratic

[21] Indeed, Wales, with its devolved parliament, has greater autonomy over economic policy than much larger English city regions. This has raised debate as to whether England's cities and regions need a new settlement (Centre for Cities).

[22] In line with Sen's (1999) concept of substantive freedom which embodies 'the freedom to participate in the social, political and economic life of the community'.

involvement in the economy needs to be developed at the city level but must extend outward to the European level, otherwise actors (such as transnational corporations) with a pan-European perspective and competence will undermine any local autonomy.

REFERENCES

Alcorso, C. and Windsor, K. (2008). *Skills in Context: A Guide to the Skill Ecosystems Approach to Workforce Development*, Sydney: Department of Education and Training.

Asheim, B. T., Boschma, R., and Cooke, P. (2011). 'Constructing Regional Advantage: Platform Policies Based On Related Variety and Differentiated Knowledge Bases', *Regional Studies* 45(7), 893–904.

Bailey, D. (2003). 'Globalisation, Regions and Cluster Policies: The Case of the Rover Task Force', *Policy Studies* 24(2/3), 67–85.

Bailey, D., Chapain, C., Fauth, B., and Mahdon, M. (2008). *Life after Longbridge: Three Years On. Pathways to Re-Employment in a Restructuring Economy*. London: The Work Foundation.

Bailey, D. and Cowling, K. (2011). 'Rebuilding the City: A Focus for European Industrial Policy?', *Policy Studies* 32(4), 347–64.

Bailey, D. and de Ruyter, A. (2007). 'Globalisation, Economic Freedom and Strategic Decision-Making: A Role for Industrial Policy?', *Policy Studies* 28(4) 383–98.

Bailey, D., de Ruyter, A., and Clarke, I. (2010). 'Private Equity and the Flight of the Phoenix 4? The Restructuring, Collapse and Impact of MG Rover in the West Midlands', *Cambridge Journal of Regions, Economy and Society* 3(3), 367–82.

Becattini, G. (1990). 'The Marshallian Industrial District as a Socioeconomic Notion', in F. Pyke, G. Beccatini, and W. Sengenberger (eds), *Industrial Districts and Inter-Firm Co-operation*, pp. 37–51. Geneva: International Institute for Labour Studies.

Becattini, G., Bellandi, M., and De Propris, L. (2009). 'Critical Nodes and Contemporary Reflections on Industrial Districts: An Introduction', in G. Becattini, M. Bellandi, and L. De Propris (eds), *A Handbook of Industrial Districts*, pp. xv–xxxv. Cheltenham: Edward Elgar.

Becattini G., Bellandi M., Dei Ottati G., and Sforzi, F. (2003). *From Industrial Districts to Local Development*. Cheltenham: Edward Elgar.

Bellandi, M. (2003). 'Industrial Clusters and Districts in the New Economy: Some Perspectives and Cases', in R. Sugden, R. H. Cheng, and G. R. Meadows (eds), *Urban and Regional Prosperity in a Globalised Economy*, pp. 196–222. Cheltenham: Edward Elgar.

Bellandi, M. (2011). 'Perspectives on Mature Marshallian Industrial Districts', in P. Cooke, B. T. Asheim, R. Boschma, R. Martin, D. Schwartz, and F. Todtling (eds), *Handbook of Regional Innovation and Growth*, pp. 78–88. Cheltenham: Edward Elgar.

Best, M. H. (1990). *The New Competition*. London: Polity Press.

Blöchliger, H. and Petzold, O. (2009). *Taxes of Grants: What Revenue Source for Sub-Central Governments?*, OECD, France, Economics Department Working Paper No. 706.

Boschma, R. and Lambooy, J. (2002). 'Knowledge, Market Structure and Economic Coordination: Dynamics of Industrial Districts', *Growth and Change* 33(3), 291–311.

Branston, J. R., Cowling, K., and Sugden, R. (2006). 'Corporate Governance and the Public Interest', *International Review of Applied Economics* 20(2), 189–212.

Branston, J. R, Tomlinson, P. R., and Wilson, J. R (2012). ' "Strategic Failure" in the Financial Sector: A Policy View', *International Journal of the Economics of Business* 19(2), 169–89.

Brenner, T. and Schlump, C. (2011). 'Policy Measures and Their Effects in the Different Phases of the Cluster Life Cycle', *Regional Studies* 45(10), 1363–86.

Brusco, S. (1982). The Emilian Model: Productive Decentralisation and Social Integration, *Cambridge Journal of Economics* 6(2), 167–84.

Camagni, R. (1991). 'Local "Milieu", Uncertainty and Innovation Networks: Towards a New Dynamic Theory of Economic Space', in R. Camagni (ed.), *Innovation Networks: Spatial Perspectives*, pp. 121–42. London: Belhaven.

Centre for Cities (2014). *City Outlook 2014*. <http://www.citiesoutlook.org/> (accessed 9 February 2014).

Christopherson, S. (2010). 'Building "Phoenix Industries" in Our Old Industrial Cities', in J. Tomaney (ed.), *The Future of Regional Policy*, pp. 78–87. London: The Smith Institute/ Regional Studies Association.

Christopherson, S. and Clark, J. (2007). *Remaking Regional Economies: Power, Labor and Firm Strategies in the Knowledge Economy*. London: Routledge.

Clayton, N. (2011). 'The Spatial Impacts of Recession', in D. Bailey and C. Chapain (eds), *The Recession and Beyond: Local and Regional Responses to the Downturn*, pp. 27–44. London: Taylor & Francis.

Coase, R. H. (1937) 'The nature of the firm', *Economica*, 4(16), 386–405.

Coffey, D. and Tomlinson, P. R. (2006). 'Multiple Facilities, Strategic Splitting and Vertical Structures: Stability, Growth and Distribution Reconsidered', *The Manchester School* 74(5), 558–76.

Cooke, P. and Morgan, K. (1994). 'Growth Regions Under Duress: Renewal Strategies in Baden-Wurttemberg and Emilia-Romagna', in A. Amin and N. Thrift (eds), *Globalisation, Institutions and Regional Development in Europe*, pp. 91–117. Oxford: Oxford University Press Centre for Cities, <http://www.centreforcities.org/>.

Cooke, P. and Morgan, K. (1998). *The Associational Economy: Firms, Regions and Innovation*. Oxford: Oxford University Press.

Cowling, K. and Sugden, R. (1998). 'The Essence of the Modern Corporation: Markets, Strategic Decision-Making and the Theory of the Firm', *The Manchester School* 66(1), 59–86.

Cowling, K. and Sugden, R. (1999). 'The Wealth of Localities, Regions and Nations: Developing Multinational Economics', *New Political Economy* 4, 361–78.

Cowling, K. and Tomlinson, P. R. (2000). 'The Japanese Crisis: A Case of Strategic Failure?', *The Economic Journal* 110(464), F358–81.

Cowling, K. and Tomlinson, P. R. (2005). 'Globalisation and Corporate Power', *Contributions to Political Economy* 24(1), 33–54.

Cowling, K. and Tomlinson, P. R. (2011). 'Post the Washington Consensus: Economic Governance and Industrial Strategies for the 21st Century', *Cambridge Journal of Economics* 35(5), 831–52.

Cuddas, J. (2014). 'Power and One Nation', Speech to the New Local Government Network's Annual Conference, 12 February, <http://www.joncruddas.org.uk/sites/joncruddas.org.uk/files/power%201%20%282%29.pdf>.

De Propris, L. (2001). 'Systemic Flexibility, Production Fragmentation and Cluster Governance', *European Planning Studies* 9(6), 739–53.

De Propris, L. and Cooke, P. (2011). 'A Policy Agenda for EU Smart Growth: The Role of Creative and Cultural Industries, *Policy Studies* 32(4), 365–75.

Dicken, P. (2010). *Global Shift: Mapping the Changing Contours of the Global Economy*. London: Sage.

Dixon, T. (2005). 'The Role of Retailing in Urban Regeneration', *Local Economy* 20(2), 168–82.

Finegold, D. (1999). 'Creating Self-Sustaining High Skill Ecosystems', *Oxford Review of Economic Policy* 15(1) 60–81.

Fothergill, S. (2009). *The Impact of Recession on Unemployment in Industrial Britain*. Barnsley: Industrial Communities Alliance.

Frenken, K., Van Oort, F., and Verburg, T. (2007). 'Related Variety, Unrelated Variety and Regional Economic Growth', *Regional Studies* 41, 685–97.

Glaeser, E. L. (1994). 'Cities, Information and Economic Growth', *Cityscape* 1(1), 9–47.

Glaeser, E. L. (2010). 'America's Revival Begins With Its Cities', *The Boston Globe* 30 December.

Glaeser, E. L., Kallal, H., Scheinkman, J., and Shleifer, A. (1992). 'Growth in Cities', *Journal of Political Economy* 100, 1126–54.

Glasmeier, A., Martin, R., Tyler, P., and Dorling, D. (2008). 'Editorial: Poverty and Place in the UK and the USA', *Cambridge Journal of Regions, Economy and Society* 1(1), 1–16.

Glazyrina, V. (2000). 'Krasnoiarsk—26: A Closed City of the Defence Industry Complex', in J. Barber and M. Harrison, *The Soviet Defence Industry Complex from Stalin to Khrushchev*, pp. 195–204. Houndmills: Palgrave Macmillan.

Gospodini, A. (2009). 'Post-Industrial Trajectories of Mediterranean European Cities: The Case of Post-Olympics Athens', *Urban Studies* 46(5/6), 1157–86.

Grabher, G. (1993). 'The Weakness of Strong Ties, the Lock-In of Regional Development in the Ruhr Area', in G. Grabher (ed), *The Embedded Firm*, pp. 255–77. Routledge: London.

Grabher, G. and Stark, D. (1997). 'Organizing Diversity: Evolutionary Theory, Network Analysis and Post-Socialism', *Regional Studies* 31, 533–44.

Heseltine, M. (2012). *No Stone Unturned: In Pursuit of Growth*. London: Department of Business, Innovation and Skills, <https://www.gov.uk/government/uploads/system/uploads/attachment_data/file/34648/12-1213-no-stone-unturned-in-pursuit-of-growth.pdf>.

Hill, E. W., Wial, H., and Wolman, H. (2008). *Exploring Regional Economic Resilience*, Institute of Urban and Regional Development, University of California Working Paper No. 200-08.

Huggins, R., Johnston, A., and Steffenson, R. (2008). 'Universities, Knowledge Networks and Regional Policy', *Cambridge Journal of Regions, Economy and Society* 1, 321–40.

Hutton, W. and Lee, N. (2012). 'The City and the Cities: Ownership, Finance and the Geography of Recovery', *Cambridge Journal of Regions, Economy and Society* 5, 325–37.

Hymer, S. (1972). 'The Multinational Corporation and the Law of Uneven Development', in J. N. Bhagwai (ed.), *Economics and World Order: From the 1970s to the 1990s*, pp. 113–40. London: Macmillan.

Jacobs, J. (1961). *The Death and Life of Great American Cities*. London: Jonathan Cape.

Jacobs, J. (1969). *The Economy of Cities*. Harmondsworth: Penguin.

Jacobs, J. (1984). *Cities and the Wealth of Nations*. Harmondsworth: Penguin.

Jessop, B. (1998). 'The Rise of Governance and the Risks of Failure: The Case of Economic Development', *International Social Science Journal* 50(155), 29–45.

Kemp, P., Bradshaw, J., Dornan, P., Finch, N., and Mayhew, E. (2004). *Routes Out of Poverty: A Research Review*. York: Joseph Rowntree Foundation.

Klepper, S. (1997). 'Industry Life Cycles', *Industrial and Corporate Change* 6, 145–81.

Le Gales, P. and Voelzkow, H. (2001). 'Introduction: The Governance of Local Economies', in C. Crouch, P. Le Gales, C. Trigilia, and H. Voelzkow (eds), *Local Production Systems in Europe. Rise or Demise?*, pp. 1–24. Oxford: Oxford University Press.

Lenihan, H. and Bailey, D. (2009). 'Intervention Essential for Those Who Lose Dell Jobs', *Irish Times* (opinion), 27 October, Dublin

MacKinnon, D., Cumbers, A., and Shaw, J. (2008). 'Rescaling Employment Relations: Key Outcomes of Change in the Privatised Rail Industry', *Environment and Planning A* 40, 1347–69.

Maillat, D. (1995). 'Territorial Dynamic, Innovative Milieus and Regional Policy', *Entrepreneurship and Regional Development* 7(2), 157–65.

Marshall, A. (1919). *Industry and Trade*. London: Macmillan.

Martin, R. (1988). 'The Political Economy of Britain's North–South Divide', *Transactions of the Institute of British Geographers* 13(4), 389–418.

Martin, R. and Sunley, P. (2011). 'Conceptualising Cluster Evolution: Beyond the Life Cycle Model?', *Regional Studies* 45(10), 1299–318.

Massey, D. (1979). 'In What Sense A Regional Problem?', *Regional Studies* 13, 233–43.

Massey, D. (1984). *Spatial Divisions of Labour, Social Structures and the Geography of Production*. London: Macmillan.

Massey, D. (1986). 'The Legacy Lingers On: The Impact of Britain's International Role on Its Internal Geography', in R. L. Martin and R. E. Rowthorn (eds), *The Geography of De-Industrialisation*, ch. 2. London: Macmillan.

Menzel, M. P. and Fornahl, D. (2010). 'Cluster Life Cycles: Dimensions and Rationales of Cluster Evolution', *Industrial and Corporate Change* 19, 205–38.

Neffke, F., Henning, M., and Boschma, R. (2011). 'How Do Regions Diversify Over Time? Industry Relatedness and the Development of New Growth Paths in Regions', *Economic Geography* 87(3), 237–65.

Nolan, P. (2004). 'Editorial: Shaping the Future: The Political Economy of Work and Employment', *Industrial Relations Journal* 35(5), 378–87.

Office of National Statistics (2004). *Life Expectancy Tables*. London: HMSO.

ODPM (Office of the Deputy Prime Minister) (2006). *State of the English Cities. Volume 1*. London: ODPM.

Peoples, J. and Sugden, R. (2001). 'Divide and Rule by Transnational Corporations', in C. N. Pitelis and R. Sugden (eds), *The Nature of the Transnational Firm*, pp. 174–91. London: Routledge.

Pike, A., Dawley, S., and Tomaney, J., (2010). 'Resilience, Adaptation and Adaptability', *Cambridge Journal of Regions, Economy and Society* 3, 59–70.

Piore, M. and Sabel, C. F. (1984). *The Second Industrial Divide*. New York: Basic Books.

Polese, M. (2005). 'Cities and National Economic Growth: A Reappraisal', *Urban Studies* 42(8), 1429–51.

Porter, M. E. (1998). *On Competition*. Boston: Harvard Business School Press.

Powell, W. W. (1990). 'Neither Market Nor Hierarchy: Network Forms of Organisation', *Research in Organizational Behaviour* 12, 295–336.

Ravenscraft, D. J. and Scherer, F. M. (1989). 'The Profitability of Mergers', *International Journal of Industrial Organization* 7, 101–16.

Sacchetti, S. and Sugden, R. (2003). 'The Governance of Networks and Economic Power: The Nature and Impact of Subcontracting Relationships', *Journal of Economic Surveys* 17(5), 669–91.

Sacchetti, S. and Tomlinson, P. R. (2009). 'Economic Governance and the Evolution of Industrial Districts Under Globalization: The Case of Two Mature European Industrial Districts', *European Planning Studies* 17(12), 1837–51.

Sassen, S. (1991). *The Global City*. London: Princeton University Press.

Sassen, S. (2006). *Cities in a World Economy*. 3rd edn. Thousand Oaks, CA: Pine Forge Press.

Sen, A. (1999). *Development as Freedom*. Oxford: Oxford University Press.

Sugden, R. and Wilson, J. (2002). 'Economic Development in the Shadow of the Consensus: A Strategic Decision-Making Approach', *Contributions to Political Economy* 21, 111–34.

Swann, P. and Prevezer, M. (1996). 'A Comparison of the Dynamics of Industrial Clustering in Computing and Biotechnology', *Research Policy* 25(7), 1139–57.

Swann, P., Prevezer, M., and Stout, D. (1998). *The Dynamics of Industrial Clustering: International Comparisons in Computing and Biotechnology*. Oxford: Oxford University Press.

Tomlinson, P. R. (2010). 'Co-operative Ties and Innovation: Some New Evidence for UK Manufacturing', *Research Policy* 39(6), 762–75.

Tomlinson, P. R. and Branston, J. R. (2014). 'Turning the Tide: Prospects for an Industrial Renaissance in the North Staffordshire Ceramics District', *Cambridge Journal of Regions, Economy and Society* 7, 489–507, doi:10.1093/cjres/rsu016.

Turok, I. (2010). 'Social Inclusion: Mixed Progress, Uncertain Prospects', in J. Tomaney (ed.), *The Future of Regional Policy*, pp. 40–9. London: The Smith Institute/Regional Studies Association.

Turok, I. and Edge, N. (1999). *The Jobs Gap in Britain's Cities: Employment Loss and Labour Market Consequences*. Bristol: Policy Press.

van Winden, W. (2008). 'Urban Governance in the Knowledge-Based Economy: Challenges for Different City Types', *Innovation: Management, Policy & Practice* 10, 197–210.

Webster, D. (1999). *Employment Convergence in 1999s Britain: How Real?* Glasgow: Glasgow City Housing.

Wills, J. (2009). 'Subcontracted Employment and its Challenge to Labor', *Labor Studies Journal* 34(4), 441–60.

Young, C., Diep, M., and Drabble, S. (2006). 'Living with Difference? The "Cosmopolitan City" and Urban Reimaging in Manchester, UK', *Urban Studies* 43(10), 1687–714.

Zeitlin, M. (1974). Corporate Ownership and Control: The Large Corporations and the Capitalist Class, *American Journal of Sociology* 79(5), 1073–119.

CHAPTER 15

···

MIND THE GAP! WHAT MIGHT A PLACE-BASED INDUSTRIAL AND REGIONAL POLICY LOOK LIKE?

···

DAVID BAILEY, PAUL HILDRETH, AND
LISA DE PROPRIS

15.1 INTRODUCTION

A recent study by the Organisation for Economic Co-operation and Development (OECD) showed that strong growth is possible in all types of regions, from capital cities to less developed towns and rural areas (OECD, 2012). Whilst a relatively small number of key centres (big 'hubs') (such as London) account for a disproportionate share of economic growth, even less developed regions make a vital contribution to national growth, accounting for 43 per cent of aggregate OECD growth between 1995 and 2007. Far from being a drag on national economic performance, less well performing regions, such as in the North of England, should be viewed as important sources of potential growth. However, to realize that potential requires a new approach, moving away from traditional policies.

In particular, this chapter along with other contributions (e.g. Barca, 2009; OECD, 2009a, 2009b, and 2012) sets out the foundations for new 'place-based' approaches to sub-national economic development policy.[1] These offer the possibility of realizing new opportunities in developing the potential of currently less well performing places. But in doing so, they may raise questions about the framework that has been adopted by the

---

[1] 'A "place-based policy" is a long-term strategy aimed at tackling persistent underutilisation of potential and producing persistent social exclusion in specific places through external interventions and multilevel governance. It promotes the supply of integrated goods and services tailored to contexts, and it triggers institutional change' (Barca, 2009, p. vii).

UK government towards sub-national economic growth, in the English context at least. Indeed, these questions start at a basic level before actually considering the policies themselves: how do we understand the role of 'knowledge' in an economy and what is the function of 'institutions' (across the public and private sectors) in development? This chapter focuses on these two issues to show how they might impact on the design of sub-national economic policy in England.

In May 2010, the newly elected Conservative–Liberal Coalition government claimed to offer a 'new approach to local growth' (*local growth*) (HMG, 2010) that would shift power away from central government to local communities. At the centre of this approach, Local Enterprise Partnerships (LEPs) were created through a relatively 'bottom-up' process across England, largely reflecting local partners' perceptions of the natural economy of their area (and/or the real politics of local cooperation). A first round of City Deals was then negotiated with the eight English Core Cities,[2] followed by a second round of City Deals. Claims are made by the government that this approach is 'place-based'. The intention was to create 'a more balanced economy' that 'recognises that places have specific geographic, historic, environmental circumstances that help to determine the prospects for growth and the most suitable approach to support the private sector and residents' opportunities' (HMG, 2010, p. 7).

But is policy 'place-based' in practice? Firstly, there are limitations in taking the 'rhetoric' (what Ministers and government publications say that a policy is all about) and even the 'policies' at face value (Hildreth and Bailey, 2013). The 'rhetoric', the 'policy' (the policy initiatives themselves) and the 'base' (the underlying framework of ideas from which the policies are derived or influenced) may be connected or disconnected in practice. Claims are made by both the Coalition and previous Labour governments for their sub-national policies being 'place-based', for example, in seeking to realize the potential of all places (e.g. HM-Treasury et al., 2007; HMG, 2010) or 're-balancing the economy' (HMG, 2010), the validity of which should be carefully examined (Hildreth, 2009; Froud et al., 2011a; Hildreth and Bailey, 2012, 2013).

Secondly, it is important to know whether it actually matters. If *local growth* is not in fact really 'place-based', then what is the alternative? In the UK (and particularly English) context the contrast is made with 'people-centred' (also referred to as 'space-neutral') approaches (Crowley et al., 2012). In domestic sub-national policy, the distinction between 'place-based' and 'people-centred' approaches has been framed narrowly as about appropriate policy solutions; is it better to prioritize investment in place ('place-based') or invest in people ('people-based') (e.g. Crowley et al., 2012)? The issue has come to a head after more than a decade of active urban and regional policy under Labour, with investment into the English regions through Regional Development Agencies (RDAs) and spatially targeted programmes, such as New Deal for Communities. Commentators questioned how effective this spending was in practice (Overman and Gibbons, 2011; Crowley et al., 2012), and in doing so highlighted what they perceive as the limitations of 'place-based' investments.

---

[2] Birmingham, Bristol, Leeds, Liverpool, Manchester, Newcastle, Nottingham, and Sheffield.

At the same time, economic and social disparities, which have been a long-standing feature of the regional and local geography of the UK, have widened still further (Gardiner et al., 2013). Despite this, the case for a more 'people-centred' approach has been arguably more vocal in the UK than the case for any 'place-based' alternative. This is despite the acknowledged risk of (already considerable) spatial disparities in England widening still further, by centring economic activity and people even more in already successful places (Gill, 2010; Overman and Gibbons, 2011). In England, this would concentrate growth yet further on London and the Greater South East (GSE), and potentially some Core Cities.[3]

Nevertheless, most recently, arguments in favour of a case for 'place-based' approaches have been articulated in a UK context (e.g. Heseltine, 2012; IPPR and the Northern Economic Futures Commission, 2012). These focus on alternative approaches towards realizing economic and social potential more broadly across places in the UK (and England) and raise basic questions about 'institutions' and 'knowledge'. However, even then such arguments risk the retort of being more appropriate to the past than to today's circumstances: 'The Heseltine report isn't all bad. But it is hard to shake the feeling that Mr Heseltine is arguing for a return to policies, many of them not particularly successful, that were developed in different times, to tackle different challenges' (Overman, 2012).

There is the question, at least in the UK context, as to whether there is some confusion around what 'place-based' really means in practice and whether it really matters. Part of the problem is the remarkably narrow way in which the debate has been framed nationally. As already indicated, this contrasts markedly with the international debate. It is surprising that the lively debate (see e.g. Barca and McCann, 2010; Gill, 2010) outside the UK between proponents of 'place-based' and 'people-based' (or 'space-neutral') policy approaches has been largely ignored in the UK. This is especially surprising given that the next round of EU Cohesion Policy from 2014 is largely shaped around a 'place-based' framework (Barca, 2009) and, as already indicated, is central to OECD policy towards 'regions' (OECD, 2009a, 2009b, and 2012). Furthermore, with the UK government seeking to both restore economic growth and reduce the budget deficit, in a context of ongoing global economic crises and austerity at home, how limited resources are spent to maximum impact becomes increasingly important. This includes, crucially, the contribution that places outside London and the South East can make to national economic prosperity; an approach in line with the international 'place-based' debates and approaches.[4] It may indeed be

---

[3] On media coverage of this, see for example 'London's Precarious Brilliance' in *The Economist*, 30 June 2012, which argues that 'Britain lives off London' and that 'if it were not for London, Britain would be off the map'. It goes on to argue that 'anything that jeopardises London endangers the country'.

[4] On this, see for example ESPON (2013) on the role of second tier cities in growth, which notes that 'there are many concerns about the dominance of capital cities, especially the costs and negative externalities of agglomeration' (p. 2). See also the IPPR and the Northern Economic Futures Commission (2012) which notes that in spite of the strongest growth being in London, some '57 per cent of net aggregate growth in the UK was generated by its lagging regions in the decade to 2008' (Garcilazo 2010 cited in IPPR and the Northern Economic Futures Commission, 2012, p. 6).

time that the broader issues raised by this literature were given appropriate focus in the UK context.

However, this represents a challenge in the English context for three reasons. Firstly, as already indicated, governments (both Coalition and former Labour ones) use the 'rhetoric' of 'place-based' policy, even when its 'policies' and 'base' may not come close to fitting them in practice (Hildreth and Bailey, 2013 and 2014). Loose 'rhetoric' like 'rebalancing the economy' (HMG, 2010) is used by Ministers without any real substance behind it (Froud et al., 2011a; Hildreth and Bailey, 2013). Secondly, differences between the approaches are open to misunderstanding (Barca, 2011). Both start from a primary concern for the welfare of people, although they then diverge around different underlying assumptions. Also, both are founded on logical economic principles, and both recognize spatial agglomeration as a reality. However, in practice there are significant points of divergence between the two approaches that are somewhat different to those that have been explored so far, at least in the UK literature. Thirdly, some of the differences between the two approaches are not entirely straightforward to comprehend. In particular, the 'place-based' approach draws on its own distinctive language (e.g. 'communities of interest' and 'local and capital city elites') that requires further explanation before being understood in a UK (or English) context.

This chapter considers the implications of a 'place-based' framework in the UK (or English) context, focusing on two key issues: the role of '(national and local) institutions' and the role of 'knowledge'. The chapter is organized around the following sections to address the question: What would a genuinely 'place-based' strategy mean in the English context? Section 15.2 outlines the basic foundations of 'place-based' policy approaches, drawing on the international literature. It draws out in particular the two key features of a 'place-based' approach, particularly as they relate to 'institutions' and to 'knowledge', recognizing that a more comprehensive coverage of the foundations of 'place-based' policy are offered elsewhere (see e.g. Barca et al., 2012; Hildreth and Bailey, 2013 and 2014). Section 15.3 examines more closely the role played by 'national' and 'local' institutions. It introduces key concepts in the 'place-based' policy literature, such as 'communities of interest' and 'capital city and local elites' and shows how they might be interpreted in a UK policy context. It also demonstrates that whilst Whitehall has ostensibly been focused on the performance of the 'local', whilst simultaneously either centralizing functions or imposing a 'conditional' form of localism (Hildreth, 2011), it may be that reform of the Centre is more critical to a 'place-based' framework. Section 15.4 introduces a 'place-based' approach towards an understanding of the role of knowledge. In doing so it shows why there is an important 'missing space' in *local growth* between the 'national' and the 'local' and how that space might be filled through appropriate institutions and policy responses. Section 15.5 reaches conclusions on what a 'place-based' approach might mean in particular for:

- Whitehall, in changing its approach towards sub-national places;
- Local places, in seeking to realize their own potential;
- What the 'missing space' is and how it might be filled; and therefore
- What a 'place-based' sub-national economic strategy might address.

15.2 Foundations of 'Place-Based' Policy

Several recent influential publications advocate 'place-based' approaches towards sub-national economic policy (Barca, 2009; OECD, 2009a, 2009b, 2012; Barca et al., 2012). Two contrasting images might be used as a basic introduction to distinguish between 'place-based' and 'space-neutral' approaches. First, the 'space-neutral' world is one where spatial adjustments occur relatively smoothly between levels of equilibrium in response to market-based price and cost signals in an urban system that is both homo-genous and predictable. In pictorial terms it might be thought of as being like a smooth free-flowing river system.[5] The alternative, a 'place-based' world, is somewhat different. It is one where the combination of geography, history, culture, and institutions create unpredictability, heterogeneity, and uncertainty in the urban system and market out-comes. Pictorially, it is more like a river system with big boulders and rapids that cause many disruptions to the natural flow of the market system. In summary, distinctions between the two approaches are:

> In essence, the differences between the space-neutral and the place-based ap-proaches centre on the question of whether the territorial systems in evidence today are the result of a unique first-best solution to efficiency and space or rather of path dependency, sunk costs, and institutional issues. As such, the two approaches repre-sent a different reading of the relationships between economic history and eco-nomic geography, giving rise to fundamentally different approaches. (Barca et al., 2012, p. 141)

However, as Barca (2011) points out, it is necessary to go beyond this to identify the es-sence of the case around 'place-based' policy approaches. Barca (2011) identifies five dif-ferent approaches taken towards development policy, to distinguish what is both common and divergent amongst them. From this analysis there are important lessons which are of relevance for understanding what 'place-based' approaches might mean in a UK/English context.

First, the case for 'people-based' (or 'space-neutral') approaches is not always framed in the same way. As Barca points out, a classic report that presents a 'space-neutral' approach based on a particular reading of the New Economic Geography (NEG) framework is the 2009 *World Development Report* (World Bank, 2009). This draws on a mix of three of the five approaches: a particular emphasis on the role of 'unique' institutions, agglomeration-driven development, and a market-led approach towards economic redistribution. In a UK context, the case for 'people-based' approaches (e.g. Overman and Gibbons, 2011) puts a stronger emphasis on the role of efficient mar-kets in promoting agglomeration within a NEG-type framework (what Barca calls an 'agglomeration driven approach') and a significantly lesser emphasis on 'unique' institutions.

---

[5] The authors would like to thank Professor Philip McCann for this metaphor of a river system to illustrate the differences in approach between a 'place-based' and 'space-blind' economic system.

Second, it becomes apparent that the distinction between 'people-based' and 'place-based' approaches is not after all centred on choices between investing in people or places. As Barca states: 'Any attempt to read the current debates if some approaches were concerned with persons and others were concerned places is preposterous' (Barca, 2011, p. 221). Both approaches are actually concerned with both people and place. What distinguishes the 'place-based' approach is that it puts greater emphasis on arguing that 'the well-being of each person, given its individual characteristics, also depends on the context in which he/she lives' (Barca, 2011, p. 221).

Third, Barca goes on to identify the core of the argument around 'place-based' approaches. In effect, it boils down to two key hypotheses concerning the role of 'knowledge' and 'local (and national) elites' in institutions that arise out of the significance of the impact of geography, history, culture, and institutions to development:

> First, the 'place-based' approach argues that no actor knows in advance 'what should be done'. It posits that sensible and reasonable decisions can emerge as the innovative result of a process of interaction and even conflict between endogenous and exogenous forces i.e. between the knowledge embedded in a place and external knowledge. In conjunction with this assumption, it also stresses the role played in producing under-development by the failure on the part of local elites, even when democratically elected, and their innate tendency to seek rents from public interventions. For these two reasons, the place-based approach ... assigns a much greater role of exogenous institutions—their knowledge, preferences and values—and therefore advocates multi-level governance. (Barca, 2011, p. 223)

Of course, there is more to the 'place-based' framework (on this, see Barca, 2009; OECD, 2009a, 2009b, and 2012; Barca et al., 2012). However, for the purpose of this chapter the two key issues of 'institutions' and 'knowledge' are explored further below to begin to offer an illustration of how a 'place-based' framework might begin to challenge the present policy paradigm.

Sections 15.3 and 15.4 explore the two issues that have been highlighted here around the role of 'institutions' and 'knowledge' within a sub-national economic framework.

15.3 NATIONAL AND LOCAL: THE ROLE OF INSTITUTIONS

We now focus on institutional issues relating to the national and local dimensions of 'place-based' policymaking.

15.3.1 National

A good place to start is to consider whether the state itself may be part of the problem as well as part of the solution. A 'place-based' framework identifies two potential institutional weaknesses in the national government (the 'national') as it conducts sub-national economic policy. The first is that the 'national' has a tendency to lack both an understanding and knowledge of local places—it lacks a 'sense of community'. In the literature, this is identified as a form of social capital that understands the local institutional context in which development takes place (Tabellini, 2010; Barca et al., 2012). It is argued that the 'national' has a consequent weakness in its capacity both to adapt its approach towards local places and to mediate local consensus and trust between local actors as well as mobilize local resources effectively (Rodríguez-Pose and Storper, 2006). If this is not appropriately understood, or adapted to, it might become a serious problem undermining the 'national' design and conduct of sub-national policy. The second argument is that the 'national' is also prone to the influence of 'capital city' elites in policy-making, favouring infrastructure, innovation, and sectoral investment for the capital city over other sub-national places (Barca et al., 2012). As a result, national policy decisions may divert resources to promote unnatural agglomerations, as well as supporting natural ones.

How might this be relevant to UK government departments in London (Whitehall)? It appears that there are key reasons why, as Heseltine (2012) points out, Whitehall might have a built-in tendency towards addressing economic issues in a 'place-less' or 'space-blind' context. This is despite its active use of 'place-based' language. Some key reasons why this might be a problem are summarized as follows:

First, there is a long-standing culture of centralism (Heseltine, 2012). England is one of the most centralized countries in the Western world. Arguably, despite the government's 'rhetoric' of localism, very little has changed in substance of the distribution of powers between the 'national' and 'local' under the Coalition. Furthermore, historically, at the first sign of trouble or when the opportunity so arises, powers tend to be taken back into Whitehall, illustrated by the re-centralization of RDA functions back into the Department of Business and Innovation, following their abolition.

Second, there is an entrenched culture of 'conditional localism' (Hildreth, 2011). This is a model where the 'national' approach to decentralization is conditional on the 'local' supporting the national policy objectives and/or performance priorities and standards. This can be compared with the 'representative' localism model, which is much closer to a Western European approach based on strong local leadership and a clear separation of responsibilities between the 'national' and the 'local'. Arguably, England has shifted from a 'conditional' model enforced through top-down inspection and performance regimes put upon the 'local' by Whitehall under Labour, to one enforced through increasing austerity in local resources (Featherstone et al., 2012). It is also seen in the language of Whitehall reports. For example, it is reflected in the 'conditional' language of 'Cities', where cities, rather than Whitehall, are seen as the potential barrier to effecting change (HMG, 2011).

Third, Whitehall lacks a holistic perspective of 'place' (Heseltine, 2012). Whitehall is organized around themed policy departments, which in turn are shaped around functions and largely 'space-blind' initiatives that focus on policy specifics. As Heseltine points out, with this fragmentation, no one is tasked to look holistically at the full range of issues facing particular places (Heseltine, 2012). This culture is reflected in the National

Policy Planning Framework (DCLG, 2011), which unusually for a Western European country offers a largely un-spatial approach to spatial planning.

Fourth, Whitehall operates around short-term policy cycles. Policy is geared, in place development terms, around 'short-term' electoral cycles of up to five years. These are subject to frequent institutional and policy changes reflecting the policy priorities of the current administration. The newly elected Coalition government swept away regional institutions with little regard for how institutional learning, knowledge, and experience in regions had been developed and how it might be retained. No apparent consideration was given to the longer timescales involved in the economic transition of places and the requirement to embed institutional learning, investment, and development over the longer term. This possibly reflects Whitehall's blindness to this being an important real issue in the development of places.

Fifth, institutional memory is absent in Whitehall. This point is related to the previous one. In view of the nature of the 'national' political cycle, Whitehall puts particular value on general policymaking expertise in response to the immediate political requirements of the governing administration, with frequent movement between roles. This is valued over embedding institutional memory. This may adversely impact in Whitehall under-valuing why it is critically important in a local context.

Sixth, the 'national' is subject to a process of 'hollowing out'. A longer-term process of 'hollowing out' of the 'national' is reinforced by continuing austerity cuts on depart-ments. However, it is a weakness that when resources are scarce, proposals to reform the Civil Service fail to address how the 'national' might engage more strategically with sub-national places with more limited resources or devolve responsibilities to the 'local' (HMG, 2012).

Seventh, the 'national' economic framework is largely un-spatial. In government, the long-standing neoclassical economic framework reinforces the dominance of a 'space-neutral' perspective that is clouded in an apparently 'place-based' 'rhetoric' (Hil-dreth, 2009; Froud et al., 2011a; Hildreth and Bailey, 2013). It also constrains Whitehall's openness to new evidence, challenging its validity if it does not conform to the param-eters of its favoured framework.

Eighth, London is given undue influence in policy and resource allocation. London (and the Greater South East (GSE) and its banking and financial sector) is prioritized at all costs, against other places and sectors. As a result, institutional and investment deci-sions are London/GSE-centric (spatially and sectorally), with London provided with a unique model of government in England not on offer elsewhere. As a result, statements regarding the spatial and sectoral 're-balancing' of the economy become empty 'rhet-oric' without any real substance behind them (Froud et al., 2011a).

For these reasons, a barrier to realizing the potential of currently weaker places—such as the Northern economy—may lie not in the North but in Whitehall itself. A 'place-based' approach predicts:

> It is wholly unrealistic to expect that central government decision-makers have ei-ther the knowledge or expertise regarding North East Local Enterprise Partnership

area issues—of a technological, skills-related, or institutional nature—in order to make sound judgments appropriate to context. (McCann, 2013, p. 4)

Part of the problem is that Whitehall is presently largely failing to both understand and do something about it. When the 'national' has prioritized 'place-based' initiatives, for example in City Deals, it has done so by establishing a special unit outside the usual departmental structure to do so, but which is then left fighting its corner between other departments and the 'local'. The reform of the 'national' is therefore a key to a 'place-based' approach. But this needs to go alongside changes in the 'local', to which we now turn.

15.3.2 Local

A 'place-based' perspective does not just raise questions about the Centre. It also acknowledges that there are potential weaknesses that relate to the 'local' that need to be addressed. In particular, the possibility of 'under-development traps' occurring is highlighted, which may inhibit the growth potential of regions and localities or perpetuate the presence of social exclusion (Barca, 2009; Barca et al., 2012). A 'place-based' approach argues that this may not just be a consequence of the market. Rather, it may also relate to a failure by 'local elites' to act effectively or to local institutional weaknesses (Barca, 2009).

There may be two sets of problems. Each may arise out of different understandings of 'place'. 'Place' is a dynamic concept. It is the subject of an extensive literature offering a diverse range of meanings (see e.g. Hubbard and Kitchin, 2011). A challenge for economic geography is that places do not stand still. Places are not islands, but interact both within and with other places around them through the market-influenced behaviours of their key foundational elements of people and firms (Hildreth, 2007b). They are shaped by history, their geographical and social setting, and their institutional characteristics, making each place distinctive and different (Barca et al., 2012). As we have already noted, a key difference between a 'place-based' and a 'people-centred' approach is whether this really matters in the design of policy.

The first set of problems might relate to an understanding of place that relates to 'how we are governed'. This relates to the area administered by the (city or town) local authority (see Bailey et al., Chapter 14, this volume). It is important, because it is usually associated with the civic, cultural, and historical identity of the 'place' which is shaped by events and transitions over long periods of time (Hildreth, 2007a). This concept of 'place' has significance within the Coalition's localism agenda (Hildreth, 2011).

These may impact on the effectiveness of 'local elites' (local authorities and their partners) both within 'places' and across neighbouring 'places' to enable effective change. This has implications for how the city sees itself and its relationships with other places around it, for example politically in matters of 'trust', 'control', and 'respect' of its neighbours (Tabellini, 2010). Key issues are therefore:

First, there may be a lack of trust—There may be long-standing historical rivalries between 'places' that lie within the same 'natural economy' that are acted out by political leaderships through lack of effective cooperation across boundaries. This may occur, for example: (1) within a single local authority; (2) across two (or more) local authorities within a 'natural economy'; or (3) between two overlapping authorities in a two tier situation.

Second, serious under-bounding may impact on capacity—Where a city is seriously under-bounded in relation to its physical footprint, it may constrain its capacity to act strategically in relation to its economic area, particularly if there is an absence of 'trust' between neighbouring authorities. A few English city local authorities are so well bounded to capture part of their economic area, beyond the physical footprint of the city. Leeds is one example. However, many are well under-bounded. The physical city of Nottingham, for example, is crossed by the boundaries of five district councils and two county councils, as well as by the city council itself.

Third, a culture of 'conditional localism'—In the context of a dominant culture 'conditional localism', there is constant pressure on the 'local' to conform to the demands and priorities of the Centre over local needs and priorities. This may stifle local innovation and lead to an inappropriate allocation of local resources in relation to local development needs (Hildreth, 2011).

The second issue relates to an economic understanding of 'place', which is defined by 'how we live and work', by the ways in which people and firms operate their lives between the city and towns and villages that surround it. It might be referred to as the 'natural economic area' (HMG, 2010), or sub-region, or in appropriate cases, city-region. It is a dynamic concept expressed in terms of the connections and flows from home to work, home to shop, home to home in housing moves, home to cultural entertainment as well as the way that businesses relate to their customers and suppliers (Hildreth, 2007b). This is central to the Coalition's case for the establishment of LEPs as 'natural economic areas' (HMG, 2010).

'How we live and work' is a loosely defined or fuzzy concept. There are different ways of understanding a 'natural economic area' (HMG, 2010). The most common is to relate it to the containment of labour markets beyond the boundary of a city into its surrounding area. This might be interpreted in a narrow sense, such as in a functional urban region (FUR), or more widely, within the context of a city-region as expressed in the POLYNET study, which identified 50 FURs within the London Mega-City-Region (Hall and Pain, 2006). In most cases, the concept of a LEP has been interpreted more narrowly rather than broadly. A total of 39 LEPs have been created, some based on limited sub-regional geographies, sometimes influenced by who partners get on with or not, rather than any systematic economic analysis of spatial economies (e.g. Greater Birmingham and Solihull). Also, the idea of a 'natural economy' based on labour markets has limitations outside the bigger city agglomerations. It works well for Manchester and Leeds, where there clearly is a city-regional geography. But for 'gateway' cities like Hull, and 'industrial' cities like Blackburn and Burnley (Hildreth, 2007a), the geography of their labour markets is contained within a limited space and their economies 'isolated' in relation to other places (see e.g. Work Foundation et al., 2009). This undermines the value of a 'natural economy' as a loosely used concept. To an extent, the LEP boundaries for these cities do acknowledge this. However, a question is: Do they go far enough? Further, the geography of firms, for example, in supply chain relationships or broader cluster relations may go far wider than that captured by travel to work areas. The relevant 'economic' scale for the automotive cluster, for instance, covers at least five English regions (the East Midlands, North West, South East, South West and the West Midlands) (Hildreth and Bailey, 2013).

The consequential outcome is likely to be a widening institutional capacity gap between places in responding to the challenges of their local economies.[6] As an example, Leeds and its partners have been building city-regional capacity since the early 2000s. Progress has been gradual rather than spectacular, but the city-region was able to absorb the 'best' features of the new LEP (such as gaining the input of able private sector leaders new to working with the public sector) and to carry on building on an existing capacity-building trajectory. Contrast this with the North East LEP. Despite the encouragement of the 2006 OECD Territorial Review to form effective city-regional collaboration (OECD, 2006), the local authority partners found it difficult to maintain progress due to lack of trust, particularly, but not wholly, between Newcastle and Sunderland. Efforts to establish a Tyne & Wear city-region foundered following the abolition of the RDA, and the new North East LEP was started with limited resources almost from scratch and is left having to work very hard to try to catch up, although the most recent moves to form a 'combined authority' show that progress can be made.

The issue of trust does not arise just because of the factors outlined above relating to 'how we are governed'. Also, crucially they relate to the impact of economic linkages between places which may operate in a way that are either 'complementary' or 'less complementary' (Lucci and Hildreth, 2008; Work Foundation et al., 2009; Overman et al., 2010). In other words, if one city grows, its neighbour within the same 'natural economy' may not benefit. Locally understood perceptions of this are likely to impact on the willingness or otherwise to collaborative effectively, what can be seen as a problem of collective action in economic terms.

It can therefore be seen that in a 'place-based' framework, institutional weaknesses might be identified in both the 'national' and the 'local', which potentially act as barriers to the successful realization of the potential of different places. Part of the answer in a 'place-based' framework is to develop a multilevel governance framework to bridge the 'national' and the 'local'. For the 'national' it is about recognizing its weaknesses—in particular its inability to make sound judgements appropriate to local context and having

---

[6] In a similar vein, see Bailey and De Propris (2002) on the 1988 reform of the EU Structural Funds, which gave EU regions an *entitlement* to participate in the design and implementation of regional policy. They found that some of the weakest regions lacked the institutional capacity to access and implement the structural funds allocated to them, and as a result regional inequalities initially increased and only later started to narrow. Only after a process of institutional capacity-building and learning were some regions able to interact with the European Commission and national governments on regional policy issues, and only then where Member States allowed it.

no ability to foster the engagement of the local stakeholders (public or private) to drive economic development (McCann, 2013). On the other hand, it has an important role to foster trust between the 'national' and 'local', in the design of devolution of responsibilities and resources to maximum effect, and to incentivizee collaborative behaviours. For the 'local' it is about seeking an exogenous input to support locally based collaboration to enable the targeting of places with appropriate bundles of public good investments and overcome issues of 'trust'.

However, as already indicated, the spatial gap between the 'local' (including the LEP) is wide, not just in geography but also in 'trust'. In addition, this is not just about the public sector. The significance of the multilevel governance approach is not that it is just public to public, but rather recognizing that in a 'place-based' framework different actors—public and private—inter-dependently contribute towards the success of the sub-national economy. In that context, much of the action and collaboration may take place in what we have termed the 'missing space'. It is to this that our attention now turns.

15.4 The 'Missing Space' and the Role and Uncertainty of Knowledge

As a result, there is a 'missing space' or gap between the 'national' and the 'local' which, we argue, present policy (in England at least) does not fully address, either in the sense of spatial scale or of institutional arrangements. On the scale aspect, it is argued here that this 'missing space' occurs for at least three reasons, particularly outside the larger city-regions (such as Manchester and Leeds). First, the 'local' (including the LEP) often lacks sufficient scope, depth, and capacity to be effective. Linked to this, there is the risk that local elites may capture policy and funding for their own benefit, so exogenous challenge is required (this is a point picked up in international policy debates and which also links to the need for a multilevel governance framework). Second, outside the larger city-regions, LEPs commonly lack appropriate geography, being fragmented and effectively incomplete (see Heseltine, 2012, on the need to review LEP boundaries).[7] Third, there remains the absence of effective multilevel governance from the 'national' to the 'local' based on the key principles of 'trust' and 'respect'. Labour sought to fill this 'missing space' in a top-down way with administrative regions and regional institutions, particularly RDAs. Few might argue for going back to that top-down administrative

---

[7] Major criticisms of the 'old' RDAs were that that they were imposed in a top-down manner, bore little relationship with functional economic geographies, and were not accountable to localities. RDAs had the 'wrong geography', it was argued. In contrast, the creation of LEPs has been very much a bottom-up process, and while potentially helpful in terms of accountability, there is no guarantee that the resulting configuration of LEPs has the 'right geography' either. In fact, the new configuration of new LEPs may have just as severe problems of scale and boundaries as the old RDAs, albeit in a different form (see Townsend, 2012; Hildreth and Bailey, 2013).

geography. However, given the fragmentation and significant capacity variation in the subsequent LEPs which were created in a bottom-up way, the critical question is: Is there a 'missing space' that present policy does not fill, and does it matter? This in fact relates to a long-standing debate in industrial policy design as to the appropriateness of 'top-down' versus 'bottom-up' designed interventions and institutions (see e.g. De Bandt, 1999).

Under a 'space-neutral' framework none of this would seem to matter, as such industrial and regional policy interventions are anyway of limited value and may be seen as counterproductive. Rather, under a 'space-neutral' approach, key elements of policy should instead focus on: first, to support disadvantaged people to achieve better individual outcomes, through education, skills, and welfare policy, regardless of where they live; second, to enable greater geographic mobility to make it easier for people to move to growing areas; and third, to reduce the barriers to the expansion of economically successful places (Overman and Gibbons, 2011; Crowley et al., 2012). The basic argument presented is that left to themselves, markets will adjust if the barriers preventing them doing so are addressed. Hence, it is more important to focus on spatially blind universal institutional solutions, rather than seeking to fill a 'missing space' with institutionally based or related solutions. However, giving local authorities greater local discretion is supported to some extent, because it does facilitate experimentalism and innovation. Nevertheless, in terms of industrial and economic development, the view is taken that it is better to allow the market to work by itself, rather than for the state to actively intervene, for example through an industrial policy. Indeed, a smaller public sector is seen as potentially creating more space for the private sector to grow (Faggio and Overman, 2012) and hence is seen as beneficial. The spatially blind approach is in fact highly critical of anything more than a limited market-failure role for state intervention, seeing industrial and regional policies and their accompanying institutions as ineffective (Overman, 2012).

A 'place-based' approach sees things rather differently. In part this is because, as noted earlier, under such a perspective knowledge is seen as critical for effective policy development (Barca, 2011; Barca et al., 2012). Yet within this perspective, it is recognized that such knowledge is not already known either by the state, firms, or local stakeholders. As a result there is a positive role for policy in aiming to stimulate new knowledge and ideas through interactions between local groups (endogenously) and external actors (exogenously) (Barca, 2011; Barca et al., 2012). Linked to this, the 'smart specialization' approach has been closely linked with place-based approaches to regional development policy, at least in how they have been developed in the European Union (Barca, 2009: European Commission, 2011).[8] In particular, in terms of

---

[8] See Barca (2009, p. xvii): 'Place-based interventions, building on the strengths and taking account of the weaknesses of previous experience as regards cohesion policy in this area, could complement policies aimed at developing a European Research Area, by selecting in each region a limited number of sectors in which innovation can most readily occur and a knowledge base built up. Through such an approach—defined in the current policy debate as "smart specialisation"—the most could be made of the present diversity of industrial agglomerations and networks, while their "openness" beyond regional or national boundaries would be promoted...'

regional policy it has been used to emphasize the need to exploit related variety, build regional embeddedness, and enable strategic diversification (McCann and Ortega-Argilés, 2011). In so doing, it stresses the need for regional actors (government, firms, universities, research institutions) to collaborate, recognizing the current starting point for the region in terms of skills, technologies, and institutional governance and then to build on these capabilities rather than trying to start 'from scratch' (Wolfe, 2011).

This approach thus sees the capacity of territories to root their economic activity into the local institutional fabric as being at the heart of their economic success, through the generation, acquisition, and exchange of knowledge. Yet such knowledge is in turn uncertain, and it is embedded in localities and needs to be uncovered through participatory and bottom-up processes to build consensus and trust (Barca et al., 2012). Indeed, as noted earlier, the tendency of the 'state' is to lack both an understanding and knowledge of local places. It lacks a 'sense of community' (e.g. Barca et al., 2012), with a consequent weakness in its capacity to adapt its approach towards local places and mediate local consensus and trust between local actors as well as to mobilize local resources effectively.

This place-based smart specialization approach has strong parallels with Rodrik's (2004) perspective of industrial policy as a *process* of discovery requiring strategic collaboration between the private sector and state in unlocking growth opportunities, but set within a framework of multilevel governance so as to enable a process of local collaboration and discovery, while enabling external challenge to local elites engaging in rent-seeking behaviour. So industrial and regional policies which facilitate this process of discovery through strategic collaboration are seen as relevant under place-based/smart specialization perspectives and require appropriate institutions to engender this.

In fact, this is largely how intelligent industrial policy design is conceived of in contemporary debates (see Rodrik, 2004, 2008 and various contributions in this volume), with industrial policy ideally having the quality of 'embedded autonomy', whereby it is not captured by firms and sectors, but where, as noted, it focuses on the discovery process, where firms and the state learn about underlying costs and opportunities and engage in strategic coordination. So, for example, in the context of onshoring possibilities for UK manufacturing, it might mean government working with industry to identify key fractures in the supply chain and how to address them.[9] This is no longer about 'picking winners' or propping up failing firms or industries but rather, as the IPPR and Northern Economic Futures Commission (2012, p. 9) notes, about 'seeking to identify and support the elements of comparative advantage within the economy that enable innovation and new technologies to take root and companies to grow'.

---

[9] The latter has been identified as a key weakness of the UK's manufacturing base. Froud et al. (2011a), for example, note that in the UK's largely foreign-owned branch assembly plants, broken supply chains effectively undermine high British content and limit domestic backward linkages.

In this regard, there is an institutional and capacity failure inherent at the national level in terms of the lack of resources to design industrial policy interventions. As Froud et al. (2011b, p. 20)[10] note, on industrial policy there is a

> ... large gap between the old interventionism of 'picking winners' on the one hand, and the generic neo-liberal enterprise policies that have failed us for the last thirty years. But this is a gap that urgently needs to be bridged. It's an area of ignorance, a knowledge space that needs to be fashioned, if the UK is to start to create the successful industrial policies needed for regeneration.

In this sense, given the lack of resources at a national level to develop such policies, and given the capacity constraints of many LEPs outside of major cities, there would appear to be a role for an intermediate tier in bringing 'place' and 'sectors' together in terms of industrial and regional policy development, a point which has been highlighted by the IPPR and Northern Economic Futures Commission (2012). This has examined what a 'northern' industrial strategy might look like, identifying sectoral trends, analysing emerging strengths and opportunities identified by LEPs, and carrying out analysis of the export potential of key sectors in which the North already holds emergent strengths and which can be built on in a 'smart specialization' sense. Indeed, as the report notes, the results of this analysis offer some cause for optimism: despite an ongoing decline in traditional sectors such as manufacturing and extraction, new sectoral strengths are seen as emerging in related fields such as advanced manufacturing, pharmaceuticals, and bio-health. The report goes on to note that LEPs and local authorities need to continue to develop their intelligence on key sub-sectors that are seen as having potential locally, but that between the LEP level and the national level there is scope (or space in our terms) for 'a clear northern innovation agenda that is based on a small number of priorities and strategic assets and which addresses some of the North's cross-cutting innovation challenges' (IPPR and Northern Economic Futures Commission, 2012, p. 9).

The wider point is that filling this missing space requires regionally based industrial development strategies promoting 'related diversification'. Such strategies need to recognize (1) the need to bring together different but related activities in a region and (2) the differing potentials of regions to diversify, due to different industrial, knowledge, and institutional structures linked to specific regional historical trajectories. Rather than 'starting from scratch' or applying 'one-size-fits-all policies', regional industrial strategies instead require tailor-made policy actions embedded in, and linked to, the specific needs and available resources of regions, starting with the existing knowledge

---

[10] Froud et al. (2011b, p. 18) see the Bombardier case as 'an exemplary instance of how things go wrong in the absence of industrial policy. Generic pro-enterprise policies plus neglect of sectoral specifics about demand management and ownership has decimated British manufacturing capacity in key sectors, destroyed the supply chains that sustain successful industries, and deskilled core sections of the labour force. In the aggregate, neglect has thrown hundreds of thousands out of work, and undermined the economies of the ex-industrial regions whose service based private sectors are clients of the state.'

and institutional base in that region. These need to capitalize on region-specific assets, rather than attempting to apply policies that may have worked in quite different places.

This 'missing space' can also be seen in terms of the industrial policy capacity that has been lost with the abolition of the RDAs. In particular, the removal of RDAs has effectively removed a tier of governance that was—in some cases at least—engaged in attempts to exploit related variety, build regional embeddedness, and enable strategic diversification. As one leader of a combined authority stated to us, 'LEPs talk place but BIS talks sectors'.

In essence the subsequent policy 'base' here is 'space-neutral', emphasizing the importance of London and the GSE (Hildreth and Bailey, 2013). It is difficult to see how this shift to a policy of 'centralized localism' will actually help, for example, clusters in mature industrial regions like the West Midlands (or the North) to compete in the high-skill and high-technology niches that they increasingly occupy (Bentley et al., 2010). Indeed, it is in the areas of cluster and innovation policy that there may be particular challenges (Centre for Cities, 2014). Part of the problem is that what remains of industrial policy post-RDAs is based in London, where civil servants are removed from events on the ground and—as noted—generally lack the capacity to develop appropriate industrial policies for the reconstruction of the manufacturing base (Froud et al, 2011a, 2011b). The key point here is that RDAs were often better positioned to make sound judgements about how best to offer support and to which clusters (and/or technologies), as they had a superior information base to that of central government. By way of example, the RDA Advantage West Midlands supported the Niche Vehicles Network, comprising a network of stakeholders across the region which collaborates on the application of new technologies in low-volume vehicle production. This classic open innovation-type approach (MacNeill and Bailey, 2010) is too fine-tuned in scale to have visibility and relevance in Whitehall, yet offers much opportunity for this region's automotive cluster in shifting from low-value, high-volume work to niche high-value low-carbon activities. Here, regional-level industrial policy was critical in helping to develop a 'phoenix industry' linked to trends in open innovation, and which might be seen as a good example of place-based 'smart specialization' in operation (Amison and Bailey, 2014).[11]

An important lesson is that there remains a key role for the coordination of LEPs' economic and cluster strategies, most obviously via some sort of intermediate tier infrastructure. The need for joint LEP working can also be evidenced in the regional data and intelligence legacy of the RDAs. Whilst this is being retained in core cities such as Birmingham and Manchester after the abolition of RDAs, it is not clear whether other parts

---

[11] An opposing challenge may also be evident, in that excessive decentralization may see an 'all hands in the pork barrel' approach, with a fragmentation of RDAs into much smaller LEPs leading to limited public resources effectively being wasted on a myriad of micro-scale and uncoordinated projects. For example, as Swinney et al. (2010) note, only a small number of cities will actually be able to develop specialist clusters in sectors identified as 'high-growth' industries, and they identified a serious 'reality gap' in policy. The danger is that many such projects are likely to fail as they will not actually be building on natural historical bases with genuine skill sets that can be reorientated towards new growth or 'phoenix' clusters (Swinney et al., 2010) in a smart specialization sense.

of their regions will have access to such data and intelligence. The key point is that if smart specialization is an important element of place-based approaches, then questions remain as to whether LEPs have the powers, resources, and governance arrangements necessary to deliver such an approach. This is especially pertinent if, as Barca et al. (2012) suggest, 'place-based' development strategies require mechanisms which build on local capabilities and promote innovative ideas through the interaction of local and general knowledge and of endogenous and exogenous actors.

An interesting question is to what extent Whitehall has responded to the recommendations of the Heseltine (2012) report and is prepared to change so as to allow this 'missing space' to be filled.[12] While the government announced they are 'accepting in full or in part 81 of Heseltine's 89 recommendations', the reality is less encouraging, as a detailed examination of Annex A of the government response (HM-Treasury, 2013) indicates. Marlow (2013), for example, shows that of the 15 Heseltine proposals relating to 'local growth deals', the government 'accepts' just nine of them. Furthermore, Marlow (2013) notes that, as regards local leadership of innovation, 'even "accept" means, de facto, enduring top down control of this vital agenda'. Marlow goes on to highlight that the 'inability of LEPs and (local authorities) to position innovation and knowledge-economy at the centre of local growth strategies in cities and areas seeking to be globally competitive will leave a massive hole which no amount of single local growth fund is likely to fill'. Similarly, the response points to continued top-down control of innovation funding (HM-Treasury, 2013, p. 43, para 2.26) even though no justification is offered for this stance.[13]

More recently, the Labour Party, via the 2014 Adonis report, has welcomed much of the Heseltine report (Adonis, 2014). Under the Labour plans, LEPs would gain control over skills budgets currently allocated in a top-down way at a national level, and combined authorities would gain powers over transport, housing, and other infrastructure spending. It appears that only 'city and county regions' that meet strict tests established by the Adonis report will be given new powers over transport and housing infrastructure funding, as well as over the Work Programme and skills.

However, it seems that regions will still have to take part in a bidding process into the Local Growth Fund, with the government ultimately deciding which cities receive devolved powers and how much they can spend.

This is disappointing, as the bidding process itself eats up huge amounts of time and effort. Combined authority 'super-councils' should simply be allocated resources and powers when they show that they have met certain criteria and that their economic strategies are predicated on creating high-skilled, well-paid jobs in the private sector.

---

[12] Insofar as Heseltine (2012) actually proposes filling this space. His review can anyway be criticized, for example, in terms of a failure to embrace multilevel governance and hence a genuine place-based smart specialization approach, or for really proposing an industrial policy for the regions (for a critique on the latter, see Williams, 2012).

[13] The government response (HM-Treasury, 2013, p. 43, para 2.26) does state that on innovation, 'where local areas make the case that they can deliver better results if funding was devolved, then government will listen'. Listening is one thing, doing something is quite different.

Moreover, in looking at the detail of Labour's policy, the £30 billion on offer is in fact over five years, with just £6bn a year to be devolved. This is still far short of what was envisaged by Heseltine.

In summary, we suggest that there is a 'missing space' or 'governance gap' and this has a number of dimensions. In the 'boulder-strewn' river of sub-national geography, the design of institutions and interventions at appropriate spatial levels really does matter. What is more, they need to overcome potential weaknesses that operate at and between both the 'national' and 'local', which constitute barriers to the realization of enterprise, innovation, and potential across the economic system as a whole.

15.5 CONCLUSIONS

Given that 'the "place-based" approach is the "new paradigm" of regional policy' (Barca, 2011, p. 225), this chapter has sought to answer the question: What might a genuinely place-based approach in England look like? Having highlighted the basic foundations and key concepts of 'place-based' policy approaches, this chapter has interpreted and applied them in an English context. Using this analysis adds value to policy debates, as it highlights that in a 'place-based' framework, institutional weaknesses can be identified in *both* the 'national' and the 'local', which potentially act as barriers to the successful realization of the potential of different places. Indeed, part of the policy solution in a 'place-based' framework is to develop a multilevel governance framework to bridge the 'national' and the 'local'.

For the 'national' it is about recognizing its weaknesses—in particular its inability to make sound judgements appropriate to local context and having no or limited ability to foster the engagement of local stakeholders (public or private) to drive economic development. Yet it also has an important role to foster trust between the 'national' and 'local', in the design of the devolution of responsibilities and resources to maximum effect, and to incentivize collaborative behaviours. For the 'local' it is about seeking an exogenous input to support locally based collaboration to enable the targeting of places with appropriate bundles of public good investments and overcoming issues of 'trust'.

The significance of the multilevel governance approach is not that it is just public to public, but rather recognizing that in a 'place-based' framework different actors—public and private—interdependently contribute towards the success of the sub-national economy. In that context, much of the action and collaboration may take place in what we perceive as the 'missing space' between the 'national' and the 'local' which present policy (in England at least) does not fully address, either in the sense of spatial scale or institutional arrangements.

Filling this 'missing space' or 'governance gap' requires regionally based industrial development strategies which bring place and sectors together and which recognize (1) the need to bring together different but related activities in a region and (2) the differing potentials of regions to diversify, due to different industrial, knowledge, and institutional structures linked to specific regional historical trajectories. Such an approach also calls for the recognition that knowledge is not already known either by the state, firms, or local stakeholders. As a result, there is a positive role for policy in aiming to stimulate new knowledge and ideas through interactions between local groups (endogenously) and external actors (exogenously) (Barca, 2011). This has similarities with modern conceptions of industrial policy, whereby the latter is perceived as a *process* of discovery requiring strategic collaboration between the private sector and state in unlocking growth opportunities. Rather than 'starting from scratch' or applying 'one-size-fits-all policies', regional industrial strategies instead require tailor-made policy actions embedded in, and linked to, the specific needs and available resources of regions, starting with the existing knowledge and institutional base in that region. These need to capitalize on region-specific assets, rather than attempting to apply policies that may have worked in quite different places.

In summary, the 'missing space' in the English context has a number of dimensions. In the 'boulder-strewn' river of sub-national geography, the design of institutions and interventions at appropriate spatial levels matters. Moreover, such 'place-based' institutions and interventions need to overcome potential weaknesses that operate at and between both the 'national' and 'local', which constitute barriers to the realization of enterprise, innovation, and potential across the economic system as a whole. This, we argue, has yet to be realized properly in policy debates over industrial and regional policy in the English context.

References

Adonis, A. (2014). *Mending the Fracture Economy. Smarter State, Better Jobs. Final Report of the Adonis Review*. London: Policy Network.

Amison, P. and Bailey, D. (2014). 'Phoenix Industries and Open Innovation? The Midlands Advanced Automotive Manufacturing and Engineering Industry', *Cambridge Journal of Regions, Economy and Society* 7(3) 397–411, doi: 10.1093/cjres/rsu007.

Bailey, D. and De Propris, L. (2002). 'The 1988 Reform of the Structural Funds: Entitlement or Empowerment?', *Journal of European Public Policy* 9(3), 408–28.

Barca, F. (2009). 'An Agenda for a Reformed Cohesion Policy: A Place Based Approach to Meeting European Union Challenges and Expectations', Brussels: DG Regio.

Barca, F. (2011). *Alternative Approaches to Development Policy: Intersections and Divergences*, in *OECD, OECD Regional Outlook 2011*, pp. 215–25, Paris: Organisation for Economic Co-operation and Development.

Barca, F. and McCann, P. (2010). 'The Place-Based Approach: A Response to Mr Gill', VoxEU. org, 9 October, <http://www.voxeu.org/article/regional-development-policies-place-based-or -people-centred>.

Barca, F., McCann, P., and Rodríguez, P. (2012). 'The Case for Regional Development Intervention: Place-Based Versus Place-Neutral Approaches', *Journal of Regional Science* 52(1), 134–52.

Bentley, G., Bailey D., and Shutt, J. (2010). 'From RDAs to LEPs: A New Localism? Case Examples of West Midlands and Yorkshire', *Local Economy* 25(7), 535–57.

Centre for Cities (2014). *Industrial Revolutions: Capturing the Growth Potential.* London: Centre for Cities/McKinsey.

Crowley, L., Balaram, B., and Lee, N. (2012). *People or Place? Urban Policy in the Age of Austerity.* London: The Work Foundation.

DCLG (Department for Communities and Local Government) (2011). 'National Planning Framework', <http://www.communities.gov.uk/publications/planningandbuilding/nppf>.

De Bandt, J. (1999). 'Practical Issue of Networking and Cooperation', in K. Cowling (ed.), *Industrial Policy in Europe: Theoretical Perspectives and Practical Approaches*, pp. 152–63. London: Routledge.

ESPON (2013). 'SGPTD Second Tier Cities and Territorial Development in Europe: Performance, Policies and Prospects', <http://www.espon.eu/export/sites/default/Documents/Projects/AppliedResearch/SGPTD/SGPTD_Final_Report_-_Final_Version_27.09.12.pdf>.

European Commission (2011). *Proposal for a Regulation of the European Parliament and of the Council*, COM (2011) 615 Final, 6/10/2011, Brussels, European Commission.

Faggio, G. and Overman, H. (2012). 'The Effect of Public Sector Employment, LSE Research Laboratory', <http://www.spatialeconomics.ac.uk/textonly/serc/publications/download/sercdp0111.pdf>.

Featherstone, D., Ince, A., Mackinnon, D., Strauss, K., and Cumbers, A. (2012). 'Progressive Localism and the Construction of Political Alternatives', *Transactions of the Institute of British Geographers* 37(2), 177–82.

Froud, J., Johal, S., Law, J., Leaver, A., and Williams, K. (2011a). *Rebalancing the Economy (or Buyer's Remorse)*, Manchester University, CRESC Working Paper No. 87.

Froud, J., Johal, S., Law, J., Leaver, A., and Williams, K. (2011b). Knowing What to Do? How Not to Build Trains. Manchester University, CRESC Research Report.

Gardiner, B., Martin, R., and Tyler, P. (2013). Spatially Unbalanced Growth in the British Economy, *Journal of Economic Geography* 13(6), 889–928, doi: 10.1093/jeg/lbt003.

Gill, I. (2010). 'Regional Development Policies: Place-Based or People-Centred?', VoxEU.org, 9 October, <http://www.voxeu.org/article/regional-development-policies-place-based-or-people-centred>.

Hall, P. and Pain, K. (2006). *The Polycentric Metropolis: Learning from Mega-City Regions.* London: Earthscan.

Heseltine, M. (2012). *No Stone Unturned in the Pursuit of Growth.* London: BIS, <https://www.gov.uk/government/uploads/system/uploads/attachment_data/file/34648/12-1213-no-stone-unturned-in-pursuit-of-growth.pdf>.

Hildreth, P. A. (2007a). 'Understanding Medium-Sized Cities', *Town & Country Planning* 76(5), 163–7.

Hildreth, P. A. (2007b). The Dynamics of 'Place-Shaping': The Changing Rationale for Urban Regeneration, *Journal of Urban Regeneration and Renewal* 1(3), 227–39.

Hildreth, P. A. (2009). 'Understanding 'New Regional Policy': What is Behind the Government's Sub-National Economic and Regeneration Policy for England?', *Journal of Urban Regeneration and Renewal* 2(4), 318–36.

Hildreth, P. (2011). 'What is Localism, and What Implications Do Different Models Have for Managing the Local Economy?', *Local Economy* 26(8), 702–14.

Hildreth, P. and Bailey, D. (2012). 'What Are the Economics behind the Move to LEPs', in M. Ward and S. Hardy (eds), *Changing Gear. Is Localism the New Regionalism?*, pp. 25–34. London: Smith Institute and Regional Studies Association.

Hildreth, P. and Bailey, D. (2013). 'The Economics Behind the Move to "Localism" in England', *Cambridge Journal of Regions, Economy and Society* 6(2), 233–49.

Hildreth, P. and Bailey, D. (2014). 'Place-Based Economic Development Strategy in England: Filling the Missing Space', *Local Economy* 29(4–5), 363–77.

HMG (HM Government) (2010). *Local Growth: Realising Every Place's Potential*, Department of Business Innovation and Skills, London, No. Cm 7961.

HMG (HM Government) (2011). 'Unlocking Growth in Cities', <http://www.dpm.cabinetoffice.gov.uk/sites/default/files_dpm/resources/CO_Unlocking%20GrowthCities_acc.pdf (last accessed 25/04/2014)>.

HMG (HM Government) (2012). *The Civil Service Reform Plan*. London: Civil Service Cabinet Office.

HM-Treasury (2013). *Government's Response to the Heseltine Review*, HM Treasury, London, Cm8587.

HM-Treasury, BERR, and CLG (2007). *Review of Sub-National Economic Development and Regeneration*. London: HM-Treasury.

Hubbard, P. and Kitchin, R. (eds), (2011). *Key Thinkers in Space and Place*. London: Sage.

IPPR and the Northern Economic Futures Commission (2012). *Northern Prosperity is National Prosperity: A Strategy for Revitalising the UK Economy*. London: Institute for Public Policy Research.

Lucci, P. and Hildreth, P. (2008). *City Links: Integration and Isolation*. London: Centre for Cities.

McCann, P. (2013). 'The North East (NELEP) Area in the Context of the Global Economy', Newcastle, North East LEP.

McCann, P. and Ortega-Argilés, R. (2011). *Smart specialisation, regional growth and applications to EU cohesion policy*, Economic Geography Working Paper 2011, Faculty of Spatial Sciences, University of Groningen.

MacNeill, S. and Bailey, D. (2010). 'Changing Policies for the Automotive Industry in an "Old" Industrial Region: An Open Innovation Model for the UK West Midlands?', *International Journal of Automotive Technology and Management* 10(2/3), 128–44.

Marlow, D. (2013). 'Is There a Big Hole in the Innovation "Stone" in the Government's Response to Heseltine?', *Regeneration & Renewal*, 25 March.

OECD (Organisation for Economic Co-operation and Development) (2006). *Territorial Reviews: Newcastle in the North East, United Kingdom*. Paris: OECD.

OECD (Organisation for Economic Co-operation and Development) (2009a). *How Regions Grow: Trends and Analysis*. Paris: OECD.

OECD (Organisation for Economic Co-operation and Development) (2009b). *Regions Matter: Economic Recovery, Innovation and Sustainable Growth*. Paris: OECD.

OECD (Organisation for Economic Co-operation and Development) (2012). *Promoting Growth in All Regions*. Paris: OECD.

Overman, H. (2012). 'Heseltine's Report is a Return to the Unsuccessful', *Financial Times* 31 October.

Overman, H. G. and Gibbons, S. (2011). 'Unequal Britain: How Real Are Regional Disparities?', *CentrePiece* 16(2), 23–5, <http://cep.lse.ac.uk/pubs/download/cp353.pdf>.

Overman, H. G., Rice, P., and Venables, A. J. (2010). 'Economic Linkages Across Space', *Regional Studies* 44(1), 17–33.

Rodríguez-Pose, A. and Storper, M. (2006). 'Better Rules or Stronger Communities? On the Social Foundations of Institutional Change and its Economic Effects', *Economic Geography* 82(1), 1–25.

Rodrik. D. (2004). *Industrial Policy for the 21st Century*. Cambridge, MA: John F. Kennedy School of Government.

Rodrik, D. (2008). *One Economics, Many Recipes: Globalization, Institutions, and Economic Growth*. Princeton, NJ: Princeton University Press.

Swinney, P., Larkin, K., and Webber, C. (2010). *Firm Intentions: Cities, Private Sector Jobs and the Coalition*. London: Centre for Cities.

Tabellini, G. (2010). 'Culture and Institutions: Economic Development in the Regions of Europe', *Journal of the European Economic Association* 8, 677–716.

The Economist. (2012). 'London's Precarious Brilliance', *The Economist* 30 June.

Townsend, A. (2012). 'The Functionality of LEPs: Are They Based on Travel to Work?', in M. Ward and S. Hardy (eds), *Changing Gears. Is Localism the New Regionalism?*. London: The Smith Institute/Regional Studies Association.

Williams, K. (2012). 'What Lord Heseltine Doesn't Say about the Regions', *The Guardian* 31 October, <http://www.guardian.co.uk/commentisfree/2012/oct/31/lord-heseltine-britain-ex-industrial-regions>.

Wolfe, D. A. (2011). Regional Resilience and Place-Based Development Policy: Implications for Canada. Wilfred Laurier University, Waterloo, Ontario, Paper Presented to the Canadian Political Science Association.

Work Foundation, SURF, and Centre for Cities (2009). 'City Relationships: Economic Linkages in Northern City Regions', <http://www.theworkfoundation.com/Reports/227/City-Relationships-Economic-linkages-in-Northern-city-regions>.

World Bank (2009). *World Development Report 2009: Reshaping Economic Geography*. Washington DC: World Bank.

PART 5

REGULATION, FDI, AND INDUSTRIAL POLICY

CHAPTER 16

....

REGULATION AND GOVERNANCE OF PUBLIC UTILITIES

....

MICHAEL WATERSON

16.1 INTRODUCTION

ONE of the underlying political reasons behind the initial drive to privatization in the UK thirty years ago was the attempt to depoliticize such industries. Actually, in examples as diverse as energy and rail transport, this has not happened. If energy prices rise, it is seen by the public to be the government's role to tackle the issue. The government is also, of course, intimately involved in decisions about HS2, the proposed new high-speed rail link to the West Midlands and North of England. Originally, a mix of competition amongst private firms and regulation was intended to tackle the governance issues of the public utilities. In this context, it is salutary to look back at what was written by one of the principal architects of the structure, Stephen Littlechild, in his analysis of the case. One key theme was 'Competition where possible, regulation where necessary', and of regulation being a 'means of "holding the fort" until competition arrives' (Littlechild, 1983, para 4.11). Littlechild was right about many things, but the brave warriors in the fort must be getting somewhat weary now.

Actually another main driver, and ultimate source of problems, was the perceived need for private money to fund necessary infrastructure improvements in the various utilities. This inevitably led to conflicts between providing sufficient incentives for firms to take part and tightness of constraints on their operation. There was a third, unspoken, driver: most nationalized industries were heavily unionized and the government of the day wished to reduce union power; it was thought that by privatizing the industries, the role of unions would be reduced.

Examining the scoresheet, it is clear that there are examples where no sensible commentator would want to go back to the framework prior to privatization and regulation or anything resembling it. It is now difficult to remember the control exercised by BT over such simple things as the telephone instrument in our home, the long wait for a phone line, and so on. Competition in the mobile phone industry, without the national operator BT as a competitor unlike in many other Western European countries, has given us a modern, well-operated system providing people with considerable utility, at least on a revealed preference basis. It would also be difficult to imagine going to the British Gas showroom as the only place to buy our cooker. These examples exhibit a failing of the public utility, disguising self-interest through safety considerations. But they also reveal a deeper truth, still valid today. Whereas we could not trust our nationalized industries fully to serve the public interest, no more can we now trust our privatized industries with this.

On the other side of the scoresheet, there are real difficulties in financing certain long-term activities through private money without substantial public involvement. There seems no way for one government to bind the next and its successors in such a way that gives sufficient confidence for investors in major capital projects to put their own money at risk for extended periods within the existing system. Britain is moving into a potential real shortage of power plants. Initially, private firms were happy to build gas-fired power stations—a turnkey construction job, plus a long-term contract for gas and a long-term contract for power output, de-risks such a project, and long term in this case might mean only ten years. They are nowhere near as happy to finance a new nuclear power plant, they know they are in a strong position in making an agreement to go ahead, and the government knows they know this. So, the only agreement that de-risks this project sufficiently appears to drive a hole right through the current wholesale power market, with guaranteed prices (massively above current prices) for forty years into the future.

There is a further force of general significance. Over the period since the first privatizations, Britain has experienced substantial increases in inequality across consumers (Cribb, 2013). At the same time, implicit subsidies that were commonly built into many of the operations of public utilities have been stripped away, meaning that the distribution of entitlements to rather basic services by the poor has been severely impacted. As a result, growth in fuel poverty, for example, has been marked.

In this chapter, I will to some extent discuss each of the major industries, pointing out particular features of their development as privatized concerns worthy of note—each has its peculiarities. In doing this, I focus almost exclusively on Great Britain.[1] However, since a large proportion of the innovations were first tried in Britain, this focus is not as parochial as it might seem. In this, I shall not cover postal services; in my view it is too early to be reflective on the area. I discuss telecoms under the general context of RPI-X, then develop themes for each of the other cases, concluding with a few brief, more general thoughts.

---

[1] That is, Northern Ireland, which has significantly different regimes in almost all industries considered below, is not discussed.

16.2 RPI-X REGULATION

It is thirty years since the UK moved into the arena of economic regulation, through the privatization of British Telecom (BT) in 1984. At the time, the idea of privatization was extremely controversial, and the regulatory approach was viewed as very novel, whereas now both are seen as quite routine. But now is a suitable time for an assessment, albeit a personal one. How has it been, for us? Luckily, few mistakes were made in this first foray into privatization. This was a mixture of caution and design. Caution was exercised by engineering an initial partial sell-off of BT, rather than the whole business. In designing the framework for regulation, Littlechild (1983) produced an excellent blueprint.

It is worth dwelling on the nature of the task on which Littlechild was engaged. He was asked, in short order, to write a report on an appropriate form of control over BT. He was given a set of potential objectives and a pair of models to consider. In the event, he changed both the ranking and the scope of the objectives, as well as (at literally the last moment) adopting a basic framework substantially different from either of those he was supposed to compare.[2] Despite the assumptions made being demonstrated significantly at error, the underlying model has proven resilient enough to be adopted in some form or another in all subsequent UK privatizations of industries with a natural monopoly character as well as being widely adopted in other jurisdictions.

The mechanism Littlechild proposed, RPI-X, as a formula for regulating a basket of prices of products coming from the regulated firm has been significantly complicated in subsequent cases, yet retains its basic appeal. For him, this was the measure that scored better overall than others, including no explicit controls (the one he initially favoured), on the five criteria: protection against monopoly (which included BT abuse of its dominant position), encouraging efficiency and innovation, minimizing the burden of regulation, the promotion of competition, and (a poor last, in his opinion) maximizing the proceeds to the Treasury.

He proposed this as a short-term solution, regulation 'holding the fort' because, in the light of the times, he saw facilities competition in telecoms as an imminent possibility. In practice, this has not materialized, or at least not in the way envisaged. But then, of course, he was writing before the advent of the Internet. The only practical way in which most consumers can get stable and extensive access to the Internet is through a fixed-line telephone connection that otherwise lies for the most part unused. In order to do this, they need to pay a line rental and for all but the small minority of consumers who are supplied by cable, this in turn means using BT's Openreach division's services. Without access to the Internet, tablets such as the iPad would, frankly, be boring; TV would be limited for most people to programmes broadcast terrestrially; and nifty new devices such as can control central heating remotely would not function. Absent the Internet, mobile phones plus services such as Skype would provide the functionality of fixed lines in competition with BT. So, Littlechild was overly optimistic about facilities

---

[2] See the discussion in Bartle, 2003.

competition developing, even in telecoms, let alone in, say, water, where he clearly viewed it as being more problematic (Beesley and Littlechild, 1989).

This question of what would happen at the end of a (five-year) period in a regulatory regime was always going to be a vexed one. It was optimistic to expect facilities competition to develop rapidly, and yet it was clear that an unchanged price cap could not be a long-term solution because of the tendency to lead either to politically unacceptable levels of profit or, at the other extreme, to difficulties in operation and potential need for bailouts. So, in periodic revision of the formula, an obvious approach is to tighten it if earnings appear excessive, to loosen it if earnings are too low to fund necessary investments. But this means in turn that decisions about revision to the formula turn on the rate of return being earned on capital, compared with a benchmark rate calculated for that industry, and on the cost trends in the industry. This is a far cry from the initial anticipation that '[The regulator] does not have to make any judgements or calculations with respect to capital, allocation of costs, rates of return, future movements of costs and demand, desirable performance, etc' (1983, para. 13.20). In fact, at the time of a five-yearly review, regulators do find the need to make judgements about all these issues, in telecoms just as in other industries.

Littlechild also reckoned without the lawyers. The early regulators (including Littlechild himself) had a much-admired independence of spirit, able to take tough decisions that were firmly opposed to their regulated company charges in many cases. They did not feel the need to explain, in detail, every move they made. How different this has become, with the possibility of judicial review of every aspect of a decision seen, for example, in telecoms appeals cases, where vast quantities of materials are provided by the relevant parties to justify a position and explain why the regulator is wrong, in turn leading to considerable volumes of paper from the regulator justifying their decisions. Thus, rather than a five-yearly decision process, there are continual skirmishes between telecoms operators and the regulator, OFCOM, on just such matters for judgement as likely trends, for example, in costs and demand, valuation of existing long-lived assets, and so on. This brings with it the ever-present potential problem of 'capture' of the regulator by those it is supposed to be regulating independently. The regulator always needs to take an independent line, despite the difficult life this can create.

Here there is an important but indirect link between the valuation of long-lived assets and the issue of returns to the Treasury. Many privatizations, from the earliest (BT) to the latest (Royal Mail) at time of writing, have generated a substantial furore regarding the price at which the business was sold. This may well be a justifiable concern. The initial governmental aim, of making sure that privatization was a 'success' in the narrow terms of being able to place the shares on the market and therefore being extremely conservative about pricing the initial offering, is lamentable (and press comment upon it similarly so). In a capitalist system, if investors with cash see a bargain they will go for it; giving these people a bargain is not a success in any sensible terms.[3] But there is, or should be, a clear distinction between selling off a business around which competition

---

[3] Of course, this was probably one of the political aims at the time, to create a society in which a wider range of people felt confident in investing in the stock market.

will develop and selling off monopoly rights, a long and disreputable tradition in British (and other) political systems.[4] The sale of a business with long-lived assets for a particular price implies a valuation on the assets of that business, *if* they can be separately identified. Thus a high initial price carries with it the danger that, when the time comes for a five-yearly review, implications are drawn about the anticipated return to shareholders (or, as it would be put, shareholders' legitimate expectations) on those long-lived assets. Surprisingly, this can be an issue even thirty years after the event.

One novel feature of the regulatory regime developed has survived and proved its long-term worth, albeit subject to substantial changes. The standard pattern of regulated industries in the US was that the whole business was regulated. Littlechild's novel approach was that what should be regulated is those parts of the business unlikely to be subject to competition. Thus he proposed a tariff basket approach, where a basket of business and residential rentals of the phone line, plus local call charges, would be regulated, but not other types of call, where he saw competition developing. In practice, the final blueprint included a wider basket of goods, and indeed the basket was changed over time in the light of experience, but the idea has been retained.

A further point is relevant here. If price is regulated, the regulator needs at the same time to ensure that service quality does not slip, because one obvious way for a monopoly provider to reduce costs is by relaxing on service quality. Here, the early decision by the telecoms regulator to collect, publish, and make use of quality information is to be commended.

In many respects, the Littlechild report was a leap into the theoretical darkness. Because rate-of-return regulation had been around for some time, its potential limitations were well known, most famously the Averch-Johnson (1962) effect meaning that there is a tendency for 'gold-plating' of capital.[5] There was also, of course, the famous Ramsey (1927) result, although it had probably not been thought of in the regulatory context at that stage and, much nearer to time, Baron and Myerson's (1982) well-known paper on the problem of regulating a firm with unknown cost. But most of the academic literature discussing the positive and negative features of price cap regulation post-dates the Littlechild report, rather than providing useful input into the initial thinking.

As an example, one major issue that arises when part of an industry is subject to regulation and another part is not is that of access. If competition is to develop and, as is very common, in order to compete effectively that competition needs access to monopolized facilities owned by the regulated firm, then competition will not develop if means are found to limit access or make it unprofitable. For example, in telecoms, a competitor to BT needs access to the BT system in order to provide a complete service—if the person

---

[4] As a historical note, the taxation of salt as a revenue-raising device has in Britain, France, India, Russia, and China led to substantial health problems and many severe protests. Thus by analogy, it is important to see the difference between selling off a particular salt works and selling off the right to sell salt in a country. The latter would maximize returns to the seller, but ossifies the structure of the industry.

[5] This tendency can persist in an RPI-X-type scheme once the scheme is up for review and the capital base is being considered. A trenchant view on this, with evidence of 'gold-plating' at Stansted Airport, was given in Ryanair's evidence to CC (2009a; see para 7.71) in respect of Stansted.

I want to phone is on BT, my operator needs to make use of the BT network (at least the 'final mile' to that customer's landline phone) in order to terminate my call. But if the access cost is high, my chosen operator may find it very difficult to provide a service that is competitive with BT's own.[6] Thus one common issue facing a regulator is how to price access to the monopoly elements of a service. There is some acknowledgment of this problem in the Littlechild report, in the form of advocacy (para 13.15) of 'tough non-discrimination clauses in BT's licence to prevent predatory behaviour against competitors', plus the requirement to publish its tariffs. Access pricing is a complex issue, more complex than the 'efficient component pricing rule' (ECPR) originally set out in Willig (1979) and Baumol (1983), both relatively obscure sources that were available at the time Littlechild wrote. It was not until some years later that Laffont and Tirole (1994) and Armstrong et al. (1994) set out a comprehensive analysis of the main issues. Put loosely, mandated access at the marginal cost of providing access creates incentives on the part of the monopolist to find non-price means of restricting access, whilst providing access on the basis of the opportunity cost (including foregone revenues) of that access (the ECPR) is too unsubtle—the opportunity cost of course contains a monopoly rent. In fact, the access issue is one that relates not only to cases where essential facilities are supplied by a firm that competes in the same final market as the firm seeking access, but also in a different form to situations where there is vertical separation between the essential facility and the competitive sector (as in electricity).

Indeed, the access pricing difficulties are significant as regards BT retail and BT Openreach, despite an accounting separation between the two. This is partly because they share many facilities, for example office premises and ductwork; indeed some facilities such as telephone exchange buildings are shared also with other providers such as TalkTalk and Sky; therefore issues arise regarding services provided to the facility (such as cooling), rather than provided to any party in particular.

One general issue that access pricing raises, but which manifests itself in most sectors, is the need for a great deal more measurement at various stages than was undertaken whilst the industry was in state hands. In a state monolith, there is only limited need for measurement at intermediate stages, and often there was only vague information on where costs were incurred. Once a number of separate players enter the picture, the need to understand costs in some detail becomes much more apparent. In turn this creates a significant need for measurement. Often flow volume, which is commonly assumed in economic models to be the primary driver of costs, plays only a small part in the overall cost structure, yet costs are not truly fixed. For example, many facilities (e.g. trunk networks) where continuous service is required generate costs proportional to maximum throughput, rather than average flows. This requires measurement of at least peak flows, but often also measurement at many points, in order to determine bottlenecks in the paths taken by the service, the impact of exogenous

---

[6] It is in this sense that what I wrote about earlier in the context of the Internet should be read. If everyone I need to call has a mobile phone, then a competitor to BT need not use BT's final mile to terminate their call.

factors, and so on, together with efficient means of collecting and interpreting these measurements in real time, so as to take decisions. This becomes most obvious in the energy sector.

16.3 THE NETWORK ENERGY INDUSTRIES

The next activity to be privatized following BT was the gas industry. Network energy industries (i.e. electricity and gas) exhibit many features in common with each other,[7] although the development was initially quite different. A significant compromise was made in the case of gas, so that initially it was privatized as a whole, from well head to appliance supply, on somewhat spurious arguments. It was not until ten years after its privatization that it came to resemble the current vertically separated structure, with supply companies being separate from transmission activity. To a large extent, in terms of their current structure and regulation, both industries can be discussed as one, and indeed many of the participants are active in both markets.

First though, some crucial technical differences. Gas is an industry with one-way flows, from producer to consumer, whereas electricity has the potential for two-way movements, although the network has not normally been set up to facilitate these, so it requires adjustment. Gas also has some leeway on the match between demand and supply, because it can be stored and the transmission network can itself act as storage, through variable line-packing. In electricity it is crucial that supply is equated with demand at all times. In addition, electricity is generated through a variety of technologies, whereas gas comes (in more or less homogenous form) from a small number of locations. Hence electricity requires a greater degree of control, with more sophistication built into the economic regulatory system. The regulator, whilst initially separate, is now the same body. Thus the discussion below focuses on electricity, since it raises the issues of both. This is also one of the most controversial industries.

Initially a very bold move was made in electricity, to separate the industry in England and Wales vertically into four layers: generation, transmission, distribution, and supply.[8] Of these, transmission and (local) distribution were seen as naturally monopolistic activities (particularly the former, given the strong need for coordination imposed by the technical need to equate demand and supply at all times). The transmission system operator (TSO) has a quasi-command and control role, buying or selling electricity in near time (less than one hour in advance of delivery) in order to balance the

---

[7] There is a clear distinction between electricity and gas, where the network is an integral part of the delivery process, and oil, where the ease of handling, high value, and energy content to weight means that decentralized road transport is an efficient means of delivery. This industry has not been in state hands since the Second World War.

[8] This was probably the first conceptual separation between distribution and supply. It took place in Scotland somewhat later.

system.[9] Thus, separating it out avoids one of the potential errors in restructuring an industry on privatization, namely that the separation becomes fixed into the structure even if it outlives its usefulness; it is difficult to see how technological change would render this particular separation subject to change within the medium-term future, at least. Nevertheless, it may be that along with the increased growth of two-way electricity movements at distribution level, together with the growth of storage technologies, there will be some need for replication of this function also at local level. Initially, suppliers were the same companies as distributors, and were regulated as regards both activities. However, since 2002 all supply across both electricity and gas has been deregulated, so in discussing supply we refer only to the structure in place currently.

One of the main functions of a supplier is absorption of pricing risk. The exact technical link between supply and demand, coupled with the substantially inelastic short-run relationship between demand and price, means that very large wholesale pricing movements are experienced over short time intervals in order to equate supply and demand. It is neither technically possible (at present) nor socially feasible to pass these wild fluctuations on to consumers. Therefore, the supplier in effect acts like an insurance company (or, perhaps more exactly, a bookmaker) to tackle the issue. Suppliers purchase a portfolio of contracts for future delivery, in order to balance certainty against price given their expected supply commitments. Only a small amount of electricity (perhaps 3 per cent) is traded directly through the balancing mechanism (Simmonds, 2002). This is in contrast to the situation prior to 2001, which is when the New Electricity Trading Arrangements (NETA) commenced. Previously, in common with the systems operating in most other countries and electricity regimes, most electricity was traded through the Pool, a central market mechanism.

A key feature of the Pool was that generators were paid the system marginal price (SMP) for the relevant time period. Therefore, generators with low marginal cost would bid into the system, knowing that they would be selected and paid significantly above their bid. For example, nuclear plants would be bid in on this basis. Of course, these low marginal cost plants commonly had high fixed costs, so that the gap between SMP and their marginal cost provided a return to past investment and also a signal as to the profitability of new investment in generation. Thus, by comparing the Pool price path with the cost of a fuel to generate electricity (allowing for a given efficiency in generation), together with likely construction costs, a good indication of the potential profitability of a new plant could be developed.

The context of the move to NETA was the concern about market power in generation in England and Wales, stemming from the concentrated nature of the market at privatization (with two strategic players) and the origin of the firms' key decision-makers in a single firm, the Central Electricity Generating Board (see Green and Newbery, 1992). This implied that collusion, or at least knowledge of likely responses by the other party, was a clear possibility. The regulator was concerned enough about limited competition

---

[9] For useful details, see the following explanatory guide: <http://www.elexon.co.uk/wp-content/uploads/2013/11/beginners_guide_to_trading_arrangements_v4.0_cgi.pdf>.

in generation to persuade the two major strategic generators to divest 4GW and 2GW of capacity respectively to a third force by mid-1996. Indeed, these concerns prompted another move by the regulator, namely to allow the limited integration between generators and suppliers in return for further divestment in 1999. This started a rush to integrate between generators and suppliers, so that by around 2002, all six major suppliers had developed or purchased significant generation capacity as well as capturing around 99 per cent of the domestic supply market, leaving only a very small independent supply sector. Independent generators remained important, but suffered from their weakened bargaining power once NETA was implemented and, in the case at least of Nuclear Electric and one of the other merchant generators, led to a 're-capitalization' in order that they continue to operate.[10]

Arguably, supply is a rather competitive business. Indeed, when supply competition was first mooted, it was envisaged that companies in industries entirely different from energy but with strong reputations for consumer service and significant knowledge of their customers' requirements (such as supermarkets) would be significant players. This happened only to a limited extent. However, the combination of two separate decisions (NETA and allowing vertical integration), both of which might well have been innocuous in their own right, and carried out for the best of motives, has in practice proven problematic. The problem stems from the opacity of the wholesale market. For example, a House of Commons committee inquiry (2008) received significant evidence from small entrants to the supply business that they were unable to create a sufficiently attractive offer because so much of the wholesale market involved internal transactions between different parts of the same integrated businesses. In the days of the Pool, the evidence of pricing was there for all to see; following NETA (and its extension to Scotland in 2005 under BETTA), prices except for a very small amount of near-to-close pricing became something of a matter of guesswork (or assessments) available from price discovery agents such as Heren and Pratts—at a price, of course.

The problem is that customers and the media express disbelief (and in the case of some customers, face real hardship) when energy suppliers swiftly raise prices by significant double-digit percentages at fairly short intervals. Of course, sometimes they lower them, but the suspicion remains that they are slower to lower prices than to raise them. And the key question—To what extent are these prices reflecting costs?—is almost impossible for an outsider to answer accurately. Remember that suppliers are purchasing a portfolio of futures-dated contracts in often opaque markets at various prices. It is difficult for the regulator to discover, or for the big six to refute, the potential for profit-taking when prices to consumers rise sharply. Because energy prices are such a sensitive consumer issue, politicians on all sides are keen to wade in with their own (in my view) simplistic 'solutions' to the problem. Thereby, one of the potential benefits of privatization, the de-politicization of the energy markets, has disappeared.

---

[10] Clearly, if you own an asset whose debt is expensive to service, but you can operate at low marginal cost so you have a revenue stream into the indefinite future, then if the capital and hence the debt servicing costs are written down enough, you can continue to operate.

There is another aspect of this issue. The opacity of prices means that independent merchant generators are extremely reluctant to engage in new investment in generation plant. Thus the UK has been walking into a problem of declining margins of safety between likely maximum loads on the system and available generation capacity, a problem that will worsen as old nuclear plants are retired and old and relatively dirty coal plant is forced into retirement. Here we have a classic political problem—lead times for new generation, particularly nuclear generation, are long, longer than the political cycle. Therefore governments have a tendency to shelve problems until they become urgent. The saga over building a new nuclear facility at Hinkley Point is a good example. This has been mooted for some time, but it is an immensely costly investment, and therefore risky in a market where output prices fluctuate significantly. Thus guarantees have been sought, and obtained, from the government for long-term price support for the project, in which EDF, one of the big six suppliers, is the key partner. This is not a desirable basis on which to conduct long-term energy policy, nor a good basis for the regulator to work from. The regulator is in a hard place between being captured by the industry and being captured by the government of the day.

There are additional factors to be brought into the mix, both concerning climate change. One is the policy, driven by the need for greater renewable power, to develop strategies to supply it. The British are not as naturally 'green' as many other European countries—the Germans have made huge (and somewhat costly) strides in the direction of both wind and solar power, and the presence in particular of photovoltaics has smoothed out the German midday peak in demand; Italy and Spain also have moved significantly into solar power. France has a very substantial nuclear fleet, which is 'green' by some people's standards, and much of Scandinavia relies heavily on Norwegian hydropower. Everyone in Britain likes to have electricity available, but few people like to be surrounded by wind turbines. A cynic would suggest that people of southeast England were happy when much of our power was generated through giant coal-fired plants situated along the river Trent, because they could use electricity but not see it being produced. They are now happy to have wind farms, so long as they are somewhere else. The upshot of this is that offshore wind, an inherently expensive technology, is politically likely to be most easily developed.

The other aspect of wind and solar power is that it is unbiddable, unlike conventional thermal power. Thus increased renewables of this type require either significant development of storage technology or, more likely in the medium run, increasingly intermittent, and therefore less efficient, use of gas-fired technologies. This is not widely appreciated. But it is a factor in the discussions of developing the capacity market—a market for payments to power stations to be available, rather than paying them only when they produce power.

The overall impact of these policies is that we are moving rapidly away from a model of generation as a competitive market system towards one where, paradoxically, almost all types of power plant are in some sense subsidized—nuclear, wind, photovoltaic, biomass, plus coal and gas via payments for capacity availability. This in an industry where the externalities are generally negative; not a good recipe for efficient regulation!

Of course the other alternative, or complementary, aspect of electricity is demand side management. It has always struck me as a somewhat strange idea that the energy supply companies have been pushed into the 'turkeys voting for Christmas' role of attempting to promote energy-saving measures. Unfortunately also, the approaches adopted by their agents have been badly managed, so that no records appear to be kept of who has installed significant loft insulation, who has solid walls and is therefore annoyed by constant calls from companies offering to install cavity wall insulation, and so on. In retrospect, it would have been better if parties with a more genuine incentive to reduce and smooth customer consumption could have been put on to this activity.

16.4 WATER AND SEWAGE

It was always acknowledged that the scope for competition in the water and, particularly, sewage sector was very limited. The less famous Littlechild report on water (1986) acknowledges that in an industry where regulation is inherently long lived, considerations of rate of return loom much larger, because most of the investments are long term and investors need some assurance that the assets will not be stranded. Initially on privatization in 1989 at least, the industry was also subject to an above-RPI form of price regulation, because purity standards in water and sewage needed to be increased to Continental European levels. In this sense, the industry inherited and needed to remedy a dubious recent past, despite the Victorians' early advances both in water and sewage services.

Here an interesting new concept was developed, that of 'yardstick competition'. The industry was reorganized into river basin catchment areas, so far as the ten water and sewage companies were concerned, plus a number of usually much smaller water-only companies that often relied on idiosyncratic local supplies, either from rivers or from boreholes into aquifers. In total, there were approximately thirty water supply businesses, and although there were only ten sewage companies, because economies of scale in sewage are modest, this involved a much larger number of individual sewage works. Thus in both water and sewage, there was (just) enough scope for statistical comparison across companies, in order to identify relatively efficient and relatively inefficient operation, and to penalize the latter. Also, many investment tasks are essentially standard, such as laying a particular length of trench, installing a pump, and so on, so in evaluating investments, these standardized tasks can be (and have been) developed into standardized allowed costs for the task, so enabling cross-company comparison and control.

As far as continuing operations are concerned, water provision is somewhat idiosyncratic. Some sources and treatment requirements are inevitably more costly to work than others. Some involve a rather denser network of pipes than others, some involve substantially more pumping than others. This leads to regression models of output on costs in which control variables such as population density, pipework density, pumping heights, and so forth are inserted. The regression residuals then hopefully indicate relatively efficient and inefficient operators. In practice, although these comparisons might be seen as moderately sophisticated, they have not been significantly enhanced to encompass developments in econometrics, since they were instituted in the early years of privatized water companies. Therefore, in my view they do not make the best use of the information in the regulator's hands, for reasons which are understandable but not convincing. There is also a tendency to make *ex post* adjustments, rather than building these into the regression framework.

There is also an unfortunate side effect on the industry structure. In any other industry, if two small companies operating in non-contiguous areas of the country were to find good reasons to merge, this would not trouble the competition authorities. However in water, this can mean the loss of a vital datapoint. Hence the case is examined in detail, with costly consequences. Finally, there have been more recent attempts, first in Scotland, to develop competition in water supply (for example different grades of water for industrial use). This is only ever going to be a small element of the overall industry, in my opinion.

16.5 TRANSPORT

The final sector I will consider is transport. Here the main aspects I will look at are rail and local bus services. First, however, a few words on airports. Whoever first designed the system of ownership of privatized airport facilities in Britain certainly seems not to have had competition at the back of their mind. It seems odd that the British Airports Authority, when privatized as a whole in 1987, had a monopoly both of the three main London airports and the two main Scottish airports, and one plausible competitor for the London airports in the form of Southampton, together with Aberdeen in Scotland. Since there is no good reason for the London airports or the Scottish lowland airports to be under the same control, it is unsurprising that the Competition Commission, in a trenchant landmark report in 2009 (CC, 2009a), recommended and eventually (after a long and hard-fought battle in respect of Stansted) was able by early 2013 to enforce divestiture of two of the three London airports. It is a little early to see the full fruits of this action, but it is clear that the incentives of the three different parties who now hold the three London airports will be substantially different from the incentives of the set of airports taken together.

Rail privatization was a somewhat untidy affair, developed at speed against a background of significant opposition prior to the 1997 election and in some parts insignificant recognition both of the idiosyncratic nature of the rail network as it exists in Great Britain and of the limited scope for on-rail competition. A complex vertical structure with a web of contractual relationships was developed, including a complex system of regulation, with the best of intentions perhaps, but certainly vulnerable to criticism.

In retrospect, one of the main issues turned out to be a significant knowledge deficit so far as the state of the infrastructure was concerned, made worse by the loss of skilled employees to contractors or other sectors. This infrastructure was severely tested and found wanting as a result of the substantial growth in patronage, leading to a series of extremely damaging incidents in the late 1990s to early 2000s. The infrastructure operator (Railtrack, a private company) was seen as incompetent and over-interested in profit at the expense of other things. Key upgrade projects proved difficult and cost overruns were legendary. As a result, Railtrack was put into administration and what is effectively a nationalized company, Network Rail, has assumed the role. However, it is still the case that by far the majority of delays to services are attributable to infrastructure failings.

Most operations so far as passenger services are concerned are carried out by franchised operators. It was seen that the rolling stock to be used by these was both expensive and long lived. Because the franchises could not plausibly cover more than a small part of the likely life of the rolling stock (which might be forty years) three leasing companies were developed, from whom the necessary vehicles could be rented. However, although three suppliers might seem enough to get broadly competitive pricing in many industries, given the idiosyncratic nature of much of the network, for many lines at most two suppliers would have appropriate equipment and for some, only one. Thus the leasing structure, although it allowed investment in new stock and allowed a range of competitors for a franchise, was far from perfect and has been much criticized as well as the subject of a Competition Commission report (2009b).

Rail fares have been raised in real terms for many years, but despite this, there has been a substantial and sustained increase in rail travel from privatization onwards, even through the considerable macroeconomic fluctuations in the late 2000s. To this extent, the experiment should be judged a success. However, there are two connected caveats regarding operators that are significant. Operating franchises are awarded on the basis of competitive tenders, for relatively long periods of time. It is important to note that these do not represent 'Chadwick auctions' of the type proposed by Demsetz (1968). Rather, the competition is won by the supplier (subject to quality constraints) which offers the largest payment schedule to the government. Also, because of the growth in expected passenger numbers, franchise proposals commonly consist of a schedule of payments rising over the life of the contract. However, the assumptions underlying these, which may themselves derive from Department for Transport (DfT) forecasts, can be over-optimistic and lead to franchise operators 'walking away' from franchises early in the period. This has brought the process, and with it the DfT, into some disrepute. Indeed, it has successfully been legally challenged, by Virgin Trains. What happens when a franchisee walks away? The answer is that Directly Operated Railways, a government body, takes over for a while. Unfortunately, in many eyes, this same body is ruled out of competing directly for the award of franchises, despite its good record in cases such as the East Coast where it has stepped in.

In the main, the operators of services are companies also active in the bus market, although several have significant input from Continental European operators. In this sense, the franchise structure has succeeded in creating a system in which companies expert in transport in other contexts play a significant part. There has been significant consolidation amongst the firms, but at least for the present there probably remains sufficient competition between them.

There is quite a marked contrast within local bus transport. One cannot help a suspicion that the contrasts between the system devised for buses in London as opposed to outside London is suggestive that the rest of the country is of little interest to those in government. The well-organized system of five-year (Chadwick auction) franchises within London is well respected outside the country and leads to a system with attractive network properties, significant monitoring of service quality, and a rising patronage. Outside London, apart from the relatively small fraction of those services viewed as socially necessary which are franchise operations,[11] the model is completely competitive.

The introduction of competition in buses has some benefits,[12] but until the subsidization of fares for those of pensionable age bus patronage had been declining, quality of service remains variable, and network benefits have commonly been lost so far as passengers are concerned. This is not a model that is the envy of Continental European cities. In the case of relatively rural routes and small towns, where network benefits (the ability to complete a journey using more than one bus) are rather unimportant and obviously poor operations can be supplanted by better services (as has happened in some notable instances), the completely free competition on fares and routes works reasonably well. But in the larger urban centres, as a result of various benefits of large-scale operation, even poor-quality operators survive for many years. In certain cases, this is boosted by the important role of operator-only weekly and monthly passes, which commonly have a much stronger role in the market than the all-singing-all-dancing variants rather indifferently marketed at higher prices by local passenger transport authorities. In the case of some large metropolitan areas, there have been sustained attempts to introduce a local franchise framework similar to that which exists in London; so far, however, these have not borne fruit. One significant issue is the possibility of legal challenge to the change to a franchise scheme—it is unclear what exactly the current operators 'own' in a particular location. Thus the bus market outside London exhibits the problem of ossification of a structure that may well be sub-optimal, created by the initial design of the privatization.

16.6 Conclusions

The point just made is one of wider importance. In organizing the structure of an industry for privatization, certain decisions are made which then become irreversible in practice. Therefore it is important, in making structural changes, to think them through

---

[11] Some authorities appear to be much better at eliciting tenders for these than are others; clearly local practices differ. This can be, and has been, a useful route for smaller operators into larger service provision.

[12] Here it may be useful to note that Oxford is in the almost unique position of having a stable, largely duopolistic structure to its bus services and, given the nature of the city, this structure works well.

carefully. There have been examples of changed structures *ex post*, most significantly perhaps in the case of British Gas, but these are undoubtedly difficult to engineer, particularly when the industry has now become fragmented.

A final thought: Devising a market remedy is not like devising a remedy for a crime, such as a prison sentence, because the latter can be enforced. In redesigning a market, the difficult lesson is that given a set of incentives, firms will act in a strategic manner. They will optimize subject to those incentives or remedies. This is a difficult lesson, because it is tempting for a regulatory body to see a problem and devise a remedy for that problem without seeing what the firm(s) might do in relation to the remedy; several examples could be cited. Not only may firms prevaricate, they may also see through to a solution that satisfies the 'remedy' but does not have the intended effect on the industry. This suggests that proposed remedies, or changes to a system, should be tested on cynical industry insiders who cannot themselves benefit from the change, but can nevertheless see how others could benefit, and can therefore caution against particular proposals towards others that have a similar effect but without similar problems. Easy to say, but no doubt difficult to put into action!

Note: Michael Waterson has been a Member of the Competition Commission, but he was not involved in any of the Inquiries specifically cited in the text. He would like to acknowledge the opportunity offered to air some of the ideas expressed here in a short lecture series delivered at the University of Verona in April 2014.

References

Armstrong, M., Cowan, S., and Vickers, J. (1994). *Regulatory Reform: Economic Analysis and the British Experience*. London: The MIT Press.

Averch, H. and Johnson, L. L. (1962). 'Behavior of the Firm under Regulatory Constraint', *American Economic Review* 52(5): 1052–69.

Baron, D. and Myerson, R. (1982). 'Regulating a Monopolist with Unknown Costs', *Econometrica* 50, 911–30.

Bartle, I. (ed.) (2003). *The UK Model of Utility Regulation*, University of Bath CRI Proceedings No. 31.

Baumol, W. J. (1983). 'Some Subtle Issues in Railroad Deregulation', *International Journal of Transport Economics* 10, 341–55.

Beesley, M. E. and Littlechild, S. C. (1989). 'The Regulation of Privatized Monopolies in the United Kingdom', *RAND Journal of Economics* 20, 454–72.

CC (Competition Commission) (2009a). *BAA Airports Market Investigation*. CC: London.

CC (Competition Commission) (2009b). *Rolling Stock Leasing Market Investigation*. CC: London.

Cribb, J. (2013). *Income Inequality in the UK*. London: Institute for Fiscal Studies.

Demsetz, H. (1968). 'Why Regulate Utilities', *Journal of Law and Economics* 11, 55–66.

Green, R. J. and Newbery, D. J. (1992). 'Competition in the British Electricity Spot Market', *Journal of Political Economy* 100(5), 929–53.

House of Commons Business and Enterprise Committee (2008). *Energy Prices, Fuel Poverty and OFGEM HC293*. London: HMSO.

Laffont, J.-J. and Tirole, J. (1994). 'Access Pricing and Competition', *European Economic Review* 38, 1673–710.

Littlechild, S. C. (1983). *Regulation of British Telecommunications' Profitability: Report to the Secretary of State for Industry*. London: HMSO.

Littlechild, S. C. (1986). *Economic Regulation of Privatised Water Authorities, Report to the Secretary of State for Industry*, London: HMSO.

Ramsey, F. P. (1927). 'A Contribution to the Theory of Taxation', *Economic Journal* 37, 47–61.

Simmonds, G. (2002). 'Regulation of the UK Electricity Industry', CRI Industry Brief, <http://www.bath.ac.uk/management/cri/pubpdf/Industry_Briefs/Electricity_Gillian_Simmonds.pdf>

Willig, R. (1979). 'The Theory of Network Access Pricing', in H. B. Trebing (ed.), *Issues in Public Utility Regulation*. Michigan: Michigan State University Public Utilities Papers.

CHAPTER 17

REFINING INWARD INVESTMENT POLICY

Maximizing the Returns to Limited Funds

NIGEL DRIFFIELD, SANDRA LANCHEROS, AND YAMA TEMOURI

17.1 INTRODUCTION

THE attraction of internationally mobile capital has been at the cornerstone of UK industrial and regional policy for a generation. While the UK has held an open door stance on inward investment since the Second World War, the emphasis on attracting foreign investors coincided with the decline of traditional manufacturing industries in the 1980s. For a long time the focus of UK foreign direct investment (FDI) policy was to generate employment for the available labour force in the less developed regions of the UK.

However, the emphasis in more recent policy documents has begun to catch up with the academic literature concerned with the wider benefits of attracting internationally mobile capital, including 'raising productivity through technology transfer and spillover effects' (Driffield et al., 2013). Despite the desirability of these two policy goals, 'evidence suggests that FDI projects that create large-scale employment typically do not involve much technology transfer, and vice versa' (Driffield et al., 2013).

One of the questions that we therefore intend to address in this chapter is the suitability of the instruments that have been used to attract internationally mobile capital. We argue that, in general, the policy instruments used in the UK have been rather a 'blunt instrument' and applications of more general policy initiatives, rather than bespoke policies to attract, and more importantly maximize, the potential benefits of inward investment to the host region.

Section 17.2 sketches broad trends in the FDI policies in the UK during the last three decades. Section 17.3 discusses the potential benefits of inward FDI and the role of direct interventions to attract internationally mobile capital. Section 17.4 comments on other areas of economic policy necessary to attract FDI. Section 17.5 concludes.

17.2 FDI Policy in Britain

For some thirty years inward investment policy has become synonymous with both industrial and regional policy in the UK. There are numerous papers that plot out the first twenty years or so of industrial and regional policy in the context of inward investment (see for example Armstrong and Taylor, 1993; Wren and Taylor, 1999; Bailey and Driffield, 2007). We do not therefore intend to discuss this in any detail, but to point out two themes that have emerged. The first has been the steady decrease in central government expenditure to finance the regional and FDI policy in the UK, reflecting the continuous changes in regulations within the European Union as well as the political stance of recent governments. The second (not unrelated to the first) has been the ongoing changes in the organizational structure to coordinate and deliver the regional and FDI policies within the UK and the extent to which regions of the UK have been able to pursue their own agendas. We discuss these themes in the following section.

17.2.1 The Policy Setting

The Conservative government of the 1980s was very open to attracting inward investment, but more sceptical about intervention. It could be argued, therefore, that while there was little in terms of a national policy, due to the prevailing view that support for inward investment amounted to unwarranted subsidies that were market distorting, there was far more support offered through regional agencies of the UK. The Regional Development Agencies (RDAs) in Scotland and Wales became champions of inward investment attraction in the UK, while the other Government Office regions promoted Regional Selective Assistance (RSA—later Strategic Finance for Investment in England—SFIE), Regional Development Grants, and EU funding, to compete for internationally mobile capital. This led to a number of high-profile examples of UK regions competing with each other for the same investment, often to the benefit of the firm concerned. There was equal concern expressed through this period that such policies were merely moving jobs around the UK, such that jobs in assisted areas where the subsidies were greatest were displacing jobs elsewhere (Taylor and Wren, 1997).

This approach to regional policy essentially assumed that unemployment was the issue that had to be addressed, and therefore by stimulating exogenous increases in labour demand, this would alleviate regional inequality. However, this presumes, as argued by Morgan (1997), that unemployment is the cause of regional decline rather than a symptom of the wider problem of low levels of productivity and innovation. The extent to which inward investment policy has been able or even genuinely sought to address the latter issue is a matter of some debate.

There are two reasons for considering the importance of this argument. The first is the contentious and somewhat varied literature that seeks to determine the *cost-per-job* of inward investment support (for a discussion of the earlier literature, and of earlier analysis of the relative returns to such interventions, see Taylor and Wren, 1997; Hart et al., 2008; Jones and Wren, 2008). While it is not the purpose of this chapter to discuss the variability in the cost-per-job estimates that are provided by this literature, one inescapable conclusion can be drawn, which is, in the absence of any wider beneficial effects of attracting foreign investment, the costs of RSA provided to foreign firms appear high. This argument links to the wider point made by Morgan (1997) and Driffield (2001), who illustrate that the rationale of attracting inward investment has been firmly based on the assumption that certain indirect benefits from FDI will accrue to the domestic sector, in the form of technological or productivity externalities. If this is the case, then the social returns to such investments are significant and may justify the large subsidies.

Thus, inward investment policies have been based on the assumed causal link between inward investment and regional development. The argument for subsidizing inward investment is based on 'superior' multinational enterprises (MNEs) entering the domestic industry and their advantages that can be assimilated by the domestic sector through various channels. Part of this explanation is based on inter-industry adjustment, including a reallocation of resources to industry sectors of above average industry comparative advantage. On a regional level, new foreign manufacturing investment can also have beneficial economic consequences. In addition to job creation and resource transfer, foreign inward investments can also provide technology and skills transfer to supplier and customer sectors. MNEs may then provide a basis for technology spillovers and the development of innovatory capacity in domestically owned sectors (Blomström and Kokko, 1996).

With the change of government in 1997, regional policy was given a higher profile, with views to this effect set out in the 2001 and 2003 White Papers. These paid lip service to an argument that has been advanced by the Treasury since the mid-1970s, which is that the focus of regional policy is to maximize the economic potential of all regions, through addressing market failure. On the one hand, this recognizes the interdependencies between regions, both in terms of competing for resources and also recognizing that a zero-sum game between regions is highly sub-optimal, given the number of supply chains that cross regions of the UK. On the other hand, the government recognized the need to be more proactive in seeking to attract inward investment, not merely with capital incentives but with a more coherent package, seeking to effectively market the UK and its regions and stress the potential benefits of links between inward investment and domestic capacity. The Department for Trade and Industry (2006) recognizes this explicitly, that without intervention the UK is likely to experience a sub-optimal level of inward investment.

The 'Local Growth White Paper' in 2010 represents perhaps the biggest single change in the regional nomenclature in this country over the past thirty years, namely the demise of the RDAs and the creation of Local Enterprise Partnerships (LEPs). While others in this volume will comment in more detail on what that will mean for regional policy and regional governance, we can say that with respect to inward investment policy this has meant three things. Firstly, the LEPs do not have the budgets of RDAs to support investment directly, though in practice the RDAs mostly channelled money that was made available through other initiatives. Secondly, the LEPs, starting from a very low base, are having to generate inward investment strategies in the new climate of austerity. This has caused a real polarization of inward investment policy in the UK, with far more emphasis on the role of UKTI, with hitherto city-based council inward investment teams taking a remit of a wider area, and linking inward investment strategies to the LEPs' economic strategy more generally, along with use of EU money, and wider initiatives on skills and innovation. At the time of writing this chapter, the areas that are successful in terms of attracting inward investment are those that have pursued a more targeted approach, focused on certain sectors and the value proposition of the local economy. Thirdly, within LEPs the focus shifted to the value proposition that regions are able to put to inward investors, even before the recent austerity, and the demise of RDAs meant that support for inward investment was declining in real terms.

Figure 17.1 illustrates the slight rebalancing of business support interventions away from inward investors towards indigenous firms. There are many good reasons, highlighted for example by the various reviews of RSA that emphasize the greater social benefits to supporting domestic firms rather than inward investors. Indeed, the work for the Manchester Independent Economic Review (MIER, 2009) also highlights the greater social

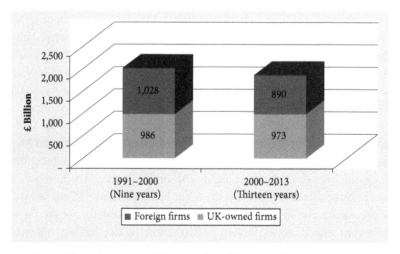

FIGURE 17.1 Financial Assistance to UK-Owned and Foreign Firms in the Assisted Areas of Great Britain: 1991–2000 and 2001–13.

Source: Industrial Development Act, 1982; Annual Reports 2001–13

returns to supporting domestic rather than inward investment. Nevertheless, the attraction of inward investment remains a key element of most local economic strategies, largely because of the potential scale of these investments, but attracting this needs to be based on the long-term value proposition of the region rather than subsidy.

17.3 BENEFITS FROM FDI AND THE ROLE OF POLICY

As we have discussed in section 17.2, there is a clear distinction between maximizing inward investment and maximizing the benefits of inward investment. For a long time, the focus of inward investment policy was to generate employment for the available labour force. In practical terms this meant a supposed matching between the pool of unemployed in a given region, and the type of jobs one was able to attract to a region. However, with a series of reports suggesting that the cost-per-job simply did not merit this degree of intervention, along with concerns over the longevity of some of the employment, the emphasis within policy documents began to catch up with the academic literature concerned with the wider benefits of attracting internationally mobile capital to a region. Cynically, one may suggest that such analysis was merely an attempt to justify *ex post* the rather large subsidies that were paid. One may be more generous and argue that this has led to a better understanding of the economic strengths of the region, and the extent to which inward investment in certain sectors can enhance the region.

There is a large literature on each of these areas, but essentially the argument is that inward investment produces goods for export as well as for sale locally and introduces new technology into the host region. The basis for this argument is the essential premise that in order to succeed in a foreign environment, the firm must have some inherent advantage over the domestic competition. In turn, these firm-specific advantages are interpreted (perhaps erroneously) in terms of technological advantages, which are then transferred into the host country. These advantages lead to an increase in average productivity, increased competition and competitiveness, and increase in the demand for skilled labour as this technology is skilled labour augmenting. The empirical literature then simply finds disagreement over the magnitude of these effects.

The more important question, however, is whether policy interventions, in the form of the type of intervention or support, will impact on the magnitude of the beneficial effects? Here we essentially lean on two literatures. The first demonstrates that when seeking to determine the effect of inward investment on the host country, it is impossible to divorce the effect from the motivation of the firm to enter a given location (Driffield and Love, 2005, 2007; Driffield et al., 2010). The second is the literature which stresses the importance of linkages between the inward investors and host country firms, both at the sectoral level (Javorcik, 2004) and within and across regions within a regional science setting (Driffield et al., 2004).

Apart from *resource-seeking* FDI, the standard distinction is between *market-seeking* FDI—where the firm seeks to exploit existing firm-specific assets in a new environment—and *asset-seeking* FDI, which is where the firm invests in a location in order to access the technology or knowledge which exists there, either in domestic firms or other inward investors. Driffield and Love (2005, 2007) and Driffield et al. (2010) show that this distinction is important in terms of both the productivity and employment effects of such investment. To summarize, these papers find that some inward investment does indeed generate significant technology transfer effects that boost productivity, beyond the private gains to the firm. The new investment in itself increases average productivity, and in addition there are significant spillovers into the domestic sector. This effect, however, is limited to cases where the inward investment has significant technological advantages over the domestic sector, or itself generates significant productivity growth in its affiliate in the host country. Equally, there are other cases where the UK is an attractive location for certain assembly-type operations, typically for firms from outside the EU looking to sell into the single market. In such cases, relatively low labour costs (compared with other parts of Northern Europe) and a much more flexible labour market make the UK attractive, and this investment tends to generate low- and medium-skill employment, both in the firm and with positive demand effects into the domestic sector. However, what is clear is that these two effects are independent of each other, in that one either achieves technology transfer or employment creation, but not both.

This presents two issues for policy-makers. Firstly, they need to be able to identify *ex ante* the types of investments that will generate the desired results, whether that is productivity growth and technological upgrading, or whether it is employment creation; and secondly, the instruments available need to be sufficiently sophisticated to distinguish between different investors and produce the desired outcome. Hitherto the broad brush approach to this issue has been unable to do this (Bailey and Driffield, 2007; Jones and Wren, 2008).

A particular issue is what policy measures can be used to attract high-technology FDI. Driffield et al. (2010) carried out an evaluation of the support that the United Kingdom Trade and Investment (UKTI) offers to support R&D, both to inward investors and potential exporters. As this report points out, the essential problem with attempting to derive a policy framework to stimulate or attract foreign-owned R&D faces the same issues as we discussed above. Assuming that MNEs are more R&D intensive than average firms, irrespective of where the R&D is carried out, attracting inward investment should *ceteris paribus* improve the innovative capacity of the host region, depending on how embedded the affiliate is into the global production system of the parent. This may occur as a result of entry of higher R&D MNEs which increases the average level of R&D in the economy, also known as the 'batting average' effect. The internationalization of MNEs' R&D activities (Cantwell, 1991) is part of this process, although there is mixed evidence on whether developed OECD countries gain or lose by this process (Onodera, 2008). The assumption of net benefits from foreign entrants' R&D activities is also consistent with the standard OLI model of FDI (Dunning, 1988).

The situation is complicated, however, by the possible interaction between MNE subsidiaries and domestic firms. Most high-technology sectors in the UK suffer significant skill shortages, so while attracting high-technology inward investment is always attractive to local policy-makers, there is always the concern over where new firms will find suitably qualified employees, often leading to more activity in already overheated labour markets. Driffield (2001), for example, shows a degree of crowding out between foreign-owned R&D and domestic R&D, with the R&D undertaken in domestic firms.

As a result, one would expect both a complementary or substituting relationship between R&D and innovation undertaken by MNE subsidiaries and that of domestic enterprises, so that the net effect of entry of R&D-producing MNEs is uncertain. Competition from MNEs may stimulate the R&D activities of domestic enterprises, encouraging them to be more innovative in order to compete both domestically and abroad. In addition, the ability of domestic enterprises to benefit from both intra- and inter-industry spillovers from MNEs depends on their absorptive capacity, an important element of which is in-house R&D (Cohen and Levinthal, 1989).

However, there may be a substitute relationship between domestic and foreign R&D. In part this may arise from a *direct substitution* effect: if domestic enterprises recognize that the R&D and technology produced by MNE subsidiaries is available at a lower cost and less risk than they can produce themselves, firms may opt to obtain technology this way, with a result that foreign R&D substitutes for domestic R&D. Note that while this may result in a reduction in total R&D carried out in the economy, it may nevertheless be beneficial if access to improved technology is achieved by market means rather then (relatively inefficient) R&D carried out by domestic enterprises.

There is also the possibility of a *crowding out effect* occurring via the market, and involves foreign subsidiaries' R&D spending increasing the demand for R&D and hence its price. This may occur through bidding up the wages of researchers or other investment inputs, which may lead to firms altering their investment priorities. The net result of this may be that even if MNE research spending raises the total amount of R&D in the economy, the real amount of R&D (after adjusting for the higher cost of research) will actually be reduced.

This suggests that even where the UK is able to effectively target high-tech firms and attract foreign R&D to the UK, foreign-owned R&D to the UK may do little to increase the overall innovatory capacity of the UK. This again requires an evaluation of the project on a case by case basis.

17.3.1 Foreign Acquisition of Domestic Companies

Possibly the most contentious form of FDI is inward investment by M&A. The issues of contention typically involve whether this is surrendering economic sovereignty, and whether this makes their longevity subject to strategic decisions taken abroad.

Some two-thirds of global FDI flows are M&A rather than greenfield FDI. Typically, however, at least initially, inward investment by acquisition does not attract the same forms of incentives as greenfield FDI, though there are plenty of examples of high-profile inward investors being granted RSA or SFIE as part of subsequent investments or capital upgrading. However, in general, any policy questions surrounding the initial acquisition tend to focus on competition policy rather than other forms of industrial policy or regional policy.

As such, the academic literature tends to focus on the *ex post* performance of both the target and acquirer (see for example Harris and Robinson, 2002; Girma and Görg, 2003). Typically this literature sets up the issue as a test of foreign firm-specific advantage. The argument follows that if MNEs are superior to domestic firms, and if MNEs then take over a domestic plant, that plant will increase productivity as it absorbs superior knowledge or technology from the parent. The literature recognizes that of course there may be significant sample selection effects (better-performing firms may be acquired) and allows for this. Of course, the mechanism described is at least a two-stage process, relying not merely on the presence of firm-specific advantage but also the desire of the parent to transfer knowledge into the newly acquired affiliate, and in turn the affiliate being in a position to acquire this knowledge. If this is the case, then there may be an argument for encouraging this activity, despite the criticism that foreign firms acquiring UK businesses often attracts in the popular press. However, most evidence suggests that such acquisition generates little in terms of productivity growth at the firm level, little in terms of spillovers, and a small but significant decline in employment. The question, then, perhaps should be whether such activity should be restricted rather than encouraged, and indeed the editors of this volume have argued on a number of occasions, and in a number of both academic and policy-related articles, that there is an argument for this.

This analysis again, however, ignores a fundamental question: What was the motive for the acquisition in the first place? If, for example, the motivation is the acquisition of a high-performing firm that is crucial to the parent's supply chain, then why would one expect any subsequent performance increase? This is very different from the acquisition of an underperforming firm and seeking to turn it round, and just as the outcome is different, so should be the policy response. Since the crisis, however, what we are observing is possibly another phenomenon, which is investment in the UK by emerging market MNEs who are cash rich, derived typically from significant scale economies in medium-tech activity at home, who are therefore able to provide badly needed investment for UK firms. Typically the popular press, and even sometimes business commentators, object vociferously to this up to the point where the firm is seen to be thriving, and then it is lauded as a huge success for inward investment policy. Our view is that the UK should certainly be open to such investments and support investment in physical capital in the same way as other firms are supported, and that they should certainly not be discouraged; and further, that 'aftercare' should be provided to these firms in the same way as it is for other inward investment.

17.4 The Wider Policy Agenda Impacting FDI Flows

Thus far we have discussed the policy options with respect to direct intervention to attract internationally mobile capital. It is important to stress, however, that many other areas of economic policy influence a country's ability to attract FDI. Some of the major factors include corporate tax rates, labour market flexibility and aftercare.

17.4.1 Corporate Tax Rates

- Higher effective average tax rates have a negative influence on inward FDI.
- The literature has shown varying degrees of tax influence, depending on the type of tax rate, country, and time period considered. However, for the UK a modest estimate is that a 1 per cent increase in EATR will reduce the probability of a firm locating in the UK by 1.29 percentage points.
- The UK's main rate of corporation tax stood at 24 per cent in 2012, which was considerably lower than its main rivals' tax rates, such as the US, France, and Japan.

17.4.2 Labour Market Flexibility

- Labour market flexibility is seen as a key determinant for attracting FDI.
- Labour market flexibility is seen by policy-makers as facilitating better firm performance and higher levels of firm productivity, and is generally considered to be a precondition for economic strength (HM Treasury, 2003; Anderson et al., 2006). However, labour market flexibility is multifaceted and goes beyond factor cost differentials. It includes, for instance, labour market regulation (employment protection) and institutional arrangements with regard to wage bargaining. Whether and to what extent changes to labour market conditions affect inward FDI is the focus of a large literature (Pain, 1993; Bajo-Rubio and Sosvilla-Rivero, 1994; Cooke, 1997; Pain and Lansbury, 1997; Cooke and Noble, 1998; Barrell and Pain, 1999; Love and Lage-Hidalgo, 2000; Dewit et al. 2003; Love, 2003; Wei and Balasubramanyam, 2006; Haaland and Wooton, 2007; Gheasi et al., 2012).
- In terms of the World Economic Forum index on labour market flexibility, the UK scores 2.51 and thus is more flexible than most countries in the world, particularly among the OECD member countries. Countries which score lower (i.e. more flexible labour markets) are the US, Denmark, and Switzerland.
- Studies which examine the link between FDI and migration show that large diaspora populations attract investment from the home country, and this may explain the high proportion of Indian FDI that targets the UK. More generally, migration of skilled labour influences FDI flows in both directions.

17.4.3 Institutions

- The literature shows that institutional quality differences impact significantly on the ability of a country to attract FDI. It also influences the type of investment that is attracted.
- The UK system of institutions is well placed to attract inward FDI. Numerous indicators from different sources show that the UK compares favourably with its main competitors in the OECD.

17.4.4 Aftercare

- There is survey evidence that some inward investors find the UKTI support in giving information and network contact beneficial in their decision to locate in the UK or in other aspects of their investment. This is also related to the issue of aftercare, which is seen to become more important in the future, not only for retaining existing stock of FDI but also because doing this well can help sustain high levels of new inward FDI.
- The practitioner-based literature in this area focuses much more on the 'softer' side of inward investment promotion, such as aftercare and marketing of locations, rather than simply subsidies. UNCTAD (2007) produced a report on the importance of aftercare, which maps very closely onto the various UKTI publications on aftercare (see for example UKTI 2006, 2009). Both see aftercare as essentially a location-marketing activity. The UNCTAD report, however, highlights some differences in the way aftercare is implemented across countries, with, for example, in the case of the UK, responsibility traditionally being divided between the national agency, UKTI, and the now defunct RDAs. While UKTI does have a network of regional offices, it is not clear that the functions previously being performed by the RDAs are now being performed. The newly established LEPs have no similar responsibility, so this may be an area of disadvantage for the UK going forward.
- The same can also be said of promotion activities in general, with regions, either through LEPs or through the regional growth funds, having to bid for money. This raises the possibility of regional agents not being as flexible in response mode to inward investors as the RDAs had been previously.
- What is clear, however, is that the UNCTAD report argues that in a world of scarcer resources for investment promotion, aftercare is becoming more important. Further, they argue that in countries which have historically attracted significant FDI, such as the UK, Singapore, or Malaysia, a high proportion of current flows are strongly linked to existing stocks, such that retention of the existing stock is as important for new investment as it is for retaining existing employment. Perhaps the best-known study that highlights the strategic importance of aftercare is Birkinshaw (1998), which argues that aftercare needs to be sustained, rather than simply

reacting to potential relocations. The UK strategy on this is cited by UNCTAD as an exemplar, with UKTI's 'Investor Development' programme aimed at helping established investors grow, expand, and add higher value-added activities to their UK-based operations. A sub-region in London operates a 'Business Development' programme to support growth and expansion of firms, in collaboration with Think London, a sub-national IPA. An issue for speculation, however, is the extent to which this will be maintained with the current regional nomenclature recently established in the UK. The current emphasis on localities bidding for support from a centrally established source may place the emphasis on efficiency and timeliness rather than on strategic considerations.

17.4.5 Exchange Rates

- The literature on currency fluctuations shows that a relatively stable exchange rate offers certainty for foreign investors and may increase inward FDI. Sterling has depreciated against the dollar and appreciated against the euro since the onset of the recent financial crisis, which will at the margin have had positive effects on inward investments from the US and been less of an incentive for EU FDI.

17.4.6 Agglomeration

- The literature on spatial agglomeration shows that FDI inflows are significantly affected by agglomeration economies.
- For the UK, evidence shows that past success is a determinant of future success in attracting foreign FDI inflows, in the sense that previous FDI inflows act as a stimulus for future FDI inflows. This is particularly the case for regional concentrations of given industries which produce goods and services using world-leading technology, thus adding support to the importance of agglomeration for the maintenance of industrial advantages.

The UK compares well with its European counterparts with regard to agglomeration economies, having established world-renowned clusters in both manufacturing and services sectors across different regions of the UK.

All of the above evidence, based on anecdotal discussions with inward investment promotion agencies, case studies, and large-scale econometric estimation highlights, above all else, the importance of stability and predictability. Our work, for example, on developing and transition economies, as well as the UK, highlights the importance not only of good quality institutions, but also the certainty that these provide (Driffield et al., 2013). This can be considered in terms of policy consistency relating not only to inward investment but also, for example, to fiscal and monetary policy. There is a large body of work that, while emphasizing the importance of institutions and governance, also high-lights the scale of international business that is willing to invest in emerging or devel-oping countries, providing there is a degree of certainty about policy responses.

In the UK context, this was perhaps best highlighted in the various debates con-cerning currency unions or other exchange rate regimes. Dating back to the exchange rate mechanism, and then more recently concerning the euro, most policy pronounce-ments by inward investors in the UK were not so concerned with whether the decision was 'in or out', but that the decision be made, and be stuck with for the long term.[1] This issue can be seen more starkly in terms of the debate concerning the UK's continuing membership of the European Union. While there is not scope here to debate this issue fully, it is clear that the UK would be far less attractive for inward investors from both within and outside the EU were the UK to leave, for the very reasons outlined above.

17.5 CONCLUSION

Governments intervene when markets fail. Market failure can be specified in many dif-ferent forms. In the context of this evaluation, the most important elements are: incom-plete markets, externalities, and information asymmetries. These principles should be weighed up and expressed in every investment subsidy scheme.[2]

Incomplete markets are interpreted as the existence of a gap in the availability of private sector external finance (e.g. formal or informal equity capital) to firms for start-up and expansion activity in particular regions. This can be related to unwillingness of the private sector to become involved in projects which they deem to be 'high risk'. Externalities are viewed as the positive indirect effects that result from firms being located together. Posi-tive externalities include collaboration and networking opportunities (technological externalities such as spillovers, linkages), information transfer, the freeing up of internal human and financial capital (that can be utilized in other innovative actions within the firm), the leverage of additional private sector financial support, and the range of per-ceived or actual benefits associated with large urban labour markets (e.g. skill sets). Infor-mation asymmetry arises when firms are unaware of sources and mechanisms to access the necessary amounts of external finance required for new plants and/or the expansion of existing operations.

In this context, this chapter has sought to highlight a number of issues. Firstly, inward investment policy cannot be a blunt instrument where the same policy is applied to all cases. The major restriction here, however, is competition policy and the extent to which

---

[1] Perhaps the one exception to this were the Japanese car manufacturers, who expressed a preference at the time for the UK to join the euro, essentially because so many of their internal transactions within Europe take place in euros. This again, however, is a plea for certainty, notably over currency fluctuations, rather than a desire to influence exchange rate decisions from a political standpoint.

[2] An example of this is the recently revised business case for the SFIE scheme.

different firms can receive different treatment. Secondly, improved policy requires that the inward investment agencies tie in the needs of the investor to the strategic priority of the region, and this is one area where smaller regions, in the form of LEPS, may be better placed than the RDAs to do this. Evidence is emerging that city-regions are communicating their value proposition to potential inward investors in this way, and by focusing on certain sectors, getting the desired results.

Policy-makers are now putting the onus on firms to justify the need for subsidy, not merely in terms of employment generation but also in terms of the wider economic benefits discussed. On at least one level, this places firms in a relatively difficult position, of having to examine what spillovers may come from their investment. At the same time, policy-makers seek to maximize any informal technology transfer away from the firm.

This suggests, therefore, that there needs to be more discrimination in policies designed to attract FDI. There is clearly a place for seeking investment that will create employment for lower-skill workers. There are also clear benefits to the UK economy of attracting frontier technology and the world's leading firms, in both high-tech manufacturing and knowledge intensive services. It is important, however, to recognize that these are essentially mutually exclusive. The first may be attracted by some form of employment subsidy, the second almost certainly not. The latter is more likely to be attracted by high-quality facilities and infrastructure, a well-educated workforce, and not least strong protection of intellectual property rights at the country level. There may well be technology transfer or spillovers from this type of investment, but it is also important to understand that the firm will do all it can to prevent this.

Thus, emphasis needs to shift from maximizing inward investment flows to maximizing the benefits of inward investment. As discussed in 17.2, the beneficial effects of inward investment are many and varied. There are many examples of foreign acquisitions leading to greatly increased performance. The current example of the acquisition of Jaguar Land Rover by TATA, for example, would contrast with the econometric literature which suggests on average little gain from foreign acquisition. Equally, most of the literature suggests that while on average the productivity spillover effect from inward investment is 'significant but small' in cases where the inward investors introduce new technology and generate productivity growth internally, the social return to the investment is much higher. This is enhanced where there are direct links and complementarities between the foreign and domestic sector. This places the onus on local policy-makers to establish not only the value proposition that their region wishes to convey, but also what added value the inward investment offers.

With the demise of the regional development agencies and the development of LEPs, one potential advantage is that this makes the decision-making process more local, with the emphasis being on the gains from inward investment, not simply the investment flows. The challenge for local policy-makers is therefore to develop a framework by which projects can be evaluated for the overall contribution to jobs, competitiveness, and growth, and this is what we have tried to offer here.

Finally, while the focus of this chapter is on inward investment policy, we make a plea not to ignore the domestic sector. It is important to stress here that, formally, there is no form of capital subsidy or investment incentive that is available to inward investors in the UK that is not available to domestic firms. However, it is commonly argued that it is easier for inward investors in any country to show additionality from their investment, and that their investment is unlikely to cause distortions in either goods or capital markets, than it is for domestic firms. It is also generally argued by inward investment agencies that they simply cannot find investment projects at a large enough scale from domestic firms. For example, one of the comments from local policy-makers on our research as part of the Manchester Independent Economic Review (<http://www. manchester-review.org.uk/>), in which we argued that local agencies should place more emphasis on domestic firms because expansion or new investment by local agents generated higher social returns, was simply that local firms cannot be found. It remains the case, however, that the final evaluation of Regional Selective Assistance for England and Wales, Northern Ireland, and Scotland all points to the returns being greater for support for local firms, compared with inward investors.

Other chapters in this volume focus on industrial policy in general in more detail, but investments by large domestic establishments are equally likely to be embedded with new technology, to be skilled labour-augmenting, and to generate spillovers as inward investment projects of a similar size. Large, domestically owned firms can be an important engine of growth in the UK, both in capital investment and employment terms. Historically, however, this investment has been positively associated with long-term debt, and this funding has to an extent dried up since the financial crisis, threatening the capacity of the domestic sector to maintain its position as a driver of investment growth, and suggesting why there has again been a focus on inward investment.

References

Anderson, J., Grahl, J., Jefferys, S., and Tasiran, A. (2006). *Labour Market Flexibility and Sectoral Productivity: A Comparative*, Employment Relations Research Series No. 66.

Armstrong, H. and Taylor, J. (1993). *Regional Economics and Policy*. 2nd edn. New York/ London: Harvester Wheatsheaf.

Bailey, D. and Driffield, N. (2007). 'Industrial Policy, FDI and Employment: Still a "Missing a Strategy"?', *Journal of Competition, Industry and Trade* 7(3), 189–211.

Bajo-Rubio, O. and Sosvilla-Rivero, S. (1994). 'An Econometric Analysis of Foreign Direct Investment in Spain, 1964–89', *Southern Economic Journal* 61(1), 104–20.

Barrell, R. and Pain, N. (1999). 'Foreign Direct Investment, Technological Change and Economic Growth within Europe', *Economic Journal* 107, 1770–86.

Birkinshaw, J. (1998). 'Foreign Owned Subsidiaries and Regional Development: The Case of Sweden', in J. Birkinshaw and N. Hood (eds), *Multinational Corporate Evolution and Subsidiary Development*, pp. 268–98. Basingstoke: Palgrave Macmillan.

Blomström, M. and Kokko, A. (1996). *Multinational Corporations and Spillovers*. Stockholm School of Economics, CEPR Discussion Paper No. 1365.

Cantwell, J. A. (1991). 'The International Agglomeration of R&D', in M. C. Casson (ed.), *Global Research Strategy and International Competitiveness*, pp. 216–32. Oxford: Blackwell.

Cohen, W. M. and Levinthal, D. A. (1989). 'Innovation and Learning: The Two Faces of R&D', *Economic Journal* 99 (397), 569–96.

Cooke, W. N. (1997). 'The Influence of Industrial Relations Factors on U.S. Foreign Direct Investment Abroad', *Industrial and Labor Relations Review* 51(1), 3–17.

Cooke, W. N. and Noble, D. S. (1998). 'Industrial relations systems and U.S. foreign direct investment abroad', *British Journal of Industrial Relations* 36(4), 581–609.

Department of Trade and Industry (2006). *International Trade and Investment: The Economic Rationale for Government Support*, Economics Paper No. 18, <https://www.gov.uk/government/uploads/system/uploads/attachment_data/file/32106/11-805-international-trade-investment-rationale-for-support.pdf>.

Dewit, G, Görg, H., and Montagna, C. (2003). 'Should I Stay or Should I Go? A Note on Employment Protection, Domestic Anchorage, and FDI', IZA Working paper No. 845.

Driffield, N. (2001). 'The Impact on Domestic Productivity of Inward Investment in the UK', *The Manchester School* 69(1), 103–19.

Driffield, N. and Love, J. H. (2005). 'Who Gains from Whom? Spillovers, Competition and Technology Sourcing in the Foreign-Owned Sector of UK Manufacturing', *The Scottish Journal of Political Economy* 52(5), 663–86.

Driffield, N. and Love, J. H. (2007). 'Linking FDI Motivation and Host Economy Productivity Effects: Conceptual and Empirical Analysis', *Journal of International Business Studies* 38(2), 460–73.

Driffield, N., Love, J. H., and Menghinello, S. (2010). 'The Multinational Enterprise as a Source of International Knowledge Flows: Direct Evidence from Italy', *Journal of International Business Studies* 41 (2), 350–9.

Driffield, N., Mickiewicz, T., and Temouri, Y. (2013). 'Institutional Reforms, Productivity and Profitability: From Rents to Competition?', *Journal of Comparative Economics* 41(2), 583–600.

Driffield, N., Munday, M., and Roberts, A. (2004). 'Inward Investment, Transactions Linkages, and Productivity Spillovers', *Papers in Regional Science* 83(4), 699–722.

Dunning, J. H. (1988). 'The Eclectic Paradigm of International Production: A Restatement of Some Possible Extensions', *Journal of International Business Studies* 19(1), 1–29.

Gheasi, M., Nijkamp, P., and Rietveld, P. (2012). 'Migration and Foreign Direct Investment: Education Matters', *Annals of Regional Science* 51(1), 73–87.

Girma, S. and Görg, H. (2003). *Evaluating the Causal Effects of Foreign Acquisition on Domestic Skilled and Unskilled Wages*, Institute for the Study of Labor (IZA) Discussion Papers No. 903.

Haaland, J. I. and Wooton, I. (2007). 'Domestic Labour Markets and Foreign Direct Investment', *Review of International Economics* 15(3), 462–80.

Harris, R. and Robinson, C. (2002). 'The Effect of Foreign Acquisitions on Total Factor Productivity: Plant-Level Evidence from UK Manufacturing, 1987–1992', *Review of Economics and Statistics* 84(3), 562–8.

Hart, M., Driffield, N., Roper, S., and Mole, K. (2008). *Evaluation of Regional Selective Assistance (RSA) and Its Successor, Selective Finance for Investment in England (SFIE)*, BERR Occasional Paper No. 2.

HM Treasury (2003). *Pre-Budget Report: Appendix C—Flexibility in the UK Economy*. London: HM Treasury.

Javorcik B. S. (2004). 'Does Foreign Direct Investment Increase the Productivity of Domestic Firms? In Search of Spillovers through Backward Linkages', *American Economic Review* 94(3), 605–27.

Jones, J. and Wren, C. (2008). 'Foreign Inward Investment and Regional Prospects', *Northern Economic Review* 38, 61–79.

Love, J. H. (2003). 'Technology Sourcing Versus Technology Exploitation: An Analysis of US Foreign Direct Investment Flows', *Applied Economics* 35, 1667–78.

Love, J. H. and Lage-Hidalgo, F. (2000). 'Analysing the Determinants of US Direct Investment in Mexico', *Applied Economics* 32, 1259–67.

MIER (2009). Growing Indigenous and Domestic Investment in Manchester. Report for Manchester Independent Economic Review.

Morgan, K. (1997). 'The Learning Region: Institutions, Innovation and Regional Renewal', *Regional Studies* 31, 491–503.

Onodera, O. (2008). *Trade and Investment Project: A Synthesis Paper*, OECD Trade Policy Working Papers No. 72. Paris: OECD.

Pain, N. (1993). 'An Econometric Analysis of Foreign Direct Investment in the United Kingdom', *Scottish Journal of Political Economy* 40(1), 1–23.

Pain, N. and Lansbury, M. (1997). 'Regional Economic Integration and Foreign Direct Investment: The Case of German investment in Europe', *National Institute Economic Review* 160, 87–99.

Taylor, J. and Wren, C. (1997). 'UK Regional Policy: An Evaluation', *Regional Studies* 31(9), 835–48.

UKTI (2006). *Study of the Relative Economic Benefits of UK Trade and Investment Support for Trade and Inward Investment.* London: UKTI.

UKTI (2009). *UKTI Inward Investment Evaluation Case Studies: Final Report to UKTI*, SQW Consulting. London: UKTI.

UNCTAD (2007). Aftercare: A Core Function in Investment Promotion. Geneva: UNCTAD.

Wei, Y. and Balasubramanyam, V. N. (2006). 'Diaspora and Development', *The World Economy* 25(11), 1599–1609.

Wren, C. and Taylor, J. (1999). 'Industrial Restructuring and Regional Policy', *Oxford Economic Papers* 51, 487–516.

CHAPTER 18

....

TAKEOVERS AND TAKEOVER POLICY

....

AJIT SINGH, GURMAIL SINGH, DAVID BAILEY,
AND HELENA LENIHAN

18.1 INTRODUCTION

THIS chapter provides an overview of the literature on the market for corporate control and nature of takeovers before offering some suggestions as to how takeover policy might be developed in the UK context. The chapter first examines the dynamics of takeovers and mergers by charting six great historical takeover 'waves'. It examines why takeover waves exist and why they rise and fall. It then examines the market for corporate control in civil law and non-civil law countries before discussing the determinant of share prices, the market for corporate control, and nature of the takeover mechanism. It finishes by examining the recent debates on takeover policy in the UK stimulated by the Cadbury and AstraZeneca cases before offering some suggestions as to how takeover policy might be developed in the UK context, for example through 'throwing some sand' in the wheels of the takeover machine and through the adoption of a new 'Public Interest Test'.

18.2 THE DYNAMICS OF TAKEOVERS AND MERGERS: TAKEOVER WAVES

Most of the theoretical and empirical literature on mergers and acquisitions (M&A) is static in nature and focuses on the causes and consequences of takeovers. Very little evidence is available on its dynamics dimensions. This section presents available evidence from a historical perspective of the occurrence of merger waves over the last century and attempts to explain the emergence, rise, and demise of the merger waves. At the end, we shall appeal to Hyman Minsky's (1986 and 1992) 'Financial Instability Hypothesis' to explain the rise, boom, and busts of merger waves. It should be noted that takeovers are neither a random phenomenon nor a random walk. Rather, the most prominent feature of takeovers, revealed by the global empirical evidence over more than a century, is that acquisitions come in waves. The merger waves emphasize the dynamics of the takeover process. It is therefore surprising that this aspect of the subject has not been given greater attention in the literature. This chapter will help fill this lacuna.

Empirical evidence compiled by researchers (Jarrell et al., 1988; Bruner, 2002; Martynova and Renneboog, 2008) reveals that since the late nineteenth century the world has experienced six major takeover waves, and researchers visualize the formation of a powerful seventh wave since 2013. The first takeover wave (1890–1903) was confined to the United States, fuelled by radical changes in technology, the development of the New York Stock Exchange (NYSE), and legislation on incorporation, and was characterized by horizontal mergers leading to the formation of monopolies in basic manufacturing industries, dominated by textiles, steel, and hydraulic power. The second wave (1910–29) was again confined to the US and originated in the end of the First World War and the enforcement of anti-monopoly laws; it was characterized by fewer monopolies, more oligopolies, vertical mergers, and conglomerates in the primary metals, petroleum, chemicals, steel, and transportation industries. This wave ended in the 1929 stock market crash and the Great Depression.

The third takeover wave (1950–73), besides the US, included the UK and Europe and originated in the post-Second World War economic recovery and a tightening of the anti-trust regime; it was characterized by conglomerate mergers and equity-financed mergers in aerospace, electricity, industrial machinery, and railway equipment. The worldwide energy crisis of 1973, a crackdown on conglomerates, new legislation (such as the Williams Act and the Tax Reform Act), plus the stock market crash, ended the third wave.

The fourth takeover wave (1981–9), besides the US, UK and Europe, also extended to Asia and began with changes in anti-trust policy, the deregulation of the financial services sector, and technological breakthroughs in electronics, and was dominated by hostile mergers characterized as mega-mergers in petrochemicals (oil and gas and pharmaceuticals), electronics and communication, and aviation industries. The wave ended with financial institution reforms, the 1989 Recovery and Enforcement Act, anti-takeover legislation, the Gulf War, and a stock market crash. The fifth wave (1993–2001), also known as the 'strategic restructuring', was dominated by cross-border transactions and coincided with an economic and financial boom, liberalization, globalization, deregulation, and privatization, and was characterized by consolidation on path-breaking revolutionary changes in information and communication technology and banking industries. This fifth wave came to an end with the economic slowdown, the 9/11 attack, and another stock market crash.

The sixth takeover wave (2003–7) began with the global economic recovery and was characterized by cross-border mega-mergers and a preference for friendly negotiations over aggressive hostile takeovers across steel, pharmaceuticals, banks, and airline industries. The wave witnessed the joining of Indian and Chinese companies in some of the biggest cross-border deals (Tata Steel–Corus; Arcelor–Mittal; and IBM–Lenovo as examples). The wave ended with the onset of the sub-prime lending crisis at the end of 2007 and consequent stock market crash, and in global recession.

These six waves exhibit distinct characteristics and underlying motives rendering each wave different from its predecessor wave. Nonetheless, some common characteristics run through all of these waves. First, takeovers generally occurred in periods of economic recovery. Second, the waves coincided with rapid credit expansion and ended with the crash of the stock markets. Third, takeover waves were often driven by industrial and technological shocks like technological and industrial innovations, and foreign competition. Fourth, takeovers were frequently fuelled by regulatory changes such as anti-trust legislation, liberalization, deregulation, and globalization.

18.3 WHY WAVES?

Major external economic, technological, financial, regulatory, and political shocks no doubt coincide with the emergence and demise of takeover waves, but these events are not adequate to fully understand why acquisition deals swell, peak, and tumble so dramatically. Researchers put forth various explanations to understand why the frequency of mergers and acquisitions greatly increases at a particular point in time. The main hypotheses in this context are: the q-theory hypothesis, the industrial shock hypothesis, the managerial discretion hypothesis, and the overvaluation hypothesis. The first two are based on neoclassical assumptions of managers maximizing shareholders' wealth and capital market efficiency, whereas the latter two are characterized as behavioural, in that these relax the neoclassical assumption of market efficiency.

On the first hypothesis, Jovanovic and Rousseau (2002) extended Tobin's q-theory of investment to merger waves. They argued that the wave pattern is due to technological shocks generating the profitability of the investment, leading to an increase in many firms' Tobin's qs (the ratio between the market value and replacement value). Firms with rising qs can expand profitably by acquiring other firms. Consequently, technological shock generates a stock market boom and merger wave. The q-hypothesis, however, permits only horizontal mergers and also does not synchronize with the empirical observation of lesser merger frequency in unlisted companies compared with listed ones, even though the major technological event made merger equally profitable for both of them. On the second hypothesis, Mitchell and Mulherin (1996) and Harford (2005), in their 'industrial shock hypothesis', assume numerous different technological, regulatory, and other forms of shocks. These industry-specific shocks require a large-scale reallocation of assets and raise the merger profitability in the specific industry. A clustering of merger waves in a number of industries simultaneously aggregates into an economy-wide merger wave. Harford (2005) further argued that these shocks as such are not enough. There must be adequate liquidity in the economy for a shock to accommodate asset reallocation and to propagate a wave. Like the q-theory, the industrial shock hypothesis also fails to identify waves in unlisted companies.

The managerial behaviour (managerial hubris and herding behaviour) theories posit that the increased optimism in the equity market leads to a boom in the stock market. The managerial discretion hypothesis by Marris (1964) and Mueller (1969) recognizes the principal–agent conflict between managers and shareholders. Managers are assumed to sacrifice profit to size and the growth of their firms (Gugler et al., 2012). This is mainly due to the fact that either their own income is tied to the growth of their firms, or they drive to acquire 'psychic income' from managing a bigger firm. The thesis claims that the increased optimism, a boom in the share prices, and cash flow tend to reduce the constraints on managers in pursuing their goal of high growth and/or bigger size through mergers, thereby permitting them to undertake wealth-destroying mergers. The overvaluation theory of mergers assumes that some firms' share prices are overvalued during stock market booms (Shleifer and Vishny, 2003). Aware of overvaluation and wishing to protect their shareholders from future downslides, managers of these firms exchange their overvalued shares for the real assets of another company. Merger waves occur as the number of overvalued companies peaks during a stock market boom. Yet why do target managers accept overvalued shares? Rhodes-Kropf and Viswanathan (2004) proposed that it becomes difficult for the target managers to judge whether the high premium is due to over-optimism or due to expected merger synergies, and thus they become willing partners in mergers. Both of these behavioural theories are consistent with the higher frequency of mergers in companies listed on the stock market. However, none of them fully explains all types of merger waves (Gugler and Yurtoglu, 2008; Gugler et al., 2012).

18.4 WHY DO WAVES RISE AND FALL?

Major external economic, technological, financial, regulatory, and political shocks no doubt coincide with the emergence and demise of takeover waves, but these events are not adequate to fully understand why acquisition deals swell, peak, and tumble so dramatically. Clark and Mills (2013) argue that merger waves have four distinct phases, which are frequently manifestations of changing business confidence. During the first phase, the economy is not in good shape, business morale is low, and only a few deals are struck. In the second phase, the improving economy makes finance available, deals pick up albeit slowly as most deals are still regarded as risky, thus scaring away less confident buyers. In the third phase, activity accelerates sharply and the takeover boom is legitimized; this in turn builds the overconfidence of chief executives and the takeover wave enters its fourth phase. This is when the number of acquirers willing to pay the takeover price rises rapidly. Besides explaining the rise and fall of waves, the phase analysis explains temporal variations in the acquisition premium in a particular wave. Evidence suggests that the bid premium in the first phase averaged 10–18 per cent, rising to 20–35 per cent in the second phase, to over 50 per cent in the third phase, and to a catastrophically frothy premium above 100 per cent in the fourth phase. The chances of a profitable marriage, Clark and Mills (2013) argue, fall significantly once the target premium exceeds 40 per cent.

Clark and Mills' (2013) rationalization of the rise and fall of takeover waves is analogous to Minsky's 'Financial Instability Hypothesis'. Minsky (1986 and 1992) envisaged that the financial system swings between stability and fragility and that the booms and busts that accompany them are endogenous to unregulated market economies. He argued that the mechanism of crisis mainly lies in the accumulation of debt by the non-government sector, the division of ownership and management of big corporations and financial institutions, financial innovations, ever-growing and massive debt financing of uncertain projects, and fundamental uncertainty. He distinguishes three types of borrowers in this context: hedge borrowers, speculative borrowers, and 'Ponzi' borrowers. The hedge borrowers can pay their debt liabilities (both interest and principal) from their current cash flows, whereas the speculative borrowers' cash flow from investment can only service the debt and they have to borrow to re-borrow and roll over the principal. For the 'Ponzi' borrowers, the cash flow from operations is not sufficient to make interest payments or the repayment of principal, as their borrowing operations are based on the belief that the appreciation in the value of assets will be adequate to refinance the debt and keep them afloat.

Over the protracted period of good time, it is argued, the financial structure in market economies moves from hedgers to speculators and Ponzi units and the system transits from stable to unstable stages. This happens specifically when an economy with a substantial proportion of speculative borrowers is in an inflationary state and the attempt of the monetary authority to exert control leads to the end of rising asset prices. Consequently, many speculative borrowers are unable to refinance and become Ponzi units, and the net worth of previous Ponzi borrowers evaporates. Subsequently, the baton of the crisis passes on from speculators to the hedge borrowers and the situation ultimately leads to the collapse of asset values under an unsustainable level of debt burden.

In the context of takeovers and mergers, Minsky's hedge borrowers are akin to the acquisition firms paying target premiums of up to 40 per cent (the first two waves); speculator borrowers to acquiring firms paying target premium in the range of 40–100 per cent (third wave); and Ponzi units to those acquiring firms who pay target premiums exceeding 100 per cent. In Minsky's progression of three stages of borrowers, the sequencing and transition of merger waves from the first phase to the fourth takes the stock market from stable to boom and from boom to busts of takeover waves. Minsky's hypothesis is also in line with empirical observations by Kolev et al. (2012, p. 35) that 'early movers fare better than later movers in merger waves'.

18.5 THE MARKET FOR CORPORATE CONTROL IN CIVIL LAW AND NON-CIVIL LAW COUNTRIES

The above analysis of takeover waves has not yet led to any startling theoretical, empirical, or policy results. These waves are nevertheless important to the takeover process and the function of the market for corporate control. This section will discuss the issue of the market for corporate control in civil law and non-civil law countries. The main argument of this section is that support for an active market for corporate control is neither a core principle of company law nor an essential argument of financial and economic development.[1] As Deakin and Singh (2009, pp. 4–6) observe:

> Too close a focus on the supposed efficiency of prevailing institutions is liable to make us forget the often tortuous and uneven path by which they came to acquire their apparent dominance. Britain's industrial revolution took place during a period when few businesses enjoyed limited liability. In the US, many states allowed personal claims to be brought against shareholders for corporate debts late into the nineteenth century and some, including California, into the twentieth. Yet corporate law scholars today assert that limited liability and the positioning of corporate from personal assets are essential parts of the legal 'bedrock' supporting enterprise... This view arguably ascribes 'survival value' to institutions whose endurance may have more to do with historical contingency than efficiency... Is the same true of today's norm of shareholder value?
>
> It is surprisingly difficult to find support within our company law for the notion of shareholder primacy. It cannot be found by referring to the rhetorical claim, associated with today's pension funds and other institutional investors, that shareholders 'own the company'. No legal system acknowledges the claims that shareholders 'own the company'. If we understand the company to be the fictive legal entity which is brought into being through the act of incorporation, it is not clear in what sense such a thing could be 'owned' by anyone. But more pertinently, nor does the ownership of a share entitle its holder to a particular segment or portion of the company's assets, at least while it is a going concern...
>
> It is important to note, the law on directors' duties is no more helpful. In the English-law based common law systems, with only a few exceptions, directors' fiduciary interests of loyalty and care are owed to the company, not directly to the shareholders. In practice, the company's 'interests' will often be synonymous with those of its members, that is, the shareholders. However, shareholders are not entitled to engage directly in the management of the enterprise; this is the responsibility of the board. According to Delaware corporate law, 'the business and affairs of every corporation... shall be managed by or under the direction of a board of directors'... Many of the formative cases of English company law, dating from the nineteenth and early twentieth centuries, make the same point. (Deakin and Singh, 2009)

---

[1] This subsection of the paper is based on Deakin and Singh (2009), which is revised and reviewed here.

Deakin and Singh (2009, p. 6) go on to say:

> The proposed statement of directors' duties requires directors to act in the collective best interests of shareholders, but recognizes that this can only be achieved by taking due account of wider interests. The transparency element provides the information needed to underpin this approach to governance. Just as importantly, we believe that [a] wider reporting requirement—particularly for large companies—will be an important contribution to competitiveness. Companies are increasingly reliant on qualitative and intangible, or 'soft' assets such as the skills and knowledge of their employees and their corporate reputation. The reporting framework must recognize this and ensure that companies provide the market and other interests with the information they need to understand their companies' business and assess performance.

More broadly, it should be noted that Section 172 of the Companies Act 2006, which is headed the 'Duty to promote the interests of the company', now provides that:

(1) A director of a company must act in the way he considers, in good faith, would be most likely to promote the success of the company for the benefit of its members as a whole...
(2) In fulfilling the duty imposed by this section a director must (so far as reasonably practicable) have regard to:
   (a) The likely consequences of any decision in the long term,
   (b) The interests of the company's employees,
   (c) The need to foster the company's business relationships with suppliers, customers and others,
   (d) The impact of the company's operations on the community and the environment,
   (e) The desirability of the company maintaining a high reputation for high standards of business conduct, and
   (f) The need to act fairly as between the members of the company.

18.6 THE DETERMINATION OF SHARE PRICES

The orthodox paradigm of share price determination postulates that share prices are efficient because they emanate from perfect markets involving large numbers of well-informed buyers and sellers in which no one buyer or seller can influence the price and where there is a homogenous product, namely shares. There is, however, an alternative paradigm indicated by the quotation from Keynes cited earlier that characterizes stock markets essentially as gambling casinos dominated by speculators. Stiglitz (1994), Allen and Gale (2001), Shiller (2001), Baker and Wurgler (2007), Hong and Stein (2007), and not least students of behavioural finance (see for example Barberis, Huang, and Thaler, 2006) formalize the various elements of this paradigm. In brief, this literature suggests that, in the face of a highly uncertain future, share prices are likely to be influenced by the so-called 'noise traders' and by whims, fads, and contagion. For similar reasons of psychology, investors may attribute much greater weight to near-term price forecasts rather than historical long-term performance. This line of reasoning is taken further in the growing literature on behavioural finance.

Until recently, the empirical literature on share prices was dominated by the so-called 'efficient markets hypothesis' (EMH), which argues that real world share prices are efficient in the sense that they incorporate all available information (Fama, 1970). In the 1970s, evidence in favour of this hypothesis was thought to be overwhelming, with enthusiasts regarding it as the best-documented hypothesis throughout the social sciences (Jensen, 1978). In the 1980s and 1990s, with (a) the 1987 stock market crash, (b) the meltdown in the Asian stock markets in the 1990s, and (c) the bursting of the technology stocks bubble in 2000, the EMH suffered fundamental setbacks. Alan Greenspan (1998) commented as follows on the reasons for (a) and (b): 'At one point the economic system appears stable, the next it behaves as though a dam has reached breaking point, and water (read confidence) evacuates the reservoir. The United States experiences such a sudden change with the decline in stock prices of more than 20 percent on October 19, 1987. There is no credible scenario that can readily explain so abrupt a change in the fundamentals of long-term valuations on that one day...' But why do these events seem to erupt without some readily evident precursors? Certainly, the more extended the risk taking, or more generally the lower the discount factors applied to future outcomes, the more vulnerable are markets to a shock that abruptly triggers a revision in expectations and sets off a vicious cycle of contraction. Episodes of vicious cycles cannot be easily forecast, as our recent experience with Asia has demonstrated. Kindleberger and Aliber (1989) similarly documented about thirty cases of unwarranted euphoria and excessive pessimism on the stock markets since the South Sea bubble of 1720. He termed these episodes manias, panics, and crashes.

Tobin (1984) made an analytically useful distinction between two kinds of efficiency of stock markets: (a) the information arbitrage efficiency that ensures that all information concerning a firm's shares immediately percolates to all stock markets participants, ensuring that no participant can make a profit on such public information; (b) fundamental valuation efficiency, that is, share prices accurately reflect a firm's fundamentals, namely the long-term expected profitability. The growing consensus view is that, in these terms, stock markets may at best be regarded as being efficient in the sense of (a) but far from being efficient in the economically more important sense of (b). Thus EMH, as identified in (a), is compatible with share prices not reflecting fundamental values.

The latter proposition may be illustrated by considering the case of the recent dot-com boom and burst in the US. The main stock market for technology company shares there is NASDAQ. In 1995, the value of the NASDAQ index was 1052.1; by 1998, it doubled to 2192.7; in the next twelve months, it nearly doubled again to 4069.3 on December 31 1999. At its peak in March 2000, the value of the index was 5063.3. Over the following three years, NASDAQ crashed to 1335.5, less than a quarter of its value at the peak. This pattern of share price movement on NASDAQ looks *prima facie* like a classical share price bubble, followed by a bust. These prices could not be efficient in the fundamental valuation sense, simultaneously both at the top of the boom and in the trough. This is because there was little evidence of a change of the required magnitude in the economic fundamentals during this period. True, the US economy had a trend increase in long-term productivity growth rate, but there were no dramatic changes in the growth of corporate earnings and dividends. While the share prices soared, the latter continued to expand at their normal, far slower pace (Shiller, 2001).

A more detailed discussion, as well as other examples of share prices evidently departing from their fundamentals, is provided in Singh et al. (2005). It is generally accepted that such mis-pricing of shares is a common occurrence on the stock market and it may persist for a considerable period, some would say for as long as ten to twenty years. The Nikkei stock market index in Japan reached a value of approximately 38,000 in the mid-1980s. Over twenty-five years later, it has not recovered to even half the 1980s value. Evidence suggests a share price bubble on the Tokyo stock market in the mid-1980s. Similarly, UK and US stock markets did not recover to their pre-Great Depression index values until the mid-1950s. To sum up, analyses and evidence suggest that the average firm share prices may depart from the fundamentals for prolonged periods. Many friends of the stock market, while acknowledging the likelihood of mis-pricing, suggest that the latter persists only for three or four years rather than ten or twenty (Jensen, 2005).

18.7 THE TAKEOVER MECHANISM AND THE MARKET FOR CORPORATE CONTROL

The market for corporate control is thought to be the evolutionary end point of stock market development. The ability of an outside group of investors to acquire a corporation, often through a hostile bid, is the hallmark of the stock market-dominated US and UK financial systems. The textbook interpretation of takeovers is that they improve efficiency by transferring corporate assets to those who can manage them more productively. Consequently, more effective managers emerge who can raise the firm's profitability and share price. Even if current managers are not replaced, an active market for corporate control presents a credible threat that inefficient managers will be replaced and thus ensures that the incumbent management is 'kept on its toes' and actively seeks to maximize shareholder value and thereby raises corporate performance. Even if quoted firms are not directly susceptible to changes in share prices because they finance themselves almost exclusively from internal finance (as the pecking order theory implies), the market for corporate control can still discipline managers. Furthermore, even if all firms are on the efficiency frontier, the amalgamation of some through the act of takeovers may lead to a better social allocation of resources via synergy, it is argued.

However, a critical school has developed a multifaceted critique that has increasingly questioned the above textbook version of the market for corporate control. Firstly, a number of analysts in the critical school have pointed out that in the real world the market for corporate control, even in advanced economies, has an inherent flaw in its operation: it is far easier for a large firm to take over a small one than the other way round (Singh, 1971, 1975; Singh and Hamid, 1992). In principle, while it is possible that a small, efficient firm may take over a larger and less efficient company (and to a degree this occurred in the US takeover wave of the 1980s through 'junk bonds'), its incidence is very small (Cosh and Hughes, 1989). In a takeover battle, it is the absolute firepower (absolute size) that counts rather than the relative efficiency. Therefore, the development of an active market for corporate control may encourage managers to 'empire-build' not only to increase their monopoly power, but also to progressively shield themselves from takeover by becoming larger (see Singh, 1975, 1992).

Secondly, the efficient operation of the takeover mechanism requires that enormous amounts of information are widely available. Specifically, market participants require information on the profitability of corporations under their existing management and what their prospective profitability would be under an alternative management if they were taken over. It has been noted that such information is not easily available even in advanced countries, and this informational deficit is likely to be greater in developing countries.

Thirdly, takeovers are a very expensive way of changing management (Peacock and Bannock, 1991). There are huge transactions costs associated with takeovers in countries like the US and UK which hinder the efficiency of the takeover mechanism. It should also be borne in mind that highly successful countries such as Japan, Germany, and France have not had an active market for corporate control and have thus avoided these costs, while still maintaining systems for disciplining managers. Furthermore, there is no evidence that corporate governance necessarily improves after takeovers. This is for the simple reason that all takeovers are not disciplinary; in many of them the acquiring firm is motivated by empire-building considerations or even by asset-stripping.

Fourthly, there is theoretical work (see for example Stein, 1989) which suggests that even if managers wish to maximize shareholder wealth, it would pay them to be myopic in a world of takeovers and signal-jamming. Thus, takeovers could exacerbate the already present tendencies towards short-termism in a stock market-based system.

Fifthly, it has been argued that takeovers can be used as a device to avoid honouring implicit contracts developed between workers and the former management (Shleifer and Summers, 1988). This abandonment of implicit contracts can be argued to be socially harmful in that it discourages the accumulation of firm-specific human capital by workers. The absence of strong worker-protection laws in many developing countries means that such considerations may be significant.

In view of the foregoing considerations, it is not surprising that although there exists a very active market for corporate control in the major Anglo-Saxon countries, it is seriously inefficient. Two kinds of evidence support this conclusion. Firstly, studies of the takeover selection process indicate that selection in the market for corporate control takes place only to a limited extent on the basis of the target firm's performance and much more so on the basis of its size. A large, relatively unprofitable firm has a much smaller chance of being acquired than a small, profitable firm. Secondly, controlling for other relevant variables, studies of post-merger profitability of amalgamating firms indicate that there is at best no improvement on average in post-merger profits but most likely a decline (Ravenscraft and Scherer, 1987; Singh, 1992; Tichy, 2002; Pallazo and Scherer, 2006).[2] To the extent that an increase in market power is associated with mergers, the lack of such an increase suggests a microeconomic inefficiency in resource utilization, certainly not an improvement.

A related set of financial studies, so-called 'event studies', also suggests that in US takeovers the acquiring firms suffer a sizeable decline in share prices in the period of six months to three years following the merger. The gainers are mainly the acquired firms, whose share prices may rise by up to 20 per cent on average (Jensen, 1988). This poses serious incentive problems as potential acquiring firms stand to lose rather than to gain. Equally importantly, in order to classify these gains to the shareholders of acquired firms as being social gains, the analysis has to assume that share prices are always efficient in the fundamental valuation sense, which, as indicated above, is far from being the case. The rise in the share price of the acquired firm may reflect simply the price for control which empire builders are willing to pay, even to the detriment of their own share-holders (Singh and Weisse, 2000).

Furthermore, a priori analysis as well as evidence indicates that in practice the imper-fections of the pricing and the takeover processes together may lead to 'short-termism' on the part of corporate managements. This is reflected in the fact that the latter are obliged to fulfil the market analysts' short-term (quarterly or six-monthly) expectations of the firms' earnings per share (Cosh et al., 1990). Evidence suggests that if such short-term targets are not met, there is a fall in share prices, making the firm *ceteris paribus* vulnerable to takeover.

The existence of takeover mechanisms not only induces short-termism but also, as Jensen (2005) emphasizes, a change in the culture and operations of the corporations, leading to such pathological cases as Enron and WorldCom. Jensen (2005) seeks to explain the 'forces' bearing on the many firms who experienced large rises in share prices and subsequent declines during the ICT bubble in 2000. He blames the mis-pricing of shares which is ubiquitous in stock markets on deficiencies in corporate governance, and regards overvalued equity as being a bigger problem than undervalued equity (Jensen, 2005). In so doing, Jensen (2005) notes that although the market for corporate control could solve the problem of undervalued equity, it cannot solve the agency prob-lems of overvalued equity; 'this is because it is difficult to buy-up an overvalued com-pany, eliminate its overvalue and make a profit'. He cites many examples of subsequent value destruction because of overvaluation of equity by analysts, stock brokers, and others during the stock market euphoria.

---

[2] There has been a vast amount of research on this subject, particularly for the UK and US economies. See also Meeks (1977), who came to the conclusion that there was either no changing profitability due to takeovers or a decline. He called for a more stringent policy towards mergers. Cowling et al. (1980) came to the conclusion that efficiency is rarely increased by mergers but is actually often reduced.

18.8 AFTER CADBURY: CURRENT DEBATES AND POLICY OPTIONS IN THE UK CONTEXT

The 2010 takeover of Cadbury by the larger US-based food conglomerate Kraft raised a number of concerns which link with the wider academic literature examined above on the nature of the takeover process, in the UK context (House of Commons, 2010). Cadbury had a strong record on investment and corporate social responsibility and was seen as an 'efficient' company with little need for a change in management (Bailey and Clancy, 2010). Yet after a lengthy period of vulnerability during which Cadbury was seen as 'in play', the much larger Kraft conglomerate succeeded in acquiring Cadbury after a protracted hostile bid process. During the 'end game' hostile bid, the offer bid was increased from around £10.2 billion to £11.5bn, with a significant 'bid premium' offered. So as to win over support, Kraft's Chief Executive Irene Rosenfeld made various 'assurances', including that of keeping open Cadbury's Somerdale plant. After the completion of the takeover, it was almost immediately announced that the factory would be closed and production shifted—as previously planned by Cadbury—to Poland (Bailey and Clancy, 2010). While then Secretary of State for Business, Innovation and Skills Lord Mandelson protested over the takeover, he had no legal power on which to intervene, as powers had been effectively removed in 2002, as will be seen below. In a telling comment in the *Financial Times*, Hutton and Blond (2010) noted that 'the current regime is a charter for a great sell-off of British assets. The rules of the game are tilted to favour hostile takeovers. Too many great UK companies have disappeared.'

The Cadbury takeover led to reviews by the Takeover Panel (2011), the Department for Business, Skills and Innovation (BIS, 2011), the House of Commons BIS Select Committee in the House of Commons (House of Commons, 2010), as well as catalysing the later Kay (2012) and Cox (2013) reviews. The Kay Review (2012), for example, was critical of the UK's takeover regime but only went as far as to suggest a number of measures to improve trust and to encourage more shareholder engagement. Such measures would not pass a 'Cadbury Test' in the sense of having enabled Cadbury to defend itself from the hostile takeover. There were calls from some within Labour and Liberal Democrat ranks for the reinsertion of a more general public interest test, although at the time this was rejected by Lord Mandelson. Similarly, the Conservative–Liberal Democrat Coalition government from 2010 rejected calls for change, notably in response to Lord Heseltine's (2013) 'No Stone Unturned' report which had suggested that the government could use powers in the Enterprise Act 2002 to 'allow ministers to consider takeovers and mergers to ensure our long-term industrial capabilities are given proper consideration', with the government acting 'in exceptional cases to discourage unwanted investments'. The Coalition government firmly rejected the idea and opposed any substantive change, including the introduction of a wider public interest test (BIS, 2012). The only changes undertaken have been cosmetic changes in terms of how self-regulation by the Takeover Panel works.

Just a few years after the Kraft takeover of Cadbury, the proposed takeover of British pharma giant AstraZeneca in 2014 by the US-based Pfizer again stimulated a debate over takeovers. This time, the £63bn offer would have made this the largest-ever foreign takeover of a British company. Despite not going ahead, as AstraZeneca stood firm against the takeover bid, the proposed takeover was illustrative on a number of levels. Firstly, even members of the Conservative–Liberal Democrat Coalition government realized that AstraZeneca had 'strategic' value, being the second-biggest UK pharma company. At the time of the takeover bid, Astra employed 6,700 workers and accounted for 2.3 per cent of British exports, investing some £2.8bn in research and development. That 'strategic' value had a degree of resonance in the context of a government claiming to want to 'rebalance' the economy.

Secondly, the takeover bid was also unusual in that the usual pattern did not hold. Usually the story went something like this: the board of the target firm plays 'hard to get', driving up the offer price; eventually the 'white flag' goes up and shareholders approve the deal. The bid may be considered by competition agencies in the UK and Brussels but usually is not blocked. Rather, it will be waved through, in main part because the government has no legal power at all to intervene even if it wanted to, other than on competition grounds. Some so-called 'assurances' may be given by the bidding firm as a political escape valve for the government. These are usually forgotten about as soon as the takeover is completed, and will anyway never be monitored by the government (Bailey et al., 1994). On this, defenders of the status quo and free markets argue that governments anyway do not have the necessary skills to intervene in such cases and are bad at 'picking winners'; 'leave it to the market' is the usual refrain. But that all ignores the evidence presented in earlier sections of this chapter; for example, numerous studies have shown that most big takeovers fail to deliver benefits, even for shareholders. As seen, after takeover, profits often stay the same or go down, despite huge amounts having been spent on the acquisition.

As a 2013 Policy Network report has highlighted, takeovers in the UK are more common, more likely to be hostile, and more likely to go ahead than in any other major economy (Davis et al., 2013). Evidence suggests that a significant proportion of takeover activity is not beneficial to the creation of long-term shareholder value, the industrial base, the national economy, or society as a whole. In addition, as seen in the case of the Kraft takeover of Cadbury, shareholders are increasingly driven by short-term value. It was hedge funds buying up Cadbury shares on a 'one-way bet' which in part helped undermine long-term shareholder commitment, in turn pushing up the share price, before voting for the takeover and then 'cashing out' at a profit once the deal was done (Bailey and Clancy, 2010).

Meanwhile, as noted, the situation is rather different elsewhere, where governments are much more likely to intervene. The French government often intervenes in takeovers it does not see as in the national interest (Bailey et al., 1994), the GE bid for Alstom in 2014 being the most recent case. A usual tactic is to slow things down to find a French 'white knight'. Similarly, in 2010 the Canadian government stopped a proposed takeover by BHP Billiton of a Canadian mining firm, the Potash Corporation, with the Canadian industry minister stating that he was unconvinced that a BHP Billiton takeover would create a 'significant net improvement in the level and nature of economic activity', which is a key test required under the Investment Canada Act. In the UK, however, the government has been reducing the power to intervene. A key change came under the Labour government's 2002 Enterprise Act, which critically removed the Public Interest Test from examining such takeovers (except in relation to defence, the media, water companies, and—added later—with regard to financial stability). Politicians now seem willing to re-examine the merits of such a test, having previously rejected change.

Even those against outright government intervention via such a test might note that takeovers—especially hostile ones—are anyway often more difficult in other countries (as seen above). For example, in the US, firms can use 'poison pill' defences to resist corporate raiders, while in Germany the key threshold for gaining control is 75 per cent, not 50.1 per cent as in the UK. Meanwhile, in Japan, the prevalence of cross shareholdings make hostile takeovers very difficult. So even without direct government intervention, takeovers are more difficult anyway because of institutional arrangements. The Kraft takeover of Cadbury changed perceptions in this regard and it now appears that a wider range of actors are converging on some sort of rule change—witness Lord Heseltine's intervention on AstraZeneca in 2014. That could involve reforms on a number of levels so as to promote greater long-term commitment and give defending firms a greater degree of protection from hostile takeover.

The first two sets of reforms could change the broader environment within which takeovers occur. A first set of reforms could amend the tax system and wider financial system so to promote more long-term commitment amongst investors. For example, capital gains tax and dividend tax could be tapered with each year that shares are held (Cox, 2013), thus reducing the incentives for hedge funds to buy up shares in takeover situations then 'cash out' on completion of the takeover. In addition, quarterly reporting could be eliminated and changes could be made to codes of governance so as to ensure that long-term incentives are central in executive pay deals (Cox, 2013). Similarly, more committed shareholding might be encouraged by only allowing dividend payments after a minimum period of shareholding (Bootle, 2009). Finally, a financial transactions—or Tobin—tax could reduce the amount of speculative financial activity while also offering the possibility of raising revenue (Cosh et al., 1990; see also Sawyer, Chapter 6, this volume). A second set of reforms could make changes to the wider nature of corporate governance. These might involve, for example, better provision for employee representation on the boards of companies, in line with a 'German model', so that workers have a say in takeover situations, as well as the reform of the ownership of companies and a broadening of the scope of directors' obligations.

Turning to the nature of takeovers directly, a third set of reforms could involve 'throwing some sand in the wheels' of the takeover machine via significant changes to the Takeover Code. These could involve, for example, raising the 'bar' in takeover situations (for example, raising the threshold for gaining control to two-thirds of shareholders rather than 50.1 per cent) and only allowing longer-term shareholders (who have held shares in the firm for at least a year) to have a vote in takeover situations. Taken together, these two changes may have been enough to enable Cadbury to remain independent, and could have a useful impact in giving target firms a greater degree of protection from hostile bids without preventing such takeovers completely.

Finally, a fourth set of reforms could reactivate a form of the Public Interest Test which was largely abolished in 2002.[3] This new test could be applied by reference to a statutory list of factors, in a manner similar to that adopted for the key duties of a company director as defined in Section 172 of the 2006 Companies Act. What remains of the public interest test could be retained and built upon, for example extending the scope of the test to utilities beyond water, banks, national security (as in the United States), and key areas of infrastructure (see Davis et al., 2013). A wider interpretation of the 'public interest' would need to be redeployed, going beyond pure competition grounds. On takeovers, the requirement would be on bidders and targets (where a takeover had been agreed) to effectively demonstrate that the proposed takeover took into account a range of factors. In line with Davis et al. (2013), these might comprise the longer-term financial sustainability of the company, as well as commitments to growth, research and development, retaining core assets, and to other stakeholders (such as employees, suppliers, the local community, and environment). Whatever the precise mix of factors, a range of indicators could be developed to test takeovers, with the Public Interest Test triggered in cases where any takeover was over a certain threshold size, whether in terms of value, employment, and/or market share, and would not be targeted at foreign takeovers per se.

In order to avoid risks of 'picking winners' and the waste of resources on lobbying, such a public interest test would not be applied by existing regulator bodies or the Secretary of State.[4] A number of options exist in terms of institutional arrangements around such a test, such as setting up a new Public Interest Commission independent of the existing Takeover Panel and Competition and Markets Authority (CMA), or replacing the Takeover Panel with a larger body with public interest responsibilities, or a revised CMA with powers to investigate on public interest issues (Davis et al., 2013). Whichever path is taken, the composition and remit of the new body could be underpinned by statute and have a wider balance of stakeholders, including shareholders and investment companies, business representatives, and employee and consumer organizations.

Overall, reforms to the nature of the Takeover Code (raising the bar and limiting voting rights to longer-tem shareholders), along with the reintroduction of a new Public Interest Test, would have the effect of throwing some sand in the wheels of the takeover machine to mitigate against the negative effects of an overly active market for corporate control and to better protect long-term stakeholders.

---

[3] There are, of course, a number of criticisms of such an approach. Lord Mandelson argued against bringing back a Public Interest test in 2010 as this would be seen as protectionist and as anti-foreign investment. Such concerns were echoed by Vince Cable in 2012 in rejecting Lord Heseltine's takeover proposals in 'No Stone Unturned'. These are countered by Davis et al. (2013).

[4] Cowling and Sawyer (1990) argued that to avoid wasted resources on such lobbying, mergers over a certain size should simply be prohibited. Given that this is highly unlikely in the current environment, we instead argue for a range of reforms that minimize such risks while also serving to reduce the probability of takeovers and their negative effects.

18.9 CONCLUSIONS

This chapter has provided an overview of the literature on the market for corporate control and nature of takeovers before offering some suggestions as to how takeover policy might be developed in the UK context. The chapter first examined the dynamics of takeovers and mergers by charting six great historical takeover 'waves'. It argues that the world today is on the verge of another gigantic takeover movement which is likely to do more harm than good to the competitive process and international economy. The chapter went on to examine why takeover waves exist, and why they rise and fall. The latter discussion was followed by an examination of the market for corporate control in civil law and non-civil law countries, the determinant of share prices, and the market for corporate control and nature of the takeover mechanism.

As has been explored throughout this chapter, a multifaceted critique has developed which has increasingly questioned the textbook version of the market for corporate control. This critique has, for example, stressed that in the real world, the market for corporate control has an inherent flaw in its operation in that it is far easier for a large firm to take over a small one than the other way round. Therefore, the development of an active market for corporate control may encourage managers to 'empire-build', not only to increase their monopoly power but also to progressively shield themselves from takeover by becoming larger. In addition, there is no evidence that corporate governance necessarily improves after takeover. This is for the simple reason that all takeovers are not disciplinary; in fact, in many of them the acquiring firm is motivated by empire-building considerations or even by asset-stripping. Furthermore, even if managers wish to maximize shareholder wealth, it would pay them to be myopic in a world of takeovers and signal-jamming. Thus, takeovers could exacerbate the already present tendencies towards short-termism in a stock market-based system.

Given such failures, the market for corporate control in the major Anglo-Saxon countries can be seen as being seriously inefficient. This is backed up by evidence on the takeover selection process and studies of post-merger profitability of amalgamating firms (which indicate that there is at best no improvement on average in post-merger profits but most likely a decline) as well as studies suggesting that acquiring firms suffer a sizeable decline in share prices post-merger. Furthermore, a priori analysis as well as evidence indicates that in practice the imperfections of the pricing and the takeover processes together may lead to 'short-termism' on the part of corporate managements.

It is in such a context that the chapter ended by examining the recent debates on takeover policy stimulated by the Cadbury and AstraZeneca cases before offering some suggestions as to how takeover policy might be developed in the UK context. We suggest reforms across four broad areas: by reforms to the tax system and financial system to encourage longer-term commitment; by broader corporate governance changes; by amendments to the Takeover Code to give greater protection to defending firms, such as through 'raising the bar'; and finally, through the reinsertion of a Public Interest Test to policy to enable an independent body to examine the public interest impact of takeovers above certain thresholds. Taken together, we argue that such measures could 'throw some sand' in the wheels of an inefficient and costly takeover machine.

References

Allen, F. and Gale, D. (2001). *Comparing Financial Systems*. Cambridge, MA: MIT Press.

Bailey, D. and Clancy, J. (2010). *Blogs from the Blackstuff*, vol. 1: *The Case for Rewiring the Economy*. Birmingham: Fifth Way Press.

Bailey, D., Harte, G., and Sugden, R. (1994). *Transnationals and Governments: Recent Government Policies in Japan, France, the United States, Germany and Britain*. London: Routledge.

Baker, M. and Wurgler, J. (2007). 'Investor Sentiment in the Stock Market', *Journal of Economic Perspectives* 21(2), 129–51.

Barberis, N., Huang, M., and Thaler, R. H. (2006). 'Individual Preferences, Monetary Gambles, and Stock Market Participation: A Case for Narrow Framing', *American Economic Review* 96(4), 1069–90.

BIS (Department of Business, Innovation and Skills) (2011). *Consultation on Failures in Corporate Governance and the Markets: Response*. London: Department of Business, Skills and Innovation.

BIS (Department of Business, Innovation and Skills) (2012). *Growth, Competition and the Competition Regime: Government Response to Consultation*. London: Department of Business, Skills and Innovation.

Bootle, R. (2009). *The Trouble with Markets: Saving Capitalism From Itself*. London: Nicholas Brealey.

Bruner, R. F. (2002). 'Does M&A Pay? A Survey of Evidence for the Decision-Maker', *Journal of Applied Finance* 12, 48–68.

Clark, P. J. and Mills, R. W. (2013). *Masterminding the Deal: Breakthroughs in M&A Strategy and Analysis*. London: Kogan Page.

Cosh, A. and Hughes, A. (1989). *Ownership, Management Incentives and Company Performance: An Empirical Analysis for the UK 1968–80*. Melbourne: La Trobe University School of Economics.

Cosh, A., Hughes, A., and Singh, A. (1990). *Takeovers and Short-Termism in the UK*. London: IPPR.

Cowling, K. and Sawyer, M. (1990). 'Mergers and Monopoly Policy', in K. Cowling and R. Sugden (eds), *A New Economic Policy for Britain: Essays on the Development of Industry*, pp. 72–86. Manchester: Manchester University Press.

Cowling, K., Stoneman, P., Cubbin, J., Cable, J., Hall, G., Domberger, S., and Dutton, P. (1980). *Mergers and Economic Performance*. Cambridge: Cambridge University Press.

Cox, G. (2013). *Cox Review: Overcoming Short-Termism within British Business: The Key to Sustained Economic Growth*. London: The Labour Party.

Davis, A., Offenbach, D., Stevens, R., and Grant, N. (2013). *Takeovers and the Public Interest*. London: Policy Network.

Deakin, S. and Singh, A., (2009). 'The Stock Market, The Market for Corporate Control and the Theory of the Firm: Legal and Economic Perspectives and Implications for Public Policy', in P. Bjuggren and D. Mueller (eds), *The Modern Firm, Corporate Governance and Investment*, pp. 185–223. Cheltenham: Edward Elgar, <http://mpra.ub.uni-muenchen.de/53792/1/MPRA_paper_53792.pdf>.

Fama, E. (1970). 'Efficient Capital Markets: A Review of Theory and Empirical Work', *Journal of Finance* 25(2), 383–417.

Greenspan, A. (1998). *Statement of Alan Greenspan, Chairman, Board of Governors of the Federal Reserve System Before the Committee on Banking, Housing, and Urban Affairs, US Senate, July 21, 1998.* Washington DC: Federal Reserve Board.

Gugler, K. and Yurtoglu, B. (2008). *The Economics of Corporate Governance and Mergers.* Cheltenham: Edward Elgar.

Gugler, K., Mueller, D. C., and Weichselbaumer, M. (2012). 'The Determinants of Merger Waves: An International Perspective', *International Journal of Industrial Organisation* 30(1), 1–15.

Harford, J. (2005). 'What Drives Merger Waves?', *Journal of Financial Economics* 77(3), 529–60.

Heseltine, M. (2013). *No Stone Unturned in Pursuit of Growth.* London: Department of Business, Innovation and Skills.

Hong, H. and Stein, J. C. (2007). 'Disagreement and the Stock Market', *Journal of Economic Perspectives* 21(2), 109–28.

House of Commons (2010). *Mergers, Acquisitions and Takeovers: The Takeover of Cadbury by Kraft.* London: Business, Innovation and Skills Select Committee, HMSO.

Hutton, W. and Blond, P. (2010). 'End This Charter for Selling Off Top British Companies', *Financial Times* 21 January.

Jarrell, G. A., Brickley, J. A., and Netter, J. M. (1988). 'The Market for Corporate Control: The Empirical Evidence Since 1980', *Journal of Economic Perspectives* 2(1), 49–68.

Jensen, M. C. (1978). 'Some Anomalous Evidence Regarding Market Efficiency', *Journal of Financial Economics* 6, 95–101.

Jensen, M. C. (1988). 'Takeovers: Their Causes and Consequences', *Journal of Economic Perspectives* 2, 21–48.

Jensen, M. C. (2005). *A Theory of the Firm: Governance, Residual Claims and Organizational Forms.* Cambridge, MA: Harvard University Press.

Jovanovic, B. and Rousseau, P. (2002). *The Q-Theory of Mergers*, NBER Working Paper No. w8740, < http://ssrn.com/abstract=298264>.

Kay, J. (2012). *The Key Review of UK Equity Markets and Long-Term Decision-Making.* London: Department of Business, Innovation and Skills.

Kindleberger, C. and Aliber, R. (1989). *Manias, Panics and Crashes: A History of Financial Crises.* Basingstoke: Palgrave Macmillan.

Kolev, K., Haleblian, J., and McNamara, G. (2012). 'A Review of the Merger and Acquisition Wave Literature', in D. Faulkner, S. Teerikangas, and R. J. Joseph (eds), *The Handbook of Mergers and Acquisitions*, pp. 19–39. Oxford: Oxford University Press.

Marris, R. (1964). *The Economic Theory of Managerial Capitalism.* New York: Free Press of Glencoe.

Martynova, M. and Renneboog, L. (2008). 'A Century of Corporate Takeovers: What Have We Learned and Where Do We Stand?', *Journal of Banking & Finance* 32(10), 2148–77.

Meeks, G. (1977). *Disappointing Marriage. A Study of the Gains from Merger.* Cambridge: Cambridge University Press.

Minsky, H. P. (1986). *Stabilizing an Unstable Economy.* New Haven: Yale University Press.

Minsky, H. P. (1992). *The Financial Instability Hypothesis*, The Jerome Levy Economics Institute Working Paper No. 74, <http://dx.doi.org/10.2139/ssrn.161024>.

Mitchell, M. and Mulherin, J. H. (1996). 'The Impact of Industry Shocks on Takeovers and Restructuring Activity', *Journal of Financial Economics* 41(1), 193–229.

Mueller, D. C. (1969). 'A Theory of Conglomerate Mergers', *Quarterly Journal of Economics* 83, 643–59.

Pallazo, P. and Scherer, A. (2006). 'Corporate Legitimacy as Deliberation: A Communicative Framework', *Journal of Business Ethics* 66, 71–88.

Peacock, A. and Bannock, G. (1991). *Corporate Takeovers and the Public Interest*. Aberdeen: Aberdeen University Press.

Ravenscraft, D. J. and Scherer, F. M. (1987). 'The Profitability of Mergers', *International Journal of Industrial Organization* 7(1), 101–16.

Rhodes-Kropf, M. and Viswanathan, S. (2004). 'Market Valuation and Merger Waves', *Journal of Finance* 59(6), 2685–718.

Shiller, R. (2001). *Irrational Exuberance*. New York: Broadway Books.

Shleifer, A. and Summers, L. (1988). *Breach of Trust in Hostile Takeovers*. Chicago: University of Chicago Press.

Shleifer, A. and Vishny, R. W. (2003). Stock Market Driven Acquisitions, *Journal of Financial Economics* 70(3), 295–311.

Singh, A. (1971). *Take-Overs, the Stock Market and the Theory of the Firm*. Cambridge: Cambridge University Press.

Singh, A. (1975). *An Essay on the Political Economy of Chinese Development. Thames Papers in Political Economy*. London: Thames Polytechnic.

Singh, A. (1992). 'Corporate Takeovers', in John Eatwell, Murray Milgate, and Peter Newman (eds), *The New Palgrave Dictionary of Money and Finance*. Macmillan: London and New York.

Singh, A. and Hamid, J. (1992). *Corporate Financial Structures in Developing Countries*. Washington DC: The World Bank.

Singh, A. and Weisse, D. (2000). *Information Technology, Venture Capital and the Stock Market*. Cambridge: University of Cambridge, Department of Applied Economics.

Singh, A., Zammit, A., De Hoyo, R., Singh, A., and Weisse, B. (2005). *Shareholder Value Maximisation, Stock Market and New Technology: Should the US Corporate Model be the Universal Standard?*. Cambridge: University of Cambridge, Centre for Business Research.

Stein, J. (1989). 'Efficient Capital Markets, Inefficient Firms: A Model of Myopic Corporate Behaviour', *Quarterly Journal of Economics* 104, 655–69.

Stiglitz, J. (1994). *The Role of the State in Financial Markets*. New York: Columbia.

Takeover Panel (2011). *RS 2011/1 Review of Certain Aspects of the Regulation of Takeover Bids. Response Statement by the Code Committee of the Panel Following the Consultation on PC 3 2011/1*. London: Takeover Panel.

Tichy, N. (2002). *The Cycle of Leadership*. New York: HarperCollins.

Tobin, J. (1984). *On the Efficiency of the Financial System*. Lloyds Bank Review.

PART 6

INDUSTRIAL POLICY AND SUSTAINABLE DEVELOPMENT

CHAPTER 19

INDUSTRIAL POLICY FOR A SUSTAINABLE GROWTH PATH

KARL AIGINGER

19.1 OUTLINE AND OBJECTIVE

INDUSTRIAL policy has again become a major issue in industrialized countries, as this volume itself indicates. We analyse why this has happened and to what extent a 'new' industrial policy should be different from the old, discredited policy, which often tended to decelerate structural change. Academic scholars (Rodrik, 2004; Aiginger, 2007, 2012; Aghion et al., 2011) offer concepts of a 'new' or 'systemic' industrial policy, which should be based on new technologies and support society's long-term targets. This rationale for government intervention goes well beyond the traditional market failure arguments, such as monopolies, and is based on international externalities and coordination failures. The US government, the European Commission, and the Organisation for Economic Co-operation and Development (OECD) have advocated re-industrialization and industry-oriented 'integrated' policies since at least the financial crisis of 2009.[1] The European Commission has initiated WWWforEurope, a European research programme involving thirty-three European research teams and supporting US economists (e.g. Philippe Aghion, Kenneth Arrow, Graciela Chichilnisky, Barry Eichengreen, Jeffrey Sachs) to analyse the feasibility of a new path for growth in Europe based on social and ecological innovation.[2] In the meantime, US industrial policy is lured by the prospect of cheap energy, which it hopes will—together with rising wages in China—reduce its large current account deficit. The UK, which also has twin deficits in its trade and public budgets, is pondering how to revive its industrial sector. At the same time, the UK protects its financial

[1] European Commission (2010, 2012); OECD (2012); Veugelers (2013).
[2] See <http://www.foreurope.eu/>.

sector, which has been a more powerful job generator than manufacturing in the past two decades. France is undecided whether and how to shelter its remaining industry from globalization, relying either on *grand projets*, regional innovation centres (*pôles industriels*), or public–private sector networks, or alternatively fostering employment and new businesses by reducing social charges and corporation tax. Southern Europe has lost a substantial part of its industrial base and is trying to stop its decline in GDP by revitalizing exports to global markets,[3] but forfeiting its change to organize 'industrial zones', encouraging start-ups and inward foreign direct investment with different administrative rules.

An important question is whether industrial policy and climate policy are partners or adversaries. The European Commission started this discussion by moving 'sustainability' (together with 'competitiveness') to the 'centre stage' of industrial policy (European Commission, 2010). Renewable energy was declared one of the 'enabling technologies'. But Europe also envies the US's cheap, new energy sources and fears that energy-intensive industries in particular will relocate to the US for lower energy prices, or to Asia for lower environmental standards. These arguments limit the 'greening' of Europe's industrial policy. If the second line of arguments wins, Europe will lose the first-mover advantage of becoming a test bed for clean technologies which could be exported to other countries in the future as worldwide environmental ambitions increase.

We discuss the challenges of a 'low-road' answer to the US's new competitive advantage of low energy prices, and contrast it to a 'high-road' strategy for competitiveness. This strategy connects industrial policy proper with innovation and climate policy, to generate a new, 'systemic' industrial policy. It supports society's long-term goals and is based on the comparative advantages of industrialized countries. The alternative, a low-road strategy aimed at lower standards and wages, would bring the similar short-term relief for troubled companies as 'old' industrial policy used to do, reducing the long-term dynamics of manufacturing in rich countries.[4]

19.2 RE-EMERGING ATTENTION FOR MANUFACTURING

19.2.1 The Hypothesis of Rise and Fall

The eventual decline of the share of manufacturing in industrialized countries' GDP is well established in economic theory (e.g. as the second phase of the so-called three-sector hypothesis, Fourastier, 1954 and Clark, 1940). It is driven both by demand forces

---

[3] See Aiginger, Firgo et al. (2012).

[4] For an overview on definitions of 'industrial policy' see Aiginger (2007) and other papers in the Journal of Industry, Competition and Trade (2007). If not otherwise stated, the term 'industry' is used synonymously with 'manufacturing'.

(the preference for services increases with rising income) and by supply forces (techno-logical progress lowers manufacturing cost). This sectoral shift—after a first phase of industrialization—has been welcomed as a sign of a mature society, because service jobs are less strenuous and subject to less cyclical variation.[5] It has been argued that this transformation should not happen too soon or too quickly (see the criticism of the UK's premature de-industrialization in the 1960s), *inter alia* because the lion's share of technological innovation occurs in manufacturing. Product-cycle theory and trade theory stress that it is a particular feature of the international division of labour that industrialized countries have advantages in the invention and innovation phase, while developing countries have advantages in manufacturing mature products with standardized production. The transfer of parts of the value chain to lower-income countries provides rents for higher-income countries. At the same time, services have changed from personal and government services to 'production-related' services, the crown jewels being IT and financial services, which offer dynamic employment and high wages.

19.2.2 Renewed Interest

Increasing attention towards the manufacturing sector, and calls to limit or reverse its decline, have arisen since 2000 for at least two reasons: firstly, emerging market coun-tries' inroads into global manufacturing; and secondly, industrialized countries' experi-ence that bubbles in non-trade related sectors had aggravated the severity and length of the financial crisis.

Competitive pressure from emerging markets: industrialized countries are losing market share to emerging market manufacturers, which are making inroads in ever more sectors, and not only in traditional, labour-intensive ones. China now has the lar-gest industrial sector in absolute terms. Trade deficits of several large industrialized countries have ballooned and can no longer be offset by service exports. This has resulted in large current account deficits (especially in the US, as well as in the UK, France, and Italy).

Experience before and during the financial crisis: economic growth in non-manufacturing was particularly strong in the run-up to the crisis; bubbles occurred in the construction sector, in property prices, and in financial markets, often driven by low interest rates or public support. Evidence has mounted that economic growth is no longer positively affected by the size of the financial sector, as bubbles in finance and construction have destabilized economies (Cecchetti and Kharroubi, 2012; Schneeweiß, 2012). Looking for indicators to explain different national performance during the financial crisis has

---

[5] This argument was more convincing when most service jobs were permanent and full-time and many jobs in manufacturing were dirty or even dangerous. Today manufacturing jobs, especially those in industrialized countries, are full-time, while service sector jobs have become more volatile and, in part, precarious.

shown the current account balance as the most important determinant of the depth of the crisis across countries (Aiginger, 2011b).[6] Countries with current account deficits at the start of the crisis together with a small manufacturing base endured a particularly long crisis, and output is often still lower than in 2007 (see Figures 19.1, 19.2, 19.3). In Southern Europe,[7] where the share of manufacturing declined to 11 per cent (2012) from 16 per cent (1960), and current account deficits amounted to 13 per cent of GDP before the crisis, GDP is today still more than 10 per cent below its pre-crisis peak (Aiginger et al., 2012).[8] Ireland, which also had a severe crisis resulting from bubbles in the construction and finance sectors, recovered more quickly *inter alia* by boosting exports through its large industrial base.

In summary, it is difficult to explain differing national performance during the recent financial crisis with one single factor, but if there is a candidate it is pre-crisis balance

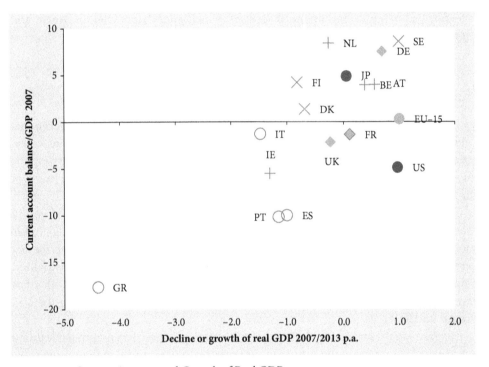

FIGURE 19.1 Current Account and Growth of Real GDP.

Source: Eurostat (AMECO)

[6] Robustness checks show that this relation is not dependant on outliers (like Greece at the one end or China at the other end). However, the current account balances may signal deeper and more complex problems of an economy which cannot be proxied easily by other variables.

[7] Defined as Greece, Spain, and Portugal; unweighted average.

[8] In Greece, the industrial sector declined to 8 per cent (2011) from 15 per cent (1980) and the current account deficit reached 18 per cent of GDP (2008). Similar developments occurred in Portugal, Spain, and Latvia.

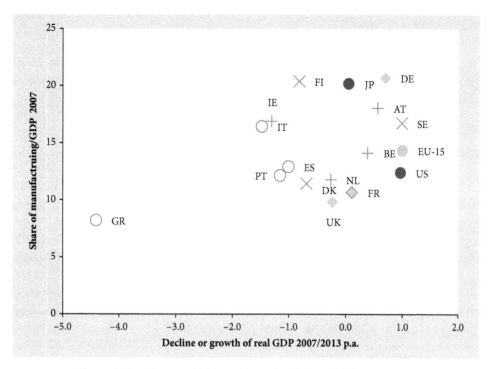

FIGURE 19.2 Share of Manufacturing (Current Prices) and Growth of Real GDP.

Source: Eurostat (AMECO)

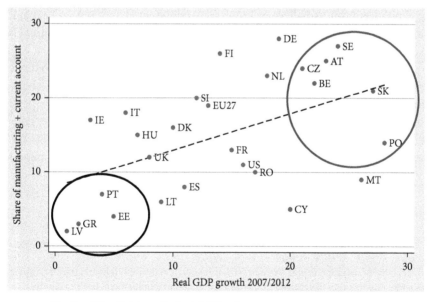

FIGURE 19.3 Depth of the Crisis vs 'Industrial Base'.

Ranked by performance and industrial base

Remark: industrial base = share of manufacturing/GDP 2007 plus share of current account; the sum is ranked (low sum of shares = 1); output performance = change in real GDP growth 2012/2007 (lowest rate = 1)

Source: Eurostat (AMECO)

of current account.[9] The importance of manufacturing as a basis for growth is well known. This sector conducts the largest share of R&D and many sophisticated services are based on or connected to production.[10]

19.2.3 Stylized Facts on the Share of Manufacturing

In the US, manufacturing currently generates only 12 per cent of GDP, less than half its share in 1960. The financial sector's contribution to GDP is increasing, approaching 10 per cent of value added and 40 per cent of all corporate profits (Wolf, 2014). A new argument for the declining manufacturing base in the US is provided by recent MIT studies (Berger, 2013), namely that although new products' invention phase still starts in the US, the offshoring of production to low-cost countries occurs earlier (Berger, 2013). As a consequence, the learning process from new products in the late innovation and early production phases is transferred to other countries. This reduces positive spillover effects to other companies and subsequent innovations. Cooperation in the US manufacturing sector is less developed than in Europe. US companies are 'alone at home', instead of being part of a cluster of related companies or embedded in industrial ecosystems.

In Western Europe (EU-15) manufacturing's declining share of GDP, to 14 per cent (2012) from 21 per cent (1960), is less dramatic.[11] But Europe is unable to eliminate the gap in per capita income and labour productivity compared to the US (which is larger in per capita terms and smaller per hour; see Aiginger et al., 2013). R&D expenditure particularly by companies is lower in Europe, and Europe lacks top universities (Janger et al., 2011).

Overall, it appears that in the US spending on innovation—and resulting productivity—is high, although this is not used to produce enough goods or services to balance trade. In contrast, Europe has a balanced trade position, with low dynamics and a persistent productivity deficit[12] compared to the frontier economy. At the same time, emerging market countries are gaining market share in both regions.

These trends have led to calls for a new industrial policy in academic papers and policy documents (see Table 19.1).

---

[9] Budget deficits and the debt/GDP ratio were far less able to explain country differences during the crisis. There is no easy relationship between the share of manufacturing at current prices in 2007 and the changes in countries' GDP thereafter (see Figure 19.2).

[10] The decline of manufacturing's share in GDP is higher, if measured in nominal terms (which reflects wages and incomes generated in manufacturing) and in employment, less in volumes.

[11] Country differences are large. In the UK, the share of manufacturing in GDP dropped to 10.5 per cent (average over 2001 to 2012, from 25.7 per cent (average over 1961 to 1970, nominal terms); in France it fell to 10.8 per cent, from 21.1 per cent. It was stable in Finland (due to the ICT boom) and in Ireland.

[12] This holds more for per capita productivity than for per hour productivity.

Table 19.1 Share of Manufacturing and the Dynamic of Industrial Production

	Share of manufacturing at current prices								Increase of production index	
	1960	1980	1990	1995	2000	2009	2011	2012	2000/2008	2008/2012
	In %								% p.a.	
Germany	29.9	26.1	24.7	19.9	20.0	17.4	20.3	20.0	2.3	−0.3
Ireland	11.5	14.9	19.3	20.6	23.1	19.5	21.4	21.0	4.5	0.3
Greece	12.4	15.3	12.8	10.6	9.6	7.9	8.1	8.5	−0.6	−6.9
Spain	14.8	23.7	18.8	16.4	16.2	11.4	12.2	12.2	0.1	−6.2
France	22.2	18.4	15.8	14.4	13.6	9.6	9.2	8.9	−0.3	−2.7
Italy	23.8	26.2	20.5	19.4	18.0	14.3	14.7	14.0	−0.2	−4.9
Austria	26.7	20.7	19.1	17.5	18.1	16.2	16.7	16.4	4.0	0.1
Portugal	20.3	21.5	19.7	16.0	15.0	11.1	12.0	12.3	−0.9	−3.6
United Kingdom	26.2	19.9	17.3	17.1	13.8	9.3	9.1	9.0	−0.8	−2.7
USA	25.2	20.0	16.3	15.8	14.3	11.1	11.6	−	0.6	0.1
EU–15	21.3	20.2	18.2	17.6	16.4	12.7	13.5	13.5	0.8	−2.2
Euro area				17.7	17.1	13.3	14.4	14.2	−	−
EU–27				17.6	16.5	13.0	−	−	−	−

1) Increase of production index EU–15 2008/2011
Source: Eurostat (AMECO)

19.3 Industrial Policy: From the Bottom to the Top of the Agenda

We have shown that the renewed emphasis on manufacturing in industrialized countries is based on two economic arguments: (1) emerging market countries' increasing share of global GDP; (2) the evidence from the financial crisis that a decline in the manufacturing sector combined with a current account deficit aggravated the financial crisis or delayed recovery; we had known before that the manufacturing sector is necessary for research and innovation, which are the main growth drivers in industrialized countries. But this line—known before the financial crisis—has attracted increased attention following evidence from the US that early offshoring can lead to a loss of learning and skills in frontier technologies. We may add the political argument that public budgets, which were used to rescue banks and finance unemployment and pensions, were not subsequently directed towards job creation and growth in the real economy. As a result, politicians and policy documents are now unanimously calling for a new industrial policy in countries from the US to the UK and France. This section gives an overview first on 'old' industrial policy, and then on calls of academia and economic policy for a new one.

19.3.1 Past Policy: Diversity and Demise

Industrial policy in Europe has been implemented differently over time and across countries. As far as a timeline is concerned, European industrial policy began with the European Coal and Steel Community. For a while thereafter, it remained primarily a national policy with a predominantly sectoral focus (French style, large projects, national champions); this was followed by a period of horizontal competitiveness policies (German style, broad 'measures' that did not discriminate between sectors). The European Community failed to mention industrial policy at all in the 'Treaty of Rome' and its successor, the EU, mainly followed the horizontal approach. In the 1990s, it looked as if interest in industrial policy was dying in the EU, as well as at national level (Aiginger, 2007). An early revival was attempted by defining a 'matrix-type' approach (European Commission, 2005; the term was proposed in Aiginger and Sieber, 2006): Here it was argued that industrial policy should be predominantly horizontal, complemented with sector-specific measures, because horizontal measures have different impacts across sectors.

As far as the success of different instruments of industrial policy is concerned, empirical analyses of previous strategies reveal that countries relying on state aid and regulation as their main policy instruments registered an inferior macroeconomic performance,[13] whereas countries focusing on promoting positive externalities as their main instrument of industrial policy had superior macroeconomic results (Aiginger and Sieber, 2006). A group of Scandinavian countries (Sweden, Finland, and Denmark) invested heavily in R&D and education, focusing especially on ICT industries, thus implementing an industrial policy with the aim of promoting a knowledge-driven economy. These Scandinavian countries could be the benchmark for a future-oriented industrial and innovation policy, since they managed to achieve a broad selection of economic goals (income, social inclusion, ecological excellence, fiscal prudence) by a high-road strategy.

Overall, industrial policy was landed with the image of a 'born loser'. All too often governments intervened to preserve old structures or national interests. 'Old' industrial policy often implicitly decelerated structural change and slowed technological progress. It even impeded policy goals, such as improving energy efficiency and green technologies, while sheltering large, ecologically disastrous businesses, ranging from petrochemicals companies to steelmakers (e.g. U.S. Steel in the twentieth century or polluting plants in southern Italy today). Industrial policy in this mode was ineffective, since its goals contradicted other policies (competition or employment policy) and did not create synergies with innovation, education, regional, or climate policy. 'No industrial policy is the best industrial policy' was the conclusion in the US, and 'horizontal industrial policy only' was Germany's mantra, before later gaining acceptance at EU level.

---

[13] As measured by a set of indicators on economic dynamics, employment, and the stability of the economy.

19.3.2 Academia Defining Elements of a 'New Industrial Policy'

Academic literature took the lead in defining how, in a globalized world, a future-oriented industrial policy could be different from the past. Many proposals exist, and here we mention only three: Rodrik (2004) first offered the perspective of industrial policy for developing countries, and later a 'manufacturing imperative' (Rodrik, 2011) and recently a blueprint for a 'green industrial policy' (Rodrik, 2013). Aghion et al. (2011) present a pro-market approach for an industrial policy in frontier economies. In addition, Aiginger (2012) introduces the concept of a systemic industrial policy, based on the finding that the European countries that fared best during the financial crisis had strategies combining innovation, education, and openness.

The following elements seem to be common to these 'new approaches':

- Industrial policy should be a state of mind…create a climate of cooperation between government and the private sector…a discovery process…generate positive spillovers to other sectors and not be based on purely financial incentives…not picking winners (Rodrik, 2011). It should target activities and broad sectors, never firms; it should promote new activities not prevent exit…follow markets instead of leading them (Aghion et al., 2011).

- Industrial policy is necessary to prevent 'lock-in' situations, of investing in old technologies. Producers of 'dirty products' tend to innovate in 'dirty programs'. In a nutshell, Aghion et al. (2011) argue that new research follows old paradigms and that companies invest where they have been successful in the past. The task of industrial policy is to prevent conservative path-dependent decisions.

- Industrial policy should create new comparative advantages and help developing countries to diversify; it should stimulate exports, not prevent imports. New industrial policy should favour competition, instead of being an adversary of competition policy. Industrial policy should not protect non-viable domestic firms (a criticism of older industrial policy) (Aghion et al., 2011).

- Governments should only intervene where they have a long-term interest (not just short-term goals such as saving jobs in distressed regions or during the depths of a recession); it has to be connected with societal needs. Industrial policy should benefit society as a whole, not just individual companies (Aiginger and Guger, 2006; Rodrik, 2008, 2011; Aghion et al., 2011; Reinstaller, 2013).

- Industrial policy should no longer be an isolated policy. It has already merged with innovation policy…it has to build up and be supported by education policy. It has to be systemic, pushed by competition, pulled by 'beyond-GDP' goals (Aiginger, 2012; see also Box 19.1). Industrial policy should start from the vision of where an economy wants to be in twenty or thirty years in the future, of which factors (income, social goals, ecological sustainability) will define welfare, and of which capabilities will provide competitiveness and growth on a path aligned with these pillars (Aiginger et al., 2013).

Box 19.1 A Systemic Industrial and Innovation Policy: Driven by Vision, Pushed by Competition and Openness (Aiginger, 2012)

A future-oriented industrial policy has to be systemic in the sense that it needs to be derived from society's goals. If the European citizen's welfare function gives a large weighting to rising incomes, more social inclusion (less wage dispersion), a stable financial system, and sustainability, then industrial policy has to promote these goals. Innovation should be shifted to social and ecological innovation (a feasible task given the scope of government involvement in R&D). Industrial policy should also make use of forces that promote change and foster higher incomes, e.g. competition, globalization, education, and training. Thus a 'Systemic Industrial Policy' is pulled by a vision and pushed by competition.

The Systemic Industrial and Innovation Policy (SIIP) in a nutshell.

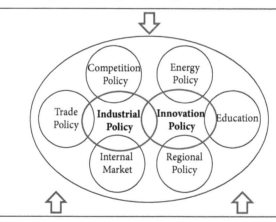

Mazzucato (2011)—focusing on the interface of industrial and innovation policies—advocates a procurement policy that actively promotes innovation, specifically innovation in non-technical fields, that is, social and ecological innovation. The state is an important source and catalyst in virtually all new technologies. The vision of an entrepreneurial state facilitating the emergence of new generic technologies may be a little over-optimistic, nonetheless, because of path dependency, government decisions are vital if big changes in technology or society are to occur. Meanwhile, Johnson (2009) calls for industrial policy to rebalance the economy towards non-financial sectors (such as manufacturing) and away from the financial sector.

Rodrik (2013) makes the case for a green industrial policy, describing in detail green growth policies in the US (including the spectacular rise and fall of the public-subsidized Californian solar cell company 'Solyndra'), in Germany, China, and India. He stresses that we have to understand that failures are a necessary 'part and parcel' of successful industrial policy efforts. Among better rules required for green industrial policy he mentions interaction with the private sector ('embeddedness, but not in bed' or—in other words—between 'arm's length and capture'). A new industrial policy needs discipline; firms must know they cannot 'game government'. Further principles are that underperformance has to result in removal of assistance and accountability, meaning that the public agencies must explain what they are doing and how. Industrial policy is one plank of a strategy to avert catastrophic climate change, and subsidy wars are far better than tariff wars since they expand the global supply of clean technologies.[14]

There are caveats to all of these calls for industrial policy. Procurement policy with specific goals can result in disguised protectionism. 'Following the market' versus 'concentration on new activities' can be a trade-off; enforcing exports can be an argument for preventing imports with some mercantilist or anti-globalization perspectives and so on. Companies will behave strategically and lobby for public support, which limits any industrial policy based on dialogue and cooperation between government and industry, if government does not have the experts who are willing and able to distinguish between companies' superior knowledge and their short-term interests. To minimize some of these risks, there should be benchmarks and the criteria for success and failure should depend on productivity and exports; if goals are not attained by the policy measures, subsidization should end, following clearly defined rules.

In summary, the 'new industrial policy' should be forward-looking, favour competition, and support long-term societal needs (like e.g. 'green industrial policy'). It should be an integrated or systemic policy, not an isolated policy strand in conflict with other policies. Policy measures should have a clearly communicated goal and the results of intervention should be carefully monitored. The concept of a systemic industrial and innovation policy (SIIP) is summarized in Box 19.1.

19.3.3 Policy Documents: Following Academia and Overtaking

This section analyses concepts for a new industrial policy, from policy documents that were inspired first by the challenges of globalization and then by the financial crisis.

---

[14] Other papers calling for a new industrial policy are Aiginger (2009, 2011a); Criscuolo et al. (2012); OECD (2012, 2014); Owen (2012); Wade (2012); O'Sullivan et al. (2013); Stiglitz et al. (2013).

Due to space constraints we shall concentrate on Europe and on European Commission documents, with some reference to an OECD document at the end of the section. Attempts to reformulate industrial policy have been made for industrialized countries and for developing countries, for Europe, for the US and for Asian countries.

19.3.3.1 *New Industrial Policy in Recent EU Documents*

The European Commission's new industrial policy developed in phases and through several documents (European Commission, 2005, 2009, 2011a, 2011b, 2012, 2013, 2014a, 2014b).

In a first stage (after the impact of globalization became visible and before the financial crisis set in) these documents sidestepped the old divide between the horizontal and the vertical approach, by declaring both necessary. The horizontal approach continued to dominate, while sectoral ideas entered through different sector-specific effects of horizontal policies (and the necessity to fine-tune or complement them).[15] The documents also call for 'key enabling technologies', 'flagship initiatives', and 'priority lines', which all have a certain sectoral or thematic 'ring'.

In a second stage, the Commission attempted to resolve old trade-offs and conflicts, for example between competition policy (which is critical of very large companies and national champions) and industrial policy proper (sheltering incumbent champions and looking for new ones), by calling for an 'integrated' industrial policy. Competition, trade, internal markets, regions, innovation, and resource and energy policies should cooperate and develop synergies to arrive at a 'wider industrial policy'. All these policy documents refer to the Europe 2020 strategy goals for smart, inclusive, and sustainable growth as their background framework.

In the third stage, pressure for a 'greener' industrial policy arises from the 20/20/20 energy goals and from the roadmap for 2050, which sets European goals to reduce greenhouse gases by 80 to 95 per cent by 2050. Hurdles to 'greening' come from the repeated assertion that all industries are important and that all parts of the value chain—from resource extraction to after-sales services—are relevant for competitiveness. In addition, the threat that energy-intensive industries could relocate to regions with lower energy prices and lower environmental standards (including the carbon leakage argument) is used to limit ambitions for higher fossil fuel taxes. This results in documents where different goals for industrial (and energy) policy are merely accumulated or listed, without addressing the conflicts between them or establishing any priorities. Setting 'competitiveness' *and* 'sustainability' at the 'centre stage' is one such compromise (European Commission, 2010). If competitiveness is understood as cost competitiveness (which is the dominant implicit interpretation in some documents), this calls for low energy costs, while sustainability requires higher energy prices for fossil energies to incentivize greater efficiency or switching to renewable energy sources.

---

[15] For an overview see Aiginger and Sieber (2006) and Peneder (2009, 2010).

19.3.3.2 *Resilient Manufacturing Plus Ambitious New Target*

All documents[16] show the European Commission's confidence in the performance of Europe's manufacturing sector. It is frequently mentioned that Europe's share of world trade was relatively stable (at least in the decade before the financial crisis) and that the manufacturing sector (excluding energy and raw materials) had a large trade surplus. The importance of manufacturing is highlighted by evidence that one in four private sector jobs is created in manufacturing (and one further job in associated services; European Commission, 2010), and that 75 per cent of exports and 80 per cent of private R&D originates in manufacturing. The Commission further states that Europe is a world leader in many strategic sectors such as car-making, aeronautics, engineering, aerospace, chemicals, and pharmaceuticals (European Commission, 2012).

On the other hand, a 'fresh approach' (European Commission, 2010) is seen as necessary, because 3 million jobs have been lost in manufacturing since the start of the crisis, and because recovery in Europe has been generally slow. Together with the past experience of the decline of the share of manufacturing in GDP, this motivated the European Commission to set the goal to 'reverse the declining role of industry in Europe from its current level of around 16% of GDP to as much as 20% by 2020'. This ambitious statement is complemented by calls for higher levels of investment, greater intra-European trade, and a significant increase in the number of SMEs (small- and medium-sized enterprises) and exports to third (non-EU) countries.

Given the reasons for the declining share of manufacturing (higher productivity, lower relative price increases, as well as a lower income elasticity of demand for manufactured goods compared to services, Figures 19.4, 19.5, 19.6), this goal is unlikely to be achieved without a dramatic change in the general economic growth path. If Europe wishes to improve the competitiveness of its manufacturing sector in the traditional sense, it must raise productivity or lower costs, actions which are both likely to lead to declining shares of industrial goods produced for the home market (see Peneder, 2014). Lower costs and higher productivity could improve Europe's trade position, although given Europe's existing export surplus, this is neither pressing nor is it a strategy that would be left unchallenged by other regions.[17]

The picture changes only if we take into consideration the fact that core manufacturing products are combined ever more with production-related and value-enhancing services. If products become more durable, more consumer-specific (e.g. via digitalization) or ecologically sustainable, and if production is aligned with training, social innovations, and larger resource efficiency, this could allow price increases in line with increasing consumer valuation. These are the features of a new growth path which

---

[16] This refers to policy documents. They often refer to basic scientific work done for the annual Competitiveness Reports (e.g. European Commission, 2009, 2011a, 2011b), which are prepared by a research network under the coordination of WIFO (Austrian Institute of Economic Research) (see Janger et al., 2011).

[17] With the exception of southern European countries, which need more exports to restart growth. On the other hand, Germany's large surplus is clearly not maximizing German welfare.

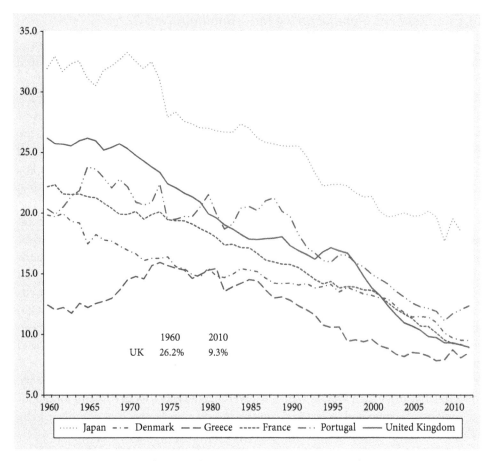

FIGURE 19.4 Share of Manufacturing from 1960 to 2012: Countries with a Strong Decline Nominal Value; in % of GDP.

Source: Eurostat (AMECO)

requires new incentives and changing consumer preferences, and where the costs involved have to be assessed by domestic and international markets as increasing consumer value. Whether this increasing 'service component' will be included statistically in the measurement of value added by the manufacturing sector, or in related services or government accounts, is another question. What the European Commission intends with its goal—if taken literally—is to dampen the decline of the share of industry and to limit other regions' inroads into European domestic markets.

19.3.3.3 OECD's Call for a 'Soft Industrial Policy'

The OECD, formerly the fiercest critic of the old industrial policy, views clean technologies as essential elements of the 'soft industrial policy' strategy (OECD, 2012).[18]

---

[18] For an overview of OECD documents, see Warwick (2013).

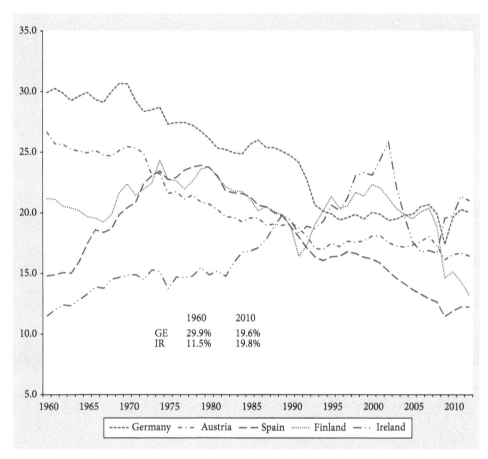

FIGURE 19.5 Share of Manufacturing 1960 to 2012: Countries with a Smaller Decline Nominal Value; in % of GDP.

Source: Eurostat (AMECO)

OECD advocates an industrial policy based on a 'more facilitating, co-ordinating role for government, consistent with the systems approach' (networks, strategies, priorities). Warwick (2013) adopts a broad and inclusive definition of industrial policy. Industrial policy has moved from a traditional approach based on product market interventions (subsidies, state ownership, tariff protection), through a phase of correcting market failure by taxes and subsidies, operating mainly on factor markets (R&D, training, access to finance), to a third stage of helping to build up systems, create networks, develop institutions, and align strategic priorities. He summarizes recent experience with industrial policy in France, UK, the Netherlands, as well as in Japan, India, China, and other Asian countries, and offers a new typology for industrial policy by policy domains (product markets, labour and skills, capital markets, technology, and systems/institutions) and by policy orientation (horizontal, selective). Warwick (2013) distinguishes between policies for catching up and frontier countries (each developing or following comparative advantages). Analysing industrial policy in action, he analyses

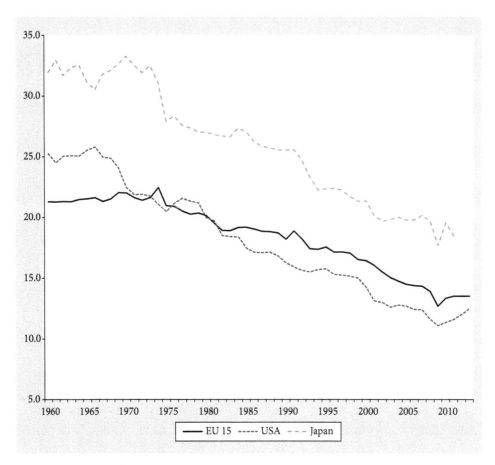

FIGURE 19.6 Share of Manufacturing 1960 to 2012: EU–15, USA, Japan Nominal Value; in % of GDP.

Source: Eurostat (AMECO)

green growth policy describing policy instruments for a green industrial policy. All important for the future success are better evaluation techniques and monitoring.[19]

19.3.3.4 *'Remaking' vs 'Alone at Home' in the US*

In the US, discussion is labelled as the 'remaking' or the 'second spring' of manufacturing, with highlights like the declaration by Jeff Immelt (General Electric CEO) of 'outsourcing as the most outdated model', furthermore the praise for Lenovo for restarting computer production in North Carolina and for General Electric for returning washing machine manufacture to Kentucky.[20] For a broader approach highlighting the principal reasons

[19] The discussion of a new industrial policy is still an ongoing debate. See Warwick (2013) also for risks and possible failures in future industrial policy.

[20] Notice that these popular examples are related to qualified labour in the US or to wage increases in China, not to energy prices.

for the decline of US manufacturing as being the lack of cooperation across US companies and the loss of learning capacity due to early offshoring, see Berger (2013). The hope to base the 'renaissance' on cheap energy prices and its impact on the structure of US manufacturing is analysed in Section 19.5.

19.4 EUROPE—A SUCCESS STORY IN NEED OF A VISION AND BENCHMARKS

19.4.1 A Successful Experiment in a Midlife Crisis

Much analysis of Europe's low dynamics over the past decade forgets that the European Union has been a tremendously successful integration experiment. It started with only six members fifty years ago. It now has twenty-eight members with ten more countries applying for membership or neighbourhood contracts. Europe has integrated former communist countries at such a high speed that the World Bank labelled it an 'integration machine' (World Bank, 2012). A once divided and fractured continent is now united as a peaceful region (rewarded with the Nobel Prize). Europe is lauded for its 'soft' foreign policy and for spreading the rule of law (Sachs, 2008).

The current EU-28 is the largest economic region in the world, as measured by Gross National Product. Its share of world trade is more stable than the US's, albeit falling slightly due to the impact of the newly industrialized countries. Europe takes the lead in pushing for environmental goals (Kyoto Protocol, EU-2020 energy goals) and has promoted a system of carbon emissions trading.[21] Europe has lower shares of poverty and less income inequality than other economic areas.

19.4.2 Low Dynamics and Conventional Remedies

Nevertheless there are also indications of weaknesses. Economic output in the eurozone in 2014 is still lower than it was in 2008.[22] Europe has a double-digit unemployment rate, its banks are undercapitalized, and its Member States pay higher interest rates for their sovereign debt (despite lower debt/GDP ratios) than the US and Japan. There are internal trade disequilibria, with large surpluses in Germany, the Netherlands, and Austria, and deficits in some big countries (UK, France) and in Southern Europe (the deficits in the latter region are now declining, in part due to reduced imports). Europe will miss its

[21] The system broke down since too many energy-intensive sectors were exempted, and other energy-intensive companies were able to buy extremely cheap permits from ailing Eastern European companies or from companies severely hit by the financial crisis.

[22] In contrast to the US, where it is 9 per cent higher; world output exceeds its pre-crisis level by 20 per cent compared with 2008.

employment, R&D, and poverty reduction goals set out in the Europe 2020 strategy (and adapted by national policy decisions). It will not reach its goals for energy efficiency and curbing CO_2 by 2020, and it will grossly miss the trajectories of the energy roadmap to 2050.

Lower dynamics[23] and large disequilibria are partly a consequence of the problem that the European institutions (which were adequate for a small number of countries and an integration process limited to trade) are no longer adequate for twenty-eight countries, the majority of which also share a common currency.

Five rather conventional policies are needed to revive Europe's dynamics (Aiginger, 2014; Aiginger and Glocker, 2015, forthcoming): (1) reducing the disequilibria by joint responsibility[24] of the debtor and the creditor countries; (2) increasing domestic demand either by boosting consumption via higher wages or less income inequality, or, in a climate of reduced uncertainty, by encouraging companies to reinvest their profits; (3) restructuring government expenditure and taxes so that they become more growth-friendly; (4) boosting investment in education, retraining, innovation, and young people; and (5) making use of higher market growth—albeit also higher volatility—in the neighbourhood for exports and investment, including the Black Sea region, Russia, and North Africa.

19.4.3 Towards a New Growth Path: Four Game-Changing Proposals

However, changes need to go further. Europe must develop its existing socio-economic model into a role model for a dynamic, inclusive, and ecological society in a globalizing world.[25] Social expenditures and ecological ambitions should be turned from costs into drivers of new dynamics (e.g. through an activating labour market policy or an innovation-based sustainability strategy). A new European model could be attractive for young people, as well as for countries climbing up the income ladder, which are looking for alternatives to the Chinese catch-up model or the US frontier model based on individualism, with low priority for social goals and sustainability.

The European Commission—reacting to this need for a new and far-reaching strategy—tendered a large socio-economic research programme (WWWforEurope) to develop a new growth path that, on the one hand, extends the goals of Europe 2020 into the future and on the other targets a much deeper socio-ecological transition.[26] Tentative results indicate that several important changes have to be made if Europe wishes to

---

[23] Of employment, GDP, and productivity.

[24] See Aiginger et al. (2012).

[25] Of course the European model is not itself monolithic today (see Aiginger, 2006). Different European models share common elements, particularly when compared to the models in Asia and the US.

[26] A team of thirty-three European research groups, coordinated by WIFO, won the DG Research tender. The project is now halfway into its four-year term, with about 100 research articles available at <http://www.foreurope.eu/>.

develop its socio-economic model into a compelling vision. We start by noting some of the overarching changes needed, then discuss some 'barriers' to change.

19.4.3.1 *Game Changer 1: From GDP to Beyond-GDP*

Economists have always understood that GDP is not a welfare indicator—both for technical reasons and for the concept. GDP and its growth nevertheless dominate the discussion of economic policy and are seen as the single overarching measure of success of an economy or region. The criticism of this indicator and its alternatives were summarized by the so-called Stiglitz–Sen–Fitoussi Commission, leading to the 'beyond-GDP goals' (Stiglitz et al., 2009; Stiglitz et al., 2010). These are now widely accepted as a superior theoretical approach. The OECD has published a corresponding set of 'Better Life Indicators', which many countries have started to use as a measure of performance.

Income per capita and income growth will remain important goals particularly for low-income individuals, regions, and countries. Other goals receive greater priority, as the marginal utility of income declines. This does not preclude GDP dynamics from remaining an instrument for reaching other ultimate goals, such as full employment, social security, health, consumer choice, and so on—the key point is that we should measure the achievement of the ultimate goals, not of the instruments used to reach them.

For a new European growth path and industrial policy, this change from GDP to beyond-GDP is particularly important. The industrial sector is one of the largest production sectors and is responsible for the lion's share of research and development. If the innovations developed in manufacturing do not help attain welfare (as defined by the beyond-GDP goals), the potential of the economic system is not fully utilized. Industrial policy should enforce and accelerate manufacturing's welfare orientation, should support also non-technical innovation, and it should be systemic and forward-looking.

19.4.3.2 *Game Changer 2: Redefining Competitiveness*

The term 'competitiveness' has been used over and over again in the narrow sense of cost competitiveness, calling for lower wages and other production costs as policy instruments to 'stay' competitive or 'regain' competitiveness. In its enlightened version, productivity is acknowledged as a second element of cost competitiveness, leading to unit cost approaches. The cost focus has been criticized for a long time, spawning approaches that emphasize technological or qualitative competitiveness, and measuring 'outcome competitiveness' using a combination of targets (e.g. income, employment).[27] Finally, competitiveness should be based on capabilities like skills, innovation, institutions, an empowering social system, and ecological ambitions. Outcomes should be defined by the achievement of broad, socio-economic goals. Aiginger et al. (2013) therefore propose defining competitiveness as the 'ability to deliver beyond-GDP goals'. This definition could end the preoccupation of economic policy with costs instead of capabilities.

---

[27] See concepts used by the OECD and the European Commission analysed in Aiginger (2006) and several other papers in the special issue on competitiveness in the Journal of Industry, Competition and Trade (2006).

19.4.3.3 *Game Changer 3: Distinguishing between a Low Road and a High Road*

In principle, countries have two ways to close current account deficits, to increase dynamics of the economy, or to reduce unemployment. One is to lower costs (wages, taxes, energy prices); the other is to raise productivity, by boosting capabilities (education, innovation), and by becoming a leader in energy efficiency and renewable energy.[28] We label the first path to regain competitiveness a 'low-road strategy' and the second a 'high-road strategy'. It is difficult for countries with high wages to increase per capita GDP by reducing wages, because low-income countries have greater competitive advantages in this aspect. Industrialized countries can more successfully compete on quality, innovation, and new services (see Aiginger, 1997).

19.4.3.4 *Game Changer 4: Industrial Policy as a Strategy for High-Road Competitiveness*

Academic literature and commentary provide many definitions of industrial policy,[29] without an agreement on a common definition. We propose to define industrial policy as economic policy to promote the competitiveness of a country or region, where competitiveness is defined as the ability to deliver the beyond-GDP goals.[30] For industrialized countries with high per capita incomes, industrial policy should therefore explicitly be a high-road strategy of competitiveness based on capabilities, good institutions, and high ambitions for social and ecological behaviour. For Europe and its vision of a socio-economic system with a strong emphasis on inclusion and sustainability, this high-road strategy explicitly includes equality and green goals.

This definition should end (or at least mitigate) the conflict between industrial policy favouring on the one hand specific sectors, and on the other hand activities with positive external effects like innovation and education. It should also mitigate the conflict between industrial policy calling for low energy prices and environmental policy aimed at significantly reducing carbon emissions. Society's ultimate goals determine the direction in which it should move, and the weighting of these goals will differ according to income levels, preferences, and cultural attitudes. These ultimate goals should set the direction of policy interventions and the instruments of industrial policy.

19.4.4 Status Quo Bias and Political Rebound Effects

We have defined four game-changing proposals that are far from easy to implement: (1) a new yardstick for performance; (2) a new definition of competitiveness; (3) the choice between a low and a high road to competitiveness (suggesting that welfare increases in industrialized countries require a high-road strategy); and (4) a broader industrial

---

[28] We could label this as a multiple equilibrium point of view.
[29] For an overview, see Aiginger (2007, 2012).
[30] Of related interest, see Peneder (2014).

policy encompassing goals that were considered beyond its ambit until now. We have to expect hurdles on this path. Some resistance comes from the traditional inefficiency of governments in reaching their goals, some from the fact that voters tend to vote for their short-term interests, often influenced by lobbying groups that benefit from the status quo. Discussion of these hurdles is part of WWWforEurope's remit and can be found on <http://www.foreurope.eu/> (Aiginger, 2013; Arrow, 2013; Geels, 2013; Aiginger, 2014). In Section 19.5 we will highlight some barriers and political 'rebound effects'[31] at the interface of industrial and energy policy.

In general, government and old industrial policy tend to support the status quo. Political rebound effects usually set in once transition has started and some low-hanging fruit has been harvested.

19.5 INTERFACE OF INDUSTRIAL AND ENERGY POLICY: PROGRESS AND BARRIERS

19.5.1 The New Consensus

The need for and the success of a new industrial policy, which promotes 'high-road' competitiveness in industrial countries and explicitly takes societal goals into account, can be illustrated through the measures taken for reaching climate goals and the industrial sector's contribution to this path.

Global warming and the need to limit temperature change to a 2°C increase (relative to the pre-industrial age) until 2100 are now well understood. This holds also for the contribution of human activities and the extent to which greenhouse gases have to be curbed (Stern, 2007; IPCC, 2014). Europe has established a roadmap, according to which emissions should be reduced between 80 per cent and 95 per cent by 2050.[32] Worldwide negotiations led to the Kyoto Protocol in 1997 and there is still hope that this could be extended in 2015. Europe has set a shorter-run goal to reduce its greenhouse emissions by 20 per cent by 2020 and plans exist to possibly increase this target to 30 per cent or 40 per cent. The European Commission puts sustainability at the centre stage of its industrial policy (see Section 19.3.3.1). The US at the federal level is reluctant to accept ambitious climate targets in international negotiations, but some states have their own sustainability strategies and President Obama agreed with the Chinese government about individual climate targets. While not agreeing to contractual limits, China acknowledges the 'big city

---

[31] Political rebound effects mean successful lobbying by defenders of the status quo, after there had initially been strong political support for change.

[32] Simulations by the PRIMES energy system model show that this very ambitious target is in principle feasible without reducing economic growth, although this would require radical technological innovations (energy efficiency improvement greatly above the historical trends) and de-carbonization initiated by a carbon price of 250€/t (European Commission, 2011a; Kupers, 2012; Schleicher and Köppl, 2013).

problem' and has carbon emission targets for 200 cities (*Financial Times*, 15 April 2013). China is also leading the development of electrical cars.

19.5.2 Signs of Change

There are encouraging signs that energy policy is on a new path:

- The EU-27's greenhouse gas emissions for 2010 are 10 per cent below their 1990 levels.
- Material consumption was 14 per cent lower in 2000 than in 1970, and further declined by 13 per cent between 2000 and 2010 (Fischer-Kowalski and Hausknost, 2014).[33]
- Nearly all industrialized countries show signs of relative decoupling, insofar as energy consumption (and in particular fossil energy use) is increasing at a lower rate than GDP.
- Denmark succeeded in achieving an absolute decoupling of its energy consumption: while GDP more than doubled between 1970 and 2010, fossil fuel consumption decreased by 23 per cent.
- The share of energy derived from renewables is increasing. In Portugal, Sweden, and Austria 50 per cent or more of electricity comes from renewable sources.

19.5.3 Resistance to Change

There are also backlashes and rebound effects:

- The European CO_2 emission trading system collapsed and there is little political will to re-establish it—let alone to deepen its ambitions. The new Australian government abolished its CO_2 tax (in contrast, China introduced such a tax in seven cities).
- In energy policy, the focus is shifting backwards, away from supporting energy efficiency and renewable energy, and towards the old strategy of emphasizing 'affordable' prices and security of supply. Germany's *Energiewende*—the plan to phase out nuclear energy—is under pressure and has already been softened in a new coalition agreement. In Europe, coal use has increased after the collapse of CO_2 emission trading, as it has become cheaper than gas. It is also used to complement renewable energy at times of low supply. Nuclear energy is also returning via the so-called 'neutrality approach'; the UK has openly requested new subsidies, based on the argument that nuclear energy is too expensive without such subsidies.

19.5.4 Low Energy Prices in the US

The availability of new energy sources, especially liquefied gas and gas extracted via new technologies such as fracking, has caused US energy prices to plummet; this is regarded as

---

[33] For differences in decoupling between production and consumption, see Munoz and Steininger (2010). Thanks to Angela Köppl for this reference.

a chance to revitalize US manufacturing.[34] Spillover effects to Europe exist as US coal is now exported, causing European gas prices to decline. Europe's energy-intensive industries are calling for the region to match the US's renewed (and now amplified) comparative advantage in energy prices: Europe should copy the US in exploiting similar new energy sources (such as fracking for gas). At the same time, Europe has already been assisting its energy-intensive industries with free allowances for CO_2 emissions. It has also postponed restoring the CO_2 emission trading system or taxing fossil fuels and kerosene (see Table 19.2).

19.5.5 Two Strategic Answers

In principle, European industrial policy has two options to answer the challenge of lower US energy costs: the first, to try to lower its own energy costs; and the second, to boost energy efficiency so as to limit the cost difference, plus provide additional measures to improve high-road competitiveness, if improvements in energy efficiency alone cannot bridge the gap. The first answer follows the logic of 'old' industrial policy. If some input costs are too high, try to get cheaper inputs too or subsidize the firm (low-cost

Table 19.2 European and US Sector Balances and Export Share

	EU				US			
	1999	2011	1999	2011	1999	2011	1999	2011
	Trade in bn €		Shares of exports		Trade in bn €		Shares of exports	
Energy-intensive industries								
Exports	77.7	247.4	11.3	15.5	57.3	123.1	9.7	16.0
Imports	64.1	216.9	9.3	13.6	79.0	106.0	13.3	13.8
Trade balance	13.6	30.5	2.0	1.9	−21.7	17.1	−3.7	2.2
Technology-driven industries								
Exports	252.1	530.9	36.6	33.2	280.0	246.3	47.2	32.0
Imports	250.1	436.8	36.3	27.3	371.1	424.3	62.5	55.1
Trade balance	2.1	94.1	0.3	5.9	−91.1	−178.0	−15.3	−23.1
Resource-intensive industries								
Exports	76.1	192.2	11.1	12.0	50.2	76.0	8.5	9.9
Imports	72.0	198.1	10.5	12.4	121.6	116.2	20.5	15.1
Trade balance	4.1	−5.8	0.6	−0.4	−71.4	−40.1	−12.0	−5.2
Engineering industries								
Exports	365.1	767.8	53.1	48.1	379.7	367.9	64.0	47.7
Imports	328.5	580.8	47.7	36.3	490.7	576.3	82.7	74.8
Trade balance	36.6	187.0	5.3	11.7	−111.0	−208.5	−18.7	−27.1

Source: Eurostat (AMECO), WIFO database

---

[34] Focusing on cheap energy as the main characteristic of the new industrial policy in the US may not tell the whole story since there are also several innovation and technology initiatives. For a critical assessment of the new US strategy see Rattner (2014).

Box 19.2 Carbon Leakage

Carbon leakage addresses the problem that ambitious standards and emission taxes in one country may shift the production of resource-intensive products to countries with lower standards, thus raising worldwide greenhouse gases. This argument is used to oppose higher energy prices or standards in Europe.

The carbon leakage argument is not completely wrong in the short run, but not convincing in the long run. Actual shifts in production depend on broader strategies, innovation efforts, spillover effects, and policy measures.

- If a company is forced to reduce emissions due to higher prices, it may introduce a better technology, not only in respect to energy but also labour or capital efficiency. This 'innovation effect' may exceed the 'relocation effect'.
- Emission trading can provide an 'efficiency discount' to the three most efficient companies (e.g. half price per ton emitted). Then innovating companies receive a double dividend from innovation: first, lower costs from the advanced technology; and second, a lower price for the remaining emissions. Furthermore, research funds like those in the EU framework programme could promote technologies radically reducing emissions. A programme to develop an ultra-low carbon technology in steel production exists, the technology has been developed, however a site for a test factory still needs to be built.
- Carbon leakage could be reduced if companies are urged to deploy the 'best technology' to plants in countries with lower standards. Incentives range from moral suasion or stakeholder activism, to trade or investment agreements. A minimum requirement would be that multinational firms have to report plant-specific emissions.
- A tax or import duty could be levied on the difference between minimal and actual emissions. Such 'border adjustment schemes' should, however, be treated carefully, as duties reduce trade, are open to protectionist misuse, and may provoke counter-measures. 'Climate funds' accelerating the global diffusion of the best technology, financed by emission trading or by a financial transaction tax, are a better alternative.

The carbon leakage argument stresses the short-run decision where to locate a *new* plant at a given point of time; it is less convincing for relocations if plants already exist. And worldwide emissions in the longer run depend firstly on technological progress in frontier countries and secondly on the speed of the global diffusion of clean technologies. Higher prices and standards in frontier countries will shift the frontier of efficiency, and trade and investment policy, political, moral, and legal pressure and technology transfer funds will decide about the speed of diffusion of best technology. Recall that total subsidies for fossil fuels are estimated to equal €400bn,[1] and could be used to boost technology transfer.

Summing up, a strategy to slow technological progress via cheaper energy and emissions prices in the countries at the frontier will probably increase worldwide emissions in the long run.[2] A green industrial policy will dynamically push *all* countries up the environmental quality ladder.

---

[1] This is six times as much as the subsidies for renewable energy sources.

[2] The carbon leakage element is restricted to a few industries. Only four industries have energy costs of 10 per cent of total costs; for most industries, energy costs are between 1 per cent and 2 per cent of total costs (Aiginger, 2013).

strategy). The second answer is to try to increase productivity and/or to foster factors which increase tomorrow's competitive advantages, specifically those fitting to the long-run goals of the society. It is not even evident that low energy prices will help to decrease the US trade deficit. The US currently has a surplus in trade with energy-intensive goods and a large deficit in technology-driven industries (€178 billion). Energy costs are very low in technology-driven industries, and only in these sectors can a rich country be successful in the long run. Investment in skills and research thus would promote the long-run specialization of a rich country much better (see Box 19.2).

19.6   Summary: A Systemic Policy, Aligned with Beyond-GDP Goals

(1) Industrial policy is back on the political agenda, driven by fear (globalization, de-industrialization) and hope (increasing employment, sustainability). Bubbles in non-manufacturing sectors (finance, construction, housing) have fuelled the financial crisis, and recovery is especially difficult in countries with a small manufacturing sector, particularly when it is combined with a current account deficit.

(2) Academia suggests that a new industrial policy must be different from the past. It should promote competition and be a discovery process in a cooperative climate between government and companies. It should align industrial policy with the long-term interests of the society. It has to be systemic and driven by a wider vision, instead of a stand-alone policy in conflict with other strands of government policy. It should stop extending the life of non-viable industries or artificially creating national champions requiring shelter from global competitors.

(3) A new industrial policy requires three new yardsticks and a redefinition of industrial policy.

- First, economic performance should be measured by a broader set of goals or a more comprehensive indicator, instead of GDP (or GDP growth). This could be the 'beyond-GDP goals' or some overall indicator of well-being like life satisfaction, happiness, or life expectation.
- Second, it should downgrade or abandon the concept of price competitiveness, which emphasizes low costs (or in its enlightened version low unit labour costs). Competitiveness should be defined as 'ability to achieve beyond-GDP goals'.
- Third, in trying to increase welfare (beyond-GDP goals), countries may pursue a low-road strategy (emphasizing low costs, taxes, social and ecological standards) or a high-road strategy based on research, skills, ecological ambition, an empowering employment policy, and excellent institutions. Industrialized countries have to pursue a high-road strategy, if they want to maintain their frontier position.

- Industrial policy for high-income countries should be defined as the sum of policy measures to achieve 'high-road competitiveness'. By targeting high-road competitiveness and achieving society's wider aims (including social and ecological goals), industrial policy thus merges into a systemic socio-economic strategy.

(4) Policy documents developed by international organizations, the European Commission, and national governments have defined new goals for industrial policy that partially follow the ideas of academia. All proposals directly or indirectly focus on the structure of the economies as a whole, not only on a narrowly defined manufacturing sector, since the borders between manufacturing and services are ever more blurred. The OECD's 'New Perspectives Program' promotes the inclusion of social and ecological goals into economic models and thinking.

(5) The European Commission puts sustainability 'at the centre stage' of industrial policy (unfortunately, jointly with a rather conventionally defined cost competitiveness). Its Energy Roadmap 2050 sets the goal to reduce greenhouse gas emissions by as much as '80 to 95%'. Radical innovation projects—for example, on ultra-low carbon steel—have been started. Recently, the European Commission set a goal to increase manufacturing's share of nominal value added GDP to 20 per cent by 2020 (from 16 per cent currently), which is realistic only if quality of production is significantly upgraded and service components are added into the definition of 'manufacturing'.

(6) The renewed interest in industrial policy in the US was motivated by the current account deficit. Reducing energy imports and becoming a net exporter for energy seem to be the overarching policy priorities. But a large share of the US deficit—€180bn—stems from a US trade deficit in technology-driven industries (where energy costs are about 1 per cent of total costs). Reducing energy prices will not boost the US's share of manufacturing in global trade, as keeping the median wage constant for fifty years did not help.

(7) The new intentions of industrial policy are still on trial. Europe's fear of losing cost competitiveness relative to the US is reducing its determination to put sustainability at the 'centre stage'. On the positive side, the share of renewable energy has increased strongly, with some countries producing 50 per cent of electric energy from 'green' sources. But new energy sources need complementary fossil fuels and investment in the power-grid infrastructure. Coal use in Europe increased after the collapse of the European emissions trading scheme. Increasing US coal exports made coal cheaper in Europe than gas. At the same time, China is undertaking a deep transformation, trying to increase resource and energy efficiency—albeit from a very low initial level. It has set goals to increase R&D investment to 2 per cent of GDP (the current EU share) and is making advances in electric vehicles and alternative energies.

(8) Europe has in principle two choices to cope with high energy prices: to go for lower energy prices itself (by exploiting shale gas or by reducing taxes on energy)

or to further its lead in energy efficiency *plus* to increase investment in innovation and top education. Given a vision of a system encompassing social and ecological goals, the only viable choice is to pursue an industrial policy to encourage energy efficiency and social and ecological innovation.

(9) Going for a socio-ecological transition can make Europe a 'role model' for other countries, even if different preferences and circumstances will always call for some heterogeneity. Industrial policy should foster the long-run transition, not decelerate structural change. This is a demanding challenge, given vested interests and the traditional role of governments to preserve the status quo and national champions.

(10) Refocusing on the economy's industrial base makes sense, particularly after the experience of bubbles in financial and real estate markets. New industrial policy should support the transition of traditional, narrowly defined manufacturing selling tangible 'goods' to a sector producing greater consumer value, supporting the economy's long-term goals. We therefore define an industrial policy for high-wage countries as strategy to promote high-road competitiveness where competitiveness is defined as the ability of an economy to provide 'beyond-GDP goals'.

Acknowledgements

The author thanks David Bailey, Heinz Handler, Jürgen Janger, Christian Ketels, Peter Mayerhofer, Michael Peneder, Gunter Tichy, Johanna Vogel, and Ken Warwick for their helpful suggestions and comments and Dagmar Guttmann and Eva Sokoll for research assistance.

References

Aghion, P., Boulanger, J., and Cohen, E. (2011). *Rethinking Industrial Policy*. Bruegel Policy Brief, April.

Aiginger, K. (1997). 'The Use of Unit Values to Discriminate between Price and Quality Competition', *Cambridge Journal of Economics* 21, 571–92.

Aiginger, K. (2006). 'Competitiveness: From a Dangerous Obsession to a Welfare Creating Ability with Positive Externalities', *Journal of Industry, Competition and Trade* 6(2), 161–77.

Aiginger, K. (2007). 'Industrial Policy: A Dying Breed or a Re-Emerging Phoenix', *Journal of Industry, Competition and Trade* 7(3/4), 297–323.

Aiginger, K. (2009). Evaluation of the Finnish National Innovation System. Policy Report.

Aiginger, K. (2011a). 'The Inefficiency of Industrial and Innovation Policy in France', VOX 3, October, <http://www.voxeu.org/article/inefficiency-industrial-and-innovation-policy-france>.

Aiginger, K. (2011b). 'Why Growth Performance Differed across Countries in the Recent Crisis: The Impact of Pre-Crisis Conditions', *Review of Economics and Finance* 4, 35–52.

Aiginger, K. (2012). *A Systemic Industrial Policy to Pave a New Growth Path for Europe*, WIFO Working Paper No. 421/2012.

Aiginger, K. (2013). European Industrial Policy: Systemic and Integrated or Isolated Again? European Parliament, Brussels, Industrial Policy Roundtable, 24 April.

Aiginger, K. (2014). *Towards New Dynamics: A Science Based Vision for Europe*. WWWforEurope Working Paper.

Aiginger, K., Bärenthaler-Sieber, S., and Vogel, J. (2013). *Competitiveness Under New Perspectives*, WWWforEurope Working Paper No. 44.

Aiginger, K., Cramme, O., Ederer, S., Liddle, R., and Thillaye, R. (2012). *Reconciling the Short and the Long Run: Governance Reforms to Solve the Crisis and Beyond*, WWWforEurope Policy Brief No. 1.

Aiginger, K., Firgo, M., and Huber, P. (2012). *Policy Options for the Development of Peripheral Regions and Countries of Europe*, WWWforEurope Policy Brief No. 2.

Aiginger, K. and Glocker, C. (2015, forthcoming). 'Restarting Growth in Europe', *Applied Economics Quarterly*.

Aiginger, K. and Guger, A. (2006). 'The European Socio-Economic Model', in A. Giddens, P. Diamond, and R. Liddle, (eds), *Global Europe, Social Europe*, pp. 124–50. Cambridge: Polity Press.

Aiginger, K. and Sieber, S. (2006). 'The Matrix Approach to Industrial Policy', *International Review of Applied Economics* 20(5), 573–603.

Arrow, K. (2013). 'Knowledge, Belief and the Economic System', *WIFO-Monatsberichte* 12, 943–51.

Berger, S. (2013). *Making in America. From Innovation to Market*. Cambridge MA: MIT.

Cecchetti, St. and Kharroubi, E. (2012). *Reassessing the Impact of Finance on Growth*, BIS Working Paper No. 381.

Clark, C. (1940). *The Conditions of Economic Progress*. London: Macmillan.

Criscuolo, C., Martin, R., Overman, H., and Van Reenen, J. (2012). *The Causal Effects of an Industrial Policy*, NBER Working Paper No. 17842.

European Commission (2005). *Implementing the Community Lisbon Programme: A Policy Framework to Strengthen EU Manufacturing—Towards a More Integrated Approach for Industrial Policy*, Brussels, No. COM(2005) 474 final.

European Commission (2009). *Preparing for Our Future: Developing a Common Strategy for Key Enabling Technologies in the EU*, Brussel, No. COM(2009) 512.

European Commission (2010). *An Integrated Industrial Policy for the Globalisation Era Putting Competitiveness and Sustainability at Centre Stage*, Brussels, No. COM(2010), 614.

European Commission (2011a). *Impact Assessment, Energy Roadmap 2050*, Brussel, Commission Staff Working Paper No. SEC(2011) 1565.

European Commission (2011b). *A Resource-Efficient Europe: Flagship Initiative Under the Europe 2020 Strategy, Communication from the Commission to the European Parliament, the Council, the European Economic and Social Committee and the Committee of the Regions*, No. COM(2011) 21 final, <http://eur-lex.europa.eu/LexUriServ/LexUriServ.do?uri=COM:2011:0021:FIN:EN:PDF>.

European Commission (2012). *A Stronger European Industry for Growth and Economic Recovery, Industrial Policy Communication Update*, Brussels, No. COM(2012) 582 final.

European Commission (2013). 'European Competitiveness Report 2013: Towards Knowledge Driven Reindustrialisation', Brussels.

European Commission (2014a). *For a European Industrial Renaissance*, Brussels, No. COM (2014) 14.

European Commission (2014b). *A Vision for the Internal Market for Industrial Products*, Brussels, No. COM(2014) 23.

Fischer-Kowalski, M. and Hausknost, D. (2014). *Large Scale Societal Transitions in the Past*, WWWforEurope Working Paper No. 55.

Fourastier, F. (1954). *Die große Hoffnung des 20*. Köln: Jahrhunderts.

Geels, F. W. (2013). *The Impact of the Financial-Economic Crisis on Sustainability Transitions: Financial Investment, Governance and Public Discourse*, WWWforEurope Working Paper No. 39.

Intergovernmental Panel on Climate Change (2014). Climate Change 2014: Mitigation of Climate Change.

Jaeger, C. C., Paroussos, L., Mangalagiu, D., Kupers, R., Mandel, A., and Tabara, J. D. (2011). *A New Growth Path for Europe*. Potsdam.

Janger, J., Hölzl, W., Kaniovski, S., Kutsam, J., Peneder, M., Reinstaller, A., Sieber, S., Stadler, I., and Unterlass, F. (2011). *Structural Change and the Competitiveness of EU Member States*, European Commission Final Report No. CR 2011.

Johnson, S. (2009). The Economic Crisis and the Crisis in Economics. Revised Version of a Speech Prepared for the Presidential Address to the Association for Comparative Economics, San Francisco, 4 January.

Journal of Industry, Competition and Trade (2006). 'Special Issue on Competitiveness', *Journal of Industry, Competition and Trade* 6(2).

Journal of Industry, Competition and Trade (2007). 'Special Issue on the Future of Industrial Policy', *Journal of Industry, Competition and Trade* 7(314).

Kupers, R. (2012). A New Growth Path for Europe. WWWforEurope Lecture at WIFO, 22 January.

Mazzucato, M. (2011). *The Entrepreneurial State*. London: Demos.

Muñoz, P. and Steininger, K. W. (2010). 'Austria's CO2 Responsibility and the Carbon Content of its International Trade', *Ecological Economics* 69(10), 2003–19. doi:10.1016/j.ecolecon.2010.05.017, doi: 10.1016/j.ecolecon.2010.05.017.

O'Sullivan, E., Andreoni, A., and López-Gómes, C. (2013). 'What is New in the New Industrial Policy? A Manufacturing Systems Perspective', *Oxford Review of Economic Policy* 29(2), 432–62.

OECD (Organisation for Economic Co-operation and Development) (2012). *Beyond Industrial Policy: Emerging Issues and New Trends*, Draft STI Working Paper on Industrial Policy, No. DSTI/IND(2012)19. Paris: OECD.

OECD (Organisation for Economic Co-operation and Development) (2014). *Evaluation of Industrial Policy*. Paris: OECD.

Owen, G. (2012). *Industrial Policy in Europe since the Second World War: What Has Been Learnt?*, The European Center for International Political Economy, Brussels, ECIPE Occasional Paper No. 1.

Peneder, M. (2009). *Sectoral Growth Drivers and Competitiveness in the European Union*. Brussels: European Commission.

Peneder, M. (2010). 'Technological Regimes and the Variety of Innovation Behavior: Creating Integrated Taxonomies of Firms and Sectors', *Research Policy* 39, 323–34.

Peneder, M. (2014). *Warum die Neue Industriepolitik die Deindustrialisierung beschleunigen wird*, FIW Policy Brief No. 23.

Rattner, S. (2014). 'The Myth of Industrial Rebound', *New York Times* 26 January.

Reinstaller, A. (2013). *An Evolutionary View on Social Innovation and the Process of Economic Change*, WWWforEurope Working Paper No. 43.

Reinstaller, A., Hölzl, W., Kutsam, J., and Schmid, C. (2013). *The Development of Productive Structures of EU Member Countries and Their International Competitiveness, Study for the European Commission, DG Enterprise and Industry*. Vienna: WIFO.

Rifkin, J. (2012). 'The Third Industrial Revolution: How the Internet, Green Electricity, and 3-D Printing are Ushering in a Sustainable Era of Distributed Capitalism', *World Financial Review*, 3 March.

Rodrik, D. (2004). Industrial Policy for the Twenty-First Century. Paper prepared for UNIDO, <http://www.hks.harvard.edu/fs/drodrik/Research%20papers/UNIDOSep.pdf>.

Rodrik, D. (2008). 'Industrial Policy: Don't Ask Why, Ask How', *Middle East Development Journal* Demo Issue, 1–29.

Rodrik, D. (2011). The Manufacturing Imperative. Project Syndicate. <http://www.project-syndicate.org/commentary/rodrik60/english>.

Rodrik, D. (2013). *Green Industrial Policy*. Paper written for the Grantham Research Institute project on 'Green Growth and the New Industrial Revolution'.

Rodrik, D., Subramanian, A., and Trebbi, F. (2004). 'Institutions Rule: The Primacy of Institutions over Geography and Integration in Economic Development', *Journal of Economic Growth* 9(2), 131–65.

Sachs, J. (2008)., 'Europe as a Soft Power', *Financial Times* 19 August.

Schleicher, S. and Köppl, A. (2013). *Energieperspektiven für Österreich Zielorientierte Strukturen und Strategien für 2020 und 2030*.

Schneeweiß, S. (2012). *Wieviel Finanzmarkt braucht die Realwirtschaft?*. Vienna: Thesis Wirtschaftsuniversität Wien (Vienna University for Economics and Business).

Stern, S. (2007). *Stern Review: The Economics of Climate Change*. London: HM Treasury.

Stiglitz, J. E., Lin, J. Y., and Monga, C. (2013). *The Rejuvenation of Industrial Policy*, The World Bank, Washington, Policy Research Working Paper No. 6628.

Stiglitz, J., Sen, A., and Fitoussi, J.-P. (2009). Report by the Commission on the Measurement of Economic Performance and Social Progress.

Stiglitz, J., Sen, A., and Fitoussi, J.-P. (2010). *Mismeasuring Our Lives*. New York: The New Press.

Veugelers, R. (ed.). (2013). 'Manufacturing Europe's Future', *Bruegel Blueprint Series*, XXI.

Wade, R. H. (2012). 'Return of Industrial Policy?', *International Review of Applied Economics* 26(2), 223–39.

Warwick, K. (2013). *Beyond Industrial Policy: Emerging Issues and New Trends*, OECD Science, Technology and Industry Policy Papers No. 2.

Wolf, M. (2014). Introduction to the Session: Integration, Currency Unions, and Balance of Payments at INET Conference, Toronto.

World Bank (2012). *Golden Growth: Restoring the Lustre of the European Economic Model*, Washington: The World Bank, Working Paper No. 68168.

....

CHAPTER 20

INDUSTRIAL POLICY

A Green Agenda

....

DAN COFFEY AND CAROLE THORNLEY

20.1 INTRODUCTION

....

POLICY in Britain towards industry, if uncertain, is evolving. It is poised to move away from one-sided preoccupations with 'horizontal' policy, in the sense of generic measures intended to apply broadly across sectors, to include a new role for policies targeting specific sectors; and the reduction of carbon emissions is now expressly on the policy agenda. But at the same time, there are significant contra-indications about intent. Despite a now secure scientific consensus on greenhouse gases and global warming, and the impetus provided by the Stern Review (HMG, 2006), there are risks of a backward lurch towards re-carbonizing strategies even in the midst of efforts to regulate to reduce carbon emissions. Official policy in Britain is in any case rhetorically wedded to a comparatively narrow vision of low carbon industrial development that will be achieved by successful commercial exploitation of improving technologies. And it is constrained by a powerful lobby faction hostile even to the mildest efforts to rethink policy relationships and the role of the state vis-à-vis industry.

In this chapter, we first review political contexts before considering at a quite general level the significant difficulties low carbon development poses for traditional industrial policy perspectives on what it is hoped will be gained by a more interventionist role for the state. For this purpose we critically appraise a seemingly innocuous formulation which attempts to bridge questions of national economic balance and business competitiveness vis-à-vis traditional industrial policy goals like improvements to the balance of trade, employment, and growth; we emphasize the stresses that appear when sustainability confronts these traditional policy objectives. We next consider the prospective reorientation in Britain towards policy measures targeting industries which are preselected as strategic, and explain why this is a potential gain for policy design for sustainability; but at the same time we warn that in seeking to supplement a horizontal policy framework there are risks that policy outcomes will be unduly 'vertical', in the sense of eliding the critical importance of cross-sector linkages, and that a preoccupation with industrial growth will trump sustainability. We illustrate this with a short review of policy towards Britain's car industry—branch-arm of a global industry and a major source of carbon emissions that will worsen steadily in its environmental impact as worldwide fleets of fossil fuel-powered vehicles grow—where sustainability is a major theme. We close with some short notes on the UN Environmental Programme (UNEP) initiative on new business models favouring product service systems, and call for further research on market redesign for sustainability.

20.2 POLICY CONTEXTS

The shock of the economic and financial crisis of 2008–9 caused soul-searching amongst at least some policy-makers about the causes of the ongoing shrinkage of Britain's manufacturing industries. While output indices for real estate, retail, and financial services ballooned, comparisons suggested that the country's national output in manufactures was less in absolute terms for 2009 than during Britain's first full year inside Europe's common market, in 1973 (Griffiths and Wall, 2012, p. 4). In the same year, jobs in manufacture fell to 10 per cent of the national.[1] This provided a context for reawakened concerns about de-industrialization.

Of particular note is how the then Labour government, led by Prime Minister Gordon Brown, responded. A new industrial strategy was launched—*The UK Low Carbon Industrial Strategy* (HMG, 2009a)—predicated on the potential benefits of low carbon policy. While cast in somewhat general terms, areas looked at included energy and resources management, products, skills, and infrastructures, as well as information and communications technology; highlighted sectors included aerospace, automotive, chemicals, and construction. The document was co-produced by the Departments for Business, Innovation and Skills (BIS) and Energy and Climate Change (DECC), with a foreword from Peter Mandelson, architect of the New Labour project, and Ed Miliband, now Labour leader. An association was thus posited between industrial redevelopment to correct sectoral imbalances, and the promotion of low carbon initiatives. Set against the record of previous decades, the arrival of this document could be, and should be, seen as a potentially significant policy departure.

Pressure for this move had been building before the crash. Regulatory measures to reduce carbon emissions, reflecting international commitments and undertakings and the developing stance of the EU vis-à-vis Member States, were lending substantial impetus

---

[1] See Social Trends (2010, p. 49) (and bearing in mind of course the well-known problems of delineating between sectors and gauging relative employment weightings).

at sector levels to business requests from government for financial and infrastructures support. The British Trades Union Congress (TUC), sensitive to union memberships, favoured low carbon policy themes to revivify industrial policy (TUC, 2005) (its concern with socially just low carbon transitions is acknowledged in the new low carbon strategy: see HMG, 2009a, p. 87, citing TUC, 2008). The TUC also supported transitional assistance schemes, while pressing for credible long-term government commitments on investment. The low carbon industrial policy initiative did not emerge without contexts.

It is perhaps incidental, but nonetheless worthwhile, to pause at this juncture to note that the role of unions should certainly not be underestimated in questions of industrial policy formulation going forward. They possess their own international networks, understandings, and expertise, and collectively span the public and private sectors. Individual trade unions, whether of the general kind like Unite in manufacture or UNISON in public services, or industry-specific like the construction workers union UCATT and its campaigns for greener social housing, have been highly active in identifying areas of policy relevance (see Coffey and Thornley, 2015a, forthcoming). For its part, the TUC has pressed the government to heed its own Committee on Climate Change, which independently advises on carbon emissions, and made the case for a new economic model incorporating a green revolution in 'skills, jobs and industries' (O'Grady, 2013). There is joint TUC–industry work on the 'energy-intensive industries'—aluminium, oil and chemicals, steel, glass, cement, ceramics, paper-making (Burke, 2012).[2]

The identity of these particular industries also throws light on the extent of the conundrums facing traditional industrial policy models. The ceramics industry in Britain, for instance, clusters in the potteries district of Stoke-on-Trent in the English West Midlands; it has redevelopment potentials (see Tomlinson and Branston, 2014; also Hervas-Oliver et al., 2011), but promoting an energy-intensive sector requires consideration of measures on energy use. Or consider the recession-hit construction industry, with its potential to create demands on all seven industries listed above: building materials include aluminium, steel, glass, and cement; work, including fabrication, transport, mixing, and assembly, requires power; a new housing programme produces homes to be lit, heated, and adorned.

Returning to wider policy themes and their political contexts, the inconclusive general election of 2010 saw the formation of a new Coalition government comprised of the Conservatives and Liberal Democrats. Despite immediate talk of a 'march of the makers' by the new Chancellor of the Exchequer and Conservative Party strategist George Osborne, impetus for a change of policy direction was almost as quickly lost. A disappointing Coalition 'Plan for Growth' (HMG, 2011) simply reiterated a supply side, deregulatory and low corporate tax agenda for Britain. Likewise, a Treasury-run austerity programme has favoured public spending cuts and reduced transfer payments to the

---

[2] See also TUC (2013).

unemployed and disabled, over the kind of growth-oriented 'greening' strategies favoured by critics. The impression of a lost moment is not lessened by seeming efforts to win the next election by recreating the conditions of the last economic crisis, with measures to spur private house sales stoking fears of another asset bubble.[3]

The Treasury, perennially unsympathetic to industrial policy, has also acted to curtail the ambitions of Michael Heseltine, the Conservative Party's most senior champion of state mobilization in support of local and regional industrial development and economic renewal. In a report commissioned by Prime Minister David Cameron (see Heseltine, 2012), Lord Heseltine called for, amongst other things, a £49 billion transfer of existing central government money into a single developmental 'pot'—the Single Local Growth Fund—to go to local areas over a four-year period, with immediate pump-priming to kick-start 'strategies' and 'structures'. Instead, the Treasury has opted to allocate just £2 billion for 2015/16, as well as in each subsequent year of the next Parliament, to a total of about one-sixth that recommended. While a large number of smaller recommendations by Lord Heseltine have been accepted or partially accepted by the government, the manifest blockage here, as in other important areas (including keener oversight of foreign acquisitions of assets held in Britain), has been aptly described as 'disappointingly timid' (Brinkley, 2013).

There is certainly more than a hint of déjà vu to this. When Heseltine served in John Major's post-1992 government as President of the Board of Trade he was known to favour 'selective intervention'; he was blocked accordingly from chairing the Cabinet Industrial Policy Committee, saw the then National Economic Development Council (NEDC) which he proposed to chair abolished, and encountered a Treasury 'flexing its muscles' by signalling tighter spending limits (Theakston, 1996, p. 171). The TUC, welcoming Heseltine's recent Review, correctly warned of likely resistance from quarters including the Cabinet and the Treasury, antipathetic to efforts to reorient government industry policies (Barber, 2012). What is different this time is the extent to which the struggle over policy is now enmeshed in the case for low carbon economic development, with campaigners against what might be called the 'Treasury line' favouring an investment-led recovery focusing on green jobs, technologies, and infrastructures. It is a time of flux in policy alignments: on the one hand there is the recently inaugurated Associate Parliamentary Manufacturing Group (since re-labelled the All-Party Parliamentary Manufacturing Group)—a cross-party organization seeking open debate and welcoming all comers—and on the other sizeable policy camps deeply hostile to a more activist state.

If the Treasury line is hostile, on the more positive side the Coalition's Secretary of State at the Department for Business, Innovation and Skills (BIS), the Liberal Democrat Vince Cable, has tried to at least maintain previous policy trajectories. Alongside familiar, and now well-worn if not dog-eared, promises to plan long term and tackle market failures, support sector partnerships, encourage emerging technologies, and develop 'pipelines' of skilled workers (see Cable, 2012), Cable has overseen the publication of a more

---

[3] This is still an unresolved point of public debate at time of writing.

explicitly formulated proposal—in *Industrial Strategy: UK Sector Analysis* (HMG, 2012)—to move to sector-targeted industrial policies alongside existing policy frameworks. This has been accompanied by a call from Michael Heseltine to underpin a national growth strategy with ten sector councils,[4] recalling an earlier Labour ambition for 'ten industrial forums' (Coates, 2005, p. 105). The Automotive Council, established by Labour in 2009, and discussed in more detail in a later section of this chapter, is now seen as a 'model case'. This body is tasked with facilitating profitable but sustainable development.

Similar hopes for an environmentally sounder industrial trajectory can also be seen as partly included in aspirations for a more effective use of state procurement policies as a transformative policy tool—another longer-standing proposal predating the Coalition—as well as more innovative approaches to questions of securing business finance. On this latter point, a Green Investment Bank was formed in 2012 as a public company, although as yet it is hardly positioned to be more than a peripheral influence.

Yet against even such first steps there are further, and global, contra-indications. As the slump in oil and energy prices that commenced from the mid-1980s petered out, price and cost structures became less favourable to fossil fuel use. However, a concerted effort is now under way to redevelop oil and gas. The current live controversy over shale oil and gas is a case in point.[5] As an article by the Global Head of Commodities Research at Citi, Edward L. Morse, published in a recent issue of *Foreign Affairs*, puts it, a 'paradigm shift' beckons:

> It is clear that vast amounts of hydrocarbons have migrated from their original source rock and become trapped in shale and tight rock, and the extent of these rock formations, like the extent of the original source rock, is enormous—containing resources far in excess of total global conventional proven oil reserves, which are 1.5 trillion barrels. And there are already signs that the technology involved in extracting these resources is transferable outside the United States, so that its international spread is inevitable. / In short, it now looks as though the first decades of the twenty-first century will see an extension of the trend that has persisted for the past few millennia: the availability of plentiful energy at ever-lower cost and with ever-greater efficiency, enabling major advances in global economic growth. (Morse, 2014, pp. 3–4)

The publishing venue in which this article appears conveys a salient point: energy resourcing is inseparably linked to the geopolitical. The current realignment of American energy policy vis-à-vis exports; its hopes of contesting Russia and other energy exporters on the world stage; its exhortations to the EU to get with the project; all of these involve considerations going beyond mere economy or environment. The author of the piece does identify three main problem areas yet to be fully resolved. One is the rapid tail-off in production at each well site, a geological feature of the extraction process, producing

---

[4] See Heseltine (2012).

[5] For pre-financial crisis British energy policy, see Rutledge (2007). This gives a broad sense of how British policy reacted first to falling then rising prices.

uncertainties on production volumes; another is fear of negative cash flows, in which investors fail to see a return on their money. On each, the assessment is sanguine. The third comprises a set of environmental concerns: water resource drainage or pollution; waste spillage; and seismic activity (see Morse, 2014, pp. 5–6). Here a recommendation is made for a clearer steer to the industry on 'best practices'. But amidst such points of controversy—which *are* recognized—it is notable that nothing is said per se about the implications for greenhouse gas emissions.

But the issues here, and over and above the obvious point that shale oil and gas when combusted will release carbon, are immense, and the potential for exacerbating industrial greenhouse problems profound. The key point is delivered clearly and accessibly in Sperling and Gordon (2009), an excellent survey, principally from a US perspective, of the problems posed by the growing worldwide fleet of motorized vehicles powered by fossil fuels. They consider the link between fossil fuel-dependent transport systems and 'Big Oil', viewed as a closely related commercial interest. Experienced in handling large-scale fossil fuel projects, and accomplished at organizing distribution networks, they see Big Oil in the West as a highly active sector increasingly engaged with developing unconventional oil sources: dense and viscous heavy oils, of the kind found in Venezuela; tar sands, of the kind found in (Alberta) Canada; coal oil, converted from coal to oil through gasification and synthesizing or by direct liquefaction; and shale.[6] The point these writers make is that developing unconventional oil sources not only represents environmentally damaging retrenchment for Big Oil—'in most cases [the unconventional oil source] contains high levels of nitrogen, sulphur and heavy metal contaminants, and its mining and processing consumes huge quantities of water and energy and causes extreme damage to surrounding ecosystems.... [with] perhaps 15 percent more CO_2 per gallon of gasoline from very heavy oils and tar sands to at least 100 percent more for fuels made from coal' (Sperling and Gordon, 2009, p. 129)—but also a global lock-in for the worldwide transport energy system, back into fossil fuels.

In the particular case of shale gas and shale oil extraction, energy sector enthusiasts seem as likely to point to the 'Darwinian competition' which has seen more than 6,000 independents in oil and gas compete in the US for the new shale business, and Chesapeake surpass ExxonMobil as 'largest U.S. natural gas supplier' (Hefner, 2014, pp. 10–11). But as the sector shakes out, the newer large interests that will compete and co-exist with existing large interests will push just as hard on policy, at home and abroad.

The spillover into domestic British politics of the drive for 'fracking'—the hydraulic fracturing of shale rocks to free up hydrocarbons—has left environmental campaigners here, as in the US, aghast. But it has nonetheless emerged as a major policy plank for energy. It is enough simply to recall that a British jury had to be convened in order to declare Parliament's only Green Party MP, Caroline Lucas, innocent of a serious public order defence by dint of peaceful participation in a protest to wonder whether, in an odd

---

[6] See Sperling and Gordon (2009, pp. 123–30) for summary descriptions.

reversal of history, the state powers that were used to close down Britain's coal mines will open up its shale. In terms of policies for industry, the political signals could hardly be more mixed.

20.3 Balance and Sustainability

The contradictions of policy formulation are not eased by the general difficulties environmental sustainability poses for industrial policy. In this section we consider the chief of these complications—the unavoidable fact that those who have traditionally advocated industrial policy, and whatever else their reasoning, have usually done so in order to see higher national levels of industrial capacity and output, not least in manufacture. At the same time we warn against the policy-maker predilection for selling sustainability as if this was nothing more than a way of describing more effective business practices within existing market trajectories, cutting energy costs in production (say) or making serial improvements in products to reduce carbon footprints while improving customer experience.

20.3.1 Internal and External Balance

One way of viewing a well-balanced economy is to say that a national economy has achieved a satisfactory sectoral balance when enabled to grow at rates and in ways consistent with something akin to full employment, while earning enough from exports to pay for imports at something like stable exchange rates, subject (of course) to various *ceteris paribus* clauses. This would mean that the overall composition of the economy is such that inadequately developed industrial capabilities do not impede. Should this prove to be a problem, a space exists for the state to adopt a proactive industrial policy stance to promote industrial development. Something like this vision underpins a framework of analysis which has proved particularly influential in past British industrial policy debate. In particular, and assuming a growing world economy, balance in an open economy requires an appropriate level and mix of sectoral capabilities to maintain desired rates of employment and output growth at more or less stable, and certainly not continuously depreciating, exchange rates.[7]

It has long also been proposed that one reason why domestic industrial performance fails is that the individual business units within lack commercial capabilities like innovativeness, and as such are unable to capture world income growth to a sufficient degree:

---

[7] For applications to Britain in the 1970s and to America in the 1990s see, inter alia, Singh (1977) and Howes and Singh (2000) (and references in each). For a comment, see also Coffey and Thornley (2009, ch. 2). The best introduction to the 'de-industrialization' literature for Britain remains Coates (1994).

> Basically in a growing world economy the growth of exports is mainly to be explained by the income elasticity of demand of foreign countries for a country's products; but it is a matter of the innovative ability and adaptive capacity of its manufacturers whether this income elasticity will tend to be relatively large or small. (Kaldor, 1981, p. 603; cited in Howes and Singh, 2000, p. 5)

The income elasticity of demand abroad for exports is the determinant of how much a country like Britain, for example, would be able to sell overseas in an assumed context of rising world incomes, to balance national expenditures on imports of goods produced abroad. In this connection, manufactures have been considered commercially important because they are a highly tradable branch of production, as well as strategically important for any national economy structurally dependent on imports of commodities like food and fuel—both relevant to historic British experience. Where there is a growing world market for manufactured goods it is therefore important to match rival economies for attractive products. And this is not simply a question of cost-competitiveness; even with relatively competitive exchange rate-weighted labour costs, for instance, proper attention to a range of other sales dimensions for products—'quality, marketing, design, reliability and service' (Howes and Singh, 2000, p. 4)—is necessary to ensure that sufficiently attractive and hence internationally saleable goods are produced.

The perspective thus offered is one that marries a view on good business practices, sensitive to more than just common currency costs, with a policy emphasis on working to achieve sectoral balance in the wider economy. As an approach to what industrial policy should aim to achieve, it tends accordingly to favour constructive improvements, driven by public measures to support private business investment, and a significant research and development (R&D) effort for products aided by technology policy and funding for infrastructures, focusing on key export sectors. Conversely, poorly designed policy can have perverse effects on industry. The view is one of cumulative causal processes interacting over time: success in innovation today breeds conditions for success tomorrow. One feature of this approach is that exchange rate devaluation on its own is not a lasting solution to the problem of engendering industrial dynamism.[8]

Summarized thus, and stripped of policy features like temporary import controls, at one point widely recommended by supporters of state industrial intervention to support re-industrialization, there is little to frighten any but the most obdurate followers of the 'market forces' cannon, especially faced with the problems exposed by the 2008–9 crisis. A number of key assumptions, applied to Britain, resonate with current thought:

(1) There is an assumption that promoting business competitiveness, and winning markets abroad for Britain, is a central policy endeavour.

---

[8] Which is not to say that an overvalued exchange rate is never a problem, but rather that there is more to winning markets than competing on cost. Note that the very substantial currency devaluation in Britain since 2008–9 has not had the positive effects on the structure of British production many first expected.

(2) There is an assumption that worldwide growth is the expected norm, so that the problem for the nation is to capture its benefits by exporting.
(3) Competitive cost in common currencies is important, but investments in new product technologies and infrastructures are also essential.

Indeed, it is hard to see any of the major political parties voicing even the suspicion of an objection to these points, on grounds of reasonableness.

20.3.2 Enter the Dragon: Injecting Sustainability

However, things look less reasonable if sustainability is a goal. It becomes more problematic to think of industrial policy as a tool to improve the alignment between public goals and private aims by helping commercial businesses win markets and thereby grow industries. And things remain difficult even in the presence of so-called 'eco-innovation'— 'innovation that reflects the concept's explicit emphasis on a reduction of environmental impact, whether such an effect is intended or not' (OECD, 2009, p. 13; cited in Kesidou and Demirel, 2012, p. 862).[9] Eco-innovation, described in these terms, is environmentally benign; business contexts may not be.

Consider in the first instance a cost-of-business example, based for illustration's sake on a single-firm single-output industry with two contrasting production regimes. Regime A generates lower marginal production costs and lower per unit carbon emissions than regime B, achieved through adoption of energy-saving production methods. While it might seem axiomatic that regime A is environmentally preferable, there are in fact two contrasting forces to consider. The obvious one is the reduction in per unit emissions of carbon. If for regime A it is E_A and for regime B it is E_B, the per unit reduction is E_B minus E_A. Easily overlooked are the increased emissions from any extra units of industry output produced and sold as a result of the regime change. However, under reasonable assumptions about final customer demand for the product, profit-seeking behaviour (unless constrained) will lead the firm under regime A to fully exploit the cost benefit and produce more units. Let output with regime A and B be Q_A and Q_B respectively, with $Q_A > Q_B$. Evidently, net carbon emissions are only lower if the emissions released on the extra units produced is less than the emissions otherwise saved. In other words, it requires that $(Q_A - Q_B)E_A - Q_B(E_B - E_A) < 0$. Were the sign reversed, net carbon emissions would be highest with the low carbon technology.

The point is not entirely unsubtle. Small cost savings with large emissions reductions are a priori better for the environment than large cost savings with small emissions reductions, although businesses acting on purely commercial grounds would choose the latter; and if the costs of business reorganization are substantial then so too must be

---

[9] Social and institutional changes, as well as aspects more specific to business firms, are included in 'innovation' (see Kesidou and Demirel, 2012, p. 862).

the cost benefits if innovation is justifiable on a profitability basis.[10] This basic issue also applies naturally when the assumption of a single-firm single-output industry is developed to include more realistic cases. Its crux is not the presence of an improving technology but rather the business propensity to only exploit such changes as will facilitate profit-making, in which connection there is a predisposition to growth ($Q_A > Q_B$). What should be immediately apparent is that if public goals incorporate sustainability, then even in the presence of 'improving technology' there is no axiomatic coincidence between what is wanted and what commerce delivers.

Looking at the bigger picture, firms are in any event most likely to innovate when they see a buoyant future demand for their products. The example above is for static demand conditions: reducing the price of the product because of lower energy costs generates more sales, but the sales level at any price is a given and (for simplicity) certain quantity. In a growing world economy, sales at any price will be expected to rise. Now while such a scenario is certainly conducive to energy-saving innovations, it is also one in which, year on year, production quantities rise. Output is expanding because of growth conditions on the demand side, and energy-savings innovations reinforce that output expansion on the cost side. From the perspective of traditional approaches to industrial policy, it is precisely this kind of cumulative interaction between demand, innovation, and cost that policy-makers are assumed to be seeking, generating growth. But if eco-improving innovation of the type that reduces production cost through energy savings occurs in contexts where the growth experienced is comparatively large, then from a sustainability perspective victory could be pyrrhic.

Consider in the second instance the question of what it is that private commerce does to cultivate markets through clever product design. In other words, what it is that businesses do when applying 'innovative ability' and 'adaptive capacity' to develop products, sometimes at least. For this purpose a real world illustration is drawn from the car industry, where the marketing of design features, equipment loadings and ratings, and post-sale services provision is an immediately recognizable industry feature.

Following the oil shocks of the 1970s it was widely predicted that smaller, fuel-efficient models would push out large cars, most notably in America, then experiencing rising Japanese import penetration. Moving thirty-plus years ahead, this is not what happened. As Sperling and Gordon (2009)—already encountered in connection with Big Oil and oil-fuelled transport—show, falling energy prices from the 1980s saw previous marketing trajectories in America reassert: the Honda Accord, for instance, chosen because Honda is a 'better' environmental performer, underwent a 75 per cent weight increase between 1976 and 2008; by the end of this period, it travelled 15 miles (24km) less to the gallon (Sperling and Gordon, 2009, p. 19). Moreover, as the American giants led an industry

---

[10] The possibility that net energy savings from 'greener' business organization generate higher overall carbon releases because of the promotion of output is an area of study on both sides of the Atlantic, including computable general equilibrium (CGE) modelling. Note that because lower energy costs reduce the marginal costs of production, output will expand once an innovation is made regardless of the initial size of the investment cost or reorganization cost initially required, if these are (correctly) treated as fixed costs.

charge into light trucks—'minivans, pickups and SUVs'—things got 'heavier and bigger' still; from around 1985 improvements in average vehicle efficiency were more or less completely annulled by the larger tonnage of the average vehicle driven (Sperling and Gordon, 2009, pp. 20–1). Over this period production volumes increased, as did vehicle fleets. What is particularly ironic is that through these years, and as Sperling and Gordon stress, the industry saw many eco-improving innovations: reduced material weight, aerodynamic drag, and tyre friction; electronics and computer-driven driving and monitoring systems; greater fuel combustion efficiency.

Once again, there is no necessary coincidence between what businesses seeking profits deliver and what environmental protection requires. In each example, innovation is consistent with what advocates past and present have demanded of industrial policy: industrial growth. If the aim of policy is simply to promote industrial innovation and capabilities, in order to capture income benefits by selling domestically or via exports, there is no case per se for objecting to scenarios like those above. But if sustainability is a serious objective, traditional purviews on industrial policy goals and the policy visions which follow are no longer adequate: growth, if sustainably achieved, is likely to be as much contingent on restraining commercial energies as on encouraging and promoting them; and growth cannot be posited as an outcome that can *always* be made sustainable. This poses particularly stringent challenges for policies towards manufacture.

In many circumstances, even where an innovation can plausibly be said to reduce the environmental impact of a production process or a product, it will simply not be true that the overall business context is a benign one. This does not mean that eco-innovation research is unimportant. A recent empirical study by Kesidou and Demirel (2012), for example, surveying contributions from a range of literatures on factors promoting eco-innovation, adds valuable insights by separating out factors influencing initial firm decisions to eco-innovate from factors which then help determine the level of the investments which are made.[11] Using a database of more than 1,500 UK-based manufacturing firms, they find amongst other things that while corporate social responsibility and customer demands might influence decisions to innovate, actual investment levels reflect other factors, including regulatory pressures on the least innovative firms. They conclude that stricter environmental regulation is essential. If the academic contribution to industrial policy formulation is to achieve anything, it will be to consider how best innovations at firm level can be channelled into scenarios with overall trajectories that are positive for the environment vis-à-vis the interplay of firms, industries, and national economies.

In one area alone there is an obvious plus side to the intrusion of sustainability concerns into traditional industrial policy thought. Where firms operate as transnationals, a redistribution of their investment profiles across national borders might well see them improve their private competitive position in the marketplace, but at the absolute or relative expense of at least some host economies; for this reason alone, the social effectiveness of a nation's industrial base is not a simple corollary of the competitiveness in

---

[11] The authors in part explore the 'Porter' hypothesis, that regulation exerts a positive effect on eco-innovation. See also Demirel and Kesidou (2011).

the marketplace of individual business units.[12] Supra-national rules and binding international commitments offer one route towards mitigating the risks of loss of international business for individual states, subject to comparative differences in credible enforcement.[13] Moves to bring carbon footprints for consumption into line with carbon footprints for production—and to block corporations selling in Western markets from outsourcing dirty operations to countries where environmental rules are either laxer to begin with or less effectively enforced—could give greater scope for a restoration of local controls over investment.

20.4 HORIZONTAL VERSUS SECTOR-SPECIFIC POLICY

Perhaps the most important shift in Britain's industrial policy thinking, coming just after acceptance of at least the principle of sustainability, is the reappearance of arguments advocating sector-specific policy efforts. Policies intended to apply more or less equally across many industrial sectors are conventionally referred to as horizontal, whereas sector-specific policies are tailored to target particular industries. Much is being made in this connection of seeking 'spillover' effects, running from targeted sectors through to related industries, as a basis for policy selection. We begin our assessment of a potentially positive policy development by warning that growth preoccupations are already overshadowing sustainability.

20.4.1 Britain's Horizontal Policy Framework

We have outlined elsewhere our view on British predispositions on the horizontal plane, drawing on Coates's (2005) policy survey.[14] The overall thrust of thinking about industry has for some decades been to make Britain an attractive venue for foreign investors, to draw in large corporations and to create, by this means, a thriving business environment within which smaller and medium-sized enterprises (SMEs) also flourish.[15] The character of policy thus conceived has been of a general kind. A stable macroeconomic environment, with clear rules for inflation targeting and government borrowing over the cycle;

---

[12] In the 1970s, for example, Britain was destabilized by industrial hollowing out as a number of large American and British firms developed operations on the continental mainland of Europe at the expense of operations in Britain. Similar later observations have been made on hollowing out (kūdōka) in Japan.

[13] The car industry, further discussed in Section 20.5, is a case in point. Britain's policy framework conforms to EU environmental legislation on emissions, energy efficiency, reclamation, and waste, as well as international obligations. But once outside the common ground of the EU, legislative frameworks, enforcement rates, and penalties for lack of compliance can be seen to differ. Working by international treaty and assistance to eliminate differences is one route ahead.

[14] For further discussion see Coffey and Thornley (2015a).

[15] For an empirical critique of casual thinking, see Kitson et al. (2003).

ample reserves of labour, based on high labour market participation and migrant workers drawn from EU Member States; state investment in skills and education; all were conceived, like low corporation tax and weak employment rights (Tony Blair's aversion to 'overburdensome regulation': see HMG, 1998, p. 2), as a general policy framework working for the business community at large. While certain policies required tailoring at the point of application—directing extra resources to areas of educational disadvantage and basic skills training to the long-term unemployed, evolving sector skills councils from the old industrial training boards (see Coates, 2005, pp. 96–101)[16]—policy thought tended nonetheless to run towards the horizontal.

That events have since tarnished the package hardly needs saying. For present purposes what is more important is that a policy apparatus conceived of in these terms is not conducive to policy measures aimed at promoting industrial sustainability alongside growth. Placing a policy premium on pleasing prospective inward investors does not produce the most favourable context for environmental regulation. More prosaically, a government and civil service culture mainly versed in broad-brush policy initiatives is ill-suited to detailed industry work of the kind implied by industrial heterogeneity: the 'energy-intensive industries', listed in an earlier section, are a good case in point, as are the particular issues generated, for example, by the automotive industries, including cars. Analogies can be drawn with the specificities of the policy mixes needed to tackle problems of river management, soil erosion, and poor city air quality. A commitment to tailored policy design is a positive policy step.

20.4.2 The New Sector Strategy

At the same time, it is also evident that in any pending contest industrial growth is going to trump the requirements of environmental sustainability. The traditional defence of sector-specific industrial policy is that by targeting particular industries and projects it facilitates a better allocation of scarce government (public) resources, and helps avoid policy misdirection. It implies a more active policy positioning, informed by an awareness of key industry features like growth potentials, product tradability, technological opportunities, and the costs of effective assistance, all carefully weighed in a calculus of overall pay-offs (see Cowling et al., 1999, pp. 18–20). Such themes certainly receive a sounding in the new sector strategy. But it also makes clear that the principal policy aim is to identify sectors best able to facilitate capture of 'high value added opportunities', as a prelude to committing resources to lever support; industries targeted for support should also be in position to benefit from rising incomes (implying high income elasticities of demand) and changing consumer patterns (HMG, 2012).[17] Environmental

---

[16] As Cowling et al. (1999) observe, there will always be an overlap between policies conceived of on the horizontal plane and sector-specific measures, not only in skills and training but in disbursing industry aid and assistance.

[17] A perspective consistent in significant ways with that reviewed in Section 20.3.

products are cited, alongside changing business practices and new technology, demography, and lifestyle changes (HMG, 2012, p. 20); but it is tacit throughout that 'sustainability' is most important to the new industrial analysis where it can act as a future selling point for new industrial outputs.

This is illustrated by the use made of spillover analysis. The new sector policy ranks twenty industries in Britain on the basis of where to direct support for R&D and with a view to generating positive spillover effects (HMG, 2012, p. 20). The manufacturing industry, following the standard industrial codes, which organizes the processing, marketing, and distribution of agricultural produce ('food, beverages and tobacco') fails to make it into the top ten priority sectors, while agriculture itself is placed just second from the bottom in order of strategic import. While the particular emphasis is on R&D (in any case being viewed through a distorting lens, if sustainability is a priority), carried through to a general set of sector priorities this is environmentally absurd.

The on-road freight sector, for example, is both a major contributor to carbon emissions and a notoriously difficult regulatory case, with standards and targets complicated by a mix of vehicle types, variable tonnages and distances, and cross-border travel. One serious step which can be taken, however, to mitigate environmental impact is to economize on loads and distances, and hence on the HGV fleet size and (per tonne) mileages.[18] One way to do this in Britain would be to look at how food is produced and processed, where consumed, and how marketed and distributed. Rethinking linkages running from agriculture through to people has the potential to generate a positive 'spillover' for the environment.[19] A revitalized agriculture, hollowed out in Britain much like manufacture, would also change the balance of necessities in the flows of trade. But these are perhaps not the right kind of spillover effects: they are not growth oriented.

On the other side of the coin, in the list of twenty industries, pharmaceuticals, automotive ('motor vehicles and parts'), and aerospace hold the top three spots, followed by electronics, computers, chemicals, machinery, and equipment (HMG, 2012, p. 20). While the spillover effects, in terms of growth potentials, are here quite evident, from the viewpoint of sustainable development there are other issues. In particular, the most advanced sector-specific industrial policy package in Britain, targeting a sector at the forefront of the world's greenhouse dilemma, has the surprising demerit of appearing unduly vertical in conception, with critical cross-sector linkages not sufficiently incorporated in the policy mix. With this in mind, we therefore turn next to the difficult case of the car industry.

---

[18] The SMMT reports that much effort has been required to make progress on appropriate methodologies and metrics to gauge the effectiveness of partial technological options on fuels and propulsion in the heavy goods (HGV) transport sector, more limited than for lighter vehicles (see SMMT, 2010).

[19] After the Second World War, when greater food self-sufficiency was deemed important, a series of marketing boards and other bodies were tasked with providing support to farmers to implement a new national agricultural policy. Their functions have since been transferred to the purchasing divisions of large supermarket chains. The consequences of this are illustrated in Bowman et al. (2012) for meat products. A redeveloped and remodelled agriculture would have to change this.

20.5 The Car Industry: A Case Study in Contrariness

The car industry, as it evolved through the larger part of the twentieth century, came to be possessed by dominant product architectures: an internal combustion engine (ICE) reliant on fossil fuels housed in an all-steel body, supported by a massive pre- and post-production service industry. Some writers speak of an industrial monoculture, extending from these most visible features of the dominant car design into an entire 'landscape': 'tangible and fixed features such as fuel stations for petrol and diesel, legal requirements and regulatory regimes . . . popular culture and public acceptance . . . a vast support infrastructure' (Wells, 2010, p. 309). The transition towards sustainable forms of mobility is often thought—and perhaps this is what most government policy-makers also think—to entail first and foremost the introduction of alternative vehicle technologies supported by the enabling efforts of governments to facilitate access to university research capabilities and new fuelling infrastructures.

20.5.1 The Industry Composition in Britain

According to the Society of Motor Manufacturers and Traders (SMMT),[20] and excluding construction and agricultural equipment, seven volume car manufacturers and seven commercial vehicle manufacturers presently operate in Britain, not including bus and coach production, split between a slightly larger number of businesses; a range of niche producers of more specialist cars and vehicles includes a major motorsport cluster centring around (but not exclusive to) the Oxford area. The industry is a major direct and indirect employer: recent estimates by the SMMT, with a current membership of over 600 UK-based automotive companies, claims close to three-quarters of a million employees in jobs spread across the manufacturing, retail, and aftermarket parts of the sector, with just under one-fifth employed in manufacture for vehicles and parts. There is some strength in engines: over 2.5 million engines, compared with just over 1.5m cars, and less than 100,000 commercial vehicles, were produced in Britain last year. Ford, which no longer assembles cars in Britain, is the largest engine manufacturer, splitting between sites for diesel engines (Dagenham) and petrol (Bridgend). The industry is export oriented: in 2013 more than three-quarters of all vehicles built were exported (an historically high share, accounted for at least in part by the effects of the crisis); half went to the EU, with China followed by Russia and America accounting for the bulk of the remainder. However, for decades now the balance of automotive trade has been negative; a recently

---

[20] The SMMT Ltd is the industry's main trade body in Britain. It plays an important role in the work (described in this section) of the British Automotive Council. The brief industry sketch partly follows SMMT Ltd (2014). On some counts there are eight volume car makers operating in Britain—Ford, GM, Toyota, Honda, Renault-Nissan, Tata, BMW, and VW (Bentley)—although the last of these is not properly described as engaging in volume activity.

recorded surplus in cars, the first in over thirty years, tended if anything to highlight the extent to which deficits are an expected norm.

A structural feature of the industry is its dominance by foreign-owned transnationals in most of its branches, and certainly in cars where there are no large domestic corporations. Niche players, and small business start-ups seeking to exploit present technological uncertainties, provide the exception which proves the industry rule. Attracting inward investment, as with other manufacturing branches, is viewed as paramount for policy. A recent summary of Britain's automotive policy (HMG, 2013),[21] while highlighting sustainability, makes clear that a main goal of sector policy ambition is to win a bigger share in international value chains (HMG, 2013, p. 5).

British production is comparatively strong for larger luxury cars, including off-road utility vehicles, as with Jaguar Land Rover (Tata). Rolls-Royce (BMW) has recently seen strong sales, likewise Bentley (VW). Somewhat paradoxically, given growing sensitivities to a possible transformation in the sector to favour lower carbon vehicles, this is seen as a defining future strength by many commentators. For its part, the new sector strategy for Britain, reviewed in the last section, sees car exports, ideally in high value added product categories, as strategically critical; and particularly so exports to emerging market economies, driven by rising world incomes and marketing advantages for the cleanest cars. Transport expenditures are predicted to rise faster than world income, with large populations, notably in China and India, promising large markets (see HMG, 2012).

20.5.2 The British Automotive Council

In the year in which Britain's Low Carbon Industrial Strategy was launched an Automotive Council was established, following the recommendations of a government-sponsored policy review that was an offshoot of earlier reviews of automotive and aerospace (see HMG, 2009b).[22] The Council is organized as an industry–government deliberative body, jointly chaired by the Cabinet Minister heading BIS (currently Vince Cable) and an industry leader. In addition to a CEO, the Executive is principally comprised of industry representatives drawn mainly from car and truck manufacture and large supply groups, with other automotive sectors (and a bank) also represented. The largest manufacturing union, Unite, supplies one member. The Engineering and Physical Sciences Research Council (EPSRC), which disburses research grants, favouring collaborative projects, to university engineering and science departments, is also represented. The Council's intent is to improve communications and planning and facilitate commercial exploitation of more sustainable vehicle technologies, thereby building a platform to win inward investment for Britain. The Council's activities are divided between two main subgroups,

---

[21] The document in question was produced by BIS but in collaboration with automotive industry branches active in Britain via the British Automotive Council.

[22] Space prohibits description of other institutions developing, initiating, and facilitating policy in Britain. The Department for Transport (DfT) and Office for Low Emission Vehicles (OLEV) are very important, as too the Technology Strategy Board (TSB). The Council interfaces with these and others.

a Technology Group and a Supply Chain Group, tasked with working on technology and supply chain policy formulation and (still evolving) industry 'road maps'.

As earlier noted, the Automotive Council is now seen as something of a flagship policy institution in an industry widely regarded as a model case for the application of Britain's sectoral strategy, endorsed by senior Coalition figures like Vince Cable and Michael Heseltine (see Section 20.2). The Labour Party likewise continues to be supportive (Umunna, 2012). There are some, albeit not exact, parallels with developments in France, where another operating structure, the Plateforme de la Fillière Automobile (PFA), has been established; and there are moves afoot in Italy to establish something along British–French lines (Calabrese et al., 2013). On an EU plane, these developments can be seen as part defensive as well as proactive.

20.5.3 The Current Policy Mix

Over the past decade or so a targeted set of policy tools and applications has fallen into place to encourage alternative vehicle technologies. Running through these briefly, a range of measures is at once apparent: tax instruments, matched funding awards, grants for consumers and providers, public procurement initiatives, and infrastructure schemes. The main array, by policy type, target vehicle category, and goal, is shown in Table 20.1. (This reproduces a table in Coffey and Thornley (2013), the one change being that the term 'van' is used here to denote light commercial vehicles.)

A distinction can be made between one-shot measures and continuing policies. The first two table entries belong to the former category. A time-limited loans guarantee scheme ('automotive assistance programme'), based on a £2.3bn fund to assist projects passing a minimum size criterion and contributing to reduced carbon emissions, and a matched-funds scrappage scheme, offering subsidies for new vehicle purchases by drivers handing in older cars, were introduced in 2009 (ending 2010) to provide short-term support. Like the first, the second scheme was justified partly by net carbon efficiencies, as 'dirtier' vehicles exited the fleet (for further details, see Coffey and Thornley, 2013, pp. 136–8). Similar measures were deployed throughout the EU (Calabrese 2015; Calabrese et al., 2013). For continuing policies, complementarities are important: actions to promote sales, whether through gradated vehicle excise duties imposing higher liabilities on higher emissions vehicles, or discriminatory tax exemption thresholds for capital allowances on company cars, or by direct subsidy, interact positively with actions to sponsor research and provide civil infrastructures (comment is also made in Coffey and Thornley, 2013, pp. 138–41). However, a fuel duty escalator, on an inflation plus basis to price out the most polluting classes of engine, has for now been abandoned as an option.

Of further interest is the regional dimension to policy. The low carbon industrial strategy for Britain as a whole has seen cities and regions designated Low Carbon Economic Areas (LCEAs) that will channel resources into low carbon industrial development. Three are relevant to the car industry (others include areas for marine energy, the built

Table 20.1 Alternative Vehicle Technology Policy Array

	Policy	Target Category	Goal
matched-funds subsidy	[1]scrappage scheme	cars, *vans	support: employment income reduce: CO_2 emissions
time-limited loans guarantees	[1]automotive assistance scheme	larger automotive businesses and investment projects	support: employment income reduce: CO_2 emissions
tax policies	vehicle excise duty (discriminatory)	cars, vans, **HGVs	support: electric cars, electric vans, plug-in hybrids
	[2]capital allowances (discriminatory)	cars, vans	reduce: CO_2 emissions
	fuel duties	private and commercial vehicles	government revenue
	R&D tax credits	all businesses	support: innovation
matched-funds awards + projects	Low Carbon Vehicles Innovation Platform (LCVIP)	all vehicles/supporting technologies	support: low carbon innovation
grants for buyers	Plug-In Car/Van Grants	cars, vans	support: plug-in cars and vans
	Green Bus Fund	bus fleets	support: lower carbon emission buses/vans
	Low Carbon Vehicles Public Procurements Programme (LCVPPP)	public sector fleets (trials and buyers)	reduce: CO_2 emissions
infrastructure	Plugged-In Places	cars, vans	support: plug-in vehicles reduce: CO_2 emissions
regional policy	Low Carbon Economic Areas (LCEAs)	(1)–ultra-low carbon vehicles; (2)–advanced automotive engineering; (3)–hydrogen and low carbon fuels	exploit comparative regional advantages: (1)–North East (2)–Midlands (3)–Wales

* vans or light commercial vehicles–no more than 3.5 tonnes
** HGVs–Heavy Goods Vehicles
[1] scheme ended 2010;
[2] electric/plug-in hybrid company tax exemption scheduled to end
Source: reproducing Table 1 from Coffey and Thornley (2013)

environment, and nuclear energy): the North East of England, for ultra-low carbon emissions vehicles; the Midlands, for advanced automotive technology; and Wales, for hydrogen and low carbon fuels. In the North East, for example, the LCEA is dominated by Nissan and projects like the Nissan Leaf electric car and production of lithium-ion electric vehicle battery cells at the company's Sunderland site; but there are other smaller manufacturing specialists in electric vehicle technologies, as well as local university research strengths: clustering is evident (see Figure 20.1).

A decision by the Coalition government to abolish Regional Development Agencies (RDAs), established in 1998 to give support to the regions, has to some extent

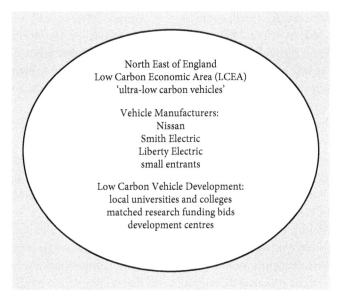

North East of England
Low Carbon Economic Area (LCEA)
'ultra-low carbon vehicles'

Vehicle Manufacturers:
Nissan
Smith Electric
Liberty Electric
small entrants

Low Carbon Vehicle Development:
local universities and colleges
matched research funding bids
development centres

FIGURE 20.1 North East LCEA Electric Vehicle Cluster.

overshadowed this initiative, and invited criticism. For example, the RDA for the North East helped position the region by securing an early place in the 'Plugged-in Places' scheme—which offered matched funding opportunities to public–private partnerships to instal charging points for battery-dependent cars around Britain—as well as using its own financing capability to prime the region's electric charging infrastructure; it contributed to matching funding on other low carbon projects; helped involve local universities in a low carbon vehicle research centre; and was instrumental in mobilizing resources for automotive development (from sources including the European Investment Bank). The jury is out on the ultimate consequences of abolition (for further discussion see Bailey, 2010; Berkeley et al., 2012; and Harper and Wells, 2012).[23]

20.5.4 The Limits to Technology

Putting this concern aside, there are more fundamental problems of long-term viability for this development programme. Perhaps the most basic point of note is that at present levels of technological know-how there is no such entity as a 'green'—and hence sustainable—car. In this respect policy-makers, like the industry, use language with licence. The main technology road map adopted by the Automotive Council for cars envisages a developmental trajectory which will see a series of breakthroughs in energy storage systems and propulsion mechanisms; hybrid technologies will advance,

[23] RDAs have been replaced by a larger number of more localized Local Enterprise Partnerships (LEPs), less visibly funded and less experienced. As noted in Section 20.2, the Treasury has stymied resourcing efforts by Michael Heseltine.

mass electric vehicles (EVs) will come online commercially, fuel cell technologies will become practicable. As the middle of the century approaches, the world will be transformed. Each breakthrough will feed others—there will be 'hops' across technologies— and at each stage infrastructures will expand and be refined. The big breakthroughs are not really anticipated before 2030. In the meantime, improvements to conventional (ICE) technologies can and will continue.[24]

Now even this is not quite what it seems. There is no such thing, for example, as a 'green' electric car, or at least, not per se. Rather, the carbon released moves from the tailpipe to the power station. Powered by the dirtier class of coal-fired power station, of the kind abounding (say) in China, the pure electric car will be dirtier than an efficient conventional car. Powered by a nuclear power station, of the kind abounding in France, then the electric car is a less dirty technology, at least in carbon terms. In France, with a strong nuclear lobby, electric is seen as the future. Great hopes also reside in fuel cell technologies, using hydrogen[25] as fuel, as an alternative pathway to low carbon emission forms of personal transport; but obstacles, including competition not only from conventional car designs powered directly by fossil fuel combustion but also electric cars, and questions of fuel storage and refuelling, are substantial (Sperling and Gordon, 2009, pp. 31–7). The prognosis on the technology front is not simple.

20.5.5 The Limits to Vertical Thinking

What is also abundantly clear is that rational policy towards the car industry is not readily separated from energy policy. While a shift from a preoccupation with generic or horizontal policy design must be welcomed, it is also important that sector-specific policy is not conceived of in terms which treat industrial sectors as separable vertical blocs. It is not plausible to engage a debate on the merits or otherwise of electric vehicle technologies for the environment without debating too wider energy policies and priorities, as for example on the merits and demerits of nuclear energy when discussing the pros and cons of resourcing electric cars.[26] These critical cross-sector linkages are inadequately represented in policy. As with the lowly status given the agriculture–food

---

[24] It is notable that the five main designated research priorities identified by the Automotive Council Technology Group for Britain include internal combustion engines alongside electric motors and power electronics, light vehicle and power-train structures, and intelligent mobility. The car industry in Britain is a proportionately substantial sector contributor to total R&D.

[25] Notwithstanding the role allotted the Welsh LCEA, hydrogen pathway development in Britain (as in other countries) is small. Other initiatives include formation (in 2012) of the UK H_2 Mobility Group, to investigate technology, infrastructure, and refuelling as well as future business. There has also been matched funding for demonstrator projects and a hydrogen and fuel cell research funding competition to spur firms to build capabilities. But there are no cheap or easy routes towards environmentally sound fuels for cars, as Sperling and Gordon (2009) (see ch. 4) explain in a clear and unbiased way.

[26] This broadening of popular understanding should include initiatives like the new Advanced Propulsion Centre (APC) (HMG, 2013, pp. 30–1) for vehicles.

industry nexus in Britain's new sector strategy, with no priority for environmental 'spillover', the cross-sector linkages that seem to matter most are those driving growth—or to put it differently, those making further demands on resources.

It is in much this same vein that the present British government enthusiasm for shale is being borne along, on the back of American proclamations that the years of expensive fossil fuel are over—decades of cheapness beckon. This is being linked to a US 'manufacturing renaissance': the laying down of more than 150,000 well sites for fracking, worked more than 2 million times in total, is juxtaposed with new and growing demands on 'chemical, steel and aluminium plants', with support for jobs (Hefner, 2014, pp. 9–12). But these latter industries, fracking aside, are in another world amongst the leading instances of the so-called 'energy-intensive industries'. The head of commodities research at Citi, earlier cited, observes that:

> declining production costs... [combined with] the spread of shale gas and tight oil production globally... suggest a sustainable price of around $5.50 per thousand cubic feet for natural gas in the United States and a trading range of $70–$90 per barrel for oil globally by the end of this decade. (Morse, 2014, p. 4)

To this is added that, in the case of oil, 'adequate returns' on investment are realizable on 'most drilling' at prices below $50 per barrel, and on a declining trajectory that points to less than $40 (Morse, 2014, p. 6). Yet as Sperling and Gordon (2009) show, such sporadic flare-ups of car industry innovation in alternative vehicle technologies as have previously occurred have foundered and sputtered when energy prices fall. Oil has for some years repeatedly traded, and comfortably, at prices in excess of $100 per barrel. It is an open secret that within the car industry many have looked towards significantly higher oil prices than this when pondering transitions. It is true, perhaps, that a cheap natural gas source might spark industry interest in natural gas as a fuel source for cars and trucks (Hefner, 2014, p. 14).[27] But its advantages for the environment come largely in comparisons with the dirtier class of older petrol and diesel engines (Sperling and Gordon, 2009, p. 94), while fracking for gas is also a source of greenhouse accelerants as a by-product.[28]

20.5.6 The Limits to Growth

The underlying problem posed by the car industry is the same as that posed by the lurch towards shale in the fuel and energy sectors. This is the desire for industrial (and services) related growth, with attendant profit opportunities for businesses, employment

[27] In Europe, Italy has been the leader in natural gas engine technologies (a point noted in Sperling and Gordon, 2009, p. 93; also Calabrese, 2015). There has been little comparative interest in Britain, at least prior to fracking.

[28] A point made in Krupp (2014, pp. 17–19), like Morse (2014) and Hefner (2014) one of several comment pieces assembled by *Foreign Affairs*. A fourth article, by Levinson (2014), posits shale as a natural gas fuel source for automotive.

opportunities for populations, and trade advantages for economies[29]—with fear of disadvantage for late-movers. It is the problem posed more generally by the otherwise intelligent and welcome move towards sector-specific policy measures targeting strategic industries, a break from recent (and failed) policy fixations. If sustainability is seriously intended, then the fundamental task of industrial policy analysis must be to look across sector linkages and see not only growth opportunities but growth problems, areas requiring curtailment or redirection. It must identify ways to progress other objectives *with* sustainability.

20.5.7 Product Service Systems and the Case for Market Reform

One potentially interesting line of thought has been proposed by the United Nations Environmental Programme (UNEP), which envisages a different kind of environmental impact life cycle management for industrial goods. With examples ranging from chemical products to community solar energy, the new product-service systems (PSS) model thus entailed would move from traditional business forms to new forms in which businesses retain the principle property rights in manufactured products but lease their use to customers, who are also supplied with supporting services:

> Product-Service-Systems (PSS)—promotes a focus shift from selling just products to selling the utility, through a mix of products and services while fulfilling the same client demands with less environmental impact. (UNEP, 2002, p. 3)

When applied to the car industry, 'selling mobility', businesses would organize individual leasing schemes, car-sharing and pooling schemes, and pay-as-you-go ventures (see Ceschin and Vezzoli, 2010).

As we argue elsewhere, to imagine this extended to the volume car market is to imagine an industry transformed. Car makers, the key strategic interest, would have to realign profit centres, providing access to cars through arrangements including leasing as part of a parcel including access to a full range of ancillary services extending to include fuels and maintenance. The critical point would be that car ownership titles would stay with their manufacturers, or with the product-supply groups that organize the nexus with final car users; customers for their part would not expect to own the cars stored in their driveways or garages, even where thought of as a household fixture; business fleets similarly would be on lease.

In practice, it would entail a radical vertical restructuring of a major manufacturing sector, with car makers forward integrating into services that are also reorganized around a product-service system. An alternative business model organized on this scale would remove a generally little noticed but possibly critical market impediment to change: car makers currently generate a large part of their income from selling replacement parts to

---

[29] For energy there are also loudly proclaimed national security dimensions.

large fleets of ageing conventional vehicle technologies; alternative vehicle technologies do not offer the same kind of business.[30] The traverse between states could conceivably generate temporary but potentially meaningful growth in short- to medium-term production, as one kind of vehicle fleet is run down and replaced with another, while still reducing net carbon emissions (see Coffey and Thornley, 2012, 2013). But this requires identifying the appropriate energy sector policy mix as well as the most appropriate business model for an otherwise intractable industry. And much research is needed still on market redesign for sustainability.

20.6 CONCLUSIONS

Policy in Britain today stands unevenly at a crossroads. Along one route a more sustainable developmental path beckons, inviting costs and difficulties as well as scope for economic and social regeneration. The weight of policy, however, is already tacking downhill, towards cheap energy based on a project that cannot but further sustain already unsustainable carbonized forms of industry in areas of global import like personal transport. Few advocates of a more interventionist industrial policy stance from the British government have anything in mind other than a more vibrant manufacturing base, and much the same holds true outside Britain. While it is tempting to suggest that technological fixes beckon for difficult environmental issues, provided there is due government sponsorship promoted by market incentives for eco-innovation and supporting infrastructures, in the flagship case of the car and truck sector, this is wishful thinking. Talk of green cars must give way to more rational assessments of the industry's interface with the energy sector, which in turn requires a wider dialogue; government should act to engage with a wider citizenry and informed media. The market form itself must change, moving from a traditional manufacturing model supported by a service sector to a service sector providing a utility; and as with cars, so too must manufacture at large be rethought. The creation of new forums for policy debate, nationally—as with the Automotive Council—and locally, must certainly be welcomed: but engaging expertise and devolving decisions cannot be a substitute for facing up to the extent and depth of the structural problems facing industrial economies. The latest dash for gas—this time shale gas, followed by oil—represents a global disaster in waiting, not only for policies to break with a worldwide transport energy system locked into fossil fuel consumption, including cars, but for environmental conservation at large: it is remarkable that the Anglo-American policymaking culture, which places so much faith in the laws of supply and demand and the power of the marketplace, seems suddenly incapable of linking energy price structures to business choices.

There is a welcome move in Britain towards the first steps of implementation of a low carbon industrial strategy. There has been a positive change in direction at another level,

---

[30] This theme is further developed in Coffey and Thornley (2015b, forthcoming).

with the new willingness to think of industrial policy in sectoral as well as horizontal terms. There is a risk that policy thinking devolves too far in the direction of treating industries in ways which understate cross-sector linkages, and with spillovers sought only insofar as growth, jobs, and trade are concerned. But the larger problem is that the parameters for intelligent policy design are changing in ways and in degrees that are still not admitted to. The balance of policy is still skewed towards 'larger', 'more', and 'global', with little sense that their contrary quality vis-à-vis the environment is recognized. The goal of industrial policy analysis, if these words are to be more than an umbrella term for anything that applies to 'policy' and to 'industry', must be to help identify ways in which development contexts are created that are socially acceptable, economically viable, and (ultimately) sustainable.

ACKNOWLEDGEMENTS

We wish to thank the editors of this book for suggestions.

REFERENCES

Web document dates refer to publication: all sites were checked on July 5 2014.

Bailey, D. (2010). 'After RDAs: Look Before You LEP', *Birmingham Post* Business Blog.

Barber, B. (2012). 'TUC Press Release: Heseltine Review must be embraced across government' <http://www.tuc.org.uk/economy/tuc-21584-fo.cfm>.

Berkeley, N., Jarvis, D., and Bailey, J. (2012). 'Phoenix from the Ashes: Can Low Carbon Vehicles Ensure the Long-Term of the West Midlands Automotive Cluster', *International Journal of Automotive Technology and Management* 12(2), 137–52.

Bowman, A., Froud, J., Johal, S., Law, J., Leaver, A., and Williams, K. (2012). *Bringing Home the Bacon: From Trader Mentalities to Industrial Policy.* CRESC Public Interest Report.

Brinkley, I. (2013). 'Spending Review Will Have "Little Impact" On Growth and Jobs', *Guardian* 2 July.

Burke, T. (2012). 'TUC Press Release: Tony Burke's speech at the Green is Good for Growth conference: 23 October 2012' <http://www.tuc.org.uk/workplace/tuc-21596-fo.cfm>.

Cable, V. (2012). 'Industrial Strategy: Cable outlines vision for future of British industry'. <https://www.gov.uk/government/speeches/industrial-strategy-cable-outlines-vision-for-future-of-british-industry>.

Calabrese, G. (2015). 'Outlining Policy Responses to Stimulate Automotive Car Demand by Environmental Impact Reduction', *Journal of Environmental Planning and Management* 58(1), 2 January 2015, 55–68(14).

Calabrese, G., Coffey, D., and Pardi, T. (2013). *New Industrial Policies for the Automotive Industry in Europe*, Working Paper CNR-Ceris No. 21.

Ceschin, F. and Vezzoli, C. (2010). 'The Role of Public Policy in Stimulating Radical Environmental Impact Reduction in the Automotive Sector: The Need to Focus on Product-Service System Innovation', *International Journal of Automotive Technology and Management* 10(2/3), 321–41.

Coates, D. (1994). *The Question of UK Decline: Economy, State and Society*. London: Harvester.

Coates, D. (2005). *Prolonged Labour: The Slow Birth of New Labour Britain*. Basingstoke and New York: Palgrave Macmillan.

Coffey, D. and Thornley, C. (2009). *Globalization and Varieties of Capitalism: New Labour, Economic Policy and the Abject State*. Basingstoke and New York: Palgrave Macmillan.

Coffey, D. and Thornley, C. (2012). 'Low Carbon Mobility versus Private Car Ownership: Towards a New Business Vision for the Automotive World?', *Local Economy* 27(7), 732–48.

Coffey, D. and Thornley, C. (2013). 'Nurtured Competition and Optimal Vehicle Life: A Missing Theme in Public Policy Formulation for Alternative Vehicle Technologies', *International Journal of Automotive Technology and Management* 13(2), 134–54.

Coffey, D. and Thornley, C. (2015a, forthcoming) 'Industrial Policy: The British Case', in F. Gerlach, M. Schietinger, and A. Ziegler (eds), *Industrial Policy in Europe*. Marburg: Schüren Verlag.

Coffey, D. and Thornley, C. (2015b, forthcoming). *Capitalism, Crises, Transnationals and the State: An Alternative Political Economy of the British Car Industry*. Basingstoke and New York: Palgrave Macmillan.

Cowling, K., Oughton, C., and Sugden, R. (1999). 'A Reorientation of Industrial Policy? Horizontal Policies and Targeting', in K. Cowling (ed.), *Industrial Policy in Europe: Theoretical Perspectives and Practical Proposals*, pp. 17–31. London and New York: Routledge.

Demirel, P. and Kesidou, E. (2011). 'Stimulating Different Types of Eco-Innovation in the UK: Government Policies and Firm Motivations', *Ecological Economics* 70(8), 1546–57.

Griffiths, A. and Wall, S. (2012). *Applied Economics*. Harlow, Essex: Pearson Education Ltd.

Harper, G. and Wells, P. (2012). 'Diverse Regional Sustainability Strategies: Template for the Future or Squandered Resources?' *International Journal of Automotive Technology and Management* 12(2), 143–71.

Hefner III, R. A. (2014). 'The United States of Gas: Why the Shale Revolution Could Have Happened Only in America', *Foreign Affairs* 93(3) May/June, 9–14.

Hervas-Oliver, J. L., Jackson, I., and Tomlinson, P. R. (2011). '"May the Ovens Never Grow Cold": Regional Resilience and Industrial Policy in the North Staffordshire Ceramics Industrial District with Lessons from Sassoulo and Castellon', *Policy Studies* 32(4), 377–95.

Heseltine, M. (2012). 'No Stone Unturned: In Pursuit of Growth', <https://www.gov.uk/government/publications/no-stone-unturned-in-pursuit-of-growth>.

HMG (1998). *Fairness at Work*. London: HM Government, Department for Trade and Industry.

HMG (2006). *Stern Review: The Economics of Climate Change*. London: HM Government, HM Treasury.

HMG (2009a). *The UK Low Carbon Industrial Strategy*. London: HM Government, Department for Business, Innovation and Skills and Department for Energy and Climate Change.

HMG (2009b). *New Automotive Innovation and Growth Team: An Independent Report on the Future of the Automotive Industry in the UK*. London: HM Government, Department for Business Enterprise and Regulatory Reform (BERR).

HMG (2011). *The Plan for Growth*. London: HM Government, British Treasury, and Department for Business, Innovation and Skills.

HMG (2012). *Industrial Strategy: UK Sector Analysis*. London: HM Government, Department for Business, Innovation and Skills.

HMG (2013). *Driving Success: A Strategy for Growth and Sustainability in the UK Automotive Sector*. London: HM Government, Department for Business, Innovation and Skills.

Howes, C. and Singh, A. (2000). 'Introduction: Competitiveness Matters', in C. Howes and A. Singh (eds), *Competitiveness Matters: Industry and Economic Performance in the US*, pp. 1–28. Ann Arbor: The University of Michigan Press.

Kaldor, N. (1981). 'The Role of Increasing Returns, Technical Progress and Cumulative Causation in the Theory of International Trade and Economic Growth', *Economie appliquée* 34(4), 593–617.

Kesidou, E. and Demirel, P. (2012). 'On the Drivers of Eco-Innovations: Empirical Evidence from the UK', *Research Policy* 41(5), 862–70.

Kitson, M., Michie, J., and Sheehan, M. (2003). 'Markets, Competition, Co-operation and Innovation', in D. Coffey and C. Thornley (eds), *Industrial and Labour Market Policy and Performance: Issues and perspectives*, pp. 29–44. London and New York: Routledge.

Krupp, F. (2014). 'Don't Just Drill Baby – Drill Carefully: How to Make Fracking Safer for the Environment', *Foreign Affairs* 93(3) May/June, 15–20.

Levinson, D. M. (2014). 'Electric Avenue: How to Make Zero-Emissions Cars Go Mainstream', *Foreign Affairs* 93(3) May/June, 21–6.

Morse, E. L. (2014). 'Welcome to the Revolution: Why Shale Is the Next Shale', *Foreign Affairs* 93(3) May/June, 3–7.

O'Grady, F. (2013). 'TUC Press Release: Frances O'Grady's Atlee Memorial lecture' <http://www.tuc.org.uk/union/tuc-22151-fo.cfm>.

OECD (Organisation for Economic Co-operation and Development) (2009). *Sustainable Manufacturing and Eco-Innovation: Framework, Practices and Measurement—Synthesis Report*. Paris: OECD.

Rutledge, I. (2007). 'New Labour, Energy Policy and "Competitive Markets"', *Cambridge Journal of Economics* 31(6), 901–25.

Singh, A. (1977). 'UK Industry and the World Economy: A Case of De-Industrialization?', *Cambridge Journal of Economics* 1(2), 113–36.

SMMT Ltd (2010). *The Society of Motor Manufacturers and Traders: Heavy Goods Vehicle (HGV) Ultra Low Carbon (ULC) Strategy*. London: Society of Motor Manufacturers and Traders Ltd.

SMMT Ltd (2014). *The Society of Motor Manufacturers and Traders: Motor Industry Facts 2014*. London: Society of Motor Manufacturers and Traders Ltd.

Social Trends (2010). *Social Trends No. 40: Labour Market*. London: Office for National Statistics.

Sperling, D. and Gordon, D. (2009). *Two Billion Cars: Driving Towards Sustainability*. Oxford and New York: Oxford University Press.

Theakston, K. (1996). 'Whitehall, Westminster and Industrial Policy', in D. Coates (ed.), *Industrial Policy in Britain*, pp. 159–81. Basingstoke and London: Palgrave Macmillan.

Tomlinson, P. R. and Branston, J. R. (2014). 'Turning the Tide: Prospects for an Industrial Renaissance in the North Staffordshire Ceramics District', *Cambridge Journal of Regions, Economy and Society* 7(3), 489–507, doi:10.1093/cjres/rsu016.

TUC (2005). *An Industrial Strategy for the United Kingdom*. London: Trades Union Congress.

TUC (2008). *A Green and Fair Future for a Transition to a Low Carbon Economy*. London: Trades Union Congress.

TUC (2013). *Industrial Policy for the Green Economy*. London: Trades Union Congress.

Umunna, C. (2012). 'Automotive for the People', *New Statesman* 16 July, 14.

UNEP (2002). *Product-Service Systems and Sustainability: Opportunities for Sustainable Solutions*. Paris: United Nations Environmental Programme.

Wells, P. (2010). 'Sustainability and Diversity in the Global Automotive Industry', *International Journal of Automotive Technology and Management* 10(2/3), 305–20.

Author index

A

Abernathy, W.J. 175
Acemoglu, D. 174
Acs, Z.J. 131, 143
Adams, J. 49, 52
Adonis, A. 303
Aghion, P. 20, 86, 373
Aiginger, K. 3, 12, 368, 370, 372, 373, 382, 383, 384, 385
Alcorso, C. 280
Alemany, L. 131
Aliber, R. 350
Allen, F. 349
Allsopp, C.J. 21
Amel, D. 112
Amison, P. 302
Amsden, A.H. 19, 22, 23, 46, 83
Angell, M. 173, 176
Aoki, M. 23
Applebaum, E. 230
Arestis, P. 122, 126
Armour, J. 134, 143
Armstrong, H. 328
Armstrong, M. 316
Arouzo-Carod, J-M. 2, 4
Arrow, K. 170, 385
Asheim, B.T. 266
Atkinson, A.B. 32–3
Audretsch, D.B. 22, 131, 141, 143
Auerswald, P.E. 134
Aujac, H. 49
Averch, H. 315
Ayadi, R. 124

B

Baer, H. 124
Bailey, D. 2, 4, 10, 11, 263, 267, 275, 277, 288, 290, 294, 295, 297, 302, 328, 332, 354, 355, 413

Bailey, T. 61, 127, 199
Bajo-Rubio, O. 335
Baker, M. 349
Balasubramanyam, V.N. 335
Bannock, G. 352
Barber, B. 398
Barberis, N. 349
Barca, F. 287, 289, 290, 291, 292, 293, 295, 299, 300, 303, 304, 305
Baron, D. 315
Barrell, R. 185, 335
Barry, C. 151
Bartlett, B. 56
Baumol, W.J. 19, 316
Bayo-Moriones, A. 185
Becattini, G. 268, 277, 278
Beck, T. 124
Becker, G. 206, 208
Beecroft, A. 241
Beesley, M.E. 314
Bellandi, M. 268
Benavot, A. 207
Bennett, T. 252
Bentham, J. 63, 71
Bentley, G. 302
Bergemann, D. 138
Berger, A.N. 131, 141
Berger, S. 370, 381
Berkeley, N. 413
Berle, A. 74
Best, M.H. 22, 268
Bester, H. 141
Bevan, S. 231
Bianchi, P. 4
Bingham, L.B. 252
Bingham, M. 44, 45, 46
Birkinshaw, J. 336
Black, B.S. 144
Blankenburg, S. 82, 92
Blöchliger, H. 281

Block, F. 111, 113, 171, 172, 175
Blomström, M. 185, 329
Blond, P. 354
Bloom, N. 191
Bluestone, B. 208
Bologna, P. 124
Boltho, A. 21
Bolton, J.E. 143
Bootle, R. 356
Boschma, R. 278
Boulanger, J. 20
Bowman, A. 5, 62, 63, 71, 72, 73
Bradley, C. 250
Brander, J. Du. Q. 132, 136
Branscomb, L.M. 134
Branston, J.R. 27
Braudel, F. 70-1, 76
Brinkley, I. 398
Brogaard, J. 109
Brown, P. 8, 207, 211, 212, 213, 217,
    220, 221
Brown, R. 185, 186
Bruner, R.F. 344
Brusco, S. 268
Brynin, M. 212
Brynjolfsson, E. 217
Bryson, A. 252
Buigues, P-A. 55
Burgess, S. 245
Burke, T. 397
Burt, S.L. 119
Bygrave, W.D. 131, 143

C
Cable, V. 56-7, 398
Calabrese, G. 411
Camagni, R. 265
Cantwell, J.A. 332
Carnoy, M. 208
Carpenter, R.E. 144
Carter, M. 208
Cecchetti, S. 367
Ceschin, F. 416
Chang, H.-J. 2, 4, 22, 23
Chang, S.J. 151
Chesier, S. 23

Christensen, J. 107
Christopherson, S. 268, 277, 278, 280, 281
Cihak, M. 124
Cimoli, M. 4, 20, 23
Clancy, J. 354
Clark, C. 366
Clark, J. 268, 277
Clark, K.B. 175
Clark, P.J. 346, 347
Clarke, S. 209
Clayton, N. 276
Clifton, R. 249
Coase, R.H. 22, 32, 33, 266
Coates, D. 4, 5, 41, 42, 45, 46, 47, 50, 52, 399,
    406, 407
Coffey, D. 12, 127, 219, 268, 397, 411, 417
Cohen, E. 20
Cohen, S. 53
Cohen, W. 185, 333
Colling, T. 246-7, 252
Cook, P.J. 211, 216
Cooke, P. 265, 278
Cooke, W.N. 335
Corby, S. 241, 248, 249, 255, 256
Cosh, A. 352, 356
Cowling, K. 1, 4, 10, 18, 19, 22, 23,
    24, 29, 33, 61, 127, 263, 264, 267,
    280, 407
Cowling, M. 7, 131, 141
Cox, A. 199, 200
Cox, G. 354, 356
Cressy, R. 141, 143
Cribb, J. 312
Crotty, J. 103
Crowley, L. 288, 299
Cumming, D.J. 134, 143, 144, 152, 154,
    159, 162

D
Da Rin, M. 134, 143
Davies, R. 112
Davila, A. 131, 143
Davis, A. 355, 357
Dayson, K. 113
Deakin, S. 348, 349
De Bandt, J. 299

De Dreu, C. 250
Dedrick, K. 220
Deeg, R. 23
De Jonghe, O. 124
de la Cuesta, M. 71
de la Mothe, J. 23
Demirel, P. 403
Demsetz, H. 323
Denis, D.J. 143
De Propris, L. 10, 265, 267, 278
de Ruyter, A. 277
Dewit, G. 335
De Young, R. 112
Dicken, P. 268
Dickens, L. 245, 255
Dimov, D. 131, 134, 135, 141
Di Tommaso, M. 45
Dix, G. 245, 251
Dixit, A. 19
Dixon, T. 275
Doeringer, P. 208
Dolder, C. 253
Dolton, P. 187
Dore, R. 175
Dormois, J-P. 52
Dosi, G. 3, 86, 88
Driffield, N. 11, 327, 328, 329, 331, 332,
    333, 337
Drinkwater, S. 253
Dromey, J. 251
Duhigg, C. 175
Dunning, J.H. 332

E
Edgerton, D. 43
Egeln, J. 143
Eisinger, P. 44
Elias, P. 216
Epstein, G. 102, 103
Evans, P. 217

F
Fagerberg, J. 23, 24, 28
Fama, E. 350
Featherstone, D. 293

Federico, G. 48, 54
Feldenkirchen, W. 48, 55
Felstead, A. 190, 192
Fersterer, J. 186
Fine, B. 20, 122
Finegold, D. 208, 280
Fischer, M. 386
Florin, J. 144
Foray, D. 171
Foreman-Peck, J. 48, 54
Fornahl, D. 265, 266, 278, 279
Forth, J. 200
Fothergill, S. 276
Fourastier, F. 366
Foxon, T.J. 121
Frank, Robert H. 211, 216
Freeman, C. 21, 22, 23, 28, 170
Frenken, K. 265, 278
Froud, J. 5, 61, 63, 288, 290, 294, 301, 302
Fukuyama, F. 119
Fuller, A. 196

G
Gale, D. 349
Gallie, D. 250
Galvez-Nogales, E. 18
Gangl, M. 186
Gardiner, B. 289
Geels, F.W. 385
Genn, H. 255, 256
George, G. 185
Gheasi, M. 335
Ghoshal, S. 27
Gibbons, S. 246, 288, 289, 291, 299
Gifford, S. 131
Gill, I. 289
Gilson, R.J. 144
Girma, S. 334
Glaeser, E.L. 263, 265
Glasmeier, A. 275
Glocker, C. 382
Glyn, A. 119
Goda, T. 118
Godley, W. 107
Gold, M. 235
Goldfarb, Z. 57

Goldin, C. 209, 220
Gompers, P.A. 131, 138, 143, 144, 151, 152
Gordon, D. 208, 400, 404, 405, 414, 415
Gordon, R. 66
Görg, H. 334
Gospel, H. 200
Gospodini, A. 275
Grabher, G. 266
Grabowski, R. 23
Graham, O. 45
Grant, W. 45, 51
Green, A. 191, 192
Green, F. 8, 185, 187, 189, 192, 193, 194
Green, R.J. 276, 318
Greenspan, A. 350
Greenwald, B. 82
Greenwood, R. 55
Griffiths, A. 396
Guger, A. 373
Gugler, K. 346

H
Haaland, J.I. 335
Hacker, J.S. 174
Haldane, A.G. 112
Hall, M. 252
Hall, P. 49, 50, 52, 55, 296
Hamid, J. 352
Hanushek, E. 206, 208, 220
Harford, J. 345
Harper, G. 413
Harris, L. 122
Harris, R. 334
Harrison, R. 143
Hart, M. 329
Hausmann, R. 20, 88
Hayek, F.A. 25, 28, 33
Heffernan, S. 124
Hefner, R.A. 400, 415
Hege, U. 138
Hein, E. 102
Hellwig, M. 141
Hepple, B. 241, 245, 247, 248
Hervas-Oliver, J.L. 397
Heseltine, M. *see* main index

Hesse, H. 124
Hildreth, P. 10, 288, 290, 293, 294, 295, 296,
    297, 302
Hillage, J. 192
Hill, E. 266
Hill, S. 154
Hillier, B. 141
Hodgen, J. 195
Hollenstein, H. 185
Hong, H. 349
Howes, C. 402
Huang, M. 349
Hubbard, P. 295
Huggins, R. 277
Hughes, A. 183, 352
Hunt, T. 64
Hutton, W. 1, 263, 276, 354
Hymer, S. 269, 270
Hyytinen, A. 131

I
Ibrahimo, W. 141
Irwin, D.A. 2

J
Jääskeläinen, M. 132, 135, 136
Jackson, G. 23
Jacobs, J. 264–5, 269, 278, 281
Jarrell, G.A. 344
Javorcik, B.S. 331
Jeng, L. 144
Jensen, M.C. 350, 351, 353
Jessop, B. 268
Johal, S. 5
Johnson, C. 22, 53
Johnson, L.L. 315
Johnson, S. 375
Jomo, K.S. 23
Jones, C. 250
Jones, J. 329, 332
Jones, R. 67
Jordan, E. 249
Jorde, T.M. 19, 20
Jovanovic, B. 345

K

Kaldor, N. 19, 21, 22, 402
Kaplan, S.N. 135, 141
Karakitsos, E. 122
Katz, L. 209, 220
Kay, J. 354
Keasey, K. 124
Keep, E. 194
Keilbach, M. 131, 141, 143
Keller, M.R. 171, 172, 175
Kesidou, E. 403
Keuschnigg, C. 131, 134
Kewin, J. 199
Keynes, J.M. 109
Khan, M. 6, 82, 85, 86, 87, 89, 92, 93, 94, 95
Kharroubi, E. 367
Kindleberger, C. 350
Kitchin, R. 295
Kitschelt, H. 47
Kitson, M. 120, 122
Klein, P.G. 25, 27, 30
Knight, F.H. 174
Kocieniewski, D. 175
Kokko, A. 185, 329
Kolev, K. 347
Kozul-Wright, R. 45
Krauss, E.S. 46
Krippner, G.R. 175
Krueger, A.O. 85
Krueger, D. 186
Krugman, P.R. 21, 23, 24, 56, 63
Kumar, K. 186
Kupfer, A. 219

L

Laffont, J.-J. 170, 316
Lage-Hidalgo, F. 335
Lall, S. 30
Lambooy, J. 278
Lancheros, Sandra 11
Lansbury, M. 335
Lash, S. 47
Latrielle, P. 9, 241, 246, 248, 249, 250, 251, 252, 253, 255, 256

Lauder, H. 8, 218
Lazonick, W. 173, 174, 175
Leaver, A. 5
Lee, N. 1, 263, 276
Lee, S. 43, 50, 53
Le Leslé, V. 124
Leleux, B. 134
Lenihan, H. 2, 4, 11
Lera-López, F. 185
Lerner, J. 131, 134, 135, 136, 138, 141, 143, 144, 151, 152
Levinson, K. 235
Levinthal, D. 185, 333
Lin, J. 22, 23
Lin, Y. 23
Lindbeck, A. 249
Lipsky, D. 253–4
List, F. 21
Littlechild, S.C. 311, 313–16, 321
Llewellyn, D.T. 117
Love, J.H. 331, 332, 335
Lucas, R.E. 21
Lucci, P. 297
Lundvall, B.A. 23, 185
Lynch, J.F. 254
Lysandrou, P. 118

M

McAfee, A. 217
McArdle, L. 252
McCann, P. 65, 289, 295, 298, 300
Machin, S. 187
MacIntosh, J.G. 143
McIntosh, S. 187
MacKinnon, D. 263, 270
MacNeill, S. 302
Mahoney, J.T. 20
Maier, J.B. 131
Maillat, D. 265
Majluf, N. 141
Mangan, D. 241, 247, 249
Manigart, S. 134
Marcotte, D. 197
Marglin, S.A. 121
Marlow, D. 303

Marques, P. 69
Marriott, R. 135, 143
Marris, R. 346
Marshall, A. 265
Marti, I. 131
Martin, R. 265, 270, 273
Martynova, M. 344
Mason, C. 141
Mason, G. 8, 184, 185, 186, 188, 195, 199, 276
Mathonet, P.Y. 143
Matsumoto, G. 46
Matthias, M. 53
Maula, M. 134, 135
Mazzucato, M. 7, 8, 56, 63, 65, 67, 170, 171, 172, 173, 174, 175, 176, 177, 374
Menzel, M.P. 265, 266, 278, 279
Metcalfe, S. 24
Meyer, D. 207
Meyer, T. 141
Michie, J. 7, 111, 117, 120, 121, 122, 124, 125
Milberg, W. 31
Mills, R.W. 346, 347
Milne, S. 119
Mina, A. 183
Mincer, J. 213
Minsky, H.P. 344, 347
Mishel, L. 208, 213
Mitchell, M. 345
Moran, P. 27
Morelli, S. 32–3
Morgan, K. 265, 328, 329
Morris, G. 245
Morse, E. 399, 400, 415
Mote, L.R. 124
Mueller, D.C. 346
Mulherin, J.H. 345
Murphy, K.M. 88
Murray, G. 7, 131, 132, 134, 135, 141, 143
Myers, S.C. 141
Myerson, R. 315

N
Nathan, M. 63, 65, 69, 184
Nelson, R. 20, 22, 23, 24, 170
Newbery, D.J. 318
Newfield, C. 216

Nielsen, S.B. 131, 134
Nightingale, P. 132, 135, 141, 143
Noble, D.S. 335
Nolan, P. 23, 275
Norden, L. 124
North, D.C. 22
Nubler, I. 20
Nurkse, R. 88

O
Obstfeld, M. 63
O'Grady, F. 397
Olofsson, C. 143
Olson, M. 32
Onodera, O. 332
Ortega-Argiles, R. 65, 300
Ostrom, E. 32
Oughton, C. 121, 124, 125
Overman, H. 63, 65, 69, 288, 289, 291, 297, 299

P
Page, Tim 9
Pain, K. 296
Pain, N. 185, 335
Pallazo, P. 353
Paquet, G. 23
Pasinetti, L. 20, 21, 22
Peacock, A. 352
Pelikan, P. 86
Peneder, M. 377
Penrose, E. 20, 28
Penrose, J. 23
Peoples, J. 268
Petersen, B.C. 144
Petersen, K. 185
Petzold, O. 281
Pickett, K. 174
Pierrakis, Y. 132, 134
Pierson, P. 174
Pike, A. 266, 279
Piketty, T. 174, 218
Piore, M. 208, 268
Pisano, G.P. 31, 172
Pitelis, C. 5, 18, 19, 20, 21, 22, 23, 24, 25, 26, 27, 28, 29, 30, 31, 33

Polese, M. 278
Pondy, L.R. 254
Porter, M. 24, 29, 30, 65, 265, 268
Pourvand, K. 64
Powdthavee, N. 187
Prais, S. 186, 190
Prassl, J. 247
Prestowitz, C. 54–5
Purcell, J. 251, 252, 256
Purcell, K. 212, 213, 216
Putnam, R.D. 27

Q

Qian, Y. 83

R

Rahim, N. 253
Ravenscraft, D.J. 353
Reich, S. 44
Reinstaller, A. 373
Renneboog, L. 344
Rhodes-Kropf, M. 345
Ricardo, D. 21
Richard, D. 196
Richardson, G. 20
Ritter, J.R. 152
Robinson, C. 334
Robinson, J. 21
Roche, W. 254
Rodriguez-Pose, A. 293
Rodrik, D. 3, 18, 20, 22, 23, 88, 300, 373, 375
Romer, P.M. 21
Rose, C. 235
Rosenstein-Rodan, P.N. 88
Ross, D. 19
Rousseau, P. 345

S

Sabel, C.F. 268
Sacchetti, S. 267, 268, 278
Sachs, J. 381
Sahlman, W.A. 134
Saks, A. 251
Samuelson, P.A. 21

Sanders, A. 245
Sassen, S. 263, 270
Saunders, A. 112
Saundry, R. 246, 249, 250, 251, 252, 253
Sawyer, M. 6, 103, 126, 228, 356
Saxenian, A. 185
Scharfstein, D. 55
Scherer, F.M. 19, 353
Schor, J.B. 121
Schultz, T. 207
Schumpeter, J. 20, 220
Schweitzer, S. 45
Scitovsky, T. 88
Seargeant, J. 253, 255
Sekkat, K. 55
Serra, N. 22
Shackleton, J.R. 245
Shapiro, H. 23, 29
Shaxton, N. 107
Shih, W. 31
Shiller, R. 349, 351
Shipman, A. 176, 177
Shleifer, A. 346, 352
Shonfield, A. 48
Sieber, S. 372
Sikka, P. 111, 113
Simmonds, G. 318
Singh, A. 11, 47, 348, 349, 351, 352, 353, 402
Singh, G. 11
Sin Yi Cheung 8
Skedinger, P. 249
Skidelsky, R. 177
Slivinski, S. 54
Smith, E.O. 48
Sohl, J.E. 134
Solow, M.R. 21
Soskice, D. 208
Sosvilla-Rivero, S. 335
Sparks, L. 119
Sperling, D. 400, 404, 405, 414, 415
Stanfield, C. 200
Stark, D. 266
Steedman, H. 196
Stein, J. 349, 352
Stern, S. 385
Stiglitz, J. 3, 20, 22, 82, 86, 118, 119, 131, 141, 217, 349, 383

Stoffaës, C. 49, 50, 52
Storey, D.J. 131, 134, 143
Storper, M. 293
Streek, W. 48, 246
Stromberg, P. 141
Sugden, R. 4, 267, 268, 280
Summers, L. 352
Sundry, R. 9
Sunley, P. 265
Surlemont, B. 134
Swann, P. 266, 278

T

Tabellini, G. 293, 295
Tamkin, P. 200
Tatton-Brown, C. 249
Taylor, J. 328, 329
Taylor, L. 23, 29
Teague, P. 254
Teece, D.J. 19, 20, 24
Temori, Y. 11
Thaler, R.H. 349
Theakston, K. 398
Thompson, G. 53, 54
Thornley, C. 12, 126, 397, 411, 417
Thurow, L. 208
Tichy, N. 353
Timmons, J.A. 131, 143
Tirole, J. 316
Tobin, J. 350
Tomaney, J. 69
Tomlinson, P.R. 1, 10, 18, 22, 23, 24,
    29, 33, 61, 127, 219, 264, 267,
    268, 278
Toner, P. 186
Tracey, B. 112
Tulum, Ö 173
Turner, A. 56
Turok, I. 275
Tuselman, H.F. 231

U

Udell, G.F. 131, 141
Umunna, C. 411
Unwin, L. 196

Urry, J. 47
Urwin, P. 246, 250, 255

V

Väänänen, L. 131
Vallascas, F. 124
van Dijk, F. 255
van Reenen, J. 191
van Wanrooy, B. 242, 248
van Winden, W. 275
Vedder, R. 216
Venables, A.J. 30
Vernier-Palliez, B. 49
Vezzoli, C. 416
Vignoles, A. 187
Vishny, R.W. 346
Viswanathan, S. 346
Vitols, S. 231
Vives, X. 124
Vogel, D. 45, 46

W

Wade, R. 1, 23, 83, 219, 221
Wagner, K. 186
Walker, D.A. 131
Walker, I. 187
Wall, S. 396
Warwick, K. 18, 20, 379
Weber, M. 124
Webster, D. 275
Wei, Y. 335
Weingast, B.R. 83
Weiss, A. 131, 141
Weiss, L. 56
Weisse, D. 353
Weixi Liu 7
Welch, I. 152
Wells, P. 144, 409, 413
Westhead, P. 134
Whitley, R. 89
Wickham-Jones, M. 53
Wignaraja, G. 24
Wilkinson, R.G. 174
Williams, K. 5
Williams, M. 253

Williamson, J. 9, 22, 119
Williamson, O.E. 88
Willig, R. 316
Wilson, J.R. 267, 280
Wimmer, A. 209
Windsor, K. 280
Winkelmann, R. 186
Winter, S.G. 20, 22, 24
Winterbotham, M. 188, 191, 192
Winter-Ebmer, R. 186
Woessmann, L. 206, 208, 220
Wolf, M. 370
Wolfe, D.A. 300
Wong, P. 131
Wood, S. 253

Wooton, I. 335
Wren, C. 328, 329, 332
Wurgler, J. 349

Y
Yurtoglu, B. 346

Z
Zahra, S.A. 185
Zakaria, F. 17
Zhu, Y. 187
Zingales, L. 33
Zysman, J. 53

General Index

A

Acas (Advisory, Conciliation and Arbitration Service) 245, 246, 254, 255
Acas Code of Practice on Disciplinary and Grievance Procedures (2009) 246, 253
ACCA (Association of Chartered Certified Accountants) 28, 253
access pricing 315–16
adaptive capacity 404
administrative guidance 47
ADR (Alternative Dispute Resolution) 246–7
ADR Pledge 246
adversarial political culture vii
AEIC (American Energy Innovation Council) 173
agglomeration driven approach 291
agro-business clusters 18
Airbus 67
airports 322
Alfred Herbert 51
All-Party Parliamentary Manufacturing Group 398
Alstom 355
Alternative Economic Strategy 53
Amazon 31
American School (of capitalist economies) 2
Amgen 173
anti-trust 18, 19
Apple Inc. 31, 175, 221
apprenticeships viii, 191–2, 196, 196–7, 199
Arcelor-Mittal 345
architectural innovations 175
ARPA-E (Advanced Research Projects Agency for Energy) 173
Asia, industrial policy 79–97
Asian consensus 21
asset ownership, importance of 118–20, 121

AstraZeneca 11, 343, 355, 358
asymetric return distributions 136
Australia
    follow-on venture capital investments 150
    IIF (Innovation Investment Fund) *see* IIF
    market gap 137
    risk capital investment statistics 147
    venture capital market, and IIF 137–40
AVCAL (Australian Venture Capital Association) 133, 138, 145, 162
Averch-Johnson effect 315

B

Bank of England
    and bank failures 123–4
    and corporate diversity 127
    monetary policy 4
bank failures 123–4
Bank of France 50
Banking Disclosure Act 113
banking sector reform 123
banking sector structure 110–12
banking system diversity 111
banks
    balance sheet structures 124
    business funding ix, 7
    and capital investment 111
    commercial 7
    competitiveness 124
    concentration reduction 111–12, 125
    credit controllers 210
    disclosure 113
    geographic spread 124–5
    government role 111
    guided lending 112–13
    investment/commercial ring fencing 7, 61, 110

banks (*cont.*)
  key roles 104
  large bank domination 124
  ownership diversity 124
  product mis-selling 73
  regional development 7
  sector resilience 124
  separation of roles 110
  size of 112
  taxation 33
  TBTF (too big to fail) *see* TBTF
Barnett formula 274
Beecroft Report 241, 248–9
Beijing Consensus 21, 23
Bell Labs 173
Bentley 410
Berry index of bank diversification 124
BHP Billiton 355–6
biotechnology industry 174
BIS (Department for Business, Innovation
      and Skills) 62, 63, 65, 354, 396
  Employment Law Review 249
Blair-Thatcher economic policies 60–1, 76
Blair, Tony 407
BNDES national development bank 177
bolt-on auxiliary policies 61, 63
borrower types 347
bottleneck assets 28, 30, 31
Braeburn capital 175
Branson, Richard 117
BRICs (Brazil, Russia, India, China), success
      of 1, 17, 31
Bristol-Myers Squibb 176
Britain *see* UK
British Aerospace 50
British Automotive Council 410–11
British Business Bank proposal ix
British Gas 325
British Leyland 50–1
Brown, Gordon 56, 61, 396
BT (British Telecom) 72–3, 312, 313, 314,
      315–16
BT Openreach 313, 316
Building Societies Act (1986) 123
business clusters 18, 23, 30
business competition 24
business ecosystems 30

business/employee interests consensus 9
business funding ix
business, and the regulatory burden 248–50
business taxation viii
bus services *see* transport

C
Cable, Vince 56–7, 63, 197, 398–9, 410, 411
CA (competitive advantage) 26, 28,
      29, 33–4
Cadbury 11, 343, 354–7, 358
Callaghan, James 50, 61
Cambridge School 20
Cameron, David 20, 56, 60, 398
capital gains tax 175
capital gold-plating 315
capitalism, six periods in 120–2
capitalism unleashed 119, 120, 122
carbon emissions 12
carbon leakage 388
car industry 409–17
  alternative vehicle technology policy 412
  British Automotive Council 410–11
  composition in UK 409–10
  current policy mix 411–13
  electric vehicles 413–14
  growth limits 415–16
  market reform 416–17
  product service systems 416–17
  technology limits 413–14
  vertical thinking limits 414–15
carried interest 136
Catapult Innovation Centres 280
Catapult technology centres viii, 64
CBI (Confederation of British Industry) 63
CDO (colateralized debt obligation)
      products 118
Central Electricity Generating Board 318
centralism 293
centralized localism 302
Centre for Cities 275, 276, 277
ceramic cities 280
Chadwick auctions 323, 324
China
  DIP 23
  higher education 219

industrial policy 23, 83
middle-class salaries 221
state capitalism 23
Christian Democrats (West Germany) 47
Chrysler 51
Churchill, Winston 122
CIMA 253
Cisco 31
cities 263–82
City Deals 288
City of London dominance 116, 122, 126
Civilization and Capitalism 70
Civitas 64
climate change 127
cluster competition 219
cluster paradox 278
cluster policy 3, 23, 302
CMA (Competition and Markets
        Authority) 357
Coalition Agreement (2010) 117
Coalition Agreement 116–17
Coalition Government 61, 123, 194
    austerity measures 242, 397–8
    and employment protection 241, 246,
        249, 256
    and local growth 288
    and place-based policies 288–90
    Plan for Growth 397
Coca Cola 253
co-created value 31
codified knowledge 89
colateralized debt obligation *see* CDO
commercial general partner *see* GP
Commission for Employment and Skills
        (UK) 199
Communist Manifesto 120
Companies Act (2006) 228, 349, 357
company decision-making, workers' voice
        in 225–39
company directors' duties 228, 348, 349, 357
comparative advantage 26, 28, 34, 90
competition
    in business model 73–4
    with cooperation 20, 27
    and financialization 71
    and globalization 71
    perfect/contestable 19

quality-cost revolution 209–10
Competition Commission 322, 323, 325
competition policy 338
Competitive Advantage of Nations
        Diamond 24
competitive deregulation 250
competitive manufacturing 80
competitiveness 79, 84, 86, 87, 90, 402–3
    in Europe 383, 385
competitor policies 63–5
conditional localism 293, 296
Conservative Party Conference (1992) 2
Conservative Party (UK) 50, 51, 53
contestable competition 19
contingency contracts 90
contracting failures 81, 87, 91
conventional framing, limits of 66–70
Co-operative Bank 117
Co-operative Group 117, 119
co-opetition 20, 27
coordinated capitalism 44
corporate control 11, 348–9, 351–3
corporate diversity 116, 117, 127
    Michie-Oughton diversity index 7,
        122–6, 127
corporate governance 9, 76, 226–9
    reform 239
    in UK 226–9
    workers' representation on European
        boards 232–6
corporate income tax 175
corporate investment 105
corporate takeovers 11
corporate venture capital funds 154
Corporation Tax viii
corruption 34
cost/differentiation framework 29
cost-per-job 329
counter-cyclical lending 177
country differentiation branding 28–9
CPs (competition policies) 18–20
CRA (Community Reinvestment Act)
        (USA) 112–13
creative destruction 19–20
credit controllers 210
credit rationing 104
crowding out effect 333

D

DARPA (Pentagon procurement division) 45

DECC (Department for Energy and Climate Change) 396

decentralization 302

De Gaulle, Charles 50

degree places, engineering/ manufacturing viii–ix

de-industrialization 6, 43–4, 55, 79, 80, 86, 273

demand management approach 3

democracy, in workplace 225

demutualization 123

Denmark
  country differentiation branding 28–9
  graduate-level courses 198

Department of Energy (USA) 54

Department of Trade (UK) 55

deregulation 22, 53

derivatives 6, 109–10

development banks 91, 113–14

DfT (Department for Transport) 323

digital Taylorism 210–11, 212, 217

DIISR (Department of Innovation, Industry, Science and Research) 132, 133, 144, 145, 151, 162

DIPs (development industrial policies) 5
  China 23
  and ITPs 21–4
  and market failures 18
  perspectives on 18–24
  PPPPs (public-private-polity-based partnerships) 27, 29, 30, 34
  top-down-bottom-up approach 27, 32, 33

DIPs-ITPs myths 24–7

directed lending 114

Directly Operated Railways 323

directors' duties 228, 348, 349, 357

direct returns to the state 175

direct substitution effect 333

discovery investment 88

Dispute Resolution Commitment 246

Dispute Resolution Regulations (2004) 245

division of labour, and market failure 25

domestic industrial performance 401

domestic innovation 86

Donovan Report 242, 251

double dualism 269–70

Dutt Committee 93, 94

E

East Asia
  ex ante rents for learning 94
  ex post rents for learning 94–5
  industrial (chaebol) subsidy 91, 92–3
  industrial policy 83, 90, 92
  political settlements 93

EAT (Employment Appeal Tribunal) 247, 256

ECFs (Enterprise Capital Funds) 136

eco-innovation 403

economically active households, real income growth 68

economic development, and financial development 103

economic diversification 26

economic governance 121, *see also* strategic decision-making
  asymmetries in 267

economic power, asymmetries in 267

economic regional imbalances 125

economic sectoral balance 402

economic sustainability, and SCA (sustainable competitive advantage) 18, 24

EDF 320

education
  and global labour market 218–19
  graduate-level courses 198, 212
  and human capital theory 207–8, 209
  and productivity 218
  returns to 220
  and skills 186–7, 194, 206–8

EEF (Engineering Employers Federation) 63

electoral cycle vii

electricity industry *see* network energy industries

embedded mercantilism 46

EMH (efficient market hypothesis) 350

employability skills 194–5

employee engagement 8, 127

employee representation 9
  on corporate boards 8, 9

employment
  global competition for 207–8
  higher education 8

skills and training 8
  and takeovers 362
Employment Act (2002) 245
Employment Act (2008) 246
employment contracts, and takeovers 352
employment disputes 250
  adjudication 255–6
  competitive deregulation 250
  early case assessment 254
  Early Conciliation 246, 254
  external resolutions 254–5
  internal resolutions 251–4
  PCC (pre-claim conciliation) 246, 254
  peer review 254
  policy debate 250–6
  resolution gap 251
  in SMEs 253
employment issues, and industrial
      policy 8–10
employment law 9
employment litigation 249
employment rights 8, 9, 241–56
Employment Rights (Dispute Resolution) Act
      (1998) 245, 255
The End of the Experiment? 72
endogenous growth theory 21
energy industries 317–21
energy-intensive industries 407
energy policy, and industrial policy
      385–9
energy prices, USA 386–7
Energy Roadmap 390
Engaging for Success report 250
Enterprise Act (2002) 356
entrepreneurial finance 135
entrepreneurship
  finance for 6–8
  youth 32
EOPs (Employer Ownership Pilots) 197
equity trading 109
ESPRC (Engineering and Physical Sciences
      Research Council) 410
ESVCLP (Early-Stage Venture Capital
      Limited Partnerships) 137
ETs (Employment Tribunals) 241, 245–8,
      250, 256
  fees 247–8

EU
  Cohesion Policy 289
  in GFC 2
  Maastricht Treaty 54
  structural policy 65
  workers' representation on European
      boards 232–6
EUNIP (European Network on Industrial
      Policy) 4
Europe
  competitiveness 383
  economic dynamics, proposals to
      revive 381–2
  energy policy, and industrial policy
      385–9
  export share 387
  growth and GDP 383
  industrial policy 372, 383, 385–9
  integration of former communist
      countries 381
  low road/high road strategy 384
  trade balances 387
European Commission
  industrial policy documents 375–81
  integrated industrial policy 2–3
  and sustainability/competitiveness 366
European Investment Bank 114
European Participation Index
      231–2
European Union *see* EU
European Working Time Directive 242
eurozone economic output 381
event studies 353
evergreen funds 163
evolutionary/systems-based views 3
exchange rates 108
  devaluation 402
exogenous technical change 21
exports 3
externalities 32
ExxonMobil 400
EZ (economic zones) 30

F
Facebook 31
Fair Trade Movement 127

FDI
  and agglomeration economies 337–8
  asset-seeking 332
  by multinationals 55
  and corporate tax rates 335
  and exchange rates 337
  foreign acquisition of domestic
      companies 333–4
  inward 28, 29–30
  knowledge-intensive 30
  and labour market flexibility 335
  market-seeking 332
  policy 11, 101, 328–31, 339
  in private sector capital growth 53
  promotion 3
  resource-seeking 332
  and skills 185
  and UKTI support 336–7
  see also investment; inward investment
      policy
Federal Ministry for Research and
    Technology 48
Ferranti 51, 67
FESSUD (Financialization Economy Society
    and Sustainable Development) 101
fictitious capital 109
finance, and industrial strategy 101–14
financial architecture 6–8, 116–28
financial bolt-on 61
financial innovations 6
Financial Instability Hypothesis 344, 347
financial institutions 55–6, 108–14
financialization 102, 109
financial reform 175–6
financial restructuring 7
financial risk 104
financial sector
  diversity 7
  and industrial strategy 107–8
  and industry 102
  reforms 108–14
  roles 104, 109
  size 103
financial services factory 210
financial transactions taxes 7, 104, 109–10
financing, SMEs (small and medium-sized
    businesses) 7

financing gaps 133
Finland, and Nokia 218
FIRE (finance, insurance and real estate) 103
firm competitiveness 86
firm organization 89
firm staging 154
FirstGroup 235–6
fiscal deficit limits 177
fiscal policy 4
flagship initiatives 376
follow the money sectoral analysis 72
follow-on venture capital investments 150
Ford 409
foreign direct investment see FDI
fossil fuel 400, 415
foundational economy 5–6, 71–2, 74–7
France
  credit control 50
  grand projets 366
  higher education courses 198
  industrial policy 49–50, 51–2
  industrial subsidy 52
  nationalization 50
  sustainable growth 366
  workers' voice below board level 238
free market capitalism 119
free markets 22, 34
free-riding 32, 88, 268
free trade 21, 22
FRG (Federal Republic of Germany)
    see Germany
Froud, Julie 5
funding escalator 135, 153
fund managers' costs 138
FUR (functional urban region) 296

G
GAJ (global auction for jobs) 207, 209, 212,
    213, 216
  demand issues 219–20
  and global labour market restructuring
      218–21
  returns 220–1
  supply issues 218–19
Gandhi, Indira 93–4
gas industry see network energy industries

GDP
  and bank deposits 103
  current account and growth of real 368
  growth distribution 67
  growth goal 65, 66
  and investment 105
  manufacturing share and growth of real
    GDP 369
  and market valuation 103
  and public sector debt 54
GEC 61
General Electric 253, 355
*General Theory of Employment, Interest and
  Money* 119
geography, in national policy 65
Germany
  apprenticeships 199
  banking system 111
  deindustrialization policy for 43–4
  graduate-level courses 198
  higher education 219
  industrial policy 1
  industrial subsidy 55
  Mittelstand SMEs 31
  post-Second World War policies 43–4
  West German (FRG) industrial
    policy 47–8
  workers' voice below board level 237–8
GFC (global financial crisis)(2008) 1, 2, 5, 17,
  110, 118, 119, 123, 396
Gibbons Review 246
Gini-Simpson index 124
Giscard d'Estaing, Valery 49
Glass-Steagall Act 110
global auction for jobs *see* GAJ
global capital 6
global cities 269–70
  double dualism 269–70
global financial crisis *see* GFC
global financial institutions 6
globalization 32
global labour market restructuring 218–21
global value chains 30, 33
global warming 385
Golden Age of Capitalism 120–1
Google 31, 175
governance gap 298–305

governance structures 5
government failures 25, 91
government financial leverage 135–6
government investment 64
government objectives, in neoclassical
  economics 19
government policy cycles 294
GP (commercial general partner) 132, 162
graduate income 213, 214, 215, 216
graduate premium 212–13
graduates
  in non-graduate roles 216–17
  see also GAJ
graduate underemployment 212
Grameen bank 279
Gramm-Leach-Bliley Act 110
Great Recession (2008–13) 1, 212–17, 222,
  242, 263
  and early career graduates 216–17
Greece, country differentiation
  branding 28–9
green industrial policy *see* IP (industrial
  policy)
green investment 114
Green Investment Bank 64, 113, 399
Green New Deal 121, 125–6
Green Party 400
green power 320
green technology 12
growth theory 21
GVA (gross value added) measure 69, 70

H

Hamilton, Alexander 2, 45
Heath, Edward 50–1, 61
hedge borrowers 347
Heseltine, Michael 2, 55, 56, 263, 289, 293,
  303, 304, 354, 356, 398, 399, 411
HES model 21
HFT (high frequency trading) 109
hierarchical relations 267
higher education 8, 9
high frequency trading *see* HFT
high-skill ecosystems 280
High-tech Gründerfonds 136
high value added opportunities 407

Hirshmann-Herfindahl index of
    concentration 124
HM Treasury and Small Business Service 143
Honda 61
horizontal industrial policy 12, 25–7, 33, 82,
    372, 376, 395, 406–7
HR (human resources) function 251
HRST (Human Resources in Science and
    Technology) 189, 190
human capital prescription, and industrial
    policy 217–18
human capital theory 206–9, 212–17
    coincidence of interests within 217
hybrid intervention structures 134
hybrid schemes 132
hybrid VC funds, operating
    characteristics 142, 162, 163
hybrid venture capital 7

I
IBM 18, 67
IBM-Lenovo 345
ICE (Information and Consultation of
    Employees Regulations)(2005) 225
ICI 61
ICMSs (Integrated Conflict Management
    Systems) 253, 254, 256
ICT bubble 353
ICTs (Information and Communication
    Technologies) 185
IF Metall 236
IIF Affiliate Fund 133
IIF (Innovation Investment Fund) 7, 131–64
    and Australian venture capital
        market 137–40
    data sources 145–52
    early-stage focus 141, 154–6, 163
    effectiveness evaluation criteria 140–4,
        162–3
    exit performance 143, 150, 159–61
    external finance 148
    individual business amounts 141–3
    industry choice 150
    investment size 156–7
    investment stages for IIF supported
        businesses 148

investment value 145
investor types/investment effectiveness
    relationship 148–9
IPO (initial public offering) 143–4
    methodology 144–5
    multinomial logistic regression 158
    multiple funding rounds supply 141, 152–4
    new knowledge industry investments 143,
        157–9
    objectives 137
    portfolio firms 148
    probit regressions exit outcomes 160
    research limitations 162
    statistics 145–52
    variables 146, 155
    VC funds 132, 133–6
IMA (Investment Management
    Association) 227
IMF (International Monetary Fund) 51, 119
inclusive growth 174
income dispersal, within occupations 216
income elasticity of demand 402
income inequality 118
Independent Banking Commission
    (UK) 110–11
India
    automobile industry 95–6
    industrial policy 96–7
    middle-class salaries 221
    political settlement 96
    rent 93
    tariff protection 96
    Tier 1/2 component production 95, 96
Indonesia, industrial policy 23
industrial decline 61
industrial finance 101–2
industrial innovation 80
industrialization 210
industrial policy see IP (industrial policy)
industrial production dynamic, and
    manufacturing 371
industrial shock hypothesis 345
Industrial Strategy: UK Sector Analysis 399
industrial strategy see IP (industrial policy)
industrial subsidy 51, 52, 55, 79, 91
industry, finance for 6–8
industry sector councils viii

infant industries, rent allocation to 87
inflation 51
Information and Consultation of Employees
        Regulations (2005) *see* ICE
infra economy 71
innovation
    architectural innovations 175
    eco-innovation 403
    finance for 6–8, 171
    financial 6
    in industrial strategy 200
    open 8
    and skills 201
    smart 8
    state-funded 67, 176
    ten-year horizon vii, ix
    use of term 184
    see also IP (industrial policy)
innovation capabilities 31
innovation clusters 28
innovation funding 303
Innovation Investment Fund *see* IIF
innovation-led growth
    funding for 7–8
    smart 170–8
innovation policies 3, 6, 86
innovation programmes vii
innovation reviews, five-yearly vii, ix
Innovation Survey (UK) 184
innovation system vii, 24
innovation systems/eco-systems 170
innovation union 170
innovative ability 404
insideout production model 219, 221
institutional memory 294
intellectual framing 66
inter-employment networks 200
international competitiveness 24
Internet 313
investment 80, 105–7
    by TNCs (transnational companies) 206
    private 339
    and savings 105–7
    and tax 175
    Tobin's q-theory 345
    transnational mobile 264
    see also FDI; inward investment policy

investment-averse firms 72
Investment Canada Act 356
investment coordination 88
investment limitations 136
investment problems 87
    developing countries 87
investment risk 174
investors, and shares 228
investor types/investment effectiveness
        relationship 148–9
inward investment policy 206, 327–40
    aftercare 336–7
    agglomeration 337–8
    corporate tax rates 335
    exchange rates 337
    FDI benefits 331–3
    FDI as foreign M&A 333–4
    FDI policy in UK 328–31
    institutions 336
    labour market flexibility 335
    and MNEs 329, 332, 333, 334
    White Papers on 329
    see also FDI; investment
iPhone funding 172, 175
iPhone production 221
IP (industrial policy) vii, 50–1, 52, 54, 65, 80,
        371–81
    academic proposals 373–5
    agenda vii, 50–1, 52, 54, 65, 80, 371–81
    at its peak 48–52
    in context 83
    coordination 88
    definition of 18, 41–3
    dimensions of 81–5
    DIP (development industrial policies)
        see DIPs
    discriminatory 82
    and employment issues 8–10
    and energy policy 385–9
    exchange rates 108
    and financial sector 101–14
    five-yearly reviews ix
    green industrial policy 366, 375, 376,
        395–418
    horizontal 12, 25–7, 33, 82, 372, 376, 395,
        406–7
    and human capital prescription 217–18

IP (industrial policy) (*cont.*)
  and implementation 84
  industrial policy activism 63, 207
  innovation oriented 193
  integrated 376
  internal/external economic balance 401–3
  international experiences 41–59
  long-term vii
  matrix type 372
  new approaches to 373–5
  new industrial strategy 63–5
  past policy 372
  perspectives on 5–6
  place-based 287–305
  placing 41–3
  policy design 82–5
  policy documents 375–81, 390
  policy failure 85
  policy instruments 4
  post-Second World War 5, 6, 43
  in practice 44–8
  re-emergence of 56–7
  reframing 60–78
  and regional development 10–11
  regional policy 411
  and regulation 11
  rents 87
  retreat from 52–6
  rise of 43–4
  role of 79–97
  sector-specific 407
  shared framing 63–5
  skills *see* skills
  smart 8
  soft 378–80
  state-led 207
  state monitoring and enforcement 81, 85,
      86–7
  state role in 1, 207
  success of 17
  and sustainable development 12, 390
  for sustainable growth 365–91
  systemic 3
  types of 42
  vertical 26–7, 82, 376
  wider 376
  yardsticks 389–90

  see also car industry; individual countries;
      innovation; manufacturing
IPO (initial public offering) 143–4, 174
  share price performance 151–2, 164
IPPR (Institute for Public Policy
    Research) 300, 301
IP vertical approach 376
IS (industrial strategy) *see* DIPs
Italy, industrial success 277–8
ITPs (international trade policies) 5
  and DIPs 21–4
  DIPs-ITPs myths 24–7

J
Jacobs, Jane 10, 264–5
Jaguar Land Rover 339, 410
Japan
  deindustrialization policy for 43–4
  industrial organization model 23
  industrial policy 1, 22–3, 46–7
  industrial subsidy 55
  post-Second World War policies for 43–4,
      46–7
  zaibatsu companies 46
JCB 62
Jobs, Steve 172
junk bonds 352

K
Kay Review 354
key enabling technologies 376
key industry sectors vii
Keynesian demand management approach
      3, 56, 126
Keynes, John Maynard 109, 119
KfW state investment bank 177
King, Mervyn 105
knowledge, role and uncertainty of 298–304
knowledge transfer processes 185
knowledge work, stratification of 211, 212–17
Kraft 354–7
Kroger 31
KTPs (Knowledge Transfer
      Partnerships) 183–4
Kyoto Protocol 385

L

Labour Force Survey (UK) 187, 213
labour market flexibility 3
Labour Party (UK) 50, 53, 56, 69, 194, 242
labour productivity 31–2
labour skills 276
large company dominance in UK 116
LCEAs (Low Carbon Economic Areas)
        411, 412
learning rents 89
Lehman Brothers collapse 56
LEPs (Local Enterprise Partnerships) 288,
        296–9, 301, 302, 303, 330, 339
liberal capitalism 44
liberal militarism 43
light touch regulation 117
limited funds, maximizing returns to 327–40
limited partners *see* LP
liquidation 161
Littlechild Report (1983) 313–17
Littlechild Report (1986) 321
Lloyds 74, 117
Local Economic Partnerships viii
local elites 295
local growth 288, 289
Local Growth White Paper 330
local value chains 31
long twentieth century 116
LPs (limited partners) 132, 162, 163

M

Maastricht Treaty 54
MacLeod and Clarke Report 250
Macmillan Committee on Finance and
        Industry 143
macroeconomic fiscal approaches 3
Major, John 55
Malaysia, industrial policy 23
managed-trade policies 22
managerial behaviour theories 346
Mandelson, Peter 396
manufacturing
    core products 377–8
    crisis and industrial base 369
    declining 377
    emerging market competition 367, 371

and financial crisis 367–8
and GDP 366–7, 368–70
re-emergence 366–71
resilient 377–8
service component 378
share of 370–1, 378, 379, 380
in USA 380–1
and wealth creation 19
see also IP (industrial policy)
manufacturing imports (UK) 62
manufacturing investment (UK) 62
manufacturing output (UK) 61–2
manuservices 26
market competition 24
market for corporate control 351–3
market diversification 31
market failure
    and DIPs 18
    and division of labour 25
    and government intervention 338
    and horizontal measures 25–6
    key sectors 64
    perspective on 3
    and risk 170
    SMEs 134, 135
market resource allocation 218
Maruti-Suzuki 95
Marxism 120
mechanical Taylorism 210–11
mergers 11, 46, *see also* takeovers
methodological nationalism, and human
        capital theory 209
METI (Ministry of Economy, Trade and
        Industry) 22
MG Rover 275
Michie-Oughton diversity index 7, 122–6, 127
Microsoft 31, 221
Middlandstand SMEs 31
MIER (Manchester Independent Economic
        Review) 330, 340
Miliband, Ed 122, 263, 396
mining, social licence 75
Ministry for Scientific Research (West
        Germany) 48
Ministry of Technology (UK) 50
missing space 298–305
mission oriented investments 170–1

MITI (Ministry of International Trade and Industry) 22, 45–6
Mitterand, François 49–50, 51–2
MNEs (multinational enterprises) 30–1, 55
monetarist policy 53
monetary policy 4
monopoly 20
monopoly rights 315
Morrisons 72
MRTP (Monopolies and Restrictive Trade Practices) Act(India) 93–4
MSCI (Morgan Stanley Capital International Index) 145, 152
multilevel governance approach 304
multinomial logistic regression 158
multi-zonal economy 70–1, 76
mutual societies 7

N
NASDAQ 350–1
national capitalisms 42
National Coal Board 51
national economic framework, as unspatial 294
national hollowing out 294
national income accounting 70
National Minimum Wage 242
National Science Foundation 54, 175
National Statistical Office 127
natural economic area 296
NEG (New Economic Geography) 291
neo-liberal orthodoxy 56
NETA (New Electricity Trading Arrangements) 318–19
network energy industries 317–21
Network Rail 323
networks of direction 267
networks of mutual dependence 267
New Deal 121, 125–6
New Deal for Communities 288
new-knowledge-based sectors 131
New Labour see Labour Party (UK)
new trade theory 21
niche-differentiation strategies 29
NIH (National Institutes of Health)

R&D funding 171, 173, 176
risk-taking 173
Nikkei stock market 351
Nissan 412
noise traders 350
Nokia 177, 218
nominal GVA growth share 69
Northern Economic Futures Commission 300, 301
Northern Rock 117, 123
No Stone Unturned report 263, 354, see also Heseltine
NS&I 124
Nuclear Electric 319
NYSE (New York Stock Exchange) 344

O
oasis operations 210
Obama, Barack 33, 57
OECD (Organisation for Economic Co-operation and Development) 20, 54, 184, 189–90, 287, 289, 378–80
OFCOM 314
Office for Budget Responbility (UK) 62
Office for Fiscal Responsibility 4
Office for National Statistics 125
Old Labour see Labour Party (UK)
OLS (ordinary least squares) 152 regression 155
one nation politics 263
open innovation 8
organizational capabilities 81, 84, 86–91
organized capitalism 47
outsourcing 72, 86
Overman, Henry 63, 65, 69
overseas interests priority 116
Owen, Robert 118
Oxford Centre for Mutual & Employee-owned Business 123

P
pari passu structure 135
patent policy 86
path dependence 29
PCC (pre-claim conciliation) 246, 254

PDF (Pooled Development Fund) 137
PE investments 138, 139
pension funds 227
people-based policy 288–92
perfect competition 19
Pfizer 173, 174, 354
pharmaceutical funding 173–4, 176
picking winners 83–4, 177, 357
Pitelis, Christos 5
place-based policy 287–305
    foundations of 291–2
    role of local institutions 295–8
    role of national institutions 292–5
place perspective 293
planning for competition 25
platform techniques 210
pluralism 34
poison pill defences 356
Poisson regression results 153
policies targeting 26–7
policy design 82–5
    and externatities 92
Policy Exchange 64
policy failure 85
policy goals 42–3
policy-induced rents 87
policy instruments 4
    rent creating 87–8
policy levers/outcomes 66–70
policy/resource allocation, London
        priority 294
political settlements 93
political structures 5
Ponzi borrowers 347
Pool central marketing system 318, 319
population urbanization 127
positioning strategy 28
positive externalities 88
post-Second World War industrial policy
        5, 6, 43
post-Second World War reconstruction 22
post-Washington consensus 22
Potash Corporation 355–6
PPPPs (public-private-polity-based
        partnerships) 27, 29, 30
price opacity 320
pricing risk absorption 318

Primary Urban Areas 274
principal-agent problems 87
priority lines 376
private equity investment data 140
Private Equity/Management Buy-Out 134
private finance 172
private investment 339
private ownership 121
private sector efficiency 174
privatization 22, 53, 72–3, 119
proactive export policy 64
probit regressions exit outcomes 160
procurement policy 375
product-cycle theory 367
production-related services 367
productive asset ownership 118–20, 121
productive bolt-on 61
productivity 107, 229–31
    and targeted action 230
productivity puzzle 229–30
productivity/rewards link 218
psychic income 346
public entrepreneurs 30
Public Interest Commission 357
Public Interest Test 11, 343, 357, 358–9
public ownership 121
public-private-polity-based partnerships
        see PPPPs
public utilities
    regulation and governance of 311–25
        network energy industries 317–21
        RPI-X regulation 313–17
        transport 322–4
        water and sewage industries 321–2

Q
quality-cost revolution 209–10, 212

R
R&D 9, 63, 66, 67
R&D expenditure 64
R&D funding 171–4
R&D intervention 66
R&D tax deduction 176
rail franchises 73
rail services see transport

Railtrack 323
RBS 74
RDAs (Regional Development Agencies) 288,
    298, 302, 328, 330, 339, 412–13
Reagan, Ronald 53, 54, 56
real original income
    annual change in 68
    growth share 68
rebalancing the economy 122
recommendations (Wright) viii–ix
Recovery and Enforcement Act (1989) 344
REDRESS initiative 252
regional clusters 28
regional development, and industrial
        policy 3, 10–11, 48
regional development banks 7
Regional Development Grants 328
regional development policies 5–6
regional GVA as percentage of London's 70
regional imbalances, economic 125
regional industrial policy 3, 10–11
    place-based 287–305
regulation, and industrial policy 11
regulatory capture 34
re-industrialization 31, 402
Renault 50, 52
rent
    allocation 87–8
    learning rents 94
    monopolization of 131
    policy-induced 85, 87
rent-creating policy instruments 87–8
rent management, political economy of
        91–7
rent products 90
rent-seeking 34
Report from the Commission on
        Ownership 116
Report on the Subject of Manufactures 2, 45
research, public funding 86
resource creation 19
Revenge of History 119
revolving funds 163
ring fencing (banks) see banks
risk averseness 178
risk capital 172
    availability 131–2

risk landscape 170
risk-return relationship 170
risk and rewards balance 178
risk-taking 64
    state as lead risk-taker 178
Robin Hood Tax 126
ROE (return on equity) 177
Rolls-Royce 18, 26, 51, 410
Ross, Wilbur 117
Royal Mail 314
RPI-X regulation 313–17
RSA (Regional Selective Assistance) 328–9,
        330, 334, 340
RVCFs (Regional Venture Capital
        Funds) 136

S
SAAB AB 237
SAS (Survey of Adult Skills) 189–91
savings 105–7
SBIC (Small Business Investment
        Corporation) 135, 136
SCA (sustainable competitive advantage)
    business strategy-informed DIP-IS 27–33
    and economic sustainability 18, 24–33
science/technology budget viii
sector picking 64
securitization 6, 109
service sector employment 56
service sector growth 53
SFIE (Strategic Finance for Investment in
        England) 328, 334
shared framing 63–5
shareholder primacy
    in company law 348
    weakness of 226–9
shareholder value 102
shareholders
    and corporate control 226–7
    election of directors 226
share price determination 349–51
share trading 228
short-termism 9, 122, 172, 353
Siemens 61
SIIP (Systemic Industrial and Innovation
        Policy) 3, 374

Singapore
    industrial policy 23
    wage policy 30
Single European Market 54
Single Local Growth Fund 398
singular dynamic economy 70
SITRA 177
skill-based technological change 174
skill bias theory 220
skilled worker unemployment 189
skills
    apprenticeships viii, 191–2, 196, 196–7, 199
    and education 186–7
    embedding in industrial strategy 200–1
    employability 194–5
    and employment 207
    existing skills and training, UK 188–93
    and firms' absorptive capacity 185
    globalization of 209
    graduate/intermediate 198–9
    graduate-level courses 198
    and ICTs (Information and
        Communication Technologies) 185
    for improved innovation
        performance 184–8
    initial/continuing training
        balance 199–200
    innovation-relevant skills and
        education 194
    key sector 197
    management 191, 194
    policy development, new approach to 193–7
    range of 186
    state support for 219
    STEM (Science; Technology; Engineering
        and Mathematics) subjects 194–5
    and supply chains 185
    technical/generic 197–8
    training 8, 192–3
    training barrier 189
    training deficit 189
    training externality 194
skills deficit 8, 188, 189, 191, 201
skills gap 189
skills shortage 189
skills strategy 183–4
skills underutilization 189

skills updating, professions affected by 188
Sky 316
Skype 313
smart growth 174
smart industrial policy 8
smart innovation 8
SMART objectives viii, 183
SMEs (small and medium-sized enterprises/
        businesses) 7, 30–1, 131, 253, 406
SMMT (Society of Motor Manufacturers and
        Traders) 409
SMP (system marginal price) 318
Social Chapter 242
social elections 238
social gradients 191
social licensing 6, 74–7
soft industrial policy 378–80
South Asia
    ex ante rents for learning 94
    ex post rents for learning 94–5
    industrial policy 80, 83, 93
    technology adoption 95
South Korea, industrial policy 1, 23, 83
Soviet Union, collapse of 119
space-neutral approach 291, 299
spacially-blind approach 299
speculative borrowers 347
spillover 11, 219, 387, 408, 415
staging 154
state
    direct returns to 175
    as lead risk-taker 178
state capitalism 23
state decentralization 76
state-funded innovation 67
state interventionism 48, 56
state investment 8
state investment banks 177
state lending institutions 64
STEM (Science; Technology; Engineering
        and Mathematics) subjects 194–5
Stern Review 395
stock exchange automation 109
stock markets 351
strategic decision-making 226, 267–9, 277
        see also economic governance
strategic failure 267, 276, 281

strategic restructuring wave 344
structurally depressed industries 46
structural rationalization 11, 46
student loans 176
success fees 138
supermarkets 72, 73
supply chains 62, 72, 74, 185, 221
supply-side policies 3
supra economy 71
sustainability, and industrial policy 12, 403–6
Suzuki 95, 96
Sweden
    country differentiation branding 28–9
    good work policy 231
    trade union participation 236
    workers' voice below board level 236–7
Swedish Metalworkers Union 231
Switzerland, graduate-level courses 198
systemic industrial policy 3, 374
systems of innovation perspective 21, 23,
        24, 26

T
tacit knowledge 89
Taiwan, industrial policy 23, 83
Takeover Code 356, 357, 358
Takeover Panel 354
takeovers/takeover policy 343–59
    borrower types 347
    and employment contracts 352
    and management 352
    and market for corporate control 351–3
    Public Interest Test 11, 343, 357, 358–9
    share price determination 349–51
    strategic restructuring 344
    takeover mechanism 351–3
    takeover waves 11, 343–7, 358
    UK policy 354–7
TalkTalk 316
targeted state intervention 176
targeted subsidies 64
TATA 339
Tata Steel-Corus 345
tax concessions 55
tax incentives 53
Taxol 176

Tax Reform Act 344
tax revenue 126
tax system reform 175
Taylorism 210–11, 212, 217
TBTF (too big to fail) institutions 6, 112, 122,
        123, 124, 125
TEAC (Think-tank for Action on Social
        Change) 263
technical innovation 63
technological breakthroughs 176
technological capabilities 81
technological change, skill-based 174
technology acquisition 87–8
Technology Strategy Board viii, 280
technology transfer, and FDI 11
TechnoPartners fund 136
Tesco 72
Thailand, industrial policy 23
Thales 238
Thatcher-Blair economic policies
        60–1, 76
Thatcher, Margaret 51, 53, 54, 55, 56, 119
Think London 337
three-level economy 70–1
tiger economies 22, 23
TNCs (transnational companies) 206, 211,
        217, 219, 267–8, 269
Tobin's q-theory 345
Tobin Tax 126
Tokyo stock market 351
top-to-bottom economy reformatting 66
Town and Villages Enterprises 23
Toyota 28
trade deficits 55
trade theory 367
trade unions
    and carbon policy 397
    organizational weakness 248, 251
    participion 236, 252, 311
    power 53, 311
training 8, 189, 192–3
    see also skills
training externality 194
transport 322–4
trickle-down economics 53
trust 296
TSB 74

TSO (transmission system operator) 317
TUC (Trades Union Congress) 63, 397
TUPE (Transfer of Undertakings(Protection of Employment)) Regulations 247

U
UK
    aircraft building 43
    atomic bomb development 43
    economic decline 116
    economic performance indicators 243–4
    economic policy 5–6
    employment ptotection levels 249
    FDI policy 11, 101, 328–31
    financial architecture 6–8, 116–28
    GDP 66
    GDP growth 105
    GDP and investment 105
    GVA (gross value added) measure 69, 70
    higher education courses 198
    jobs gap 275
    large company dominance 116
    post-Second World War global
        dominance 43–4
    post-Second World War policies 60–1
    productivity 229–31
    regeneration 275
    regional structural priorities 11
    skills see skills
UK cities 263–82
    city dynamics 264–76
    diversity, importance of 264–6
    economic governance, importance
        of 266–9
    economic picture by city 271–2
    industrial strategy for 276–81
    Jacobian economies 264–6
    jobs deficit 274–6
    North-South divide 270–6
    unemployment 276
The UK Low Carbon Industrial Strategy 396
UKTI (United Kingdom Trade and
        Investment) 330, 332, 336, 337
unbalanced economy 61
under-bounding 296
under-development traps 295

UNEP (UN Environmental Programme) 12,
        396, 416
unfair dismissal 247
UNIC (Urban Network for Innovation in
        Ceramic Cities) 280
Unison 397
Unite 397, 410
United Kingdom see UK
United Nations see UN
United States see USA
unsustainable processes, in macro-economic
        balance 107
USA
    agricultural subsidy 54
    energy prices 386–7
    export share 387
    federal departments 46
    higher education courses 198
    industrial policy 1, 44–6, 54–5, 390
    post-Second World War global
        dominance 43–4
    R&D support 54, 67
    tariffs 55
    trade balances 387

V
value added 102
value capture 24
value chains 30, 31, 33
varieties of capitalism perspective 21, 23
VCLP (Venture Capital Limited
        Partnerships) 137
VC (venture capital) 131–2, 172
    corporate funds 154
    follow-on investments 150
    hybrid 7, 162
    hybrid intervention structures 134–5
    investment data 139, 140
    IPO exits 174
    markets, government intervention in 133–6
    public VC interventions 143
    and SMEs 7
    see also IIF
vehicles 28, 29–30
venture capital see VC
Vernier-Palliez, Bernard 49

vertical industrial policies 26–7, 82, 376, 396
VET (vocational education and training) 186
Vietnam, industrial policy 23
Virgin Trains 323
Volkswagen 237–8

W
wage differentials 211
wage earner funds 127
Warren Buffet 33
war for talent 211–12
Washington consensus 21, 22
water and sewage industries 321–2
wealth creation 19
wealth inequality 118
Williams Act 344
Wilson, Harold 50–1, 61
winner-takes-all ideology 32
winner-takes-all markets 211
winter of discontent 51
workers' representation on company
        boards 232–6

workers' voice
    below board level 236–8
    economic benefits of facilitating 229–32
    and productivity 229–31
working knowledge 211
work practices, high performance 230
World Bank 119
World Development Report (2009) 291
Wright Review (2014) 4

X
Xerox 18
Xerox Parcs 173

Y
yardstick competition 321
Yozma programme 136, 163

Z
zaibatsu companies 46